THE MACMILLAN ANTHOLOGY OF
AUSTRALIAN LITERATURE

THE MACMILLAN ANTHOLOGY OF AUSTRALIAN LITERATURE

EDITED BY

KEN GOODWIN AND ALAN LAWSON

UNIVERSITY OF QUEENSLAND, AUSTRALIA

WITH THE ASSISTANCE OF

BRUCE BENNETT • GERRY BOSTOCK • SNEJA GUNEW
BRIAN KIERNAN • SUSAN McKERNAN • THOMAS SHAPCOTT
KEN STEWART • JENNIFER STRAUSS • ELIZABETH WEBBY

PUBLISHED WITH THE ASSISTANCE OF THE AUSTRALIA COUNCIL

First published 1990 by
THE MACMILLAN COMPANY OF AUSTRALIA PTY LTD
107 Moray Street, South Melbourne 3205
6 Clarke Street, Crows Nest 2065

Associated companies and representatives
throughout the world

National Library of Australia
cataloguing in publication data

The Macmillan anthology of Australian literature.

ISBN 0 333 50159 4.
ISBN 0 333 50158 6 (pbk.).

1. Australian literature. I. Goodwin, K. L. (Kenneth
Leslie), 1934– . II. Lawson, Alan, 1948– . III.
Bennett, Bruce, 1941– IV. Title: Anthology of
Australian literature.

A820'.8

Cover painting: *The Landing of
Captain Cook* by William
John Hughes, 6 October 1985.
© William John Hughes.

Set in Linotron 202 Sabon by
Graphicraft Typesetters, Hong Kong
Printed in Hong Kong

CONTENTS

B   *Living in Aboriginal Australia*   75

C   *Convictism*   133

D   *The Migrant Experience*   168

E *Cultural Intersections* 213

x   *Contents*

F   *The Vision Splendid*   238

G *Mapping and Naming*   292

K   *Person to Person*

L   *Writing the Self*   526

ACKNOWLEDGEMENTS

The editors and publishers are grateful to the following for permission to reproduce copyright material:

Allen & Unwin Australia for 'Johnny Blue' from *Going Home* by Archie Weller, and for 'Colony or Nation' from *The Foundations of Culture in Australia: An Essay Toward National Self Respect* by P. R. Stephensen; Angus & Robertson Publishers for 'Towards Abstraction/Possibly a Gull's Wing' from *Selected Poems* by Robert Adamson, (© Robert Adamson, 1977), for the extract from the poem 'Golden Builders' from *Selected Poems* by Vincent Buckley, (© The Estate of Vincent Buckley, 1981), for 'Oracles for a Childhood Journey' from *Selected Poems* by Rosemary Dobson, (© Rosemary Dobson, 1980), for 'Quayside Meditation' and 'The Wind at Your Door' from *Forty Years' Poems* by R. D. FitzGerald, (© Estate of R. D. FitzGerald, 1965), for 'Australia' from *Selected Poems* by Mary Gilmore, (© Estate of Dame Mary Gilmore, 1948), for 'Thought is Surrounded by a Halo' and 'Carnal Knowledge 1' from *Selected Poems* by Gwen Harwood, (© Gwen Harwood, 1975), for 'Dialogue' from *The Lion's Bride*, (© Gwen Harwood, 1981), for 'Australia', 'Pyramis, or The House of Ascent' and 'The Planctus' from *Collected Poems 1930–70* by A. D. Hope, (© A. D. Hope), for 'Country Places' from *Antechinus: Poems 1975–1980* by A. D. Hope, (© A. D. Hope, 1981), for 'Shall then another' from *The Poems of Kenneth Mackenzie* by Kenneth Mackenzie, (© E. Little, H. S. Mackenzie, 1972), for 'Terra Australis', 'Envoi' and 'Because' from *Collected Poems 1936–70* by James McAuley, (© Norma McAuley, 1971), for 'Second Essay on Interest: The Emu', 'The Quality of Sprawl' and 'The Steel' from *The People's Otherworld* by Les A. Murray, (© Les A. Murray, 1983), for 'Clancy of The Overflow' and 'An Answer to Various Bards' from *The Collected Verse of A. B. Paterson* by A. B. Paterson, (© Retusa Pty Limited, 1921), for 'Deep Well 10: I had no human speech' from *Selected Poems* by Roland Robinson, (© Roland Robinson, 1989), for 'Nuremberg' from *Selected Poems* by Kenneth Slessor, (© Paul Slessor, 1944), for 'Terra Australis' from *Selected Poems* by Douglas Stewart, (© Douglas Stewart, 1967), for 'The Singing Bones' from *Selected Poems — A Counterfeit Silence* by Randolph Stow, (© Randolph Stow, 1969), for 'Eyre All Alone' from *Collected Poems* by Francis Webb, (© A. L. Meere, C. M. Snell, M. A. Webb-Wagg, 1973), for 'For New England', 'The Cycads' and 'Woman to Man' from *Collected Poems* by Judith Wright, (© Judith Wright, 1971), for 'Eyes' from *Phantom Dwelling* by Judith Wright, (© Judith Wright, 1985), for 'A Snake Down Under' from *The Hottest Night of the Century* by Glenda Adams, (© Glenda Adams, 1970), for 'The Love-nest; or, Which Sin Is That?' from *Tales of Parramatta and India* by Ethel Anderson, (© Betha Ogden,

1973), for the extract from *The Wells of Beersheba* by Frank Dalby Davison, for the extract from *My Brilliant Career* by Miles Franklin, (© Estate of Miles Franklin, 1901), for the extract from *The Boys in the Island* by C. J. Koch, (© C. J. Koch, 1958, 1974, 1986), for the extract from *The Pea-Pickers* by Eve Langley, (© K. M. Clark, A. Clark, R. L. Clark, 1942), for the extract from *Letters 1890–1922* by Henry Lawson, edited by Colin Roderick, for the extract from *Think—or be Damned* by Brian Penton, (© Estate late Brian Penton), for 'House-Girl' by Hal Porter, from *Happiness* by Katharine Susannah Prichard, (© Ric Throssell, 1967), for 'Three in a Row' from *The Adventures of Cuffy Mahony* by Henry Handel Richardson, (© Margaret Capon), for the extract from *Josh* by Ivan Southall, (© Ivan Southall, 1971), for 'Making a Living' from *Alien Son* by Judah Waten, (© Mrs H. Waten), for the extract from *The Magic Pudding* by Norman Lindsay, (© Janet Glad, 1918), for the extract from 'Where the Cooler Bars Grow' from *The Best of Lennie Lower* edited by Cyril Pearl, (© Mrs P. M. Pearl), and for the extract from 'Sydney in The Seventies' from *Song of the Pen* by A. B. Paterson, (© Retusa Pty Limited); Professor Ronald M. Berndt for 'A Wonguri-Mandjigai Song Cycle of the Moon Bone' (Song 2) from *Oceania*, XIX (1), 1948, for 'The Djanggawul Song Cycle' (Song 1 and Song 2) from *Djanggawul: An Aboriginal Religious Cult of North-eastern Arnhem Land*, Longman Cheshire, Melbourne, Routledge and Kegan Paul, London, 1952, and for 'The Goulburn Island Cycle' (Song 3 and Song 4) from *Love Songs of Arnhem Land*, Nelson, Melbourne, 1976; Chatto & Windus for the extract from *An Imaginary Life* by David Malouf; Moya Costello for 'An Imaginary Conversation about Brian "Squizzy" Taylor' from *Kites in Jakarta*, Sea Cruise Books; Anna Couani for 'Remember to Forget' from *Were All Women Sex-Mad? and Other Short Stories* by Anna Couani; Cunnamulla Australian Native Welfare Association and Hazel McKellar for the extract from *Matya-Mundu: A History of the Aboriginal People of South West Queensland* by Hazel McKellar; Currency Press for the extract from *No Sugar* by Jack Davis, the extract from *The Humour of Barry Humphries* by Barry Humphries, the extract from *Kullark* by Jack Davis, the extract from *Summer of the Seventeenth Doll* by Ray Lawler, the extract from *The Golden Age* by Louis Nowra, and the extract from *The Removalists* by David Williamson; Curtis Brown (Aust.) Pty Ltd for the extract from *Poor Fellow My Country* by Xavier Herbert, (© Robyn Pill); David Higham Associates Limited for the extract from *My Brother Jack* by George Johnston; Equity Trustees for the extracts from *Fourteen Years: Extracts from a Private Journal* by Nettie Palmer, Meanjin Press, 1948; Faber and Faber Ltd for the extract from *The Tilted Cross* by Hal Porter; Fremantle Arts Centre Press for the extract from *Lines of Flight* by Marion Campbell, and for 'Daisy Corunna's Story' from *My Place* by Sally Morgan; Dorothy Hewett for 'Grave Fairytale' from *Rapunzel in Suburbia*, New Poetry, 1975; Hodder & Stoughton Limited for the extract from *The Playmaker* by Thomas Keneally; Hyland House Publishing Pty Ltd for the extract from *Doctor Wooreddy's Prescription for Enduring the Ending of the World* by Colin Johnson, and for 'Song Twenty-Three' and 'Song Thirty' from *The Song-Circle of Jacky and Selected Poems* by Colin Johnson; Jacaranda Wiley Ltd for 'Old Girl' from *Children of the Dragon* by Oodgeroo of the tribe of Noonuccal, custodian of the land Minjerribah, and for 'We are Going', 'No More Boomerang' and 'Gifts' from *My People* by Oodgeroo of the tribe of Noonuccal, custodian of the land Minjerribah; Jonathan Cape Ltd for the extracts from *Voss* by Patrick White; Sylvia Kantaris for 'The Tenth Muse' from *The Tenth Muse* by Sylvia Kantaris, Menhir, 1986; Antigone Kefala for 'Memory' by Antigone Kefala; Longman Cheshire Pty Limited for 'Pioneers and Arboraphobes' from *The Australian Ugliness* by Robin Boyd, for 'Pleasant Sunday Afternoon', 'A Victorian Hangman Tells His Love' and 'Homecoming' from *Sometimes Gladness, Collected Poems* by Bruce Dawe, for 'The Djang-gawul Song Cycle' from *Djanggawul: An Aboriginal Religious Cult of North-eastern Arnhem Land*, and for 'The Cultural Cringe' from *The Australian Tradition: Studies in a Colonial Culture*, 2nd edition by A. A. Phillips; Lothian Books for 'The Orange Tree' and 'The Poor Country' from *Collected Poems of John Shaw Neilson* by John Shaw Neilson, and for 'Australia' and the Introduction from *The Poems of Bernard O'Dowd*; David Malouf for 'A First Place: The Mapping of a World' by David Malouf from *Southerly;* Martin Secker & Warburg for the extract from *Visitants* by Randolph Stow; McPhee Gribble Publishers and Penguin Books Australia for 'Civilisation and its Discontents' from *Postcards from Surfers* by Helen Garner, and for 'Melpo' from *Milk* by Beverley Farmer; Barbara Mobbs for 'The Prodigal Son' and 'Miss Slattery and Her Demon Lover' by Patrick White; Drusilla Modjeska for 'The Emergence of Women Writers since 1975' by Drusilla Modjeska from *Australian Feminist Studies* 4, Autumn 1987; Finola Moorhead for 'The Landscape of the Egg' by Finola Moorhead; Bill Mudie for 'They'll Tell You About Me' by Ian Mudie; Oxford University Press (Australia) for 'Standing, naked, feet apart' from *Late Winter Child* by Vincent Buckley; Oxford University Press (UK) for 'On First Looking into Chapman's Hesiod' from *Collected Poems* by Peter Porter; Penguin Books (Australia) for the extract from *Woman in a Lampshade* by Elizabeth Jolley, for 'From a Bush Log Book' from *State of the Art* by Frank Moorhouse, for 'The Nightshift' from *North Wind* by John Morrison, for 'A Little Demon' from *Ocean of Story* edited by R. G. Geering, and for 'The Words She Types' from *The Man of Slow Feeling* by M. Wilding; Penguin Books Australia Ltd for the extract from *The White Stag of Exile* by Thomas Shapcott; Reed Books Pty Ltd for 'The Great Australian Larrikin' from *The Yarns of Billy Borker* by Frank Hardy, and for 'Bees' from *Altjeringa and Other Aboriginal Poems* by Roland Robinson; Scribe Publications Ptd Ltd for 'Our House' by Lily Brett; Sun Books for the extract from *Tirra Lirra by the River* by Jessica Anderson; Thomas Nelson Australia for the extract from *A Kindness Cup* by Thea Astley; University of Queensland Press for the extract from *Oh Lucky Country* by R. Cappiello (1984), for the extract from *War Crimes* by Peter Carey (1979), for 'Geography III' from *Collected Poems* by Michael Dransfield, edited by R. Hall (1987), for 'Mister Man' from *People ARE Legends* by K. Gilbert (1978), for 'The Space Between' from *Bearded Ladies* by Kate Grenville (1984), for 'Mrs Macintosh' from *Selected Poems* by R. Hall (1975), for 'Hypothesis' from *Tactics* by J. Maiden (1974), for 'The Crab Feast' from *First Things Last* by D. Malouf (1980), for 'A Good Marriage' from *The Home Girls* by Olga Masters (1982), for 'The Tree: Convict Monologue I, III' from *Begin with Walking* by Thomas Shapcott (1972), for 'The Elegy Fires' from *Welcome!: Poems* by Thomas Shapcott (1983), for 'Feliks Skrzynecki' from *Immigrant Chronicle* by P. Skrzynecki (1975), for 'Developing a Wife' from *Selected Poems 1960–1980* by A. Taylor (1982), for 'Lufthansa' from *Under Berlin: New Poems 1988* by John Tranter (1988), for 'Seventh Poem' from 'A Rhapsody of Old Men' from *The Observatory* by Dimitris Tsaloumas (1984), and for 'The Journey' from *The Book of Epigrams* by Dimitris Tsaloumas (1985); Ania Walwicz for 'Wogs' from *Mattoid* by Ania Walwicz and for 'Australia' from *Island in the Sun: An Anthology of Recent Prose* by Ania Walwicz (Sea Cruise Books); Judith Wright for 'Australia's Double Aspect' from *Preoccupations in Australian Poetry* by Judith Wright, Oxford University Press, 1966;

Illustrations: William Hughes for the painting *The Landing of Captain Cook* by William Hughes, 6 October 1985 on the cover and p. 11, © William Hughes; The *Age* for the photograph on p. 75; the cartoon on p. 133 'The Glorious Twenty-Sixth' is from *The Bulletin*, February 1899; the cartoon on p. 168, 'Australia and the Immigrant'; is from *Punch*, 23 April 1923; Peter Lyssiotis and *Arena* for the photograph on p. 213, 'Missiles' from 'Shadows' by Peter Lyssiotis, *Arena* 76, 1986; the cartoon 'Australia Faces the Dawn' on p. 238 is from *The Bulletin*, 2 January 1901; Bruce Petty for the cartoon on p. 292 from the cover of *The Australian Author* 8(2), Autumn-April 1976; Art Gallery of New South Wales for the painting *The Expulsion* by Margaret Preston, 1952, on p. 331; Sydney gouache stencil on black card, 60×48 cm, gift of W. G. Preston 1967; Elizabeth Jolley, *Scripsi* and the State Library of New South Wales for the manuscript on p. 377; National Library of Australia for the photograph on p. 409, 'Goldfields of Reno', O.I. Bell Collection; Art Gallery of South Australia, Adelaide for the painting on p. 463, *The Lovers* by Joy Hester, c1956–8, gouache, ink and oil on paper mounted on composition board, 101.5×63.4 cm, South Australian Government Grant 1972, and for the painting on p. 526, *The Letters* by Emma Minnie Boyd, 1889, oil on canvas, 45.8×30.7 cm, M.J.M. Carter Collection.

INTRODUCTION

To select, to group, to arrange—these are common, perhaps natural, human desires and activities, and without them our minds would become overloaded and anarchic and our ability to understand anything at all would atrophy. Societies too, like individual minds, exercise the same kinds of choosing, discarding and ordering processes. The telling of history or the value placed on cultural beliefs and objects are matters requiring high degrees of selectivity. The comfortable European eighteenth-century notion that one could provide 'A Complete Account of...' anything at all is untenable. We may still cherish the delusion of comprehensiveness, of course, or attempt the impossible, as in the Parliamentary *Hansard* or the *Historical Records*, but such efforts are fated to be imperfect and incomplete.

Selection, whether personal or cultural, is never a once-and-for-ever activity: it is subject to continual revision. One should not think, for instance, that the Arnhem Land songs opening Section B represent some immutable traditional culture. They may be twentieth-century creations or they may be a twentieth-century form of songs which have existed over thousands of years. What is certain is that, like any cultural discourse, they have been subject to change. Even in a relatively simple process such as the selection and arrangement of works to include in this Anthology, many successive stages of change occurred. What is actually printed is, in both its selection and ordering, only one of a multitude of possibilities. This inescapable fact might have been best represented by a set of loose sheets which each reader on a particular occasion could shuffle arbitrarily or rearrange for a specific set of purposes, rather like some French *nouveau roman* or multiple-adventure story. But such a format poses house-keeping problems. The commonest solution is to privilege either chronology or authorship as an organising principle. What we have done instead is twofold: first, we have arranged the material in an order that should provide illumination, delight, and surprise through juxtaposition; and secondly we have provided at the end of this Introduction a few suggestions for creating different personal pathways.

An anthology, the word meaning, originally, a collection of flowers, is a gathering of what one or more people consider worth drawing attention to and preserving. In English-speaking Australia, the first anthologies appeared at the end of the 1840s and in the 1850s. They were endowed with titles like *The Southern Euphrosyne and Australian Miscellany* (a volume that included 'examples of the native aboriginal melodies, put into modern rhythm, and harmonized as solos, quartettes, &c') and *The Australian Souvenir for 1851*. The first anthology to make a retrospective selection from what had been written in Australia was G.B. Barton's *Poets and Prose Writers of New South Wales* (1866). Commissioned for the

Paris Exhibition of 1867 (one of many nineteenth-century international expositions where the Australian colonies exhibited), the volume included work by William Charles Wentworth, J. D. Lang, Charles Harpur, Henry Parkes, D. H. Deniehy, Henry Kendall, Sir Thomas Mitchell, J. L. Michael and a number of others. Barton was eclectic in the genres he included: there were poems, fictional sketches, exploration narratives, newspaper accounts, speeches and historical and biographical material.

This Anthology takes a similarly eclectic approach. It is distinct, then, from those confined to a single genre, typically poetry or the short story, or those that give a privileged position to the 'literary' or 'high cultural' genres of lyric poetry and fiction. All of G. B. Barton's genres will also be found in this Anthology together with some extracts from novels and plays, and rather more emphasis on satiric and comic works.

It also adopts a fairly inclusive and flexible interpretation of 'Australian'. Birth, citizenship or residence are all taken as qualifying an author for inclusion—and even a brief visit to Australia if the text is concerned in some way with the 'being' of Australia or Australianness. The range is, then, from Aboriginal songs translated into English to the writing of those who have only recently arrived in the country.

In every instance an attempt has been made to print the text from as authorised and uncorrupt a source as possible. A debt is thus due to the many previous authors and editors on whose textual judgment reliance has inevitably had to be placed. Where publishing conventions of capitalisation and spelling have changed over the years, preference has been given to the form in which the earliest readers of a text would have seen it, though there has been a regularisation in such matters of punctuation as single and double inverted commas. Where an author uses a mark of ellipsis (...) it has been simply reprinted; where the editors have omitted a passage, it is indicated by ellipsis marks within square brackets [...] or, where one or more stanzas of verse have been omitted, by the use of three vertical full points. Where the original text contained single brief footnotes, these have been printed within square brackets.

The date given at the end of each piece is usually the date of first publication or, where that was uncertain, the date of first publication in volume form. In a few instances the delay between writing and publication was so long that to have given simply the date of publication would have distorted the sense of chronology relative to other items.

Some of the groupings of material (notably Sections A, F and G) draw attention to Australia as a subject—or image or 'construct'. Others are concerned with sub-groups of that broad subject: Aboriginal Australia or Convictism, for instance. Others again draw no particular attention to Australia at all, but are concerned with The Writing Process or with the verbal simulation of relationships between one human being and another. These groupings can be undone and the items regrouped as required with the aid of the material in Alternative Ways of Seeing, at the end of this Introduction. This includes a table of all the items in the chronological order of their publication (or writing, when that is known), so one obvious way of rearranging the contents would be to read them in the order of this table. But a number of other suggestions, involving alternative themes, modes, styles, and genres are also included.

Each Section is introduced by a brief essay that raises some theoretical questions (of both a sociological and a literary kind), explains the basis of selection and arrangement within it, and provides comments on most of the text items. Help with difficulties in the texts can be found in these sectional introductions; by this procedure the texts themselves have been kept free of distracting editorial notes.

The material at the end of the volume includes a chronological table of events in Australian history and literary history, so that it is possible to gain a quick impression of the context in which literary works were written and published. There is also a set of brief biographies of all the authors whose work is represented.

The compilation of this Anthology would not have been possible without the many helpful suggestions and responses of the Contributing Editors. It is with a deep sense of gratitude that we thank them for their unstinting help. This was always conceived as a work that would be usable by a wide range of students and general readers. It was therefore crucial to the enterprise to seek advice on the selection and arrangement of the contents from as wide a group of people as possible. The Contributing Editors were invited to participate in this project because of the variety and extent of their experience as writers, readers, teachers, critics, administrators, reviewers and anthologists, across the range of Australian literary culture. In the first stage of the compilation of the volume they contributed hundreds of items for inclusion, as well as suggesting individual writers and kinds of writing that should be represented. From these the General Editors made a large preliminary selection which was then commented upon by the Contributing Editors; very extensive additions and deletions were then made and further drafts circulated before the General Editors made this final selection. We believe that this has been a rewarding and productive procedure and has resulted in an Anthology of greater diversity and discrimination than could have been the product of our unaided labours. The Contributing Editors provided a multitude of ideas and suggested the remedying of many of the infelicities of earlier drafts. Three of them provided sectional introductions: Ken Stewart (Section C), Sneja Gunew (Section D), Brian Kiernan (Section J). Responsibility for the other sectional introductions, for the final choice of items and for the arrangement of material is, however, ours, and no blame should be attributed to the Contributing Editors.

No undertaking of this kind could be completed without access to the resources of the major Australian public collections of printed books and manuscript material. We are grateful for the helpful suggestions and co-operation of many public and university librarians throughout the country. Our special thanks are due to Ms Margaret O'Hagan, Fryer Librarian in the University of Queensland Libraries who, with her staff, provided consistent and cheerful support for the project.

The University of Queensland, through one of its Humanities Special Project Grants and through support made available by Mr Ron Marks, Head of the Department of English, assisted the Editors in the assembling of the material for this Anthology. It is a pleasure to record our thanks for this invaluable help.

We were fortunate to have the services as a Research Assistant of Ms Shane Rowlands. Her meticulousness, efficiency and ingenuity were matched by her unfailing cheerfulness and forbearance.

It is also a pleasure to record our thanks to the following for their advice and assistance on particular matters: Debra Adelaide, Patricia Barton, Maryanne Dever, Richard Fotheringham, Gün Gencer, Doug Hall, Cliff Hanna, Veronica Kelly, Brian Matthews and Stephen Torre. The untimely death of Barry Andrews prevented him from taking an active part in a project to which he generously contributed enthusiasm and wise counsel during its preliminary stage.

ALTERNATIVE WAYS OF SEEING

Extending the Sections

Most of the Sections in this Anthology have a close relationship to at least one of the others. Section A (Place and People), for example, is closely related to Section F (The Vision Splendid) and Section G (Mapping and Naming). All three are concerned with the interaction between human beings and the land of Australia. One could, for instance, group the extract from Cook's *Account* with Douglas Stewart's 'Terra Australis', Webb's 'Eyre All Alone', Jackey Jackey's account of the death of Kennedy and Randolph Stow's *Visitants*, as texts about exploration—and in some instances texts *of* exploration in language. Or one might group material from these three Sections according to whether an individual item took an optimistic (utopian) or pessimistic (dystopian) view of the human and topographical relationship.

Section B, Living in Aboriginal Australia, offers some writing by Aborigines (or Murris, Kooris, or Noong-ahs), but there are other items by Black Australians in Sections D, F, and K. Similarly, migrant writers whose first language was not English are not confined to Sections D and E, but can be found also in Sections A, G, H, I, and J.

Reordering the Sections

The order that we have adopted is not, as we have already noted, immut—able. Perhaps by explaining its logic we may make it easier for users to read the Anthology in other ways that best suit their own purposes. The first Section takes as its organising principle the significant experience of Australia as a physical and metaphysical place. The three that follow are broadly arranged by subject: Section B by the more particular experience of that place by Aboriginal Australians; Section C by the historical antece-dents of much European-Australian experience, namely the convicts, and by the imaginative legacy of that experience; and Section D by those more distinctively defined by the dominant Australian ethos as 'migrants'. The next three Sections focus more closely on the way in which those (and other) kinds of experience have been rendered into distinctive literary forms, tropes and images. The discursive formations that they have been given all have their own ideological functions: they include the evolution of new forms, languages and styles as the culture (and therefore its arti-culation) is hybridised (Section E); the expression of the sometimes high-nationalist Vision Splendid (Section F); and the more metaphysical privileging of the imagination in the Mapping and Naming of a 'new' country (Section G).

Questions of Cultural Politics are then addressed more explicitly in Section H, and the following Section I, shows how they are often contiguous with certain kinds of literary politics, in which writers reflect and argue about appropriate modes, styles and subjects. The tenth Section, Realism and Romance, illustrates a particular argument about literary form and subject that has been especially persistent and significant in Australia over a long period. The final two Sections, K and L, address more personal concerns and the ways in which they may be written. Person to Person concerns itself with the way in which writers have adapted the forms of writing to interpersonal relations, romantic love, sexual relations and familial ones, while Writing the Self engages with the solipsism which is the subject of so much writing.

It might be just as instructive to consider the Sections in reverse order. Then one might see a sense of writing the world evolve out of concern with the self and with the immediate relationship to other close individuals; a reflection on the act of writing itself could lead to an engagement with the nature of one's cultural environment and the way it constructs itself through writing; and that might lead to an examination of the way in which the experience of groups is reflected or produced and the way in which attempts are made to image the nation in the material that is given in Place and People, The Vision Splendid and Mapping and Naming. One might also read Realism and Romance in conjunction with these Sections, to see how the debate about the way in which the nation is imaged can be seen as a particular argument about writing; or one might put it alongside Convictism to see how that subject has raised those very same generic questions.

Inventing New Groupings

If convictism and the bush seem hackneyed themes, it is possible to construct a grouping concerned with experiences of the shoreline and coastal regions of Australia. It might include Cook's *Account*, the *Djanggawul Song Cycle*, Mudrooroo Narogin's [Colin Johnson's] *Dr Wooreddy*, Keneally's *The Playmaker*, the ballads 'Botany Bay' and 'Moreton Bay', Brennan's 'Each day I see the long ships coming into port', Jean Curlewis' 'Sydney Surfing' and so on.

Various kinds of non-fictional prose are represented in the Anthology. Explorers' accounts, journalistic pieces, cultural commentary and polemic, political writing, literary criticism and history, biography and diary extracts all appear. It would be possible to group items of the same genre, mode, circumstance or purpose together, to make, for instance, a collection of items of political writing or of literary criticism. Alternatively, it would be possible to compare non-fictional prose accounts with fictional or poetic items having a similar purpose. Social criticism and satire, for instance, are not confined to non-fictional prose: Barbara Baynton's fictional 'The Chosen Vessel' might be considered more telling than Henry Lawson's journalistic piece, 'Crime in the Bush'; Les Murray's poem, 'The

Quality of Sprawl', might be considered quite as enlightening as Marcus Clarke's 'The Future Australian Race'; both the Baynton and the Murray could be read alongside the pieces by Anna Couani and Rosa Cappiello, which subvert form as well as subject.

If it is plausible that oppressed or neglected groups tend to express themselves in modes of speech or writing that subvert standard authorised modes, it would be worth looking for the evidence in this Anthology. Are women writers perhaps drawn towards melodrama, particularly in the Gothic mode, because it is subversive of narrative realism and linear logic, or because it represents the dislocation of their own lives? Works by 'Tasma', Rosa Cappiello, Moya Costello, Anna Couani, Gwen Harwood, Elizabeth Jolley, Lesbia Harford, Eve Langley and Dorothy Hewett provide ample material to test the theory.

The Section on The Writing Process offers examples of various non-realistic modes, including surrealism and post-modernism, but other Sections provide examples too. It would, for instance, be instructive to make comparisons between the different uses of irony, or of the vernacular speaking or narrating voice, or of the unreliable narrator. For such re-groupings, much material could be found in the works of Joseph Furphy, Murray Bail, Lily Brett, Ania Walwicz, Π O, Louis Nowra, Moya Costello, Anna Couani, Finola Moorhead, Marion Campbell, Dal Stivens, Peter Carey, Michael Wilding, Frank Moorhouse and Helen Garner.

Comic (or perhaps more precisely comedic) writing is another grouping that can be extracted from the Anthology. Apart from a small number of items that are unintentionally humorous, those deliberately cast in this mode, one that covers a vast range of tones, include Murray Bail's 'Home Ownership', Bruce Dawe's 'Pleasant Sunday Afternoon', Barry Humphries' 'Days of the Week', Patrick White's 'Miss Slattery', Oodgeroo's 'No More Boomerang', Wenz's 'Advice to New Chums', the ballad 'Botany Bay', Lennie Lower's 'Where the Cooler Bars Grow', Frank Hardy's 'The Great Australian Larrikin', Ian Mudie's 'They'll Tell You About Me' and the piece by 'Ern Malley'.

Reading according to place or region is also possible. There are obviously clusters of items about Sydney, but there are also items set in other capital cities, regional cities, the islands of Bass Strait, and—with a notably strong sense of place—the Aboriginal lands of Western Australia and Arnhem Land.

Chronological List of Items

Finally, to move from space to time, it is possible to read in chronological groupings with the aid of the following table of items:

Section A

PLACE AND PEOPLE

'Australia', 'literature' and 'Australian literature' exist as subjects in discourse by virtue of substantial agreement about certain conventions. In order to talk at all we have to begin with some assumptions: assumptions about the general or rough-and-ready meaning of key terms and assumptions about what is worth discussing. While it is obvious that the value judgments of someone who has never heard of Australia will differ from those of someone who is either proud or ashamed of living in Australia, and equally obvious that the value judgments of a dispossessed Aborigine will differ from those of a large white mining or pastoral company, discourse can nevertheless proceed through agreement about the significance (if not the exact meaning or implication) of certain concepts. Geographical concepts such as the land, its features and contents may be referred to; historical concepts such as convictism, colonialism, pastoralism, or the gold rushes; sociological concepts such as urbanisation, racism, ethnic origin or multiculturalism; psychological concepts such as exile, loneliness, renewal and self-discovery; moral concepts such as mateship, endurance and fair play; socio-legal concepts such as equality and democracy; or linguistic and literary concepts such as laconicism, scepticism, the dismantling of expectations and hyperbole or the tall story. Qualities or demands (or, perhaps, inventions) such as these go to make up what is said to be Australian culture, and this culture is assumed to be overt or latent in writing in and about Australia.

Whether these qualities or features exist outside the assertion that they do, or the demand that they should, or outside the images in which they are signified is a matter of substantial cultural debate. Many of the disputants *want* certain features to be considered typical of, or essential to, 'the Australian identity'—because that makes them feel more secure or more powerful. But the demands are in conflict, they change over time, and the strength of support for them waxes and wanes.

'The bush' is a concept that can aptly illustrate such divergences. Marcus Clarke, in his 1876 Preface to Adam Lindsay Gordon's *Poems*, described the 'Australian forests as characterised by 'Weird Melancholy', a phrase quoted by Henry Lawson in the report of his own travels, 'In a Wet Season' in 1892. D. H. Lawrence, writing to Katharine Susannah Prichard in 1922, said that he loved Australia's 'weird, far-away natural beauty', which for him had 'a great fascination, but also a dismal grey terror, underneath'. Jeannie (Mrs Aeneas) Gunn, in *We of the Never-Never*, published in 1908, by which time 'the bush' had almost entirely displaced 'the forest' as the appropriate term, expressed the belief that:

The bush can be cruel at times, and yet, although she may leave us alone with our beloved dead, her very cruelty brings with it a fierce, consoling pain; for out-bush our dead are all our own.

Yet this is not at all the view taken in Harpur's 'A Mid-Summer Noon in the Australian Forest', in Kendall's 'Bell-Birds' or 'The Barcoo', in much of A. B. Paterson or in Hugh McCrae. Nor is it consonant with the painter Tom Roberts' view, expressed in a speech of 1926: 'I would much rather speak of its witchery than its melancholy.' That sense of reverence can also be found resuscitated in the writing of the Jindyworobaks.

Writers and painters project on to the bush, as we all tend to do with all of these concepts, their own natures, demands and needs. It is a favourite European tactic, evident from the very first, and very varied, European reports of the continent of Australia and its inhabitants.

Lieutenant James Cook's *Account* indicates a willingness to believe well of the land that he had almost accidentally encountered. He notes that it is inhabited, speaks of anchoring in Botany Bay opposite 'a small village', is surprised when his landing is met with determined and courageous opposition, and hopes to buy himself into favour with the gift of 'nails, beads, and other trifles'. The nails, quite valuable to Europeans, proved to be of no special interest to 'the natives' (as Cook called them), though this is not something he appears to have anticipated. Cultural, including verbal, communication proved to be a problem. Cook seems to have hoped that Tupia (or Tupaia) might understand the language of the Aborigines. (Tupaia, whose navigational skills Cook much admired, was a priest from Raiatea in the Society Islands.)

Cook presumably had little knowledge of the great antiquity of the culture he observed. Even Mary Gilmore, writing some 150 years later, can summon up only the Greek Heroic Age as a marker by which to date the culture of the Arunta (or Aranda) people as being already ancient. Henry Kingsley, in his novel *Geoffry Hamlyn*, also relies on Old World comparisons for his description: 'A new heaven and a new earth'. This is a cry from the biblical Book of Revelation, and the notion of patriarchs moving on to new pastures with vast herds is conveyed in the Old Testament image of Lot and Abraham. Even Judith Wright, in a poem concerned with her joint heritage from Europe and Australia, refers to an Australian native tree as 'Gothic'—perhaps because of the irregularity of its branches.

The German traveller, Friedrich Gerstaecker, comments on how 'the bush' means different geographical regions to the city-dweller and the squatter. For him it is essentially the semi-arid mallee scrub.

For Henry Lawson the bush is almost a state of mind—and a depressed and depressing one at that. It is a breeding place for tyranny, madness, and crime. Its 'awful monotony' breaks down all ties of respectability, loyalty, and mateship; in the concluding words of his story, 'The Bush Undertaker', it is 'the nurse and tutor of eccentric minds'.

Something of the same mood is evident in Vance Palmer's early sketch, 'The Hermit'. But the narrator exaggerates the mood. He is miserable and wants to project that mood on to Joe and his home. What he actually conveys is, in fact, largely at odds with the gloomy interpretation he places on it.

The moral disapproval evident in Vance Palmer's story is derived from a feeling about the bush. In Chapter 9 of Catherine Helen Spence's novel, *Clara Morison*, the moral disapproval stems from a feeling about an historical event, the finding of gold. Margaret Elliot, Clara Morison's cousin, is full of reproof for Mrs Tubbins' behaviour, which she attributes to the evil effects of sudden wealth. Everything the Tubbins family touches they degrade in Margaret's (and the narrator's) view. The piano is a good one, but ruined; the music (a popular song by Charles William Glover and part of an early opera by Rossini) is good but useless; the children are indulged and spoilt; their secular and spiritual education is neglected; and avarice affects them all.

Caroline Atkinson's sentimental novel, *Cowanda*, has a similarly high moral tone. Like Catherine Spence's work, the suggestion is that human goodness will not find itself handicapped in Australia, a country in which opportunities for good and evil are equally to hand.

In Patrick White's *Voss*, the erratic central character is always apt to project his feelings onto the landscape. In this extract, Voss, in the early stages of his doomed effort to cross the continent, is travelling from Newcastle to Mr Sanderson's station at Rhine Towers. For him 'It was a gentle, healing landscape', one that did not, like some rougher territories, drive him in upon himself. As the narrator says, his transitory illusions at this moment made him 'ready to believe that all men were good'. But by the time, a few days later, that they reach Rhine Towers, Voss detects tragedy and sin, and the young poet, Frank Le Mesurier, also sees that the brief moment of Edenic innocence is broken.

Many Australian works depict white pioneers (such as those in *Geoffry Hamlyn* or in Mary Durack's 1959 family history, *Kings in Grass Castles*) in heroic terms. They are said to combine adventurousness and daring; to battle drought, flood, and fire; and to raise worthy successors. Henry Lawson's stories present a different view of the squatter class, the perspective of the small selector or the itinerant worker. Robin Boyd's very influential sociological study of the city and suburbia, *The Australian Ugliness*, turns 'pioneer', 'progress', and 'development' into pejorative terms. He too makes a psychological projection onto the Australian landscape: it was 'made in one of nature's more relaxed, even casual, moods'. For him that is a virtue, compared with the obsessive neatness of the European landscape.

The Australian Ugliness, first published in 1960, may well have had an influence on some of the landscaping ideas espoused in George Johnston's novel, *My Brother Jack* (1964). In the extract given here the narrator, David Meredith, has trouble, shortly after the end of the 1939-45 war, in buying a gum tree, still an unfashionable acquisition for the suburban block.

Hostility to native trees is even more overt in Thomas Shapcott's poem, 'The Trees: A Convict Monologue'. The convict habitué of the 'lovely broken-mouthed slut city' is unnerved by the bush, and vows to 'cut down every tree'. There could hardly be a more striking contrast between this attitude and that in Harpur's 'A Mid-Summer Noon in the Australian Forest' or Kendall's 'Bell-Birds'.

Like the others in this group of poems about the poet and nature, Judith Wright's 'Eyes' distinguishes between the human being and nature. The fox has his ways that the human being cannot fathom, but neither fox nor pea-flower can match the human being's inward eyes that relate chicken-feathers to fox to the need for a gun.

'Eyes' is followed by a group of poems about suburbia, beginning with part of Vincent Buckley's 'Golden Builders' sequence. The poet is wandering among the industrial streets interspersed with garden squares on the city side of the University of Melbourne. Some are named after British lords. This fact, together with the sight of an old nineteenth-century Sunday-School building and his sense of evening, causes the poet to meditate on whether there is in this environment any sense of Christianity, any presence of the Lord Christ.

Murray Bail's story, 'Home Ownership', concerns a different kind of diminishing presence. Parker retreats into his home, the home diminishes into a collapsed pile. So much for development and progress; so much for the ultimate controlling effect of humanity on the environment.

Bruce Dawe's 'Pleasant Sunday Afternoon', like many of Patrick White's stories (though not 'Miss Slattery') is set neither in suburbia nor in the countryside, but on the outskirts of a city or town. A barely-educated man, with an untidy house and unruly children (reminiscent of the Tubbinses in the extract from *Clara Morison*), is visited on a Sunday afternoon by an encyclopaedia salesman. One of the children, Stewart, seems to vomit over the pages. Another, Graham, defecates on the floor and uses the encyclopaedia to wipe himself. In the end the defeated salesman bolts from the disaster, leaving his ruined set of encyclopaedias behind. Packaged learning and the Australian sprawl have found no common ground.

Satire, particularly when it is in a good-natured mode, is often ambivalent in its values. Just as one can feel sympathy both for the encyclopaedia salesman and for Eth and her husband, so in Barry Humphries' Sandy Stone monologue one can feel sympathy for the regulated life of Sandy and Beryl and at the same time enjoy the satire on a mindless form of Australian behaviour.

White's story, 'Miss Slattery and her Demon Lover', raises questions about Australian culture even more sharply. What is civilisation? What is civilised behaviour? To what extent is it a matter of relativity or local convention? Is wit, as distinct from the less intellectual forms of humour, evident in Australian society? Is Australian society provincial, and if so in what sense? Are Australians capable of passionate and theatrical forms of sex? These are the questions raised in the story. In the end Miss Slattery emancipates herself from the insidious and distinctly European power of Tibby Szabo, but the questions remain unresolved. And they remain relevant to many of the subsequent pieces in this Anthology.

Ken Goodwin/Alan Lawson

James Cook
from AN ACCOUNT OF A ROUND VOYAGE OF THE ENDEAVOUR IN THE YEAR MDCCLXX ALONG THE EAST COAST OF AUSTRALIA

1770 April

Friday 20

We brought to for the night, and at four in the morning made sail along shore to the northward. At six, the norther-most land in sight bore NNW and we were at this time about four leagues from the shore. At noon, we were in latitude 36°51'S longitude 209°53'W and about three leagues distant from the shore. The weather being clear, gave us a good view of the country, which has a very pleasing appearance: it is of a moderate height, diversified by hills and vallies, ridges and plains, interspersed with a few lawns of no great extent, but in general covered with wood: the ascent of the hills and ridges is gentle, and the summits are not high. We continued to sail along the shore to the northward, with a southerly wind, and in the afternoon we saw smoke in several places, by which we knew the country to be inhabited. [. . .]

Saturday 28

After dinner the boats were manned, and we set out from the ship, having Tupia of our party. We intended to land where we saw the people, and began to hope that as they had so little regarded the ship's coming into the bay, they would as little regard our coming on shore: in this, however, we were disappointed; for as soon as we approached the rocks, two of the men came down upon them to dispute our landing, and the rest ran away. Each of the two champions was armed with a lance about ten feet long, and a short stick which he seemed to handle as if it was a machine to assist him in managing or throwing the lance: they called to us in a very loud tone, and in a harsh dissonant language, of which neither we nor Tupia understood a single word: they brandished their weapons, and seemed resolved to defend their coast to the uttermost, though they were but two, and we were forty. I could not but admire their courage, and being very unwilling that hostilities should commence with such inequality of force between us, I ordered the boat to lie upon her oars: we then parlied by signs for about a quarter of an hour, and to bespeak their good-will, I threw them nails, beads, and other trifles, which they took up and seemed to be well pleased with. I then made signs that I wanted water, and, by all the means that I could devise, endeavoured to convince them that we would do them no harm: they now waved to us, and I was willing to interpret it as an invitation; but upon our putting the boat in, they came again to oppose us. One appeared to be a youth about nineteen or twenty, and the other a man of middle age: as I had now no other resource I fired a musket between them. Upon the report, the youngest dropped a bundle of lances upon the rock, but recollecting himself in an instant he snatched them up again with great haste: a stone was then thrown at us, upon which I ordered a musket to be fired with small shot, which struck the eldest upon the legs, and he immediately ran to one of the houses, which was distant about an hundred yards: I now hoped that our contest was over, and we immediately landed; but we had scarcely left the boat when he returned, and we then perceived that he had left the rock only to fetch a shield or target for his defence. As soon as he came up, he threw a lance at us, and his comrade another; they fell where we stood thickest, but happily hurt nobody. A third musquet with small shot was then fired at them, upon which one of them threw another lance, and both immediately ran away: if we had pursued, we might probably have taken one of them; but Mr Banks suggesting that the lances might be poisoned, I thought it not prudent to venture into the woods.

(1773)

Mary Gilmore
AUSTRALIA

I

There was great beauty in the names her people called her,
Shaping to patterns of sound the form of their words;
They wove to measure of speech the cry of the bird,
And the voices that rose from the reeds of the cowal.

There, when the trumpeting frog boomed forth in the night,   5
Gobbagumbalin! he said, *Gobbagumbalin!*
And even as Aristophanes heard, in the far-off deeps
Of his Grecian marshes, the frogs, so we in that word.
'*Gobbagumbalin! ... Gobbagumbalin! ...*'
Harken, and measure the sound!   10

II

Mark where, fallen, the tribes move in the shadow;
Dark are the silent places where Arunta walks—
Dark as the dim valleys of Hades where stalk,
Grey-shaped, the Gods and heroes of the Greeks.
These were the young; for even then Arunta was old.   15
Very old was Arunta when Alexander wept;
Old, old was Arunta when over Bethlehem
Was seen the star that told the birth of Christ;
Old, old was Arunta when upward from the deep
Was swung the hammer-symbol of Poseidon.   20
Troy rose and fell, but Arunta lived on.
Then was Arunta put out in a night.

(1932)

Wurleys: gunyahs, or shelter places
Moolpa: the spoonbill
Cowal: a coolamon-hole or small lake
Weenyah: 'whither'
Arunta: a tribe of Central Australia, the name being used here as a general designation for reasons of the drama and poetry

Henry Kingsley
THE RECOLLECTIONS OF GEOFFRY HAMLYN

from CHAPTER 18

THE FIRST PUFF OF THE SOUTH WIND

A new heaven and a new earth! Tier beyond tier, height above height, the great wooded ranges go rolling away westward, till on the lofty sky-line they are crowned with a gleam of everlasting snow. To the eastward they sink down, breaking into isolated forest-fringed peaks, and rock-crowned eminences, till with rapidly straightening lines they fade into the broad grey plains, beyond which the Southern Ocean is visible by the white sea-haze upon the sky.

All creation is new and strange. The trees, surpassing in size the largest English oaks, are of a species we have never seen before. The graceful shrubs, the bright-coloured flowers, ay, the very grass itself, are of species unknown in Europe; while flaming lories and brilliant parroquets fly whistling, not unmusically, through the gloomy forest, and over head in the higher fields of air, still lit up by the last rays of the sun, countless cockatoos wheel and scream in noisy joy, as we may see the gulls do about an English headland.

To the northward a great glen, sinking suddenly from the saddle on which we stand, stretches away in long vista, until it joins a broader valley, through which we can dimly see a full-fed river winding along in gleaming reaches, through level meadow land, interspersed with clumps of timber.

We are in Australia. Three hundred and fifty miles south of Sydney, on the great watershed which divides the Belloury from the Maryburnong, since better known as the Snowy-river of Gippsland.

As the sun was going down on the scene I have been describing, James Stockbridge and I, Geoffry Hamlyn, reined up our horses on the ridge above-mentioned, and gazed down the long gully which lay stretched at our feet. Only the tallest trees stood with their higher boughs glowing with the gold of the departing day, and we stood undetermined which route to pursue, and half inclined to camp at the next waterhole we should see. We had lost some cattle, and among others a valuable imported bull, which we were very anxious to recover. For five days we had been passing on from run to run, making inquiries without success, and were now fifty long miles from home in a southerly direction. We were beyond the bounds of all settlement; the last station we had been at was twenty miles to the north of us, and the occupiers of it, as they had told us the night before, had only taken up their country about ten weeks, and were as yet the furthest pioneers to the southward.

At this time Stockbridge and I had been settled in our new home about two years, and were beginning to get comfortable and contented. We had had but little trouble with the blacks, and having taken possession of a fine piece of country, were flourishing and well to do.

We had never heard from home but once, and that was from Tom Troubridge, soon after our departure, telling us that if we succeeded he should follow, for that the old place seemed changed now we were gone. We had neither of us left any near relations behind us, and already we began to think that we were cut off for ever from old acquaintances and associations, and were beginning to be resigned to it.

Let us return to where he and I were standing alone in the forest. I dismounted to set right some strap or another, and, instead of getting on my horse again at once, stood leaning against him, looking at the prospect, glad to ease my legs for a time, for they were cramped with many hours' riding.

Stockbridge sat in his saddle immoveable and silent as a statue, and when I looked in his face I saw that his heart had travelled further than his eye could reach, and that he was looking far beyond the horizon that bounded his earthly vision, away to the pleasant old home which was home to us no longer.

'Jim,' said I, 'I wonder what is going on at Drumston now?'

'I wonder,' he said softly.

A pause.

Below us, in the valley, a mob of jackasses [Dacelo Gigantea] were shouting and laughing uproariously, and a magpie was chanting his noble vesper hymn from a lofty tree.

'Jim,' I began again, 'do you ever think of poor little Mary now?'

'Yes, old boy, I do,' he replied; 'I can't help it; I was thinking of her then—I am always thinking of her, and, what's more, I always shall be. Don't think me a fool, old friend, but I love that girl as well now as ever I did. I wonder if she has married that fellow Hawker?'

'I fear there is but little doubt of it,' I said; 'try to forget her, James. Get in a rage with her, and. be proud about it; you'll make all your life unhappy if you don't.'

He laughed. 'That's all very well, Jeff, but it's easier said than done.— Do you hear that? There are cattle down the gully.'

There was some noise in the air, beside the evening rustle of the south wind among the tree-tops. Now it sounded like a far-off hubbub of waters, now swelled up harmonious, like the booming of cathedral bells across some rich old English valley on a still summer's afternoon.

'There are cattle down there, certainly,' I said, 'and a very large number of them; they are not ours, depend upon it: there are men with them, too, or they would not make so much noise. Can it be the blacks driving them off from the strangers we stayed with last night, do you think? If so, we had best look out for ourselves.'

'Blacks could hardly manage such a large mob as there are there,' said James. 'I'll tell you what I think it is, old Jeff; it's some new chums going to cross the watershed, and look for new country to the south. If so, let us go down and meet them: they will camp down by the river yonder.'

James was right. All doubt about what the new comers were was solved before we reached the river, for we could hear the rapid detonation of the stock-whips loud above the lowing of the cattle; so we sat and watched them debouche from the forest into the broad river meadows in the gathering gloom: saw the scene so venerable and ancient, so seldom seen in the Old World—the patriarchs moving into the desert with all their wealth, to find a new pasture-ground. A simple primitive action, the first and simplest act of colonization, yet producing such great results on the history of the world, as did the parting of Lot and Abraham in times gone by.

First came the cattle lowing loudly, some trying to stop and graze on the rich pasture after their long day's travel, some heading noisily towards the river, now beginning to steam with the rising evening mist. Now a lordly bull, followed closely by two favourite heifers, tries to take matters into his own hands, and cut out a route for himself, but is soon driven ignominiously back in a lumbering gallop by a quick-eyed stockman. Now a silly calf takes it into his head to go for a small excursion up the range, followed, of course, by his doting mother, and has to be headed in again, not without muttered wrath and lowerings of the head from madame. Behind the cattle come horsemen, some six or seven in number, and last, four drays, bearing the household goods, come crawling up the pass.

We had time to notice that there were women on the foremost dray, when it became evident that the party intended camping in a turn of the river just below. One man kicked his feet out of the stirrups, and sitting loosely in his saddle, prepared to watch the cattle for the first few hours till he was relieved. Another lit a fire against a fallen tree, and while the bullock-drivers were busy unyoking their beasts, and the women were clambering from the dray, two of the horsemen separated from the others, and came forward to meet us.

Both of them I saw were men of vast stature. One rode upright, with a military seat, while his companion had his feet out of his stirrups, and rode loosely, as if tired with his journey. Further than this, I could distinguish nothing in the darkening twilight; but, looking at James, I saw that he was eagerly scanning the strangers, with elevated eyebrow and opened lips. Ere I could speak to him, he had dashed forward with a shout, and when I came up with him, wondering, I found myself shaking hands, talking and laughing, everything in fact short of crying, with Major Buckley and Thomas Troubridge.

'Range up alongside here, Jeff, you rascal,' said Tom, 'and let me get a fair hug at you. What do you think of this for a lark; eh?—to meet you out here, all promiscuous, in the forest, like Prince Arthur! We could not go out of our way to see you, though we knew where you were located, for we must hurry on and get a piece of country we have been told of on the next river. We are going to settle down close by you, you see. We'll make a new Drumston in the wilderness.'

'This is a happy meeting, indeed, old Tom,' I said, as we rode towards the drays, after the Major and James. 'We shall have happy times, now we have got some of our old friends round us. Who is come with you? How is Mrs Buckley?'

'Mrs Buckley is as well as ever, and as handsome. My pretty little cousin, Mary Hawker, and old Miss Thornton are with us; the poor old Vicar is dead.'

'Mary Hawker with you?' I said. 'And her husband, Tom?'

'Hardly, old friend. We travel in better company,' said he. 'George Hawker is transported for life.'

'Alas, poor Mary!' I answered. 'And what for?'

Coining,' he answered. 'I'll tell you the story another time. To-night let us rejoice.'

I could not but watch James, who was riding before us, to see how he would take this news. The Major, I saw, was telling him all about it, but James seemed to take it quite quietly, only nodding his head as the other went on. I knew how he would feel for his old love, and I turned and said to Troubridge,—

'Jim will be very sorry to hear of this. I wish she had married him.'

'That's what we all say,' said Tom. 'I am sorry for poor Jim. He is about the best man I know, take him all in all. If that fellow were to die, she might have him yet, Hamlyn.'

We reached the drays. There sat Mrs Buckley on a log, a noble, happy matron, laughing at her son as he toddled about, busy gathering sticks for the fire. Beside her was Mary, paler and older-looking than when we had seen her last, with her child upon her lap, looking sad and worn. But a sadder sight for me was old Miss Thornton, silent and frightened, glancing uneasily round, as though expecting some new horror. No child for her to cling to and strive for. No husband to watch for and anticipate every wish. A poor, timid, nervous old maid, thrown adrift in her old age upon a strange sea of anomalous wonders. Every old favourite prejudice torn up by the roots. All old formulas of life scattered to the winds!

She told me in confidence that evening that she had been in sad trouble all day. At dinner-time some naked blacks had come up to the dray, and had frightened and shocked her. Then the dray had been nearly upset, and her hat crushed among the trees. A favourite and precious bag, which never left her, had been dropped in the water; and her Prayer-book, a parting gift from Lady Kate, had been utterly spoiled. A hundred petty annoyances and griefs, which Mary barely remarked, and which brave Mrs Buckley, in her strong determination of following her lord to the ends of the earth, and of being as much help and as little incumbrance to him as she could, had laughed at, were to her great misfortunes. Why, the very fact, as she told me, of sitting on the top of a swinging jolting dray was enough to keep her in a continual state of agony and terror, so that when she alit at night, and sat down, she could not help weeping silently, dreading lest any one should see her.

Suddenly, Mary was by her side, kneeling down.

'Aunt,' she said, 'dearest aunt, don't break down. It is all my wicked fault. You will break my heart, auntie dear, if you cry like that. Why did ever I bring you on this hideous journey?'

'How could I leave you in your trouble, my love?' said Miss Thornton. You did right to come, my love. We are among old friends. We have come too far for trouble to reach us. We shall soon have a happy home again now, and all will be well.'

(1859)

Judith Wright
FOR NEW ENGLAND

Your trees, the homesick and the swarthy native,
blow all one way to me, this southern weather
that smells of early snow:
                        And I remember
The house closed in with sycamore and chestnut   5
fighting the foreign wind.
Here I will stay, she said; be done with the black north,
the harsh horizon rimmed with drought.—
Planted the island there and drew it round her.
Therefore I find in me the double tree.

And therefore I, deserted on the wharves,   10
have watched the ships fan out their web of streamers
(thinking of how the lookout at the heads
leaned out towards the dubious rims of sea
to find a sail blown over like a message
you are not forgotten),   15
or followed through the taproot of the poplar...
But look, oh look, the Gothic tree's on fire
with blown galahs, and fuming with wild wings.

The hard inquiring wind strikes to the bone
and whines division.
                        Many roads meet here   20
in me, the traveller and the ways I travel.
All the hills' gathered waters feed my seas
who am the swimmer and the mountain river;
and the long slopes' concurrence is my flesh
who am the gazer and the land I stare on;   25
and dogwood blooms within my winter blood,
and orchards fruit in me and need no season.
But sullenly the jealous bones recall
what other earth is shaped and hoarded in them.

Where's home, Ulysses? Cuckolded by lewd time   30
he never found again the girl he sailed from,
but at his fireside met the islands waiting
and died there, twice a stranger.
                        Wind, blow through me
till the nostalgic candles of laburnum
fuse with the dogwood in a single flame   35
to touch alight these sapless memories.
Then will my land turn sweetly from the plough
and all my pastures rise as green as spring.

                                            (1944)

Frederick (Friedrich) Gerstaecker
THE TWO CONVICTS

from CHAPTER 4

THE BUSH

The newly-arrived immigrant in the United States of North America is frequently tantalized with the 'far west', which he seeks to reach by railway, steamer, or on horseback, still following the sun. The farther west he goes, the more the 'far west' seems to retire before him; and this is the case even in the endless forests west of the Mississippi. In the marshes, where no trace is seen but that of the hunter and the game he is pursuing, he still says he is going *to the west*, because bears are getting scarce, and buffaloes may be classed among the natural curiosities of the locality.

Exactly the same kind of thing happens to the newly-arrived stranger in the Australian *bush*, although he need not go so far in search of it. The inhabitants of Sydney, or of one of the other seaports, are apt to denominate whatever is situated beyond the precincts of their townships as *bush*. But the traveller soon discovers, as he journeys onward, that it lies farther off; and at the stations in the wildest parts of the interior, the squatters do not consider whatever is within the precincts of their fences or roads—that is to say, cart-tracks—to be bush. Beyond that boundary, at least, they cannot deny that it exists. There, indeed, commences that dreary solitude of sand and malley-bushes, prickly grass, and salt-bush, and whatever may be the names of the monstrosities of Australian vegetation.

Vast, fearfully vast and endless distances stretch out in hills and plains; but without the pleasant and definite character usually imparted to a country by undulating scenery. Not a drop of water flows through these wastes; no clear brook bubbles along the valleys, offering to the hunter or wanderer a fixed and definite course which he can follow as a guide out of these wastes. As the waves of the sea, to which the word of the Almighty has assigned their place, spread out in all directions, so, for hundreds of miles, do the malley-bushes extend over desert salt tracts, upon which even the native blacks dare not venture. Heat, and a fine, salt, sandy dust, threaten to deprive the traveller of his sight; and no water is to be found to save the exhausted wanderer from a miserable death. With camels it might, *perhaps*, be possible to penetrate for some distance into this desert; but, under existing circumstances, the attempt would be useless, and such experiments have already led to a sacrifice of many lives. If some habitable oasis does exist in the interior, it could scarcely be turned to any account, even if once reached. It must certainly be unfit for cultivation. The hot wind which blows from the interior is sufficient to burn up all vegetation of the distant colonies, over which it passes with its withering breath: and much less could its processes go on under its influence, in spite of any amount of labour or any sacrifice.

(1857)

Henry Lawson
CRIME IN THE BUSH

The average city man's ignorance concerning the nearer bush—to say nothing of 'Out Back'—and the human life therein, is greater even than the average new-chum's, for the new-chum usually takes pains to collect information concerning the land of his exile, adoption or hope. To the city mind the drovers, the shearers, the station hands, the 'cockies' or farmers, the teamsters and even the diggers, all belong to one and the same class, and are accepted in the street under the general term of 'bushies'—and no questions asked. The city mind is too much occupied by the board-and-lodging or rent problems, etc., to have any but the vaguest ideas concerning the unique conditions of the life that lies beyond the cities. And, in return, the Sydney or Melbourne man is regarded out back as a jackeroo or new-chum—little or no distinction being made between the Australian-born 'green-hand' and the newly-arrived cockney; which is just. But it is with the farmer or 'cockie' class that the writer is here chiefly concerned, for it is mostly in the so-called 'settled' districts that are committed the crimes which seem so brutally senseless or motiveless to city people.

The shearer is a social animal at his worst; he is often a city bushman—*i.e.*, a man who has been through and round and between the provinces by rail and boat. Not unfrequently he is an English public school man and a man of the world; so even the veriest out-back bushie, whose metropolis is Bourke, is brought in touch with outside civilisation. But there are hundreds of out-of-the-way places in the nearer bush of Australia—hidden away in unheard-of 'pockets' in the ranges; on barren creeks (abandoned by pioneering farmers and pastoralists 'moving up country' half a century ago); up at the ends of long, dark gullies, and away out on God-forsaken 'box', native-apple, or stringy-bark flats—where families live for generations in mental darkness almost inconceivable in this enlightened age and country. They are often in a worse condition mentally than savages to the manner born; for natural savages have a social law, a social intercourse—perhaps more or less inadequate, but infinitely better than none at all. Some of these families live from one year's end to another without seeing a face except the face of somebody of their own class, and that of an occasional stranger whose character or sanity must at least be doubtful, to explain his presence in such places. Some of these families are descended from a convict of the worst type on one side or the other, perhaps on both; and, if not born criminals, are trained in shady ways from childhood. Conceived and bred under the shadow of exile, hardship or 'trouble', the sullen, brooding spirit which enwraps their lonely bush-buried homes will carry further their moral degradation. You may sometimes see a dray or spring-cart, of antiquated pattern, dragging wearily and unnoticed into the 'township', and containing a woman, haggard and spiritless-looking, or hard and vicious-faced—or else a sullen, brooding man—who sells produce for tea, flour, and sugar, and goes out again within the hour, without, perhaps, having exchanged half-a-dozen words with anyone. This is the only hint conveyed to the outer fringe of God's country—and wasted on apathetic neighbours—of the existence of such a people.

These places need to be humanised. There are things done in the bush (where large families, and sometimes several large families, pig together in ignorance in badly partitioned huts) known well to neighbours; or to school-teachers—mere lads, going through their martyrdom in such places—and to girl-teachers too, God forgive us!—or even to the police; things which would make a strong man shudder. Clean-minded people shrink from admitting the existence of such things, until one, bolder than the rest, and with the certainty of having his or her good name connected with, perhaps, one of the dirtiest cases known to police annals, speaks up for the sake of outraged nature and reason, and 'horrifies' Australia. But too often the informant is one of the brooding, unhealthy-minded ruck who speaks up only from motives of envy or revenge.

We want light on these places. We have the crime of the Dederers—the two brothers who killed their father and burned the body as they would have burned a log, and yet seemed quite unconscious of having done anything out of the common. To those who know the conditions under which many families like the Dederers exist in Australia, their crime is neither inexplicable nor particularly astounding. The Dederers, if I remember rightly, were reported as never having been even to the nearest 'township' in their dark lives. No doubt they were incapable of expressing, in any sort of language, bush or otherwise, what they felt; if, indeed, they felt anything.

Such dark ignorance is especially dangerous because it is ape-like in its 'emotions', in its likes and dislikes. There are families in the bush with the male members of whom an intelligent and experienced bushman would never trust himself alone—if he had reason to be satisfied with the natural shape of the back of his head; nor yet with the female members—if he valued his neck and the *post mortem* memory of him. You might be mates with a man in the bush for months, and be under the impression that you are on the best of terms with him, or even fancy that he has a decided liking for you, and yet he might brood over some fancied slight or injury—something you have said or done, or haven't said or done— anything, in fact, that might suggest itself to an ignorant, morose, and vindictive nature—until his alleged mind is in such a diseased condition that he is capable of turning on you any moment of the day or night and doing you to death.

So the respectable farmer—too outspoken and careless, perhaps, but good-hearted, and never dreaming of the existence of an enemy—turning to slumber again after the 'cock-crow' hitch in his sleep, hears a furtive whistle and the clatter of retreating hoofs on slanting sliprails and thinks it is some over-late or early neighbours passing through; but starts wide enough awake next time to see the glare, sniff the smoke, and hear the roar and crackle of fire, and, rushing out, white-faced and with heart standing still, finds a shed or stack—the stack of unthreshed wheat, perhaps—in flames. The crime of arson used to be very, very common in Australia—and no 'land laws' or 'wrongs of Ireland' to explain its prevalence. Such malice is terrifying to those who have seen what it is capable of. You never know when you are safe, no matter how carefully you guard your words, looks, or actions; and the only remedy—for the application of which the law would promptly hang you—would be to sit up nights with a gun with a chalked sight, until you get a glimpse of your ape-minded and unprovoked enemy, and then carefully shoot him.

There are places in Australia where the existence of the evil eye and of witches is believed in; and where national, religious, and clan hatreds, which perhaps have died out in the old-world countries from which they came, are preserved in their original intensity; where is all the ignorant suspicion and distrust of a half-savage peasantry. The police, whose duty it is to collect returns for harmless agricultural statistics, can tell you of the difficulty they experience—and not in such out-of-the-way localities either—and of the obstacles thrown in their way when trying to obtain the barest reliable information. 'Experienced great difficulty in obtaining information from landholders'; 'Declines to supply necessary information'; 'Still refuses', etc., are common on the margins and 'remark' spaces of returned and re-returned schedule-forms. Perhaps the cruellest of all the bad sights of the bush is the case of the child born to a family with which it has nothing in common mentally (possibly physically)—the 'throw-back' to original and better stock—whose bright mind is slowly but surely warped to madness by the conditions of life under which the individual is expected to be contented and happy. Such warped natures are often responsible for the worst sexual crimes. There are brutally selfish parents in the bush who regard and work their children as slaves—and worse. Any experienced bush school-teacher could bear me out in this, with heart-rending stories of child slavery and ill-treatment almost past belief. I remember the case of a boy who attended night-school with me for a few months in the bush. His parents sent him under pressure of 'public opinion'. He had to work from daylight until after dark, and do the work of a man—or be starved and beaten to it. He was nineteen, and an idiot. But some people said that he was only an adopted son.

Democractic Maoriland, with its natural and geographical advantages over Australia, is yet not free from the dark spot I refer to. I have known three white children at a Maori (native) school who belonged to a family of (originally) seventeen children. Two or three of the family were alleged to be the children of the eldest unmarried daughter. Of the three who attended school, two girls and a boy, the boy was over fourteen; the girls eight and nine. The boy was ignorant even of the existence of an alphabet. He had the face of a weazened, vicious little old man; and a good deal of the nature. The girls' faces were little masks of what their mother's might have been were she twenty or thirty years older. Both parents looked younger and fresher than the children. Boy and girls rose at daylight, cooked their parents' breakfast (bacon, eggs, etc.), carried it in to them, had a meal of bread and fat, and, when necessary, went into the bush to cut and get together a load of firewood. And the girls were eight and nine. The boy's physical development was naturally abnormal, but his head didn't seem to belong to his body. Sons can be over-worked, starved, stunted mentally, and otherwise cruelly treated to such an extent that they are capable of turning upon and killing a brutish parent—just as savage slaves will, when they get the chance, kill their savage masters.

Then there is the unprovoked, unpremeditated, passionless, and almost inexplicable bush murder, when two mates have lived together in the bush for years, until they can pass days and weeks without exchanging a word, or noticing anything unusual in the circumstance—till the shadow of the over-hanging, brooding ridge, or the awful monotony of the horizonless plain, deadens and darkens the mind of one so that the very presence of his mate, perhaps, becomes a constant source of vague but haunting irritation. Then, one day, being behind the other with an axe or an adze to his hand, he suddenly, but dispassionately, smashes his skull, and is afterwards utterly unable to account for his action except by the muttered explanations that he 'had to do it', or 'something made me do it'. Bush loneliness has the same sort of influence on the blackfellow alone with whites—as instance the latest reported crime committed by a blackfellow, who afterwards expressed sorrow for killing the 'poor old man', but couldn't understand why he did it—unless it was because the white man, having stooped to drink, was in 'such a good position for killing'.

Such crimes as those just instanced, and worse, might be described as the ultimate result of a craving for variety—for something better or brighter, perhaps, but, anyway, something *different*—the protest of the outraged nature of the black or white savage against the—to him—unnatural conditions.

Respectability only intensifies the awful monotony of these wretched bush townships—till the women are forced to watch for dirt and holes in a neighbour's washing hung out on the line, and men to gossip and make mischief like women. Shortcomings in a neighbour are talked about and exaggerated—and invented. Even a tragedy is secretly welcomed—notwithstanding the fact that the whole community is supposed, in double-column head-lines, to be horrified. Careless remarks are caught up, disturbed, and magnified. No respectable girl can leave the township on an innocent visit without something discreditable being discovered to be connected with her departure from the wretched hole. City spielers attach themselves to local pubs, and prey with little or no disguise on idiotic cheque-men; bush larrikins—who are becoming more contemptible and cowardly than their city prototypes—openly boast of their 'successes', and give the girl's name. And both classes are accepted as commonplace—the community never dreams of giving them an hour's start to get out of reach of *men*, or stand the penalty.

Then there is the miserable bush feud which arises (perhaps started generations ago—the original cause forgotten) over a stray bull, a party fence, a girl, a practical joke, a misunderstanding or a fancied slight—anything or nothing; and is brooded over by men who have little else to think about in the brooding bush. There is the threat to 'pull yer' and have satisfaction—the miserable court case and cross action brought on the paltriest pretences that ever merited the disgust of a magistrate—intensifying hatreds to a murderous degree. And 'friends' aid and abet and fan the hell-fire in men's hearts, till at last birth is given to the spirit that sneaks out after dark and cuts a neighbour's wire-fences, or before daylight and stands a gate ajar, or softly lets down the rails that a neighbour's own cattle may get into his crop or garden, destroying the result of months of weary toil and taking the food out of his children's mouths. The spirit that shoots or hamstrings horses grazing under the starlight; that sets a match to stack or shed.

Mischief breeds mischief; malice, malice; and the tongues of the local hags applaud and chorus, and damn and exaggerate and lie, until the wretched hole is ripe for a 'horror'. Then the Horror comes.

(1897)

'Steele Rudd' (Arthur Hoey Davis)
CRANKY JACK

It was early in the day. Traveller after traveller was trudging by Shingle Hut. One who carried no swag halted at the rails and came in. He asked Dad for a job. 'I dunno,' Dad answered—'what wages would you want?' The man said he wouldn't want any. Dad engaged him at once.

And *such* a man! Tall, bony, heavy-jawed, shaven with a reaping-hook, apparently. He had a thick crop of black hair—shaggy, unkempt, and full of grease, grass, and fragments of dry gum-leaves. On his head were two old felt hats—one sewn inside the other. On his back a shirt made from a piece of blue blanket, with white cotton stitches striding up and down it like lines of fencing. His trousers were gloom itself; they were a problem, and bore reliable evidence of his industry. No ordinary person would consider himself out of work while in them. And the new-comer was no ordinary person. He seemed to have all the woe of the world upon him; he was as sad and weird-looking as a widow out in the wet.

In the yard was a large heap of firewood—remarkable truth!—which Dad told him to chop up. He began. And how he worked! The axe rang again—particularly when it left the handle—and pieces of wood scattered everywhere. Dad watched him chopping for awhile, then went with Dave to pull corn.

For hours the man chopped away without once looking at the sun. Mother came out. Joy! She had never seen so much wood cut before. She was delighted. She made a cup of tea and took it to the man, and apologised for having no sugar to put in it. He paid no attention to her; he worked harder. Mother waited, holding the tea in her hand. A lump of wood nearly as big as a shingle flew up and shaved her left ear. She put the tea on the ground and went in search of eggs for dinner. (We were out of meat—the kangaroo dog was lame. He had got 'ripped' the last time we killed.)

The tea remained on the ground. Chips fell into it. The dog saw it. He limped towards it eagerly, and dipped the point of his nose in it. It burnt him. An aged rooster strutted along and looked sideways at it. *He* distrusted it and went away. It attracted the pig—a sow with nine young ones. She waddled up, and poked the cup over with her nose; then she sat down on it, while the family joyously gathered round the saucer. Still the man chopped on.

Mother returned—without any eggs. She rescued the crockery from the pigs and turned curiously to the man. She said, 'Why, you've let them take the tea!' No answer. She wondered.

Suddenly, and for the fiftieth time, the axe flew off. The man held the handle and stared at the woodheap. Mother watched him. He removed his hats, and looked inside them. He remained looking inside them.

Mother watched him more closely. His lips moved. He said, '*Listen to them! They're coming! I knew they'd follow!*'

'Who?' asked Mother, trembling slightly.

'*They're in the wood*!' he went on. "Ha, ha! I've got them. They'll never get out; *never get out*!'

Mother fled, screaming. She ran inside and called the children. Sal assisted her. They trooped in like wallabies—all but Joe. He was away earning money. He was getting a shilling a week from Maloney, for chasing cockatoos from the corn.

They closed and barricaded the doors, and Sal took down the gun, which Mother made her hide beneath the bed. They sat listening, anxiously and intently. The wind began to rise. A lump of soot fell from the chimney into the fireplace—where there was no fire. Mother shuddered. Some more fell. Mother jumped to her feet. So did Sal. They looked at each other in dismay. The children began to cry. The chain for hanging the kettle on started swinging to and fro. Mother's knees gave way. The chain continued swinging. A pair of bare legs came down into the fireplace— they were curled round the chain. Mother collapsed. Sal screamed, and ran to the door, but couldn't open it. The legs left the chain and dangled in the air. Sal called 'Murder!'

Her cry was answered. It was Joe, who had been over at Maloney's making his fortune. He came to the rescue. He dropped out of the chimney and shook himself. Sal stared at him. He was calm and covered from head to foot with soot and dirt. He looked round and said, 'Thought yuz could keep me out, did'n' y'?' Sal could only look at him. 'I saw yuz all run in,' he was saying, when Sal thought of Mother, and sprang to her. Sal shook her, and slapped her, and threw water on her till she sat up and stared about. Then Joe stared.

Dad came in for dinner—which, course, wasn't ready. Mother began to cry, and asked him what he meant by keeping a madman on the place, and told him she *knew* he wanted to have them all murdered. Dad didn't understand. Sal explained. Then he went out and told the man to 'Clear!' The man simply said 'No.'

'Go on, now!' Dad said, pointing to the rails. The man smiled at the wood-heap as he worked. Dad waited. 'Ain't y' going?' he repeated.

'Leave me alone when I'm chopping wood for the missus,' the man answered; then smiled and muttered to himself. Dad left him alone and went inside wondering.

Next day Mother and Dad were talking at the barn. Mother, bare-headed, was holding some eggs in her apron. Dad was leaning on a hoe.

'I *am* afraid of him,' Mother said; 'it's not right you should keep him about the place. No one's safe with such a man. Some day he'll take it in his head to kill us all, and then—'

'Tut, tut, woman; poor old Jack! he's harmless as a baby.'

'All right' (sullenly); 'you'll see!'

Dad laughed and went away with the hoe on his shoulder to cut burr.

Middle of summer. Dad and Dave in the paddock moving lucerne. Jack sinking post-holes for a milking-yard close to the house. Joe at intervals stealing behind him to prick him with straws through a rent in the rear of his patched moleskins. Little Bill—in readiness to run—standing off, enjoying the sport.

Inside the house sat Mother and Sal, sewing and talking of Maloney's new baby.

'Dear me,' said Mother; 'it's the tiniest mite of a thing I ever saw; why, bless me, anyone of y' at its age would have made three of—'

'*Mind*, Mother!' Sal shrieked, jumping up on the sofa. Mother screamed and mounted the table. Both gasped for breath, and leaning cautiously over peeped down at a big black snake which had glided in at the front door. Then, pale and scared-looking, they stared across at each other.

The snake crawled over to the safe and drank up some milk which had been spilt on the floor. Mother saw its full length and groaned. The snake wriggled to the leg of the table.

'Look out!' cried Sal, gathering up her skirts and dancing about on the sofa.

Mother squealed hysterically.

Joe appeared. He laughed.

'You wretch!' Mother yelled. 'Run!—*run* and fetch your father!'

Joe went and brought Jack.

'Oh-h, my God!'—Mother moaned, as Jack stood at the door, staring strangely at her. 'Kill it!—why don't he *kill* it!'

Jack didn't move, but talked to himself. Mother shuddered.

The reptile crawled to the bedroom door. Then for the first time the man's eyes rested upon it. It glided into the bedroom, and Mother and Sal ran off for Dad.

Jack fixed his eyes on the snake and continued muttering to himself. Several times it made an attempt to mount the dressing-table. Finally it succeeded. Suddenly Jack's demeanour changed. He threw off his ragged hat and talked wildly. A fearful expression filled his ugly features. His voice altered.

'You're the Devil!' he said; '*the Devil*! THE DEVIL! The missus brought you—ah-h-h!'

The snake's head passed behind the looking-glass. Jack drew nearer, clenching his fists and gesticulating. As he did he came full before the looking-glass and saw, perhaps for the first time in his life, his own image. An unearthly howl came from him. '*Me father*!' he shouted, and bolted from the house.

Dad came in with the long-handled shovel, swung it about the room, and smashed pieces off the cradle, and tore the bed-curtains down, and made a great noise altogether. Finally, he killed the snake and put it on the fire; and Joe and the cat watched it wriggle on the hot coals.

Meanwhile, Jack, bare-headed, rushed across the yard. He ran over little Bill, and tumbled through the wire-fence on the broad of his back. He roared like a wild beast, clutched at space, and spat, and kicked his heels in the air.

'Let me up!—*ah-h-h!*—let go me throat!' he hissed.

The dog ran over and barked at him. He found his feet again, and, making off, ran through the wheat, glancing back over his shoulder as he tore along. He crossed into the grass paddock, and running to a big tree dodged round and round it. Then from tree to tree he went, and that evening at sun-down, when Joe was bringing the cows home, Jack was still flying from 'his father'.

After supper.

'I wonder now what the old fool saw in that snake to send him off his head like that?' Dad said, gazing wonderingly into the fire. 'He sees plenty of them, goodness knows.'

'That wasn't it. It wasn't the snake at all,' Mother said; 'there was madness in the man's eyes all the while. I saw it the moment he came to the door.' She appealed to Sal.

'Nonsense!' said Dad; '*nonsense*!' and he tried to laugh.

'Oh, of course it's *nonsense*,' Mother went on; 'everything I say is nonsense. It won't be nonsense when you come home some day and find us all on the floor with our throats cut.'

'Pshaw!' Dad answered; 'what's the use of talking like that?' Then to Dave: 'Go out and see if he's in the barn!'

Dave fidgetted. He didn't like the idea. Joe giggled.

'Surely you're not *frightened*?' Dad shouted.

Dave coloured up.

'No—don't think so,' he said; and, after a pause, '*You* go and see.'

It was Dad's turn to feel uneasy. He pretended to straighten the fire, and coughed several times. 'Perhaps it's just as well,' he said, 'to let him be to-night.'

Of course, Dad wasn't afraid; he *said* he wasn't, but he drove the pegs in the doors and windows before going to bed that night.

Next morning, Dad said to Dave and Joe, 'Come 'long, and we'll see where he's got to.'

In a gully at the back of the grass-paddock they found him. He was ploughing—sitting astride the highest limb of a fallen tree, and, in a hoarse voice and strange, calling out—'Gee, Captain!—come here, Tidy!—*wa-ay*!'

'Blowed if I know,' Dad muttered, coming to a standstill. 'Wonder if he *is* clean mad?'

Dave was speechless, and Joe began to tremble.

They listened. And as the man's voice rang out in the quiet gully and the echoes rumbled round the ridge and the affrighted birds flew up, the place felt eerie somehow.

'It's no use bein' afraid of him,' Dad went on. 'We must go and bounce him, that's all.' But there was a tremor in Dad's voice which Dave didn't like.

'See if he knows us, anyway'—and Dad shouted, '*Hey-y*!'

Jack looked up and immediately scrambled from the limb. That was enough for Dave. He turned and made tracks. So did Dad and Joe. They ran. No one could have run harder. Terror overcame Joe. He squealed and grabbed hold of Dad's shirt, which was ballooning in the wind.

'Let go!' Dad gasped. '*Damn* y', let me *go*!'—trying to shake him off. But Joe had great faith in his parent, and clung to him closely.

When they had covered a hundred yards or so, Dave glanced back, and seeing that Jack wasn't pursuing them, stopped and chuckled at the others.

'Eh?' Dad said, completely winded—'Eh?' Then to Dave, when he got some breath:

'Well, you *are* an ass of a fellow. (*Puff*!) What th' *devil* did y'*run* f'?'

'Wot did I run f'? Wot did *you* run f'?'

'Bah!' and Dad boldly led the way back.

'Now look here (turning fiercely upon Joe), don't you come catching hold of me again, or if y' *do* I'll knock y'r d—d head off!...Clear home altogether, and get under the bed if y'r as frightened as *that*.'

Joe slunk behind.

But when Dad *did* approach Jack, which wasn't until he had talked a great deal to him across a big log, the latter didn't show any desire to take life, but allowed himself to be escorted home and locked in the barn quietly enough.

Dad kept Jack confined in the barn several days, and if anyone approached the door or the cracks he would ask:

'Is me father there yet?'

'Your father's dead and buried long ago, man,' Dad used to tell him.

'Yes,' he would say, 'but he's alive again. The missus keeps him in there'—indicating the house.

And sometimes when Dad was not about Joe would put his mouth to a crack and say:

'Here's y'r *father*, Jack!' Then, like a caged beast, the man would howl and tramp up and down, his eyes starting out of his head, while Joe would bolt inside and tell Mother that 'Jack's getting out,' and nearly send her to her grave.

But one day Jack *did* get out, and, while Mother and Sal were ironing, came to the door with the axe on his shoulder.

They dropped the irons, and shrank into a corner and cowered piteously—too scared even to cry out.

He took no notice of them, but, moving stealthily on tiptoes, approached the bedroom door and peeped in. He paused just a moment to grip the axe with both hands. Then with a howl and a bound he entered the room and shattered the looking-glass into fragments.

He bent down and looked closely at the pieces.

'He's dead now,' he said calmly, and walked out. Then he went to work at the post-holes again, just as though nothing had happened.

Fifteen years have passed since then, and the man is still at Shingle Hut. He's the best horse Dad ever had. He slaves from daylight till dark; keeps no Sunday; knows no companion; lives chiefly on meat and machine oil; domiciles in the barn; and has never asked for a rise in his wages. His name we never knew. We call him 'Jack.' The neighbours call him '*Cranky* Jack.'

(1897)

Vance Palmer
THE HERMIT

The rain had been falling all day with a grim persistency, and the coach moved with painful slowness in spite of its five horses. There had been the plain first, a wide stretch of black soil covered by dead barley-grass, and it had taken the edge from their enthusiasm in the beginning, if indeed any keen anticipation for the road had ever filled them. They were lean animals, inured to curses and the whip, and they had to live by grazing in the hardest winter, so that they had no energy to spare for a track that had turned into glue. On that endless plain the loose grass had clung to the wheels till they looked like monstrous sheaves of wheat, increasing in size as they rolled on.

But the ridges were nearly as bad. Going uphill the unshod hoofs of the horses struggled for foothold in the slimy clay, and every descent was a peril. No one was conscious of peril, however, for the sodden dreariness of the day precluded any lively emotion. The rain fell with depressing itera-tion. It turned the ground into a sponge, and the trees into insubstantial things that might dissolve like sugar at any moment. It trickled down the back of our necks and filtered into our souls. It saturated every material object till nothing was dry or clean. And the grey sky came down close, seeming to mingle with the earth, till it was difficult to remember a world that had been lit by the sun.

There were four of us in the coach and we had a hundred miles to go, but by the time darkness finally announced itself only a third of the distance had been covered. The driver, a pessimistic man born to be covered by either mud or dust, was chiefly preoccupied by the fact that never in fifteen years had he gone so near being late with the mails. From his conversation one was led to infer that the mails were his sole point of honour. The world, flesh, and devil might claim him for their own for the three days he was not on the road, but no flooded river had ever delayed him beyond scheduled time. Drenched with mud from head to foot he worked with his hands, feet, and lungs to get the last ounce of energy out of the horses, and his dried, sun-bitten face and sinewy body conveyed the impression that he was forcing the coach along by sheer strength of will.

Of the other two men one was a saddler, a short, tubby man from the town, whose red face peeped out cheerfully from the midst of his swad-dling oilskins. No rain, cold, or fatigue could quite dry up the sources of his humour. He applied it energetically to the horses, the coach, the stretches of dripping mulga till sheer exhaustion beat him down, and he slept with his head bent forward and the rain trickling spitefully down the nape of his neck. His companion, a driller, was not supported by the same fund of inner strength. He carried instead several flasks of whisky which he produced with labour at intervals and offered to the company, but not with any of the alacrity of a man who expects a refusal. By midnight all had sunk into an uneasy sleep; all except the driver, who, astride of one of the polers, flayed and grunted, forging through swollen creeks and walls of wet darkness, as if intent on demonstrating that the human will was still a factor in the universe.

Cramped and chilled, dozing on the outer confines of sleep, one was able to grasp something of the mystery of eternity. It seemed incredible that the journey had had any beginning or would ultimately have an end. Voices that conveyed memories of a remote past fought somewhere on the edge of the outer world about a matter of no importance. Or could it be the driver persuading the fallen leader to rise from the mud? For a moment the intelligence peeped out tentatively like a snail to decide the matter and then withdrew into the warm deeps of semi-consciousness. Our bodies contracted with our minds, as if hopeful that a process of compression would squeeze sufficient heat into the blood.

At last a voice, coming evidently from a far distance, made itself finally audible:

'This is Joe's...We'll get a change of horses here but we'll have to wait a couple of hours till sunrise.'

Somehow it was annoying to be disturbed and to be reminded that life was still going on. We stretched ourselves with an effort, and climbed out to an unfriendly earth that oozed about our ankles. The coach-driver and another man were unhooking the traces, and the smell of sweat, horse-hair, and wet oilskin assailed the nostrils violently, but a few yards away stood a small, ragged shanty, its light coming cheerfully through the wide chinks of the slab walls.

This was Joe's home, apparently. A pack of lean kangaroo-dogs raised themselves from the hearth at our entrance and sniffed suspiciously at our wet clothing. They seemed to be covered with ashes instead of hair, and their eyes held a drowsy hostility, but above the smouldering fire swung a huge billy of black tea, and that at least was a cheerful sight. When the horses had been finally provided for our host came in, and without a word placed on the table four pannikins, a dried loaf, and a hunk of corned beef. We fell to eating voraciously, hardly lifting our eyes, while the wind whistled eerily through the chinks and our host walked up and down, talking to his dogs and occasionally stopping at the door to peer out into the night. With the last bite finished the coach-driver rose and put wood on the fire, wrapped his oilskins round him, and unceremoniously curled himself up on the hearth; the saddler after some meditation did likewise; and the pair of them having completed a circle round the fire there was nothing left for us but to light our pipes and wait for dawn.

It was not an enlivening prospect. Two of us were wet and unhappy, our tongues sore from too much tobacco, our minds thin and shrivelled from lack of nourishment, and our bodies chilled and bruised to a point of painful torpor. The third party, our host, had the uneasiness of a man who was not fond of his kind. A lean, crotchety old fellow with a sparse white beard, stiff limbs, and restless eyes, he walked up and down talking, now to us, now to the dogs, but never altering his tone or the direction of his head:

'You oughter been here by the afternoon if the horses had been better 'n a team of goats. But they ain't. Ol' Fahey keeps the same lot on the road till they wouldn't throw a shadow on a sunny day, and I'm ashamed to let the dogs see me putting the harness on 'em. Down, Bally, you son of a sheep-eater. Ain't that the on'y bit of beef I've got to keep me over the week-end. You know that as well as I do, so you needn't look black now. You're one of the same breed as Ol' Fahey, you are. Every quid he gets hold of is a pris'ner, an' every bit of food you see goes inter y'r mouth. I says to him "If you don't put a fresh lot of horses on the road next month..."'

It was the same thing over and over again, and he never varied his walk up and down the hut except to stop and look out of the door. Somehow he had the appearance of a man who would prefer to sleep in the day-time and spend the night in poking the fire and talking to his dogs. A strange face was his, not evil in its essence, but filled with suspicion of his kind and bleached like an unhealthy potato. Perhaps it was solitude that had twisted his mind and driven him into alliance with kangaroo-dogs, snakes, and other inhuman things; for the heap in the corner that looked like a bundle of wet rags proved to be a carpet-snake of great length and sluggish habits. It was an unpleasant-looking reptile. It had none of the decadent beauty that should rightfully belong to a snake. It seemed bleached, bloated, corrupt, bald in the matter of scales, and only fit to inhabit a glass case in a Zoo. The rain had ceased, and the wind coming keenly through the gaps in the wall made the dogs whine and move about uneasily in search of a sheltered spot. They looked grudgingly at the snake's corner and its coils seemed to move slightly whenever they approached too near.

'The rats was bad here,' said our host (apparently in explanation to the dogs). 'They come after that bit of chaff I've got in the rafters. If it wasn't for that there snake I'd get no peace at all.'

The candle had guttered down, and the remains of it were beginning to drip into the bottle that held it, but the arriving light was already penetrating the walls. Our host sauntered over to a small door and knocked three times with his knuckles. It was the first time either of us had noticed the door or the short, wet skirt hanging on it, but soon afterwards a rattle of hobble-chains and the sound of a small, shrill voice from the creek-bed assured us that Joe's was not the only human life on the place. The dogs slunk out one by one through the door in exploration and the two men by the fire rose and shook the ashes from their coats. It was nearly time to take the road again.

Within a few minutes we were hooking the plunging horses to the coach and drinking in the freshness of a world that was washed by the rain and half-warmed by the sun. The surrounding mulga seemed to have been turned into silver, and flocks of screeching galahs hung about, the clear light showing up the colour of their crimson breasts. But the owner of the short, wet skirt was nowhere in evidence. When the horses had leapt off towards the main track, and the coach was swinging down the ridge at a perilous rate our host turned and went back to his hut, accompanied by his file of dogs, and his manner was that of a hermit who has rid himself of an unpleasant manifestation of life.

'Married a black woman, Joe did,' said the driver at last, 'At least... She died when he was doing time. He must have done about twenty years altogether, one way and another. Young calves! Never could keep his hands off a cleanskin that came near the place. It's dead certain he'd be in there now if it wasn't for leaving them there dogs. They keep him straight... Then there's the girl.'

We looked back to see a small figure astride the top rail of the yard. She was hatless and bootless, and her body, though still, had something wild and eager about it. The sun was behind her as she perched on the high rail, and somehow she had the aspect of a fierce young bird poising itself for a flight.

(1915)

Catherine Helen Spence
CLARA MORISON

from VOLUME 2, CHAPTER 9

SIGNS OF COLONIAL PROSPERITY!

Never had such an incongruous-looking abode greeted the eyes of the cousins. Into one room, which had a clay floor, and was indeed the only room in the house, there was crammed so much furniture, that there was scarcely standing room. A piano, by Collard and Collard, stood in one corner; a cheffonier, with a great array of decanters and glasses, graced another; there were two chests of drawers, wedged between a common stretcher and a heap of bedding, which seemed intended for a nightly shakedown. There was, in truth, an abundance of everything but chairs, and that deficiency was made up by a number of three-legged stools, which the children liked to lift on to the drawers, and, climbing by the handles, to perch themselves where they could reach the rafters of the unceiled house. A very small piece of matting lay under the table, but the legs of the piano and of all the valuable furniture rested on the earthen floor.

'Rather a change of days for us,' said Mrs Tubbins, glancing complacently from her furniture to her visitors. 'Aint we snug now, Miss Marget? This is a prettier piany than yours, and cost more money too, I expect, for my master gin sixty guineas for it the week before he left me, that I might have something cheerful in the house; but the children are for ever strumming on it, and broke three of the prettiest of the brass wires no further gone than last night. They tear at the wires with their fingers, and scrape across them with an iron hoop they picked up, which aint doing justice to the piany. Just play us a tune, Miss Marget, to let them see how it should be done.'

Margaret found that the piano had suffered very much from the course of treatment which the young Tubbinses had pursued; she played very softly, in order to spare her own ears.

'Just try now, Fanny, if you can play like that,' said Mrs Tubbins.

Fanny struck the notes at random, more gently than her wont, and her mother smiled approvingly, and said she knew she would come on if she had any one to tell her how to play. Then Clara was asked to give a tune, and as she was but a tyro, she could not moderate her style to the piano, but played as hard as she did on her cousin's.

'Your cousin beats you, Miss Marget; but if she would just put her foot on the stick below, it would make a wonderful improvement. It sounds quite grand, and booms in your ears; but I think there ought to be two sticks, one for each foot, that folk may have all their limbs helping the music; but yours had only one. Do you know anybody who would come in for a few hours every day to teach me and Fanny, for it would be grand to be able to play to Mr Tubbins when he comes back?'

'Have you any music?' asked Clara, wondering at the extraordinary tones of the handsome and apparently new piano.

'Oh! I beg your pardon, Miss. I should have given you the books. I never play without them myself.' And Mrs Tubbins handed her a leaf of

Jeannette and Jeannot, and another which had formed part of the overture to Tancredi, saying that she really ought to buy another book or two. 'I went to Platts' last week, and they wanted to sell me an instruction book, as they called it, and asked a guinea for it, but I saw they thought me green, for the book was more words than music; so I told the young man as served me that I knew chalk from cheese, and that was not the book for my money, and did not spend a brass farthing in the shop after all. You'll stop and have a glass of wine with me, Miss Marget? Fanny, run across to the public-house for a pint of sherry, the best they have got.'

'I wish Annie had been with us,' said Margaret, unable to repress a smile. 'She has not been well or in good spirits lately, and it would have done her good to have seen you in the midst of all your splendour.'

'I expect her young man is at the diggings, and she is pining about him; but it's far worse to have to pine after one's old man;' and Mrs Tubbins heaved a sigh, but controlled her feelings at the sight of her piano.

'All our young men are at the diggings—George, Gilbert, and Henry Martin,' observed Margaret.

'That's the young man Miss Grace has married,' said Mrs Tubbins.

'Only going to marry '

'Dear, dear! how long you two misses have been in settling for yourselves! But here's Fanny with the wine and biscuits.'

'Give me my fourpenny, mother, for going your message.'

'I only said I'd give you twopence, and I can see you have been nibbling, and don't deserve a brass farthing, you little good-for-nothing! Oh, how I wish I had not lost my keys!'

'Bob has planted them somewhere, mother, to get at the plums and sugar. I've got my fourpenny, so I don't mind how soon you find them.' And Fanny ran away to the nearest lolly shop, and all her brothers and sisters followed her.

'Don't you send the children to school?' asked Margaret. 'It is very bad for them to be running about idle.'

'I did send them a bit, but Fanny got scolded, and Bob got thrashed; and the little ones were kept in, and got no dinner at all one day; so they just hate the school, and won't go to it no more.'

'You should make them go, whether they will or not,' said Margaret. 'You will ruin your children if you allow them to do as they please, and all the gold and all the fine furniture in the world will never make up to you for the misery disobedient children will give you. I speak seriously to you, Mrs Tubbins; for I see great evils coming on this colony from money being thrown into the hands of people who, instead of teaching their children the uses and duties of wealth, indulge them in everything they ask for. Send your children to school regularly, and insist upon their obeying you at home, that their father may be proud of them when he returns, and may find, after all his toil and hardships, a happy fireside and an orderly family.'

'What you say is all very true, Miss Marget, but you are over hard on the likes of us, who never got no learning, and don't quite see the use of it.'

'If you don't see the use of their learning, make them work as they used to do.'

'They ain't got no call to work, for I have lots of clothes for them, and a silk gown for myself to go to town with; and where is the use of them slaving just as if we had not a penny.'

'I have not seen you at church for a long time,' said Margaret. 'Do you go to chapel now?'

'Indeed, I ain't got a sitting anywheres just at present, and I don't like getting my religion for nothing now, when I can afford to pay for it. Your church is not ours, and I am just wondering which one to join; but, after all, I never get time to go to church, for there is the dinner to make ready in the morning, and the children to put to bed at night, so it is ill convenient for me to get away.'

'But don't the children go to church or Sunday school? I remember your telling me how fond Fanny was of learning hymns and catechism.'

'So she was then, and I was glad to get an old frock of yours to make down for her, to look decent to go to school in; but we are much smarter now.'

And Mrs Tubbins took from a very miscellaneous lot of things Fanny's pink satin bonnet and dress of green and lavender silk, saying that she thought them very genteel, and that they took her fancy in the shop at first sight. Then her own gorgeous attire for Sundays was brought out for Margaret's inspection and admiration; and she was busy telling how much every article had cost, when her two nieces, Sarah and Lucinda Hagget, came in.

'Oh, aunt, how vain you are of your finery!' said Miss Lucinda. 'You never let anybody miss the sight of it if you can help. I fancy you are prouder of that fine silk dress than you are of your piany, though it's the piany I envy,'—but the speaker looked very hard at the gown too.

'Have you left your places, girls, that you are both here at this time of day?—and such good places you had too,' said Mrs Tubbins.

'I hadn't enough of wages,' said Sarah. 'How do people expect one to dress on seven shillings a-week? I sha'n't take a place again under eight, if I have washing to do. Lucinda had no washing, so she might have stopped.'

'Stopped at such a place! Why, it was so dull that you could hear the grass growing, for want of anything else to hear. If I could get a good cheerful place, I shouldn't mind taking six shillings a-week till we hear from father.'

'I know a lady who wants a girl; she would give you an easy place, and she is a good mistress—Mrs Trueman,' said Margaret.

'A grass widow!—I won't go there,' cried Lucinda. 'It is enough to pull down any creature's spirits, to live with such whining people. You, aunt, are the cheerfullest of the lot, and me and Sarah have come to stop with you till we get suited.'

'Where are you all to sleep?' asked Margaret.

'Oh! I make up a bed on the piany every night,' replied Mrs Tubbins; 'and it holds a good many of the little ones, and Sarah may go beside them. It is quite handy for a bed. I can manage, I warrant.'

Miss Lucinda meanwhile was busily engaged trying to make out a nigger melody, but could not manage it. She was just going to ask Margaret to tell her what notes should be struck, when the cousins rose to depart. Clara could not get over the idea of the handiness of the large square piano, and its being strummed on and raked with hoops all day, and slept on all night: she hurried out of hearing of the people inside, and indulged in a long and hearty fit of laughter.

'It is all very well for you to laugh,' said Margaret; 'but I must say it is no laughing matter. I remember Mrs Tubbins a hard-working honest woman, who brought up her family better than the average of her class; and now this suddenly-acquired wealth is ruining them all. When his gold is spent, I suppose Tubbins will set off for more; and until the diggings are worked out, South Australia is none the better for that family.'

'Are you longing to see the end of the gold, Margaret?'

'Heartily!' was the answer.

(1854)

Caroline Atkinson
COWANDA, THE VETERAN'S GRANT: AN AUSTRALIAN STORY

from CHAPTER 5

A brilliant-flowered creeper had been trained across the verandah, throwing a grateful shade; and the pure white blinds, which were drawn, cast a softened light within the very small drawing-room, where already a simple china tea-service was arranged upon a round table, near the French window. Welton had pushed it open, and then stepped back to secure the garden wicket, and Gilbert found himself thus unceremoniously ushered into the presence of Miss Welton. She rose to receive him with an easy composure, which at once calmed his trepidation; she might have been his own age; rather tall and well-formed, with a graceful carriage; her complexion was spotlessly fair, and her mild brown eye had nothing of the restlessness of fever in its glances; she appeared to have forgotten herself, and to think only of those about her; you knew that the white dress was fitted with such precision from a good taste rather than vanity, and the brown hair, smoothly parted across the fair brow, might have been fastidiously simple on anyone else. It was a happy evening: Gilbert was not treated as a stranger, and he did not feel one, as he offered Clare his arm, and took the fish basket from her hand, or when he guided her to her seat in the boat. She was not so handsome as Rachel, nor so clever or deep-feeling, perhaps; but she looked so calm and happy, and made everyone else feel so happy near her. He found, too, by a few remarks which passed between the brother and sister, that they were Christians, and instinctively began to talk to them of his sister, warming as he spoke of her, and recalled her generous loving nature. The rich sunset tinting the waves, the rocky shores of the harbour—how she would have admired them!—the sight would have thrilled the warm pulses of that sensitive heart. His companions listened, and smiled kindly; and from that time he was elevated far beyond his previous standard in their estimation.

The moon rose before the fish basket was filled, and they turned the bow homewards. Lighted up by the soft lunar beams, the scene was inexpressibly lovely: the waves dancing in the light, and rippling round the boat;—the rocky shores, casting a deep shadow at their feet, and the glistening white walls and metal roofs of houses among the wooded summits;—the lamps in the distant city, and the masts of shipping rising up round the wharves, combined to form a pleasing scene, and under the impression of the moment Gilbert exclaimed, 'After all, Sydney is not so bad. I do believe I shall get used to it in time.'

'And like it,' Welton added.

'I don't say that. What do you think, Miss Clare?'

'That it is possible to become attached to any place, if we seek the good, not evil of it, and are at peace with ourselves.'

'That latter clause puts contentment beyond the reach of many.'

'Why should it? No one is *forced* to do evil. We have a promise from the highest source that a "way of escape" is before us, and surely nothing but a sense of unworthiness can make us at enmity with ourselves.'

'But suppose we cannot see the "way of escape"?'

'I can only reply to that by a quotation—"Do the Duty which lies nearest thee, which thou knowest to be a Duty; thy second Duty will already become clearer." I believe that that is the safe way to find the road, if we seek light on our duties from Christ.'

Gilbert looked gravely into the calm, pale face; he had rested on his oar, and bent forward, for her voice was low, and perhaps then more than usually so. For a moment the serious impression lasted, and then he threw it off, and began an attack upon city life. Welton had always lived in a town, and had little idea of life beyond it; to exist remote from the morning's paper at the breakfast table, and the cries of the vendors of luxuries or necessaries, appeared problematical, and a question he was not disposed to solve; but though their tastes were thus opposed, the evening had strengthened their friendship, and this was the first of a series of visits which were a source of mutual pleasure; but they were viewed with bitter jealousy by Blackmore, and he used every effort to prevent them, and often successfully. He had once accompanied Gilbert on a visit to his friends, but the ex-superintendent was uneasy in the presence of the calm, quiet girl; her very silence reproved him, and with many an inaudible expletive he vowed never to 'catch himself there again', under penalties which are readily evoked by the profane and thoughtless. Gilbert, on the contrary, mixing for the first time in his life with a refined and pretty girl in his own station of life, and with the unrestraint of a relative, insensibly attached much importance to Clare's words and movements, and a smile was dwelt on with considerable pleasure.

(1859)

Patrick White
VOSS

from CHAPTER 6

The country was by no means new to Voss, who had returned by land from Moreton Bay and the North, yet, on this significant occasion, he observed all things as if for the first time. It was a gentle, healing landscape in those parts. So he was looking about him with contented eye, drinking deep draughts of a most simple medicine. Sometimes they would leave the road, from the stones of which their horses' feet had been striking little angry sparks, and take short cuts instead along the bush tracks, walking on leaves and silence. It was not the volcanic silence of solitary travel through infinity. The German had experienced this, and been exhausted by it, winding deeper into himself, into blacker thickets of thorns. Through this bushland, men had already blazed a way. Pale scars showed in the sides of the hairy trees. Voss was merely following now, and could almost have accepted this solution as the only desirable one. The world of gods was becoming a world of men. Men wound behind him, heads mostly down, in single file. He was no longer irritated by their coughing. Ahead of him sat the long, thin, civilized back of his host.

'The country round here is divided up, for the greater part, into small holdings. That is to say, until we reach the boundaries of Rhine Towers, and Dulverton, which is the property of Ralph Angus,' explained Sanderson, who would sometimes become embarrassed by silence, and feel it his duty to instruct his guests.

At places, in clearings, little, wild, rosy children would approach the track, and stand with their noses running, and lips curled in natural wonder. Their homespun frocks made them look stiffer. An aura of timelessness enveloped their rooted bodies. They would not speak, of course, to destroy any such illusion. They stood, and looked, out of their relentless blue or hot-chocolate eyes, till the rump of the last horse had all but disappeared. Then these children would run along the track in the wake of the riders, jumping the mounds of yellow dung, shouting and sniffing, as if they had known the horsemen all along, and always been brave.

Only less timid by a little were the mothers, who would run out, shaking the structure of a slab or wattle hut, dashing the suds from their arms, or returning to its brown bodice the big breast that had been giving suck. In spite of their initial enthusiasm, the mothers would stop short, and stand in the disturbed silence, after mumbling a few guilty words. It was for husbands to speak to emissaries from the world. So the squatters themselves would come up, in boots they had cobbled during winter nights. Their Adam's apples moved stiffly with some intelligence of weather, flocks, or crops. As they had hewn, painfully, an existence out of the scrub and rocks, so they proceeded to hew the words out of a poor vocabulary.

Voss appeared to glow.

'These are good people. One can see,' he said. 'Have they all been free settlers?'

'Some. Some are emancipists,' Sanderson replied from over his shoulder.

'There are both kinds. And there are good and bad of each.'

Because he was a better man than Voss, he also had fewer transitory illusions. Just then, exalted by hopes of regeneration, the German was ready to believe that all men were good.

'It goes without saying there are such distinctions,' he agreed, but with the air of suffering of one who has been misunderstood by a superficial companion. 'If you will look into the skin of a beautiful young lady, you will see perhaps one or two blemishes: a patch of slight inflammation, let us say, the holes of the pores, even a pimple. But this is not to deny the essence of her beauty. Will you not concur?'

'If it is a question of essence,' Sanderson replied, with appropriate gravity.

The way he was placed, Voss could see only his host's back, which was that long, discreet, civilized one already mentioned.

Sanderson was a man of a certain culture, which his passionate search for truth had rid of intellectual ostentation. In another age the landowner might have become a monk, and from there gone on to be a hermit. In the mid-nineteenth century, an English gentleman and devoted husband did not behave in such a manner, so he renounced Belgravia for New South Wales, and learned to mortify himself in other ways. Because he was rich and among the first to arrive, he had acquired a goodish slice of land. After this victory of worldly pride, almost unavoidable, perhaps, in anyone of his class, humility had set in. He did live most simply, together with his modest wife. They were seldom idle, unless the reading of books, after the candles were lit, be considered idleness. This was the one thing people held against the Sandersons, and it certainly did seem vain and peculiar. They had whole rows of books, bound in leather, and were forever devouring them. They would pick out passages for each other as if they had been titbits of tender meat, and afterwards shine with almost physical pleasure. Beyond this, there was nothing to which a man might take exception. Sanderson tended his flocks and herds like any other Christian. If he was more prosperous than most, one did not notice it unduly, and both he and his wife would wash their servants' feet in many thoughtful and imperceptible ways.

'We are how many miles now from your property?' Voss would ask on and off.

And Sanderson would tell.

'I am most anxious to see it,' Voss said invariably.

Places yet unvisited can become an obsession, promising final peace, all goodness [...]

Late in the afternoon of their arrival, the party descended from the hills into a river valley, of which the brown water ran with evening murmur, and brown fish snoozed upon the stones. Now the horses pricked their ears, and arched their necks tirelessly. They were all nervous veins as they stepped out along the pleasant valley. They were so certain. Which did, indeed, inspire even strangers with a certain confidence and sense of home-coming.

Soon domestic cows had run to look, and horned rams, dragging their sex amongst the clover, were being brought to fold by a youthful shepherd. But it was the valley itself which drew Voss. Its mineral splendours were increased in that light. As bronze retreated, veins of silver loomed in the gullies, knobs of amethyst and sapphire glowed on the hills, until the horsemen rounded that bastion which fortified from sight the ultimate stronghold of beauty.

'*Achhh!*' cried Voss, upon seeing.

Sanderson laughed almost sheepishly.

'Those rocks, on that bit of a hill up there, are the "Towers" from which the place takes its name.'

'It is quite correct,' said the German. 'It is a castle.'

This was for the moment pure gold. The purple stream of evening flowing at its base almost drowned Voss. Snatches of memory racing through him made it seem the more intolerable that he might not finally sink, but would rise as from other drownings on the same calamitous raft.

Sanderson, too, was bringing him back, throwing him simple, wooden words.

'You can see the homestead. Down there in the willows. That is the shed where we shear our sheep. The store, over by the elm. And the men's cottages. We are quite a community, you see. They are even building a church.'

Skeins of mist, or smoke, had tangled with the purple shadows. Dogs dashed out on plumes of dust, to mingle with the company of riders, and bark till almost choked by their own tongues. The men were silent, however, from the magnificence through which they had passed, and at the prospect of new acquaintanceships. Some grew afraid. Young Harry Robarts began to shiver in a cold sweat, and Turner, who had now been sober several days, feared that in his nakedness he might not survive further hazards of experience. Even Palfreyman realized he had failed that day to pray to God, and must forfeit what progress he had made on the road where progress is perhaps illusory. So he was hanging back, and would not have associated with his fellows if it had been possible to avoid them.

A woman in grey dress and white apron, holding a little girl by the hand, approached, and spoke, with gravity and great sweetness.

'Welcome, Mr Voss, to Rhine Towers.' To which immediately she added, not without a smiling confusion, 'Everybody is, of course, welcome.'

Sanderson, who had jumped down, touched his wife very briefly, and this woman, of indeterminate age, was obviously strengthened. For a second, it was seen, she forgot other duties. Then her husband called, and two grooms came, parting the fronds of the willows, to take the horses.

'Come on, Voss. They will be seen to,' Sanderson announced. 'Are you so in love with the saddle? Come inside, and we shall hope to make you comfortable.'

'Yes,' said Voss.

But he continued to sit, thoughtful, with his mouth folded in.

The serpent has slid even into this paradise, Frank Le Mesurier realized, and sighed.

Everyone was expecting something.

'I did not think to impose upon you to this extent, Mr Sanderson,' the German released his lip and replied. 'It would embarrass me to think such a large party should inconvenience you by intruding under your rooftree. I would prefer to camp down somewhere in the neighbourhood with my men, with our own blankets, beside a bivouac fire.'

Mrs Sanderson looked at her husband, who had turned rather pale.

'It would not enter my head,' said the latter.

Since it had entered the German's, his eye shone with bitter pleasure. Now the beauty of their approach to Rhine Towers appeared to have been a tragic one, of which the last fragments were crumbling in the dusk. He had been wrong to surrender to sensuous delights, and must now suffer accordingly.

(1957)

Robin Boyd
THE AUSTRALIAN UGLINESS

from CHAPTER 4

PIONEERS AND ARBORAPHOBES

The failure of Australia to come to terms with herself—worse: her failure to have the least desire to come to terms with herself—can be largely explained in a phrase: the cult of pioneering. The early period of discovery, exploration and taming of the country coloured the national outlook till long after the frontier was pushed back out of sight of the corner window of Mon Repos in Hydrangea Crescent. And when Australia grew a little too long in the tooth to cling any more to the blanket excuse of youth a new pioneering period opened and revived the spirit.

The second period of pioneering, starting about the beginning of the second half of the twentieth century, is less romantic than the first was, since it involves factories and sub-divisions instead of sheep, gold and limitless acreages of the bush, but it is no less affecting to the participants. After half a century of coasting Australia is now a pioneer land again, conscious of her enormous potential and of the challenging work waiting to be done. As a pioneer land she has little time for introspective questioning, no patience with conservation, and little or no sentiment for hereditary possessions. As a pioneer, she adds to the indecisive quality of her new culture the devastating extra element of destructiveness. This ranges from spendthriftiness to arrant vandalism, and is directed against the various irreplaceable assets provided by nature and the nineteenth century and, in Sydney, the eighteenth century.

Despite the comparative flatness of the continent, the absence of high ranges and the lack of dramatic scenic contrasts, the object of the pioneering cult is to reduce everything possible to the same level. If sometimes this object is beyond the scope of bulldozers, at least cemeteries can be placed on the highest promontories and factories can fill the winding valleys.

Despite the lack of water, and the national fear of drought, and the general agreement that dryness could be the worst impediment in Australia's boundless future, the object of the pioneering cult is to remove all sight and sound of water from everyday life. The city waterfront is the place only for wharves and warehouses. Factories have always gravitated

to the river valleys where they had wonderfully convenient natural drains
for the disposal of dyestuffs, sewerage and industrial refuse. The lowness
and the thicker undergrowth beside rivers and creeks also recommended
their valleys as official or unofficial dumping grounds for suburban refuse.

Despite the natural tendency of the country to overheat, despite the
blistering outback legend and the constant search for relief even in the
milder areas during the hottest weeks of summer, the object of the pioneering cult is to banish all shade from everyday life. Every lot is cleared for
yards in all directions before it is considered safe for building.

Despite the nation's lack of attractive, dramatic historic background,
and the temporary look of most of man's feeble efforts to subjugate the
natural elements, despite the political advantages of national symbols at a
time when the northern Asian waters are growing uncomfortably warm,
the object of the pioneering cult is to push aside old buildings, whatever
their historic or architectural interest, without a moment's misgivings—
without the knowldge that there is any cause for a moment's misgivings, if
the space is required for a car park or an unloading dock.

The object of the pioneer cult, in short, is to clear all decks for action, to
reduce everything to the same comprehensible level so that something new
can be put on it. The pioneer has never a moment's doubt that what he
puts up will be better than what he tears down. In fact all he achieves is a
more intense reduction of character in the background culture, allowing
him even more freedom for the application of momentarily satisfying
features.

Any sensitive visitor should be warned. He will be perplexed by the
apparently senseless destruction of some old structures. He will ask what
madness is it that causes the real estate agents to direct a complete
devastation of land before it is offered for sale, not content even to leave
the degree of destruction to the individual tastes of the home-builders. One
can perhaps understand the mass destruction in the case of cheap land in
the outer suburbs on the fringe of the bush. The gum trees here are
probably too plentiful to command any respect, and the job of clearing is
considered as inevitable for a home-builder now as it was last century for a
farmer. Once the Housing Commission in Perth was persuaded by a
tree-lover group to spare some of the native bush in an outer-suburban
subdivision. The commission agreed to leave two gums in each front
garden. But six months after the estate was opened every tree had been
removed by the occupiers.

Modern Australians have no especially psychopathic fear of the gum or
the wattle, but no two trees could have been designed to be less sympathetic to the qualities of tidiness and conformist indecision which are desired
in the artificial background. The Australian bush was made in one of
nature's more relaxed, even casual moods. Everything is evergreen, yet this
term is often ironic, at least in relation to the ubiquitous gum tree.
Certainly the eucalypt is not deciduous, but it is sometimes blue, often
olive-grey, and occasionally brown. Measured against a fresh green European ideal, the Australian bush presents a slovenly scene. The grass grows
long, ochre and rank. Most eucalypts are undisciplined in the extreme,
their branches straggling wildly with disconnected tufts of leaves. It is
quite impossible to trim one into the shape of a rooster or a kangaroo.
They do not drop their leaves suddenly and predictably, but all through

the year in a slummocky way, and are likely at unexpected moments to add to the dry brown mess at their feet a dead branch or length of bark which one of them has discarded, having finished with it. The wattle and other native trees are almost as indolent in their habits, lounging at drunken angles on the shabby, crackly, threadbare ochre carpet. The vertical limp leaves and the hungry earth consume whatever water they receive so avidly that within minutes after a rainstorm everything looks as dry as before and the yellow dust is free to rise again. It is all most unpleasant, measured against the European ideal. It is faintly frightening: not that it menaces, but simply because it is so unfamiliar, so strangely primeval: as different again from the European or North American landscapes as a tropical jungle. It disturbs the white Australian, the expatriate European, remembering, it seems, even at generations removed, his own northern lands where even the wild woods are civilised, with neat, compact trees changing beautiful hues, yellow and red, as bright as any painter's colour-card, and a layer of moist leaves, green grass and daisies on the weedless ground like a lovely Axminster carpet.

(1960)

George Johnston
MY BROTHER JACK

from CHAPTER 13

I did clean the car the following Sunday morning, though, and altogether there were seven cars out along Beverley Grove, all being hosed or polished or rubbed at, and Wally Solomons came across from the big cream company Plymouth he had taken out for the week-end, with a handsome yellow polishing-cloth of a new sort, impregnated with something or other, which he presented to me because General Motors were sending them out with their country salesmen as a little goodwill stunt, and he said, 'It's this chemical stuff that's in the cloth, it just shifts the road-scum like that,' and I said, 'Oh?' and he said, 'It's windscreens and hub-caps that give the final touch to a polish job, you know, if they're not sparkling the whole vehicle looks like nothing on earth.' And under my breath I said, 'Go and get stuffed.'

And then Phyland the chartered accountant came up from his neat black Hillman wiping the dipstick on a clean pull of cotton-waste, Phyland the accountant with his pale, pinched-up little widowed woman's face, the sort of face, I found myself thinking, that he must take out from a locked filing-cabinet each day and put on very carefully and accurately like a company audit. Solomons showed him the new impregnated polishing-cloth and explained it, and Phyland said, 'By Jove, that sounds pretty good,' and Solomons promised to try to get one for him too, and then for five minutes they just stood there beside the red MG discussing whether Karkleen Rapid was a better polish than Caldwell's Hi-Gloss, and I thought of the balanced, audited Phyland turds flowing down the plumbing outlet outside my study window, and under my breath I said, 'You can *both* go and get stuffed,' and turned my back on them and pretended to be busy on something to do with the front-suspension. But even from there I could see old Treadwell pottering among his dahlias, and looking rather critically across the dividing fence at Helen's cinerarias.

It was worse the Sunday after that. Two days previous to this the van had delivered our new console-radio, which Helen and I had chosen after hours of poring over catalogues, and which had been delivered from the same company which had made my desk and much of the furniture in the house. Although the wood was plain and waxed and solid, the contraption was deceptively elaborate, for in addition to the sunken wireless it contained a record-player and a compact cocktail-cabinet with a coloured cut-glass set for twelve, and I hated it from the moment it was delivered to our house, although I had thoroughly approved of it at the beginning and had signed the time-payment agreement without a qualm.

On this Sunday morning I had to get up on the roof to fit the stubby tubular mast which would take the new long aerial, and it had to be made fast to the chimney with the bolted metal straps which had come with the set, and for this I borrowed the Solomons' ladder. When I had finished the job—which didn't take long because the pamphlet which had come with the radio gave detailed illustrated instructions for fixing what was called the Quicktite Patent Antenna Clamp, and added, 'Even a child can do it!'—I stayed up on the roof, sitting on the sloping, terracotta tiles with my back wedged against the chimney because for the first time in weeks I had an odd feeling, not only of being alone and away from everything, but of being in some way unassailable as well, and I had not been up on the roof of a house since the time, more than twenty years before, when I had looked down in the rain on old Grandma Emma raging around the back garden brandishing the castor-oil bottle.

This second experience was even m___ ___if___ ___
because my elev___
look out over al___
all around me, a___
three forms of p___
of lawns interse___
cars out in Bev___
reflected, they h___
here in the 'good___
gardens, and th___
clipped and law___
mignonette were
things were so n___
hearts, or what s___
tised behind the l___
door-knobs and t___
course, the public
people might be
existence where a___

I stayed up on t___
other things begar___
things. (I could ev___
the suburbs, on t___

ruminate on all the problems of the world. The ancient Stylites had liked desert places for their meditations.)

The realisation that I did not love Helen, and never had loved her, came to me quite dispassionately at first; so dispassionately that I was able to examine the revelation with a kind of clear careful logic, and find it sound, and put it aside for later. 'Later', of course, would be another thing altogether, when I would want to blame *her* for the predicament we were in, and then passion and anger would need to be invoked. But not yet.

Still, it was the thought of Helen, busy at her casserole in the kitchen, that diverted my reflections at once to all the disturbing little problems and quandaries which up until so recently had baffled and troubled me— politics and Spain and the German ships and the interviews on the liners— because I saw that I had been wrong to allow Helen to work these things out for me. I should have seen for myself that a lot of the dissonance of the world had nothing whatever to do with 'downtrodden masses' or any of Helen's other clichés, but was there because half the world lived in mental deserts very much like the Beverley Park Gardens Estate, and that the real enemy was not the obvious embodiment of evil, like Hitler or his persecu- tion of the Jews or the Russian purges or the bombs on Guernica, but was this awful fetish of a respectability that would rather look the other way than cause a fuss, that hated 'scenes', that did not *want* to know because *to know* might somehow force them into a situation which could take the polish off the duco and blight the herbaceous borders and lay scabrous patches across the attended lawns.

But there were gradations of this respectability—this was the next thing I worked out as Meredith Stylites of the Garden Suburb—and I knew that there had been more things of true value in the shabby house called *Avalon*, from which I had fled, than there ever would be, or could be, in this villa in Beverley Grove. This was where my meditations began to turn in and maul me. I stared around over the whole of the sterile desolation, and I realised with a start of panic that I had got myself into the middle of this red and arid desert, and there was nobody to bring me water.

I had chosen it, of my own free will. I had planned for it, approved of it, connived at it, worked for it, and paid for it. But no!—I winced as the mauling became more brutal—the whole point was that *I had not paid for it!* Oh no, I had not *paid* for it, not yet...I had mortgaged my life and my career for years ahead simply for the privilege of living between Mr Phyland and Mr Treadwell and directly opposite Wally and Sandra Solo- mons!

And the console-radio, the hated new acquisition of the console-radio, inclusive of the Quicktite Patent Antenna Clamp against which my back rested, was another seventy-five pounds, thirteen shillings and elevenpence to be added to all those other precise and handsomely-printed documents with which the top drawer of my desk was stuffed. My guarantees! Diplomas! Some of them even looked like diplomas, with their Old English type and the copperplate flourishes and the big red impressive seals. Diplomas conferred in testimony of some inalienable right to live on in the soft warmth of these empty plains where heads could always be hidden in the comforting granular sand of an unimpeachable respectability. Gavin Turley's guarantees...

(This was the point where Meredith Stylites of the Garden Suburb abandoned his red brick chimney-pillar and eased himself down the pitch *both* go and get stuffed,' and turned my back on them and pretended to be busy on something to do with the front-suspension. But even from there I could see old Treadwell pottering among his dahlias, and looking rather critically across the dividing fence at Helen's cinerarias.

It was worse the Sunday after that. Two days previous to this the van had delivered our new console-radio, which Helen and I had chosen after hours of poring over catalogues, and which had been delivered from the same company which had made my desk and much of the furniture in the house. Although the wood was plain and waxed and solid, the contraption was deceptively elaborate, for in addition to the sunken wireless it contained a record-player and a compact cocktail-cabinet with a coloured cut-glass set for twelve, and I hated it from the moment it was delivered to our house, although I had thoroughly approved of it at the beginning and had signed the time-payment agreement without a qualm.

On this Sunday morning I had to get up on the roof to fit the stubby tubular mast which would take the new long aerial, and it had to be made fast to the chimney with the bolted metal straps which had come with the set, and for this I borrowed the Solomons' ladder. When I had finished the job—which didn't take long because the pamphlet which had come with the radio gave detailed illustrated instructions for fixing what was called the Quicktite Patent Antenna Clamp, and added, 'Even a child can do it!'—I stayed up on the roof, sitting on the sloping, terracotta tiles with my back wedged against the chimney because for the first time in weeks I had an odd feeling, not only of being alone and away from everything, but of being in some way unassailable as well, and I had not been up on the roof of a house since the time, more than twenty years before, when I had looked down in the rain on old Grandma Emma raging around the back garden brandishing the castor-oil bottle.

This second experience was even more terrifying, in a different way, because my elevation provided me with the first opportunity I had had to look out over all the Beverley Park Gardens Estate, and there was nothing all around me, as far as I could see, but a plain of dull red rooftops in their three forms of pitching and closer to hand the green squares and rectangles of lawns intersected by ribbons of asphalt and cement, and I counted nine cars out in Beverley Grove being washed and polished. In the slums, I reflected, they had a fetish about keeping front door-knobs polished, but here in the 'good' respectable suburbs the fetish was applied to cars and to gardens, and there were fixed rituals about this, so that hedges were clipped and lawns trimmed and beds weeded, and the lobelia and the mignonette were tidy in their borders, and the people would see that these things were so no matter what desolation or anxiety or fear was in their hearts, or what spiritless endeavours or connubial treacheries were practised behind the blind neat concealment of their thin red-brick walls. The door-knobs and this more elaborate ritual were part of a similar thing, of course, the public 'front', but it occurred to me suddenly that the door-knob people might be a worthier tribe, really, because they still grappled with existence where audacities were possible, and even adventure.

I stayed up on the roof because once I had worked this out a great many other things began to follow. Strange things. Terrifying things. Wondering things. (I could even stay up here for years, I thought, like some Stylite of the suburbs, on terracotta building tiles in place of a Syrian pillar, and ruminate on all the problems of the world. The ancient Stylites had liked desert places for their meditations.)

The realisation that I did not love Helen, and never had loved her, came to me quite dispassionately at first; so dispassionately that I was able to examine the revelation with a kind of clear careful logic, and find it sound, and put it aside for later. 'Later', of course, would be another thing altogether, when I would want to blame *her* for the predicament we were in, and then passion and anger would need to be invoked. But not yet.

Still, it was the thought of Helen, busy at her casserole in the kitchen, that diverted my reflections at once to all the disturbing little problems and quandaries which up until so recently had baffled and troubled me—politics and Spain and the German ships and the interviews on the liners—because I saw that I had been wrong to allow Helen to work these things out for me. I should have seen for myself that a lot of the dissonance of the world had nothing whatever to do with 'downtrodden masses' or any of Helen's other clichés, but was there because half the world lived in mental deserts very much like the Beverley Park Gardens Estate, and that the real enemy was not the obvious embodiment of evil, like Hitler or his persecution of the Jews or the Russian purges or the bombs on Guernica, but was this awful fetish of a respectability that would rather look the other way than cause a fuss, that hated 'scenes', that did not *want* to know because *to know* might somehow force them into a situation which could take the polish off the duco and blight the herbaceous borders and lay scabrous patches across the attended lawns.

But there were gradations of this respectability—this was the next thing I worked out as Meredith Stylites of the Garden Suburb—and I knew that there had been more things of true value in the shabby house called *Avalon*, from which I had fled, than there ever would be, or could be, in this villa in Beverley Grove. This was where my meditations began to turn in and maul me. I stared around over the whole of the sterile desolation, and I realised with a start of panic that I had got myself into the middle of this red and arid desert, and there was nobody to bring me water.

I had chosen it, of my own free will. I had planned for it, approved of it, connived at it, worked for it, and paid for it. But no!—I winced as the mauling became more brutal—the whole point was that I *had not paid for it!* Oh no, I had not *paid* for it, not yet...I had mortgaged my life and my career for years ahead simply for the privilege of living between Mr Phyland and Mr Treadwell and directly opposite Wally and Sandra Solomons!

And the console-radio, the hated new acquisition of the console-radio, inclusive of the Quicktite Patent Antenna Clamp against which my back rested, was another seventy-five pounds, thirteen shillings and elevenpence to be added to all those other precise and handsomely-printed documents with which the top drawer of my desk was stuffed. My guarantees! Diplomas! Some of them even looked like diplomas, with their Old English type and the copperplate flourishes and the big red impressive seals. Diplomas conferred in testimony of some inalienable right to live on in the soft warmth of these empty plains where heads could always be hidden in the comforting granular sand of an unimpeachable respectability. Gavin Turley's guarantees...

(This was the point where Meredith Stylites of the Garden Suburb abandoned his red brick chimney-pillar and eased himself down the pitch of the tiled roof, and was transformed into the qualified Meredith, Bachelor of Deserts, Doctor of Sterile Studies, Master of the Empty Soul, by the time he reached the point where the borrowed Solomons' ladder poked two rungs above the eaves, and there he sat for a few more minutes with his long legs dangling over the guttering, staring around at the desert of his choice as if he might memorise forever its every shade and contour, and this was when the really forceful realisation came to him . . .)

There was not one tree on the whole estate.

Yet there must have been trees once, I thought, because when you closely examined the layout of the estate there were little folds to it and faint graceful rises and declivities, not anywhere near definite enough to be thought of as hills or gullies, but the place was not really *flat*, that was the point, and at one side, a little distance beyond Dr Felton Carradine's house, there was almost a real knoll. Once—I felt absolutely sure about this—there would have been trees growing here and there, and I pictured this knoll as having two or three good sturdy blue-gums or stringybarks on the crest, and slopes brown with bracken, and some sandy chewed-out patches where rabbits would have made little squats scattered with the liquorice-black pellets of their droppings and where they would have hopped about at dusk, flickering the pale cotton tufts of their tails. The place could have been really beautiful at one time in a tranquil sort of way, I thought—before Bernie Rothenstein came in with his bulldozers and graders and grubbed out all the trees and flattened everything out so that the subdivision pegs could be hammered in and his lorries could move about without hindrance—because there was a blur of higher ground much farther out, and beyond that the bluish bulk of the Dandenongs sat up there against a good bright sky in nice shapes and colours. And now there was nothing but a great red scab grown over the wounds the bulldozers had made, and not a single tree remaining, because by no stretch of the imagination could anybody count the spindly little sticks which had been stuck in at intervals along the footpaths, because they really were only sticks, and too hidden behind their ugly little tree-guards for anyone to know whether they were leafing or whether they were dead.

I climbed down the Solomons' ladder at once and went straight out to the car and just drove off. It was only about a mile to Goodenough's Nurseries, and we had bought our seedlings there so I knew he stayed open on Sunday mornings, because that was when a lot of suburban gardeners who were tied up at their offices through the week would come to pick up shrubs or seedlings, or to arrange for top-dressing, or to discuss pruning or spraying, or just to talk with him or his gardeners about mulching and tilth and compost-heaps and reinvigoration of their lawns and beds.

I parked the car outside and went in through the gate beneath the painted sign that simply said GOODENOUGH NURSERIES—Jos. Goodenough, Prop.—Est. 1907, and there was Jos. Goodenough himself standing beside the potting-sheds, looking square and reddish and sort of flatly cut out against the slow cool sweep of the sprinklers over the flower-beds, like the Jack of Hearts in a pack of playing cards, and I felt renewed at the very sight of him because there was something earthy and true and reliable about his presence as he stood there in the smell of damp loam and blood-and-bone manure, with a felt hat on his head, his Sunday hat, and his thick braces up over his grey flannel undershirt, and I remember that his braces were striped the way men's winceyette pyjamas used to be and the words POLICE AND FIREMEN were stamped on each of the little metal clips that adjusted them, and I have often wondered since what sort of a guarantee *that* was supposed to be.

I told him I wanted to buy a tree, and he rubbed at his nose and said, 'Well, mister, that's a bit broad and sweepin' like, ain't it? You know, a tree. Which district do you live in, can you tell me that to give me an idea?' So I told him and this brightened him up, because at once he nodded knowingly and said, 'Beverley Park Gardens, eh...yeah, well up there they're goin' in fer the more decorative type of thing, aren't they? You know, the camellia, like, or the hardier sort of hibiscus, or gardenia, even a good well-developed double-fuchsia. Or some of the nice ornamental shrubs an' that.'

'No,' I said. 'A tree. I want a *proper* tree. Something that'll grow into a real tree very quickly.'

'Well...' He went back to rubbing at his nose, harder than before. 'It wouldn't be something like a decorative cypress you got in mind, one each side of a front entrance porch, like...although they *are* pretty slow comin' on, you know, they do look well in the long run but they're slow old growers.'

'Listen, Mr 'Goodenough,' I said patiently. 'It's quite simple. I want something you can put in the ground now and look at it in, say, two years' time and say, "There, that's a real bloody tree!"'

He had both hands busy now, one scrubbing at his nose and the other scratching pensively at his backside.

'It ain't a *gum* you got in mind, is it?' he asked at last, rather dubiously. 'One of them quick-growin' eucalypts...you wouldn't be thinkin' of them, though?'

'Why not? Do they grow quickly?'

'Some of 'em. Some of 'em shoot up like billy-oh. The sugar-gum 'ld be about the best taker, I'd say. The sugars won't get to the size of some of the others, mind you, not at the mature growth, but in the early stages I reckon it's the sugar 'ld give you the best show. Oh, I reckon you could get a tree say thirty foot high or so within a couple of years if you gave her a bit of encouragement early. Maybe even up to forty foot if the spread's there for the roots.'

'But that sounds exactly what I want.'

'Sugar-gum, eh?' He scratched away at his bottom and shook his head. 'Yeah, well you're the customer, mister, an' if that's what you got your mind set on...Matter of fact, I got a pretty fair sort of a sapling round behind the sheds there—I keep a few of 'em on hand just in case there's a call for wind-breaks, you know. I c'ld let you have her for six bob. I wouldn't like you to regret it later, though, mister, and be complainin' so I better warn you. Plants an' trees are just like anythink else, you know, an' you can't never expect anythink to come on well unless it's at the expense of somethink else, an' these gums they do tear a pretty solid amount of nourishment out of the soil. I mean you'd have to expect strife with your lawn growth and your flower-beds.'

(1964)

Thomas Shapcott
from THE TREES: A CONVICT MONOLOGUE

I

I move sharp, not too fancy or nice—a lurch,
a curse, a getaway. They called me mudsplash
but I was quicker: my eyes have been everywhere
two jumps before you.
What a laugh to be flicked in for passing forged currency!   5
I'm still laughing—rather laugh than dance, I tell you.
The others were fools on the convictship, but I rubbed close in
just for the mansmell, to remind myself we were still living.
My guts ache most for the people-breath of streets:
while I was free I never left the city but once—   10
shit, the stink of countryside! air to blast your snotholes
fill you full of bush and breeze and bloody distances.
The only good thing was it taught me, then,
that even air is special: one gulp and you know
you are home in my lovely broken-mouthed slut city   15

.
.
.

III

But, after the barracks and good crush of quarters, the open
unnerved me, I had not planned on that—the just nothing
of hills, hollows, ridges. Nobody told me trees watched,
connived, were not still, were never still.
They rubbed, they grew blisters like their blistered leaves.   20
At first, night-time, listen, something about aloneness,
but later, even at day, it was voices no one could live with,
not human: earth, decay, silences. That was it—silence
speaking to me. I did not scream. Rubbing. Suddenly
to awake trapped, held down in nothing but emptiness   25
and to run screaming, voice rattling to drown that foreignness
till the cavities of the head were cities of yell myself myself
all through the too bright moonsilence and the hallways.
And then ropes and then whips beat me sensible.
I am recovered. I will cut down every tree,   30
every one. I will be invincible.

(1972)

Charles Harpur
A MID-SUMMER NOON
IN THE AUSTRALIAN FOREST

Not a bird disturbs the air,
There is quiet everywhere;
Over plains and over woods
What a mighty stillness broods.

  Even the grasshoppers keep   5
Where the coolest shadows sleep;
Even the busy ants are found
Resting in their pebbled mound;
Even the locust clingeth now
In silence to the barky bough: 10
And over hills and over plains
Quiet, vast and slumbrous, reigns.

  Only there's a drowsy humming
From yon warm lagoon slow coming:
'Tis the dragon-hornet—see!   15
All bedaubed resplendently
With yellow on a tawny ground—
Each rich spot nor square nor round,

But rudely heart-shaped, as it were
The blurred and hasty impress there,   20
Of a vermeil-crusted seal
Dusted o'er with golden meal:
Only there's a droning where
Yon bright beetle gleams the air—
Gleams it in its droning flight   25
With a slanting track of light,
Till rising in the sunshine higher,
Its shards flame out like gems on fire.

  Every other thing is still,
Save the ever wakeful rill,   30
Whose cool murmur only throws
A cooler comfort round Repose;
Or some ripple in the sea
Of leafy boughs, where, lazily,
Tired Summer, in her forest bower   35
Turning with the noontide hour,
Heaves a slumbrous breath, ere she
Once more slumbers peacefully.

O 'tis easeful here to lie
Hidden from Noon's scorching eye,   40
In this grassy cool recess
Musing thus of Quietness.

(1858)

Henry Kendall
BELL-BIRDS

By channels of coolness the echoes are calling,
And down the dim gorges I hear the creek falling;
It lives in the mountain, where moss and the sedges
Touch with their beauty the banks and the ledges;
Through brakes of the cedar and sycamore bowers   5
Struggles the light that is love to the flowers.
And, softer than slumber, and sweeter than singing,
The notes of the bell-birds are running and ringing.

The silver-voiced bell-birds, the darlings of day-time,
They sing in September their songs of the May-time.   10
When shadows wax strong, and the thunder-bolts hurtle,
They hide with their fear in the leaves of the myrtle;
When rain and the sunbeams shine mingled together
They start up like fairies that follow fair weather,
And straightway the hues of their feathers unfolden   15
Are the green and the purple, the blue and the golden.

October, the maiden of bright yellow tresses,
Loiters for love in these cool wildernesses;
Loiters knee-deep in the grasses to listen,
Where dripping rocks gleam and the leafy pools glisten. 20
Then is the time when the water-moons splendid
Break with their gold, and are scattered or blended
Over the creeks, till the woodlands have warning
Of songs of the bell-bird and wings of the morning.

Welcome as waters unkissed by the summers   25
Are the voices of bell-birds to thirsty far-comers.
When fiery December sets foot in the forest,
And the need of the wayfarer presses the sorest,
Pent in the ridges for ever and ever,
The bell-bird directs him to spring and to river,   30
With ring and with ripple, like runnels whose torrents
Are toned by the pebbles and leaves in the currents.

Often I sit, looking back to a childhood
Mixt with the sights and the sounds of the wildwood,
Longing for power and the sweetness to fashion   35
Lyrics with beats like the heart-beats of passion—
Songs interwoven of lights and of laughters
Borrowed from bell-birds in far forest rafters;
So I might keep in the city and alleys
The beauty and strength of the deep mountain valleys,   40
Charming to slumber the pain of my losses
With glimpses of creeks and a vision of mosses.

(1867)

Judith Wright
EYES

At the end of winter my self-sown vine sends up
sprays of purple flowers, each with two green eyes.

Driving home in the night I startled a fox.
The headlights fixed him staring and snarling back.

There's altogether too much I know nothing about: 5
my eyes slide over signals clear to the fox.

But what I do see I can fix meanings to.
There are connections, things leave tracks of causation.

The fox-trot marks in the hardened silt of the road
led to those chicken-feathers caught in the fence.   10

The fox's two green eyes echo his universe;
he can track rabbits better than I can foxes.

But I saw the chicken-feathers caught in the fence;
and fox, I know who's looking for you with a rifle.

You know no better than the two green eyes on the pea-flower   15
the link between the feathers and the sound of the shot.

(1985)

Vincent Buckley
from GOLDEN BUILDERS
For Leonard French

I

The hammers of iron glow down Faraday.
Lygon and Drummond shift under their resonance.
Saws and hammers drawn across the bending air
shuttling like a bow; the saw trembles
the hammers are molten, they flow with quick light   5
striking; the flush spreads and deepens on the stone.
The drills call the streets together
stretching hall to lecture-room to hospital.

But prop old walls with battens of old wood.

Saturday work. Sabbath work. *On this day*   10
we laid this stone
to open this Sabbath School. Feed My Lambs.

The sun dies half-glowing in the floating brickdust,
suspended between red and saffron.
The colours resonate like a noise; the muscles of mouth   15

neck shoulders loins arm themselves against it.
Pavements clink like steel; the air soft,
palpable as cork, lets the stone cornices
gasp into it. Pelham surrenders. Grattan
runs leading forward, seeking the garden's breadth, the fearful   20
edge of green on which the sexes lay.

We have built this Sabbath School. Feed My Lambs.

Evening wanders through my hands and feet
my mouth is cool as the air that now thins
twitching the lights on down winding paths. Everything   25
leans on this bright cold. In gaps of lanes, in tingling
shabby squares, I hear the crying of the machines.

O Cardigan, Queensberry, Elgin: names of their lordships.
Cardigan, Elgin, Lygon: Shall I find here my Lord's grave?

(1971)

Murray Bail
HOME OWNERSHIP

The insidious habit of thrift was proclaimed by the churches and the home-purchase pamphlets: '13,690 homes have been provided, another 605 are under construction.' That was year ending June 30, 1934. All you needed was a deposit of £35. The houses were built on cedar stilts, Brisbane being such a humid city. It's the stilts and the galvanised iron which give Brisbane its temporary air as if the whole lot could be quickly dismantled or swept away.

The street began like all the rest littered with sharp-smelling sawdust and bent nails not yet rusty or trodden into the ground. The sewerage came later. All white, the row of wooden houses exuded a kind of transparent hope, definitely, like new glass. The ground all around was bare.

That was what? Goodness, forty years back.

Like everything else the street has changed.

Number 17 has the front porch converted into a sleepout with louvred windows. Next door there, 'EMOH RUO', has the yellow carport leaning against the side.

Plenty of others have tacked on if not another bedroom, something. There are metal blinds galore, housenames in inlaid mulga, portholes, lantern lights near the doorbell, various weather-vanes and ornamental flyscreens.

After the war the street went through a slack phase; nothing much moved (changed). A nomadic period followed, rented accommodation, the appearance of solitary strangers.

And now—must be due to the exorbitant cost of new housing—young couples have returned, and there's been a spate of further extensions, 'improvements', shouting children at dusk and power-saws biting into the night. Only one house, Parker's there over the road, has remained as it was, motionless on its stilts, while the street and time passed it by. Parker couldn't be better named! Since he moved in the week after he married he hasn't budged.

As a young man he rode a bike to work, the future before him. In those days he had yellow hair and an open blank expression. With their new house in the background Joyce would run out and wave, after first wiping her hands on her thighs: funny characteristic habit of hers. Then she'd remain for several minutes leaning over the gate, looking up and down. Other times, early in their marriage, she could be seen digging in the garden with a heart-shaped trowel.

Joyce cut back the wild grass and muck; carted away the builder's rubbish; and one weekend had Parker out there pouring concrete borders. Here she planted several cactus plants which threw geometric shadows at dusk. It was an attempt to impose order on the harsh elements, as if their lives would become ordered accordingly. This is common in Queensland. People dress very neatly.

Yet Joyce certainly wasn't the person one normally associates with cactus. The house wore brightly-coloured curtains. On certain afternoons the windows reflected the trees and passing clouds just like her sunglasses, while the door in between kept opening and closing. With the step painted verandah-red the house had a look...very conscious of itself. Joyce had this other funny habit, noticeable even from a distance: after saying something, usually to a man, she'd roll her lips back as if she'd committed an error or was applying lipstick. A nervous habit. She was short, firm-breasted. She had large eyes. Oh, she was something! Joyce always liked to laugh. At the same time she was serious. She could be hard on Parker some days—waiting for him the minute he stepped in. He, the pedalling Methodist, without a tie but with the top button done up. He had a simple wooden expression. It implied stubbornness. Where did they meet? A ludicrous, doomed pair. Couldn't everyone see that?

Brisbane hummed with a kind of humid emptiness. It drove people with a perfectly sound mind to drink. The slow-moving days were punctuated at metronomic intervals by door-to-door salesmen. The ring on Parker's bell was the signal, though often as not the house would be wide open.

The house breathed through the door.

'I say, anybody home? You-who!'

And then came the murmur of Joyce's time-consuming, idle questions; at intervals her sudden high laugh.

There was nothing else to do in Brisbane.

Raising one trousered leg on the step, arms and jaws all working in unison, the reps altered the geometry of the foreground. Most of them were hard-working with mortgages of their own, and it was noticeable how after a while most of them took to avoiding Joyce's door. She never bought anything.

There was one particular regular who peddled American pens and propelling pencils, all colours, in rows like picket fences. His narrow sample-case was lined with them.

This man had a hungry tanned neck, wiry wrists—loose gold watch—and wore brown suit-trousers. He had lizard eyes. The eyes of a lizard:

sliding off while selling half-heartedly, more interested in her over the road bending in the garden. He let out a loud conspiratorial laugh without foundation, and Joyce glanced up. You could see what he was up to. Few weeks later, sure enough, he was in there, leg up on the step, his suitcase of pens not even opened. Shielding her eyes, Joyce had a way of squinting: her hand apexed over her eyes duplicated the shape of the peaked roof sheltering the windows.

Every second Thursday he called. Regular as clockwork.

He liked to say, 'I'll toddle off now to Mrs Cactus,' and wink. He called her Mrs Cactus.

And a familiarity did grow between them. He was a traveller of sorts. He had endless stories. She took to sitting casually, ostentatiously, on his suitcase, exposing the red step of the open door. Clasping one knee as they did in those days, she leaned back and laughed. Some afternoons she wore pale blue shorts.

He told lies about himself, lies a woman recognises and yet laughs. They were for her.

She liked to laugh.

With Parker she didn't have much of a chance.

Some Friday afternoons he began appearing without calling on other houses; and every other Thursday Joyce would be there wandering casually around near the gate, expectant. Coatless in summer, leaning against the house, that shirt of his merged into the white weatherboard. All that was visible then was his tanned head. She'd come out with what looked like lime cordial or tea. For several hours he'd stay. Parker usually worked overtime on Fridays. And the house with its picket fence maintained a dental smile, no sign of decay.

There was nothing much wrong with what they were doing—sitting on the steps—yet the women who'd liked Joyce before seemed to think so. They shied away and pulled faces at the slightest pretext. Perhaps they were right; because Joyce took no notice. And he no longer bothered even bringing his sample-case. It turned out later he had lost his job.

Strange how 1939, fateful year for the world, was on a smaller scale, a fateful year for the Parkers.

Underneath these Brisbane houses people store their tools and ladders, fruits for preserves, bits of timber and junk in shadows bordered by the stilts. To camouflage the mess, white lattice covers the front and sides, perforating the shadows. It's dark and cool underneath.

At about four one afternoon he emerged from there, and returned casually to his place on the steps. A little later Joyce followed and went inside. He turned to say something but she had shut the door. The exact day is easily remembered. Hitler's armies had poured into Poland, a Friday. Emptied, made plain, devastated by the war, the streets like many others in Brisbane took an age to recover. The street seemed wider, but of course it wasn't.

Parker's house was still there; it seemed to have tilted slightly. This was another optical illusion. The undergrowth and the turbulent dead sticks which had been allowed to go wild after Joyce's death formed shoulders across the foreground, obliterating the stilts and lattice, one shoulder higher than the other. It came as a shock: it had overwhelmed Joyce's cacti, darkened the face of the house. Nothing had been done to lift the fallen front gutter, and the first time it rained, in 1945, it shed three separate streams of water.

Joyce had been pregnant, as everybody knew. Poor girl. She was found in the bathroom, some time early 1940. Circumstances remain vague. But complications occurred more in those days. Parker of course had always wanted children, actually talking about five. He was a fool.

Joyce was twenty-eight.

The front door opened and closed a few times, then it remained shut. There was no light. Parker preferred the back, the kitchen, at night.

His punctuality became a joke. He hardly spoke.

With its hooded eyes, jowls, resting on its dry shoulders, the house stubbornly gazed. It was always there. Lily-white in Joyce's day, its complexion began to deteriorate, the former pinkish glow at the end of the day assuming a kind of ashen-grey. Unattended, the paint-skin began falling away, in Parker's case revealing raw patches; it can be the problem with weather-boards. The red step, that characteristic spot alive in the centre, chafed and faded. No longer was it the focal point. Nothing was. At five o'clock a slate-coloured shadow grew below the windows and spread, and over the years darkened considerably.

Parker stopped going to church. He over-reacted, it was said.

Dandruff spotted his shoulders. He had filled out considerably: wide dark shoulders. His hair thinned and turned a kind of rust-brown. Short, back and sides. When he came out and stumbled along unshaven, unkept, it was with his kitbag to buy groceries. Some of his front teeth had gone.

It was said he had gone soft in the head.

The eyebrows darkened as weeks grew and withered in the gutters, drooping over the twin miniature roofs shading the windows. These jutted either with stubbornness or a kind of blindness. The windows beneath retreated into the shadows, never cleaned. The frown which developed was caused there by the line of wooden slats above the windows, and the angle of the fallen main gutter. Slowly the picket fence lost its smile. It had always been inane, irritating, anyway. Palings turned grey and here and there loosened by humidity and time angled and fell away: dark spaces, gaping holes, were displayed. Some time in the fifties Parker had to wear glasses. Parker had an unusually lined and weathered face for his age. As time passes, it takes an effort to maintain appearances.

Grey weeds appeared here and there, most noticeably out of the chimney.

The nose seemed to lengthen. They do with age. It grew dark, a blue-grey, and in the morning dripped for several hours.

Parker didn't seem to care.

Parker seemed merely to continue, passing through the house and time. It was a life.

Perhaps inevitably, the plumbing gave trouble. Quite an operation digging around the foundations; quite a stench too, of soaked earth and ruptured pipes. It had to be done.

Parker had hardly missed a day's work in his life.

Certainly, the roof showed signs of age. Apart from the gutters which suddenly overflowed without control or warning, a few of the corrugated sheets and the ridge-cap lifted in the slightest breeze, and rust, first freckles, then beer-coloured streaks became dark scabs: another darkening process. The roof was egg-shell thin. And of course early on parts of the lattice had gaping holes, evidently rotten below the shoulders, like one of Parker's Swedish singlets.

He withdrew further into the house, so it seemed, retreating behind shadows and that shemozzle in the foreground, and small boys sometimes crept up and rang the bell or threw stones on the roof. It naturally attracted attention, increasingly so, as the other houses became renovated. A sign in green biro, 'NO HAWKERS', appeared on the gate, although door-to-door salesmen, if you don't count the Mormons, haven't appeared in years, and even if any had it's doubtful they would have called.

The various horizontal lines had filled with dirt and moved apart, no longer parallel but wandered and concentrated around the shut mouth and the dull windows, and what with additional cracks and unexpected shadows, formed a network of wrinkles, a stubborn complexity. A kind of weariness grew as the house brooded, which was not obvious before. More and more it drooped. After all, he couldn't care less. It was futility. It happened gradually until one day it became clear and stayed that way. The steps, now grey, blurred into a jutting chin.

So he passed the years, inside.

Suddenly registering one morning, like the rare appearance of Parker along the footpath, was the bulge on the right-hand side, quite a rupture, a weakness there. And it's still there today. That can be a problem with the old weatherboards.

Parker put his bike away (under the house). Not long after, he retired. That was only a few years ago.

He kept his thoughts to himself.

Dark birds as small as flies buzzed around the mouth. A blocked chimney became a recurring minor trouble, and beginning around March, the bathroom became incontinent, quite unreliable. Other gutters slipped at the side. It settled on its shoulders, its eyes almost closed. A vibration, a tic, developed and accelerated even in the still conditions of Brisbane. It was that loose downpipe, the skinny elbow on the right.

And now this, or at last: unknown to Parker, or to anyone else in the street, white ants had been at the insides, destroying and multiplying, attacking beneath the surface. Evidently it had been going on for some time. The collapse when it came was sudden and complete. It has come as a shock. For a long time, almost since the War, it seemed no one had really been living there, and now there's only a house.

(1980)

Bruce Dawe
PLEASANT SUNDAY AFTERNOON

You mean we get this here Thingummy-thon
of   of   World Knowledge yeah that's it Jeez
a man's half-educated already
for nothing you might say   well practically
TWENTY-EIGHT MAGNIFICENT FULLY ILLUSTRATED VOLUMES   5
hey Eth here a minute and have a look at this
well you could have wiped your hands a bit first
(we're not auditioning for the Black and White Minstrels)
she won't leave that bloody stove of hers alone
no of course it won't rub off the page that's grease you silly   10
                                                sorry mate
now where's she off to   what the bloody hell
not with a red-hot knife   you've scorched it up
to buggery   ah well   you were saying
the kids Ethel the kids what do you mean   15
not quite suitable mate   these kids of mine
Eth what's young Stewart up to get him quick
starving for knowledge   use the mop love
ah there we are   a bit of the old sticky-tape
and good as new   *Graham*   ah   Ethel   looks like Graham   20
is getting set to   what's that son   you already *have*
alright son alright I'll take your word for it
no not the bloody encyclopaedia   old feller   here Eth
do something   well   what's the odds   you might as well
finish him off on this   err Contents page   25
talk about Tim Tyler   you married by any chance well
there's a treat in store   no don't get up no worries mate
we'll sort this little lot out now
what have we here   page sixty-three
I see what you mean by Magnificently Illustrated   30
now where is sixty-two   here's fifty-four
works fast doesn't he
                            well   alright mate
if you've got to go   but call in anytime
you won't believe this but we hardly ever have   35
a visitor from one year's end to the next

hey   hey there mate hey   what about your books
his books   he's left his bloody books!

                                                      (1973)

Barry Humphries
DAYS OF THE WEEK

SANDY, *in pyjamas and dressing gown, is discovered seated in a shabby armchair. He addresses the audience.*

I went to the RSL the other night and had a very nice night's entertainment. Beryl, that's the wife, came along too. Beryl's not a drinker but she had a shandy. She put in quite a reasonable quantity of time yarning with Norm Purvis's good lady and I had a beer with old Norm and some of the other chappies there. I don't say no to the occasional odd glass and Ian Preston, an old friend of mine, got up and sang a few humorous numbers—not too blue, on account of the womenfolk—so that altogether it was a really nice type of night's entertainment for us both. We called it a day round about ten-ish; didn't want to make it too late a night as Beryl had a big wash on her hands on the Monday morning and I had to be in town pretty early, stocktaking and one thing and another.

Well, we got back to Gallipoli Crescent about twenty past and Beryl and I went to bed.

We were very glad we hadn't made it too late a night on the Sunday because the Chapmans were expecting us over on the Monday night for a couple of hours to look at some slides of their trip. They're a very nice type of person and some of the coloured pictures he'd taken up north were a real...picture. Vi Chapman had gone to a lot of trouble with the savouries and altogether it was a really lovely night's entertainment for the two of us. Educational too. Well, round about ten I said we'd have to be toddling. You see, we didn't want to make it too late a night because Tuesday was the Tennis Club picture night and Beryl had a couple of tickets.

Well, there's not much I can say about the Tuesday, except that it was a really lovely night's entertainment. We're not ones for the pictures as a rule but when we do go we like to see a good bright show. After all, there's enough unhappiness and sadness in the world without going to see it in the theatre. Had a bit of strife parking the vehicle—you know what it's like up around that intersection near the Civic. Anyway, we found a possie in the long run just when we were beginning to think we might miss the blessed newsreel. The newsreel had a few shots of some of the poorer type of Italian housing conditions on the Continent and it made Beryl and I realise just how fortunate we were to have the comfort of our own home and all the little amenities round the home that make life easier for the womenfolk, and the menfolk generally, in the home. We left soon after interval as the next show wasn't the best and I was feeling a bit on the tired side. Besides, Beryl was expecting her sister and her husband over for five hundred on the Wednesday and we didn't want to make it too late a night.

So, Beryl and I went to bed.

Had to slip out of the office on the Wednesday lunch hour to get a few cashews to put round the card table. Beryl was running up a batch of sponge fingers with the passionfruit icing. There's no doubt about it, Beryl makes a lovely sponge finger.

Well, the card night went off very nicely indeed, except that Beryl's sister Lorna got a bit excited during the five hundred and knocked over a cup of tea and a curried egg sandwich on the new carpet. Oh, she was very apologetic, but as I said to Beryl later, being sorry won't buy you a new wall-to-wall. And you know what curried egg does to a burgundy Axminster.

By and large though, all things considered, and taking everything into account, it was a pretty nice night's entertainment.

They left early-ish. And Beryl and I went to bed...

Thursday was a bit quiet at the office and I was just as glad because I'd been feeling a bit more on the tired side than usual. Beryl had another fitting that night. She's having a new frock made for Geoff and Janice's wedding at Holy Trinity on the twenty-first and she wants to wear something a bit special—you know what the womenfolk are like. Anyway, I dropped her off at the dressmaker's on the way to Lodge.

It was a bit on the lateish side when I got home and I went straight to bed and we had a very nice night's...rest.

Always glad when Friday comes. Beryl and I usually have a nice quiet night in the home. It's the only chance I get to view the TV. There's usually a good story on of a Friday night—or else an educational quiz. Beryl had been down to the Town Hall library and got herself a good mystery so that, between the two of us, we had a nice night's home entertainment. We'd had a run of late nights and we were both pretty fagged so round about ten I filled the hottie and Beryl and I went to bed.

I was glad we hadn't made it too late a night as we had to be down the junction pretty early on the Saturday morning for the weekend shopping. Had a bit of strife parking the vehicle though. You know what it's like at the junction of a Saturday morning. However, I found a nice possie in the long run just when we were beginning to think we might miss the blessed butcher. I had a few minutes' worry, though. I lost Beryl in the Foodorama but she had the good sense to go back to the car.

I got home in time for a bite of lunch and then I had to whiz out again to the football. Beryl stayed at home to do the weekend baking.

Had the usual trouble parking the vehicle. You know what it's like at Memorial Park on a Saturday arvo. However, found a possie in the long run just when I was thinking I'd be late for the bounce. Oh, you wouldn't catch me missing an important semi. Beryl had packed me a nice thermos of Milo and I was pretty glad of it. It's very cold and blowy in the outer.

Had a bit of trouble shifting the vehicle. You know what it's like at Memorial Park after a big match—utility wedged right there in front of me. However I got out in the long run, just when I was beginning to think Beryl would have to wait tea. By the time I got home it was *that* blowy, the *Herald* was all over the front lawn.

Next door had invited us in to hear their *My Fairy Lady* record but I'd had a very nice afternoon's entertainment and Beryl wasn't that keen, so we made an early night of it and went to bed.

I always clean the car of a Sunday morning and do a bit of pottering in the garden. Bit worried about those rhodies.

Had the roast midday as we only like a light tea if we're going out of a Sunday night. Saves a big wash-up.

I'm really looking forward to the RSL tonight because—if you can go by experience—it ought to be a very nice night's entertainment.

(1958)

Patrick White
MISS SLATTERY AND HER DEMON LOVER

He stood holding the door just so far. A chain on it too.

'This,' she said, 'is Better Sales Pty Ltd.' Turning to a fresh page. 'Market research,' she explained. 'We want you to help us, and hope, indirectly, to help you.'

She moistened her mouth, easing a threat into an ethical compromise, technique pushed to the point where almost everyone was convinced. Only for herself the page on her pad would glare drearily blank.

Oh dear, do not be difficult, she would have said for choice to some old continental number whose afternoon sleep she had ruined.

'Faht do you vornt?' he asked.

'I want to ask you some questions,' she said.

She could be very patient when paid.

'Kvestions?'

Was he going to close the door?

'Not you. Necessarily. The housewife.'

She looked down the street, a good one, at the end of which the midday sun was waiting to deal her a blow.

'Housevife?'

At least he was slipping the chain.

'Nho! Nho! Nho!'

At least he was not going to grudge her a look.

'No lady?' she asked. 'Of any kind?'

'Nho! Nefer! Nho! I vould not keep any vooman of a permanent description.'

'That is frank,' she answered. 'You don't like them.'

Her stilettoes were hurting.

'Oh, I *lihke*! How I *lihke*! Zet is *vhy*!'

'Let us get down to business?' she said, looking at her blank pad. 'Since there is no lady, do you favour Priceless Pearl? Laundry starch. No. Kwik Kreem Breakfast Treat? Well,' she said, 'it's a kind of porridge that doesn't get lumps.'

'Faht is porritch?'

'It is something the Scotch invented. It is, well, just *porridge*, Mr Tibor.'

'Szabo.'

'It is Tibor on the bell.'

'I am Hoongahrian,' he said. 'In Hoongary ze nimes are beck to front. Szabo Tibor. You onderstend?'

He could not enlist too much of himself, as if it were necessary to explain all such matters with passionate physical emphasis.

'Yes,' she said. 'I see. Now.'

He had those short, but white teeth. He was not all that old; rather, he had reached a phase where age becomes elastic. His shoes could have cost him a whole week's pay. Altogether, all over, he was rather suède, brown suède, not above her shoulder. And hips. He had hips!

But the hall looked lovely, behind him, in black and white.

'Vinyl tiles?' Her toe pointed. 'Or lino?'

After all, she was in business.

'Faht? Hoh! Nho! Zet is all from marble.'

'Like in a bank!'

'Yehs.'

'Well, now! Where did you find all that?'

'I brought it. Oh, yehs. I bring everysing. Here zere is nossing. Nossing!'

'Oh, come, Mr Tibor—Szabo—we Australians are not all that uncivilized. Not in 1961.'

'Civilahsed! I vill learn you faht is civilahsed!'

She had never believed intensely in the advantages of knowledge, so that it was too ridiculous to find herself walking through the marble halls of Tibor Szabo Tibor. But so cool. Hearing the door click, she remembered the women they saw into pieces, and leave in railway cloak-rooms, or dispose of in back yards, or simply dump in the Harbour.

There it was, too. For Szabo Tibor had brought a View. Though at that hour of day the water might have been cut out of zinc, or aluminium, which is sharper.

'You have got it good here,' she said.

It was the kind of situation she had thought about, but never quite found herself in, and the strangeness of it made her languid, acting out a part she had seen others play, over-lifesize.

'Everysing I hef *mosst* be feuhrst class,' Szabo Tibor was explaining. 'Faht is your nime, please?'

'Oh,' she said. 'Slattery. Miss Slattery.'

'Zet is too match. Faht little nime else, please?'

Miss Slattery looked sad.

'I hate to tell you,' she said. 'I was christened Dimity. But my friends,' she added, 'call me Pete.'

'Vitch is veuorse? Faht for a nime is zet? Pete!'

'It is better than going through life with Dimity attached.'

'I vill call you nossing,' Szabo Tibor announced.

Miss Slattery was walking around in someone else's room, with large, unlikely strides, but it made her feel better. The rugs were so easy, and so very white, she realized she hadn't taken her two-piece to the cleaner.

'A nime is not necessary,' Szabo Tibor was saying. 'Tike off your het, please; it is not necessary neither.'

Miss Slattery did as she was told.

'I am not the hatty type, you know. They have us wear them for business reasons.'

She shook out her hair, to which the bottle had contributed, not altogether successfully, though certain lights gave it a look of its own, she hoped: tawnier, luminous, dappled. There was the separate lock, too, which she had persuaded to hang in the way she wanted.

An Australian girl, he saw. Another Australian girl.

Oh dear, he was older perhaps than she had thought. But cuddly. By instinct she was kind. Only wanted to giggle. At some old teddy bear in suède.

Szabo Tibor said:

'Sit.'

'Funny,' she said, running her hands into the depths of the chair, a habit she always meant to get out of, 'I have never mixed business and pleasure before.'

But Szabo Tibor had brought something very small and sweet, which ran two fiery wires out of her throat and down her nose.

'It is goot. Nho?'

'I don't know about *that*'—she coughed—'Mr Szabo. It's effective, though!'

'In Australien,' Mr Szabo said, and he was kneeling now, 'peoples call me Tibby.'

'Well! Have you a sense of humour!'

'Yehs! Yehs!' he said, and smiled. '*Witz!*'

When men started kneeling she wanted more than ever to giggle.

But Tibby Szabo was growing sterner.

'In Australien,' he said, 'no *Witz*. Nho! Novair!'

Shaking a forefinger at her. So that she became fascinated. It was so plump, for a finger, banana-coloured, with hackles of little black hairs.

'Do you onderstend?'

'Oh, yes, I understand all right. I am nossing.'

She liked it, too.

'Then faht is it?' asked Tibby Szabo, looking at his finger.

'I am always surprised,' she answered, 'at the part texture plays.'

'Are you intellectual girl?'

'My mind,' she said, re-crossing her legs, 'turned to fudge at puberty. Isn't that delicious?'

'Faht is futch?'

'Oh dear,' she said, 'you're a whale for knowing. Aren't there the things you just accept?'

She made her lock hang, for this old number who wouldn't leave off kneeling by the chair. Not so very old, though. The little gaps between his white teeth left him looking sort of defenceless.

Then Tibby Szabo took her arm, as though it didn't belong to her. The whole thing was pretty peculiar, but not as peculiar as it should have been. He took her arm, as if it were, say, a cob of corn. As if he had been chewing on a cob of corn. She wanted to giggle, and did. Supposing Mum and Wendy had seen! They would have had a real good laugh.

'You have the funniest ways,' she said, 'Tib.'

As Tibby Szabo kept on going up and down her arm.

When he started on the shoulder, she said:

'Stoput! What do you think I *am*?'

He heard enough to alter course.

A man's head in your lap somehow always made you feel it was trying to fool itself—it looked so detached, improbable, and ridiculous.

He turned his eyes on then, as if knowing: here is the greatest sucker for eyes. Oh God, nothing ever went deeper than eyes. She was a goner.

'Oh God,' she said, 'I am not like this!'

She was nothing like what she thought she was like. So she learned. She was the trampoline queen. She was an enormous, staggery spider. She was a rubber doll.

'You Austrahlian girls are visout *Temperament*,' Tibby Szabo complained. 'You are all gickle and talk. Passion is not to resist.'

'I just about broke every bone in my body not resisting,' Miss Slattery had to protest.

Her body that continued fluctuating overhead.

'Who ever heard of a glass ceiling!'

'Plenty glass ceiling. Zet is to see vis.'

'Tibby,' she asked, 'this wouldn't be—mink?'

'Yehs. Yehs. Meenk beds are goot for ze body.'

'I'll say!' she said.

She was so relaxed. She was half-dead. When it was possible to lift an arm, the long silken shudders took possession of her skin, and she realized the southerly had come, off the water, in at the window, giving her the goose-flesh.

'We're gunna catch a cold,' she warned, and coughed.

'It is goot.'

'I am glad to know that something is good,' she said, sitting up, destroying the composition in the ceiling. 'This sort of thing is all very well, but are you going to let me love you?'

Rounding on him. This fat and hairy man.

'Lof? Faht execkly do you mean?'

'Oh, Tibby!' she said.

Again he was fixing his eyes on her, extinct by now, but even in their dormancy they made her want to die. Or give. Or was it possible to give and live?

'Go to sleep,' he ordered.

'Oh, Tibby!'

She fell back floppy whimpery but dozed. Once she looked sideways at his death-mask. She looked at the ceiling, too. It was not unlike those atrocity photographs she had always tried to avoid, in the papers, after the War.

It was incredible, but always had been.

By the time Miss Slattery stepped into the street, carrying her business hat, evening had drenched the good address with the mellower light of ripened pears. She trod through it, tilted, stilted, tentative. Her neck was horribly stiff.

After that there was the Providential, for she did not remain with Better Sales Pty Ltd; she was informed that her services would no longer be required. What was it, they asked, had made her so unreliable? She said she had become distracted.

In the circumstances she was fortunate to find the position with the Providential. There, too, she made friends with Phyllis Wimble.

'A Hungarian,' Phyllis said, 'I never met a Hungarian. Sometimes I think I will work through the nationalities like a girl I knew decided to go through the religions. But gave up at the Occultists.'

'Why?'

'She simply got scared. They buried a man alive, one Saturday afternoon, over at Balmoral.'

When old Huthnance came out of his office.

'Miss Slattery,' he asked, 'where is that Dewhurst policy?'

He was rather a sweetie really.

'Oh yes,' Miss Slattery said, 'I was checking.'

'What is there to check?' Huthnance asked.

'Well,' Miss Slattery said.

And Huthnance smiled. He was still at the smiling stage.

Thursday evenings Miss Slattery kept for Tibby Szabo. She would go there Saturdays too, usually staying over till Sunday, when they would breakfast in the continental style.

There was the Saturday Miss Slattery decided to give Tibby Szabo a treat. Domesticity jacked her up on her heels; she was full of secrecy and little ways.

When Tibby asked:

'Faht is zet?'

'What is what?'

'Zet stench! Zet blue *smoke* you are mecking in my kitchenette. Faht are you prepurring?'

'That is a baked dinner,' Miss Slattery answered. 'A leg of lamb, with pumpkin and two other veg.'

'Lemb?' cried Tibby Szabo. 'Lemb! It stinks. Nefer in Budapest did lemb so much as cross ze doorways.'

And he opened the oven, and tossed the leg into the Harbour.

Miss Slattery cried then, or sat, rather, making her handkerchief into a ball.

Tibby Szabo prepared himself a snack. He had *Paprikawurst*, a breast of cold paprika chicken, paprikas in oil, paprika in cream cheese, and finally, she suspected, paprika.

'Eat!' he advised.

'A tiny crumb would choke me.'

'You are not crying?' he asked through some remains of paprika.

'I was thinking,' she replied.

'So! *Sink*-ing!'

Afterwards he made love to her, and because she had chosen love, she embraced it with a sad abandon, on the mink coverlet, under the glass sky.

Once, certainly, she sat up and said:

'It is all so *carnal*!'

'You use zeese intellectual veuords.'

He had the paprika chicken in his teeth.

There was the telephone, too, with which Miss Slattery had to contend.

'Igen! *Igen!* IGEN!' Tibby Szabo would shout, and bash the receiver on somebody anonymous.

'All this *iggy* stuff!' she said.

It began to get on her nerves.

'Demn idiots!' Tibby Szabo complained.

'How do you make your money, Tib?' Miss Slattery asked, picking at the mink coverlet.

'I am Hoongahrian,' he said. 'It come to me over ze telephown.'

Presently Szabo Tibor announced he was on his way to inspect several properties he owned around the city.

He had given her a key, at least, so that she might come and go.

'And you have had keys cut,' she asked, 'for all these other women, for Monday, Tuesday, Wednesday, and Friday in all these other flats?'

How he laughed.

'At last a real *Witz*! An Austrahlian *Witz*!' he said on going.

It seemed no time before he returned.

'Faht,' he said, 'you are still here?'

'I am the passive type,' she replied.

Indeed, she was so passive she had practically set in her own flesh beneath that glass conscience of a ceiling. Although a mild evening was ready to soothe, she shivered for her more than nakedness. When she stuck her head out the window, there were the rhinestones of Sydney glittering on the neck of darkness. But it was a splendour she saw could only dissolve.

'You Austrahlian girls,' observed Tibby Szabo, 'ven you are not all gickle, you are all cry.'

'Yes,' she said. 'I know,' she said, 'it makes things difficult. To be Australian.'

And when he popped inside her mouth a kiss like Turkish delight in action, she was less than ever able to take herself ın nand.

They drove around in Tibby's Jag. Because naturally Tibby Szabo had a Jag.

'Let us go to Manly,' she said. 'I have got to look at the Pacific Ocean.'

Tibby drove, sometimes in short, disgusted bursts, at others in long, lovely demonstrations of speed, or swooning swirls. His driving was so much the expression of Tibby Szabo himself. He was wearing the little cigar-coloured hat.

'Of course,' said Miss Slattery through her hair, 'I know you well enough to know that Manly is not Balaton.'

'Balaton?'

Tibby jumped a pedestrian crossing.

'Faht do you know about Balaton?'

'I went to school,' she said. 'I saw it on the map. You had to look at *some*thing. And there it was. A gap in the middle of Hungary.'

She never tired of watching his hands. As he drove, the soft, cajoling palms would whiten.

Afterwards when they were drawn up in comfort, inside the sounds of sea and pines, and had bought the paper-bagful of prawns, and the prawn-coloured people were squelching past, Tibby Szabo had to ask:

'Are you trying to spy on me viz all zese kvestions of Balaton?'

'All these questions? One bare mention!'

Prawn-shells tinkle as they hit the asphalt.

'I wouldn't open any drawer, not if I had the key. There's only one secret,' she said, 'I want to know the answer to.'

'But Balaton!'

'So blue. Bluer than anything we've got. So everything,' she said.

The sand-sprinkled people were going up and down. The soles of their feet were inured to it.

Tibby Szabo spat on the asphalt. It smoked.

'It isn't nice,' she said, 'to spit.'

The tips of her fingers tasted of the salt-sweet prawns. The glassy rollers, uncurling on the sand, might have raked a little farther and swallowed her down, if she had not been engulfed already in deeper, glassier caverns.

'Faht is zis secret?' Tibby asked.

'Oh!'

She had to laugh.

'It is us,' she said. 'What does it add up to?'

'Faht it edds up to? I give you a hellofa good time. I pay ze electricity end ze gess. I put you in ze vay of cut-price frocks. You hef arranged sings pretty nice.'

Suddenly too many prawn-shells were clinging to Miss Slattery's fingers. 'That is not what I mean,' she choked. 'When you love someone, I mean. I mean it's sort of difficult to put. When you could put your head in the gas-oven, and damn who's gunna pay the bill.'

Because she did not have the words, she got out her lipstick, and began to persecute her mouth.

Ladies were looking by now into the expensive car. Their glass eyes expressed surprise.

'Lof!' Tibby Szabo laughed. 'Lof is viz ze sahoul!' Then he grew very angry; he could have been throwing his hand away. 'Faht do zay know of lof?' he shouted. 'Here zere is only stike and bodies!'

Then they were looking into each other, each with an expression that suggested they might not arrive beyond a discovery just made.

Miss Slattery lobbed the paper-bag almost into the municipal bin.

'I am sursty,' Tibby complained.

Indeed, salt had formed in the corners of his mouth. Could it be that he was going to risk drinking deeper of the dregs?

'This Pacific Ocean,' Miss Slattery said, or cried, 'is all on the same note. Drive us home, Tibby,' she said, 'and make love to me.'

As he released the brake, the prawn-coloured bodies on the asphalt continued to lumber up and down, regardless.

'Listen,' Miss Slattery said, 'a girl friend of Phyllis Wimble's called Apple is giving a party in Woolloomooloo. Saturday night, Phyllis says. It's going to be bohemian.'

Szabo Tibor drew down his lower lip.

'Australhlian-bohemian-proveenshul. Zere is nossing veuorse zan bohemian-proveenshul.'

'Try it and see,' Miss Slattery advised, and bitterly added: 'A lot was discovered only by mistake.'

'And faht is zis Epple?'

'She is an oxywelder.'

'A vooman? Faht does she oxyveld?'

'I dunno. Objects and things. Apple is an artist.'

Apple was a big girl in built-up hair and pixie glasses. The night of the party most of her objects had been removed, all except what she said was her major work.

'This is *Hypotenuse of Angst*,' she explained. 'It is considered very powerful.'

And smiled.

'Will you have claret?' Apple asked. 'Or perhaps you prefer Scotch or gin. That will depend on whoever brings it along.'

Apple's party got under way. It was an old house, a large room running in many directions, walls full of Lovely Textures.

'Almost everybody here,' Phyllis Wimble confided, 'is doing something.'

'What have you brought, Phyl?' Miss Slattery asked.

'He is a grazier,' Phyllis said, 'that a nurse I know got tired of.'

'He is all body,' Miss Slattery said, now that she had learnt.

'What do you expect?'

Those who had them were tuning their guitars.

'Those are the Spanish guitarists,' Phyllis explained. 'And these are English teddies off a liner. They are only the atmosphere. It's Apple's friends who are doing things.'

'Looks a bit,' the grazier hinted.

Phyllis shushed him.

'You are hating it, Tib,' Miss Slattery said.

Tibby Szabo drew down his lip.

'I vill get dronk. On Epple's plonk.'

She saw that his teeth were ever so slightly decalcified. She saw that he was a little, fat, black man, whom she had loved, and loved still. From habit. Like biting your nails.

I must get out of it, she said. But you didn't, not out of biting your nails, until you forgot; then it was over.

The dancing had begun, and soon the kissing. The twangling of guitars broke the light into splinters. The slurp of claret stained the jokes. The teddies danced. The grazier danced the Spanish dances. His elastic-sides were so authentic. Apple fell upon her bottom.

Not everyone, not yet, had discovered Tibby Szabo was a little, fat, black man, with serrated teeth like a shark's. There was a girl called Felicia who came and sat in Tibby's lap. Though he opened his knees and she shot through, it might not have bothered Miss Slattery if Felicia had stayed.

'They say,' Phillis Wimble whispered, 'they are all madly queer.'

'Don't you know by now,' Miss Slattery said, 'that everyone is always queer?'

But Phyllis Wimble could turn narky.

'Everyone, we presume, but Tibby Szabo.'

Then Miss Slattery laughed and laughed.

'Tibby Szabo,' she laughed, 'is just about the queerest thing I've met.'

'Faht is zet?' Tibby asked.

'Nossing, darling,' Miss Slattery answered. 'I love you with all my body, and never my soul.'

It was all so *mouvementé*, said one of Apple's friends.

The grazier danced. He danced the Spanish dances. He danced bareheaded, and in his Lesbian hat. He danced in his shirt, and later, without.

'They say,' whispered Phyllis Wimble, 'there are two men locked in the lavatory together. One is a teddy, but they haven't worked out who the other can be.'

'Perhaps he is a social-realist,' Miss Slattery suggested.

She had a pain.

The brick-red grazier produced a stockwhip, too fresh from the shop, too stiff, but it smelled intoxicatingly of leather.

'Oh,' Miss Slattery cried, 'stockwhips are never *made*, they were there in the beginning.'

As the grazier uncoiled his brand-new whip, the lash fell glisteningly. It flicked a corner of her memory, unrolling a sheet of blazing blue, carpets of dust, cattle rubbing and straining past. She could not have kept it out even if she had wanted to. The electric sun beating on her head. The smell of old, sweaty leather had made her drunker than bulk claret.

'Oh, God, I'm gunna burn up!' Miss Slattery protested.

And took off her top.

She was alarmingly smooth, unscathed. Other skins, she knew, withered in the sun. She remembered the scabs on her dad's knuckles.

She had to get up then.

'Give, George!' she commanded. 'You're about the crummiest crack I ever listened to.'

Miss Slattery stood with the stockwhip. Her breasts snoozed. Or contemplated. She could have been awaiting inspiration. So Tibby Szabo noticed, leaning forward to follow to its source the faintest blue, of veins explored on previous expeditions.

Then, suddenly, Miss Slattery cracked, scattering the full room. She filled it with shrieks, disgust, and admiration. The horsehair gadfly stung the air. Miss Slattery cracked an abstract painting off the wall. She cracked a cork out of a bottle.

'Brafo, Petuska!' Tibby Szabo shouted. 'Vaz you efer in a tseerkoos?'

He was sitting forward.

'Yeah,' she said, 'a Hungarian one!'

And let the horsehair curl round Tibby's thigh.

He was sitting forward. Tibby Szabo began to sing:

> *'Csak egy kislány*
> *van a világon,*
> *az is az én*
> *drága galambo-o-om!'*

He was sitting forward with eyes half-closed, clapping and singing.

> *Hooray for love,*
> *it rots you,...'*

Miss Slattery sang.

She cracked a cigarette out of the grazier's lips.

> *'A jó Isten*
> *de nagyon szeret,'*

sang Tibby Szabo,

> *'hogy nékem adta*
> *a legszebbik-e-e-et!'* [1]

Then everybody was singing everything they had to sing, guitars disintegrating, for none could compete against the syrup from Tibby Szabo's compulsive violin.

While Miss Slattery cracked. Breasts jumping and frolicking. Her hair was so brittle. Lifted it once again, though, under the tawny sun, hawking dust, drunk on the smell of the tepid canvas water-bags.

Miss Slattery cracked once more, and brought down the sun from out of the sky.

It is not unlikely that the world will end in thunder. From the sound of it, somebody must have overturned *Hypotenuse of Angst*. Professional screamers had begun to scream. The darkness filled with hands.

'Come close, Petuska.'

It was Tibby Szabo.

'I vill screen you,' he promised, and caressed.

When a Large Person appeared with a candle. She was like a scone.

'These studios,' the Large Person announced, 'are let for purposes of creative art, and the exchange of intellectual ideas. I am not accustomed to louts—and worse,' here she looked at Miss Slattery's upper half, 'wrecking the premises,' she said. 'As there has never been any suspicion that this is a Bad House, I must ask you all to leave.'

So everybody did, for there was the Large Person's husband behind her, looking as though he might mean business. Everybody shoved and poured, there was a singing, a crumbling of music on the stairs. There was a hugging and a kissing in the street. Somebody had lost his pants. It was raining finely.

Tibby Szabo drove off very quickly, in case a lift might be asked for.

'Put on your top, Petuska,' he advised. 'You vill ketch a colt.'

It sounded reasonable. She was bundling elaborately into armholes.

'Waddayaknow!' Miss Slattery said. 'We've come away with the grazier's whip!'

'Hef vee?' Tibby Szabo remarked.

So they drove in Tibby's Jag. They were on a spiral.

'I am so tired,' Miss Slattery admitted.

And again:

'I am awful tired.'

She was staring down at those white rugs in Tibby's flat. The soft, white, serious pile. She was propped on her elbows. Knees apart. Must be looking bloody awful.

'Petuska,' he was trying it out, 'vill you perhaps do vun more creck of ze whip?'

He could have been addressing a convalescent.

'Oh, but I am tired. I am done,' she said.

'Just vun little vun.'

Then Miss Slattery got real angry.

'You and this goddam lousy whip! I wish I'd never set eyes on either!' Nor did she bother where she lashed.

'*Ach! Oh! Aÿ-yaÿ-yaÿ! Petuska!*'

Miss Slattery cracked.

'What are the people gunna say when they hear you holler like that?' As she cracked, and slashed.

'*Aÿ!* It is none of ze people's business. *Pouff! Yaÿ-yaÿ-yaÿ-yaÿ!*' Tibby Szabo cried. 'Just vun little vun more!'

And when at last she toppled, he covered her very tenderly where she lay.

'Did anyone ever want you to put on boots?'

'What ever for?' asked Phyllis Wimble.

But Miss Slattery found she had fetched the wrong file.

'Ah, dear,' she said, resuming. 'It's time I thought about a change,' she said. 'I'm feeling sort of tired.'

'Hair looks dead,' said Phyllis Wimble. 'That is always the danger signal.'

'Try a new rinse.'

'A nice strawberry.'

Miss Slattery, whose habit had been to keep Thursday evening for Tibby Szabo, could not bear to any more. Saturdays she still went, but at night, for the nights were less spiteful than the days.

'Vair vas you, Petuska, Sursday evening?' Tibby Szabo had begun to ask.

'I sat at home and watched the telly.'

'Zen I vill install ze telly for here!'

'Ah,' she said, 'the telly is something that requires the maximum of concentration.'

'Are you changing, Petuska?' Tibby asked.

'Everything is changing,' Miss Slattery said. 'It is an axiom of nature.' She laughed rather short.

'That,' she said, 'is something I think I learned at school. Same time as Balaton.'

It was dreadful, really, for everyone concerned, for Tibby Szabo had begun to ring the Providential. With urgent communications for a friend. Would she envisage Tuesday, Vensday, Friday?

However impersonally she might handle the instrument, that old Huthnance would come in and catch her on the phone. Miss Slattery saw that Huthnance and she had almost reached the point of no return.

'No,' she replied. 'Not Thursday. Or any other day but what was agreed. Saturday, I said.'

She slammed it down.

So Miss Slattery would drag through the moist evenings. In which the scarlet hibiscus had furled. No more trumpets. Her hair hung dank, as she trailed through the acid, yellow light, towards the good address at which her lover lived.

'I am developing a muscle,' she caught herself saying, and looked round to see if anyone had heard.

It was the same night that Tibby Szabo cried out from the bottom of the pit:

'Vhy em I condemned to soffer?'

Stretched on mink, Miss Slattery lay, idly flicking at her varnished toes. Without looking at the view, she knew the rhinestones of Sydney had never glittered so heartlessly.

'Faht for do you *torture* me?'

'But that is what you wanted,' she said.

Flicking. Listless.

'Petuska, I vill gif you *any*sink!'

'Nossing,' she said. 'I am going,' she said.

'*Gowing?* Ven vee are so suited to each ozzer!'

Miss Slattery flicked.

'I am sick,' she said, 'I am sick of cutting a rug out of your fat Hungarian behind.'

The horsehair lash slithered and glistened between her toes.

'But faht vill you do visout me?'

'I am going to find myself a thin Australian.'

Tibby was on his knees again.

'I am gunna get married,' Miss Slattery said, 'and have a washing-machine.'

'*Yaÿ-yaÿ-yaÿ! Petuska!*'

Then Miss Slattery took a look at Tibby's eyes, and re-discovered a suppliant poodle, seen at the window of an empty house, at dusk. She had never been very doggy, though.

'Are you ze Defel perheps?' cried Tibby Szabo.

'We Australians are not all that unnatural,' she said.

And hated herself, just a little.

As for Tibby Szabo, he was licking the back of her hand.

'Vee vill make a finenshul arrangement. Pretty substenshul.'

'No go!' Miss Slattery said.

But that is precisely what she did. She got up and pitched the grazier's stockwhip out of the window, and when she had put on her clothes, and licked her lips once or twice, and shuffled her hair together—she went.

(1963)

---

[1] 'Only one little girl
in the world,
and she is
my dear little dove!

The good God
must love me indeed
to have given me
the most beautiful one!'

LIVING IN ABORIGINAL AUSTRALIA

Land, people, religion and culture are more closely integrated in the
societies of Aboriginal Australians than in white societies. The distinctions
commonly made by whites between owners of land and the land itself, the
secular and the spiritual, the individual author and the text he or she has
created, are alien to Aboriginal society. Invading Europeans displacing
indigenous people may, however, aspire to be part of the land in a spiritual
sense. In his poem 'The land was ours before we were the land's' the
United States poet Robert Frost admitted that the European notion of
possessing the land preceded any sense of belonging to the land. In Australia the Jindyworobaks had a dream by which whites might appropriate

both the land and its Aboriginal spirituality. But such white hopes and dreams are unlikely to be as powerful as the Aboriginal assurance, expressed in the poem 'We are going' by Oodgeroo Noonuccal [Kath Walker], that 'We are the corroboree and the bora ground...We are nature and the past.'

Traditional Aboriginal stories, songs, and poems—though these are white categories—often bring together the sacred, the legendary, the totemic, the erotic and the local in ways that resist European genre classification. In the same way as visual designs and objects may be the preserve of the people of one place, or of a particular sub-section or of one sex of such people, so stories and songs will be likely to have not only their appropriate occasions for recital but also their local or clan ownership. One story may even have its prelude or its sequel owned by another clan or subsection. In other words, while individual ownership of (or more correctly inseparable attachment to) a song or story does not occur, notions of clan ownership may be very strictly adhered to. In communities relying on oral and not written means of transmission, the opportunities for hearing a particular work may be severely limited. Sometimes only part of a story can be told because the hearers are not initiated into the ceremonies and understandings to which the concealed part belongs.

This section opens with a song about (and, as it were, sung by) the dominant Ancestral Beings, the two Djanggawul Sisters and their Brother. They travel from the mythological land of sacred Beings, via the mythological island of Bralgu (the Home of the Eternal Spirits and of departed ancestors), to populate Arnhem Land. It is part of a song cycle that was performed to the accompaniment of dancing on ceremonial ground by the leaders of the clan. Sacred symbols would have been present and various rituals of respect to the Djanggawul would have been performed. Such symbols might include a ball of feathers tied by string to a pole, representing the Morning Star as a guiding light, and the conically shaped woven mat, representative of the uterus of the Sisters—for the theme of this cycle is fertility—and the Sisters, emblematically associated with the sun, are perpetually pregnant. In the songs the singers obviously move in and out of identification with the divine Beings whose song they sing.

The songs from the Goulburn Island Cycle, from the north-east of Arnhem Land, are love songs, without sacred significance. In Song 3 the men play didjeridus and clap-sticks while the women dance, the main purpose being to bring the wind and clouds for the rainy season.

The song from the Wonguri linguistic unit of the Mandjigai (sandfly) clan also comes from Arnhem Land. It is part of a cycle telling the story of the ancestral man, Moon, who lived at the Place of the Dugong. After his death by going down into the sea, he continued to re-enact his life and death each day.

These examples of song cycles were recorded, of course, in the twentieth century, but it is reasonable to suppose that they are representative of the kind of oral culture that extended back for thousands—perhaps tens of thousands—of years. The intrusion of white settlers into a land that had been occupied by the Aborigines for forty thousand years or more severely disrupted and dislocated Aboriginal culture. The late eighteenth-century scientific curiosity about Aboriginal customs and language rapidly gave way to punitive expeditions intended to annihilate the Aboriginal population or at least drive them away from their traditional grounds. Aboriginal culture was despised and derided by white colonists: missionaries regarded it as evidence of heathendom; government officials 'wanted assimilation into white values to occur as rapidly as possible; while white pastoralists often regarded it as evidence of inferiority or depravity.

In the twentieth century, Aboriginal writers began to secure publication of their works in English. David Unaipon (1872–1967), a member of the Ngarrindjeri people of South Australia, had his collection, *Native Legends*, published. Unaipon not only was expert in his own culture but was also widely read in European culture and competent as an inventor, his best-known invention being an improved mechanism for sheep-shears. But it was not until the 1960s that Aboriginal works in English appeared in any numbers. Kath Walker (who changed her name to Oodgeroo Noonuccal in 1987) had a volume of poems, *We Are Going*, published in 1964; Colin Johnson (now known as Mudrooroo Narogin) had a novel, *Wild Cat Falling*, published in the following year; Kevin Gilbert's political analysis, *Because a White Man'll Never Do It*, was published in 1973.

These written documents present the neglected plight of Aborigines: pleas for understanding; pride in Aboriginality and the pre-white history of Aborigines; dreams for a better future; anger at white indifference or the material values that (literally and philosophically) push Aborigines to the edges of society; the re-telling of the history of white domination from an Aboriginal point of view; and the sense of being dispossessed strangers in one's own land—part of a suppressed indigenous 'Fourth World' culture worse off even than the underprivileged 'Third World' one.

In this Section examples of this literature are interspersed with white interpretations of Aborigines. It should be evident that even the most knowledgeable and sympathetic white writers, among whom should be included Katharine Susannah Prichard and Xavier Herbert, present views of Aborigines and their society which do not correspond with Aboriginal perceptions. The account of Yagan in George Fletcher Moore's *Diary of Ten Years Eventful Life of an Early Settler in Western Australia* (which also includes a vocabulary list from an Aboriginal language) is sympathetic, but very much framed by European literary experience, even to the surprising comparison of Yagan to Sir William Wallace, the Scottish nationalist leader of the late thirteenth century who defended his country against the English. The presentation of Yagan in Jack Davis' play, *Kullark* (published 1982), avoids the condescension that runs through Moore's account.

Other incidents where the black writer's view is more convincing than the white's concern the struggle of the Tasmanian Aborigines to resist the beguiling genocide offered by George Augustus Robinson and others. Colin Johnson's novel, *Dr Wooreddy's Prescription for Enduring the Ending of the World* (1983), covers much the same ground as Robert Drewe's *The Savage Crows* (1976) but from the point of view of Wooreddy, the last Aboriginal male from the Bruny Island clan in the south-east of Tasmania. Wooreddy and Trugernanna (or Truganini) are puzzled and dismayed by the strange white ghosts (*num*) who intrude on their world, Wooreddy believing them at first to be manifestations of the spirit of fateful malevolence, *Ria Warrawah*. The events of the book, as the Tasmanians allow themselves to be herded on to an inhospitable island in Bass

Strait, prove this insight to be correct.

Sally Morgan and Hazel McKellar both tell stories of the treatment of black children and families by whites. Morgan's book, *My Place*, tells of an Aboriginal girl's recognition of the Aboriginality that had been concealed from her, and of her search for her personal and family history in Western Australia. McKellar's *Matya-Mundu* records the contradictions and problems of growing up on a settlement in south-western Queensland. Jack Davis' play, *No Sugar* (1986), dramatically presents conditions on the Moore River Native Settlement in the early 1930s, where Aborigines lived in prison-like conditions. The Superintendent was Mr Neal, the Matron of the hospital his wife. Later in the play, the Chief Protector of Aborigines, Mr A. O. Neville, an authoritarian administrator with a modicum of respect for Aborigines, delivers a speech to the Royal Western Australian Historical Society in Perth. Towards the end—and Davis is quoting from a copy of the speech in the possession of the Society—he says:

> When referring to Australia's treatment of her Aborigines we are apt to refer somewhat scathingly to Tasmania's harshness in ridding herself of her natives within the first seventy years of settlement. In that time some six thousand natives disappeared and only one was left alive. Yet here, in the south-west of our State, within an area about twice the size of Tasmania between 1829 and 1901—seventy-two years—a people estimated to number thirteen thousand were reduced to one thousand four hundred and nineteen, of whom nearly half were half-caste.

In the scene included in this anthology, the translation of Jimmy's song is as follows:

> Look, who is this coming?
> Crabs, crabs, crabs, crabs
> In the river mouth,
> They are coming in the river mouth, river mouth,
> Coming in the river mouth.
> Fish coming up the river,
> Up the river, up the river,
> Fish in the river mouth,
> Fish in the river mouth,
> Coming up, coming up, coming up,
> Fish and crabs, fish and crabs, fish and crabs,
> Shout of praise!

Billy Kimberley is not one of the local Nyoongahs, but a black tracker from the Kimberley region in north-western Australia. His account of the massacre of blacks at Oombulgarri is based on an account in Randolph Stow's novel, *To the Islands* (1958).

Aboriginal theatre in English was first produced by the National Black Theatre in Redfern in the mid-1970s. *The Cake Man* (1975) by Robert Merritt (televised by the ABC in 1977) and *Here Comes the Nigger!* (1976) by Gerry Bostock were early successes, the first dealing with life on an Aboriginal mission, the second with life in the inner suburbs of Sydney In Bostock's play Sam is a blind Aboriginal poet who is being tutored for his Higher School Certificate by a white woman, Odette O'Brien. Sam's brother Billy disapproves of the affection that grows up between the two; so does Odette's brother, Neil. Verna, Billy's girlfriend, is concerned that Sam is not hurt or used in the relationship. Sam's blindness is, of course, a metaphor for the colour-blindness that the author hopes for. As Sam says

> I'm blind. There was a time when I could see people on colour lines and only on colour lines; but now I'm blind I'm forced to look inside of people to see what they're really like; to see what colour they are inside. Surely that's the important thing.

In the 1980s the number of Aboriginal prisoners who died while in police cells became so alarming that a Royal Commission was established in 1988. Jack Davis' poem, 'John Pat', commemorates one of those deaths. The poem was included in the program of his play, *Barungin*, when it premiered in Perth in 1988. *Barungin* itself forms the third in a trilogy of plays (*First Born*) about the Wallitch family, the earlier two (in chronological order of the events presented) being *No Sugar* and *The Dreamers*.

Ken Goodwin/Alan Lawson

THE DJANGGAWUL SONG CYCLE

PART ONE

SONG 1

Although I leave Bralgu, I am close to it. I, Djanggawul,
    am paddling...
Paddling with all the paddles, with their flattened tapering ends.
Close I am coming, with Bildjiwuraroiju,
Coming along from Bralgu. We splash the water as we paddle,
    paddling wearily,
With Miralaidj, undulating our buttocks as we paddle.   *5*
We paddle along through the roaring tide, paddle a long way.
I am paddling along fast, through the rough sea...
Beside me is foam from our paddling, and large waves follow us.
With Bralbral, we move our wrists as we paddle, making noise as we
    go through the sea...
We, Djanggawul, are paddling along, lifting our paddles, slowly
    going along...   *10*
All the way we have paddled. I rest my paddles now, as we glide.
On the sea's surface the light from the Morning Star shines as we
    move,
Shining on the calmness of the sea.
Looking back I see its shine, an arc of light from the Morning Star.
    The shine falls on our paddles, lighting our way.
We look back to the Morning Star and see its shine, looking back as
    we paddle.   *15*
Star moving along, shining! We saw its disc quite close,
Skimming the sea's surface, and mounting again above Bralgu.
Close to us it rises above the expanse of sea; we look back,
    seeing its shine.
Morning Star, sent by the dancing Spirit People, those people of the
    rain, calling out as they dance there with outstretched arms.
They send it for us, that we may travel along its shining path from
    Bralgu.   *20*
Close, its 'feathered ball' appears above Dangdangmi! Close is the
    Morning Star, on the end of its string and pole!
Close is the Morning Star, stretching from its pole, extending out
    from its string...
Shining from Bralgu, as we paddle through the sea.
Bubbles rise to the sea's surface; our canoe is carried on the crest of
    waves. Ah, *waridj* Bralbral!
Sound made by our splashing paddles, and the sea's roar as we rise
    to the crest of a wave!   *25*
We make our paddles sound, with the noise of the sea, sound that
    is heard far away at Bralgu.
We, the Djanggawul, make sound with our paddling, make spray as
    we paddle fast...
The salty smell! The roaring sea, and its foam! Its wide expanse
    behind us!

We paddle, with Bildjiwuraroiju, following the waves along,
Pushing our way through the waves that block us   30
Sound from our sacred *ngainmara* mat! Noise as the waters surge
    around it!
Sound, as the sacred poles are moved about with the rolling of
    the canoe!

SONG 2

We Djanggawul saw the Morning Star shining . . .,
Saw its shine on the green-backed turtle, lighting up its throat . . .!
Paddling, we saw that turtle: saw its eyes open, its flippers out-
    stretched as it floated.
Sea water lapped at its shell, spreading across its back.
Making a sound as it rose above the surface; see the dilly bag
    at its back!   5
It swam through the sea, with shell like a rock, hiding the bag
    under its flipper.
'I have another basket' (the turtle says). 'It is the cuttle fish.'

from THE GOULBURN ISLAND CYCLE

SONG 3

Get the clapping sticks and the didjeridu, for we feel the urge
    for enjoyment.
Hear the rhythmic beat, and the singing of Goulburn Island people,
    clans from the Woolen River . . .
Chests turned towards the cold west wind, and the sound of the
    didjeridu . . .
Rhythmically beating, within the huts like sea-eagle nests . . .
Sound from within the huts, spreading across the country . . .   5
Clapping-sticks at the Sandspit near Goulburn Islands, at the place of
    Western Clouds, and of Standing Clouds, and at Milingimbi
    Creek . . .
Opposite Milingimbi, at the place of Coloured Reflections . . . sticks
    clapping within the huts,
Sticks clapping, for we feel the urge for enjoyment: invoking
    the western rain clouds . . .
Sound rising like clouds, wafted across the waters to Milingimbi:
Like clouds banking up, the sound hovers over the Island of
    Clouds . . .   10
Cold wind from the west, striking their chests . . .
It is ours! With this singing the wind begins to blow, swaying
    the branches,
Cold stranger wind from somewhere, from Goulburn Islands!

SONG 4

Take clay and coloured ochres, and put them on!
They paint chests and breasts with clay, in water-designs,
Hang round their necks the padded fighting-bags.

They paint themselves, those Goulburn Island people, and clans
    from the Woolen River...
They are always there, at the wide expanse of water...   5
They take more clay, for painting the fighting-sticks...
Paint on their chests designs of water-snakes...
And paint the boomerangs with coloured ochres...
Painting the small boomerangs...
Calling the invocations...all over the country, and at the place
    of the Wawalag sisters...   10
Painting themselves at Milingimbi Point, at the place of
    Standing Clouds.
At the place of the Western Clouds, at the place of
    Coloured Reflections...

from A WONGURI-MANDJIGAI SONG CYCLE OF THE MOON-BONE

SONG 2

They are sitting about in the camp, among the branches,
    along the back of the camp:
Sitting in rows in the camp, in the shade of paperbark trees:
Sitting in rows, like new white spreading clouds:
In the shade of paperbark trees, they are sitting resting like clouds.
People of the clouds, living there like mist, like mist sitting
    resting with arms on knees,   5
In toward the shade, in the Lily Place, the shade of the paperbarks.
Sitting there in rows, those Wonguri-Mandjigai people,
    paperbarks along like a cloud.
Living on cycad nut bread, sitting there with white-stained
    fingers,
Sitting in there resting, those people of the Sandfly clan...
Sitting there like mist, at that Place of the Dugong...
    and of the Dugong's Entrails...   10
Sitting resting there in the Place of the Dugong...
In that Place of the Moonlight Clay-pan, and at the Place
    of the Dugong...
There at that Dugong Place they are sitting along in rows.

Jack Davis
from KULLARK

SCENE TWO

YAGAN *enters in ceremonial paint. He chants and dances.*
YAGAN: *Woolah!*
          You came, Warrgul,
          With a flash of fire and a thunder roar,
          And as you came
          You flung the earth up to the sky,   5
          You formed the mountain ranges
          And the undulating plains.
          You made a home for me
          On Kargattup and Karta Koomba,
          Kargattup and Karta Koomba.   10
          You made the *beeyol beeyol*,
          The wide clear river,
          As you travelled onward to the sea.
          And as you went into the sunset
          Two rocks* you left to mark your passing,   15
          To tell of your returning
          And our affinity.
          You gave me kangaroo and emu for my middens,
          Feathers for corroboree at night,
          The swan, the duck and other birds you gave me,   20
          And the waters teemed with fish a-shimmering bright.
          You gave me laws and legends
          To protect me,
          And sacred places hidden in the hills.
          Then, oh *wirilo*, *wirilo*,   25
          The *jungara* came across the deep blue waters
          To rend my soul, to decimate and kill.

        (YAGAN *exits.*)

                                    (1979)

---

* Rottnest and Garden Islands

G.F. Moore
from DIARY OF TEN YEARS EVENTFUL LIFE OF AN EARLY SETTLER IN WESTERN AUSTRALIA

YAGAN

On seeing several natives approach the house, I went towards them as usual, thinking they were my old friends...When my eyes first fell upon Ya-gan, I said immediately, 'What name?' They all answered, 'Boolgat'. I said, 'No; Ya-gan'...he came forward, avowed himself, and entered into a long argument and defence of his conduct...and I confess he had almost as much of the argument as I had. Both parties seemed to consider us as respectively arguing the question. Ya-gan...used bold and emphatic language and graceful gesture, with abundant action; he delivered himself boldly. I did not understand him, but replied,...'if black man no gydyell (kill) cow, no gydyell sheep, no gydyell pig, white man all same as brother to black man, shake hands plenty.' Here I advanced with open hands to them, which all ran eagerly to grasp, save the moody chief himself...

Ya-gan again stepped forward, and leaning familiarly with his left hand on my shoulder, while he gesticulated with his right, delivered a sort of recitative, looking earnestly at my face. I regret that I could not understand him, but I conjectured, from the tone and manner, that the purport was this: 'You came to our country; you have driven us from our haunts, and disturbed us in our occupations: as we walk in our own country, we are fired upon by the white men; why should the white men treat us so?' This reminded me of a chorus in a Greek tragedy; and the other natives seemed to act as subordinate characters to Ya-gan...

The chief approached again, and fixing his eyes as if he read my countenance, said inquiringly, 'Midgegoroo shoot? walk?' (meaning was Midgegoroo dead or alive?). I felt that the question was full of personal hazard to me, and gave no reply...I answered slowly, 'White man angry—Governor angry.' However my men assured them that both Midgegoroo and his son were gone on board a ship. Ya-gan still continued to read my countenance, and when he could obtain no answer from me, he said with extraordinary vehemence of manner, distinctness of utterance, and emphasis of tone, 'White man shoot Midgegoroo, Ya-gan kill three' (holding up three fingers). I said, "Ya-gan kill all white men, soldier man and every man kill Ya-gan.' He scowled a look of daring defiance, and turned on his heel with an air of ineffable contempt.

During the latter part of this conference, he held a beautifully tapered and exquisitely pointed spear, grasped like a stiletto, about fourteen inches from the point, while the shaft lay over his shoulder, with a seeming carelessness. He evidently suspected treachery, and was on his guard against it, taking care not to let my men press on him too closely, and keeping some of the natives between myself and them.

Nothing short of an overpowering force (which I did not possess), or a cold-blooded deliberate treachery (of which I was incapable), would have enabled me to have secured him as he then stood: it was, perhaps, my duty to have attempted his arrest, dead or alive; however, consider the circumstances of my situation,—I had gone among them unarmed, little thinking that the 'Wallace' of the tribe was there.

(1884)

Dick Roughsey
from MOON AND RAINBOW: THE
AUTOBIOGRAPHY OF AN ABORIGINAL

FACES OF WHITE PIPE-CLAY

My father had just speared a stingray when he heard the people calling out from the cliff above him. They were jumping about with excitement and pointing down the coast and he heard the words '*Yockai, walpa, walpa, dunga kial!*' 'Look out, everybody, the ships of the men with faces of white pipe-clay are coming again!' Goobalathaldin put the stingray in his hand-net with other fish and hurried off to join the small group of Lardil people on the cliff top.

For many years now my father had seen these strange ships of the pale-faced men go gliding by our home island of Langu-Narnji. They were usually well out from shore in the deeper water, and although no men could be seen paddling them, they seemed to glide majestically through the water under the shade of the great white shells tied to the poles above, until they vanished from sight around the top end of Bangubella, a big bay to the north.

The people were silent as they watched the small ship pass the northern end of Langu-Narnji, but they cried out in surprise as one of the great white shells collapsed and the ship turned to glide into a small bay in front of the Red-bill Bird story place. A loud rattling noise as something splashed into the water sent my father and all our poor naked people running away in fright, and they ran on until they were hidden by the scrub on Dinglemah Hill.

They sat in the scrub on Dinglemah and watched the strange men put out a small boat and row up to land on the sandy beach. My father's people were afraid of the strange men; they had heard stories from the Yanggarl of Denham Island, and tribes on the nearby mainland, of how these white people could kill a man with thunder that sent out invisible spears to tear a hole in his body and spill his blood on the sand.

The white men lifted objects from the boat and carried them up the beach to place them above high-water mark. One of the men stood up and looked toward Dinglemah and began shouting out; he seemed to be talking to the hidden people and kept pointing to the pile of things on the beach. Then they got back in the boat and went back to their ship.

The watchers on the hill saw the men on the ship making preparations as though they were going to stay for the night, so they gathered up their small children, weapons and seafood and set off for an inland waterhole where they could camp and cook their food, safe from surprise by the white man.

Early next morning some young boys were sent out to see what the white men were doing and report on their activities. The boys soon came running back to say that the ship was sailing away to the north and that the things put on the beach were still there.

When the ship had vanished from sight my father and the other men left the women and children on Dinglemah while they crept slowly down to the beach to see what had been left behind. They found some bags and small boxes containing strange materials.

The white people had left gifts of food on the beach so that my people would become friendly towards them. But it was all wasted on these poor people; they did not understand the strange food. A bag of flour was thought to be white pipeclay and they rubbed it all over their bodies and in their hair and threw the rest away. A bag of rice was examined and thought to be a bag of hornet or wasp eggs, and no good to eat. Some bars of yellow soap seemed better tucker and these were put in the fire to cook. My mother saw the soap getting soft in the coals and, thinking it cooked, gave some to my older brother to eat. Poor old Burrud, he still remembers the terrible pains in his stomach. He and some of the other children who ate the soap were very ill and the people decided that the food had been poisoned.

This was the first real contact with white people for those few families of the Larumbanda, or South-Wind Lardil, as we are called. They did not know then that their way of life was soon to be changed forever, a way of life that had begun away off in Dreamtime, when these three great Balombanda people first entered the land and made everything.

We will never see those times come back again, they are gone. But those happy memories will never be forgotten, or those old folks, and how they lived in the time before white men came with all their warp and nails, dinghies, ropes and other things to change our happy hunting. Now I can only write stories of those days when I used to share in that same life, shared the hunt and lived through all weather and storms with my old people, up there in my country.

(1971)

Watkin Tench
A COMPLETE ACCOUNT OF THE SETTLEMENT AT PORT JACKSON

from CHAPTER 3

TRANSACTIONS OF THE COLONY, FROM THE COMMENCEMENT OF THE YEAR 1789, UNTIL THE END OF MARCH

Pursuant to his resolution, the governor on the 31st of December sent two boats, under the command of Lieutenant Ball of the Supply, and Lieutenant George Johnston of the marines, down the harbour, with directions to those officers to seize and carry off some of the natives. The boats proceeded to Manly Cove, where several Indians were seen standing on the beach, who were enticed by courteous behaviour and a few presents to enter into conversation. A proper opportunity being presented, our people rushed in among them, and seized two men: the rest fled; but the cries of the captives soon brought them back, with many others, to their rescue:

and so desperate were their struggles, that, in spite of every effort on our side, only one of them was secured; the other effected his escape. The boats put off without delay; and an attack from the shore instantly commenced: they threw spears, stones, firebrands, and whatever else presented itself, at the boats; nor did they retreat, agreeable to their former custom, until many musquets were fired over them.

The prisoner was now fastened by ropes to the thwarts of the boat; and when he saw himself irretrievably disparted from his countrymen, set up the most piercing and lamentable cries of distress. His grief, however, soon diminished: he accepted and eat of some broiled fish which was given to him, and sullenly submitted to his destiny.

1789. When the news of his arrival at Sydney was announced, I went with every other person to see him: he appeared to be about thirty years old, not tall, but robustly made; and of a countenance which, under happier circumstances, I thought would display manliness and sensibility; his agitation was excessive, and the clamourous crowds who flocked around him did not contribute to lessen it. Curiosity and observation seemed, nevertheless, not to have wholly deserted him; he shewed the effect of novelty upon ignorance; he wondered at all he saw: though broken and interrupted with dismay, his voice was soft and musical, when its natural tone could be heard; and he readily pronounced with tolerable accuracy the names of things which were taught him. To our ladies he quickly became extraordinarily courteous, a sure sign that his terror was wearing off.

Every blandishment was used to soothe him, and it had its effect. As he was entering the governor's house, some one touched a small bell which hung over the door: he started with horror and astonishment; but in a moment after was reconciled to the noise, and laughed at the cause of his perturbation. When pictures were shewn to him, he knew directly those which represented the human figure: among others, a very large handsome print of her royal highness the Dutchess of Cumberland being produced, he called out, woman, a name by which we had just before taught him to call the female convicts. Plates of birds and beasts were also laid before him; and many people were led to believe, that such as he spoke about and pointed to were known to him. But this must have been an erroneous conjecture, for the elephant, rhinoceros, and several others, which we must have discovered did they exist in the country, were of the number. Again, on the other hand, those he did not point out, were equally unknown to him.

1789. His curiosity here being satiated, we took him to a large brick house, which was building for the governor's residence: being about to enter, he cast up his eyes, and seeing some people leaning out of a window on the first story, he exclaimed aloud, and testified the most extravagant surprise. Nothing here was observed to fix his attention so strongly as some tame fowls, who were feeding near him: our dogs also he particularly noticed; but seemed more fearful than fond of them.

He dined at a side-table at the governor's; and eat heartily of fish and ducks, which he first cooled. Bread and salt meat he smelled at, but would not taste: all our liquors he treated in the same manner, and could drink nothing but water. On being shewn that he was not to wipe his hands on the chair which he sat upon, he used a towel which was gave to him, with great cleanliness and decency.

In the afternoon his hair was closely cut, his head combed, and his beard shaved; but he would not submit to these operations until he had seen them performed on another person, when he readily acquiesced. His hair, as might be supposed, was filled with vermin, whose destruction seemed to afford him great triumph; nay, either revenge, or pleasure, prompted him to eat them! but on our expressing disgust and abhorrence he left it off.

To this succeeded his immersion in a tub of water and soap, where he was completely washed and scrubbed from head to foot; after which a shirt, a jacket, and a pair of trowsers, were put upon him. Some part of this ablution I had the honour to perform, in order that I might ascertain the real colour of the skin of these people. My observation then was (and it has since been confirmed in a thousand other instances) that they are as black as the lighter cast of the African negroes.

Many unsuccessful attempts were made to learn his name; the governor therefore called him Manly, from the cove in which he was captured: this cove had received its name from the manly undaunted behaviour of a party of natives seen there, on our taking possession of the country.

To prevent his escape, a handcuff with a rope attached to it, was fastened around his left wrist, which at first highly delighted him; he called it 'Ben-gàd-ee' (or ornament), but his delight changed to rage and hatred when he discovered its use. His supper he cooked himself: some fish were given to him for this purpose, which, without any previous preparation whatever, he threw carelessly on the fire, and when they became warm took them up, and first rubbed off the scales, peeled the outside with his teeth, and eat it; afterwards he gutted them, and laying them again on the fire, completed the dressing, and eat them.

A convict was selected to sleep with him, and to attend him wherever he might go. When he went with his keeper into his apartment he appeared very restless and uneasy while a light was kept in; but on its extinction, he immediately lay down and composed himself.

Sullenness and dejection strongly marked his countenance on the following morning; to amuse him, he was taken around the camp, and to the observatory: casting his eyes to the opposite shore from the point where he stood, and seeing the smoke of fire lighted by his countrymen, he looked earnestly at it, and sighing deeply two or three times, uttered the word 'gweè-un' (fire).

His loss of spirits had not, however, the effect of impairing his appetite; eight fish, each weighing about a pound, constituted his breakfast, which he dressed as before. When he had finished his repast, he turned his back to the fire in a musing posture, and crept so close to it, that his shirt was caught by the flame; luckily his keeper soon extinguished it; but he was so terrified at the accident, that he was with difficulty persuaded to put on a second.

1st January 1789. To-day being new-year's-day, most of the officers were invited to the governor's table: Manly dined heartily on fish and roasted pork; he was seated on a chest near a window, out of which, when he had done eating, he would have thrown his plate, had he not been prevented: during dinner-time a band of music played in an adjoining apartment; and after the cloth was removed, one of the company sang in a very soft and superior style; but the powers of melody were lost on Manly, which disappointed our expectations, as he had before shown pleasure and readiness in imitating our tunes. Stretched out on his chest, and putting his hat under his head, he fell asleep.

To convince his countrymen that he had received no injury from us, the governor took him in a boat down the harbour, that they might see and converse with him: when the boat arrived, and lay at a little distance from the beach, several Indians who had retired at her approach, on seeing Manly, returned: he was greatly affected, and shed tears. At length they began to converse. Our ignorance of the language prevented us from knowing much of what passed; it was, however, easily understood that his friends asked him why he did not jump overboard, and rejoin them. He only sighed, and pointed to the fetter on his leg, by which he was bound.

In going down the harbour he had described the names by which they distinguish its numerous creeks and headlands: he was now often heard to repeat that of *Weè-rong* (Sydney), which was doubtless to inform his countrymen of the place of his capitivity; and perhaps invite them to rescue him. By this time his gloom was chaced away, and he parted from his friends without testifying reluctance. His vivacity and good humour continued all the evening, and produced so good an effect on his appetite, that he eat for supper two Kanguroo rats, each of the size of a moderate rabbit, and in addition not less than three pounds of fish.

Two days after he was taken on a similar excursion; but to our surprise the natives kept aloof, and would neither approach the shore, or discourse with their countryman: we could get no explanation of this difficulty, which seemed to affect us more than it did him. Uncourteous as they were, he performed to them an act of attentive benevolence; seeing a basket made of bark, used by them to carry water, he conveyed into it two hawks and another bird, which the people in the boat had shot, and carefully covering them over, left them as a present to his old friends. But indeed the gentleness and humanity of his disposition frequently displayed themselves: when our children, stimulated by wanton curiosity, used to flock around him, he never failed to fondle them, and, if he were eating at the time, constantly offered them the choicest part of his fare.

February, 1789. His reserve, from want of confidence in us, continued gradually to wear away: he told us his name, and Manly gave place to Ar-ab-a-noo. Bread he began to relish; and tea he drank with avidity: strong liquors he would never taste, turning from them with disgust and abhorrence. Our dogs and cats had ceased to be objects of fear, and were become his greatest pets, and constant companions at table. One of our chief amusements, after the cloth was removed, was to make him repeat the names of things in his language, which he never hesitated to do with the utmost alacrity, correcting our pronunciation when erroneous. Much information relating to the customs and manners of his country was also gained from him: but as this subject will be separately and amply treated, I shall not anticipate myself by partially touching on it here.

(1793)

Henry Kendall
THE LAST OF HIS TRIBE

He crouches, and buries his face on his knees,
  And hides in the dark of his hair;
For he cannot look up to the storm-smitten trees,
  Or think of the loneliness there—
  Of the loss and the loneliness there.   5

The wallaroos grope through the tufts of the grass,
  And turn to their covers for fear;
But he sits in the ashes and lets them pass
  Where the boomerangs sleep with the spear—
  With the nullah, the sling, and the spear.   10

Uloola, behold him! The thunder that breaks
  On the tops of the rocks with the rain,
And the wind which drives up with the salt of the lakes,
  Have made him a hunter again—
  A hunter and fisher again.   15

For his eyes have been full with a smouldering thought;
  But he dreams of the hunts of yore,
And of foes that he sought, and of fights that he fought
  With those who will battle no more—
  Who will go to the battle no more.   20

It is well that the water which tumbles and fills,
  Goes moaning and moaning along;
For an echo rolls out from the sides of the hills,
  And he starts at a wonderful song—
  At the sounds of a wonderful song.   25

And he sees, through the rents of the scattering fogs,
  The corroboree warlike and grim,
And the lubra who sat by the fire on the logs,
  To watch, like a mourner, for him—
  Like a mother and mourner for him.   30

Will he go in his sleep from these desolate lands,
  Like a chief, to the rest of his race,
With the honey-voiced woman who beckons and stands,
  And gleams like a dream in his face—
  Like a marvellous dream in his face?   35

(1864)

Oodgeroo Noonuccal (Kath Walker)
WE ARE GOING

For Grannie Coolwell

They came in to the little town
A semi-naked band subdued and silent,
All that remained of their tribe.
They came here to the place of their old bora ground
Where now the many white men hurry about like ants.   5
Notice of estate agent reads: 'Rubbish May Be Tipped Here'.
Now it half covers the traces of the old bora ring.
They sit and are confused, they cannot say their thoughts:
'We are as strangers here now, but the white tribe are
    the strangers.
We belong here, we are of the old ways.   10
We are the corroboree and the bora ground,
We are the old sacred ceremonies, the laws of the elders.
We are the wonder tales of Dream Time, the tribal legends told.
We are the past, the hunts and the laughing games,
    the wandering camp fires.
We are the lightning-bolt over Gaphembah Hill   15
Quick and terrible,
And the Thunder after him, that loud fellow.
We are the quiet daybreak paling the dark lagoon.
We are the shadow-ghosts creeping back as the camp fires
    burn low.
We are nature and the past, all the old ways   20
Gone now and scattered.
The scrubs are gone, the hunting and the laughter.
The eagle is gone, the emu and the kangaroo are gone
    from his place.
The bora ring is gone.
The corroboree is gone.   25
And we are going.'

(1964)

Mudrooroo Narogin (Colin Johnson)
from DOCTOR WOOREDDY'S PRESCRIPTION
FOR ENDURING THE ENDING OF THE WORLD

The island and the people continued to suffer. The darkness of the night-hidden land allied itself with the hidden, green, deep fears of the ocean. Wooreddy could feel it lapping about his middle and touching him with chilly fingers, cold as the white wetness he had once felt in the inland mountains. What had that been called? *turrana*. Now always he could taste salt on his lips and deep down his throat. The sea had invaded his body! This knowledge hit him one day as he was about to step on a snake which had no right to be on the snake-free island. His foot hit the ground a metre from the coiled black body in a rush of fear imagining a hissing death. *Ria Warrawah* had extended the boundary of his domain to include Bruny Island. He knew this for certain as he watched the coughing demon attack the few remaining people. *Ria Warrawah* sucked up souls and amid the vast sighing danger what could he do but chant the old protection spells, gash into his body extra-potent strength marks, carry about relics of the long dead, and hope—hope and watch the sun rise on another cloudy day of hopelessness? Day fell into day, and his numbness became a kangaroo-skin bag to hold his ever-growing panic. He told himself over and over again that he was destined to be a survivor—but, as he cast a glazed eye over the half-dozen people still alive and suffering, even his survival came into question. To survive, yes—but into what future? It lay ahead of him as dead as a fish tossed from the ocean. Automatically, he stared at the sea as he tried to imagine that his life—though not the old traditions giving it shape and meaning—would continue on aimlessly. He sighed and stared bleakly at the *num* crawling like insects on the very body of the devil. Behind him he heard the coughing demon acknowledge the sigh of the ocean. The demon hacked at his wife's chest and he could do nothing. She might eject the demon, but the odds were against it. For some reason he thought of the female, Trugernanna and this caused his mood to lift a little. She would never come to a quick end. The boat pointed in their direction. Its wooden legs swayed the body from side to side. She was every bit a survivor as he himself was. The *num* were coming to them. She would go on and on, just as he would go on, until the end.

In the bow of the boat a *num* stood and, although his body swayed unsteadily, he still managed to impart to it an attitude of eagerness and readiness for action. Wooreddy watched uncaringly. Most *num* sat in their boats, this one did not—so what! Still, as the boat entered the surf, he felt an urge to flee into the safety of the bush. He stayed where he was examining the crew. He saw no killing sticks. This relieved him enough to wait to see what the boat would bring.

The bottom of the boat touched the ground. This was instantly followed by a shouted order from the now-sprawling *num* at the grey-clad crew who grinned as they shipped their oars. At last, obeying the order, they slipped into the surf and manhandled the craft to dry sand. The head ghost scrambled up, assumed his dignity and shouted again: 'Harder, you ruffians, pull harder there.' The watching Wooreddy repeated the sounds *sotto voce* and wondered what they meant. If he had the energy, he might learn the language. The main *num* jumped dryshod onto the beach, saw the Aborigine and stamped toward him with hand outstretched.

The Aborigine waited for the strange intruder to reach him. The *num* was short with a soft body plump from many days of good eating without hunting. Short, stubby legs marched that pot-bellied trunk over the sand with dainty, precise steps lacking the finesse of the hunter. Still there was something of the stamp of a sacred dance in the steps and this gave Wooreddy an interest in the visitor. His eyes brightened as his numbness lessened. The ghost's face, round like the moon, though unscarred, shone pink like the shoulder skin of the early morning sun. Sharp, sea-coloured eyes sought to bridge the gap between them. The ghostly eyes showed such an avid interest in him that he evaded those eyes by staring at the strange skin on the ghost's head. From under it, his hair showed rust-coloured like a vein of red ochre in grey rock.

The *num* grabbed, and succeeded in capturing Wooreddy's hand. It lay limply in the grasp, while the pink-petalled lips began fluttering out sounds which were gibberish to the man. 'Such a poor, poor creature! Such a wretched being bereft of everything we civilised people hold dear. How right I was not to listen to my wife and friends who sought to dissuade me from this charitable and necessary task. No matter what hazard, it is truly the Lord's work and I will persevere.'

Behind his back, the convict crew twisted their faces in mockery. Some of them had endured a visit from him in prison and were familiar with the style of his deliverance. They described it, in their colourful way, as a 'load of shit'. Perhaps it was their felt contempt which had driven George Augustus Robinson to the greener pastures of Aboriginal welfare.

Wooreddy's mouth hesitated on the way to a smile, then he saw the faces the convicts were pulling and grinned for the first time in months. The ghost still clung to his hand. Now he fluted: 'Me, me Mr Robinson.' Wooreddy's agile mind discarded the pronouns and he repeated: 'Mee-ter Ro-bin-un'.

While behind him the convicts mouthed the words and even went into a little dance, Robinson pushed his left index finger against Wooreddy's greasy chest and, pronouncing each word slowly and distinctly, asked: 'You, you, your, name, what?' Loud snickers from the boat crew caused him to whirl around and shout: 'Don't stand around. Get that boat up on the beach'—then he turned back to the Aborigine and repeated the words in the same fluting tone, though now edged with anger.

Wooreddy politely answered: '*Narrah warrah* (yes).'

'Pleased to make your acquaintance, I'm sure, Narrah Warrah,' the *num* burbled enthusiastically, not caring if he was understood by the poor matted-haired apparition which stood before him with its nakedness partially covered by a dirty blanket. He had come to save such creatures and they would understand this intuitively. Already, this *Narrah Warrah* knew that he was their friend.

'I am your friend,' he said slowly, his voice dropping to a silky softness which oozed. 'Have no fear, Narrah Warrah'—a snigger from the convicts whipped a snarl into his tone. 'I have come to protect you from such scum as these ruffians behind me—' and he jerked a thumb over his shoulder. Wooreddy intuitively grasped what the gesture meant. He suddenly realised that here was an ally. The self-assured, pompous little ghost before him could be used to help him survive until the end of the world.

He accepted Meeter Ro-bin-un as his very own *num* with the same readiness with which Robinson had accepted the fact that he was destined to save these poor, benighted people. Such a *modus vivendi*, lacking all the essentials of a properly understood relationship, held infinite possibilities from rich comedy to equally rich tragedy. At first, Wooreddy was overjoyed. He had found a protector and also a subject of study. He tested out the relationship by making a gesture and then walking off into the bush. He was happy to find the ghost following, but his happiness disappeared when the ghost marched past him and took the lead. Robinson was defining their relationship from the beginning.

In the camp Wooreddy's wife, Lunna, sat naked and uncaring on a piece of blanket. The coughing demon hacked at her lungs. She didn't even lift her head when the *num* bent over her, his face filled with solicitude. A short distance away, one of her sons sat chewing on a tough piece of kangaroo meat while the other sat waiting his turn. They glanced up; their eyes filled with the image of the ghost, and with a united single shriek they were away into the scrub as fast as their little legs could carry them. The father called out, ordering them to return, but the sound of their feet diminished into the distance. Now and not for the first time, he wondered how he had fathered such boys. He remembered when he was their age and the sudden deep thoughts that had slowed his feet so that he more often found himself facing danger rather than fleeing from it. They had none of the qualities he cherished. It was the fault of their foreign mother. Wooreddy refused to acknowledge that his own stuffiness and indifference might have had something to do with their behaviour patterns. He hardly ever spoke to them and often ignored his wife as well.

'*Meridee bidai lidinese loomerai*,' he said explaining the sickness of his wife, but not his lack of concern—a concern which was expressed on the face of the ghost. But even that concern vanished when Trugernanna walked into the clearing clutching in each small fist an arm of the boys. Wooreddy had not been the only one observing the *num*. Trugernanna, hidden in the scrub, had studied him and decided that he was unlike the ones at the whaling station on the other side of the island. There, all that they wanted to do was take her off somewhere. At first she had found it flattering, but now it was just one of those things.

Away from the *num* the girl often went naked, but now she wore a kangaroo skin wrapped about her full hips. This was a new style which the women had adapted. The old fashion of draping the skin over the shoulders was gone for ever. Now demure in her rough skirt she shot a glance at the ghost and caught his look of approval. They liked females to be covered below the waist for most of the time.

George Augustus Robinson, destined by God to make the Aborigines the most interesting and profitable part of his life, leered at the forbidden fruits of the bare-breasted maiden who conjured up romantic visions of beautiful South Sea islands where missionaries laboured for the salvation of delightful souls. On this island and on the larger one of Van Diemen's Land, he too would be such a missionary. He went into his 'Me, Mr Robinson' routine and this time received a better response. The girl had been around the whalers and sawyers long enough to pick up quite a few words of the ghost language. She replied that her name was Trugernanna and set Robinson right in regard to the name of Wooreddy. In return Robinson smiled an expression which held more than that of the good shepherd at long last finding an intelligent sheep.

She spoke to Wooreddy and enlightened him about the *num*. Finally he had the proof that the ghost was indeed an ally. As Robinson quaintly informed Trugernanna: 'Me look after you, give you food, clothing—bad white man no longer hurt you.' And as the girl just as quaintly echoed: 'Bad *num* no longer hurt us' as she took the protector's hand and gazed up into his face with all the adoration of a child—though the fullness of her breasts belied the pose. Wooreddy found himself ignored. It annoyed him that the woman had captured all the ghost's attention. After all Meeter Ro-bin-un was his ally too!

(1983)

Oodgeroo Noonuccal (Kath Walker)
NO MORE BOOMERANG

No more boomerang
No more spear;
Now all civilized—
Colour bar and beer.

No more corroboree,   5
Gay dance and din.
Now we got movies,
And pay to go in.

No more sharing
What the hunter brings.   10
Now we work for money,
Then pay it back for things.

Now we track bosses
To catch a few bob,
Now we go walkabout   15
On bus to the job.

One time naked,
Who never knew shame;
Now we put clothes on
To hide whatsaname.   20

No more gunya,
Now bungalow,
Paid by hire purchase
In twenty year or so.

Lay down the stone axe,   25
Take up the steel,
And work like a nigger
For a white man meal.

No more firesticks
That made the whites scoff.   30
Now all electric,
And no better off.

Bunyip he finish,
Now got instead
White fella Bunyip,   35
Call him Red.

Abstract picture now—
What they coming at?
Cripes, in our caves we
Did better than that.   40

Black hunted wallaby,
White hunt dollar;
White fella witch-doctor
Wear dog-collar.

No more message-stick;   45
Lubras and lads
Got television now,
Mostly ads.

Lay down the woomera,
Lay down the waddy.
Now we got atom-bomb,   50
End *every*body.

                                        (1966)

Sally Morgan
MY PLACE

from DAISY CORUNNA'S STORY

My name is Daisy Corunna, I'm Arthur's sister. My Aboriginal name is
Talahue. I can't tell you when I was born, but I feel old. My mother had
me on Corunna Downs Station, just out of Marble Bar. She said I was
born under a big, old gum tree and the midwife was called Diana. Course,
that must have been her whitefella name. All the natives had whitefella
and tribal names. I don't know what her tribal name was. When I was
comin' into the world, a big mob of kids stood round waitin' for to get a
look at me. I bet they got a fright.

I was happy up North. I had my mother and there was Old Fanny, my
grandmother. Gladdie 'minds me of Old Fanny, she's got the same
crooked smile. They both got round faces like the moon, too. I 'member
Old Fanny always wore a handkerchief on her head with little knots tied
all the way around. Sometimes, my granddaughter Helen 'minds me of
her, too. They both short and giggly with skinny legs. Aah, she was good
for a laugh, Old Fanny.

She loved panning for tin. All the old people panned for tin. You could see it lyin' in the dirt, heavy and dark, like black marbles. Old Fanny said I had good eyes, sometimes she took me with her for luck. We traded the tin for sugar or flour. They never gave us money.

Old Fanny went pink-eye* to Hillside one day. I never saw her again. They tell me she died on Hillside, maybe she knew she was going to die. She was a good old grandmother.

On the station, I went under the name Daisy Brockman. It wasn't till I was older that I took the name Corunna. Now, some people say my father wasn't Howden Drake-Brockman, they say he was this man from Malta. What can I say? I never heard 'bout this man from Malta before. I think that's a big joke.

Aah, you see, that's the trouble with us blackfellas, we don't know who we belong to, no one'll own up. I got to be careful what I say. You can't put no lies in a book.

Course, I had another father, he wasn't my real father like, but he looked after us just the same. Chinaman was his name. He was very tall and strong. The people respected him. They were scared of him. He was Arthur's Aboriginal father, too. He was a powerful man.

My poor mother lost a lot of babies. I had two sisters that lived, Lily and Rosie. They were, what do they call it? Full blood, yes. I was the light one of the family, the little one with blonde hair. Of course, there was Arthur, but they took him away when I was just a baby.

I 'member Old Pompee, he was the old boy that looked after the vegetable garden, he told me my mother cried and cried when they took Arthur. She kept callin' to him like. Callin' to him to come back. The people thought Arthur was gettin' educated so he could run the station some day. They thought it'd be good to have a blackfella runnin' the station. They was all wrong. My poor old mother never saw him again.

Rosie and I was close. Lily was old than me. I spent a lot of time with Rosie. I was very sad when she died. She was only young. My mother nursed her, did everything for her, but we lost her. Good old Rosie, you know I been thinkin' 'bout her lately. She was what you call a good sport.

I'll tell you a story about our white man's names. My mother was in Hedland with the three of us when an English nursing sister saw her near the well. She said, 'Have you got names for your three little girls?'

Mum said, 'No.'

She said, 'Well, I'll give you names, real beautiful ones. We'll call this one Lily, this one Rosie and this little one Daisy.' I was the short one of the family. We didn't mind being called that, we thought we were pretty flowers.

I haven't told you about my brother Albert, yet. He was light, too. He used to tease me. He'd chase me, then he'd hide behind a big bush and

---

* *pink-eye*—term used by Aboriginal people of north-west Australia, similar to the more widely known term *walkabout*. A period of wandering as a nomad, often as undertaken by Aborigines who feel the need to leave the place where they are in contact with white society, and return for spiritual replenishment to their traditional way of life. Can also simply mean a holiday, usually without leave.

jump out and pretend he was the devil-devil. Oooh, he was naughty to me. They took Albert when they took Arthur, but Albert got sick and came back to the station. He was a good worker. He liked playing with me. He called me his little sister.

They was a good mob on Corunna. A real good mob. I been thinkin' 'bout all of them lately. There was Peter Linck, the well-sinker. I think he was German, he lived at the outcamp. He had Rosie, not my sister Rosie, another one. Then there was Fred Stream, by jingoes, there was a few kids that belonged to him. He had Sarah, her children were really fair, white blackfellas, really.

Aah, that colour business is a funny thing. Our colour goes away. You mix us with the white man, and pretty soon, you got no blackfellas left. Some of these whitefellas you see walkin' around, they really black underneath. You see, you never can tell. I'm old now, and look at me, look at the skin on my arms and legs, just look! It's goin' white. I used to be a lot darker than I am now. I don't know what's happened. Maybe it's the white blood takin' over, or the medicine they gave me in hospital, I don't know.

The big house on Corunna was built by the natives. They all worked together, building this and building that. If it wasn't for the natives, nothing would get done. They made the station, Drake-Brockmans didn't do it on their own.

At the back of the homestead was a big, deep hole with whitewash in it. It was thick and greasy, you could cut it with a knife. Us kids used to mix the whitewash with water and make it like a paint. Then we'd put it all over us and play corroborees. Every Saturday afternoon, we played corroboree. We mixed the red sand with water and painted that on, too. By the time we finished, you didn't know what colour we were.

I 'member the kitchen on Corunna. There was a tiny little window where the blackfellas had to line up for tucker. My mother never liked doin' that. We got a bit of tea, flour and meat, that was all. They always rang a bell when they was ready for us to come. Why do white people like ringin' bells so much?

Every morning, they woke us up with a bell. It was only 'bout five o'clock, could have been earlier. We all slept down in the camp, a good way from the main house. Every morning, someone would light a lamp, walk down into the gully and ring a bell. When I was very little, I used to get frightened. I thought it was the devil-devil come to get me.

There was a tennis court on Corunna. Can you 'magine that? I think they thought they were royalty, puttin' in a tennis court. That's an Englishman's game. They painted it with whitewash, but it didn't stay white for long, I can tell you. I had a go at hitting the ball, once. I gave up after that, it was a silly game.

I saw plenty of willy-willies up there and cyclones, too. By jingoes, a cyclone is a terrible thing! When one was coming, my mother hid me. I wasn't allowed to move. She was worried I might get killed. Get taken away by the wind. I was only small. I 'member one time we hid in the kitchen, when my mother wasn't looking, I sneaked up to the window and peeked out. You should have seen it! There was men's hats, spinifex, empty tanks, everything blowin' everywhere. It's a funny thing, but those old tanks always ended up settlin' on the tennis court.

There was a food store on Corunna. It had tin walls, tin roof and a tiny window near the top covered with flywire. You wouldn't believe the food they had in there, sacks of apricots, potatoes, tobacco, everything. It makes my mouth water just thinkin' about it. When it was siesta time, the other kids used to lift me up and poke me through the window. I'd drop down inside as quiet as a mouse when the cat's after him. Then I'd pick up food and throw it out the window. If they heard someone coming, they'd cough, then run away. I'd hide behind the sacks of potatoes and wait for them to come back for me. I had a good feed on those days.

The people were really hungry sometimes, poor things. They didn't get enough, you see. And they worked hard. You had to work hard, if you didn't do it, then they call the police in to make you work hard. When things was like that, one of the men would put me through the window again. I suppose I should feel bad about stealin' that food. Hunger is a terrible thing.

Aah, you see, the native is different to the white man. He wouldn't let a dog go without his tea.

Of course, the men all wanted their tobacco as well. The white man called it Nigger Twist. It was a twist like a licorice, only thicker. It's terrible, when you think about it, callin' something like that Nigger Twist. I mean, we all called it that because we thought that was its name.

Sometimes, we'd pinch the eggs the chooks lay in the hay shed. Aah, that old hay shed, it's kept a lot of secrets. Now there was plenty of stockmen up North, then, and they all wanted girls. We'd be hearin' all this noise in the hay shed, the hay'd be goin' up and down, the hens'd be cluckin', the roosters crowin'. Then, by and by, out would come a stockman and one of the girls. They'd be all covered in hay. 'We just bin lookin' for eggs,' they'd say.

There was a government ration we used to get now and then. It was a blanket, we all called it a flag blanket, it had the crown of Queen Victoria on it. Can you imagine that? We used to laugh about that. You see, we was wrappin' ourselves in royalty.

Then there was a mirror and a comb, a cake of soap and a couple of big spotted handkerchiefs. Sometimes, the men were lucky and got a shirt, the women never got anything.

I 'member my mother showin' me a picture of a white woman, she was all fancied up in a long, white dress. 'Ooh, Daisy,' she said, 'if only I could have a dress like that.' All the native women wanted to look like the white women, with fancy hairdos and fancy dresses.

Later, my mother learnt how to sew, she was very clever. She could draw anything, she loved drawing. She drew pictures in the sand for me all the time. Beautiful pictures. Maybe that's where you get it from, Sally.

We were cunning when we were kids. There was a big water trough on Corunna, it was used for the animals, even the camels had a drink from it. Mrs Stone always warned us not to muck around in the trough. We'd wait till she was sleeping, then we'd sneak down to the garden and dive in the trough. It was slimy and there was a lot of goona [faeces] in the water, but we didn't care. I 'member holding my breath and swimming under the water. I looked up and I could see the faces of all the animals lookin' down at me as if to say, 'What are you doin' in our water, child?'

They had a good cook on Corunna for a while, Mrs Quigley. She was a white woman, a good woman. I think Nell and Mrs Stone, the housekeeper, were a bit jealous of her. Nell was Howden's first white wife. They were real fuddy-duddies and didn't like her talkin' to anyone.

The cook had a little girl called Queenie and it was my job to look out for her. We were 'bout the same age, ooh, we had good times! We'd laugh and giggle at anythin'. We were giggling gerties, that's what Queenie's mother used to call us.

I taught Queenie all about the bush. We'd go out after a big rain. Sometimes, the rain was so heavy up North, it hurt when it hit you. That's the kind of rain you get in the wet. One day, the place would be desert, the next day, green everywhere. Green and gold, beautiful, really. I'd take Queenie out into the bush and we'd watch a little seed grow. 'Look now,' I'd say to Queenie, 'it's getting bigger.' By the time we finished lookin', that seed'd be half an inch long.

In the evenings, I liked to sit and watch the kangaroos and other animals come down and drink at the trough. The crows and the birds would have a drink, too, and do a bit of goona. I just liked to sit and watch them all. Course, you know, Corunna has blue hills all round it. They always looked soft that time of night. Sometimes, my mother would sit and watch, too. We knew how to count our blessings, then.

I was a hard worker on Corunna. I been a hard worker all my life. When I was little, I picked the grubs off the caulies and cabbages at the back of the garden. I got a boiled sweet for that. Now the blackfellas weren't allowed to pick any vegetables from the garden. You got a whipping if you were caught. Old Pompee, he used to sneak us tomatoes. And so he should have, he was eatin' them himself.

We all loved the orphaned lambs. We were their mother and their father. We fed them with a bottle with a turkey feather stuck in it. There was one lamb I fed, dear little thing she was, she was blind. She kept bumpin' into the fence and the other lambs. Poor thing. I was so upset I told cook about it and she told me this story.

'You know, Daisy, when I was a young child in Sydney, I had very bad eyesight. One day, an old lady came to visit us and she asked my mother if she could have a go at curing me. Mother said yes. They sat down and put a single grain of sugar in each eye. Ooh, it hurt! I cried and cried, but pretty soon, I could see. I'll give you some sugar, you try that with your lamb.'

I did what she said, and pretty soon, that lamb's eyes were watering all over the place. Next thing I knew, it was runnin' around like all the other lambs, not bumpin' into anything. She was a wise woman, that cook.

Aah, we played silly games when we were kids. I always played with Rosie and Topsy. That Topsy, she was one of a kind, I tell you. One day, Mrs Stone gave her a cake of soap and told her to take a bath. You know what she did? She threw the soap back and said, 'I'm not takin' no bath!' Can you 'magine cheekin' a white woman like that? Aah, she was great fun, old Topsy.

There was a creek that cut across Corunna in the wet. We loved swimming in it and catching fish. They were like sardines, we threw them on the hot ashes and then gobbled them up. They were nice, but you had to be careful of the bones.

All sorts of wild fruit grew along the creek. There was a prickly tree with fruit like an orange, but with lots of big seeds in it. You could suck the seeds. Then there was another one shaped like a banana, that was full of seeds, too. You ate the flesh and spat out the seeds. There wasn't much food in that one, just juice. There was another prickly tree that had yellow flowers like a wattle, wild beans grew off that tree. When they swelled up, we picked them and threw them in the ashes. They were good.

The best one of all was like a gooseberry bush. Aah, if you could find a patch of that, no one saw you, you just stayed there and ate. You could smell those ones a good way away, they smell like a ripe rockmelon. We'd sniff and say, 'Aah, something ripe in there, somewhere.' We'd lift up all the bushes looking for them, they were only tiny. When we found them, we'd say, 'Hmmmn, mingimullas, good old mingimullas.' I never tasted fruit like those mingimullas. They had soft green leaves like a flannel, ooh, they were good to eat.

There was another tree we used to get gum from to chew. It grew on little white sticks. We'd collect it and keep it in a tin. It went hard, like boiled lollies. You know, jubes always 'mind me of that gum. Perhaps that's why I like jubes.

Rosie and I were naughty. We'd pinch wild ducks' eggs and break up their nests. And we'd dig holes to get lizards' eggs. We could tell where the lizards had covered up their eggs. We'd dig them all out, get the eggs and bust them. Those poor creatures. They never harmed us and there we were, breakin' up their eggs. We're all God's creatures, after all.

Rosie and I used to catch birds, too. We'd get a bit of wire netting and make a cage, then we'd take it down the creek and throw wheat around. We kept the cage a little bit lifted up and we tied a long bit of string to the wood underneath.

You should have seen all the cockies, they loved wheat. When there was a big mob of them, we'd pull the string, down would come the cage and we would have them trapped. Trouble was, we couldn't do anything with them, they kept biting us. In the end, we let them go. We did silly things in those days.

When I got older, my jobs on Corunna changed. They started me working at the main house, sweeping the verandahs, emptying the toilets, scrubbing the tables and pots and pans and the floor. In those days, you scrubbed everything. In the mornings, I had to clean the hurricane lamps, then help in the kitchen.

There were always poisonous snakes hiding in the dark corners of the kitchen. You couldn't see them, but you could hear them. Sssss, ssssss, ssssss, they went. Just like that. We cornered them and killed them with sticks. There were a lot of snakes on Corunna.

Once I was working up the main house, I wasn't allowed down in the camp. If I had've known that, I'd have stayed where I was. I couldn't sleep with my mother now and I wasn't allowed to play with all my old friends.

That was the worst thing about working at the main house, not seeing my mother every day. I knew she missed me. She would walk up from the camp and call, 'Daisy, Daisy,' just like that. I couldn't talk to her, I had too much work to do. It was hard for me, then. I had to sneak away just to see my own family and friends. They were camp natives, I was a house native.

Now, I had to sleep on the homestead verandah. Some nights, it was real cold, one blanket was too thin. On nights like that, the natives used to bring wool from the shearing shed and lay that beneath them.

I didn't mind sleeping on the verandah in summer because I slept near the old cooler. It was as big as a fireplace, they kept butter and milk in it. I'd wait till everyone was asleep, then I'd sneak into the cooler and pinch some butter. I loved it, but I was never allowed to have any.

Seems like I was always getting into trouble over food. I'm like a lamb that's never been fed. I 'member once, Nell asked me to take an apple pie to the house further out on the station. Nell's real name was Eleanor, but everyone called her Nell. Anyway, I kept walkin' and walkin' and smellin' that pie. Ooh, it smelled good. I couldn't stand it any longer, I hid in a gully and dug out a bit of pie with my fingers. It was beautiful. I squashed the pie together and tried to make out like it was all there. Hmmmnnn, that was good tucker, I said to myself as I walked on.

When I gave the pie to Mrs Stone, I had to give her a note that Nell had sent as well. If I had have known what was in that note, I'd have thrown it away. It said, if any part of this pie is missing, send the note back and I will punish her.

Mrs Stone looked at the note, then she looked at the pie, then she said, 'Give this note back when you go.' I did. And, sure enough, I got whipped with the bullocks cane again.

Nell was a cruel woman, she had a hard heart. When she wasn't whippin' us girls with the bullocks cane for not workin' hard enough, she was hittin' us over the head. She didn't like natives. If one of us was in her way and we didn't move real quick, she'd give us a real hard thump over the head, just like that. Ooh, it hurt! White people are great ones for thumpin' you on the head, aren't they? We was only kids.

Aah, but they were good old days, then. I never seen days like that ever again. When they took me from the station, I never seen days like that ever again.

They told my mother I was goin' to get educated. They told all the people I was goin' to school. I thought it'd be good, goin' to school. I thought I'd be somebody real important. My mother wanted me to learn to read and write like white people. Then she wanted me to come back and teach her. There was a lot of the older people interested in learnin' how to read and write, then.

Why did they tell my mother that lie? Why do white people tell so many lies? I got nothin' out of their promises. My mother wouldn't have let me go just to work. God will make them pay for their lies. He's got people like that under the whip. They should have told my mother the truth. She thought I was coming back.

When I left, I was cryin', all the people were cryin', my mother was cryin' and beatin' her head. Lily was cryin'. I called, 'Mum, Mum, Mum!' She said, 'Don't forget me, Talahue!'

They all thought I was coming back. I thought I'd only be gone a little while. I could hear their wailing for miles and miles. 'Talahue! Talahue!' They were singin' out my name, over and over. I couldn't stop cryin'. I kept callin', 'Mum! Mum!'

(1987)

Hazel McKellar
from MATYA-MUNDU: A HISTORY OF THE ABORIGINAL PEOPLE OF SOUTH-WEST QUEENSLAND

The camp was always kept very clean. We used to make brooms from a bush of hopbush. The branches were tied together with a piece of string or wire. This broom was much better than a straw broom because it didn't remove all the topsoil but just removed the rubbish. The women would keep a large area around the camp clean for the children to play on. On washing days, the women would always boil up their clothes in a kerosene tin, or if they were lucky, in a copper.

Most of the children from the camp went to school for the first few grades. Very few kids went past Grade Three. After doing a few years at school, Aboriginal children were in great demand as domestics and in stock camps. It was not uncommon to start work as young as eleven or twelve. My father always made sure we went to school. He wouldn't ever let Mum go into the bush because he reckoned we needed our schooling.

There were a lot of problems at school because we were from the camp. My main memories of school is fighting all the way through—fighting with girls and boys. They always referred to us as 'gins' from the camp. One of the main areas where we used to fight is where the hostel is now. That used to be our favourite boxing ground. We would go over there and settle our differences after school.

We also had problems with the staff. I remember once when my father went up to school after a certain teacher had thrown a book at one of my brothers (they were always running away from school.) He went and abused the head teacher saying, 'Here I'm f...trying to get them to go to school and here you are f...flogging them and sending them home.' I can still remember that as clear as anything.

Another time I got into trouble with the domestic science teacher. She had asked us to do an assignment on the colour scheme of our home. I couldn't do it so she kept me in. I just sat there—I suppose I was rather stubborn. I tried to tell her we didn't have a colour scheme. I tried to tell her we were only living in a one-roomed shack with a bough-shed and goat pen out the back. It was just built out of rusty kerosene tins nailed together. The bough-shed was only covered with gum leaves and we only had an old wood stove in the kitchen part, and a table to eat off. We had no chairs, only kerosene tins. In the back was like a big bedroom partitioned off with a piece of calico—the kids slept in one half while Mum and Dad slept in the other. That was in the winter, but in the summer we camped anywhere on the flat.

The teacher kept me till five o'clock but I wouldn't do it. Of course I couldn't do it and I wasn't telling a lie. I suppose I could have used my imagination but it didn't dawn on me. I could have written down my dream. She kept making it clear she wanted to know what colour the bathroom was and that some kids had cream and green kitchens. I didn't feel ashamed but it was something I couldn't even explain to myself at the time.

We also had problems on cooking days. The teacher would only allow you to cook a certain quantity and you would know in your heart that it wouldn't be fair. The little quantity you would have prepared wouldn't go around the family, so your family never got to sort out your samples of cooking. You would beg your teacher to double the quantity but she would say it wouldn't be a success, yet our mother and aunties were doing it all the time.

In the time I lived at the camp, there was not much interaction with the town. The sandhill was like a big colour bar. I can't ever remember visiting any white homes when I was a kid. On Saturday night we did go into the town for the pictures. The picture theatre was roped off in sections. The blackfellas had to sit in front of the rope. You had to go through a little alley at the side to get in. In fact, murries still go in this way—the only thing that has changed is that the rope at the front has gone.

For most of the time, we organised our own entertainment at the yumba. Rounders was a popular game with children and I remember that often the old people would even join in. Dances were a very popular activity and there was a special area set aside. Before a dance, the ground was carefully prepared. First, the area was swept clean, then water was thrown on the ground. Then the area was carefully broomed, resulting in a good hard surface to dance on. The music consisted of guitar, accordian, mouth organ and gum leaf. The dances carried on till the early hours of the morning with few fights or quarrels. Cards were another popular pastime. It wasn't that people were mainly concerned about winning money but to get together with their friends and have a chat and sort out any problems.

When I was a child I remember that when people did go up to the town, they dressed up very smartly. The men would polish their shoes or boots, carefully press their trousers and shirts. They always wore a tie. The women would always wear stockings, gloves and a hat.

Murries also went up to the town to go to the hospital. When a new maternity wing was built, a special section for Aboriginal mothers was set up. It was completely separate from the section for the whites. I had my six children in that ward and you had your own shower and toilet. However, in the ordinary part of the hospital there was no separate section for murries.

(1984)

Roland Robinson
BEES

Related by Percy Mumbulla

Abraham's Bosom was the name
the place had after the white man came.
From the holler trees in their native home
them old fellers cut the honeycomb.
On honey an' little white grubs they fed,   5
'cause them young bees was blackfeller's bread.
That's why they was so mighty an' strong
in their native home at Currarong.
An' them old fellers drink was honey-bul,
honey an' water, a coolamon full.   10
Naked through the bush they went
an' never knew what sickness meant.
Them little dark bees would do you no harm,
they'd crawl all over your honey-smeared arm.
But them Eyetalian bees, they'd bung   15
your eyes right up. When we was young
we used to rob their honey trees.
Savage! They'd fetch your blood. Them bees
would zing an' zoom an' chase a feller
from Bomaderry to Bodalla.   20
Arr, old uncle Minah, Billy Bulloo,
Jacky Mumbulla, King Merriman too,
them fierce old fellers, they're all gone now.
An' the wild honey's still in the gum tree bough.

(1951)

Katharine Susannah Prichard
MARLENE

Coming out from the trees, the camp on the hillside was almost invisible.
It crouched among rocks and wet undergrowth, with the township lying
under mists in the valley below. The wurlies of bark, bagging and matted
leaves had taken on the colouring of the rocks and tree-trunks. They were
shaped like mounds of earth: crude shells with open mouths. A breath of
smoke betrayed them. It hung in the air and drifted away among the trees.

Two women riding along the bush track detected the first humpy, then
another and another, until half a dozen were in sight about a rough open
space. Dogs flew out, barking fiercely. Two or three children, barelegged,
lean, sallow, bright-eyed, with black tousled hair, slid out from before the
wurlies. A man lying beside a fire sat up and glanced at the women.

'Hullo, Benjy,' the elderly woman on a grey horse called. 'Sleeping in
this morning? Where's Mollie?'

The man grunted, starting sullenly over the rain-sodden clearing. Men and women appeared at the open mouths of other wurlies, all dressed as they had been sleeping, in faded dungarees and khaki trousers, shirts and skirts grey with grime and grease, threadbare woollen jackets and coats—cast-off clothing of the townspeople.

'Hullo, Mrs Boyd,' some of the women called.

'This is Miss Cecily Allison,' Mrs Boyd explained, introducing the girl on the chestnut colt. 'Miss Allison's from England; going to write a book about the aborigines. She wanted to see your camp.'

'We're half-castes here—not abos,' a morose, middle-aged man replied.

'And not "at home" so early in the day,' one of the young men added sarcastically. 'It's a hell of a place to see, anyhow.'

'Y're fergettin' y'r manners, Albert—swearin' before ladies!' one of the women said.

She giggled shyly.

'How's yerself, Mrs Boyd?'

'I'm well, Tilly. But you're looking like drowned rats, the lot of you. Why don't you shift camp for the winter, George?'

Mrs Boyd sat her upstanding mount squarely, as well-conditioned as he was. A good horsewoman, capable of managing her own affairs, it was evident. Her manner was authoritative, but kind and friendly.

'Where'd we shift to?' a fat, youngish woman asked jocosely. Barefooted, she stood, a once-white dress dragged across her heavy breast and thighs, a youngster slung on one hip. A little laugh nibbled its way through the crowd.

'This is the only place we're allowed to camp in the district,' the man who had first spoken said sourly. 'You know that, Mrs Boyd.'

'The rain's been comin' down steady for two months.' One of the other women raised a flat, uncomplaining treble.

'How on earth do you manage to get a dry spot in the humpies or keep your clothes dry?'

'We don't.' The crowd laughed as though that were a good joke. 'Our clothes are all soakin'. There's not a dry blanket in the camp.'

'We ought to be ducks. The rain'd run off our backs then.'

'It's a disgrace you should have to live like this,' Mrs Boyd declared. 'But what I came about this morning is Mollie. Where is she?'

The crowd shifted uneasily. Eyes encountered and glanced aside. A wild crew they looked in their shabby clothes, the women wearing remnants of finery, a bright scarf or coloured cardigan over their draggled dresses.

Brown-eyed, black-haired, they all were, but their skin varied from sickly yellow to weathered bronze. The women were sallow and tawny, the men darker. On most of the faces, thick noses and full lips denoted the aboriginal strain; a few others had sharp, neat features, showing no trace of aboriginal origin except in their eyes.

'Where is Mollie?' Mrs Boyd demanded. 'I've been letting Mr Edward drive her in to the pictures on Saturday nights when he goes into town himself. But she didn't come back with him last week. He waited an hour for her.'

'She's fair mad about the pictures, Mollie,' Ruby burbled.

'That's all very well, but it's not very considerate of her to run away like this. She knows how busy we are just now with all the cows coming in. Mr

Phillip and Mr Edward've got their hands full. I had to ride in with the mail myself this morning. And Mollie was very useful, helping with the milking and feeding poddies.'

'She's a fine kid, Mollie,' Albert declared.

'But where is she? What's the matter?'

The crowd surged. Obviously the question was disturbing: it had to be evaded. Exclamations and suggestions clattered. There was no surprise, no consternation, although everybody seemed upset, a little nervous and amused at Mrs Boyd's query.

Mrs Boyd guessed they were hiding Mollie. The child had got a quirk about something: one of those mysterious urges to go bush with her own kind.

'Did y'know Bill Bibblemun took bad with the p'monia and died in hospital, Sunday week?' somebody asked.

Others joined in eagerly.

'It was a grand funeral, Mrs Boyd.'

'The Salvation Army captain said Bill'd go straight to glory because he was a good Christian.'

'He was, too. Testified at street meetings and sang hymns—even when he was drunk.'

'They said some beautiful prayers.'

'All about his bein' washed in the blood of the lamb and his sins bein' whiter than snow.'

'And the kids have all had measles,' Ruby boasted.

'What's happened to Wally Williams?' Mrs Boyd inquired, willing to humour them. 'He was to come over and cut fencing-posts for me last month.'

There was a lull in the rattle of voices, eyelids fell, wary glances slid under them. Coughing, a hoarse whispering, filled the pause.

'He's gone up-country,' George said.

'You mean, he's in jail. What's he been up to now?'

'Well, you see, Mrs Boyd, it wasn't hardly Wally's fault,' Tilly Lewis explained. 'Jo Wiggins said some steers had got out of his holding-paddocks, and he offered Wally two bob for every steer he could track and bring in. Wally took in a couple of cleanskins. He thought they were Mr Wiggins's steers, natcherly—'

'Naturally—at two bob apiece,' Mrs Boyd agreed.

'But when the mounted trooper found a couple of red poley steer skins in Jo Wiggins's slaughteryard, Mr Wiggins put the blame on to Wally—and Wally got two years.'

'Everybody knows Jo Wiggins's game,' Mrs Boyd admitted. 'But Wally ought to keep his hands off clean-skins.'

'Oh, he's not like that, Wally, Mrs Boyd. He's a real good stockman. But if he can't get a job, he doesn't know what to do with hisself. He's jest got to be workin' cattle—'

'I know.' Mrs Boyd laughed good-humouredly. 'I suspect he's "worked" calves from our back hills before now. We had an epidemic of milkers coming in without calves last year.'

'If a cow drops a calf in the bush, Mrs Boyd, the dingoes are as likely to get it as—'

'Wally! Of course. But my money's on Wally. I reckon Jo Wiggins has had more of our calves than the dingoes.'

Her horse, cropping the young grass, swung Mrs Boyd sideways. She saw the figure of a man sleeping before a smouldering fire at the entrance of his shack. Steam was rising from the damp blanket that covered him.

'Who's that?' she asked.

'It's Charley,' a woman who had been coughing incessantly said. 'He's not well.'

'Better put that bottle away then,' Mrs Boyd advised. 'If the trooper comes round somebody'll be getting into trouble for selling Charley plonk again. Where does he get the money to buy drink, anyhow?'

'The shopkeepers take his drawings for showcards sometimes.'

'He's quite an artist in his own way, Charley,' Mrs Boyd explained to her companion. 'Self-taught. Could you show Miss Allison some of Charley's drawings, Lizzie?'

Charley's wife slipped away, burrowed into the wurley, and returned with a black exercise-book in her hands. Miss Allison dismounted to look at the drawings, crude outlines of people and animals, a football match, the finish of a race.

Pleasure in Charley's drawings, awed interest and expectancy animated his friends and relations.

'Well'—Mrs Boyd yanked her horse's head round and straightened her back, smiling but implacable—'have you made up your minds yet to tell me about Mollie?'

The faces about her changed. There was a moment of sombre, unresponsive silence.

Then Tilly Lewis exclaimed delightedly: 'Why, it's Mrs Jackson! She's been bad with the rheumatics; but got up—and put on her hat for the visitors!'

A withered little woman, a neat black hat perched on her head, walked across the clearing, wearing a dingy black dress and frayed grey cardigan with an air of forlorn propriety.

'Good morning, Myrtle,' Mrs Boyd said. 'I'm sorry to hear you've been having rheumatism.'

'What can you expect, Miss Ann?' The half-caste held herself with some dignity: her faded eyes, ringed like agates, looked up at the pleasantly smiling, healthy, fresh-complexioned woman on the big horse. 'I'm not used to living out of doors.'

'No, of course not,' Mrs Boyd replied.

'You know I was brought up at the mission station. And I've worked in some of the best homes in the district; but now—you wouldn't keep a sow in the place where I've got to live.'

'It's not right, Mrs Boyd,' George muttered.

'No, it's not right,' Mrs Boyd agreed. 'But what can I do about it? Would you go into the Old Women's Home if I could get you in, Myrtle?'

'I've been there. The police took me from the hospital after I had rheumatic fever. But I ran away—'

'She did, Mrs Boyd!' eager voices chimed.

'She walked near on a hundred and thirty miles till she got here.'

'Cooped up in the city—with a lot of low-down old women treatin' me like dirt. I've always kept myself to myself. I've always been respectable, Miss Ann.'

'Oh, yes, she's terrible respectable, Mrs Boyd,' the chorus went up.

'Nobody can't say Mrs Jackson isn't respectable!'

'All I want's to die in my own place—like any respectable person. It *is* my own place, Miss Ann, the house your father gave Tom and me; and Mr Henry had no right to turn us out.'

'She's breaking her heart, like any old abo, for the hunting-grounds of her people,' Albert said cynically. 'They always want to go home to die, but, being half-and-half, it's a roof over her head Mrs Jackson wants, and a bed to lie on.'

'I'll see what I can do about it, Myrtle,' Mrs Boyd promised.

'Funny, isn't it?' Albert's lounging, graceful figure tilted back as he gazed at her. 'You're the granddaughter of one of the early settlers who shot off more blacks than any other man in the country. Mrs Jackson is the granddaughter of one of the few survivors, and related to the best families in the district. But you've got the land and the law on your side. They put the dogs onto her if she goes round the homesteads asking for a bit of tucker or old clothes.'

'And this is the only spot where we're allowed to camp in the district.'

'Something will have to be done about it,' Mrs Boyd declared.

'What?' Albert demanded. 'All the land about has been taken up. It's private property now. We're not allowed to work in the mines. We're not allowed to sell the fish we catch—not allowed to shoot or trap. They don't want us on the farms. They won't let us work on the roads. All we're allowed to do is draw rations and rot...though there is some talk of packing us off to one of those damned reservations "where the diseased and dying remnants of the native race are permitted to end their days in peace". Excuse me quoting the local rag.'

'You can't say I haven't tried to help you,' Mrs Boyd protested. 'I've always given you work on my farm when I could.'

A wry smile twisted the young man's mouth. 'And paid us less than half you'd have had to pay other workers.'

'Albert!' one of the women objected. 'Don't take any notice of him, Mrs Boyd.'

'You're talking like one of those crazy agitators, Albert,' Mrs Boyd cried hotly. 'If you're not careful you'll find yourself being moved on.'

'I'll remember you said so, Mrs Boyd.' Albert grinned maliciously.

'It's hard on Albert not being able to get work, Mrs Boyd,' Ruby expostulated. 'He's real clever: can read and write as good as any white man. When he went to school he could beat any of the boys.'

'Lot of good it's ever done me,' Albert sneered. 'If I'd been a myall I'd've had a better life. The blacks of any tribe share all they've got with each other. The whites grab all they can for themselves—and let even their own relations starve.'

'Do the aboriginals treat half-castes better?' Miss Allison's voice rose clear and chilly against his wrath.

'They don't treat us like vermin.' Albert might have been admiring the gleam of her hair or the horse she was holding. 'Up in the nor'-west, when I was a kid, I went around with my mother's tribe. Never knew I was any different from the rest. Then my father got interested in me. Sent me down here to school. He died—and I've been trying to get a job ever since.'

'Do you want to go back to your own people?'

Albert's anger resurged. 'My own people!' he jeered. 'Who are they? My father was as fair as you are. I couldn't live in a blacks' camp now—though this is as bad. But I don't belong there. I think differently. We all do. We like soap and clean clothes when we can get them, and books. We want to go to the pictures and football matches. I want to work and have a house to live in, a wife and kids. But this is all I've got. These are my only people—mongrels like myself.'

'You shouldn't talk bitter like that, Albert,' Mrs Jackson reproved. 'It does no good.'

'Nothing does any good.' He flung away from the crowd and stalked off behind the wurlies.

'He's sore because he can't get work and the Protector won't let Penny Carnarvon marry him,' Ruby said. 'Penny's in service, and she's such a good servant they don't want to lose her. But she's fond of Albert. She says she'll learn the Protector.'

'She will, too.'

'Stella did, didn't she?'

'Too right, she did.'

'She dropped a trayload of dishes to get herself the sack because she wanted to marry Bob. But the missus forgave her and took it out of her wages. Stella had to get herself in the family way, and make up to the boss, before the Protector decided she'd better marry Bob.'

'Penny'll be going for a little holiday soon, Albert says. Then perhaps they can get married and go up north. He's almost sure he can get a job on one of the stations.'

'But where's Mollie?' Mrs Boyd returned to the attack. The crowd closed down on their laughter and gossip. There was a disconcerted shuffling and searching for something to say.

'Mollie?'

'Yes, Mollie. It's no use pretending you don't know where she is. If she's hiding, doesn't want to come home, I'm not going to worry about her. But I'll have to let the Department know—'

'Hullo, Mrs Boyd!' A girl in a pink cotton frock stood in the opening of a wurley behind the horses. A pretty little thing, sturdy and self-possessed, but rather pale, she stood there, a small bundle wrapped in a dirty shawl in her arms.

'Mollie,' Mrs Boyd gasped. 'Have you been getting a baby?'

The girl nodded, smiling.

'But you're only a child,' Mrs Boyd cried. 'You're not sixteen.'

'I was sixteen last month,' Mollie replied calmly.

'It's scandalous,' Mrs Boyd exclaimed indignantly. 'Who's the father?'

Mollie's eyes smiled back at her. 'I been going with two or three boys in town.'

The little crowd before her quivered to breathless excitement: a sigh, as of relief, and a titter of suppressed mirth escaped.

'You ought to be ashamed of yourself,' Mrs Boyd declared furiously. 'You know, I thought better of you, Mollie. I thought you were different from the other girls. You've lived with me for so many years, and I trusted you to behave yourself.'

'Don't be angry,' Mollie said quietly. 'I couldn't help it . . . and I like the baby.'

'When did it happen?'

'Last night.'

Mrs Boyd stared at the girl. She looked a little wan, but quite well.

'Is she all right?' she asked the crone who had come out of the hut behind Mollie. 'Had I better get the doctor to come out and see her, or arrange for her to go into hospital?'

'I've never felt better in my life,' Mollie said. 'Aunty May can look after me.'

'No need to bother,' the old half-caste beside Mollie mumbled soothingly. 'She hadn't a bad time. I'd have sent her to the hospital—but everything happened in such a hurry.'

'Let me see the child,' Mrs Boyd demanded: turned her horse and rode to Mollie.

'She's very little and red,' Mollie apologized, tenderly lifting the dirty shawl that covered the baby.

Mrs Boyd leaned down from her saddle. It was the ugliest scrap of humanity she had ever seen; but there was something vaguely familiar in its tiny crumpled face. Cicely Allison dragged her horse over the grass to look at the baby, too.

'Ra-ther sweet, isn't she?' she murmured mechanically. 'What are you going to call her?'

Mollie drew the shawl over the baby's face again.

'Marlene,' she said happily.

The rain descended in a gusty squall, driving the half-castes into their wurlies, the horsewomen back among the trees. As they rode, the older woman sagged in her saddle, curiously aged and grim.

'The sooner they're cleaned out of the district the better,' she said viciously. 'They're an immoral lot, these half-castes.'

'What about the whites who are responsible for them?' the girl on the chestnut colt asked.

She wondered whether it was a tragedy or a comedy she had been witnessing. These people might live like dogs in their rotten wurlies, with the dark bush behind them and the prosperous little township spread at their feet; but their aspirations were all towards the ways and ideas of the white race. The exotic film-star, and that baby in this dump of outcasts— what an indictment! Yet Miss Allison suspected they had tried to spare the baby's grandmother, with simple kindliness, knowing the truth behind Mollie's bravado. Had they altogether succeeded?

The camp on the hillside was moved on before the end of the month.

(1941)

Jack Davis
from NO SUGAR

ACT TWO

SCENE FIVE

The Moore River Settlement, a hot morning. JIMMY *ambles about outside the Superintendent's office.* MR NEAL *approaches. He has a hangover.*

NEAL: Hey, you, you're with the Northam lot, aren't you? What are you doing here?

JIMMY: What's it look like I'm doing?

NEAL: You're supposed to be up in the quarantine camp.

JIMMY: Quarantine camp, me arse.

NEAL: You're out of bounds and you know it.

JIMMY: Come off it, you know that quarantine camp is a load of bullshit, so don't try and tip it over me.

NEAL: I'll attend to you later.

   (*He heads for his office.*)

JIMMY: You know, if fertiliser was in short supply you'd make a bloody fortune'.

   (*He sniggers.*)

NEAL: (*mumbling*) Another bloody troublemaker.

   (*He sits at his desk.* MARY *brings him tea on a tray. He leers at her body.* MATRON *enters, almost catching him.*)

MATRON: Where did you get to yesterday?

NEAL: You know very well I had to go to Moora to see about—

MATRON: (*interrupting*) To spend the day in the hotel drinking. Don't imagine no one sees you come in, the condition you were in—fine example.

NEAL: I've got to get away from the place now and again.

MATRON: What about me? I was at the quarantine camp from dawn till dusk again yesterday.

NEAL: Done them all?

MATRON: Yes, eventually.

NEAL: How many have got it?

MATRON: Scabies? Mrs Mason and her three youngsters.

NEAL: Yes.

MATRON: That's all, just the four of them. I've isolated them, put them on sulphur and regular bathing.

NEAL: Four of 'em, only cases of skin disease? Only four?

MATRON: Yes, Alf. I can recognise a case of scabies when I see one.

NEAL: And you've examined the lot of them?

MATRON: Yes, I haven't been going up the Long Pool for a picnic.

NEAL: Are you telling me out of eighty-nine dumped on me, only four of them have got the bloody disease?

   (*She puts the record book in front of him.*)

Good God, woman, what's the bloody game? Eighty-nine natives in a bloody quarantine camp I've just busted me gut to get ready on time, and there's nothing bloody well wrong with 'em?

MATRON: Alf, there's no need to lose your temper and no need for bad language. They should be cleared up in a few days

NEAL: The whole job's a waste of time. They could have been treated in Northam.

MATRON: The only health hazard in the camp are the dogs.

NEAL: What dogs?

MATRON: There's about fifty of them, and a good many in less than healthy condition.

NEAL: How did the dogs get here?

MATRON: With the road party, apparently.

NEAL: No one told me anything about dogs.

MATRON: One per family.

    (*She exits.*)

NEAL: That's one too many. (*Calling*) Billy! Billy!

    (*He unlocks the armoury cupboard and gets a rifle and ammunition.*)

BILLY: (*off*) Yeah, comin' boss.

    (NEAL *counts out the ammunition.* BILLY *enters.*)

    Yeah, Boss?

NEAL: Get the horses and a length of rope, Billy.

BILLY: Yeah, boss.

    (NEAL *takes a rifle and ammunition. They exit.*)

SCENE SIX

A clearing in the pine plantation. Moore River Native Settlement, night. A camp fire burns. JIMMY *and* SAM *are painted for a corroboree.* JIMMY *mixes wilgi in tobacco tin lids, while* SAM *separates inji sticks from clapsticks.* JOE *arrives with an armful of firewood and pokes at the fire.*

JOE: They comin' now.

BILLY: (*off*) Get no rain this place summertime.

    (BILLY *and* BLUEY *enter and remove their shirts.*)

JIMMY: Eh? Where you fellas been?

BLUEY: Aw, we been pushing truck for Mr Neal.

BILLY: He goin' Mogumber.

BLUEY: (*miming taking a drink*) Doin' this fella.

JOE: He'll be *minditj* tomorrow.

    (BLUEY *and* BILLY *paint themselves with wilgi.*)

BILLY: My word you fellas pr-retty fellas.

BLUEY: *Wee-ah*, plenty *wilgi*.

BILLY: Eh? You know my country, must be walk two, three days for this much. Your country got plenty.

(JIMMY *strikes up a rhythm on the clapsticks.* BLUEY *joins him.*)

JIMMY: (*singing*)
    Tjinnung nitjakoorliny?
    Karra, karra, karra, karra,
    Moyambat a-nyinaliny a-nyinaliny,
    Baal nitja koorliny moyambat a-moyambat moyambat,
    Moyambat nitja koorliny moyambat.
    Kalkanna yirra nyinny kalkanna,
    Yirra nyinniny, yirra nyinniny,
    Moyambat a-kalkanna moyambat a-kilkanna

Yirra nyinniny, yirra nyinniny, yirra nyinniny,
Karra koorliny kalkanna karra karra koorliny kalkanna.
Karra koorliny, karra koorliny, karra koorliny,
Woolah!

BLUEY: Eh, what that one?

JIMMY: That's my grandfather song. (*Miming with his hands*)
He singin' for the *karra*, you know, crabs, to come up the river and for the fish to jump up high so he can catch them in the fish traps.

SAM: (*pointing to* BILLY'*s body paint*) Eh! Eh! Old man, what's that one?

BILLY: This one *bungarra*, an' he lookin' for berry bush. But he know that fella eagle watchin' him and he know that fella is cunnin' fella. He watchin' and lookin' for that eagle, that way, this way, that way, this way.
(*He rolls over a log, disappearing almost magically.* BLUEY *plays the didgeridoo and* BILLY *appears some distance away by turning quickly so the firelight reveals his painted body. He dances around, then seems to disappear suddenly. He rolls back over the log and drops down, seated by the fire.*)

BLUEY, SAM and JIMMY: *Yokki! Moorditj! Woolah!*

JIMMY: Eh? That one dance come from your country?

BILLY: Nah. That one come from that way, lo-o-ong way. *Wanmulla* country. Proper bad fellas.

SAM: Well, I won't be goin' there.

JOE: Me either!
(JIMMY, JOE *and* SAM *laugh.* SAM *jumps to his feet with the clapsticks.*)

SAM: This one *yahllarah! Everybody! Yahllarah!*
(*He starts a rhythm on the clapsticks.* BLUEY *plays didgeridoo.* JIMMY, *and then* JOE, *join him dancing.*)
Come on! Come on!
(*He picks up inji sticks. The Nyoongahs,* SAM, JIMMY *and* JOE, *dance with them.* BILLY *joins in. They dance with increasing speed and energy, stamping their feet, whirling in front of the fire, their bodies appearing and disappearing as the paint catches the firelight. The dance becomes faster and more frantic until finally* SAM *lets out a yell and they collapse, dropping back to their positions around the fire.* JIMMY *coughs and pants painfully.*)
(*To* JIMMY) Eh! Eh! (*Indicating his heart*) You wannta *dubakieny*, you know your *koort minditj*.

BILLY: This country got plenty good dance, eh?

BLUEY: *Wee-ah!*

JIMMY: Ah, *yuart*, not too many left now. Nearly all finish.

BILLY: No, no, no. You song man, you fella dance men. This still your country. (*Flinging his arms wide*) You, you, you, you listen! *Gudeeah* make 'em fences, windmill, make 'em road for motor car, big house, cut 'em down trees. Still your country! Not like my country, finish...finish.
(*He sits in silence. They watch him intently.* JOE *puts wood on the fire. He speaks slowly.*)

BILLY: *Kuliyah.* (*Miming pulling a trigger, grunting*) *Gudeeah* bin kill 'em. Finish, kill 'em. Big mob, 1926, kill 'em big mob my country.
(*Long pause.*)

SAM: *Nietjuk?*

BILLY: I bin stop Liveringa station and my brother, he bin run from Oombulgarri. (*Holding up four fingers*) That many days. Night time too. He bin tell me 'bout them *gudeeah*. They bin two, three stockman *gudeeah*. Bin stop along that place, Juada Station, and this one *gudeeah* Midja George, he was ridin' and he come to this river and he see these two old womans, *koories*, there in the water hole. He says, what you doin' here? They say they gettin' *gugja*.

(*He mimes pulling lily roots and eating.*)

Midja George say, where the mans? They over by that tree sleepin', and Midja George, he get off his horse, and he bin belt that old man with the stockwhip. He bin flog 'em, flog 'em, till that *gudeeah*, he get tired. Then he break the bottle glass spear, and he break the *chubel* spear.

(*He grunts and mimes this.*)

And that old man, he was bleedin', bleedin' from the eyes, and he get up and he pick up that one *chubel* spear, and he spear that one *Midja George*.

(*He demonstrates violently.*)

And that *gudeeah*, he get on his horse, he go little bit way and he fall off...finish...dead.

JIMMY: Serve the bastard right.

BILLY: No, no, no bad for my mob. Real bad. That old man and his two *koories*, they do this next day.

(*He indicates running away.*)

Two *gudeeah* come looking for Midja George. They bin find him dead.

(*Silence.*)

(*Holding up a hand*) Must be that many day. Big mob *gudeeah*. Big mob politjmans, and big mob from stations, and shoot 'em everybody mens, *koories*, little *yumbah*.

(*He grunts and mimes pulling a trigger.*)

They chuck 'em on a big fire, chuck 'em in river.

(*They sit in silence, mesmerized and shocked by* BILLY'S *gruesome story.*)

JIMMY: Anybody left, your mob?

BILLY: Not many, gid away, hide. But no one stop that place now, they all go 'nother country.

JOE: Why?

BILLY: You go there, night time you hear 'em. I bin bring cattle that way for Wyndham Meat Works. I hear 'em. Mothers cryin' and babies cryin', screamin'. *Waiwai! Wawai! Wawai!*

(*They sit in silence staring at* BILLY *who stares into the fire. Suddenly a night hawk screeches.*)

SAM: Gawd, I'm getting out of here.

JIMMY: Me too!

BLUEY: Hm, hm, hm, hm, *wee-ah, wee-ah!*

(*They quickly pick up their things and leave.* JOE *remains alone.*)

SAM: You comin'?

JOE: Go on, I'll catch you up. Go on!

JIMMY: You watch out.

(*He pinches his throat with thumb and forefinger.*)

JOE: I'll be all right.

SAM: Don't forget the *kaal*.

JOE: Okay.

(1985)

Xavier Herbert
POOR FELLOW MY COUNTRY

from CHAPTER 1

The small boy was Aboriginal—distinctly so by cast of countenance, while yet so lightly coloured as to pass for any light-skinned breed, even tanned Caucasian. His skin was cream-caramel, with a hair-sheen of gold. There was also the glint of gold in his tow-tawny mop of curls. Then his eyes were grey—with a curious intensity of expression probably due to their being set in cavernous Australoid orbits where one would expect to see dark glinting as of shaded water. His nose, fleshed and curved in the mould of his savage ancestry, at the same time was given just enough of the beakiness of the other side to make it a thing of perfection. Likewise his lips. Surely a beautiful creature to any eye but the most prejudiced in the matter of race. Indeed, but for knowing the depth and breadth of prejudice against the very strain that gave him perfection, one might well be amazed to know that such a thing could stand up to the sight of him. Yet most people, at least of this remote northern part of the Australian Continent, would dismiss him as just a *boong*. He was aged about eight.

He was squatting beside a water-hole alone, fishing. He wore only khaki pants, the rent stern of which exposed a piece of his behind so closely matching the bleached cloth as to be scarcely noticeable. In one delicate truly Aboriginal hand he held a fishing line, in the other a fish-spear. As the Aboriginal fisherman or hunter must to ensure his catch, he was singing, softly:

> *Kowee, Tjala!*
> *Long o' me come, Old Catfish*
> *I sing you...Kowee, kowee, kowee!*
> *Old Catfish, must you come...*

It was not the mere monotone that mostly goes for Aboriginal singing, but oddly tuneful, and especially sweet as the only sound in all the small world thereabout, because everything else was sleeping out the midday heat, even the wind, so that the pool—emerald, silver, blue-enamel, gold—lay still as glass.

The pool was rockbound; by a sloping tumble on the side where the boy squatted amongst roots of a banyan that made the ruddy sandstone look as if crawling with grey snakes; on the other by a sheer wall grown with ferns and other clinging vegetation and topped with trees of which the branches mingled with those of the banyan.

> *I sing you...Kowee, kowee, kowee!*
> *Old Tjala, you got 'o come...*

A golden flicker in the emerald depths. The slack line quickened. The grey eyes fairly blazed with intensity. The golden-brown hand drew the line. Up came the shadow. The fish-spear was poised. But the line fell slack and the shadow drifted down and vanished. The line came up without bait. The perfect lips moved to a soft throaty growl: 'Bloody bastard!'

He turned, to reach for a grubby cotton flour-sack hanging in the roots—to stiffen in that attitude. Only an eye of extraordinary sharpness could so quickly have discerned anything untoward, so much a part of the background was that which had intruded into it—or materialized out of it, as seemed as likely.

It was of human shape, greyish, or blackish made grey with dust and ashes and ancient body hair, so as to appear kindred to the crawling roots. It had stick legs, with shapeless lumpy feet and knobby knees, arms like a mantis, a tuft of grey hair sticking up like the crest of an angry bird out of a grubby ochred head-band, and whiskers plaited into a long goatee about slivers of cane or grass, an almost flat nose with slit septum dangling losely from enormous nostrils. It seemed to be sightless as a death's head—till suddenly there burnt within the black caverns what looked like live coals.

The seeming apparition wore no clothing, except the ceremonial loin-covering called the Hair Belt, a wide belly-band made of cord woven from human hair with a narrow pubic apron falling to the knees. The band was no mere covering, but also served for carrying numerous objects—*gungu*, or fire-lighting kit, quartz knife, *minga-minga* sticks for clicking accompaniment to singing, and a couple of boomerangs. Other articles were carried in dilly-bags of woven fibre slung round the scrub-turkey-like neck back and front, while the skeleton left arm was crooked about an assortment of spears, and the claw-like right hand held a womera. But what was of first importance in the rig-out, from an Aboriginal point of view, were the cicatrized markings in the slaty skin. Ridges were cut and brands burnt into upper arms, shoulders, breast, belly, thighs, some of very intricate design. From these a knowledgeable eye would read the wearer's status, which in this case must have been considerable.

Not a move from either. Both might have been spellbound.

The spell was broken by slight movement of the claw holding the womera—raising of the index finger. In common sign-language that meant 'Who are you?'

It was the proper way of greeting between strangers, for the elder to ask and the younger to respond, not with personal names, but the sign for his *Skin*, meaning his place in the relationship system, literally his Substance—although nothing could be more literal than the native interpretation, Skin. This was his eternal identity with the Dream Time and the factor determining his behaviour towards others, strangers or not. However, whatever the proprieties, there are strangers and strangers, and the *wisdom* of declaring one's identity to be considered. A stranger who seemed to have materialized out of nothing might well be a *Moomboo* or Devil-devil, wanting to know your Skin only to judge the propriety of eating you. The only response to the sign was a blink of grey eyes and slight quiver of lovely lip.

The grey whiskers parted in a wide grin, then jerked to cackling speech: '*Koyada kumeri.*'

Still no response. A moment of intense exchange of staring. Then the burning coals flicked to the pool. The grey glance followed. Again the golden shadow. The fair head turned, to see the mantis claws divesting themselves of dunnage. Rather like a grey spider, the unencumbered figure came slipping through the roots, to step into the shallow water a few feet from the boy, who stood as if ready to bolt. The mantis was intent now only on what was below. Swaying, and with claw to mouth, he began to chant, thin and nasal of tone, true blackfellow singing, C-sharp, E, C-sharp, each repeated four times, to accompaniment of slapping the water:

Mah-nah, mah-nah, mah-nah, mah-nah
Gu-dah, gu-dah, gu-dah, gu-dah
Mah-nah, gu-dah, mah-nah, gu-dah
Yuk!

A resounding slap went with the last note; then up an octave to repeat; down again. All the while the shadow circled and rose. Suddenly the claw left the mouth to make the gesture of spearing, while the red eyes shot a significant glance at the watchful grey eyes—without pause in chanting and slapping: '*Mah-nah, gu-dah, mah-nah, gu-dah—Yuk!*'

The boy caught on, raised the spear, stood poised to strike.

The long dorsal fin cut the surface.

Zip! The spear flew, struck, wobbled, spun violently, vanished into a bloody whirlpool. As grey eyes glanced again at the death's head, the latter split to cackle, 'Yakkarai...Properlee...Numberr-one!'

Eyes back to the pool as the haft of the spear popped up to cut wild capers through the stained emerald, at last to collapse, to reveal its whiskery victim convulsing weakly on the barbs. The boy looked at the Master of Magic, received a nod, hesitated a moment, then slipped into the water, seized the spear, flung the fish ashore. It was a beauty, a good ten pounds in weight. Again the wide grin and the cackled comment: 'Properlee!'

The boy looked as wary as before on coming out. The death's head cackled at him, 'No-more fright!' The index finger rose again.

Again hesitation. Then a small hand gave the sign *Julama*.

Along with a still wider grin, the claw came up to give the same sign. This meant they were tribal brothers—or, because of the difference in age, paternal grandsire and grandson. Bond of blood wouldn't enter into it, not even had they been truly related, because theirs was a matrilinear social system, with male authority vested primarily in mother's brothers. Their bond would be one more of affection, no less strong for having its basis solely in tradition, their responsibility to each other simply exchange of the wisdom of age for the physical advantages of youth. This matter of responsibility was raised at once, when one of the claws reached to smooth a plump golden-brown shoulder in the Aboriginal way of expressing affection, while the cackle took on the whine customary in asking favours: 'Plenty beef you got him, eh? Goot tucker long o' dat place you sit down.' Curl of the perfect lips in a slight smile. 'Which way you sit down, Kumija?' At a questioning look in the grey eyes, the cackle added: 'Kumija...dat one Granny. Wha' nam' you call-yim?'

The answer was given in a whisper, but with breath inhaled in the native way: '*Mora.*'

'Ah! Where you sit down, *Mora?*'

To tell a stranger where one camped was to accept him. Likewise to use his language. A blink of the grey eyes first, then: 'Catfish Station...Kumija.'

A long red tongue flashed over whiskered lips: 'Ah...teeshum tucker!' The whine again: 'Too-much me hungry long o' dat one...bre'millik me like him. No-goot long o' *binji*.' A claw rubbed the brand-burnt stomach that seemed so hollow as to reveal the backbone.

Young Granny nodded understanding of what was required of him. Both looked at the fish gasping its last. Old Granny said, 'You tek him long o' teeshun, give him cook.' He pulled the quartz knife from his belt, slit a length of bark from a root, gave it to the boy. The boy slipped it through the fish's gills. Then he picked up his three small spears and the gunny-sack, and the fish, which he tossed over his shoulder. Old Granny nodded for him to go ahead. He climbed through the roots to the top of the tumble of rock. He stopped and looked back. No sign of Old Granny. He peered down. He looked around wide-eyed. Old Kumija had vanished the way he had appeared—as if by magic. The grey eyes rolled in wariness. Then with a swift movement he started away from the rocks and banyans, got out into the open. Still no sign. After a moment he set out southward, following the bank of a deep dry creek. He went with the swift easy lope of a blackfellow, but with the swift uneasy glances about of one travelling alone. In a land largely peopled by spirits one must be vigilant always. They had to materialize to do you harm. You had to be a jump ahead of them. It was probably concession to the boy's non-Aboriginal heritage that, Aboriginal enough as he seemed otherwise, he dared to be travelling alone.

The sandstone of the locality, projection of a distant Plateau to be just glimpsed through the ragged open forest to northward, and the dark red sandy soil and forest, soon gave way to grey plain with meaner growth and a profusion of small spiked grey termites' nests, or Ant Beds, as called in these parts, except along the creek-bank, where water-gums and coolibahs and the like grew stoutly, despite the dryness that would obtain for most of the year. The bed of the creek, now of white sand, blazed silver. So the boy travelled for about a mile and a half, when he came to a sharp bend in the creek, round which was revealed a very different vista. From a wide bar of rock that was the determining factor in the change of direction, shimmering blue water stretched away southward to vanishing point in the dense greenery of its banks. A ruddy smudge on the blue enamel of the sky in that direction told of dust blowing on the rising afternoon wind.

A halt to make a survey all round; then the boy climbed down to cross the bar. Galahs in the timber of the further bank spotted him, swept up like a mass of rosy blossoms torn from the trees by a freak wind, wheeled over him, screaming as if truly in frank fear of some devilish design on them—as native lore had it they always were through trouble with Tchamala, the Rainbow Serpent, back in the Dream Time, and as if the boy were thinking as he cocked his head to them and yelled in mockery, '*Yerrilgeenah, Yerrilgeenah . . . gully-gully Yerrilgeenah!*'

Legend had it that the *Yerrilgeenah*, spies of the Old Woman, the Earth Mother, Koonapippi, pursued by her enemy, Tchamala, the Snake in Arcady, had taken refuge in a hollow tree (as in fact their descendants do today) only to find themselves in the Old One's belly. Hence the tuneful little song with which the boy skipped across the rocks and up the other side:

Yerrilgeenah, Yerrilgeenah, gully-gully Yerrilgeenah
Shtinkit hide long hollit tree, find himself long Tchineke binj-ee.

The red beneath the mauve of the Galah's feathers was said to be blood shed by the Snake when the birds tore at his insides with fierce parrot bills and forced him to disgorge them. The boy looked up at the flash of crimson over him. There was a tale attached to everything in the land, just as a tail was too—except to Man, a freak mutation of the heroic creatures of the Dream Time.

(1975)

Archie Weller
JOHNNY BLUE

No one liked Johnny Blue much. They reckoned he was a larrikin, a rebel and a lout.

But I liked Johnny all the time he was here, because he was the Nyoongah's mate, and mine especially. The only person who ever understood me and the only white bloke to notice me as a human instead of just a hunk of meat who could run fast.

You see, when me old man went to jail, Mum and me moved down the country because now me old man was a crim like, us Maguires had got a bad name. So we moved to Quarranocking.

There wasn't much at Quarra: only a school, a pub, a store, and a few houses settled in the yellow dust like a flock of tired cockatoos. We went and lived down the camp, near the river with the other Nyoongahs, and Mum sent me to school.

All the other kids there, most of them off farms, was older then me, and brainier and bigger too, so, being coloured as well, I got smacked up first day out. That's what the kids down these little towns is like.

There was these two big blokes pushing me around when, out of the shadows where I hadn't seen him stepped this cruel big bloke and says, quiet like,

'Youse buggers let the kid alone and fight me.'

Well, I see the big bloke's got a name about, because the two bullies let go of me like I was a tiger snake, and scooted off. Then the big bloke said, 'What's ya name, skinny ribs?'

So I says back me name, which is Jesse Maguire, then he said, 'Well my name's Johnny Blue, but I got others what people call me, whenever they find sumpin's missin'.' Then he laughed. An' I reckon he sounded like a kookaburra.

The he tells me to come and sit in the shade and have a fag, so I do. He was me mate from that very day and us two stuck together like feathers on a bird.

He was the only white bloke ever to show any real kindness to me, except perhaps me dad. Most white blokes have always pushed me round until sports days or footie seasons come around, then they lay off and even suck up because I'm a good runner.

But in Quarranocking no one touched me while I was Johnny's mate. Once Eddie Callanan tried to fight me when he reckoned Johnny wasn't around. But he was, and he came in like a cornered boomer. He gave a right that lifted Callanan off his feet, then a haymaker to the Irish Kid's belly that laid him stiff as a board.

That was one of the things I admired about me cobber. He could fight like a bunch of wildcats and he was as game as a dozen Ned Kellys.

Like the time he jumped off Dogger's Ledge, sixty feet into the waterhole, just for something to do, or when he fought five chicken kids who reckoned they would have a chance of beating him in a mob. But he laid them flat, every one of them, on his own. Or when he kicked the priest's gate down because the father had abused his mum.

No one else would have touched the priest because most of them was Catholics anyhow. Besides, the priest would go straight to the town cop, who was another mick, if anyone even gave him so much as a dirty look. But this didn't stop Johnny after he come home and found his mum howling.

Johnny really loved his old mum, but he never liked his dad, who was always drunk, fat, dirty and vicious. He was bigger and stronger than Johnny, too, so the kid got hell. Once when he come to school with a real beaut black eye he swore to me he'd get his old man one day.

Johnny was kind to all us Nyoongahs. He was a real good carpenter and made ripper toys for us, like the hill trolley he made for the Innitts, which lasted until Riley Johns smashed it into a rock and nearly brained himself. He was a good carver too and made tons of bonzer carved things for the kids down the river. He made me a horse out of red gum on a wandoo stand. Struth, it looked good—real muritch, you know—all red and shiny and all.

He loved making us kids laugh, though he never laughed much himself. He'd get us up by the dump and dress up as Miss Raymond, our teacher for maths. He'd stick an old pillow in his shorts, put a wig of mattress stuffing on his head and, speaking in a high voice, 'teach' us maths. By Jeeze he was funny, and he had us rolling around in stitches. Sometimes he'd stick a tin on his head and put on a pair of broken glasses and, with an old piece of piping, creep stealthily among the rubbish acting like the town cop.

He was funny all right, a real good actor, and I felt pretty proud that such a clever bloke was my mate.

And I admired him because he never treated us any different. When we was all laughing and fooling around together at the dump, we was all equal and all mates. And at school or in town, in front of the other white folk, he was just the same. And that's really something. A lot of white folk are friendly if no one's looking, but when there's a crowd around, they don't want to know you if your skin's black.

Johnny Blue never had a girlfriend, but he wasn't queer.

He was handsome enough in a rugged sort of way. His eyes were black like the backs of beetles and were often hidden behind a fringe of his curly black hair that grew thick and long enough to hang over his broad brown shoulders. Sometimes his eyes squinted up with laughter but mostly they were as cold as the middle of a dam in winter, them eyes of Johnny's. His nose was flat and broken like Billy Keith the boxer's, who smacked up the shearers every year in the local show. Except when he was fooling around with us kids, his mouth was always drawn back in a half-snarl, like one of them dingoes in the South Perth zoo. But his teeth was big and white and he had a ripper whistle—better than anyone else.

Another thing about Johnny Blue, he could fight, chuck boondis, spears or boomerangs, spit and run better than anyone, but he never bragged or boasted. He let other kids think they could beat him in everything, except fighting.

Winter came and the dust turned to mud around the town. The kids had mud fights instead of using boondi or conky nuts, and the old man was due out of jail soon.

Johnny and me was sharing a fag under the tank stand when Micky Rooselett came and told me Acky wanted to see me. Acky was our nickname for Mr Ackland, the headmaster. I gave a grin to Johnny and says, 'Silly bugger'll probably cane me for not doing me maths.'

Johnny gave a snarl. There was no love lost between him and old Acky, they were always getting into yikes together like a pair of male dingoes fighting over a bitch. Acky didn't like us Nyoongahs either so, since I was the only one in his class, I got the lot, too.

I got into his room and it was dark with only a bit of light shining through the cobwebby, dusty, flyspotted window panes. Acky was in a shirty mood that day, and he grabs me shoulder and yanks it around so me neck fair gets twisted. I could smell the beer on him, so I reckons, 'Look out, Jesse, this bloke's as drunk as Johnny's old man.' I was buggered if I was going to get caned by him in such a temper, 'cos I reckoned he'd half-kill me. I was scared—so I done a silly thing.

I sticks me hand in me pockets and says, 'If you hit me, I'm gonna get my old man onto you when he comes 'ome next week.'

Well, that gets him as wild as a dog in a cat's home. He pulls me about and drags me hands out and tries to lay six across them. The thing is, only one of them hit me hand and, since me fist was clenched, it only hit me knuckles but it still felt like me fingers was cut off.

Another hit me face and fair near took me eye out, and the rest got me around the shoulders, and when he'd finished he chucked me out the door.

Me arm was numb right up to me elbow and the mark on me face starts to hurt like the time Mickey Redgum, a stockman on a station where the old man was working one time, sent his stock-whip across me face accidentally. I had to bite back the tears: it would never do for a Nyoongah to cry in front of our number one enemies, by whom I mean our loving white brothers. But when I got to Johnny I couldn't keep the tears back. He wouldn't tell, and besides he was me mate.

When he saw me hand and face, he up and goes for the head's office before I can say 'struth' and, by the time I can get after him, it's too late. I hear a cry, then Acky yelling out something about ringing up Johnny's dad and Johnny shouting out that he can do what he likes but no one is going to push his little cobber around. Then Acky tells him not to come back to school, and Johnny says he won't come back for a million quid.

So Johnny was expelled. But he didn't care.

That night me life was changed. I aren't no scholar and I don't know any big words, but I guess after that night I was never really a kid any more.

I was lying in me bag and newspaper bed, watching the lightning flash like spears across the black sky. I loved the rain pelting onto the tin roof of our home-made house, though when it came through the cracks in the rusty walls and all the old nailholes in the roof, it wasn't so good.

Suddenly, I hears a thudding on me window that's not hail, so I up and opens it and in hops Johnny, looking like the bunyip coming up out of a muddy creek. I says, surprised like, 'What's up, Johnny mate?'

And he says, in a dull voice, 'I killed me dad and you've gotta help me.'

Now Johnny never lied, and anyhow, what sort of a galah would swim through all that mud to bull to a kid? Not Johnny Blue, I can tell you. So I asks him what he wants me to do and he tells me.

What happened was, after he got home from school after the stoush with Acky, the silly old coot *had* rung up like he said he would. Johnny's dad was angrier than a wounded grizzly and told the boy all sorts of things, like he had to quit fighting, to stop going around with the Nyoongahs, and that he was going to belt Johnny good for being such a fool. Then he pulls off his belt and starts to lay into him, but Johnny's mum steps in. Now old man Blue was in a cruel, wild mood, so he pushes Missus Blue out of the way and lashes her across the face with his belt.

Then Johnny went mad, because, you see, he loved his mum. He grabbed the bread knife and stuck it into his Dad's fat belly. Johnny stuck old man Blue so full of holes he was looking like a sieve, then he took off, because he didn't want to go to jail. So he came to our place, to his only mate—to me.

And he'd worked out a bit of a plan, and it was a pretty smart idea.

He reckoned they'd be looking for him pretty soon, and they'd know, with the river in flood, he couldn't swim over, and the bridge was fifteen miles down. But us Nyoongahs had made a raft out of old four-gallon kerosene drums and bits of wood, and his plan was that we both cross over then I would bring the raft back and tie it up again and hop into bed, and don't know about anything. See, if he just took the raft they'd know straight away that he'd got over. But this way, they'd spend all day tomorrow looking on this side and by then he'd be up in East Perth with his Mum's family, and they'd hide him until maybe he could go over east or something.

Well I got out of bed and into me trousers and we went off down to where the raft was. The river was all white foam, and brown, and green; and rushing and twisting like a giant koodgeeda, dashing itself against rocks and snags. It was the only way Johnny could hide from the fuzz, else I wouldn't have even gone near it, let alone try and cross it. But Johnny was the only bloke I'd have done it for, no sweat.

So we got on and pushed off from the bank with the two poles, then we're off like a flaming rodeo steer, bucking and tossing, pigrooting and rearing. But we was getting across.

We was in the middle when it happened.

I was using the pole to keep the raft off a dirty big boulder, sticking its head above the water like a water spirit. Suddenly the pole broke and the raft rammed full pelt into the rock, smashing into a thousand pieces.

Well, I wouldn't know how many pieces, really. All I know is that there was water instead of wood under me feet, and I was being dragged along like a bleeding racing car driver. I never been so fast in me life.

I couldn't swim, and I reckoned I was done. Not a nice way to croak, thinks I, so I yell for nothing in particular. Then I feel a strong arm under me and Johnny soothing me down. He used his body to protect mine, so it was him that bumped into most of the rocks and snags, but I didn't realise that at the time. Only a horrid roaring in me ears and brain, and being tossed along by the Quarra's green-brown hands.

Then we hit the bank. I felt Johnny give me an almighty push, and that's all I remember, until morning came and there I was lying flat as a tack among the reeds, like a drowned possum.

Johnny was gone and at first I thought he'd got away, but not for long. Actually, they found him before they found me. When morning came and they found me and the raft missing too, they drove down the river and over the bridge and started to come up the other side, and they found his body wrapped around a tree about half a mile down river.

Well that was the end of Johnny Blue, the Abos' mate.

He was kind to us, he fought our battles, he made us laugh and stopped our crying, he made toys for us and shared what little he had in life with us. And for all those things I admired him.

But most of all I admired him because he really *did* treat us as equals, not just people to be kind to.

You see he was a strong swimmer, he could have made it to the opposite bank alone.

I was only a skinny little Nyoongah, a quarter-caste, a nothing. But to him I was a person and an equal and his mate, and he gave his life for me.

(1986)

Gerry Bostock
from HERE COMES THE NIGGER
ACT I, SCENE II

CHARACTERS: *Verna Lambert and Sam Mathews.*
LOCATION: *Sam's flat*

(SAM *and* VERNA *can be heard coming up the stairs laughing and joking. The door opens.* VERNA *enters carrying the groceries. She crosses the room and puts the bag on the table and looks around the room.* SAM *enters, closes the door and takes a few paces and stops. He puts the suitcase down.*)

SAM: (*smiling*) Well, don't just stand there. Go and put the tucker away, woman.

VERNA: (*She picks up the groceries and turns to him, smiling.*) Still the male chauvinist, hey, big brother?

SAM: Old Aboriginal custom.

VERNA: (*She crosses to the kitchen as* SAM *picks up the suitcase.*) You'll never change.

SAM: I hope not.

VERNA: So do I, big brother!

SAM: (*He crosses the room and places the suitcase down by the settee.*) Thanks kid. You made my day.

VERNA: (*from the kitchen*) Don't mention it. Do the same for a black-fella!

SAM: Oooh, you're all heart, kid. You're all heart.

VERNA: (*re-entering the room*) Well, how's my big-time brother, the poet?

SAM: (*grins*) Still struggling, sis. Still struggling. And how's my triple certificated nehse?

VERNA: Oh, Sam...(*She crosses the room and hugs him.*) Gee, it's good to see you, Sam. It's really good to be back home.

SAM: It's good to have you back.

VERNA: Miss me...?

SAM: I sure did...we both did. We missed you a lot. (*He holds her at arm's length.*)

VERNA: I missed you too. (*She kisses him. He hesitates and they both seem embarrassed.*)

SAM: How...anyway, how'd you like to hear some good, black music?

VERNA: Yeah...yeah, I'd like that...(*She regains her composure.*) How about something to drink...you want the usual?

SAM: Plenty o' pips in the lemon juice, hey!

VERNA: Sure thing, big brother. (*She crosses to the kitchen.* SAM *goes to the stereo.*)

SAM: Ya hear anything of Bobby Randall in Adelaide?

VERNA: Yeah. He's lecturing at the Torrensville School of Advanced Education.

SAM: Oh...? What's he doing there? (*He feels the records, searching for the one he requires.*)

VERNA: The Black Studies Course. He's teaching black kids about culture and identity.

SAM: Well, that's something ya don't get in the average school.

VERNA: Yeah. Not even the white kids can get it.

SAM: I'm glad somebody's gettin' through to our own kids...and if anyone can do it, it'll be someone like Bobby Randall. He's a really great guy.

VERNA: He sure is. And he's a real black-fella, too; not like some o' them coconuts!

SAM: Coconuts...? What do you mean?

VERNA: Brown on the outside and white on the inside.

SAM: (*finds the record and puts it on the turn-table*) I got Bobby's latest record the other day...listen to this.

VERNA: (*Enters the room with two drinks. She places one on the book-shelf and approaches* SAM *with the other as he plays the record.*) Gettin' any lately, big brother? (*She takes his right hand and places the drink in it. He gives her a smile.*)

SAM: I know love's suppose t'be blind...but I ain't found anyone that blind enough, yet!

VERNA: (*giving him a sexy hug*) Nemmine. Ah still loves ya, honey! (*He gives her a playful slap on the backside.*)

SAM: (*smiles*) Garn, ya gin. I bet ya say that t'all us handsome black-fellas!

VERNA: (*She snaps her fingers and wriggles her hips.*) Whell...white might be right, but black is beautiful! Anyway, I'd rather be a slack black than an uptight white!

SAM: (*grins*) All-a-tarm, baby. All-a-tarm! (*They both laugh.*) Come on. Let's sit down.

VERNA: Wait'll I get my drink, hey. (*She gets her drink and tastes it.*)

VERNA: Mmmm. I needed this. (*They cross to the settee.*) I see Billy's put up some new posters.

SAM: Yeah. He likes to change them now and again.

VERNA: How's he been? (*They sit down.*)

SAM: (*grins*) Bloody unbearable. Ya wouldn't believe it...(*She turns to him and smiles.*)

VERNA: I know what's wrong with him. He's sex-starved, the bastard!

SAM: This could be true!

VERNA: Too bloody right, it's true! But then, so am I.

SAM: You gins are all the same, hey?

VERNA: I don't see any of you black-fellas knockin' us back. (*They laugh as they sip their drinks.*)

SAM: By the way, I got a letter from the Aboriginal Publications Foundation yesterday.

VERNA: Yeah?

SAM: I sent them a couple o' the poems ya wrote out for me before ya went to Adelaide.

VERNA: What'd they say?

SAM: Aaagh, not much. They just sent me a cheque for fifty dollars.

VERNA: (*She smiles, then squeezes his hand.*) Gee, that's great, big brother. Fame and fortune at last, hey?

SAM: They can shove the fame. All I want's the fortune.

VERNA: Ya startin' t'sound like one o'them Black Bureaucrats from Canberra, now.

SAM: (*smiles*) How about that.

VERNA: I got me doubts about you, Sam. (*They smile warmly at each other.*)

SAM: How was South Australia, anyway?

VERNA: Why d'ya think I came home!

SAM: It's like that, hey?

VERNA: Yeah. It gave me the shits. It really did!

SAM: Billy said you were working with some black-fellas on a reserve...what were they like?

VERNA: The blacks were good. The whites were shit-house.

SAM: (*holds her hand*) Ya want t'talk about it, sis? (*She looks at him in silence.*)

SAM: Well, what about it, sis?

VERNA: Ya know, Sam, before I went to the Centre I use to think us Kuuris on the coast had it bad, but truly, you should see how some o' the country blacks have to live. It's really bad.

SAM: I thought you were suppose to be based in Adelaide?

VERNA: (*She regains her composure and sips her drink.*) I was there for a couple of weeks but then I went up to the Centre with a Medical team from Royal Adelaide.

SAM: (*smiles*) Learn a bit, did ya?

VERNA: You better believe it.

SAM: Yeah? What was it like?

VERNA: Bloody incredible! Jeeze, the whites out there reminded me of the Hitler Youth and the Pious Pioneer all rolled into one.

SAM: (*gives a short laugh*) Now that's laying it on a bit thick, isn't it?

VERNA: Oh, Sam. If only you could see, and could see just some of the kids I had to treat...

Ya know, big brother, I thought I was tough...I mean, really tough. I thought nothing, nothing at all could get under my skin until I saw our little Black babies out there.

Medical terminologies like trachoma, malnutrition, scurvy and scabies didn't mean a thing to me when I saw those kids out there. All I could think of when I saw them was that they were our future Black Nation; a Black Nation with pussed-up eyes, bloated bellies and bodies riddled with sores and bleeding scabs...if you could see something like that, Sam, you wouldn't forget it in a hurry.

SAM: But you're a trained nurse. You've seen worse things than that.

VERNA: Yes. And I tried to be cold-blooded about it at first, but seeing so many sick black babies in so many different areas just turned my gut. A person can only take so much...

SAM: What about the Department...what are they doing about it?

VERNA: Sweet F.A.! The bastards don't give a damn, and besides, the only way blacks can get anything out of the Department is to shack up with the mongrels who control the purse-strings.

SAM: But what about the blacks who work for the Department...?

VERNA: Them blacks in Canberra are all the same. They're nothing but Black Bureaucrats; Black puppets dancing to the white man's tune.

SAM: But surely some of them are at least trying to do something?

VERNA: Look brother, if by chance them Blacks in Canberra manage to get off their ahrse and go to an Aboriginal Reserve, they don't live with the grass-roots people and experience conditions for themselves; no, instead they go and stay in posh hotels where they can go to buffet luncheons and have room-service with hot and cold running women. Why should they worry about the Blacks? They've got it made.

SAM: (*placing an arm around her*) It's okay, sis. You're home now. (*He sips his drink.*) Mmmmm. You still fix a mean drop.

VERNA: (*Recovering her composure, she lifts her head and kisses him on the cheek.*) Thanks, Sam.

SAM: (*He flips the lid of his watch and feels the dial for the time.*) Well...Billy should be home soon.

VERNA: Mmmm. I might go and have a shower and get freshened up.

SAM: Good. When he comes in I'll get Billy to go up the pub and get something more to drink.

VERNA: (*getting up and preparing to leave*) Good thinking ninety-nine. And get him to pick up a flagon o' Red. (*She goes toward the bathroom door and turns.*) Ya know what they say about the Old Red Ned...puts lead in ya pencil!

SAM: S'no good having lead in your pencil if you got no bastard to write to...(*They both laugh. A pause. Sam smiles.*) Garn, peasant. Go and have ya shower.

VERNA: Okay bundji...I'm goin', I'm goin'.
(*She enters the bathroom. SAM gets up and goes over to the lounge chair and feels for the guitar, finds it, picks it up and then sits down and begins to tune it. Sound FX of flushing toilet. VERNA comes out, picks up her suitcase and goes to the bedroom. SAM sings a song. VERNA enters the room with a towel wrapped around her and goes to the bathroom as the song ends. SAM again tunes the guitar. Sound FX of shower. The bathroom door is slightly ajar.*)

VERNA: (from bathroom) How are your studies coming along? (SAM *is lightly strumming the guitar.*)

SAM: (*smiles*) Got meself a new tutor. (*He stops strumming.*)

VERÑA: What happened to the last one ya had…that nice Mr Bates?

SAM: Yates!

VERNA: What?

SAM: (*He puts the guitar aside and raises his voice.*) My old tutor was Mr Yates; not Bates! He had to leave town for a while. (*He gets up and goes to the table and pours himself another drink.*)

VERNA: Who's ya new tutor?

SAM: It's a Miss Odette O'Brien. (*He sips his drink and smiles. Sound FX of shower turns off.*)

VERNA: Who did you say?

SAM: A Miss Odette O'Brien. She's comin' around t'morra afternoon. You can meet her then, if ya like? (*He goes back to the chair.*) Hope she's a good sort. But ya never know ya luck in a big city. (*He sips his drink and almost spills it at* VERNA's *next remark.*)

VERNA: Are you another one of these black-fellas who talk black and sleep white!

SAM: (*sitting down and taking occasional sips*) What did ya say? A what?

VERNA: She a gubbah chick?

SAM: I dunno…yeah…I suppose she is…(*Sound FX of shower back on.* SAM *ponders.*) Billy asked me that too…but I wonder what makes Verna say something like that…(*Raising his voice*) Why did ya say that, Verña?

(*Sound FX off. The bathroom door opens and* VERNA *pokes her head out. She has a towel draped around her body and a smaller one covering her wet hair. She has a worried expression on her face.*)

VERNA: I just don't want t'see ya get hurt, that's all. (*She goes back into the bathroom. Annoyed,* SAM *rolls a cigarette.*)

SAM: What are ya talking about? She's only going to tutor me; nothing else…anyway, what harm could a white girl do here…(*looking hurt*) After all, I'm just a poor, helpless blind man.

VERNA: (*grinning, coming back to the door*) Helpless, my black foot! (*more tenderly*) Look, Sam. All whites want to do is to change you into a black version of themselves. They want to civilise the native, and when they've had their bit, when they've got what they wanted and ripped-off as much as they could, they'll piss you off. And what will you be then: just another screwed-up black-fella! (*She re-enters the bathroom.* SAM *is silent for a moment as he expresses disbelief at* VERNA's *comment. Sound FX back on.*)

SAM: (*chuckles*) What d'ya reckon she's gonna do? Come in here, get her gear off and say, 'Here I am, Darkie…let it all hang out!' (*SAM continues to chuckle.* VERNA *can be heard laughing in the shower.*)

VERNA: Hey, Sam! You better watch it, bud. You know what they say: 'If ya start mixing with white stuff too much it might rub off on ya!' (*SAM is about to answer when* BILLY *bursts into the room. He looks excited as he glances about. Startled,* SAM *looks toward him.*)

BILLY: Hey, Sam! Where is she?

VERNA: In here…waiting! (*BILLY gives a joyful yell.*)

BILLY: You little beauty! (*He strips off his shirt as he moves to the bathroom.* SAM *follows his every movement and smiles humorously, if somewhat uncomfortably. With a contemptuous grin to* SAM, BILLY *throws his shirt to the floor and enters the bathroom.* VERNA *squeals* with laughter as BILLY *wrestles with her.*)

BILLY: Hey, Sam! Come an' look at this! (*Both* BILLY *and* VERNA *are laughing.*)

VERNA: Billy...cut that out!

BILLY: Sam! Come on in...COME ON!

VERNA: Billy! Bill...OOoooohhh...EEeeeee...Billllly...stop that ya mongrel!

(SAM *walks across the room, feels the shirt, picks it up, folds it and puts it on the settee. He then goes to the table and begins to clear it. The laughter still continues in the bathroom.*)

(*Fade out.*)

(*End Scene.*)

(1977)

Kevin Gilbert
MISTER MAN

WRITTEN *after watching a tribal Aboriginal berate Judge Furnell for his facile cleverness and his incomprehension of the affinity of the Aboriginal and his tribal land*—(Monday Conference, ABC television, 7 April 1975)

Mister man
Have you stood on this rock
Have you come close to this ghost-gum tree
Have you stood on green fingers of grass
And felt deep their life surge like me?   5
Mister man
Have you entered the caves
And greeted your own totems there
Have they given directions to go
God-like through life's pathway like me?   10
Mister man
Have you stood on the shore
Of this land your own soul now rent bare
And discovered the hatred you wrought
The suffering the death you ploughed there.   15
Mister man
Have you looked at your face
Like mine that is mirrored in land
Yours reflects only on pools
My image goes deep in the sand   20
The soil and the rocks and the trees
The souls of my people are here
The birds and the clouds and the breeze
The sun and the moon and the stars
Talk to me are of me they dwell   25
Inside me they each are a part
Of me they live in my heart

All things all created by God
Are in me this whole universe
Are of me—we speak and we cry   30
We talk and we dance and we sing
And I bring them gifts of my soul
Of my love God has bidden me bring

Mister man
If perchance you do find   35
The essence the life force in land
All giving expression to self
To soul-force then you'll understand
The God-soul in all things around
This essence of life then you live   40
Then indeed, Mister man, you do live.

(1978)

Jack Davis
JOHN PAT

Write of life the pious said
forget the past   the past is dead
But all I see in front of me
Is a concrete floor   a cell door   and John Pat.

Aah! Tear out the page   forget his age   5
Thin skull they cried that's why he died!
But I can't forget the silhouette
of a concrete floor   a cell door   and John Pat.

The end product of Gudiya* law
Is a viaduct for fang and claw   10
and a place to dwell like Roebourne's hell
of a concrete floor   a cell door   and John Pat.

He's there   Where?   there, in their minds now
deep within
There to prance a sidelong glance   15
a silly grin
To remind them all of a Gudiya wall
A concrete floor   a cell door
. . .and John Pat.

(1988)

---

* Gudiya: Kimberley term for white man

Mudrooroo Narogin (Colin Johnson)
from THE SONG-CIRCLE OF JACKY

SONG TWENTY-THREE

1

I know that I am—
No jargon, please—
I know that I am,
Water and earth
Mixed with a little wine.   *5*

Don't tell me who I am:
A child cries in me too often;
My mouth curves too often
In sadness these days.

I know that I am   *10*
Like a lonely child,
Locked in a black closet,
Huddled in the darkest, scariest corner.

Don't tell me who I am—
A deserted hotel room,   *15*
A sink in one corner,
A wardrobe, bed and chair:
No poetry, only a Rolling Stone
Opened at random notes.

2

If you want me, try your jails,   *20*
In solitude, a bible for my love.

If you want me, walk along a street
Holding in each dark doorway,
Nothing, but your middle-class do-gooder fear;
Then stop, look down, right down—   *25*
An empty bottle, a sprawled black body,
Pink streaming urine stinking of your wine.

If you want me, follow the screaming siren
Rushing pigs to crush our anger—
Brother against brother 'till they come   *30*
And hustle away the debris of our hope.

If you want me, try your grassless parks,
In solitude, old men drinking life away.

(1986)

Mudrooroo Narogin (Colin Johnson)
from THE SONG-CIRCLE OF JACKY

SONG THIRTY

'Mummy, mummy,
What's a Naboriginal?
One came to talk to us today—
What's a Nunkanbah?
Told us Captain Cook was bad,   5
Only came to steal this land—
Mummy, what's a Nembaluk?
Said that we had spoilt the ground,
Said that time would condemn us for our crime—
Mummy, do you know about the Unguru?   10
Said it was a great big snake;
Said it struck when it was hurt;
Said that it was hurting now—
Mummy, I'm too scared to cry,
I don't want our land to die.'   15
Jacky smiles, he's getting through.

(1986)

Section C

CONVICTISM

THE GLORIOUS TWENTY-SIXTH!

More Australians today than fifty or a hundred years ago are aware of a gulf, the precise extent of which is debated amongst historians, between the historical facts of the convict past and the popular, culturally transmitted myths of convictism. Time has diminished popular anxieties concerning both the 'shame' of the convict system, and the 'taint', genealogical and cultural, of convict ancestry. Researchers have been able to offer informed interpretations of the past to a more receptive and detached audience. Historians have stressed, and schoolchildren, students and (sometimes) film and television script-writers have learnt, that the convicts were generally seasoned criminals, whose actual offences were often more serious or numerous than the petty crimes for which they were officially transported; that over half of the 160,000 convicts transported between 1787 and 1868 were assigned to masters, and had little direct contact with the most notorious rigours of the penitentiaries and chain gangs; that, by contemporary standards of criminology at least, a few administrators and overseers were temperate, judicious and occasionally enlightened, and that some criminological experiments were ahead of their time; and that many transportees fared better as convicts and emancipists than they could have hoped for in Britain.

But studied history and culturally transmitted myth are easily compartmentalised. The purchase of the myth on the minds of Australian writers and readers has not been diminished by cold historical analysis. This can be explained. There are *enough* documented horrors, as Robert Hughes' popular study, *The Fatal Shore*, has illustrated, to sustain even the most melancholy and bizarre emphases. Moreover, whereas historians often seek to evaluate convictism in relation to the criminological standards of its time, myth lives in accordance with the needs and pressures of its present sustaining culture. The myths of convictism have been nurtured and developed by later historical movements and events (Eureka and Gallipoli, for example); by ancillary myths which may incorporate anti-English, anti-capitalist, anti-authoritarian or pro-'underdog' sentiments; by perceptions of the past which impose more recent humanitarian or liberal evaluations, and which may be heightened by awareness of twentieth-century 'closed systems' and mass jailings (under Nazism or Communism, for example); and by the metaphorical or analogical application of the myth to literature depicting modern twentieth-century life, as in David Ireland's *The Unknown Industrial Prisoner*. Convictism is as well, for some (especially Irish) Australians, a surrogate 'baptism by fire', a counterpart of the war, revolution or rebellion often sought as a mark of the strengthening of national character, or as a sign of the urge to independence. In literature, the emphasis on suffering, oppression and 'experience' establishes a converse and complementary image from that of the innocence of a golden age, and from Utopian and Arcadian projections. Australia's history, geography and landscape furnish its literature with extremes, real and metaphorical.

The myth itself, in a composite, compressed and exaggeratedly inclusive form, runs something like this. The aristocratic British ruling classes established a brutal and degrading penal system, in colonies at the opposite end of the world from London, in order to accommodate, out of sight, the criminal 'dregs' of society, in particular the surplus of working class and illiterate felonry. The dominant mythical convict type exiled, severed from family and friends, is a roughened but essentially decent man (never a woman), transported for a petty crime, or on political, or trumped-up charges. His mates and peers may appear guilty, even brutal (this is an ambivalent area), but he himself has been direly maligned and victimised. Although subjected to extremes of undeserved physical and mental oppression and torture, by tyrannical overseers, corrupt military and government officials, and an indifferent, insensitive society, he and his fellow prisoners endure the System as best they can, bolstered by their own solidarity, cameraderie, mateship and dry humour. They might occasionally be fired to resistance, but generally this is useless: they are the under-dogs.

In gathering its momentum and autonomous character over a two hundred year period, this myth has shed certain associations and facts, especially those relating to convictism and literature in the early nineteenth century. If the stereotype of the convict as a rum-hardened, practically-minded illiterate is historically explicable, it is also somewhat misleading and exclusive. Convicts performed the first European play in Australia, wrote the first white drama, the first fiction and the earliest poetry. Surrounding convictism emerged many of the earliest literary records (in letters, reports, verses, sermons, descriptive literature and fiction) of white settlement. Even if the precise extent of education and literacy among the convicts was known, the conclusions to be gained from the information would have to be temperately drawn: illiterate convicts had access to readers and scribes and a heritage; to mimetic literary forms such as the ballad and story; and to a world in which the written or remembered word was more essential to entertainment and communication than it has become since the invention of film, radio and television. Mimetic literature has received relatively little attention from the academic establishment, while the 'proper' poetry of the convict Michael Massey Robinson, Macquarie's unofficial laureate, with its neo-Classical celebration of colonial progress and civilisation, is understandably not received as a reflection of convict culture and literary achievement. Several other convict and free writers wrote of convictism in a way that has since become irrelevant to the convict myth: the lessons of suffering, piety, repentance, self-help and hard work were prominent early themes.

The most enduring of the embryonic versions of convict myths are ballads, particularly those like 'Moreton Bay' which stress the pain and nostalgia of exile, the tyranny of the system and its agents, and the supportive cameraderie of its oppressed victims. The bardic gazetting and cataloguing of jails and hardships, and the intimate and poignant conversational wordiness, afford ballads of this kind an authenticating and prototypical simplicity. The version of 'Moreton Bay' printed below is the best known and most concise. An earlier rendition, 'The Convict's Arrival', has been confidently attributed to the convict 'Frank the Poet' (Francis McNamara), who is believed to have been for some time a fellow prisoner and acquaintance in Van Diemen's Land of 'Red' Kelly, the father of Ned. That link might help to explain the undeniable echoes of 'Moreton Bay' in Ned Kelly's 'Jerilderie Letter', which consolidate the convict myth in later historical circumstances, and blend it for posterity with other emergent Australian myths.

The novel which more than any other single literary work consolidated and popularised the convict legend was *His Natural Life*. Marcus Clarke's perspective on convictism had been anticipated in many respects not only in the laments of the ballads, but also in anti-transportation polemical prose, notably West's *History of Tasmania*, and, in fiction, in the anonymously published *Rebel Convicts*. But the emotionally intense and comprehensive indictment in *His Natural Life* disturbed the settled public of the 1870s just at that historical juncture when a respectable, post-convict society wanted to forget. The critique spreads from a condemnation of brutal overseers to accuse all those in positions of authority, together with their silent assistants in society, government, the Church and penal administration. The victims, as measured by their loss of humanity, are not only the convicts but also the guilty 'free' agents of the System, a point reiterated in R. D. FitzGerald's 'The Wind at Your Door', and in David Ireland's *The Unknown Industrial Prisoner*. By demonstrating the operations of 'a closed system', Clarke erects a fictional microcosm, in which wider metaphysical and ethical issues are explored. 'Breaking a man's spirit', particularly the spirit of one who is innocent, and loyal both to his mates and to the directives of a 'higher' nature, becomes the purpose and effect of the system, central to Clarke's examination of man's spiritual and ethical nature, and to his implicit indictment of any such system that disregards or annihilates human dignity. The theme recurs in Hal Porter, Thomas Keneally and many other recent prose, dramatic and film narratives. Although David Ireland has stated that when he wrote *The Unknown Industrial Prisoner* he had not read Clarke's book, its culturally transmitted influence is plain: Ireland's modern industrial workers become dehumanised 'prisoners', technically free citizens, but trapped in a system in which insuperable controls, absurdities and anomalies condition and apparently destroy the possibility of spiritual sustenance and meaningful individual or even collective resistance. Nicknames indicating the role or type of the individual underline the depersonalising control of 'Puroil'.

Although the myths of convictism are not overtly or metaphorically imposed in Williamson's *The Removalists*, their connotations infiltrate the obvious depiction of police violence. The system is again a brutalising force; but the innocents now include a policeman, the inexperienced Constable Ross, who is goaded into corruption and violence, and a woman, the ineffectual, victimised Fiona Carter. The other side of Australian, proletarian, 'under-dog' anti-authoritarianism is depicted as in fact a virtual worship and acceptance of the power of the 'top dog', represented by the insensitive, violent and complacent Sergeant Simmonds. Kenny Carter, martyred by his working class conditioning, agrees with Simmonds that Ross, who is conscientious, sensitive and idealistic, lacks the necessary qualities of 'a good cop'. A degraded masculinism (or 'mateship'), which respects brawn, beer and the abuse of authority, and which commodifies and abuses women, prevails, and triggers the tragic outcome: the system is perceived by Williamson's characters as an irresistible, even acceptable and desirable fact of Australian life.

Arguably, one effect of convict mythology on Australian literary culture is its anti-sentimental dearth of virtuous authority figures, especially amongst police and magistrates. Counterparts of the neighbourly English 'bobby', or of the trouble-shooting marshal or cleanskin sheriff of the mythic American west, are hard to find. If the American western mythology derives from an historical situation of strong outlawry and inadequate law enforcement, the Australian literary depiction of law enforcement is influenced by a tradition of bureaucratic and violent excess amongst law enforcers themselves. Recent examples of police corruption will not weaken this tradition.

Implicitly and often explicitly, the myths of convictism work, like other Australian masculinist constructions, to marginalise the importance of women. Even when the myth is employed to criticise this ethos, the literary product nevertheless foregrounds male experience, and often constructs female figures as idealised or demonised gauges of male life. In 'Tasma's' 'An Old Time Episode in Tasmania', as elsewhere in her fiction, the colonial woman writer examines 'concealed' female strategies of power. Although the 'sphinx-like' convict servant Amelia Clare is, like many female characters in Victorian colonial fiction, a mysterious, enigmatic figure, whose outward appearance conceals some strange, 'other' truth, her quiet triumph over the patriarchal convict overlord, the 'free master', is tacitly endorsed in terms of the story's pre-feminist and class ideologies.

Finally, it might be suggested that an important aspect of the literary magnetism of convictism is the virtual inseparability, within the subject matter itself, of the Gothic or grotesquely melodramatic, and the historical or 'real'. Convictism is for the Australian writer the accessible language and metaphor of oppressive evil. Although it encourages Clarke, Porter and Keneally, for example, to find language which heightens the grotesque element, they authenticate their work through an illusion of historicity gained from pertinent and 'realistic' detail and imagery. The simplest writing of the ballads is similarly, though not so 'artificially', heightened by its subject matter. More recently, Bruce Dawe's chilling satire on capital punishment uses a striking grotesquerie to construct a grim ironical scheme which, though original in its context, is familiar in the literary tradition of inhumanity that convictism initiated.

Ken Stewart

Thomas Keneally
THE PLAYMAKER

from CHAPTER 10

WRYNECK DAY

As Harry had feared, the new penal society in the South Seas worked its way towards its first hanging through a number of petty meannesses, lesser tragedies and hapless tries at escape.

In that first February, for example, the transports which had brought the lags still sat in the deep anchorages of Sydney Cove. One day the black cook of *Prince of Wales*, pulling himself ashore by means of the ship's hawser rope, which was fastened to nearby rocks, was—for a joke— shaken off it by two of the boys aboard the ship and drowned in the deep opaquely blue anchorage perhaps twenty paces from the beach.

While those who could swim splashed about looking for his body, two of the women lags were ordered—for some minor thieving—to twenty-five lashes at the tail of the cart, a punishment supervised by a reluctant Mr Provost Marshal Brewer and enacted by his convict constables. It was not that Harry questioned that such sentences were statements of public order. He was no radical, no United Englishman. It was because he did believe in retribution that his dreams *were* so coloured with punishment.

Because of his gentle spirit, he had ordered the lighter flay for the women. The rumour went around this town at the world's end that he'd instructed the constables to give a high proportion of 'sweetheart blows', blows that is which Harry's convict constables deliberately delivered with less than full force. Seven sweethearts out of each ten, it was rumoured Harry had ordered. People thought this quaint, and the women them- selves, two of the worst London criminals from *Friendship*, would later, healing around their campfires, mock him for it.

In those days too, some were fleeing HE's rational kingdom. A general muster of all the convicts on a Saturday late in that February showed that nine men and one woman had flitted beyond the boundaries of the camp and were missing.

The French were still down in Botany, refitting their two ships and waiting for their naturalist, the Abbé le Receveur, to die of the terrible wound in his side a Samoan native had given him two months before and which had now become gangrenous. You could be sure that every one of the ten escapees had been down to Botany to beg the Compte de La Perouse and his officers, in the name of French mercy, to take them aboard.

In fact, the Frenchman had recently sent two officers north to Sydney Cove, a seven-mile walk overland through the unearthly forests, still—in those days before the smallpox plague—full of playful and flitting Indians, to assure HE that he had dismissed all convicts who came out of the woods pleading with his men. He had, said the Compte, no desire to intrude in the internal justice of Britain. Ralph thought the phrase in one sense funny. The convicts were as *external* to the Kingdom of the Georges as you could get!

Omens continued to multiply. In Sydney, it was considered a cautionary sight when on a thunderous afternoon a white arm floated by the women's camp on the tide. Better, the arm signified to the women, to wait around the new township for the familiar rites of the Church of England and of the Criminal Law than to run away into the forest or expect the aid of Indians and of French scientists.

The rite of punishment then, towards which the settlement was collecting itself, and the forces both of order and darkness so clearly tending, began with the night arrest of William Murphy, a Yorkshire Irishman and highway robber found singing an indistinct Gaelic song while flat-out drunk outside his tent. Murphy's condition was the first evidence to arise from a crime which had been reported that afternoon by the Commissary. Eighteen bottles of wine, part of the hospital stores, had been stolen.

Robbie Ross, who took a particular interest in the stores, undertook the questioning of Murphy. Ralph had been at that time the officer of the day—he had been sleeping in his uniform every night, and very poorly, since Dabby Bryant had not yet delivered him from his terrible discreet dreams. So a number of times a night he still might encounter Betsey Alicia in her coffin, or bearing a louse on her forehead, or a cockroach on the hem of her dress. Thus sapped by his dreams, he went to Robbie's tent for Murphy's questioning.

Major Robbie had his quirks. The interrogation of Murphy went ahead in the redolence of attar of roses which Robbie scattered around his bed and clothing, and that of his nine-year-old son John, to ward off fevers. Harry Brewer, the Provost Marshal, was there too in Robbie's oversweet ambience. Harry got no pleasure from the fragrance of Robbie's tent. You could tell from his face that he knew he now stood—as it were—in the presence of the first capital crime of the new world.

Murphy seemed parched and remorseful, but kept on denying any wrongdoing. He claimed he had traded a shirt for the wine—he couldn't remember who had made the trade. Major Ross circled him with a savage intent that was worse than blows. In Robbie's apparent hatred of this Irishman, this idiot thief, you could see all his grievance against the country, against Cook and Banks for having recommended this place in the first instance, against Tommy Townshend the Home Secretary for taking them seriously. But all that ferocity was, for the moment, transferred to this young sallow Irishman.

'You will hang,' yelled Robbie, his voice somehow reverberating even in a canvas marquee. There was an awful Caledonian length to Robbie's vowels. 'You will be the first Christian twisted in this awful place. And when it is given over, as it will be, and when we all leave, as we will, you will rot unknown in a grave visited—from now to the first fart of doom— by no one but savages! And you a Papist! A Papist! Aren't you, laddie? Answer me! Answer!'

'I have to confess, good major,' said Murphy, hopefully courageous, as if Robbie was offering Catholic martyrdom rather than mere hanging for a criminal offence, 'I have to admit that I am indeed of the Holy Catholic and Apostolic Church.'

'Some bastard in a hedge in Ireland,' screamed Robbie at Ralph and Harry, 'trained him to say that if ever he was challenged by a filthy Presbyterian such as myself.'

Robbie placed a knuckle under the young Papist's jaw and raised the boy's face. 'And you curious people believe—isn't it so?—in the remission of sins in a yon small Hell called Purg-a-tory. From which you can be delivered only by the prayers of the just. Isn't it so?'

Murphy was panting. All at once he no longer liked this doctrinal discussion. Ralph was pretty sure that though Murphy might indeed die for his faith, he was less likely to die for his accomplices.

'Who will pray for the remission of *your* sins,' raged Robbie, 'you Papist bastard? Who here? Those natives covered in fish oil? Who will come here after we are gone? Not even the Portuguese, who share the same heresies as you, you pickpocketing bastard, you Irish pedlar. Not even them.'

But Murphy surprised Ralph by refusing to name any others. Robbie pushed his face aside and yelled for the corporal at the door. 'Take him away. Mr Brewer will hang him tomorrow morning.'

This assurance made Harry Brewer—rather than Murphy—panic. It was this specific boy Harry did not wish to hang. He would for the moment rather deal with the idea of the as yet unnamed ones who were Murphy's accomplices.

Under the thunder and lightning that afternoon, in the grotesquely named 'prison tent' near the men's camp, Murphy at last told Harry—not Robbie Ross— the names of four accomplices. They had not only stolen wine, but butter, pork and split peas. Robbie, told of the confession, was delighted that among those named by Murphy and now arrested by Ralph's Quarter Guard was an infamous young lag named Tom Barrett.

This Tom Barrett was only a youth, but the fliest of all fly boys. He had been condemned to death and reprieved twice already—first when, barely more than a child, he stole jewellery and clothing from a London spinster. He had, like Sideway, then been found wandering the West Country in the weeks after the convict mutiny aboard the transport *Mercury* in Torbay. He was tried with Robert Sideway and others at Exeter for the crime of return from transportation. There, for a second time in his scarcely sixteen years, he had been sentenced to death. When the sentence was commuted, Tom went to the hold of the hulk *Dunkirk* in Plymouth Harbour and at last sailed on the *Charlotte*.

Even so, up to the point of his transportation, Tom Barrett's criminal career had shown little of style to distinguish it from that of a hundred others aboard *Charlotte* and *Friendship*. Where he got his style from, his criminal flashness and repute, was from an incident on board *Charlotte* while the convict fleet was tied up in Rio harbour.

Canoes carrying Portuguese traders and black oarsmen made journeys out to the ships to barter, and the convicts who had money of their own, deposited with the master of the ship or a member of the crew for safekeeping, were allowed to buy food and delicacies. This was considered—by old-fashioned officers like Robbie Ross—a dangerous and faddish innovation of HE's. But Surgeon White approved the merchandise the traders had for sale—oranges, plantains, cantaloupes, limes and fancy breads.

The trade went on, on each of the convict transports, in the standard barricaded exercise yard aft of the main mast. The barricades stood three feet high and were topped with spikes. Behind them the convicts could stretch in the sunlight and have a sight of the green slopes of the city of

Rio, the Sugarloaf and the palace square.

One of the Portuguese merchants approached a Marine officer and complained to him about a quarter dollar a convict had paid him for bread. It was counterfeit. You could tell by scraping it with a knife that it had a large proportion of pewter in it.

The quarter dollar was traced back to Tom Barrett. A search of his bedspace in the convict hold showed he owned a bag full of them, manufactured of chunks of pewter, Marine belt buckles and buttons, and the occasional gold coin thrown into the brew. The coins were competently minted, using a metal mould Tom had acquired before leaving England.

Everyone—officers and convicts on other ships—had been astonished that Tom had been able to build in the convict holds the fires necessary to forge metal coins. It did not really take anyone long to conclude that he had got both the freedom to build a fire *and* the ingredients for his coins by pimping between the Marines and the thirty or so women convicts in the forrard section of *Charlotte*. In the convict view, by forging aboard ship, Tom had done honour to his canting crew and to the gods of criminality. He wore with easy carelessness the style of a man likely to hang young.

The time for *that*—it seemed—had arrived. In the Sydney Cove version of a new earth, where the new earth looked inhospitable to European grain and the London criminals proved inept at farming, the only certain supply of food could come from what was in the storehouse. No one knew if England, having shipped them to the dark, unredeemed side of things, would remember to send them the staples of life, or if these *were* sent, whether the ships that carried them could come safely to them. For it was understood even by the brutal convict mind that few sailors could manage to bring a flotilla the distance HE and his Scottish navigator, Johnny Hunter, had brought them.

Under these conditions, HE had to define the stealing of food on any large scale as the equivalent of murder, and to make it a capital offence. Harry understood this: that now Barrett—still less than twenty—was facing his third and inescapable death sentence.

(1987)

Hal Porter
THE TILTED CROSS

from CHAPTER 1

Van Diemen's Land, an ugly trinket suspended at the world's discredited rump, was freezing. From horizon to horizon stretched a tarpaulin of congealed vapour so tense that it had now and then split, and had rattled down a vicious litter of sleet like minced glass, that year, that winter, that day.

That year, that winter, that day, the terraces and cucumber frames and summer-house and stables and attic gables of *Cindermead* were also freezing. The pump had been frozen until ten o'clock; the peacocks skulked, and squawked imperial displeasure, in the barn; the gardener, as he hacked at metal clods, swore vilely as an earl. Elegance had no more been denied the icy scourgings and crystal grits from Organpipe Mountain than the gibbet staked in the heart of Hobart Town, than the gaols, the dolly-shops, the limekilns, the brickfield, the orphan school and the Jews' burial ground. At noon the sleeting had stopped.

Ladders and gallows and crucifixes of fused snow slanted up the precipices of Organ-pipe and the steeps of Knocklofty to the skylights of a firmament lacking angels to cosset anything or manna to sustain anyone. Land and sky alike seemed repelled by the English and the half-cultured urbanity they had securely established on a solid foundation of political brutality, crime, unemployment and colonial corruption.

On the mountain wall vast snow cameos pointed their profiles unseeingly east and west away from Hobart Town glued on the foothills below. It was a forty-year-old town smelling still of raw planks and sawdust and new guile. Napping hammers and the rasp of trowels sounded among boulders like loaves rolled from above in derision of the hungry. It was a town of the dispossessed; half its creatures criminal, half its creatures lower class or lower middle class. It was the privy of London; it was indeed, a miniature and foundling London, a Johnny-come-lately London, turnkey-ridden and soldier-hounded, its barracks and prisons imprisoned between a height of stone and a depthless water. Nothing and no one attempted the barricades of Organ-pipe except convict escapees blotched, like leopards, with gaol-sores. No one returned over the crags except bushrangers, crazed from suppers of human flesh, and chattering a litany learned in a hinterland of horror. There was nowhere to go in Hobart Town except Hobart Town. Since it had been planted in perversity it had taken root and grown, a weed town, perverse and obverse.

There, therefore, in that place, West End, was southerly.

(1961)

R. D. FitzGerald
THE WIND AT YOUR DOOR
To Mary Gilmore

My ancestor was called on to go out—
a medical man, and one such must by law
wait in attendance on the pampered knout
and lend his countenance to what he saw,
lest the pet, patting with too bared a claw,   5
be judged a clumsy pussy. Bitter and hard,
see, as I see him, in that jailhouse yard.

Or see my thought of him: though time may keep
elsewhere tradition or a portrait still,
I would not feel under his cloak of sleep   10
if beard there or smooth chin, just to fulfil
some canon of precision. Good or ill
his blood's my own; and scratching in his grave
could find me more than I might wish to have.

Let him then be much of the middle style   15

of height and colouring; let his hair be dark
and his eyes green; and for that slit, the smile
that seemed inhuman, have it cruel and stark,
but grant it could be too the ironic mark
of all caught in the system—who the most,   20
the doctor or the flesh twined round that post?

There was a high wind blowing on that day;
for one who would not watch, but looked aside,
said that when twice he turned it blew his way
splashes of blood and strips of human hide   25
shaken out from the lashes that were plied
by one right-handed, one left-handed tough,
sweating at this paid task, and skilled enough.

That wind blows to your door down all these years.
Have you not known it when some breath you drew   30
tasted of blood? Your comfort is in arrears
of just thanks to a savagery tamed in you
only as subtler fears may serve in lieu
of thong and noose—old savagery which has built
your world and laws out of the lives it spilt.   35

For what was jailyard widens and takes in
my country. Fifty paces of stamped earth
stretch; and grey walls retreat and grow so thin
that towns show through and clearings—new raw
   birth
which burst from handcuffs—and free hands go forth   40
to win tomorrow's harvest from a vast
ploughland—the fifty paces of that past.

But see it through a window barred across,
from cells this side, facing the outer gate
which shuts on freedom, opens on its loss   45
in a flat wall. Look left now through the grate
at buildings like more walls, roofed with grey slate
or hollowed in the thickness of laid stone
each side the court where the crowd stands this noon.

One there with the officials, thick of build,   50
not stout, say burly (so this obstinate man
ghosts in the eyes) is he whom enemies killed
(as I was taught) because the monopolist clan
found him a grit in their smooth-turning plan,
too loyally active on behalf of Bligh.   55
So he got lost; and history passed him by.

But now he buttons his long coat against
the biting gusts, or as a gesture of mind,
habitual; as if to keep him fenced
from stabs of slander sticking him from behind,   60
sped by the schemers never far to find

in faction, where approval from one source
damns in another clubroom as of course.

This man had Hunter's confidence, King's praise;
and settlers on the starving Hawkesbury banks   65
recalled through twilight drifting across their days
the doctor's fee of little more than thanks
so often; and how sent by their squeezed ranks
he put their case in London. I find I lack
the hateful paint to daub him wholly black.   70

Perhaps my life replies to his too much
through veiling generations dropped between.
My weakness here, resentments there, may touch
old motives and explain them, till I lean
to the forgiveness I must hope may clean   75
my own shortcomings; since no man can live
in his own sight if it will not forgive.

Certainly I must own him whether or not
it be my will. I was made understand
this much when once, marking a freehold lot,   80
my papers suddenly told me it was land
granted to Martin Mason. I felt his hand
heavily on my shoulder, and knew what coil
binds life to life through bodies, and soul to soil.

There, over to one corner, a bony group   85
of prisoners waits; and each shall be in turn
tied by his own arms in a human loop
about the post, with his back bared to learn
the price of seeking freedom. So they earn
three hundred rippling stripes apiece, as set   90
by the law's mathematics against the debt.

These are the Irish batch of Castle Hill,
rebels and mutineers, my countrymen
twice over: first, because of those to till
my birthplace first, hack roads, raise roofs; and then   95
because their older land time and again
enrolls me through my forbears; and I claim
as origin that threshold whence we came.

One sufferer had my surname, and thereto
'Maurice', which added up to history once;   100
an ignorant dolt, no doubt, for all that crew
was tenantry. The breed of clod and dunce
makes patriots and true men: could I announce
that Maurice as my kin I say aloud
I'd take his irons as heraldry, and be proud.   105

Maurice is at the post. Its music lulls,
one hundred lashes done. If backbone shows
then play the tune on buttocks! But feel his pulse;
that's what a doctor's for; and if it goes

lamely, then dose it with these purging blows—   *110*
which have not made him moan; though, writhing
   there,
'Let my neck be,' he says, 'and flog me fair.'

One hundred lashes more, then rest the flail.
What says the doctor now? 'This dog won't yelp;
he'll tire you out before you'll see him fail;   *115*
here's strength to spare; go on!' Ay, pound to pulp;
yet when you've done he'll walk without your help,
and knock down guards who'd carry him being bid,
and sing no song of where the pikes are hid.

It would be well if I could find, removed   *120*
through generations back—who knows how far?—
more than a surname's thickness as a proved
bridge with that man's foundations. I need some star
of courage from his firmament, a bar
against surrenders: faith. All trials are less   *125*
than rain-blacked wind tells of that old distress.

Yet I can live with Mason. What is told
and what my heart knows of his heart, can sort
much truth from falsehood, much there that I hold
good clearly or good clouded by report;   *130*
and for things bad, ill grows where ills resort:
they were bad times. None know what in his place
they might have done. I've my own faults to face.

(1958)

Anonymous
MORETON BAY

One Sunday morning as I went walking
   by Brisbane waters I chanced to stray,
And I heard a convict his fate bewailing
   as on the sunny river bank he lay:
'I am a native of Erin's island,   *5*
   though banished now from my native shore;
They tore me from my aged parents
   and from the maiden whom I do adore.

'I've been a prisoner at Port Macquaire,
   at Norfolk Island and Emu Plains,   *10*
At Castle Hill and at cursed Toongabbie,
   at all those settlements I've worked in chains;
But of all places of condemnation
   and penal stations in New South Wales
To Moreton Bay I have found no equal,   *15*
   excessive tyranny each day prevails.

'For three long years I've been beastly treated
   and heavy irons on my legs I wore;

My back with flogging is lacerated
    and often painted with my crimson gore.   *20*
And many a man from downright starvation
    lies mouldering now underneath the clay;
And Captain Logan he had us mangled
    at the triangles of Moreton Bay.

'Like the Egyptians and ancient Hebrews   *25*
    we were oppressed under Logan's yoke,
Till a native black lying there in ambush
    did give our tyrant his mortal stroke.
My fellow prisoners, be exhilarated
    that all such monsters such a death may find!   *30*
And when from bondage we are liberated
    our former sufferings shall fade from mind.'

                                      (?1830s)

Marcus Clarke
HIS NATURAL LIFE

BOOK 4

from CHAPTER 7

BREAKING A MAN'S SPIRIT

The insubordination of which Rufus Dawes had been guilty was, in this instance, insignificant. It was the custom of the newly-fledged constables of Captain Frere to enter the wards at night, armed with cutlasses, tramping about, and making a great noise. Mindful of the report of Pounce, they pulled the men roughly from their hammocks, examined their persons for concealed tobacco, and compelled them to open their mouths to see if any was inside. The men in Dawes's gang—to which Mr Troke had an especial objection—were often searched more than once in a night, searched going to work, searched at meals, searched going to prayers, searched coming out, and this in the roughest manner. Their sleep broken, and what little self-respect they might yet presume to retain harried out of them, the objects of this incessant persecution were ready to turn upon and kill their tormentors.

    The great aim of Troke was to catch Dawes tripping, but the leader of the 'Ring' was too wary. In vain had Troke, eager to sustain his reputation for sharpness, burst in upon the convict at all times and seasons. He had found nothing. In vain had he laid traps for him; in vain had he 'planted' figs of tobacco, and attaching long threads to them, waited in a bush hard by, until the pluck at the end of his line should give token that the fish had bitten. The experienced 'old hand' was too acute for him. Filled with digust and ambition, he determined upon an ingenious little trick. He was certain that Dawes possessed tobacco; the thing was to find it upon him. Now, Rufus Dawes, holding aloof, as was his custom, from the majority of his companions, had made one friend—if so mindless and battered an old wreck could be called a friend—Blind Mooney. Perhaps this oddly-assorted friendship was brought about by two causes—one, that Mooney was the only man on the island who knew more of the horrors of convictism than the leader of the Ring; the other, that Mooney was blind, and, to a moody, sullen man, subject to violent fits of passion and a constant suspicion of all his fellow-creatures, a blind companion was more congenial than a sharp-eyed one.

Mooney was one of the 'First Fleeters'. He had arrived in Sydney fifty-seven years before, in the year 1789, and when he was transported he was fourteen years old. He had been through the whole round of servitude, had worked as a bondsman, had married, and been 'up country', had been again sentenced, and was a sort of dismal patriarch of Norfolk Island, having been there at its former settlement. He had no friends. His wife was long since dead, and he stated, without contradiction, that his master, having taken a fancy to her, had despatched the uncomplaisant husband to imprisonment. Such cases were not uncommon.

One of the many ways in which Rufus Dawes had obtained the affection of the old blind man was the gift of such fragments of tobacco as he had himself from time to time secured. Troke knew this; and on the evening in question hit upon an excellent plan. Admitting himself noiselessly into the boat-shed, where the gang slept, he crept close to the sleeping Dawes, and counterfeiting Mooney's mumbling utterance, asked for 'some tobacco'. Rufus Dawes was but half awake, and on repeating his request, Troke felt something put into his hand. He grasped Dawes's arm, and struck a light. He had got his man this time: Dawes had conveyed to his fancied friend a piece of tobacco almost as big as the top joint of his little finger.

One can understand the feelings of a man entrapped by such base means. Rufus Dawes no sooner saw the hated face of Warder Troke peering over his hammock, than he sprang out, and exerting to the utmost his powerful muscles, knocked Mr Troke fairly off his legs into the arms of the in-coming constables. A desperate struggle took place, at the end of which, the convict, overpowered by numbers, was borne senseless to the cells, gagged, and chained to the ring-bolt on the bare flags. While in this condition he was savagely beaten by five or six constables.

To this maimed and manacled rebel was the Commandant ushered by Troke the next morning.

'Ha! ha! my man,' said the Commandant. 'Here you are again, you see. How do you like this sort of thing?'

Dawes, glaring, makes no answer.

'You shall have fifty lashes, my man,' said Frere. 'We'll see how you'll feel then!'

The fifty were duly administered, and the Commandant called the next day. The rebel was still mute.

'Give him fifty more, Mr Troke. We'll see what he's made of.'

One hundred and twenty lashes were inflicted in the course of the morning, but still the sullen convict refused to speak. He was then treated to fourteen days' solitary confinement in one of the new cells. On being brought out and confronted with his tormentor, he merely laughed. For this he was sent back for another fourteen days; and still remaining obdurate, was flogged again, and got fourteen days more. Had the chaplain then visited him, he might have found him open to consolation, but the chaplain—so it was stated—was sick. When brought out at the conclusion of his third confinement, he was found to be in so exhausted a condition, that the doctor ordered him to hospital. As soon as he was sufficiently recovered, Frere visited him, and finding his 'spirit' not yet 'broken', ordered that he should be put to grind maize. Dawes declined to work. So they chained his hand to one arm of the grindstone, and placed another prisoner at the other arm. As the second prisoner turned, the hand of Dawes of course revolved.

'You're not such a pebble as folks seemed to think,' grinned Frere, pointing to the turning wheel.

Upon which the indomitable poor devil straightened his sorely-tried muscles, and prevented the wheel from turning at all. Frere gave him fifty more lashes, and sent him the next day to grind cayenne pepper. This was a punishment more dreaded by the convicts than any other. The pungent dust filled their eyes and lungs, causing them the most excruciating torments. For a man with a raw back the work was one continued agony. In four days, Rufus Dawes, emaciated, blistered, blinded, broke down.

'For God's sake, Captain Frere, kill me at once!' he said.

'No fear,' said the other, rejoiced at this proof of his power. 'You've given in; that's all I wanted. Troke, take him to the hospital.'

When he was in hospital, North visited him.

'I would have come to see you before,' said the clergyman, 'but I have been very ill.'

In truth he looked so. He had had a fever, it seemed, and they had shaved his beard, and cropped his hair. Dawes could see that the haggard, wasted man had passed through some agony almost as great as his own. The next day Frere visited him, complimented him on his courage, and offered to make him a constable. Dawes turned his scarred back to his torturer, and resolutely declined to answer.

'I am afraid you have made an enemy of the Commandant,' said North, the next day. 'Why not accept his offer?'

Dawes cast on him a glance of quiet scorn. 'And betray my mates? I'm not one of that sort.'

The clergyman spoke to him of hope, of release, of repentance, and redemption. The prisoner laughed. 'Who's to redeem me?' he said, expressing his thoughts in phraseology that to ordinary folks might seem blasphemous. 'It would take a Christ to die again to save such as I.'

North spoke to him of immortality. 'There is another life,' said he. 'Do not risk your chance of happiness in it. You have a future to live for, man.'

'I hope not,' said the victim of the 'system'. 'I want to rest—to rest, and never to be disturbed again.'

His 'spirit' was broken enough by this time. Yet he had resolution enough to refuse Frere's repeated offers. 'I'll never "jump" it,' he said to North, 'if they cut me in half first.'

North pityingly implored the stubborn mind to have mercy on the lacerated body, but without effect. His own wayward heart gave him the key to read the cipher of this man's life. 'A noble nature ruined,' said he to himself. 'What is the secret of his history?'

Dawes, on his part, seeing how different from other black coats was this priest—at once so ardent and so gloomy, so stern and so tender—began to speculate on the cause of his monitor's sunken cheeks, fiery eyes, and pre-occupied manner, to wonder what grief inspired those agonized prayers, those eloquent and daring supplications, which were daily poured

out over his rude bed. So between these two—the priest and the sinner—
was a sort of sympathetic bond.

(1870–74)

'Tasma' (Jessie Couvreur)
AN OLD-TIME EPISODE IN TASMANIA

The gig was waiting upon the narrow gravel drive in front of the fuchsia-
wreathed porch of Cowa Cottage. Perched upon the seat, holding the whip
in two small, plump, ungloved hands, sat Trucaninny, Mr Paton's
youngest daughter, whose straw-coloured, sun-steeped hair, and clear,
sky-reflecting eyes, seemed to protest against the name of a black gin that
some 'clay-brained cleric' had bestowed upon her irresponsible little person at the baptismal font some eight or nine years ago. The scene of this
outrage was Old St David's Cathedral, Hobart,—or, as it was then called,
Hobart *Town*,—chief city of the Arcadian island of Tasmania; and just at
this moment, eight o'clock on a November morning, the said cathedral
tower, round and ungainly, coated with a surface of dingy white plaster,
reflected back the purest, brightest light in the world. From Trucaninny's
perch—she had taken the driver's seat—she could see, not only the
cathedral, but a considerable portion of the town, which took the form of
a capital S as it followed the windings of the coast. Beyond the wharves,
against which a few whalers and fishing-boats were lying idle, the middle
distance was represented by the broad waters of the Derwent, radiantly
blue, and glittering with silver sparkles; while the far-off background
showed a long stretch of yellow sand, and the hazy, undulating outline of
low-lying purple hills. Behind her the aspect was different. Tiers of hills
rose one above the other in grand confusion, until they culminated in the
towering height of Mount Wellington, keeping guard in majestic silence
over the lonely little city that encircled its base. This portion of the view,
however, was hidden from Trucaninny's gaze by the weatherboard cottage
in front of which the gig was standing,—though I doubt whether in any
case she would have turned her head to look at it; the faculty of enjoying a
beautiful landscape being an acquisition of later years than she had
attained since the perpetration of the afore-mentioned outrage of her
christening. Conversely, as Herbert Spencer says, the young man who was
holding the horse's head until such time as the owner of the gig should
emerge from the fuchsia-wreathed porch, fastened his eyes upon the
beautiful scene before him with more than an artist's appreciation in their
gaze. He was dressed in the rough clothes of a working gardener, and so
much of his head as could be seen beneath the old felt wide-awake that
covered it, bore ominous evidence of having been recently shaved. I use the
word ominous advisedly, for a shaven head in connection with a working
suit had nothing priestly in its suggestion, and could bear, indeed, only one
interpretation in the wicked old times in Tasmania. The young man
keeping watch over the gig had clearly come into that fair scene for his
country's good; and the explanation of the absence of a prison suit was
doubtless due to the fact he was out on a ticket-of-leave. What the
landscape had to say to him under these circumstances was not precisely

clear. Perhaps all his soul was going out towards the white-sailed wool-ship tacking down the Bay on the first stage of a journey of most uncertain length; or possibly the wondrous beauty of the scene, contrasted with the unspeakable horror of the one he had left, brought the vague impression that it was merely some exquisite vision. That a place so appalling as his old prison should exist in the heart of all this peace and loveliness, seemed too strange an anomaly. Either that was a nightmare and this was real, or this was a fantastic dream and that was the revolting truth; but then which was which, and how had he, Richard Cole, late No 213, come to be mixed up with either?

As though to give a practical answer to his melancholy question, the sharp tingle of a whip's lash made itself felt at this instant across his cheek. In aiming the cumbersome driving-whip at the persistent flies exploring the mare's back, Trucaninny had brought it down in a direction she had not intended it to take. For a moment she stood aghast. Richard's face was white with passion. He turned fiercely round; his flaming eyes seemed literally to send out sparks of anger. 'Oh, please, I didn't mean it,' cried the child penitently. 'I wanted to hit the flies. I did indeed. I hope I didn't hurt you?'

The *amende honorable* brought about an immediate reaction. The change in the young man's face was wonderful to behold. As he smiled back full reassurance at the offender, it might be seen that his eyes could express the extremes of contrary feeling at the very shortest notice. For all answer, he raised his old felt wide-awake in a half-mocking though entirely courtly fashion, like some nineteenth century Don César de Bazan, and made a graceful bow.

'Are *you* talking to the man, Truca?' cried a querulous voice at this moment from the porch, with a stress on the you that made the little girl lower her head, shame-faced. 'What do you mean by disobeying orders, miss?'

The lady who swept out upon the verandah at the close of this tirade was in entire accord with her voice. 'British matron' would have been the complete description of Miss Paton, if fate had not willed that she should be only a British spinster. The inflexibility that comes of finality of opinion regarding what is proper and what is the reverse,—a rule of conduct that is of universal application for the true British matron,—expressed itself in every line of her face and in every fold of her gown. That she was relentlessly respectable and unyielding might be read at the first glance; that she had been handsome, in the same hard way, a great many years before Truca was maltreated at the baptismal font, might also have been guessed at from present indications. But that she should be the 'own sister' of the good-looking, military-moustached, debonair man (I use the word debonair here in the French sense) who now followed her out of the porch, was less easy to divine. The character of the features as well as of the expression spoke of two widely differing temperaments. Indeed, save for a curious dent between the eyebrows, and a something in the nostrils that seemed to say he was not to be trifled with, Mr Paton might have sat for the portrait of one of those jolly good fellows who reiterate so tunefully that they 'won't go home till morning', and who are as good as their word afterwards.

Yet 'jolly good fellow' as he showed himself in card-rooms and among

so-called boon companions, he could reveal himself in a very different light
to the convicts who fell under his rule. Forming part of a system for the
crushing down of the unhappy prisoners, in accordance with the principle
of 'Woe be to him through whom the offence cometh,' he could return
with a light heart to his breakfast or his dinner, after seeing some score of
his fellow-men abjectly writhing under the lash, or pinioned in a ghastly
row upon the hideous gallows. 'Use,' says Shakespeare, 'can almost change
the stamp of Nature.' In Mr Paton's case it had warped as well as changed
it. Like the people who live in the atmosphere of Courts, and come to
regard all outsiders as another and inferior race, he had come to look upon
humanity as divisible into two classes—namely, those who were convicts,
and those who were not. For the latter, he had still some ready drops of
the milk of human kindness at his disposal. For the former, he had no
more feeling than we have for snakes or sharks, as the typical and popular
embodiments of evil.

Miss Paton had speedily adopted her brother's views in this respect.
Summoned from England to keep house for him at the death of Trucaninny's mother, she showed an aptitude for introducing prison discipline into
her domestic rule. From constant association with the severe *régime* that
she was accustomed to see exercised upon the convicts, she had ended by
regarding disobedience to orders, whether in children or in servants, as the
unpardonable sin. One of her laws, as of the Medes and Persians, was that
the young people in the Paton household should never exchange a word
with the convict servants in their father's employ. It was hard to observe
the letter of the law in the case of the indoor servants, above all for Truca,
who was by nature a garrulous little girl. Being a truthful little girl as well,
she was often obliged to confess to having had a talk with the latest
importation from the gaol,—an avowal which signified, as she well knew,
the immediate forfeiture of all her week's pocket-money.

On the present occasion her apologies to the gardener were the latest
infringement of the rule.

She looked timidly towards her aunt as the latter advanced austerely in
the direction of the gig, but, to her relief, Miss Paton hardly seemed to
notice her.

'I suppose you will bring the creature back with you, Wilfrid?' she said,
half-questioningly, half-authoritatively, as her brother mounted into the
gig and took the reins from Truca's chubby hands. 'Last time we had a
drunkard *and* a thief. The time before, a thief, and—and a—really I don't
know which was worse. It is frightful to be reduced to such a choice of
evils, but I would almost suggest your looking among the—you know—
the—in-fan-ti-cide cases this time.'

She mouthed the word in separate syllables at her brother, fearful of
pronouncing it openly before Truca and the convict gardener.

Mr Paton nodded. It was not the first time he had been sent upon the
delicate mission of choosing a maid for his sister from the female prison,
politely called the Factory, at the foot of Mount Wellington. For some
reason it would be difficult to explain, his selections were generally rather
more successful than hers. Besides which, it was a satisfaction to have
some one upon whom to throw the responsibility of the inevitable catas-
trophe that terminated the career of every successive ticket-of-leave in
turn.

The morning, as we have seen, was beautiful. The gig bowled smoothly over the macadamized length of Macquarie Street. Truca was allowed to drive; and so deftly did her little fingers guide the mare that her father lighted his cigar, and allowed himself to ruminate upon a thousand things that it would have been better perhaps to leave alone. In certain moods he was apt to deplore the fate that had landed—or stranded—him in this God-forsaken corner of the world. Talk of prisoners, indeed! What was he himself but a prisoner, since the day when he had madly passed sentence of transportation on himself and his family, because the pay of a Government clerk in England did not increase in the same ratio as the income-tax. As a matter of fact, he did not wear a canary-coloured livery, and his prison was as near an approach, people said, to an earthly Paradise as could well be conceived. With its encircling chains of mountains, folded one around the other, it was like a mighty rose, tossed from the Creator's hand into the desolate Southern Ocean. Here to his right towered purple Mount Wellington, with rugged cliffs gleaming forth from a purple background. To his left the wide Derwent shone and sparkled in blue robe and silver spangles, like the Bay of Naples, he had been told. Well, he had never seen the Bay of Naples, but there were times when he would have given all the beauty here, and as much more to spare, for a strip of London pavement in front of his old club. Mr Paton's world, indeed, was out of joint. Perhaps twelve years of unthinking acquiescence in the flogging and hanging of convicts had distorted his mental focus. As for the joys of home-life, he told himself that those which had fallen to his share brought him but cold comfort. His sister was a Puritan, and she was making his children hypocrites, with the exception, perhaps, of Truca. Another disagreeable subject of reflection was the one that his groom Richard was about to leave him. In a month's time, Richard, like his royal namesake, would be himself again. For the past five years he had been only No 213, expiating in that capacity a righteous blow aimed at a cowardly ruffian who had sworn to marry his sister—by fair means or by foul. The blow had been only too well aimed. Richard was convicted of manslaughter, and sentenced to seven years' transportation beyond the seas. His sister, who had sought to screen him, was tried and condemned for perjury. Of the latter, nothing was known. Of the former, Mr Paton only knew that he would be extremely loth to part with so good a servant. Silent as the Slave of the Lamp, exact as any machine, performing the least of his duties with the same intelligent scrupulousness, his very presence in the household was a safeguard and a reassurance. It was like his luck, Mr Paton reflected in his present pessimistic mood, to have chanced upon such a fellow, just as by his d—d good conduct he had managed to obtain a curtailment of his sentence. If Richard had been justly dealt with, he would have had two good years left to devote to the service of his employer. As to keeping him after he was a free man, that was not to be hoped for. Besides which, Mr Paton was not sure that he should feel at all at his ease in dealing with a free man. The slave-making instinct, which is always inherent in the human race whatever civilization may have done to repress it, had become his sole rule of conduct in his relations with those who served him.

There was one means perhaps of keeping the young man in bondage, but it was a means that even Mr Paton himself hesitated to employ. By an almost superhuman adherence to impossible rules, Richard had escaped hitherto the humiliation of the lash; but if a flogging could be laid to his charge, his time of probation would be of necessity prolonged, and he might continue to groom the mare and tend the garden for an indefinite space of time, with the ever intelligent thoroughness that distinguished him. A slip of paper in a sealed envelope, which the victim would carry himself to the nearest justice of the peace, would effect the desired object. The etiquette of the proceeding did not require that any explanation should be given.

Richard would be fastened to the triangles, and any subsequent revolt on his part could only involve him more deeply than before. Mr Paton had no wish to hurt him; but he was after all an invaluable servant, and perhaps he would be intelligent enough to understand that the disagreeable formality to which he was subjected was in reality only a striking mark of his master's esteem for him.

Truca's father had arrived thus far in his meditations when the gig pulled up before the Factory gate. It was a large bare building, with white unshaded walls, but the landscape which framed it gave it a magnificent setting. The little girl was allowed to accompany her father indoors, while a man in a grey prison suit, under the immediate surveillance of an armed warder, stood at the mare's head.

Mr Paton's mission was a delicate one. To gently scan his brother man, and still gentler sister woman, did not apply to his treatment of convicts. He brought his sternest official expression to bear upon the aspirants who defiled past him at the matron's bidding, in their disfiguring prison livery. One or two, who thought they detected a likely looking man behind the Government official, threw him equivocal glances as they went by. Of these he took no notice. His choice seemed to lie in the end between a sullen-looking elderly woman, whom the superintendent qualified as a 'sour jade', and a half-imbecile girl, when his attention was suddenly attracted to a new arrival, who stood out in such marked contrast with the rest, that she looked like a dove in the midst of a flock of vultures.

'Who is that?' he asked the matron in a peremptory aside.

'That, sir,'—the woman's lips assumed a tight expression as she spoke,—'she's No 27—Amelia Clare—she came out with the last batch.'

'Call her up, will you?' was the short rejoinder, and the matron reluctantly obeyed.

In his early days Truca's father had been a great lover of Italian opera. There was hardly an air of Bellini's or Donizetti's that he did not know by heart. As No 27 came slowly towards him, something in her manner of walking, coupled with the half-abstracted, half-fixed expression in her beautiful grey eyes, reminded him of Amina in the *Sonnambula*. So strong, indeed, was the impression, that he would hardly have been surprised to see No 27 take off her unbecoming prison cap and jacket, and disclose two round white arms to match her face, or to hear her sing '*Ah! non giunge*' in soft dreamy tones. He could have hummed or whistled a tuneful second himself at a moment's notice, for the matter of that. However, save in the market scene in *Martha*, there is no precedent for warbling a duet with the young person you are about to engage as a domestic servant. Mr Paton remembered this in time, and confined himself to what the French call *le stricte nécessaire*. He inquired of Amelia whether she could do fine sewing, and whether she could clear-starch. His sister had impressed these questions upon him, and he was pleased with himself for remembering them.

Amelia, or Amina (she was really very like Amina), did not reply at once. She had to bring her mind back from the far-away sphere to which it had wandered, or, in other words, to pull herself together first. When the reply did come, it was uttered in just the low, melodious tones one might have expected. She expressed her willingness to attempt whatever was required of her, but seemed very diffident as regarded her power of execution. 'I have forgotten so many things,' she concluded, with a profound sigh.

'*Sir*, you impertinent minx,' corrected the matron.

Amelia did not seem to hear, and her new employer hastened to interpose.

'We will give you a trial,' he said, in a curiously modified tone, 'and I hope you won't give me any occasion to regret it.'

The necessary formalities were hurried through. Mr Paton disregarded the deferential disclaimers of the matron, but experienced, nevertheless, something of a shock when he saw Amelia divested of her prison garb. She had a thorough-bred air that discomfited him. Worse still, she was undeniably pretty. The scissors that had clipped her fair locks had left a number of short rings that clung like trendrils round her shapely little head. She wore a black stuff jacket of extreme simplicity and faultless cut, and a little black bonnet that might have been worn by a Nursing Sister or a *grande dame* with equal appropriateness. Thus attired, her appearance was so effective, that Mr Paton asked himself whether he was not doing an unpardonably rash thing in driving No 27 down Macquarie Street in his gig, and introducing her into his household afterwards.

It was not Truca, for she had 'driven and lived' that morning, whose *mauvais quart-d'heure* was now to come. It was her father's turn to fall under its influence, as he sat, stern and rigid, on the driver's seat, with his little girl nestling up to him as close as she was able, and that strange, fair, mysterious presence on the other side, towards which he had the annoyance of seeing all the heads of the passers-by turn as he drove on towards home.

Arrived at Cowa Cottage, the young gardener ran forward to open the gate; and here an unexpected incident occurred. As Richard's eyes rested upon the new arrival, he uttered an exclamation that caused her to look round. Their eyes met, a flash of instant recognition was visible in both. Then, like the night that follows a sudden discharge of electricity, the gloom that was habitual to both faces settled down upon them once more. Richard shut the gate with his accustomed machine-like precision. Amelia looked at the intangible something in the clouds that had power to fix her gaze upon itself. Yet the emotion she had betrayed was not lost upon her employer. Who could say? As No 213 and No 27, these two might have crossed each other's paths before. That the convicts had wonderful and incomprehensible means of communicating with each other, was well known to Mr Paton. That young men and young women have an equal facility for understanding each other, was also a fact he did not ignore. But which of these two explanations might account for the signs of mutual recognition and sympathy he had just witnessed? Curiously enough, he felt, as he pondered over the mystery later in the day, that he should prefer the former solution. An offensive and defensive alliance was well known to exist among the convicts, and he told himself that he could meet and deal with the difficulties arising from such a cause as he had met and dealt with them before. That was a matter which came within his province, but the taking into account of any sentimental kind of rubbish did *not* come within his province. For some unaccountable reason, the thought of having Richard flogged presented itself anew at this juncture to his mind. He put it away, as he had done before, angered with himself for having harboured it. But it returned at intervals during the succeeding week, and was never stronger than one afternoon, when his little girl ran out to him as he sat smoking in the verandah, with an illustrated volume of *Grimm's Tales* in her hands.

'Oh, papa, look! I've found some one just like Amelia in my book of Grimm. It's the picture of Snow-White. Only look, papa! Isn't it the very living image of Amelia?'

'Nonsense!' said her father; but he looked at the page nevertheless. Truca was right. The snowmaiden in the woodcut had the very eyes and mouth of Amelia Clare—frozen through some mysterious influence into beautiful, unyielding rigidity. Mr Paton wished sometimes he had never brought the girl into his house. Not that there was any kind of fault to be found with her. Even his sister, who might have passed for 'She-who-must-be-obeyed', if Rider Haggard's books had existed at that time, could not complain of want of docile obedience to orders on the part of the new maid. Nevertheless, her presence was oppressive to the master of the house. Two lines of Byron's haunted him constantly in connection with her—

So coldly sweet, so deadly fair,
We start—for life is wanting there.

If Richard worked like an automaton, then she worked like a spirit; and when she moved noiselessly about the room where he happened to be sitting, he could not help following her uneasily with his eyes.

The days wore on, succeeding each other and resembling each other, as the French proverb has it, with desperate monotony. Christmas, replete with roses and strawberries, had come and gone. Mr Paton was alternately swayed by two demons, one of which whispered in his ear, 'Richard Cole is in love with No 27. The time for him to regain his freedom is at hand. The first use he will make of it will be to leave you, and the next to marry Amelia Clare. You will thus be deprived of everything at one blow. You will lose the best man-servant you have ever known, and your sister, the best maid. And more than this, you will lose an interest in life that gives it a stimulating flavour it has not had for many a long year. Whatever may be the impulse that prompts you to wonder what that ice-bound face and form hide, it is an impulse that makes your heart beat and your blood course warmly through your veins. When this fair, uncanny presence is removed from your home, your life will become stagnant as it was before.' To this demon Mr Paton would reply energetically, 'I won't give the fellow the chance of marrying No 27. As soon as he has his freedom, I will give him the sack, and forbid him the premises. As for Amelia, she is my prisoner, and I would send her back to gaol to-morrow if I thought there were any nonsense up between her and him.'

At this point demon No 2 would intervene: 'There is a better way of arranging matters. You have it in your power to degrade the fellow in his own eyes and in those of the girl he is after. There is more covert insolence in that impenetrable exterior of his than you have yet found out. Only give him proper provocation, and you will have ample justification for bringing him down. A good flogging would put everything upon its proper footing,—you would keep your servant, and you would put a stop to the nonsense that is very probably going on. But don't lose too much time; for if you wait until the last moment, you will betray your hand. The fellow is useful to him, they will say of Richard, but it is rather rough upon him to be made aware of it in such a way as that.'

One evening in January, Mr Paton was supposed to be at his club. In reality he was seated upon a bench in a bushy part of the garden, known as the shrubbery—in parley with the demons. The night had come down upon him almost without his being aware of it—a night heavy with heat and blackness, and noisy with the cracking and whirring of the locusts entombed in the dry soil. All at once he heard a slight rustling in the branches behind him. There was a light pressure of hands on his shoulders, and a face that felt like velvet to the touch was laid against his cheeks. Two firm, warm feminine lips pressed themselves upon his, and a voice that he recognized as Amelia's said in caressing tones, 'Dearest Dick, have I kept you waiting?'

Had it been proposed to our hero some time ago that he should change places with No 213, he would have declared that he would rather die first. But at this instant the convict's identity seemed so preferable to his own, that he hardly ventured to breathe lest he should betray the fact that he was only his own forlorn self. His silence disconcerted the intruder.

'Why don't you answer, Dick?' she asked impatiently.

'Answer? What am I to say?' responded her master. 'I am not in the secret.'

Amelia did not give him time to say more. With a cry of terror she turned and fled, disappearing as swiftly and mysteriously as she had come. The words 'Dearest Dick' continued to ring in Mr Paton's ears long after she had gone; and the more persistently the refrain was repeated, the more he felt tempted to give Richard a taste of his quality. He had tried to provoke him to some act of overt insolence in vain. He had worried and harried and insulted him all he could. The convict's constancy had never once deserted him. That his employer should have no pretext whereby he might have him degraded and imprisoned, he had acted upon the scriptural precept of turning his left cheek when he was smitten on the right. There were times when his master felt something of a persecutor's impotent rage against him. But now at least he felt he had entire justification for making an example of him. He would teach the fellow to play Romeo and Juliet with a fellow-convict behind his back. So thoroughly did the demon indoctrinate Mr Paton with these ideas, that he felt next morning as though he were doing the most righteous action in the world, when he called Richard to him after breakfast, and said in a tone which he tried to render as careless as of custom, 'Here, you! just take this note over to Mr Merton with my compliments, and *wait for the answer.*'

There was nothing in this command to cause the person who received it to grow suddenly livid. Richard had received such an order at least a score of times before, and had carried messages to and fro between his master and the justice of the peace with no more emotion than the occasion was worth. But on this particular morning, as he took the fatal note into his hands, he turned deadly pale. Instead of retreating with it in his customary automatic fashion, he fixed his eyes upon his employer's face, and something in their expression actually constrained Mr Paton to lower his own.

'May I speak a word with you, sir?' he said, in low, uncertain tones.

It was the first time such a thing had happened, and it seemed to Richard's master that the best way of meeting it would be to 'damn' the man and send him about his business.

But Richard did not go. He stood for an instant with his head thrown back, and the desperate look of an animal at bay in his eyes. At this critical moment a woman's form suddenly interposed itself between Mr Paton and his victim. Amelia was there, looking like Amina after she had awoken from her trance. She came close to her master,—she had never addressed him before,—and raised her liquid eyes to his.

'You will not be hard on—my brother, sir, for the mistake I made last night?'

'Who said I was going to be hard on him?' retorted Mr Paton, too much taken back to find any more dignified form of rejoinder. 'And if he is your brother, why do you wait until it is dark to indulge in your family effusions?'

The question was accompanied by a through and through look, before which Amelia did not quail.

'Have I your permission to speak to him in the day-time, sir?' she said submissively.

'I will institute an inquiry,' interrupted her master. 'Here, go about your business,' he added, turning to Richard; 'fetch out the mare, and hand me back that note. I'll ride over with it myself.'

Three weeks later Richard Cole was a free man, and within four months from the date upon which Mr Paton had driven Amelia Clare down Macquarie Street in his gig, she came to take respectful leave of him, dressed in the identical close-fitting jacket and demure little bonnet he remembered. Thenceforth she was nobody's bondswoman. He had a small heap of coin in readiness to hand over to her, with the payment of which, and a few gratuitous words of counsel on his part, the leave-taking would have been definitely decorously accomplished. To tell her that he was more loth than ever to part with her, did not enter into the official programme. She was her own mistress now, as much or more so than the Queen of England herself, and it was hardly to be wondered at if the first use she made of her freedom was to shake the dust of Cowa Cottage off her feet. Still, if she had only known—if she had only known. It seemed too hard to let her go with the certainty that she never did or could know. Was it not for her sake that he had been swayed by all the conflicting impulses that had made him a changed man of late? For her that he had so narrowly escaped being a criminal awhile ago, and for her that he was appearing in the novel rôle of a reformer of the convict system now? He never doubted that she would have understood him if she *had* known. But to explain was out of the question. He must avow either all or nothing, and the all meant more than he dared to admit even to himself.

This was the reason why Amelia Clare departed sphinx-like as she had come. A fortnight after she had gone, as Mr Paton was gloomily smoking by his library fire in the early dark of a wintry August evening, a letter bearing the NS Wales postmark was handed to him. The handwriting, very small and fine, had something familiar in its aspect. He broke open the seal,—letters were still habitually sealed in those days—and read as follows:—

'SIR,—I am prompted to make you a confession—why, I cannot say, for I shall probably never cross your path again. I was married last week to Richard Cole, who was not my brother, as I led you to suppose, but my affianced husband, in whose behalf I would willingly suffer again to be unjustly condemned and transported. I have the warrant of Scripture for having assumed, like Sarah, the *rôle* of sister in preference to that of wife; besides which, it is hard to divest myself of an instincctive belief that the deceit was useful to Richard on one occasion. I trust you will pardon me.—Yours respectfully, 'AMELIA COLE.'

The kindly phase Mr Paton had passed through with regard to his convict victims came to an abrupt termination. The reaction was terrible. His name is inscribed among those 'who foremost shall be damn'd to Fame' in Tasmania.

(1891)

Bruce Dawe
A VICTORIAN HANGMAN TELLS HIS LOVE

Dear one, forgive my appearing before you like this,
in a two-piece track-suit, welder's goggles
and a green cloth cap like some gross bee—this is the State's
                                      idea...
I would have come
arrayed like a bridegroom for these nuptials   5
knowing how often you have dreamed about this
moment of consummation in your cell.
If I must bind your arms now to your sides
with a leather strap and ask if you have anything to say
—these too are formalities I would dispense with: 10
I know your heart is too full at this moment
to say much and that the tranquillizer which I trust
you did not reject out of a stubborn pride
should by this have eased your ache for speech, breath
and the other incidentals which distract us from our end.   15
Let us now walk a step. This noose
with which we're wed is something of an heirloom, the last three
members of our holy family were wed with it, the softwood beam
it hangs from like a lover's tree notched with their weight.
See now I slip it over your neck, the knot   20
under the left jaw, with a slip ring
to hold the knot in place...There. Perfect.
Allow me to adjust the canvas hood

which will enable you to anticipate the officially prescribed darkness
by some seconds.   25
The journalists are ready with the flash-bulbs of their eyes
raised to the simple altar, the doctor twitches like a stethoscope
—you have been given a clean bill of health, like any
modern bride.
                    With this spring of mine
from the trap, hitting the door lever, you will go forth   30
into a new life which I, alas, am not yet fit to share.
Be assured, you will sink into the generous pool of public feeling
as gently as a leaf—accept your rôle, feel chosen.
You are this evening's headlines. Come, my love.

                                                        (1967)

David Williamson
THE REMOVALISTS

from ACT TWO

FIONA: Could you let him off the handcuffs now, Sergeant?

SIMMONDS: Mr Carter was not handcuffed for your convenience, Mrs
    Carter. Mr Carter is being detained pending arrest for offensive be-
    haviour.

FIONA: I'm not intending to press charges against him.

SIMMONDS: (*with relish*) I'm afraid the matter is out of your hands, Mrs
    Carter. The offences have been committed against myself and Constable
    Ross.

KATE: (*sharply*) Are you coming, Fiona? The taxi won't wait around all
    day.

KENNY: He's going to beat shit out of me, Fiona.

KATE: Don't be so ridiculous!

    (KATE *drags a bewildered* FIONA *out to the taxi.* ROSS *returns. There is
    a pause.*)

SIMMONDS: (*ominously*) Why would we beat shit out of you, Carter?
    (SIMMONDS *walks up to him, pushes his head against the door and
    looks into his eyes.*)
    Why would we do that? (*To* ROSS) Can you think of any reason why
    we'd do that, Ross?

ROSS: (*sullen*) No.

SIMMONDS: What's wrong with you, Ross?

ROSS: Nothing.

SIMMONDS: You've been stomping around like a constipated bear since we
    arrived, Ross. If you've got something to say then get it off your chest.
    Have you got something to say?

ROSS: (*sullen*) No.

SIMMONDS: I'll tell you what, Ross; if your attitude doesn't show a
    marked improvement I'm going to give you a rocket in your first report.
    (*Loudly*) If you've got a chip on your shoulder then knock it off, Ross,
    and knock it off right now or I'll turn it into a bloody great log. Now

knock it off, Ross. (*Bellowing*) Knock it off. Get me?

(ROSS *sulks. There is a long pause.*)

What d'you think of Ross's potential, Carter? Think he's going to make a good cop? Got what it takes?

(KENNY *remains silent.*)

Well. What d'you think?

KENNY: (*quietly*) Look, how about undoing these cuffs?

SIMMONDS: I asked you a question, Carter. Do you think Ross's going to be any great shakes as a policeman?

KENNY: I've got me doubts.

SIMMONDS: So have I. What d'you think are his main weaknesses?

KENNY: Bit hard to know where to start.

SIMMONDS: Take your time.

KENNY: (*trying to pass it off*) It's a bit hard to say on the spur of the moment.

SIMMONDS: (*feigning irritation*) I only want an opinion, Carter. I'm not asking for your balls, now am I? What do you think it is that Ross is lacking?

KENNY: He seems a bit slow up top.

SIMMONDS: Initiative, perhaps. Do you think he's lacking in initiative?

KENNY: Yeah. I had noticed that.

SIMMONDS: (*to* ROSS) Do you think we should beat the shit out of this bastard, Ross?

(ROSS *doesn't answer.*)

(*Loudly*) For Christ's sake, Ross. Show a bit of initiative. Should we beat the shit out of this bastard?

ROSS: No!

(SIMMONDS *gives a mock sigh of relief at* ROSS's *display of initiative.*)

SIMMONDS: Very good, Ross.

(*Without warning* SIMMONDS *hits* KENNY *savagely in the groin with his knee.* KENNY *doubles up in pain.*)

I think you're right, Ross. We shouldn't beat him up. He's not worth the effort.

(*He adjusts his hat.*)

Get your handcuffs.

(ROSS *unlocks* KENNY, *avoiding his eye.*)

All right, Ross. Let's go.

(*They turn to go. As they walk towards the door,* KENNY *raises himself on his elbow and yells venomously after* SIMMONDS.)

KENNY: (*still in pain*) You dead cunt!

SIMMONDS: We don't want any more trouble from you, Carter.

KENNY: I'll get you one day, boy. I'll get you, you animal. I've got a lot of mates.

SIMMONDS: Think yourself lucky I didn't charge you, Carter. Don't push your luck.

KENNY: Get out! Go on. Get out, you animal. You'll step out of your house one dark night and you'll get it, boy. Kenny Carter doesn't forget somethin' like this. Now, piss off to your police station and crawl back into the woodwork!

(*Pause.*)

SIMMONDS: (*coolly*) Book him, Ross. Abusive and threatening language.

(ROSS *hesitates.*)

Book him!

>(Ross *walks over towards* KENNY *who picks up a chair and threatens him.*)

KENNY: (*menacing*) Don't you come any closer, shithead!

ROSS: I'm placing you under arrest for abusive and threatening language, Carter. I must warn you—

KENNY: (*advancing on him*) Get out of my house you bloody great half-wit. You've had your fun, now get out!

ROSS: (*backing away*) I would advise you that any attempt—

SIMMONDS: Add deliberate obstruction and menacing behaviour, Ross.

ROSS: In addition to the earlier charges I am—(*backing away as* KENNY *advances*) charging you with deliberate—

KENNY: (*steamed up and sensing* Ross's *fear*) Do you think that uniform makes you a big man or something? Eh? Christ. A hundred bloody uniforms wouldn't do anything for you, boy. You're the bloody dregs. There's no bloody doubt about it. I've seen some cowardly fuckwits hiding behind their uniforms in my time but without a doubt you're the bottom of the bloody barrel.

>(Ross *can take it no longer. He goes temporarily berserk and launches himself at* KENNY *who is taken by surprise and drops the chair.* ROSS *knocks him to the floor, punches him and starts to bash his head against the floor.* KENNY *breaks free and backs away in terror at the ferocity of* ROSS's *attack. He breaks away and moves out into the kitchen.* ROSS *chases him offstage. There are crashes and blows offstage.* SIMMONDS *grins to himself. At last there is silence, and after a pause* ROSS *comes back. He is panting and has blood on his face.*)

SIMMONDS: Did you let him get away?

>(ROSS *is out of breath. He seems dazed.*)

Did you let him get away?

>(ROSS *is frightened. He looks at* SIMMONDS.)

ROSS: (*softly, hoarse*) I've killed the bastard, Sarge.

SIMMONDS: (*amused*) Come on, Ross. Haven't you ever knocked a man out before?

ROSS: (*frightened*) I think I've killed him.

SIMMONDS: You better not have bruised him, boy. I hope it was a nice clean punch on the chin.

ROSS: (*frightened*) No. Look, I really think I killed him.

SIMMONDS: Yes, well, I'm afraid I'm going to have to report this incident to cover myself in case anything does blow up, but if you hit him on the chin you should be right.

ROSS: I lost control, Sarge. I just lost control.

SIMMONDS: Control is something you're going to have to learn, boy. Control is the essence of the law.

ROSS: I just couldn't stop myself.

SIMMONDS: Whenever you hit a man, Ross, you should know exactly how hard you're going to hit him a full minute before you land the blow. That's a good little rule to remember.

ROSS: (*agitated*) Christ, Sarge. What's going to happen to me?

SIMMONDS: Don't worry, boy. I've got to hand in a report but I'll word it as gently as I can. I'll say that while I thought you used excessive force to detain the prisoner, it is my opinion that this mistake was almost entirely due to inexperience and certainly not to any defect of personality or the like. It'll be a good chance to have a bit of a dig at the Police School. I'll point out how inadequately they prepare recruits for the reality of their vocation.

ROSS: (*loudly*) Look, for Christ's sake, Sarge. I killed him. I really killed him!

SIMMONDS: Come on, Ross. The human being is a hell of a lot tougher than most people give him credit for. Most recruits get in a panic after their first KO.

ROSS: Go in and have a look!

SIMMONDS: I've thrown a man down a flight of concrete steps, Ross, and seen him land on his bloody head. Ten minutes later he got up and walked away. Pretty neanderthal-looking specimen, admittedly, but there you are. The only thing you've got to worry about is that Carter might rake up a bit of money and follow this through; but unless they're filthy rich they usually think twice about that one when they cool down.

ROSS: For Christ's sake go in there and have a look, Sarge!

(SIMMONDS *shrugs and walks into the kitchen. He comes back with a worried look on his face.*)

SIMMONDS: What'd you do to him?

ROSS: (*scared*) Is he dead?

SIMMONDS: He's pretty bloody white. What in the hell did you do to him?

ROSS: (*agitated*) I lost control.

SIMMONDS: What in the hell did you do? Hit him when he was down?

ROSS: No.

SIMMONDS: You didn't kick him, did you? You didn't kick him in the head?

ROSS: No. I never kicked.

SIMMONDS: But you hit him when he was down, didn't you?

ROSS: I might have. I lost control.

SIMMONDS: You idiot, Ross. You never hit a head that hasn't got some freedom of movement. For Christ's sake. Don't you know anything?

ROSS: Is he dead?

SIMMONDS: Well, he's looking pretty white.

ROSS: Why didn't you feel his pulse?

SIMMONDS: Because I came out to find out what you did to him.

ROSS: Well, for Christ's sake go and feel his pulse.

SIMMONDS: Don't order me around, boy.

ROSS: Go and feel his pulse.

SIMMONDS: I tell you what, Ross. You'll go if he's dead. I can't help you much if he's dead.

ROSS: (*wildly*) We could make it look like he committed suicide.

SIMMONDS: (*talking fast and sternly*) What? Why in the hell would we say that? To protect you? Drag myself in to protect you? Do you think we'd get away—look, his wife, the sister, the removalist—do you honestly think we'd get away with a thing like that? Headquarters may be pretty dense but I tell you what, I'm not sticking my neck out to cover up for your mistakes, Ross—your bloody lack of control. What's the training school sending out these days? Punchies? Too much adrenalin or something?

ROSS: (*hysterical*) They'd believe it, Sarge. He's had a hell of a day. You'd have to admit that. Wife walks out on him without word of warning.

Takes his television and his fridge. Just imagine if it happened to you, Sarge. Just imagine. It'd hit you right in the gut, wouldn't it? I mean to say, he had no bloody warning, the poor bastard. Did the right thing by his wife in bed the night before, loves his daughter, and we didn't even let him see the end of the movie he was watchin'. I tell you he's had a bad day. If I was him I'd be thinkin' of the best way to kick it right now!

SIMMONDS: (*pushing him away, starting to show signs of panic himself*) You're mad, Ross. You've gone right off. Do you think anyone commits suicide by beating himself to death? Gets all depressed and starts swingin' uppercuts at himself? You're in the shit, I'm afraid, Ross. There's no two ways about it and it isn't going to help you one little bit to lose your head and come up with crazy stuff like that. You're in real strife, boy, and I'm afraid—

ROSS: (*starting to forage around in the cupboard*) We could hang him. Find a bit of rope and make it look as if he bloody hung himself.

SIMMONDS: (*fast and agitated*) Don't be so bloody stupid. What about the bruises and the blood? How're you going to explain that? I've been in the force twenty-three years now, Ross, and I know what you can get away with and what you can't; and I'm telling you for sure; you won't get away with a stunt like that. Not a hope in high heaven. You've gone too far, boy, and I'm afraid you're going to have to face the consequences.

ROSS: (*wildly*) I'll say that you did it!

SIMMONDS: (*staggered*) You'll what?

ROSS: I'll say that you did it!

SIMMONDS: (*aghast*) You can't lie about a thing like this, Ross!

ROSS: You were the one who was hitting him. They all saw that. They'll believe me for sure.

SIMMONDS: (*anxious*) They all saw that I was in control, Ross. That's what they all saw. I know how hard to hit a man. That's what they all saw.

ROSS: I'll say that as soon as they left you went berserk and killed him.

SIMMONDS: No, Ross. I'm in control and people know it. They can call me all kinds of bastard but they know I'm always in control, Ross. That's my strength Ross, and that's been my strength for years and nobody's going to believe otherwise because that's the work of a raw young hot-head if ever I saw it and other people are going to see it that way too, Ross, whether you like it or not; and that's something you're going to have to face up to instead of trying to shift the blame to an area where it doesn't rightly belong and where nobody in their right senses would ever see it as belonging. I think you must be mad to think that anyone would—I think you'd best come down to the main station and confess straight away before you go getting yourself into real trouble.

ROSS: (*wildly*) No, bugger you. I'm going to lie. I'm really going to turn it on. I'm going to lie and lie and lie and lie. You wait and see. I'm sorry, Sarge, but I'm scared. I'm shit scared.

SIMMONDS: (*hysterical*) For Christ's sake don't get hysterical. Pull yourself together, man!

ROSS: I'm sorry, Sarge, but I'm scared. Shit scared.

SIMMONDS: Well, getting hysterical isn't going to help!

ROSS: They'll lock us up, Sarge! They'll lock us up for life!

SIMMONDS: They won't lock me up! I've got nothing to do with it!

ROSS: They won't put us in for life, will they, Sarge? They never put us cops away for as long as ordinary blokes, do they? (*Remembering*) Ooo, Jesus! Yes they do. Remember those two guys who knocked off the TAB? I'm sorry, Sarge, but I'm going to lie. After all, you were in charge.

SIMMONDS: (*exploding*) I didn't tell you to kill him, Ross. I didn't tell you to kill him!

ROSS: I'm no killer. I didn't join the Force to kill people. (*With a sudden idea*) Let's leave a suicide note and blast his head off with a shotgun. They won't find the bruises then.

SIMMONDS: (*yelling*) Shut up, you crazy bastard!

(KENNY, *battered and bleeding, crawls into the room unseen and hoists himself onto one of the few remaining chairs. He lights himself a cigarette and takes a deep draw.*)

ROSS: (*yelling back*) Well, good God, wouldn't you be depressed if your wife just walked out on you without a word of warning? If we blow his head off with a shotgun I won't have to lie about who killed him!

SIMMONDS: For Christ's sake shut up and pull yourself together! It isn't going to do any good to lie. They'll find bloodstains on your uniform and things like that. The best thing you could do would be to own up. The worst you'll face is manslaughter—officer in the course of his duty—and I wouldn't mind betting you'll get off on the grounds of inexperience. Yes. Loss of control due to inexperience. I'll testify to your inexperience. They probably won't let you stay in the Force but if you play your cards right you'll get your full superannuation entitlements on the grounds of psychological instability; and they can't take that away from you, boy, even if you get another job, because being unsuited to the Force doesn't mean you're not suited to something else and they—

ROSS: (*shouting*) Don't crap!

(1971)

David Ireland
from THE UNKNOWN INDUSTRIAL PRISONER

BIG DADDY   The Samurai sat watching the rest of his shift come dressed from the locker-room. Technically they were citizens, allowed to reproduce at random. A place had to be found for their children, too. As he watched, something like a fine despair seemed to spray up from somewhere inside him and shower his organs of concern with a set of patterned words, the same words that had often risen to his tongue when he saw them attacking each other openly or in secret. It was man against man at every level and the company suffered from the situation's wastefulness, but no one saw it as a blot that should be published, condemned, eradicated. Poor devils, you can't take care of yourselves, you need a father to watch over you and fight the battles you should be fighting against the false and the unfair, the cruel and the oppressive...And, as usual, he knew that although he had heart and ability for such a fight and many wanted him to be their delegate, to stand in the front line and take the company's first shots, he had never convinced himself that he had the basic inclination. Mostly the Union attracted men looking for an excuse to get off their plants when they felt like it. Those with ideas, energy and initiative got a second job outside. The Union knew only one thing: how to go for money. But what was the use of a wage increase awarded because prices had risen and industry could afford it, when as soon as the increase was awarded prices rose again because industry couldn't afford it? If the Samurai had been a man of ambition, self-seeking could have carried him through and he could have built a career on serving them, but not from love. He did not—he could not—love his brothers.

And yet he had no inherited ankle scar to scratch.

Official, pompous things amused him. He chuckled still over the name Puroil Refining, Termitary & Grinding Works painted in large letters on control block walls. Every so often it was painted out, but it always reappeared. He repeated the name aloud to the others. Few laughed. Only the Great White Father, who had written it. He met this man on his first day at the plant, as he started on afternoon shift, just before the day workers went home.

He said, 'There's our termitary,' as they passed the administration block in the company bus, and sure enough there were the little ant-people running up and down stairs, on view behind plate-glass, arguing silently with each other or sitting impassively for hours in offices equally on display. A glass box, completely enclosed except for tiny ventilation holes. He had worked there himself before transferring to the works, but he had never seen the building this way before. A great manorhouse watching over its feudal fields and wage-serfs.

'What about the grinding works?' he asked the Great White Father, who was exceedingly tall and bony and good-natured.

'The whole thing is a grinding works. Each man, if he lets it happen, is ground down a little each day until, finely and smoothly honed of all eccentricities and irregularities and the originality that could save him, the grinding suddenly stops at sixty. Then they shot you out. You wait five years to qualify for the old age pension, and when you qualify you make your choice: whether to take the government one or carry on with the company pension. They're pretty close to the same thing, in cash. Under our beneficent social system, one disqualifies you from the other. Most of us won't have to worry, we're all specially picked and processed so we peg out within a year or two of retiring. The system is further safeguarded; in the last few years of service they down-grade you so your pension won't be much, anyway, in case you escape the health hazard. You see, your pension amount is tied to your earnings in your last couple of years' service. Demote you, pay less. You're just an item of cost. The bigger the organization, the smaller the value of each man in it. And this one's huge.'

The very tall man's sea-blue eyes sparkled and danced so much during this short lecture that the Samurai kept listening attentively so as not to miss the joke, which he felt sure was coming. But no, the Great White Father was serious. He seemed to enjoy talking—the sort of man who enjoyed everything. Laughter patterned his deeply creased face, lined with the scars and lacerations of a varied, reprehensible, non-respectable, wholly enjoyable past.

'You said, if a man lets it happen...'

'If you let them grind you down, yes. You don't have to.'

'What else?'

'Fight 'em! Every step of the way!'

'They've go the whip hand. What do you fight with?'

'Smiles, a quick wit, sex, alcohol, and never say Yes to the bastards. Once you recognize the place is a prison, you're well off. The best that can be said is everyone draws an indefinite sentence. The final horror of a life behind barbed wire is mercifully withheld.' He glanced out at the high wire fence they were passing then, topped with several strands of barbed wire. 'You see, the battleground where they beat you is in here.' His long, friendly brown hand lay relaxed on his own high, resonant chest.

But just where the Samurai was expecting him to go on, he suddenly stood. The bus stopped. Their crew was decanted like a carelessly handled bacterial culture outside the host body of the low grey control block on their growing plant. Drawn by a power unseen, the human bacteria quickly made their way inside and were apparently devoured. Gunga Din, lean, brown, small and dry, went first to the urn to check the water level and turn it on ready for the first cup of tea.

The Samurai tried to catch up with the Great White Father, and did succeed, but all he would say was: 'That's where your Gallipoli is, in there.' And a long, bony finger prodded his chest, then was gone, busy with locker key and bootlaces.

'What do you mean, an indefinite sentence?' He felt foolish as he persisted, but this seemed to be a man worth talking to. The rest talked interminably of second-hand cars and overtime.

'Indefinite? You don't know when you'll get the bullet, do you?' And turned away to sniff his boots, then to scratch his right ankle. When he had his boots on, he went to wipe some dried mud on to a pile off rags in the corner, but stopped himself in time. The Glass Canoe didn't, and was busy rubbing his feet on the rags before the Great White Father tapped his shoulder.

'Humdinger,' he said. The Glass Canoe looked down. The rags stirred and stretched, yawned and looked up.

'Is that what you think of your fellow workers?'

'Christ, I'm sorry, mate,' said the Glass Canoe and everyone gaped. Perhaps he was getting sick again.

On the job, events moved slowly. On the drawing boad in the Admin block though, for eight hours a day, the pace was frantic until four, when the white-shirted multitude suddenly went home. Their effort might have been more widely spread over the twenty-four hours to take advantage of the quiet of the dark hours, but white-collar men don't yet do shifts.

The tall man had another word for him when he was dressed for work. 'No one enters those blue gates only to make gasoline, bitumen or ethylene from crude. Oil *and* excreta, that's what they fractionate here. Us and oil. With foremen, controllers, section heads, superintendents, managers and all the rest, there's maybe forty grades. Forty grades of shit. That's all any of us are. White shirts, brown shirts, overalls, boiler suits, the lot. Shit. The place is a correction centre. The purpose of giving you a job is to keep you off the streets. It's still a penal colony. All the thousands of companies are penal sub-contractors to the Government.'

Puroil's land included a stretch of what had once been parkland. Residents' petitions, questions in Parliament, real estate developers' organized, agonized pleas, no amount of democratic pressure was able to beat a foreign oil company. A few words were altered on a piece of paper somewhere, the parkland was declared industrial land and Puroil had a foothold in New South Wales. The total of 350 acres included, on the river side, some of the swampiest land this side of Botany Bay, but mangroves were cleared, swamp flats partitioned and drained and filled until only a few dozen acres on the river bank were left in their natural state. Another hundred acres of mangroves still stood on the other side of Eel River, just down from the gasoline depot of a pretended rival of Puroil: Puroil supplied them from a nice fat silver pipeline that nuzzled into the slime of the river bed and came up again out of the ground handy to their shiny white tanks.

Puroil supplied the depot of another company too, with a line that ran half a mile under cleared clay. Wagons of rival companies that ran out of their own brand, simply called in and gulped down a load of Puroil, went out and sold it as their own. Even Puroil sent out grey unmarked wagons—they had brother companies with different names. The rival companies fixed the price between themselves in the first place, the Government approved their figure then made a big deal of getting them to reduce half a cent a gallon when crude went down a cent. Then they all advertised like mad and called it competition.

At Puroil, the largest vessels of the new cracking plant were in position and complicated mazes of pipelines were being lagged with glass wool and aluminium sheet. Turbines, pumps, compressors, heaters, coolers, columns were assembled from many parts of the world; there were even a few girders and pipelines from Australia. Puroil never gave out the usual unctuous bumph about the refinery belonging to the Australian people; it was very clear that whatever faceless people owned it were a long way off. They were clever faceless people. At that distance they were able to persuade Australians to pass an Act of Parliament subsidizing their search for more oil. Even with retained profits and the help of liberal depreciation provisions they didn't feel able to bear the full cost themselves. They even persuaded Australia that Puroil's increased wealth was good for Australia. The way they put it was that it was Australia's wealth.

The plant was a new design, the first of its kind; there was a power recovery system hooked in to the catalyst reaction and regeneration cycle. Integrated, vulnerable, but designed to save half a million dollars a year on fuel bills. This one complex of twelve plant units cost forty million dollars. Even so it was an economy plant, as it said in the operators' manual. The overseas owners weren't willing to provide enough standby equipment. On two-thirds of design feed-rate the cost would be recovered in two years, after which the profit was enormous. And in seven days of twenty-four-hour running, the wages of the sixty men operating it would be paid for one year out of profit on gasoline alone, aside from sales of steam to neighbouring industries, top gas for the ethylene compressors, gas and slurry oils to the gasworks, low pressure gas for bottling, cycle oils and furnace oil to the many little oil processing factories that sprang up round the refinery. The normal cracker, they were told, ran continuously for eighteen months to two years before shutting down for inspection and repairs.

(1971)

THE MIGRANT EXPERIENCE

AUSTRALIA AND THE IMMIGRANT

Too often, in recent years, the debate over just how the migrant experience informs Australian literature has oscillated between two extreme positions: either, that all non-Aboriginal Australians are migrants, or, in effect, that only post-war settlers are migrants, leaving the rest to be simply Australians. The most significant factor governing migration before the 1940s and 1950s is that the settlers were drawn predominantly from the United Kingdom and their narratives of adjustment in a sense reinforced, both positively and negatively, the ties to 'Mother England'. The measure of difference was thus restricted to the English language and English culture, even when the writers were Irish since, in this last instance, the struggle had always been confined to England and Ireland.

However, with post-war migration there was an influx of other measures, from Europe and, more recently, from those many countries misleadingly homogenised under the term 'Asia'. These other perspectives are still often analysed in terms of a deficiency model, that is, according to a so-called lack of the English language and a lack of the cultural codes which constitute Anglophone Australia. Where they occur in the compilation which follows, it will be clear that they offer new insights, not only into their own past cultural allegiances but also into the Australian culture they encountered here.

What, then, are the dominant themes of the migrant experience? In the first place, it involves the creation of a new identity, both private and public. Inevitably, this incorporates a clash between the old self forged in other social and physical contexts and, at times, in other languages. With respect to the last element, this often constitutes an alternative conceptual structure of the self which in turn contributes to the formation of resistances to the absolutist claims made on behalf of any culture. At times such resistances take the negative turn of racism based on defensive assumptions that one's first culture is inherently superior, whereas in its positive manifestation it takes the form of a healthy scepticism towards any bid for universal truths.

Other aspects of the migrant experience include the position of mediation, particularly with respect to the children of migrants who inhabit schizophrenic existences which swing between the old culture and language at home, and the Australian codes which govern their public worlds. Finally, there is the tightrope experience of 'writing the other' which can either result in reinforcing stereotypes, thus sustaining the politics of assimilation, or break open and expose the politics of representing the other as always negative and subsidiary.

The creation of new identity, both public and private, is celebrated in the two examples first published in 1913. The poem from Christopher Brennan's Wanderer sequence recalls those early romantic narrators whose search for new selves was often projected outwards onto a quest for new worlds. Here is the outcast lost soul of High Romanticism whose voyage is more metaphysical than actual, an inner rather than outer migration. Bernard O'Dowd's poem fastens on the motif of Australia as the Promised Land, the social laboratory with Utopian potential. This was the chance to undo the Fall, to start again with the wisdom of past errors, though readers now cringe at such lines as, 'Australia wafts her sybil call wherever white men are.' In other words, this so-called Utopia functions exclusively for the redemption of white Europeans. The language is infused with Theosophical images which postulate a transcendent mystical world glimpsed through the mundane version, both heavy with allegorical portent.

A more recent and palatable fusing of new self and new land occurs in Ee Tiang Hong's 'Coming To'. As in the Brennan extract, the terrain for this narrator-in-process is the meeting place of land and sea. Again we encounter the lone voyager reborn from the sea, washed clean of old memories. Ee's narrator speaks of the self metonymically as a car out of control and this constitutes a powerful evocation of the dislocation and panic many migrants feel particularly if they cannot initially relate to the new language and thereby translate their selves into these new codes. The ambiguity of the final phrase, 'from down under', hints at a certain irony—both the self as geographically located in the antipodes, but, as well, aware of a certain reduced status. One point to note here is that it is very difficult for readers to recognise irony in the writings of so-called migrants because their texts are almost exclusively read as unproblematic autobiographical accounts. The reference to Yeats's Byzantium, that mythic Utopia of art and spirit, compounds the irony. Australia's figurative legacy of the Promised Land (explored in the O'Dowd poem) is not borne out in this poem, where its emissaries are Bruce and Eddy and an archetypal couple descending from their four-wheel drive in order to interrogate this ambiguous migrant.

When the new self is painfully reinstated in a new social environment, the biggest hurdle (explicitly so) is the detritus of the old self. David Martin's wry 'Letter to a Friend in Israel' juxtaposes a middle-aged narrator addressing, in some respects, a younger self. Youth becomes embodied in place: the Israel of pioneer Kibbutzniks who make the desert bloom each day and defend it at night. Israel/youth also incorporates the heady experience of early sexuality, incongruously surrounded by names with ancient Biblical resonances. This becomes contrasted with the narrator's present middle age ('My heart is drying on a clothes hoist') in suburban Melbourne, where the erstwhile pioneering spirit has been reduced to bathos. (Dogs did in fact make love off-stage in Patrick White's play, *A Cheery Soul*, first performed in Melbourne in November 1963.)

> And on a fine day, from the Trades Hall roof,
> The class struggle can still be clearly seen
> Beyond the university...

The last line of the poem concentrates the narrator's mixed feelings as, torn between two places and selves, he contemplates the sun whose neutrality is conceived as a form of betrayal.

Lily Brett's 'Our House' deals with the embarrassment suffered by the children of immigrants who are haunted by old selves and old ways while they stridently seek to establish themselves amongst their sharp-eyed peer group. The impossibility, or perils, of inviting one's friends home

> to
> such
> a
> crowded
> house

is a familiar theme in the writings of the second generation. I recall a Viennese friend's uncanny story of having her school mates file in for the family dinner, declining all invitations for they had come only to *observe* the what and how of this ritual.

Peter Skrzynecki's 'Feliks Skrzynecki' encompasses other common pangs experienced by the children of immigrants. Here we have another aspect of the immigrant experience, where the child becomes the mediator between the two worlds. The narrator depicts his father as an unworldly man whose interests centre on cultivating his garden and the friends from the

old country. The observing child suffers the pain of registering the prejudices directed at the father and of feeling a traitor himself when he is
unable to maintain the old language. Hadrian's Wall was built in England
to keep out the northern barbarians: just who the barbarians are now is
ultimately left ambiguous as the son retreats further into the imperial and
alien realm.

Judah Waten's 'Making a Living', from the collection *Alien Son*, is a
further example of the mediating role played by the second generation.
Again the narrator is a boy prematurely catapulted into manhood through
his encounter with the tensions and contradictions of his family's position
in a small West Australian town. The narrator becomes aware of the
differences of class, religion and culture each of which can form a basis for
varieties of oppression. Even a simple journey through town becomes an
ordeal, 'My irritation grew into anger when a group of men and women
looked at us a little too long.' As the narrator's anger explodes into shying
a bottle at the onlookers he is in turn cut off from his mother's world,
exemplified by her efforts to maintain a certain class decorum. The boy
nourishes dreams of taking over as provider, more effectively than his
impractical father, but meanwhile he explores the shades of aggression
which accumulate in response to seeing his family reduced to a freak show.
In the next episode he retaliates, verbally at first, but is again reduced to
physical threats. The end of the story finds the narrator exiled from the
town and his family abode, the old and new world, confronting adulthood
for the first time.

The disjunction between the old self and the new results also in a
resistance to the claims of any particular culture to incorporate universal
or absolute truths. Ours are the only right ways of doing things! On the
one hand this can lead to a cultural arrogance so that one takes refuge in
the certainties of one's own culture. This is exemplified by the historical
record of an anti-Chinese meeting of 1855. Here we have an early statement in which the *only* rationale for encouraging immigration is to provide cheap labour, a logic which was repeated in the justifications of
post-war immigration, where no matter what their professional status,
most non-British migrants were stamped either as 'labourer' or as 'domestic'. Here too are the roots of the rhetoric of assimilation, the notion that
legitimacy resides only in becoming the same as the Anglo-Celtic majority.
Immigrants are called '*New* Australians'. Difference is invariably equated
with a lesser status; the dominance of the white Europeans is unques-
tioned.

The narrator of Hal Porter's 'House Girl' is also assured of his own
cultural superiority. This is exemplified by his descriptions of the Japanese
society he encounters, which manage to be both racist and misogynist.
From the initial depiction of Tokyo as a latter-day whore of Babylon to
the house-girl as 'coarse, squat and neurotic' and the house-boys as 'reeking of camellia hair oil', the reader encounters a barrage of disgust and the
narrator's sense of contamination. Later in the story, he awakens to the
possibility that these factors are to some extent built into the context of
conqueror and conquered, 'the situation has taken charge of us both—
Australian and Japanese, boss and servant, conqueror and conquered,
Church of England and Shinto, man and woman'. This leads him finally to
acknowledge the house-girl's humanity and his own final insignificance.

The resistances generated in the meeting between one culture and another can also give rise to a healthy scepticism or critique of both sides. The French writer Paul Wenz's *Diary of a New Chum* directs its satire both ways. On the one hand it depicts the brutal male world of the outback and on the other it suggests a European dreamer who won't survive long if he is given to patting horse's noses, or objects to being called 'all sorts of names except your own'. Rosa Cappiello offers another type of satire in the extact from her acclaimed *Oh Lucky Country* which is, amongst other things, an outrageous rewriting of the migrant story. This text implicitly addresses the tradition of forelock-tugging accounts of 'migrant makes good' and giving due thanks to the land and its white inhabitants. Her narrator rails at everything from the architecture of Sydney to prevailing sexual mores, to the 'perfumeless flowers...the tasteless fruit'. Her anger is so excessive that its very energy becomes a positive factor and no target escapes, neither her old compatriots nor her new ones. Above all it refuses complacency. Within this torrent there are small islands of quiet, such as the sudden recollection of a line from A. D. Hope's 'Australia'.

The extract from Bandler's *Wacvie* gives a voice to the hitherto silent victims of racism. This novel recounts her father's experience of being kidnapped into the slave trade of the Queensland canefields. It employs the device of a naïve narrator whose unadorned juxtaposition of the experience of both worlds, black and white, renders the horrors experienced by the islanders all the more powerful. They receive no pay, inadequate food, and are left to die through malnutrition and exposure. The most basic requirements of human existence are denied them. Without money they cannot acquire land in order to grow their own food. The different attitude towards the land, with the whites bent on maximum exploitation, are contrasted with this. Under this onslaught, all the more effective because of its restraint, Australian culture is utterly displaced from its claims to civilisation or moral superiority.

The final element in the migrant experience is 'writing the other', exemplified by Beverley Farmer's 'Melpo' and Ania Walwicz's prose poem 'Wogs'. Farmer's story captures the ancient tensions between mother and son and mother and daughter-in-law, as told from the point of view of the Greek son rather than the Australian daughter-in-law. The filial constraints imposed by the mother on her son become indistinguishable from her xenophobia and religious prejudice against a daughter-in-law who is already a mother. The problem for the reader lies in disentangling the particularities of this mother-son bond from the generalising assumptions that this is the way *all* Greek women of Melpo's generation would feel about these issues. The evocation of the Greek family's past is to some extent offered as a background explanation for the characters' present retreat into unreality as foregrounded in the dialogue between Melpo and Kerry.

Walwicz's 'Wogs' sets out the process of dehumanisation which results from prejudice. The litany of absurdities and contradictions escalates into comedy at the same time that it echoes disconcertingly the arguments perennially mounted in newspaper attacks on migration. Here the marginalised other recreates the oppressor with devastating accuracy.

Finally, it is important to see these accounts of the migrant experience as offering not only evocations of dislocation and struggle but also a redefinition of Australian literature which comes from injecting other cultures, with their new codes, their perspectives and realities, all contributing to the place 'we' call home.

Sneja Gunew

Bernard O'Dowd
THE SOUTHERN CALL

Come hither ye, o'er all the world who seek the Altar room
  Of spacious Freedom ever lit for worshippers to be:
Come from the jaded lands to us, come from the sullen gloom,
  To sunny soils and cities sweet, to Love and Liberty!
The Truth by which ye steer by day, the Good ye pray for nightly,   5
  The Beautiful ye would be one with—here are glowing brightly!
Here ye will realise at last the Sempiternal Dream,
  Join in the Great Adventure towards the Mystic Pilgrim's goal,
And reach the summit that ye sought for following the Gleam—
  For here it is, we know, and now—the City of the Soul.   10

When men outgrew the simple fane that awed their fathers' eyes,
  And waking found the Presence gone, the Memnon music dumb,
One of the dreams they loved the best, and yearned to realise,
  Told of a star that leaps to light when new gods are to come.
Surely 'tis here Messiahs new the old world's chains will sunder,   15
  In purer skies, and genial air, and omnipresent wonder!
So, come ye all whose lighted eyes behold the star above
  The crib where waits maturing long the Hope that is to be:
And bring the gold of willing hands, the frankincense of Love,
  And, priceless o'er Golconda's gems, the myrrh of Liberty!   20

We need your grit to make the Wild the fair abiding place
  That ages have been yearning for, the Land of Heart's Desire:
Yet while we beacon hill on hill with signals to the race,
  Sorely we need your prudence old, lest reckless we aspire
To change the orbit of the world to gratify a passion,   25
  Or Kings eternal to dethrone to fit the moment's fashion.
Away so long from war's dire lore, we half forget to fight,
  Unused to hunger we despise our smiling plenty's worth,
Wrong is a stranger so to us, we scarcely know the Right,
  Yet steadied by your wisdom we were Savlours of the earth.   30

And not alone to feel the mouths of children at her breast
  Australia wafts her sibyl call wherever white men are;
But, Warden of the Boundaries, lone Outpost for the West,
  She dare not risk the paling here of splendid Europe's star.
Out in the night we seem to see piratic dangers sparkle,   35
  And on our noon's horizon growing omens grimly darkle
O'come ye of the white race hither, come ye to her call!
  'Tis not alone for us the word she sends you o'er the sea.
As ye shall rise while up we soar, our failure means your fall—
  The fall of Truth, the fall of Love, the fall of Liberty!   40

Where ancient sorrow darkens not nor ancient evils stain,
  There is no air on earth to-day gives oracles so clear;
The Creed is here that opes the Door the creeds have tried in vain;
  No secret of the universe ye may not cipher here.
Hither hath come the Holy Grail that ages long ye fared for;   45

Yea, He is here, we know, we know, the God all gods
  prepared for,
And builds for us, if but we will, millennial nationhood;
  Song for the soul, if but we call, will fill the desert hush,
His desert ravens' iron wings will bear our bodies food;
  If but we strike, the desert rock will with His fountains gush.   50

The clanking of the Iron Age grows musical at last;
  The dove replaces owl and bat, leopard becomes a fawn;
Sinister angels with the gloom are disappearing fast;
  The rumbling portents slowly change as midnight flowers in dawn
Out of the yearnings that ye sowed in centuries of sorrow   55
  Springs the fruition of your faith, Australia and To-morrow!
The Sun-burst of the Coming Age is golden on the hills;
  Shouting for joy the Sons of God amid the glory stand;
Alchemist Love elixirs new for jaded man distils;
  And Time the wizard rends the veil that hid the Promised Land!   60

*   *   *   *   *

Unto the wronged of ages singing songs of Human Rights,
  Redolent of the wattle bloom and tonic with the gum:
Into the prisons olden flashing cleansing Southern Lights,
  Unto her citizens to be, Australia cooees 'Come!'

(1913)

Christopher Brennan
EACH DAY I SEE THE LONG SHIPS
COMING INTO PORT

Each day I see the long ships coming into port
and the people crowding to their rail, glad of the shore:
because to have been alone with the sea and not to have known
of anything happening in any crowded way,
and to have heard no other voice than the crooning sea's   5
has charmed away the old rancours, and the great winds
have search'd and swept their hearts of the old irksome
    thoughts:
so, to their freshen'd gaze, each land smiles a good home.
Why envy I, seeing them made gay to greet the shore?
Surely I do not foolishly desire to go   10
hither and thither upon the earth and grow weary
with seeing many lands and peoples and the sea:
but if I might, some day, landing I reck not where
have heart to find a welcome and perchance a rest,
I would spread the sail to any wandering wind of the air   15
this night, when waves are hard and rain blots out the land.

(1902)

AN ANTI-CHINESE PUBLIC MEETING

from THE AGE

The first thing to be settled in our own minds is, whether this country is to be a British *colony* or a British *plantation*.

. . . if Australia is to be laid out in plantations, and its European inhabitants to become planters, it would be unwise to exclude the Chinese, as they are the very people that will be wanted. But, on the other hand, if our object be to found here a nation composed principally of Englishmen, and modelled after the English type, it is unnecessary for us to trouble our minds about the harshness and inconsistency of excluding a set of people, who are likely to thwart, rather than advance, that object. Any palaver about the absolute equality of man is altogether out of place, in such circumstances; for the utmost extravagance even of 'extreme democracy' goes no further than asserting equality among those who are of the same nation, and trained under the same institutions. Democrats are generally, great sticklers for nationality. Hence, their watch-words generally are, 'America for the Americans', 'Ireland for the Irish', 'Italy for the Italians', and 'Hungary for the Hungarians'. For ourselves, our 'extreme democracy' consists in claiming 'Victoria for the Victorians', and in contending that those Victorians should continue to be, what they are now—composed principally of Europeans. So long, therefore, as we are willing, on the same grounds, to concede 'China to the Chinese', we feel ourselves bound by no principle of supposed consistency to admit them here, *except in so far as it suits ourselves.*

Here lies the gist of the question:—*Politically*, we are in no difficulty. We are not obliged to admit them either within the country, or within the pale of the constitution. The question, therefore, is reduced to one of *expediency.* In this respect, there are only two points which require to be carefully considered,—first, as it bears upon the industrial, and, secondly, as it bears upon the moral, prospects of the country.

In relation to the first point, we see no cause for alarm. If we are to be a nation, we must go *forward*; and if we are to go forward, we must employ all the labor that comes in our way. If we do so, we shall take the most effectual step to create a progressive demand for unlimited supplies of labor. Had we railways spread over the country, population could not pour in too fast; and if we intend to proceed with such an enterprise, or would make a beginning with it, our present supply of labor would at once be absorbed, leaving room for as many Europeans or Asiatics as are likely to come. It is a foolish apprehension, on the part of the working classes, that they will be swamped by continued immigration, if the result of such immigration be to stimulate the development of the country. The tendency of things in a colony like this is for one stage of progress to lead to another. A certain advance in productive industry creates a necessity for other industrial pursuits, which is the grand source of that elasticity which characterises new countries. On the other hand, if we are not to go forward we have plenty of people here already for all useful purposes; but this would be an argument, not merely against Chinese immigration but against all further immigration from any quarter whatever.

There remains, then, but one view of the question which can be a source of apprehension; and that is the moral one. And here our first law is that of self-preservation. Philanthropy may say:—Let them come here, and it will give us an opportunity of lifting them out of the ditch of heathenism in which they are wallowing. Very charitable; but it is worthwhile considering whether we shall lift them out, or whether they may not as likely drag us in. If we are confident of the former, by all means let them come; but if we have a misgiving, it may prove an act of prudence, on our part, to adopt a protective policy for a time. Whether this should be in the shape of a protective tariff, as regards future arrivals, or in the shape of certain social and industrial arrangements, as regards those already landed, is a fit subject of discussion at the conference this afternoon.

(16 April 1855)

Faith Bandler
WACVIE

from CHAPTER FOUR

Wacvie woke very early. Through the crack in the barrack wall, he could see what appeared to be a white boss's house. He pressed his whole face closer to the wall, fixing one eye to the crack, his short nose flattened so hard against the slab that he felt a splinter pierce its tip.

The dawn had barely broken. The building looked grey. No doubt the new boss was in there asleep. He wondered what kind of man he would be. He could hardly be colder or more cruel than Mr Young. As he dropped back onto the pile of straw on the slab floor, Wacvie nudged Weloa in the ribs and, whispering softly so as not to waken the others, told him what he had just seen.

'Did you not sleep, Wacvie, that you have already seen where we are?'

'Yes, I slept,' Wacvie replied, 'but poorly. I was anxious to see where they've brought us.' He paused. 'Do you think we'll find John here? It's such a long time since he left us. Maybe he's working in that big house.'

'John Mully?' Weloa whispered. 'Yes, he could be here.' He raised himself and crept to the hole in the slab joints, so that he too could see the big, grey house. As he gazed at it, he saw a sudden belch of smoke rising from its roof. This was followed swiftly by a sharp whistling sound, like a bird he had once heard, but this one was so loud and penetrating that he pulled his face away from the wall, shocked by its impact. At the same time the whole barrack of bodies jolted upright from the straw. A wide door was pushed open from the outside. A voice was shouting: 'Get up, and get moving!'

Wacvie was astonished when he saw inside the 'big house'. Such big iron pots! He had been surprised when he had first seen a cast-iron camp oven, but that was very small compared with these. Sometimes the black pots were completely covered with white clouds of smoke, which the white devils called steam. The pots could not be seen until heavy crushers released a flow of sickly yellow juice, which danced around in the pots until it was thick. Then it was left to cool.

The task they hated most was putting the cooled mixture into the boxes with narrow bottoms and wide tops. These were difficult to balance so there were times, especially towards the end of the long days when they were tired, when the boxes would overbalance. Then the white devils would start screaming.

Wacvie would watch the thick and almost black syrup pour from the bottom of the boxes into the drums, leaving behind the residue of golden sugar. He remembered the sugar cane on Ambrym, its juice enriched by the dark volcanic soil. The soil was never destroyed by fire so it retained the moisture and humus so beneficial to the juice. There the cane was just a stalk that you broke off when you felt like having a cool, sweet drink. Like all other fruit, it was only picked or cut when needed. Never hoarded and changed into this.

In Queensland the rain was like the rain in Ambrym; often, when the morning was finished, heavy rain would fall. In the hot season, it was regular. Almost every afternoon, when the sun was still high, big drops fell. The people called this 'sunshowers'. It was just the kind of rain that the cane liked, but for the people it was not pleasant because they had to cover their bodies with cloth which held the water. Even if the sun shone, during the rain or afterwards, their bodies became cold. They began to cough and feel pain in their backs and legs. Sometimes their chests would ache.

In the very wet season, many died. The trenches had to be dug more deeply to hold more bodies. Tears ran down the people's brown cheeks as they dug the black soil. Lifting the lifeless bodies of their friends, they thought of the times when death had come to someone in their island village. Here there was no coming together for the farewell feasts, no unashamed wailing. At night they would speak together, recalling that back home anyone who died was almost always great in years. Yearning for freedom, they would sleep.

Wacvie was thinking a lot about freedom. One Sunday morning, as he sat on a wooden stool outside their quarters, greasing the hard boots which made his feet so sore, Weloa joined him.

'Weloa,' said Wacvie, dipping his fingers into the grease that was meant to soften the horses' harnesses, 'Weloa, perhaps after our service today, we will look for another place to work.'

'How?' asked Weloa. 'You know we can't work for another man because our second three years is not yet finished.'

'Who should care?' Wacvie retorted irritably. 'Why should we continue to let these people control us? Only people who can't look after themselves should be controlled. We have always managed without these white people. They brought us here against our wishes. And the white men who drive us are paid money but we are not paid. We should be working for ourselves as we did at home.'

'But we don't own any of this ground,' argued Weloa. 'How could we plant bananas and breadfruit for ourselves?'

Wacvie smeared more grease over the tough boot. 'Since they took us away from our land, then they should give us some of theirs.'

'We would have to pay them money for it,' Weloa insisted, starting to grease his own hard boots. 'To do that, we would need them to pay us money for our work.'

For some time now, having learned the importance of this money in the white man's world, they had been asking for payment. If only they could get it, then they would be able to save it up and buy their own land, they thought.

'We must ask them again,' said Wacvie.

Weloa agreed. It would be good to plant their own yams, taros and bananas. Perhaps too they could try growing some of these new fruits, like the one with the thick, yellow prickly peel, called pineapple, or the one that grew creeping over other trees and had a purple fruit called passion-fruit.

Wacvie was restless. Weloa thought it best to turn his thoughts to the church service about to begin.

'Who do you think will preach to us this morning?'

'Reverend McKennon,' Wacvie replied, disinterested, his thoughts still on more important matters.

'Shall we have a chance to select some of the hymns for the service?' Weloa persisted, but his friend did not reply.

For days Wacvie was preoccupied, his mind searching for a plan that would bring them freedom. He had already confronted one of the white mill henchmen, suggesting that money should be paid to him and his kin, but he had been brushed aside with a curse. What was needed was a plan that could not be thwarted by the mill masters' underlings, a plan to terminate this forced obedience, this repressive restriction to unfettered freedom. It was unreasonable. They should be able to choose their own way to live, to work and to worship. This exploitation and neglect of their physical needs must end. Time and again he asked himself: why? Why should they have to obey without right even to question? What was the reason for pouring the sweet cane juice into big bronze vats until it turned into that ugly brown sticky stuff which smelt bad and tasted bitter?

Even his body ached for freedom. He longed to plunge into cool waters and swim. Why should he be rushed every morning into the mill with no time even to greet his fellows? If only they were allowed to hold their festivals, to sing together and to use their feet to stamp out the beats of their drums! To be really together, joyful or sad, to be able to pick the fruit from the trees or the vegetables from the soil, to make a fire in the evening or to listen to children telling stories—stories of the tree spirits! Oh, why couldn't they be allowed to go and find their countrymen at other plantations, and to have celebrations with them?

But no, they could not go where they chose. They could not even wear what they chose. The women in those shapeless mother-hubbards, and the men harnessed in cloth trousers! Why, the people had almost forgotten the freedom of nakedness, and beads, and lava-lavas. Almost forgotten was the taste of fresh fish off the spear, cooked on hot stones over earth ovens! Fish with the faint flavour of bananas from being wrapped in their leaves, its flesh permeated with delicious coconut milk! And the brilliant-coloured flowers gracing the feast spread on the ground! Where was the deep black sky everlastingly lit by millions of bright stars? Why must man-made sheet iron separate them from the night skies? Once their days had been filled with all the things they needed—their ceremonies, fishing, canoeing; they had known tenderness and love for each other, compassion and respect for the aged, courage for their swift battles, and their life had been nourished by the telling of stories—stories of cyclones, storms and earthquakes, of fires and famines, stories of the imagined devil, the lesep-sep, and of the great skill of the old canoe makers...

And now! Wacvie realised that there was a feeling of ominous expectation. It seemed that the rising mill whistle sounded louder, that it was being blown a few minutes before dawn broke. The overseers were shouting more as they gave their orders and, as they held the whips more firmly in their fat hands, their knuckles were redder. Nervously they prodded the workers to hasten their walk to the mill. Those who slackened were whipped. Any who were ill or too tired were beaten that much more. The people sensed that the brutality of the white guards was being sharpened by some unknown power that was increasing their nervousness.

The megass hands were made to turn the layers more frequently. The need to dry it seemed urgent. Normally it took a day and a night to get it sufficiently dry for fuel. Now it must be dried in a day, so more turning was required. It was heavy to lift because of its moisture and it was getting too much for the yard space available. Drying was monotonous and heavy work.

'Work harder!' the white devils shouted and the brown men stretched and bent their lithe bodies, swinging the heavy spreaders with a rhythm like angry ocean waves. When it rained, all hands had to rush to the drying yard and rake the precious megass under cover. The men found themselves putting Jesus to the test, silently praying for the rain to hold off.

They worked, their breathing heavy, their legs and arms aching. As mornings dissolved into afternoons, tempers frayed and the white devils threatened more violence. Why all this extra effort for more megass to be dried? Why the need for so much work to be done in one day?

Morning, then but a few minutes to eat the saltless damper and stinking half-cooked meat, then afternoon. With the beginning of evening they were working, working the megass that made the fires to heat the water that made the steam. Steam, sugar cane and megass. It was all so much trouble and time. Yes, and sadness.

Even night did not bring peace. The women talked about the whisperings of the white women in the houses. Too tired to sleep, they talked through the night. Why this restlessness, some of the men asked. 'Big men are coming,' one of the women said, 'coming to the town and the mill, coming from places named Brisbane and Sydney.'

When Wacvie heard this, he said to Weloa: 'Look, why should we carry this load? We're not getting any money and we're working harder. We are now starting work at five o'clock in the morning,' he continued, with his new knowledge of time, 'and finishing at half-past six at night. I have heard of a better place in Queensland. They call it Maryborough. Perhaps we can find out how far away it is. If it is not too far, then we must help our people to get there.'

If only his family could go to this place, Maryborough, Weloa thought. 'Now that Emcon and our little girl are here, could I take them to this new place?' he asked Wacvie.

'If we go now to Maryborough,' Wacvie repled, 'we would have to leave too many women and children. Since they left Young's place, they have better food, so they are getting stronger. But the white devils are not going

to kill us and we must not let them kill any more of our women and
children.'

(1977)

Paul Wenz
from DIARY OF A NEW CHUM

ADVICE TO NEW CHUMS

I consider I know enough by this time to give New Chums a few tips
which may be useful:—

1. Try to keep an angelic temper and a live imagination, for you will
have to see jokes.
2. Don't be too sensitive, and don't take literally all you are told. You
will be called at times all sorts of names except your own. You will be
presented with adjectives you never met before. It is only their way of
expressing themselves.
3. Remember how to hold your gun. Don't forget that a stockwhip and
an axe are always loaded.
4. When you give them a hand in the sheep yards don't split the mob
unless you can't help it. Don't light your pipe in front of the gate when
they are trying to get 1500 wild wethers through it.
5. Don't pat horses on the nose when they are tied up to a post. It
means as a rule a broken bridle and a lot more besides.
6. Learn the pedigree of Carbine by heart. It will help you a lot.
7. When you hear a snake yarn, multiply the breadth by the length and
divide by ten. Same calculation applies to Murray cods.
8. Don't try to make them believe that we, too, have sunsets in Europe.
9. Don't dare to say that their Southern Cross is crooked.
10. Don't resent being called a New Chum. Captain Cook was a New
Chum when he landed in Australia. Most of the best men in this country
were New Chums—Ned Kelly is an exception; he was born in Australia.

(1908)

Judah Waten
from ALIEN SON

MAKING A LIVING

Another journey. But this time we went on holidays. Well, not exactly
holidays, but something near enough.

It was the summer after I had my thirteenth birthday and Father said, 'If
we don't get out of the city for a while we'll starve like dogs in an
orphanage.'

Father's affairs were going badly again; bottle dealing was worse than
bad, nobody bought bottles and no one had any to sell. Times were hard.

So Father had become a horse-dealer. He bought a few horses and all
the would-be buyers yawned, scratched themselves, looked sideways and
said, 'Things are bad. We'll do with the horses we've got.'

And those buyers who could afford more horses as soon as they set eyes on Father's decided to go in for motor-cars instead. When Father took up horse-dealing motor-cars were becoming popular. Honestly, evil fortune followed Father like a faithful hound.

Father sat about the house for days and puzzled the whole matter out. He had an idea. He would take several of his horses to the outskirts of the city and let them loose—they would finish up in a municipal pound. But his two best-looking horses could still be put to some use. He would take them to a holiday resort where he would hire them out as riding hacks to timid holiday-makers.

The more Father thought of his plan the more intoxicated he became with it and he was convinced that the timid holiday-makers were waiting for just these two horses. And of course there were many other things Father could do at the holiday resort.

Thus was born a second idea to Father. He would drive his cart round the hills buying rabbit skins and hides and tallow and what-not, while I would be responsible for the two horses, hiring them out at the guest-houses, the hotels, and in the street. After all, why shouldn't I help in making a living for the family? I was no longer a child. I had a tongue and a pair of hands. What harm would it do my mind? Father asked with passion.

Without looking at him Mother replied, 'I always said our son would have to struggle here just as I did back home. I knew it from the first day we landed in this golden kingdom.'

But despite Mother's words I was elated that it fell to me to help the family in such hard times. I could see no reason for her unhappy reflections. I felt like the other boys in the street and all of them had to do something for their families. Some of them had begun to work years ago.

Father's plan mapped out, every detail well cared for, off we went to Berrigullen, the fashionable holiday place in the hills. In such a resort Father said even if we only ate dry bread it would still be a holiday for all of us. Why, even the air in Berrigullen was noted for its wonders—it was said that the old became young, the sick healthy, and more besides. That was why so many important people in our community were beginning to go there for their holidays.

We locked up our house and loaded the spring-cart with blankets, pots and pans, saddles, spare sets of harness, three black hens, a white rooster and a part fox-terrier that, properly speaking, belonged to the whole street. The two horses that for a change were going to help feed us were tied by halters to the back of the cart.

The street turned out to see us off. Friends, acquaintances, neighbours came out of their houses as though to watch a funeral or a brawl. Some of them stood on their verandahs and waved to us. And as there were many men out of work at the time, a large crowd of people of all ages stood round the cart, laughing, gossiping, giving friendly advice, and wishing us good fortune.

It was a warm send-off, but Father was filled with gloom and his pale-blue eyes were dull and sad as though with pain. He had hardly spoken a word. He nodded his head absent-mindedly and stared unseeingly at the neighbourly men and women and barefooted children.

'Ah, these accursed journeys,' he suddenly whispered to me, 'and for what?'

His voice was filled with such sorrow that it seemed to me Father had suddenly seen through all his dreams and schemes and his heart had emptied at the prospect before him at the end of this new journey. I understood then how much Father had always hated moving.

I felt with him and I was fretful at leaving the neighbourhood. As we drove off and I waved to my companions I envied each one of them. There were Tom and Joe and Benny, and I thought of everything they would do this day—the stories they would tell each other, the games they would play, the walks through city lanes and streets.

My peevishness grew as we jogged through miles and miles of suburbs. Everywhere bystanders gazed in our direction. What was it they were looking at? Was it that the harness on the chestnut drawing our cart was threadbare and held together with wire and string, and that tufts of yellow straw stuck out of the collar? Or was it because one wheel of the cart wobbled alarmingly?

I knew it was neither. The people were looking at us. That was nothing new, for we were frequently stared at when we drove through suburban streets. But now it was different. Everything affronted me—the handsome respectable houses, the broad clean streets, the complacent, healthy faces of the people so different from those we had left behind. My irritation grew into anger when a group of men and women looked at us a little too long. There was something ironical about their gaze and one woman pointed with amusement to the two horses jogging resignedly behind the cart.

'What are you staring at?' I shouted at them. Then I picked up an empty bottle from the floor of the cart and I threw it at the group where it crashed into splinters at their feet.

Mother, startled out of her reverie, glanced in the direction of the people gesticulating at us. Then she looked at me angrily.

'Why did you behave like a hooligan?' she demanded.

I was stubbornly silent and she repeated her question. I refused to speak; it would have been impossible to explain why I had thrown the bottle. If I could have done so she might have understood and perhaps she would have ceased her bitter and ironical musings.

She said, 'You remain silent. I think I understand why. We hardly speak a common language any more. You belong to one world, I belong to another. With your new ways you have almost become a stranger to me.' And then she asked in her gentlest voice, 'Please tell me one thing—where did you acquire the cultured habit of throwing bottles at strangers?'

She went on and on but Father said nothing. He was absorbed in his own thoughts but for some reason I felt that he secretly understood my behaviour. Perhaps I had in some way expressed his feelings, too.

We were all silent when we drove into the main street of Berrigullen. We were all too moody and far away to take in the beauty of the surroundings. The township was like a garden with its rows of poplars and elms and the fruit-trees that hung over fences and hedges. On all sides in the distance tier upon tier of hills rent the fading blue sky and walled in Berrigullen.

It was not in the main street or on the heights that we lived. We had a furnished cottage in a hollow below the township where seldom any traffic passed; the sound of voices in that neighbourhood almost created a sensation.

There was an unfriendly look about our new house and at night the paper pasted over the chinks of the windows sounded in the breeze like the patter of frightened feet. It was the last cottage on the road and the bush came right up to the side fence and the back-yard was overgrown with bracken. Half a mile down the road a row of cottages similar to ours stood close to each other. There were no holiday-makers in those dwellings. There lived old-age pensioners, rabbit trappers, and fruit pickers.

I had no time to explore round the houses on our road, I had work to do. The day after we arrived in Berrigullen I was to take the two horses into the township, stand near the hotel or one of the guest-houses, preferably the biggest and best and get clients, the timid holiday-makers who were waiting for our two mounts. Father explained everything, what I was to say and how I was to say it. Apparently satisfied that I should be successful, he drove away into the hills.

Saddled and ready to be ridden, the horses ambled behind me up the steep track towards the main street. From a distance some boys called to me but I ignored them. How were they to know that I was on a most important mission? It was the first time I had taken any part in the making of a living for the family and nothing would divert me. I dreamt of the money I would bring home. In my mind I counted my earnings over and over again. I could see the coins stacked on the kitchen table so that even Mother would have to admit that she was wrong and that Father was not foolish in sending me to hire out the horses. I was filled with pride and everything round me quickened my elated feelings—the summer morning, the sweet scent of gums, the hum of insects, the cries of birds, the hot, still air. How wonderful everything seemed just then!

But as soon as I was in the main street my elation began to ebb and I saw my task in a more sombre light. Slyly fear and shame had crept into me. Where would I start? I looked round at the large houses with trees and flower bushes hiding from sight the doors and windows, and I wondered if they were the guest-houses from which I should get my customers. To make matters worse, all the words Father had carefully impressed on me vanished from my mind. I had forgotten what to say and what to do.

In despair I walked the horses up the street and then back again. The two steeds were resigned to their fate and their heads drooped in philosophical contemplation, like wise parrots in a cage.

I stopped when children's voices floated towards me from the lawn of a long, rambling house that I rightly believed must be a fashionable guest-house. In a moment I made up my mind, walked over to the gate and tied the horses to a telegraph post. Behind the low fence boys and girls played, while well-dressed men and women sat on garden benches under trees, some reading, others just chatting.

I scanned the faces of the men and women and I recognized Mr Frumkin and his wife. They were well known to me, particularly Mr Frumkin, with whom Father had for so long dealt. He was now the leading dealer in the bottle business while his wife was a notable in various ladies' societies in our community. They sat stiffly and silently and neither of them smiled or waved back to me when I shouted cheerfully, 'Hullo, Mr and Mrs Frumkin!'

And, imagining that they might be interested in my doings, I called again, 'I've got two horses here I want to hire out.'

They shifted their gaze and stared down at their feet.

For a moment I was bewildered, but the snub from the Frumkins in some unexpected way gave me strength and entirely restored my faded confidence. I thought of how I could increase their discomfiture and then I remembered the purpose for which I was outside the gate of the guest-house.

Swaggering slightly I called to the guests on the garden seats, 'Who wants to hire a good horse? Only a bob an hour.'

Nobody rose from his seat. Here and there an amused smile, a haughty stare; even the children went on with their playing. Several boys made as though to come over to me but they were stopped by the grown-ups.

I continued to call my wares as though at the market. Even there one had to shout and shout to attract customers—sooner or later someone must come over.

Without a glance in my direction the Frumkin couple left their seats and made for the veranda of the guest-house. I called insolently to Mr Frumkin. 'What about you, Mr Frumkin? The horse's back is wide enough for your behind.'

There were a few sniggers and, needing little encouragement, I continued to shout at the Frumkin couple until they disappeared into the house. Then I went on again with my business cries. Soon a man came up to the gate and he stared at me severely.

I looked him up and down and said, 'You can have your pick. Only a bob an hour.'

His face went crimson.

'Clear out,' he said angrily. 'Nobody wants your horses. Get!' he added furiously.

I edged back slowly towards the horses.

'What if I don't get?' I said.

'I'll see that you do,' he said menacingly.

'Well, I'm not going for you, anyway,' I said and turned to the guests, who had risen from their seats at the commotion.

'Who wants to hire a good horse? Only a bob an hour!' I shouted at them and out of the corner of my eye I watched the menacing gentleman.

He made as though to open the gate, and with a sudden onrush of rage, I stooped down and picked up a handful of stones. I held them in my clenched fist, ready to throw the lot at him should he but go past the gate. He stared intently at me as though to judge how serious my intentions were. He must have been quite satisfied, for he turned abruptly on his heels and walked back to the guests who were strolling towards the gate. He said something to them as he passed and they, like sheep, followed him until they all disappeared. Only a few boys remained on the lawn playing with a bat and ball.

I put my thumb to my nose and shouted derisively at them. Then, with exaggerated slowness I took the horses down the road again. There and then I decided I would have nothing more to do with guest-houses. As I passed one after another it seemed to me they were all the same, with their stiff lines and their hard, suspicious exteriors. Perhaps I attributed to the buildings something that rightly belonged to the people sitting on the well-kept lawns.

The horses stopped to drink from a trough near the hotel. The air was hot and still in the broad, sleepy road. Across the way a store rested drowsily in the shade of two poplars and the creek behind murmured gently. Overhead green and red and yellow rosellas flew with a faint hissing noise from tree to tree.

I tethered the horses to posts and walked to the veranda of the hotel. Under the open windows of the bar-room two old men sat without speaking to each other. They looked as if they were part of the wooden bench and from their ancient, shiny serge suits I guessed they were natives of the township and not holiday-makers.

One of them was idly drawing his stick over the floor and both looked up at me with expectant eyes, as though glad of any diversion.

'Do you think anyone in the hotel wants to hire a horse—cheap?' I asked.

'Well, I don't know, sonny,' one of them said. 'There's a riding school here and, besides, the hotel's got a few hacks.'

'My horses would be as good as the others,' I said.

'I wouldn't know,' the old man replied and winked slyly at his companion.

He, with a faint grin wrinkling his face, screwed up his eyes and with the air of an expert gazed at the two horses.

'They look good horses to me,' he said. 'Not as young as they used to be and a bit short of wind, but I can see they've been good workers.'

I walked with firm steps into the bar, believing my horses vouched for by the two old men, and I spoke with a full heart to the men standing at the damp, glistening counter.

'I've got the best two horses in Berrigullen for hire. Wonderful to ride and only a bob an hour.'

The drinkers turned around slowly and looked at me with lazy eyes. One of them said, 'We've got no time for riding.'

There was laughter at his words and another man said, 'Come and have a drink, lad. Lemonade, eh?'

I stood up against the counter and imitating the men I held my glass of lemonade as jauntily as they held their beer. I pushed my cap back and sipped my drink slowly as I looked around the bar. On the walls and above the shelves laden with bottles there were framed pictures of horses, boxers, and footballers. Some of them were familiar to me, others were heroes of before my time.

I could make neither head nor tail of the conversation that continued around me. There were jokes about a party that had been held in the hotel the night before. And there was talk about hang-overs and how they should be cured. I was afraid to finish my lemonade, thinking that so long as I was in the bar I still had a chance of finding at least one customer.

I turned to the man who had bought me the lemonade.

I said, 'Wouldn't you like a ride on one of the horses?'

He looked at me humorously and then put a shilling in my hand. Without a word he joined in the conversation again.

I gazed sheepishly at the shilling until the barman leaned over and, tapping me on the shoulder, pointed his thumb at the door. I hastily gulped the rest of my drink and walked out into the sunlight, my face red with the knowledge that the barman had thought I was a beggar. I was ashamed to look the two old men in the face.

'No luck?' one of them asked sympathetically.

The other said, 'These blokes in there never ride horses. They spend all their time drinking. You went to the wrong place, sonny.'

'You'll never make anything out of those blokes,' the first old man said. 'They're takers, not givers.'

I suppose the old men knew all about the holiday-makers in the hotel for they sat on the wooden bench all day. But it didn't console me and my heart was heavy when I went back to the horses and led them across the road so that they could nibble at the tufts of grass under the trees.

I blindly reproached myself with my failure and I felt guilty about my behaviour at the guest-house. I had one shilling to show for all my effort and I clutched it as if afraid that even it might fly away. Sitting on the edge of the road I stared disconsolately ahead. Only the two old men were to be seen and they looked at me with faraway eyes as if constantly turning over their memories. Silence lay over the township and the sun shone down on the rust red gravel with a fiery brilliance.

I rose from the ground to take my charges back home. The two sleepy, timid horses were stuck to me like a tail and they were my responsibility until I could return them to Father.

The main street, the guest-houses, the hotel disappeared from my sight as we descended the steep track. Nothing could now elate me. Around me was just lonely bush, grey trees and blackberry-bushes encroaching on both sides of the track. Behind the horses dust rose in tiny clouds and rolled away towards the trees. I felt my face. It was covered with dust and my fingers were black and sticky.

When I reached the bottom of the hill near our house I stopped by a tree and watched the horses nibble happily at the dry brown leaves on the ground. I couldn't face my mother just yet. I had suddenly become afraid of her intent searching eyes, her bitter words. Something had happened to me this day that would want thinking out. For the first time I had stepped out into the world and I had touched with my own hands the hard kernel of life, getting a living.

(1952)

Peter Skrzynecki
FELIKS SKRZYNECKI

My gentle father
Kept pace only with the Joneses
Of his own mind's making—
Loved his garden like an only child,
Spent years walking its perimeter   5
From sunrise to sleep.
Alert, brisk and silent,
He swept its paths
Ten times around the world.

Hands darkened   10
From cement, fingers with cracks
Like the sods he broke,
I often wondered how he existed
On five or six hours' sleep each night—
Why his arms didn't fall off   15
From the soil he turned
And tobacco he rolled.

His Polish friends
Always shook hands too violently,
I thought . . . *Feliks Skrzynecki*,   20
That formal address
I never got used to.
Talking, they reminisced
About farms where paddocks flowered
With corn and wheat,   25
Horses they bred, pigs
They were skilled in slaughtering.
Five years of forced labour in Germany
Did not dull the softness of his blue eyes.

I never once heard   30
Him complain of work, the weather
Or pain. When twice
They dug cancer out of his foot,
His comment was: 'but I'm alive'.

Growing older, I   35
Remember words he taught me,
Remnants of a language
I inherited unknowingly—
The curse that damned
A crew-cut, grey-haired   40
Department clerk
Who asked me in dancing-bear grunts:
'Did your father ever attempt to learn English?'

On the back steps of his house,
Bordered by golden cypress,   45
Lawns—geraniums younger
Than both parents,
My father sits out the evening
With his dog, smoking,
Watching stars and street lights come on,   50
Happy as I have never been.

At thirteen,
Stumbling over tenses in Caesar's *Gallic War*,
I forgot my first Polish word.
He repeated it so I never forgot.   55
After that, like a dumb prophet,

Watched me pegging my tents
Further and further south of Hadrian's Wall.

(1975)

Silvana Gardner
OLD GIRL

The French boy speaks fluent English,
the Aboriginal girl knows the latest trends,
the German doesn't wear leather any more
and the melting pot is boiling dry
of colonial British, skimming Australians   5
to the surface.
   I couldn't speak at all,
know nothing except to smile 'yes'
when my food was ridiculed.

Now I'm the old girl, the absentee
who's come back to teach what she's learnt,   10
that strange philosophy of art
as a survival kit in the same classroom
I spun steel cocoons round my eyes, ears,
arms, legs to become invisible to kindness
in the tunnel of changes growing dimmer   15
around a migrant child who ran away
in school hours to be captured
and recaptured for today's roll call of 'Present!
     Here!
     Yes!'

(1981)

Lily Brett
OUR HOUSE

In
our
shiny
square house

with
rose bushes
and
fig trees

and
handmade
up to date

tables
and
couches

you
were
never alone

a
bedraggled
pack

of
scrappy
people

lived
with
us

they
were joined
sometimes

by
people
you hardly remembered

and
I'd
never seen

at
celebrations
they sang
and danced

when
things went wrong
they jostled
to push
their point of view

on
anniversaries
of bad memories
they wept
and wailed

nothing
passed
their
comment

they
were
delighted

by technology

hadn't
lived
to see
everywhere telephones
and television

and
the food
the food
was riveting

it
was hard
to invite
people
home

to
such
a
crowded
house.

(1986)

David Martin
LETTER TO A FRIEND IN ISRAEL

You write the *khamsin* blows from Sinai
Fierce as a storm at sea. The land is brown;
You long to leave the desert for a day
To see again the hills of Galilee,
Green fields and settled country.   5
Yes, I recall the Negev after drought,
The loneliness, shirt sticking to the shoulder,
The water tower glaring at the sky,
The Arab sand that drifts under the door
Like the eighth plague of Egypt.   10

Dick's gone from the kibbutz and April too,
But you could no more think of living where
The taxis honk than Father Abraham
Could think of leaving Sarah, though at times
You dream of Haifa and Jerusalem   15
As David dreamt of naked Bathsheba.

Remember me to pioneerhood, Sam,
And to the tea-urn in the dining hall
Around which watchmen gather in the night
When guard is changed, if guard is changing yet,   20
To the red cactus blossom that the camels eat,

To children singing in the children's house;
Or if by chance you're travelling north, please give
My greetings to the little fish that swim
In the cool water of Beth Alpha's pool—　　　　　　　　　25
Beth Alpha where I had a girl.

What news
Of Melbourne, Sam? Well, Essendon's on top,
Carlton lies second, and a lad's been jailed
Who broke a bottle on the umpire's head.
The wattle's coming out in Ferntree Gully,　　　　　　30
The pubs are coming down in Swanston Street,
And on a fine day, from the Trades Hall roof,
The class struggle can still be clearly seen
Beyond the University where, lately,
The dogs of Patrick White made love off stage.　　　　35

Fondest regards to Mara and yourself:
I'd bridge this chasm if I could, but since
My heart is drying on a laundry hoist
Far from that other Israel of my youth,
You'll understand the problem that we have,　　　　　40
You there, I here...and over us together
The neutral sun, the smiling apostate.

(1964)

Beverley Farmer
MELPO

When I married Magda, Jimmy is thinking, all our family danced. We roasted kids and lambs in our whitewashed oven outside. We drank ouzo and new wine by the demijohn. The whole village was there. My mother had cooked everything. Cheese pies the size of cartwheels, meatballs, *pilafia*...In spring she picked nettles and dandelions and stewed them with rice, for Lent. In autumn she brewed thick jams from our apples and figs and windfall apricots. Tubs of yoghurt and curd cheese sat wrapped all day in blankets by our stove. On feast days an aged hen seethed, tawny and plump, in the pot. Until the Germans came, and then the Civil War.

The day I married Magda, my mother led the line of dancers holding the handkerchief, making her leaps and turns barefoot on the earth of our yard, by the light of kerosene lamps.

When our family planted out tobacco seedlings in the dry fields a long cart-ride from the village, we started at daybreak and rested in the heat of the afternoon under the oak trees at the spring. We ate hard bread, and cheese and olives, and drank spring water. Once when I was small I picked up a tortoise where it lumbered among pale clods of earth. It hissed, spurting hot urine on my hands. I dropped it, then picked it up again. *Mi,* Dimitraki! my old aunts shrieked in their black scarves. Melpo! *E,* Melpo! But my mother lay there with earthen feet, in shade as cold and thick as the spring water, fast asleep. My mother. Melpo...

'Now your mother wants to meet me,' Kerry is saying. 'Why now?'

Kerry looks taut, as if angry, Jimmy thinks; but she is only disconcerted. Flecked with brown, her pale face is blushing. A green glow off the water, wavering up, lights her bronze hair.

'Darling, she didn't say.'

'Well, why do you think she does?'

'She said so.'

'Yes, but why?'

'She didn't say.'

Jimmy, balancing his rod on the warm concrete of the pier, lies back, his head in Kerry's lap, his heavy eyes closed against the falling sun, the swathed still sea.

'You know she wouldn't hear of it before.'

'She asked me your name again and said, "Dimitri, you sure you want to marry this woman? Really marry, in our church?"'

'And what did you say?'

'Kerry.'

'Oh yes.'

'And yes, Mama, really marry.'

'What have you told her about me?'

'Nothing much. Red hair, I said, Australian, not Greek. Divorced, with one son called Ben. A teacher of maths at the same school where I teach Greek and—'

'Did you say anything about the baby?'

'No. Not yet.'

'Well, I'm not showing yet.'

'No.' He hesitates. 'Eleni and Voula have not told her either. I asked them.'

'They *know*?'

'Well, yes. I told *them*, they're my sisters. They said they'd guessed, anyway.'

'Oh, come on.'

'Yes. When they met you at the dance. They like to think they can always tell. They are pleased. A daddy at forty-five, they keep saying. Better late than never. They like you. How about after school on Thursday? Is that all right? Nothing formal. Just in and out.'

'All right.'

'You're blushing.'

'I'm nervous.'

'Try out your Greek on her.'

'I hope you're joking.'

'Me? I never joke.'

'You said she speaks English!'

'She does. She even makes us look ʾwords up for her. She hardly ever speaks Greek now, strangely enough. But very broken English. Nothing like mine. Mine is not bad, after only twenty years here. Would you not agree?'

'For a quiet life, why not?'

Shafts of sunlight are throbbing through the water as outspread fingers do, in fan-shapes.

'She wants to meet you now,' he sighs, 'because she is dying.'

'Oh! You've told her!'

'She wanted to know. I think she knew, anyway. Don't be shocked when you see her. She is wasting away, and her mind wanders. I wish you could have known her when she was young. Her life has been—*martyrio*. *Martyrio*, you know?'

'Martyrdom?'

'Yes. Martyrdom.'

'Because of the War?'

'Oh, yes, the War. Many things. The War was the worst. I was only about eight then. My sisters were too little to help. Our baby brother was sick. We were evacuated from our village. My father was a prisoner. Can you imagine it? His mother, my Yiayia Eleni, minded the little ones. I sold cigarettes, razor blades, *koulouria*—those rolls like quoits with sesame?— on the streets all day. My mother did cleaning, sewing, washing for rich women, to feed us all. But we were starving.'

'Can you remember so far back?'

'Of course. Everything. One night I remember my mother was mending by the kerosene lamp in the warehouse we were living in, in Thessaloniki. My grandmother put her hand on her shoulder.

'"Melpo," she said. "It is time you thought of yourself."

'My mother lifted her red eyes but said nothing.

'"You are young. Your whole life is ahead of you. And what about your children?"

'"Mama," my mother answered. "Don't say this."

'"It is what I would do. He is my own son, my only son. But it is what you will have to do sooner or later. He will manage somehow, he is a man. Think of yourself as a widow, Melpo. The War will go on for years. You are still beautiful. There are good men who will help you. It is not a sin. You have no money, no home, no food. I mean what I am saying."

'"No. Your son believes in me and I have always deserved it. I always will."

'Yiayia shook her scarved head and said nothing more. Her eyelids were wet. My mother went on sewing. My baby brother cried out and I rocked and hushed him back to sleep. When I looked back, my mother was still and sagging over her work, so Yiayia took it away and laid her down to sleep and pulled the flour sack over her. She saw me watching, and hugged me.

'"*Aman, paidaki mou*," she wailed, but quietly. "You must be the man of the family now."

'"I know, Yiayia," I said. "I am already."'

He lies still. Kerry bends over and kisses his brown forehead. 'I'm nervous,' she says again. Her long soft breasts nudge his ears. He feels her shiver. The gold spokes of sun have gone out of the water, leaving it black.

'Don't be.'

'Have we known each other long enough? Can we be sure? Long enough to get married?'

'Well, let me see. How long is it?'

'Ten months. No, eleven.'

'Is it eleven months?' He smiles. 'That sounds enough.'

'What will your mother think?'

'That we should wait. But I don't want to. You don't, do you?'

'No. She might like me, you never know.'

'Yes. Don't be too hard on her, will you, if she is rude? And by the way, better don't wear pants.'

'Pardon?'

'Pants. Trousers? Overalls? "Womans should wear only dresses."'

'Oh God!'

'It is her old age.'

'I don't have a dress. Or a skirt. I don't *own* one.'

'Oh. Well, never mind. Don't look like that. No, listen.' He sits up, agitated. 'Forget I said it. She can hardly see. Glaucoma.'

'What flowers does she like?'

'Oh, anything.'

'Roses?'

'Yes. Fine.'

'Oh God! I hope we come through this!'

'Darling, of course we will.'

'Do you love me?'

'Yes, of course. *Kouragio!*'

She grins back at him, pushing her fingers through the shaggy grey curls at his temples. Shadow lies all over the bay and the far city. High above, a gull hangs and sways, silent, its red legs folded, still deeply sunlit.

Eleni and Voula, exchanging looks, have served Kerry iced water, a dish of tough green figs in syrup, a glass of Marsala, then Turkish coffee. They have exclaimed over her roses and argued amiably about vases. Flustered, Kerry waits, avoiding Jimmy's eyes. She feels gruff and uncouth, awkward. A bell rings three times in another room. '*Pane*, Dimitri,' Eleni hisses. Jimmy bounds away. Kerry grins blindly at the sisters.

When he comes back and leads her to his mother's room, hot behind brown blinds and stinking of disinfectant, she misses the old woman at first among the jumbled laces and tapestries, the grey and golden faces under glass: a skull on a lace pillow, mottled, and tufted with white down. Only her thick eyes move, red-rimmed, loose in their pleated lids.

'Dimitri?' The voice a hoarse chirrup. 'This is Keri?'

'Kerry, yes. I'm glad to meet you, Mrs Yannakopoulou.'

'Good. Thank you for the roses.' Rumpled already, they sag in dim porcelain, mirrored. '*Keri* is candle in our language. *Keri* is wox.'

'Wax, Mama.'

'Yairs. Wox for candle. Dimitri, *agori mou*, put the lamp, I carn see Keri. Now leave us alone. We tok woman to woman.'

The door closes. Yellow folds of her cheeks move. She is slowly smiling.

'*Katse*, Keri, siddown.' Kerry sits in the cane armchair by the bed. 'My daughters they tell me about you.'

'They're very nice.'

'Yairs. They like you. They say good thinks about you. She hev a good heart, this *filenada* of Dzimmy, they say. She love him too much. She good mother for her little boy. Where your husband is, Keri?'

'My ex-husband. In Queensland, as far as I know. We aren't in touch.'

'Why he leave you? He hev another womans?'

'I don't know. He's been gone years.'

'You doan know?'

'No, Mrs Yannakopoulou.'

'You were very yunk.'

'Twenty-two. My son is nine.'

'How old you say?'

'Nine. *Ennea.*'

'Ach! You speak Greek!'

'I'm learning.'

'Yairs. Is very hard lenguage. How old you are, Keri?'

'Thirty.'

'Thirty. Yairs. You too old to learn Greek.'

'Oh, I'll manage. *Echo kouragio.*'

'*Kouragio!* Ah bravo.' A giggle shakes the bedcovers. 'Good. You will need *thet*, if you love Dimitri. He is quiet man. Mysterious. Always he joke. You will need to be stronk. You are, yairs. Not *oraia*, that doesun mutter. How you say?'

'*Oraia*? Beautiful. I know I'm not.'

'Better not. You not uckly. Too *oraia* no good. They fall in love with they own faces. They mek the men jealoust.' A smile bares the wires around her loose eye-teeth. 'Lonk time now Dimitri tellink me: this woman, this Keri, Mama, I want you to meet her. Keri? I say. Her name Kyriaki? No, he say, she Australian woman, she not Greek. Not Greek, Dimitri? I doan want to meet her. But he keep saying please, Mama. Orright, I say. If you thinkink to merry her, orright. Because now I hev not lonk time to live.'

'Oh , Mrs Yannakopoulou—'

'Orright. Is not secret. Everybody know.' Her hand clamps Kerry's arm. 'And before I go on my lonk, my eternity trip, I want to see my boy heppy. That is all I want now. My boy to be heppy.'

'Yes, well—'

'You are also mother. You hev a mother heart. You want what is best for your boy. You do anythink for him?'

'Yes, but—'

'You good woman. Good-heart woman. You hev *kouragio*. So mek me one favour. For *my* boy.'

'What?'

'Tell Dimitri you woan merry him. You love him. Orright. I understend love. Love him. Look after him. Live with him, orright. *Aman.* Doan merry him.'

Kerry pulls her arm away. The lamp casts a wet light on the ravelled cheeks and throat.

'So I'm not good enough.'

'You *good*. I doan say thet. But divorce woman. Not for Dimitri, no. Not for merry.'

'But he's divorced!'

'Doesun mutter. Is different. She *putana*, thet woman. He love her too much, but she go with our neighbour, our enemy. Is shame for all our femily. We come to Australia for new life. Is not Dimitri fault.'

'Yes, I know. He told me.'

'Hwat he tell you?'

'It was twenty *years* ago.'

'His heart *break*. Some children they find them one night together in the pear orchard: Magda with our enemy. They mother tell me. Dimitri was away. When Magda come home, I tok to her, I tell her I know, all the village know. I cry for my poor son. He will kill you, I say. She cry, she scream. She say she waitink baby. I say we want no *bastardo* in our femily. I pack all her *proika*. I say, go and never come back. When he come home, I tell Dimitri.'

The scaled eyes close, wet-rimmed. Kerry sighs.

'He told me about it. My divorce wasn't my fault either. And I don't play around.'

'For Dimitri next time should be only *parthena*. Veergin.'

'Isn't that up to Dimitri?'

'Is up to *you* now. You know thet, Keri. You can say no. Say *wait*.'

'And then what?'

'I know Greek girls of good femilies—'

'No. You tried that before. He told me. He wasn't interested, was he? Why arrange a marriage these days? I love Jimmy. We want to get married fairly soon. I'm going to have a baby. Jimmy's baby.'

'Hwat? You waitink baby?'

'Yes.'

'Hwen?'

'August.'

'August. I understand now.'

'So you see—'

'You should be *shame*!'

'Ashamed of a baby? Why, what's wrong with it? We aren't living in the Dark Ages. Jimmy's very happy. He likes kids. Ben adores him. He'll be a good father.'

'I understand now why he want to merry you. Apo *filotimo*! For honour. Because you trick him.'

'No. That isn't true.'

'You know hwat womans can do if they doan want baby. You know.'

'I *do* want the baby. So does he. You have no right—'

'I hev the right of mother. The right of mother who will die soon! My only livink son! Doan break my heart!'

Kerry, her face hot, pats the writhing yellow hands and stands up.

'I'd better go, Mrs Yannakopoulou. I'm sorry.'

'Wait! Listen to me: I hev money. Yes, I hev. They doan know notnink. Inside the bed.' She claws at the mattress. 'Gold pounds! Hwere they are? Take them. Hev the baby. Leave Dimitri alone. Hwere they are?'

'No, thanks.' Kerry pulls a wry face. 'I'm sorry about all this. And I was hoping you'd like me.'

The old woman is moaning. Her eyes and mouth clamp shut, and she starts shaking. Kerry shuts the door softly on the dense lamplight and goes on tiptoe to the kitchen. It is full of shrill chatter. Saucepans hiss, bouncing their lids, gushing sunlit steam. All over the table sprawl glowing red and green peppers ready to be stuffed. Jimmy, Eleni, Voula, and three children, all suddenly silent, stare with identical eyes like dates; stare up in alarm.

'Someone better go to her. Quickly.'

The sisters hurry off.

'Darling, what's wrong? What happened?'

'Ask your mother. Can you take me home?'

'Of course. Just let's wait till she—'

'It's all right, I'll get a tram. Will you come round later, though, please?'

'Yes, of course. Unless she—'

'Look, if it's all off, fair enough. But you're not to punish me. I *wasn't* hard on her.'

'Oh, Kerry, punish? Why would it be all off?'

The children are gazing open-mouthed.

'She'll tell you.'

'You tell me.'

Kerry shakes her head, reddening.

'You are punishing *me*! Why are you angry?'

'Oh, later!'

The bell rings three times. Jimmy bounds down the passage.

'Mama?' His voice breaks. 'Mama?'

'Leave me alone, all of you. And you, go with your *putana*. Leave me alone.' She struggles to turn to the shadowed wall. '*To fos. Kleis' to fos.*'

He turns off the lamp and ushers his sisters out, though they linger, he knows, whispering behind the door.

'She had to go home.'

'Good!'

'*Min klais, Mamaka.*' He smooths her sodden hair. 'No. Don't cry. Don't cry. No. No.'

'Give me a tablet. No, this ones. Water.' He slips his arm behind her knobbled back as she gulps, flinching. 'Ach. *Pikro einai.* Bitter.'

'Tell me what happened.'

But she is silent. He picks up the photograph on her dresser. It is one of the last photographs of his father. His father is sitting in the doorway, feeding Eleni's two little daughters spoonfuls of bread-and-milk. They coaxed him in baby talk for *paparitsa*. It was his *paparitsa*, not theirs. It was all he could eat by then. A white hen is tiptoeing past them. Wheat was heaped in the long room that year, a great trickling tawny mountain; the barn was too full already of barley and sesame. The best harvest since the War, his father said. Bravo, Dimitri. None of them has seen the hen yet. In the light at the door they are like three shadow puppets on a screen. He alone looks frayed, dim, melting in the air. His death is near. He regrets, Dimitri thinks, that I have had no children. No grandchild of my sowing, no grandson to bear his name. Still, he is smiling.

In the photograph the bread-and-milk bowl is white. In fact it was butter yellow and, catching the light, glowed in his father's hands like a harvest moon.

'Mama?' he says softly.

'*Nai.*'

'Tell me what happened.'

'She can tell you.'

'*Ela. Pes mou.*'

'This Keri. She hev not the right name. She not wox. Wox? She stone. Iron.'

'Why?'

'You want *her*? Hwat for? She not yunk. Not *oraia*. Not Greek. Not rich. For *proika* she hev hwat? A boy. A big boy. She zmok.'

'No.' He grins. 'She doesn't.'

'Australian womans they all zmok. Puff poof. Puff poof.'

'Kerry doesn't.'

'Dimitraki, listen to me. I know you like I know my hand. You my son. You doan love Keri.' She hesitates, then dares: 'Not like you love Magda.'

'Leave Magda out of it.'

'Thet time I save you.'

'Magda is gone. I was too young then. Forget Magda. I love Kerry now.'

'She waitink baby.'

'Yes.'

'Why you doan tok? You should be tell me this, not Keri. Is too big shock.' She sighs. 'If is your baby.'

'It is.'

'How you know? She maybe trick you. Australian womans—'

'Mama, I know.'

'*How* you know? Divorce woman!'

'Mama, I love Kerry. I trust Kerry. I need Kerry. All right?'

'*Thet* is how?' He is silent. 'You engry?'

'No.'

'Yes. You engry with me.'

'No. You will see in August if it is or not.'

'*Aman*, Dimitri,' she moans.

'Enough, Mama, now.'

'Orright, enough. Enough. Merry her, then. I am too tired for fight. Do hwat you want. But you wronk, you know?'

He waits.

'I hope so she hev a boy. For the name, your Baba name. Is good for his name to live. August, *aman*! You think I livink thet long, to see your little boy?'

'Mama, you will.' He squeezes her hand. 'My little girl, maybe. My little Melpo.'

'*Ochi*. If is girl, I doan want the name Melpo.'

'Kerry does.'

'Tell Keri if is girl, she must not call her Melpo.'

'You tell her. Next time she comes.'

'I *never* see her again.'

'Ah, Mamaka.'

'No. Sometime you askink *too* much.'

'You know,' he sighs, 'that if I have a girl, I will call her Melpo.'

'I doan want you to!'

'You do so.'

'*Aman*, Dimitri *mou*. Put me *rodostamo*.'

He tips red rosewater into his palm and sits stroking it over her cheeks and forehead and whimpering throat, the thin loose spotted skin of her forearms.

'Her heart is stone.'

'No. She is strong. Like you, she has had to be.'

'She will control your life, you want thet?'

'I *think* I can get used to it.'

'Well. I done my best. I hope so you woan be sorry, you know?'

'Thank you, Mama.'

He bends and kisses her ruffled cheek. Her eyes close.

'*Ela pio konta*,' she whispers. 'Closer. I have gold pounds inside the bed. Your Aunt Sophia's. Ach, if I had them in the War! The baby died from hunger. Take them, *paidi mou*. Doan tell the girls. Take them for your baby.'

'*Aman*, Mama. You and your gold pounds. You gave them to Magda. You drove her away. And I forgave you. Remember?'

'For your good. For honour.'

But only after years, Mama, he thinks. Bitter years.

'Sleep,' he says.

'I carn. I pain too much. Go and tell Eleni to come. Bring a clean sheet, tell her. When she goes, come back. Sit with me.'

'Can I do anything?'

'Nothink. Maybe Keri waitink you?'

'She will understand.'

'No. Go to her. When I was yunk, I was stronk. My God. Remember? And *oraia* also.'

'I know. There was not a woman like you in all Makedonia. You had a spirit like fire.'

'Hold my hend, Dimitri.'

One day when you are not tired, Mama, he thinks, I must ask you: do you remember the storm, that last summer in the .village, before the War when I was five? You sat on the porch in this cane armchair suckling Eleni. The rain was a grey wall. Hens shot past us slithering in the brown mud. The clouds were slashed by lightning and by spokes of sunlight. Afterwards I led the horse out, fighting to hold his head down, but he tore at the grape-vine, splashing rain in clusters on us all. White-eyed, his dark silver hide shivering, he munched vine leaves. I was angry. You laughed so much, Eleni lost your nipple, and kicked and wailed. Then I laughed too.

Remember how we stood in the river thigh-deep, slipping on bronze rocks. You taught me to catch little fish in my hands. We threaded them on the green stalks of water plants.

(1982)

Hal Porter
HOUSE-GIRL

At night, Tokyo, like all twentieth-century Babylons, can be seen in the sky. The city's daytime monotone—Gippsland-cow-shed-grey—has disintegrated to dazzles and blazing bars of frost and salmon, of saffron, Cape-weed, aquamarine, fuchsia and Mars-orange: colours to lure, to exaggerate, to obscure wattle-and-daub makeshift, and spangle the stench rising to the God of Poverty.

Netted miles of neons and fluorescents, hundreds of paper lanterns gross as niners, thousands of naphtha-flares, millions of sizzling bare bulbs dangling off-handedly on flex—the night-air sucks up these cheap glories and digests them to an achromatic reflection, a phosphorescent flaw in the upper dark, which can be seen for miles. It is then that the restless young, fed-up with the lightless village street, rebellious as they stumble alone along the shrine-tracks or through the camellia-groves, imagine under this distant halo a city like a vast opal, smouldering with fantastic life, and yearn to walk by its luminous walls behind which pulse the shapes of lust and all ecstasy and the future.

One by one the bravest of them, freed by their own defiance, or by domestic calamity or necessity, break the age-old village tradition, wrap all they possess in a square yard of coloured cloth, take some persimmons, and wait blank-faced by the bridge.

Jizo-san, the children's god with a dozen disease-speckled bibs about his plump stone neck, waits there too, as he has for centuries—his time-worn eyes are the only ones to see their departure. The sun is low, shines horizontally through the upreared and tattered lotus leaves, through the wing of a heron hoisting itself from an irrigation-channel. Casting a long warning shadow the bus draws near.

And so, in time, they arrive on the rim of Tokyo. Once it was called Edo, and the flames of its recurring fires the Flowers of Edo. Now the city spreads like a weed far and flat on the plain as though the fire-sprung pods had sprayed seeds farther and farther afield, as though earthquake and typhoon had scattered the multiplying tiled huts farther yet, as though cloudburst Allied bombs had splashed seeds to the very limit to infest the millet and sweet-potato fields with ramshackle factories, slums and sub-urban labyrinths.

Here then, to the rustic young, is the city of desires, and they can descend stiffly into it from the shabby bus and be lost for ever, make a fortune, commit suicide or finish up in the fetid beggars' subway near Ueno Park.

It was somehow thus, orphaned in some one-pig village, too ugly to engage the interest of brothel-suppliers, belonging, I suspect, to the un-touchable Eta sect, but with a thick personal artery of will-to-live traversing her national indifference to death, coarse, squat and neurotic, that Ikuko-san came to Tokyo and by unguessed-at ways to me.

How near her wanderings came to suicide or the Ueno tunnel I do not know; fortune to her would certainly always be the crow flying over; but she was too much of the earth ever to be lost on it. For what reason my unforeseen arrival in Tokyo, and her movements about the city seeking rice and pickled radish to sustain her ugliness, should have intersected I am at loss to say.

All I know is that a mess-sergeant who had a nervous breakdown some days later was able to produce a house-girl for me. Why and how Ikuko-san? I should like, purely for history's sake, to question him. He handed her over with dazed relief—the conjurer who finds in his hand griffin instead of rabbit. Japanese girls are very plain; she was by many points the plainest. The sergeant walked away like Oates; I never saw him again. Ikuko-san and I faced each other; she dropped a broken-winged paper sunshade and giggled repulsively. I picked it up for her, and a year of life together began.

From before six in the morning, before the shutters of the noodle-shops, curio-dealers and vegetable-markets are down, before even the bean-curd sellers have set out their trays, the house-girls awake on their threadbare rice-matting floors and buckwheat pillows, rise in the double-shuttered room among the still-sleeping others, crawl from under the mosquito-netting, and dress. They do this imagining jealous liquid glances at their American nylon stockings, English brogues, European tweeds, sweaters of Scotch wool, and solid leather handbags. They draw lips with magazine-famous sticks, clap at the house-god and give it some rice-seeds and a little bowl of chlorinated water, and leave their cell as though it were merely a dream.

They walk actressishly under the iced-water signs, each as if a happy secret lay in her tailored sleeve. They ignore the house-boys reeking of camellia hair-oil and mincing hand-in-hand and, proudly, handmaidens of the Conqueror, approach the artificial, official and hideous luxury of the Occupation Messes in which they work. Arrived elegant, they strip and redress. Now they wear the faded short work-frock that reveals too cruelly the pitiful shoulders, the flat chest, the bandy legs mottled like bamboo. On go the scrubbing-brush-grey clogs of paulownia...

She slips off her clogs in the corridor where they have been making a noise like a Shetland pony, ceases to sing loudly *Samisen Boogie*, opens the door with infinite care, tip-toes in barefoot as though I am dying, whispers:

'Will-come, Porter-san! Wake! Wake! Sivin-oh-clock-fifteen!'

She smiles the pure Japanese smile, radiant (but that need not mean she is happy), and sets my tomato-juice on the bedside table. She turns on the wireless and the electric fan, arranges my dressing-gown, slippers, bathing-and shaving-gear. She does it this morning silently, with an inward look as though the teeth of her mind chewed gristle. She has a slight droop and her mouth droops; she sighs; even her stubby feet contrive to appear distressed. Shall I be brisk, grab my things and hustle out taking no notice...or see what it is *this* time? She is doing something that seems unnecessary to two very small dahlias, one red for the male, one white for the female...does it mean anything?

'Ikuko-san!'

She acts a faint start as though roused from sorrow's lethargy and cannot quite look at me.

'*Hai*!' she says; a minute sound.

'What's the matter?' While waiting for her to enact reluctance-to-discuss-a-certain-topic the wireless plays 'I Can't See You in My Eyes Any More', and I seem to catch my ex-wife's eye from the dressing-table photograph: what was the photographer like at whom she is thrusting that absurdly heart-piercing gaze which still, in times of half-drunken nostalgia, I imagine directed at me? And why do I cart her about the world and stand her up in foreign bedrooms? Is it because she is so beautiful and a sort of diploma of manhood?

Ikuko-san hates her even more than I pretend I do; often I fish her out of strange crannies. So far there have been no pins stuck in her well-covered heart.

'What's the matter, Ikuko-san?'

'Ver-ee not happy.' Her thick-lipped pout makes her really hideous.

'Oh!' I decide to go on with it: 'Why?'

'Momma-san ver-ee sick.'

I do not side-track by inquiring into this loss of orphanship: Momma-san occasionally makes these Lazarus come-backs.

'I'm so sorry,' I say politely.

'*Hai.*' Very flat, this.

'I hope she is better soon.'

Ikuko-san mentally stamps a foot. She flashes a venomous ray at me from her seal-brown eyes. Then, with a dying fall, she accuses me: "Momma-san ver-ee, *ver-ee* poor.'

Ah!

'Cocoa?' I say.

'Thank you, Porter-san.' She is dignified, ladylike, but far from over-joyed, but at least I've started. I can feel her intensely directing my thoughts somewhere. However, there is, this morning, no time for the subtle rites of beggar's ping-pong.

'You tell me what you want, Ikuko-san, and I'll give you a canteen-order.'

Of course, of *course*—Canteen Day. I have forgotten: she is the wife who must remind, on behalf of her own rake-off if for no lesser reason.

She flashes on like a lighthouse; immediately after becomes serious, nervous, confused by visions of what she might scrounge; hoping earnestly not to ask one thing too many and suffer the face-losing humiliation of refusal; hoping most fervently not to stop asking too soon. She watches some section of my face—the treacherous corner of the mouth?—and recites meticulously and too loudly, a trial-and-error pause between each item.

'Cocoa, oh, yiss...canned milk...cak-ee...Aspro...choclit cand-ee...Lux soap...toothpast-ee...salt peanut...'

She falters, becomes pathetic and smaller; my assistance, assent or refusal, is needed. My expressionless face defeats her; moreover, a sleepless night of preparation for this has set the little flame of her mind flickering in exhaustion. I, too, have been watching—a sudden illumination makes me say with despicable magnanimity 'Go on. Whatever you want: OK. Go on, woman.'

Woman! For the first time it has struck me that, since I neither love her nor sleep with her, this necessary begging is painful for her. Indifference makes me careless of the unwritten rules. I see her fear and her woman-hood trying to veil decently what life and greed demand she must do.

Some of these delicacies may go to her own version of a Momma-san, to someone or something she, in her turn, can be magnanimous to. Some she will sell on the black market for a *presento* to me, some useless atrocity costing yen that she needs herself. Some she will arrange with antlike precision in one of the two drawers she has taken over for herself—a drawer for cosmetics, and another for supplies of food for some future drought. Alas, that her sweet tooth gnaws constantly at this future!

When I first found clothes of hers hanging beside mine in the wardrobe I was startled, irritated and had a faint feeling of repulsion: too many years of boarding-school, boarding-house life had given me that careless meticu-lousness that is the bachelor's. It was an intrusion and suggested an intimacy; but it was the custom. And as I looked at the small exquisitely darned kimonos, the couple of schoolgirlish pre-Occupation frocks in which the dye had run like tears, and the much finer attire that had been wheedled from me or given in maudlin pity or...or affection, I think I felt moved; there was certainly pathos and a sub-acid note somewhere.

Along two unbelievably different ways we had come to this temporary companionship—her broad feet had stepped for a short space from the excrement-mud of the rice-fields into a kind of film-setting; those feet would return there taking her back to the Fox Goddess, the moxa-burnings, the medicine of dried snake, the endless destructive nobility of a life of poverty. This was the one holiday between the old life and the old life she would return to with nothing to show except a hundred or so English words, some Australian slang, a taste for Aspros and Players cigarettes, a wardrobe that would wear to threads, and a collection of useless objects—a pair of old nail-scissors, shaving-cream jars, boot-polish tins, Bovril-bottles and worn-out underpants.

And, I suppose, memories of a year or so of—*de facto* motherhood? Sisterhood? Unconsummated wifehood? My room, shoes, sheets, buttons—all her special care, every day; my hangovers, tantrums, selfishness—all hers. I see her too vividly in all sorts of situations: rump in the air walking on her feet and hands to polish the floor with dark-tan shoe-polish; radiant and freshly shaved under a *permanento* one could play like a xylophone; absorbed for hours in a flower-arrangement which offends the Western eye but which one must be gracious about; filling the ash-trays with water; running across the Mess-compound in the snow—a cold-germ mask of unattractive navy-blue tied across her mouth and nose, neatly and slowly making herons, frogs, little boxes out of cunningly folded paper; teaching me the haunting age-old children's song, *Ame, ame*...

My feeling for her generally is one of the deepest pity—an unwise emotion at all times; between man and woman most unwise. Yet, for all my sympathy with her lot and all my attempts to keep on emotional no-man's-land, there are times when control slips, the gears grate:

'I told you, Ikuko-san not to wash my towel every day.'

'*Hai*.'

'That's all very well. You said "*Hai*"; you said yes; but you still wash. Now listen. Understand—no wash tower-u, no wash tower-u...You know...?'

'*Hai*.' She seems bewildered. '*Hai*. No wash Porter-san tower-u.'

I am really irritated, almost angry. She does not flinch outwardly, and her face sets at zero; her hands tremble slightly, that is all. She goes about her tasks: I see her hanging socks under the gingko-tree; I see her picking cosmos in the Mess-garden; I see her doing this and that, but like someone reluctantly hauled back to chores from the grave.

It is not until much later that I can bear her silent comings and goings no more, for they have become huge and portentous; emanations from her distress have made her a giantess. She is polishing one of her *presentos* to me—an appalling cut-glass salad-bowl the blue of a castor-oil bottle.

'Oh, for God's sake, Ikuko-san...'

There is no need for such a tone in my voice, but the situation has taken charge of us both—Australian and Japanese, boss and servant, conqueror and conquered, Church of England and Shinto, man and woman. I do not see her face, but know that a spasm of suffering cuts across it; quickly she wheels and, with a primitive animal movement, goes to the wardrobe and stands behind its half-open door, her back to me. She makes no sound, but the sounds she wrestles with disturb her body, making me aware of the strength of will which so often lends these small bodies the semblance of a physical strength they are far from possessing. I can see the hairless blotched legs quiver as her toes press into the linoleum; her body in its scanty rotten frock now and again shudders violently.

I will not look. I will not be affected. I remain sitting in the arm-chair of rhubarb-red plush and nickel like someone in Act Two; I attempt to read off-handedly, but find I am glaring at the pages. The air between is volted with misery.

Presently, from the wardrobe comes the faint rustle of a paper handkerchief—she is crying. I still make no move. The minutes float out towards the walls and moat of the Imperial Palace outside which firemen in butcher-blue Happee coats are performing marvels at the top of tall ladders.

Now that the first cruel wrestling with her pain is over she has, in the backwash of tears, begun to listen to me not taking notice of her. Human beings, East or West, know a lot of simple things about human beings. She rustles her handkerchief—and again, more loudly, and sniffs designedly. At this stage the thing could stop; she has work to do and cannot remain in the wardrobe; yet the simplicity of coming out neat, without embarrassment, is beyond her. So:

'Porter-san.' Oh, a mere sliver of voice, the voice of a naughty little daughter.

'Yes.'

'You *pisto*?'

'No, I'm not angry.'

'True?'

'Yes, true.' Pause. A Buddhist priest drives the swinging log against the temple gong. 'Ikuko-san.'

'*Hai*?'

'It's all right. You toddle off and get me some soda-water from the bar-boy. Everything's OK.'

In an instant she lands like a grasshopper by the chair, sobbing noisily. It is ultimate disgorgement. She grips my hand in her work-cracked paws.

'Me not happ-ee. Me bad girl.'

'There, there, there—everything's OK.'

'Me bad girl.'

'Come on, now. Wipe your face.'

'Oh, me die...me die...'

'Ikuko-san, soda-water, please.'

'Last night me pray for Porter-san...today bad girl...me die...'

'Soda-water, *please*. And you can ask the bar-boy for a bottle of lolly-water for yourself...'

'*Hai*?'

'Get some lolly-water from Butch...'

'*Hai*!'

She is at the dressing-table; she opens one of her drawers and powders her face, she rakes her hair with the brush with rusted wire teeth, paints her lips. She knocks over my ex-wife's photograph, but remembers not to stand it up. An accident? An expression of power over the cardboard representation of a distant woman? The smile that she turns on me has the beauty and singleness of a child's. Her eyes glitter with the ebb of tears and the dark sparkle of yet another despair hidden within, hidden deep.

'Porter-san!'

'*Hai*!....that is, yes, Ikuko-san.'

'Lolly-water and....and...'

'OK. OK. Candy, too.'

She is gone. I hear her slip into her wooden clogs outside the door and run. She is gone.

She is not anything more than a human being, which is the least of reasons for pity, love, hate or tolerance. She is only a woman in a dream between war and peace. I shall never see her again, although the finger-prints she has left on the windows of my memory are far clearer than those of people I count as necessary to the life I seem to live.

It would be difficult to recognize her again....the blurred face in the group-picture of millions, one of those forms bowed in the stinking rice-flats, in the bath-house queue at six o'clock, jammed in a bucking tram on the Ginza, waiting with endless patience on the benchless underground-railway platform, walking up the steep shrine steps past the dried-squid sellers, crossing the muddy midnight road in the jeep's headlight with a white pinafore and a bowl of shrimps.

Or, years hence, bowed to a semicircle under faggots, a towel tied over her almost hairless head—the old woman of fables, in the maple-mountains, the pheasant-woods, by the sandless shores where the stakes of the oyster-gardens and the cryptomerias of the off-shore island shrine are as black against the sunset as her black sleeves in one of which the pipe is concealed and the tobacco in a Players fifty-tin which someone she can't quite remember used years ago.

(1954)

Ee Tiang Hong
COMING TO

It was a blind corner,
I remember, I couldn't think
to brake somehow, still less in time,
That moment round the bend—
a shock of water, overwhelming sea   5
where should have been a road,
a bridge over the river,
I mean even in flood.

A sensation of floating,
car engine dumb as cork,   10
I must have passed out
as under ether, I guess,
my head just above water,

body vague as sponge, and
below the knees, adrift   15
as slush, at one with.

On *terra firma, Australis*
don't ask me how I got out, Eddy,
and, Bruce, this isn't a suicide note,
Heaven forbid! No sailing   20
to Byzantium, either. Indeed,
thankful just to have survived then
around an edge of consciousness,
new faces, fellow Australian.

And a country woman asking: 25
'Where y' from?'
Her husband stands up tall
by their four-wheel drive,
looks me up and down:
(Jesus! What on earth!)   30
And so, uncertain, 'Perth',
I said, from down under.

(1986)

Ania Walwicz
WOGS

they're not us they're them they're them they are else what you don't know
what you don't know what they think they got their own ways they stick
together you don't know what they're up to you never know with them
you just don't know with them no we didn't ask them to come here they
come and they come there is enough people here already now they crowd
us wogs they give me winter colds they take my jobs they take us they use
us they come here to make their money then they go away they take us
they rip us off landlords they rise rent they take us they work too hard
they take us they use us bosses we work in their factory rich wogs in wog
cars rich jews in rich cars they take us they work so hard we are relaxed
they get too much they own us they take my jobs away from me wogs they
don't look like you or me they look strange they are strange they don't
belong here they are different different skin colour hair they just don't
look right they take us they land on us there isn't enough space for us now
they come they work for less they can work in worse they take anything
they work too hard they want from us we have to look after our own here
not them let them go back where they come from to their own they're
everywhere they get everywhere you can't speak to them why don't you
learn to speak english properly they are not like you or me they're not the
same as everybody they change us is your child educated by an australian?
is it? do you know if? you don't know what they think you don't know
what they can do here they change us they paint their houses blue green
have you seen blue houses who ever heard of that they live too many

together they're too noisy they chatter you don't know what they say they smell funny there's something funny about them strange not like you or me i don't want to see asian tram conductors they are not us not us they're them they're else what you don't know them nobody knows them they stick together they look after one another they don't care about us they're everywhere they're everywhere every day there's more of them we work in their factories they escape here we don't have to take them in this is our home they come we didn't ask them they spoil us they take us for what they can get they're not like us they behave different they're rude they act if they own the place they look wrong too dark too squat too short all wrong ugly too fat women go to fat dark skin monkeys i want to be with my own kind people like me exactly like me they stick out you can't miss them they're everywhere they shout they're noisy they're dirty they put vegetables in their front gardens they eat garlic they shouldn't have come here in the first place they're strangers i want to be with my own kind with my brothers with people like i am there's too many of them here already you don't know how to talk to them they're not clean they annoy me funny names luigi they got their own ways they don't do as you do they're aliens they look wrong they use us they take us they take us for what they can get from us then they go away they're greedy they take our space they not us not our kind they after what they can get they stick together i don't know what they say they don't fit in they dress wrong flashy they don't know our ways they breed and breed they take what little we got what is ours what belongs to us they take ours and ours they're not us

(?1982)

Rosa Cappiello
from OH LUCKY COUNTRY

Five days sick leave a year are not enough but they are better than nothing. After the first three months' service, which is the qualifying period for sick leave entitlement, I ring the factory and tell them I'm sick. I want to enjoy them all at once, as compensation owing to me for years. It wouldn't matter if they fired me afterwards. I go to English classes two nights a week. Please speak English. Won't take notice of you if you don't. Not going this week. There's an Italian ship in port. Lella and I have taken on the task of acting as guides for two kitchen hands. Streets, buildings, restaurants, the bridge, monuments, the unfinished Opera House, museums, cathedrals—preferably with alcoves at the entrance. The odd present. I get a Japanese cigarette lighter. The other one doesn't smoke so we hurry to Circular Quay, to the ship. The second fellow dashes up to ask for a carton of cigarettes and a bottle of liqueur. Ten minutes later we see him walk down the gangplank as if he had a hernia. He rubs his hands together and asks where the toilet is so he can go and take the loot from out of his trousers. We steer him towards the toilets under the station. He comes out with a bottle of Ferro-China, a carton of Muratti cigarettes and a bundle of pornographic comic books which he waves from a distance. Lella makes a face. I don't drink much. The tonic will probably be useful for treating my ulcer. We finish up the evening drinking Ferro-China mixed with coke. In any case I was afraid it would end up like this. She asks if she can stay and sleep on the floor. Her landlords are bastards and make life difficult for her, she can't have men in. But I like to sleep in comfort. I need a big bed all to myself which is impossible when you rent a room with a family. They scarcely give you the bare essentials: a chair, sometimes a small table, a single bed with a mattress full of stains which look like blood or urine, and, if you strike it lucky, a wardrobe and a sink in your room. But I didn't have one and I couldn't let her use my bed. As I was saying, I like to be comfortable when I sleep. Lella says it's all right if she can sleep on the floor. I don't argue with her. She turns off the light.

Towards dawn, I still can't manage to get to sleep. My bedfellow has spread himself out like Christ on the cross, legs wide open, arms flung out, and he snores. Rage rises within me. I'd be capable of committing murder. To calm myself down I breathe deeply, one, two, a hundred breaths, then I start counting sheep. And by the thousandth I'm perched on the edge of the mattress, a foot and a hand on the floor to keep myself from falling. It is an impossible situation. I'm precariously balanced on a bed which is mine, the room is mine, the things around us are mine, just like the glasses and the ashtrays that they used so why the hell do I have to forfeit my well-earned rest? I'm so furious that I bite the pillow. At midday the two men go back to the ship. Lella has a quick snack and says she has to rush off home to prepare her equipment. She's begun to make good money out of her hobby and is augmenting her income by taking photographs at Greek and Cypriot weddings—like the Italians they hire receptions halls, orchestras, singers and masters of ceremony when they marry. She's often the animator, the life of the party, the court jester. She's very much in demand. Writes poems on request for the couple. And strange as it may seem, the verses give rise to admiration and debate among the guests, dull-witted and full after four, five courses irrigated with generous quantities of ethnic wine and local beer. She's the most satisfied person I've met since I emigrated. She'd rise to any occasion. A glib talker and a cynical look in her eyes which stops her from getting involved. 'Want to come?' she asks. No thanks. They pay you to put up with them. Me they don't pay. You scrounge a free meal, hors d'oeuvres and all. But do keep me in mind for the next wedding.

Towards dusk I pass by Helen's place. An unplanned visit but one I felt I had to make since I'm still smarting from the affront in the undertaker's presence. Fancy, giving him the aperitif on the sly. What a turncoat, to treat me so meanly at the smell of a male. I'm not taking this lying down. She must say it openly. I prefer to state things clearly. At least she could have put a notice on the door—'Come back later. I'm busy screwing.' And she's the one who talks about a world with its balls cut off.

I get to the front door at the same time as the girl upstairs and worm my way in like a thief. On the landing there is a cat meowing sadly. The girl pats it, says it belongs to Helen and that it's probably hungry. I'm not interested in the cat. I put my ear to the door and hear muttering. I knock in code. Silence and the angry meowing of the cat reply. I knock again. Nothing. She's in there all right. I try pushing with my shoulder.

Her timid voice asks, 'That you Rosa?'

'Who do you think it is?'

'Would you mind ringing me at the factory tomorrow at one...one o'clock, don't forget...'

In the street I bitterly regret not having gone to the Greek wedding. I don't know where to go. Downtown to look at the shops maybe. At the bus stop I change my mind. Why not visit Sofia on the North Shore? That is if I find her at the same address. She's like the wandering Jew. Persecuted by her jealous boyfriend who comes after her with a knife, she's forced to move from one end of the city to the other. It's because of her I know my way round so well. I snigger. Boyfriend isn't quite the right term. Obsessed by the concept of virginity, even though he's so young. A year younger than Sofia. He invariably brings up the subject of her defloration during copulation and only then, demanding the name and a detailed description of the vandal. For Sofia, although she would gladly tell him all, it is impossible to do so because mother nature gave her that imperfection at birth, rudely deflowering her even before she opened her eyes. And while Nicola beats her she swears again and again that he's been the only one. There's just no way to make him understand the medical explanation. There must be proof and there's no proof of virginal scent. The rose-red pigeon's blood was missing.

I go back on my tracks, hands deep in my pockets. Virile thoughts whirl round in my head. Masculine thoughts also. Since I've started reading in English with the help of a dictionary a beautiful poem has struck me to the marrow of my bones. I almost seem to have become fond of that man Hope who wrote 'The Arabian Desert of the Human Mind'. I associate with the human mind of youth, the one buried in the sand, and I've never seen a nightingale in a tree. Where have all the nightingales gone? They expect to have nightingales just as pigs expect to have their pigsty decorated with roses. They wouldn't even see a nightingale carved in wood. Yes, I confess that I'm guilty of glossing over curses and lies in my frenzy. Lies. Lies. But are they lies? Wait another day before you penetrate this mess, before you prick yourself with the splinters that are there outside. Wait another day before you become shrivelled like the fly in the stiffened cobweb. Wait, wait, before you spit out your livid breath onto the perfumless flowers, onto the tasteless fruit...

When I'm on the northbound train and after two stops the train comes out of the tunnel and clatters over the bridge suspended over an infinite expanse of transparent green water—the ferries full of people passing underneath, the lit-up Luna Park which comes towards us, the islands which seem to float in the distance, the lights in the windows which reflect the waves caught up in the foliage of the trees—it's as if friendly arms open out to welcome me. To take me in, and my hopes as well. As soon as things are fixed up again, that is, as soon as I manage to receive a weekly bonus, if the dwarf allows it, I'll look for a place to hole up in over here.

I get off at Milson's Point, ask the man at the news-stand where I can find the Miami Private Hotel. Ten minutes, climbing up and on the edge of the bay. I immediately get my bearings from the description Sofia has given me. And there it is, rising like a green and white mastodon to dominate the bay, an enormous beehive which stretches beyond the shore and stands directly on the sea. Other spurs stop at the cement wall which acts as a safeguard for the windows virtually on the water's surface. Sofia has found refuge in one of those windows and like a bobbing cork spies out the arrival of Nicola, an event both terrifying and desired. Judging by the name I had pictured something gay, touristic, possibly luxurious. Instead, starting right from the decrepit lobby—without even a coat of paint to alleviate its atmosphere reminiscent of a prison or a witches' cavern—I ask myself what sort of place this idiot has got into. The receptionist seated in her cage behind the round window favours me with a fresh angelic smile. Along the corridor, turn left, and take the stairs. I thank her. I walk along the canyon-like corridor which seems to split the huge building in two, the ceiling is so high. I get the impression of venturing out on the back of a caterpillar with its legs spread out. All the doors are wide open because it's terribly hot and the tenants in shirt sleeves enjoy the ventilation. Neon lights on the damp walls. A sanatorium would have a healthier look about it. Sofia's flat is in the depths of the basement. The spiral staircase is swallowed up in pitch darkness. Two men are climbing up, a woman and a little girl too. I climb down grasping the railing, my eyes wide open, without making way for anyone at all until I can see the bottom. The stairs are steeper at the bottom and finish up in a sort of cave, different from your usual run of the mill cave because it has three doors with rust-encrusted enamel numbers, a sign in the shape of a white hand pointing to the right and a small notice which requests that record-players should not be played too loudly. There is the sound of the sea. From number 103 come bursts of laughter, Sofia's infantile bleating, a snigger which I swear is that bitch Beniamina who with her harsh voice goes on about the faults and sexual activities of people she knows. I'm uncertain whether I should go in or not. Still, since you've come so far, take a chance. Don't tremble with apprehension for the unexpected encounter.

She opens, letting out a little cry of surprise and immediately disappears with a waddling kind of walk. She goes through the first room which is the bedroom, old broken-down furniture which a second-hand dealer wouldn't touch. In the second room the attention of Sofia and Beniamina is centred on two bowls full of rice bubbles and milk and some slices of cheese. They whirl about like a broken grandfather clock numbing the palate in this puppet-like, frothful sharing of their meal when both are short of funds. A pastoral picture, filial, maternal, paternal, biblical, consanguineous, with cheap overtones—it'll give you an idea of the harmony which true friendship still manages to generate in our time.

'Next time, come straight across the park, there's a path. You'll save yourself that horror...terrible, isn't it? But why don't you rent a room here, you'd be near to Sofia,' Beniamina advises me.

'Big deal. I don't want to give offence but what sort of million dollar view do you have from this flea-pit?'

'How much will you give me for the lease of the flat? You could even move in tonight,' says Sofia, rubbing her beautiful hands together.

'You're on the run again.'

'See,' she screams pointing the spoon at Beniamina. 'I told you so. She thinks she knows everything. Becomes suspicious straight off. Look at her, like a bloodhound at sniffing out trouble. I earn my daily bread honestly...'

Beniamina sounds off at this outburst on the subject of honesty. Honesty, a word lent to a wide and disparate variety of situations, otherwise you wouldn't be able to explain why it crops up so many times when we thrash out the differences between me and them. Them, uninterrupted seasons, wheelchairs, deposits of slime, vagrants, bottled-up feelings, thrills blended and mixed in with almonds, nutmeg, cloves, chopped garlic, pure olive oil, random flights that last for ever. But I am a cagey kind of beast, contempt is in my blood, my eyes are shut in solitude.

'I don't understand these hick provincial women,' she says. 'They keep their minds in a muff. Patched-up yokels they are, I avoid them like the plague.' She uses sophisticated phrases taken from *Epoca, Storia, L'Europeo, Look, Live*, and she repeats herself like a broken record. 'Same thing if you meet a man.' Here I've got you. 'They meddle in your affairs and in your vagina. A girl who's got an ounce of sensitivity suffers, is tormented, what an obsession! I've saved up my money, why should I share it with the first con-man to come along, the result of my labours, my sweat? Ah, bugger it, I don't go for the sluttish behaviour of these pricks, they can't fool me. I know what it means to pedal an industrial sewing machine while you're having your period and the heat's at a tropical thirty-six degrees. If I subjugate my soul to the service of a man, in exchange I want at least that he remain European, that he use that finesse to which we have been accustomed for centuries, but they don't even give you your due because by dint of killing themselves with work they've become impotent, and a man incapable of satisfying his girl might just as well go and cut his balls off because he's an enemy of the human race.'

'Good God, in that case ninety-nine per cent would go round without...' says Sofia, with a pout.

'Shut up, you put up with these types. Are we like the Australian women that we should give payment in kind for the privilege of having a little prick next to us? Remember Paolo? Sure you remember him, that bludger who always looked out the window when the conductor came round in the bus and at the pictures always shut up and made like he didn't know what was going on...'

The look on Sofia's face showed she did. 'So? You still going out with him?'

'I've dumped him. A liberated woman, available every night wasn't enough for him. He also wanted her to cook, keep his clothes in order and share the expenses. And for what? For a minute prick and a jet of tepid piss which just tickled.'

'I don't have any problems,' says Sofia.

'Me neither, since I've been going with Carmelo,' says Beniamina, and she gives a list of his sexual abilities just as she would give a list of gastronomic delights. She mutters that his favourite position is an upside down one. And he's Sicilian so he knows all about it. A master of dribbling, feint, defence and attack. He's not mean...that's real nice.

Sofia tells about her experiences. She lists all her exploits on a sheet of paper. They're both with their heads over the table, almost touching. Now and then they whisper and laugh. When she laughs Sofia puts her hand over her mouth. She's beautiful. Men turn to look at her in the street. She should have more luck but she's so stupid and such a stinker. Dangerous. A stupid, jealous and malicious woman who frightens all her friends except Beniamina whom she twists around her little finger and dominates with her cunning.

(1981)

Section E

CULTURAL INTERSECTIONS

Far from being monolithic, the culture of any society is varied, fragmented, and contradictory. That is not to say that any individual within the society or any observer from outside may not try to distinguish characteristic qualities that are complementary and internally consistent. But there is often more interest in and more psychological need to expose the oppositions. As William Blake put it, 'Without Contraries is no progression'.

Dislocation from one's original land, language, companions, or cultural environment is almost certain to bring into view the problem of cultural relativism or the conflicting demands of values and standards. In this Section the problem is considered in every item, sometimes in a quite simple way, sometimes with great intricacy.

David Malouf's novel, *An Imaginary Life*, is presented as if narrated by the Roman poet Publius Ovidius Naso (43 BC–AD 18)—the family name Naso meaning 'with the nose'. It covers the last ten years of Ovid's life, which he spent, exiled by the emperor Augustus ('our beloved leader'), among the semi-barbarous Getae people at Tomis on the shore of the Black Sea. One of the probable reasons for exile was the circulation of the salacious poem, *Ars Amatoria*, containing the suggestion that the portico dedicated by the emperor's sister in memory of her husband Marcellus was a notorious pick-up place. The official imperial culture, extending even to the subjects in the poems of Vergil (particularly the *Eclogues* and *Georgics*), is something that Malouf's Ovid finds stultifying and oppressive. In opposition to the Augustan Age he proclaims that 'I too have created an age,' existing simultaneously with the culture of Augustus: 'It is gay [a deliberate ambiguity], anarchic, ephemeral and it is fun.'

But the impiety of Ovid (for the emperor was regarded as semi-divine) led to his exile, separated from the witty company he loved, separated from the Roman language, separated from his previous self. He finds himself at the beginning of civilisation again, enraptured by the colour and the name of a little wild poppy, excited by a new life, accepting the power of words, and the inevitability of transformation (the theme of his major work, the *Metamorphoses*).

These are themes, of course, germane to white settlers in Australia and to displaced Australian Aborigines. Malouf's novel, though ostensibly set nearly twenty centuries ago and on the other side of the world, constantly makes points applicable to Australia.

The nineteenth-century English visitor to Australia, Richard Howitt, has a more naïve response to nature than Malouf's Ovid. He is concerned to take comfort in the sighting of an English phenomenon in the Australian countryside, and thus to assimilate part of an otherwise alien land to the culture he knows. It is an inward-turning gesture, very familiar in much nineteenth-century writing.

To the writers of the Jindyworobak movement, from the late 1930s to the early 1950s, such an attitude was anathema. Rex Ingamells, the founder of the group and the source of its philosophical ideals, would call it an example of Pseudo-Europeanism. By contrast, the Jindyworobaks wanted to annex or join the culture of white Australians to the culture of the Aboriginal Dreaming. One way of signalling their desire to do this was to use words appropriated (sometimes misappropriated) from Aboriginal languages, chiefly Aranda. *Moorawathimeering* is the Land of the Lost, a place of sanctuary for outcasts; *atninga* is the name given to a so-called vengeance party, charged with the task of administering Aboriginal justice; a *wurly* is a bark or tree-bough shelter; a *wilban* a cave; *tallabilla* an outlaw; *wombalunga* is the verb, to carry; *waitjurk* is murderer; *tchnidna* footprint; *karaman* leader; *wallan darenderong* strong avenger; *lilliri* shadow; *douran-douran* the north wind; and *karaworo* eaglehawk. To an English-speaking reader, the alienation of the outlaw seems to be mirrored by the alienation of the vocabulary, as if the reader were sharing the fate of the outcast.

Ingamells was the only major Jindyworobak to carry diction to such doctrinaire lengths. Roland Robinson's 'I had no human speech', though perhaps a little insistent in its use of unmistakably Australian descriptive diction, expresses the common Romantic theme of the poet's dumbness and inadequacy before the beauty and mystery of nature.

The Turkish-born Gün Gencer contrasts customs, beliefs and moods in the region of Anatolia and the city of Konya with those in Australia. This is perhaps the most evenly balanced of all the items in this Section in its responsiveness to two different cultures. It does not concern itself overtly with their intersection, but by implication anyone who has experienced both must be faced with the problems of conflicting demands.

Antigone Kefala's poem is a lament for the loss of past existence after years have passed in a foreign or newly-adopted country. The experience is even more poignant because the observers, through lack of experience, cannot share in the dimly-grasped recollection that struggles through into the alienated mind.

Dimitris Tsaloumas' poem is about an all-too-vividly recalled memory. The poem had its origin in the *coup d'état* effected in Greece by the Colonels in 1967. On Tsaloumas' home island of Leros, five thousand political prisoners were interned behind barbed wire. The poem is a lament for the feeling of shame and impotence experienced by someone who hears the news of a prisoner's arrest in a far-off country (Australia), a feeling of implication and blood-guiltiness at having deserted the politics of one's homeland.

II O's 'Schizophrenia' presents the struggle of the younger generation to sympathise with the culture and customs of one who has migrated from Europe, in this case Greece, the attitude balancing respect and amusement.

The incomprehension of one culture for another is emphasised in Louis Nowra's play *The Golden Age*. It concerns the discovery of a small white tribe living in the south-east of Tasmania. They have been cut off for generations from contact with any other human beings and they speak a strange hybrid language developed out of the conditions of their isolation. Discovered by two bushwalkers, the young Hobart professional men, Peter Archer and Francis Morris, they are in this scene displayed by Peter's mother, Elizabeth, and his father, Dr William Archer, to the Federal Minister for Health, George Ross. The conflicting senses of superciliousness, tolerance, scientific curiosity, cultural confidence and being an outcast permeate the play.

The White Stag of Exile by Thomas Shapcott is also largely concerned with the sense of being outcast and exiled. Károly Pulszky, the central (and largely historical) character, is Director of the Hungarian National Gallery at the end of the nineteenth century. His pride, self-confidence, and self-delusion result in his having to leave his position in disgrace and migrate to Brisbane, where he becomes an agent selling insurance. It is an exile from homeland, status, language, love and the civilisation that he admires, to what seems at times, despite the people, fashions and buildings, an absence of anything he can recognise as human.

Incomprehension between civilisations is also a theme of Randolph Stow's *Visitants*. Alistair Cawdor, a District Officer in the Territory of Papua in 1959, reports in his diary on one of his rare visits to the village of Wayouyo on the island of Kailuana. He tries to explain the cult that has grown up in the village, possibly encouraged by the elderly white man, Mr MacDonnell, as a form of opposition to the Christian missionaries on neighbouring islands. The cult incorporates an interpretation of a forth-coming visit by a 'space-ship', which becomes a contentious issue among rival groups seeking to seize power when the local chief, Dipapa, dies. Violence erupts and an inquiry is held. One of the witnesses is Benoni, Dipapa's nephew and an aspirant to succeed him. Another is Saliba, a domestic worker for Mr MacDonnell. From these various sources it is possible to understand something of the intensity of belief in the visitants from the stars as an alternative source of authority and leadership to what had been previously provided by the white men, the planter MacDonnell (Makadoneli) and the Australian official, Cawdor (Kodo). An internal struggle for power finds its symbols in a religious cult and in the imposed white authority. One set of visitants seems about to depose another.

This is, then, an example of a community divided internally and in its adherence to external power and symbols. The result is a double disloca-tion from harmony—cohesion and harmony being represented in the novel in images drawn from Taoism. The setting of the novel is, significantly, a country ruled by another country, Australia, itself a former colony: the colonised turned coloniser. Yet it is the values of the coloniser, 'trucks and shotguns and bombs', that are most prized by the colonised as they confidently expect the new visitants to vanquish the old. The struggle for political power has yet to be resolved; the struggle for cultural control has already been won and lost. Amid such violent opposition of cultures it is not surprising that Cawdor's grip on sanity and reality is lost. The disloca-tion from harmony is registered by the form of the novel. Instead of a single narrator or narrative there are short separate sections of narrative from different speakers. Their understanding of the circumstances and their value judgments intersect and conflict, just as their language usage does. It ranges from formal administrative English to Tok Pisin (pidgin), to the local indigenous language.

Ken Goodwin/Alan Lawson

David Malouf
from AN IMAGINARY LIFE

Called Naso because of the nose.

What my ancestor had a nose for I do not know. What I had a nose for was news—what was fashionable, what would go.

I am essentially a social creature. Some poets, Vergil for example, have an ear, perfect in every way. I have a nose. And noses are political, even when all you are putting them into are the most private places. Perhaps most political just then. Noses get you into trouble. I could sniff out too well what everyone wants to hear, has begun to think, and *will* think too, once I have said it.

After a century of war in which whole families had destroyed one another in the name of patriotism, we were at peace. I stepped right into it—an age of soft self-indulgent muddle, of sophisticated impudence, when we all seemed to have broken out of bounds at last into an enlightenment so great that there was no longer any need for belief.

'The gods are not quite dead' was my news from the universe, 'since their names are on all our lips—not to mention the monuments to them that are dedicated daily by our beloved leader. But they too have ceased to be serious. They have entered the age of play. They have abandoned the holy places and taken up residence in fables that require only our amused detachment from disbelief. They would be embarrassed by anything so glum and humourless as our grandfathers' piety. We are free at last to believe in *ourselves*. Since there are no rules, we must make some. Let them be absurd! Since there are no more restrictions, we invent them. May they be perverse!...' And so on, in the same vein.

I was discovering for my generation a new national style. No more civic virtues—since we all know where they lead. No more patriotism. No more glorification of men at arms. No more guides in verse to bee keeping and sheep drench and the loves of shepherd boys with a taste for Greek. My world was strictly personal, a guide, in good plain terms, to such country matters as can be explored in the two square metres of a bed.

The emperor has created his age. It is called Augustan, as our historians, with their eye fixed firmly on the present, have already announced. It is solemn, orderly, monumental, dull. It exists in the eulogies that are made for him (to which I decline to contribute) and in marble that will last forever.

I too have created an age. It is coterminous with his, and has its existence in the lives and loves of his subjects. It is gay, anarchic, ephemeral and it is fun. He hates me for it.

Of course in the short run Augustus wins. And the short run is now. I have been relegated—that is our nice word for it—to the limits of the known world, and expelled from the confines of our Latin tongue.

But in the shadow of a portico dedicated by his sister to her faithful husband, someone tonight is being fucked; because in a poem once I made it happen, and made that particular act, in that particular place, a gesture of public defiance. Each night now Augustus thinks of it and bites his thumb. There are places closer than the Black Sea where the emperor's power stops. The Portico of Marcellus is one of them.

But I am here, and all this, all of it, is far behind me. How foolish it now seems, my irony, my little impieties, my dancing on the tightrope over the abyss. I have smelled my way to the very edge of things, where Nothing begins. That's where a Nose gets you. I sniff and sniff and there is no news from out there, and no news from in here either. I am dead. I am relegated to the region of silence. All I can do is shout.

And that is what I am doing.

I walk up and down the stony shoreline under the cliffs, whose shadow divides the shingle into distinct segments of light and dark. I walk among the fishermen, shouting—watching them haul in their glittering surprises, their nameless catch, from out of the sea. Or I stride about in the brushwood on the cliff tops, flapping my arms against the cold, watching storms push up black out of nowhere, or great steams of thistledown and flock travelling white on the wind, and I launch my shouts.

It's a long way to Rome. If they are ever to hear me again I must raise my voice and let these torrents of dark air that flow west over the plains carry me with them. I have been silenced. But will not be stilled.

How can I give you any notion—you who know only landscapes that have been shaped for centuries to the idea we all carry in our souls of that ideal scene against which our lives should be played out—of what earth was in its original bleakness, before we brought to it the order of industry, the terraces, fields, orchards, pastures, the irrigated gardens of the world we are making in our own image.

Do you think of Italy—or whatever land it is you now inhabit—as a place given you by the gods, ready-made in all its placid beauty? It is not. It is a created place. If the gods are with you there, glowing out of a tree in some pasture or shaking their spirit over the pebbles of a brook in clear sunlight, in wells, in springs, in a stone that marks the edge of your legal right over a hillside; if the gods are there, it is because you have discovered them there, drawn them up out of your soul's need for them and dreamed them into the landscape to make it shine. They are with you, sure enough. Embrace the tree trunk and feel the spirit flow back into you, feel the warmth of the stone enter your body, lower yourself into the spring as into some liquid place of your body's other life in sleep. But the spirits have to be recognized to become real. They are not outside us, nor even entirely within, but flow back and forth between us and the objects we have made, the landscape we have shaped and move in. We have dreamed all these things in our deepest lives and they are ourselves. It is our self we are making out there, and when the landscape is complete we shall have become the gods who are intended to fill it.

It is as if each creature had the power to dream itself out of one existence into a new one, a step higher on the ladder of things. Having conceived in our sleep the idea of a further being, our bodies find, slowly, painfully, the physical process that will allow them to break their own bonds and leap up to it. So that the stone sleeping in the sun has once been molten fire and became stone when the fire was able to say, in its liquid form: 'I would be solid, I would be stone'; and the stone dreams now that the veins of ore in its nature might become liquid again and move, but within its shape as stone, so that slowly, through long centuries of aching for such a condition, for softness, for a pulse, it feels one day that the transformation has begun to occur; the veins loosen and flow, the clay relaxes, the stone, through long ages of imagining some further life, discovers eyes, a mouth, legs to leap with, and is toad. And the toad in turn conceives the possibility, now that it can move over the earth, of taking to the air, and slowly, without ever ceasing to be toad, dreams itself aloft on wings. Our bodies are not final. We are moving, all of us, in our common humankind, through the forms we love so deeply in one another, to what our hands have already touched in lovemaking and our bodies strain towards in each other's darkness. Slowly, and with pain, over centuries, we each move an infinitesimal space towards it. We are creating the lineaments of some final man, for whose delight we have prepared a landscape, and who can only be god.

I have seen the end of all this, clearly, in imagination: the earth transfigured and the gods walking upon it in their bodies' light. And I have seen the earth, as you have reader, already prepared for it, since our minds can conceive, our hands fashion, what we are not yet ready to enter: cornfields a fathom high, stacked in the sunlight, swaying under the moon; olive groves blowing from green to silver in a breeze, as if some god spoke the word *silver*, and his breath in passing over the scene transformed it with the turning of the leaves. You know all this. It is the earth as we have made it, clearing, grafting, transplanting, carrying seeds from one place to another, following no plan that we could enunciate, but allowing our bellies to lead us, and some other, deeper hunger, till the landscape we have made reveals to us the creatures we long for and must become.

I know how far we have come because I have been back to the beginnings. I have seen the unmade earth. It is flat and featureless, swamp in summer, a frozen waste in winter, without a tree or a flower or a made field, and only the wildest seeds growing together in their stunted clumps or blowing about at random on the breeze. It is a place of utter desolation, the beginning. I know it like the inside of my head. You can have no idea how far we have come, or how far back I have been to see all this; how rudimentary our life is in its beginnings.

And yet even here there are stirrings of new life. The first seeds are there to be separated and nurtured, and led on their long path to perfection.

Out walking today in my old sandals and cloak, with a straw hat to keep off the sun, stumbling about talking to myself in the muddy waste towards the river, I was stopped in my tracks by a little puff of scarlet amongst the wild corn.

Scarlet!

It is the first colour I have seen in months. Or so it seems. Scarlet. A little wild poppy, of a red so sudden it made my blood stop. I kept saying the word over and over to myself, scarlet, as if the word, like the colour, had escaped me till now, and just saying it would keep the little windblown flower in sight. Poppy. The magic of saying the word made my skin prickle, the saying almost a greater miracle than the seeing. I was drunk with joy. I danced. I shouted. Imagine the astonishment of my friends at Rome to see our cynical metropolitan poet, who barely knows a flower or a tree, dancing about in broken sandals on the earth, which is baked hard and cracked in some places, and in others puddled with foul-smelling mud—to see him dancing and singing to himself in celebration of this bloom. Poppy, scarlet poppy, flower of my far-off childhood and the cornfields round our farm at Sulmo, I have brought you into being again, I have raised you out of my earliest memories, out of my blood, to set you blowing in the wind. Scarlet. Magic word on the tongue to flash again on the eye. Scarlet. And with it all the other colours come flooding back, as magic syllables, and the earth explodes with them, they flash about me. I am making the spring. With yellow of the ox-eyed daisy of our weedy olive groves, with blue of cornflower, orange of marigold, purple of foxglove, even the pinks and cyclamens of my mother's garden that I have forgotten all these years. They come back...though there was, in fact, just a single poppy, a few blown petals of a tissue fineness and brightness, round the crown of seeds.

Where had it come from? I searched and searched but could find no other. The seeds must have blown in and taken root. But from where? From the sea—carried high up in a stream of luminous dust and let fall among us. Or in the entrails of some bird on its way north, and growing out of the bird's casual droppings as it passed.

I sit on the ground and observe it. I love this poppy. I shall watch over it.

Suddenly my head is full of flowers of all kinds. They sprout out of the earth in deep fields and roll away in my skull. I have only to name the flowers, without even knowing what they look like, the colour, the shape, the number of petals, and they burst into bud, they click open, they spread their fragrance in my mind, opening out of the secret syllables as I place them like seeds upon my tongue and give them breath. I shall make whole gardens like this. I am Flora. I am Persephone. I have the trick of it now. All it needs is belief.

And this, as I might have guessed, is how it is done. We give the gods a name and they quicken in us, they rise in their glory and power and majesty out of minds, they move forth to act in the world beyond, changing us and it. So it is that the beings we are in process of becoming will be drawn out of us. We have only to find the name and let its illumination fill us. Beginning, as always, with what is simple.

Poppy, you have saved me, you have recovered the earth for me. I know how to work the spring.

It is about to begin. All my life till now has been wasted. I had to enter the silence to find a password that would release me from my own life.

And yet the words were already written. I wrote them years ago, and only now discover what they meant, what message they had for me: 'You will be separated from yourself and yet be alive.'

Now I too must be transformed.

(1978)

Richard Howitt
TO THE DAISY

ON FINDING ONE UNEXPECTEDLY IN AUSTRALIA, 30 JULY 1840

Whence was the silvery gleam that came?
A daisy! can it be the same?
—Some fairy from my native land
For me this glad surprise has planned,
Of light and joy a sudden shower,   5
Or never had I seen this hour,
Our real English daisy-flower.

Daily I meet some shape or hue
That brings old times before me new:
Some token of life's brightest hours,   10
In streams and trees, in birds and flowers:
The past is by such spells unbound:
But never, until now, have found
What made me feel on English ground.

Of poesy thou favourite child!   15
First seen when some blest angel smiled!
O'er Britain scattered every where—
But strangely solitary here—
Yet buoyant-looking, brisk and bold,
That with like cheer do I behold   20
Thy silver rays and disk of gold.

These mosses, ferns, resemble ours:
These sundew, sorrel, speedwell-flowers:
Yet none are in all points the same
As in the isle from whence we came,   25
Save thee, dear daisy! thee alone,—
Thy crimson tips proclaim thee known;
At once we hail thee, all our own!

Now easy seems it to my mind,
I also may a primrose find   30
In some shy glen; or it may be
A cowslip nodding on the lea:
All things are possible, it seems,
To him, for whom the fairy schemes,
Whose waking hours are blest as dreams.   35

O, not miscalled the eye of day—
Sweet gowan of the Scottish brae!
Close shut at eve: with dawning light,
Opening on heathy summits bright:
When first the crimson streaks the gloom,   40
That very tint dost thou assume,
And sweetly blushest into bloom.

Flower of the dawn, and dawn of song!
O, well may grace to thee belong!
By ancient bards how blazoned wide—   45
And how by Wordsworth glorified!
And seen by Burns he could not choose
But crown thee with unfading hues—
Thou—loved of every sylvan muse!

In England thou art always seen,   50
On mead, on moor, on village-green:
In forest glen, on mountain height;
A common thing in common sight;
But here, 'midst flowers superbly dressed,
Shalt thou, and prized o'er all the rest,   55
Become our cherished garden-guest.

Australian flowers I prize nor scorn;
Let those who in this land were born
Admire them, praise them, pluck and wear
On swarthy brow, in jet-black hair: 60
I never gathered them, nor knew,
Where I a child to manhood grew;—
What have I then with them to do?

Yet flowers bloom here of loveliest dye,
Where roves and rests the enamoured eye;   65
Chaste forms, and tints of beauty rare;
For these no fondness can I spare;
Of song they have no generous dower;
No life-long memory, homely power,
Like thee, our darling English-flower.   70

(1840)

Rex Ingamells
THE WORD 'JINDYWOROBAK'

'Jindyworobak' is an Aboriginal word meaning 'to annex, to join', and I
propose to coin it for a particular use. The Jindyworobaks, I say, are those
individuals who are endeavouring to free Australian art from whatever
alien influences trammel it, that is, to bring it into proper contact with its
material. They are the few who seriously realize that an Australian culture
depends on the fulfilment and sublimation of certain definite conditions,
namely:

1. A clear recognition of environmental values.
2. The debunking of much nonsense.
3. An understanding of Australia's history and traditions, primaeval,
   colonial, and modern.

The most important of these is the first. Pseudo-Europeanism clogs the
minds of most Australians, preventing a free appreciation of nature. Their

speech and thought idioms are European; they have little direct thought-contact with nature. Although emotionally and spiritually they should be, and, I believe, are more attuned to the distinctive bush, hill and coastal places they visit than to the European parks and gardens around the cities, their thought-idiom belongs to the latter not the former. Give them a suitable thought-idiom for the former and they will be grateful. Their more important emotional and spiritual potentialities will be given the conditions for growth. The inhibited individuality of the race will be released. Australian culture will exist.

(1938)

Rex Ingamells
MOORAWATHIMEERING

Into moorawathimeering,
where atninga dare not tread,
leaving wurly for a wilban,
tallabilla, you have fled.

Wombalunga courses, waitjurk—   5
though we cannot break the ban,
and follow tchidna any further
after one-time karaman.

Far in moorawathimeering,
safe from wallan darenderong,   10
tallabilla waitjurk, wander
silently the whole day long.

Go with only lilliri
to walk along beside you there,
while douran-douran voices wail   15
and Karaworo beats the air.

(1935)

Roland Robinson
from DEEP WELL 10:
I HAD NO HUMAN SPEECH

I had no human speech. I heard
the quail-thrush cry out of stones,
reiterate its crystal word
from mountains' crumbling bones.

I had no human word, beyond   5
all words I knew the rush of ash
grey wings that gloomed in one respond
storm grey, swerved—a crimson flash.

The speech that silence only shapes:
a ruin, and the writhe of thin   10
ghost-gums against rain blue deeps
of night and ranges I drank in.

I lived where mountains moved, stood,
round me. I saw their natures change,
deepen, fire from mood to mood.   15
I found the kingfisher-blue range,

found, where dark heliotrope
shadows pied a range's power,
mauve-purple at the foothills' slope,
the parakelia, the desert flower.   20

Yet, human, with tormenting thought
tormented, I turned from these
presences, from converse sought
with deserts, flowers, stones, and trees.

(1951)

Gün Gencer
TREES II

The gumnut
puts no pressure
but
treasures
the love   5
that is the eucalypt

the water
only the blackfellow knows where
eases the walls
and the gumnut   10
full of green
bursts out of the red
into an indigo sky
over the tops
of mock tin-shed cathedrals   15
of cardboard Hollywood sets
perched tentatively along the wrong coast

and the eucalypt soars
—as the Kookaburra pecks at the props—
in fits of unadorned laughter   20

(1985)

Antigone Kefala
from MEMORY (ii)

The wind would stop abruptly and the silence
would fill with moonlight, falling unceasingly
like a blue still rain over the sleeping hills,
and in the deep of night the silk tearing
sound of waves would break over the dead sand.   5

Then from downstairs the echo of that foreign laugh
would come, surprised and unsubstantial in the stillness,
forced out of you by those black shadows
no one could exorcize.
In the strained hollowness the walls listened.   10
So you coughed to assure us that the unknown
was not so menacing,
mindful of our narrow knowledge of the dark world
and our social ways.

You that had lost the image and the way,   15
had lost now even the recollection of the way,
and wandered through the broken walls,
in that far country,
and sometimes in a stray sunray, some meaning
of the past would come to you, in strange blue shapes,   20
and then before our blind eyes,
the crystal vision òf the world would rest untouched.

(1973)

Dimitris Tsaloumas
SEVENTH POEM

They brought him one morning
O unbearable beauty
of my mornings
poppies still stain with blood
the floors of memory   5
and daisies untrodden
cover with gentle white
the paths of death.

Erect and sinless I
on the edge of vineyards   10
touched by vine-shoots—
and suddenly his eyes
demented
glance of a frightened hare
indelibly upon me.   15

They hurried him past,
he in the middle,
and above the uphill road
and the dust of wheels
the shouting of gendarmes   20
and unseemly laughter
on the birthday of my immortality.

And they handed him over in
the wilderness of prickly pear
beyond the barricade of cicadas   25
where the mind smashes
like a pigeon against a door-pane
falling
with a blood-clot on its beak.

Later, poets came   30
weaving wreaths of barbed wire
and threnodies of song,
and I was left alone with my nights
to fight, indestructible,
the look of his necessity   35
and the stigma of my shame.

                                        (1983)

Π O *(Peter Oustabasidis)*
SCHIZOPHRENIA

She tells me to tell them
'Tenk Yoo'. She tells me to t-
ell *dem* 'Tenk Yoo'. We're sitting outside (in the court-ya-
rd) of an Own-your-Own-Flat. I
t's a beautiful day. You could
almost Own-Your-Own-Life (it's
that beautiful). So she tells
me to tell *dem* 'Tenk Yoo' (cos
I'm writing everything down a-
nd what she says goes): ... so
she tells me to tell *dem* 'Tenk
Yoo'. I say if she tells me to
tell them 'Tenk Yoo' (again)
no-one'll believe me (even the
Priest gets tired of saying A-
h-men all day). So she tells
me to tell them, that she extends her thanks to all the important people in the World w-
ho told her what to do (for so
long). And that whenever we u-

se their name (in the house)
it's always with the *utmost* r-
espect and courtesy. Then she
tells me to tell *dem* 'Tenk Yoo
' and that her *son* is writing
all this down. Cos the Germans
came and closed down her school. So she never learnt to write very well. Then she tells
me to tell them, she's a very
sick woman waiting to get wel-
l. I tell her i'll be writing
all this up, in English. Cos
my Greeks not too good. She s-
ays: 'Ov'kors! Ov-kors!' I 'h
ev to.'

(1980)

Louis Nowra
from THE GOLDEN AGE

SCENE ELEVEN

*The Archers' garden of the opening scene. Twilight. A warm evening.
In the background, the Greek temple. A long table with an expensive
table setting is ready; food is on the table, as are porcelain crockery,
silverware and crystal glasses.*
ELIZABETH *escorts* GEORGE ROSS, *federal MP, into the garden.*

ELIZABETH: It was such a lovely evening we decided to have it out here.
  We expected you later.
ROSS: The Cabinet meeting took less time than I thought.
ELIZABETH: They won't be long.
ROSS: I'm most intrigued to see them. Your husband's report was extraordinary. (*Noticing the temple*) Not many of those in Australian back-
  yards.
ELIZABETH: It was built, way back in 1840 (only Australians could say
  'way back in 1840') by my great grandfather. He loved Greece, Greek
  culture; a family trait. So he built this little Olympus. It was said that he
  had a giant streak of paganism in his soul. The architect, an ex-convict,
  unfortunately used poor materials. It took the Parthenon two thousand

years to crumble, it took this less than a hundred years. Occasionally I let the spirits of the Greeks take hold of me and I put on an ancient tragedy. Last time we performed *Iphigenia in Tauris* to help a charity for unwed mothers and, do you know, some people looked down on us. But being an unwed mother is so human: one moment of passion, a lifetime of misery. Years ago, William and I could have said those speeches in ancient Greek and most of the audience would have understood; many of them were academics and artists, of course. Greek and Latin means nothing in the modern world and yet that was our greatest period of civilisation. From then on it's been all downhill. Romans conquered the world and Mussolini takes years to conquer a few Ethiopian hilltribes.

(PETER *and* FRANCIS, *both wearing tuxedos, enter.*)

Ah, Mr Ross, I would like to introduce my son, Peter. Peter, this is Mr George Ross, Federal Minister for Health.

PETER: (*shaking hands*) How do you do, sir?

ELIZABETH: And his friend, Francis Morris.

ROSS: Very glad to meet you.

(*They shake hands.*)

ELIZABETH: Francis's fascination with these people is only matched by my husband's.

ROSS: Dr Archer's report mentioned you two found this group. I couldn't not come, my curiosity about them was too great.

ELIZABETH: So is Francis's. It's the first time you've seen them since you brought them back, isn't it?

FRANCIS: Yes.

(FRANCIS *is noticeably agitated.*)

ROSS: (*looking around*) And this is where they've been staying?

ELIZABETH: William thought they would be more comfortable here and it would make studying them easier. The woman Angel is in hospital however. It was discovered that she has pulmonary tuberculosis. Her brother, Mac, is with her, it's thought he may have a touch of it too.

ROSS: So they won't be coming tonight?

ELIZABETH: No. How was Melbourne, Francis. Francis?

(FRANCIS *has been sipping a glass of wine* PETER *has poured for him to try and calm him. For a moment he is at a loss.*)

The job?

FRANCIS: I didn't get it.

ELIZABETH: Perhaps next time. Have you heard the latest about Poland, Mr Ross?

ROSS: They say Poland is about to surrender.

ELIZABETH: I can feel it in my blood. Another World War. The times are definitely out of joint. And, again, we'll send our youth off to die.

ROSS: If it's necessary to fight Nazism. Would you sign up, Francis?

FRANCIS: Yes. Fascism has to be destroyed, it's an evil philosophy. If I had been older I would have tried to fight against it in Spain.

ROSS: (*amused*) Oh, an idealist.

ELIZABETH: (*spotting people in the distance*) Ah, here they are.

(*It is an extraordinary sight.* BETSHEB *and* AYRE *are dressed magnificently.* AYRE *is wearing the dress she held in her lap and* BETSHEB *is wearing a modern evening dress.* STEF *is wearing a dinner jacket. They are escorted in by* WILLIAM, *also dressed for table, attracted by the glitter and the candles.* BETSHEB *guides* AYRE *in. Both women stop when they see* FRANCIS *and* PETER. *They are pleased to see both.*)

WILLIAM: (*to* BETSHEB) Here, I'll take Queenie Ayre.

(WILLIAM *leads* AYRE *to the central chair.* BETSHEB *and* FRANCIS *stare shyly at one another.*)

BETSHEB: 'ello.

FRANCIS: Hello.

ELIZABETH: My, how wonderful you look.

FRANCIS: You look lovely.

(BETSHEB *spins in her dress for everyone, delighted by the praise. She stops and smiles at* FRANCIS.)

BETSHEB: (*quietly*) The belle is spoonin'.

(STEF *puts his hand into one of the dips. He tastes it, then spits it out in horror.*)

WILLIAM: Mr Ross, I'm Dr Archer.

ROSS: Of course, I remember you well; that conference last year.

(STEF *sits on the grass and rocks back and forth humming to himself.*)

WILLIAM: Actually, in only a week Stef has improved out of sight.

ROSS: Did you find out who they are?

WILLIAM: These people are the last members of a group that goes back to the 1850s, during the gold rushes when everyone had the fever. Bankers, convicts, businessmen, doctors...but unlike in Victoria, the rush finished pretty quickly here. One group moved much further into the South West looking for gold than anyone else. That notebook written in animal blood, that's where I learnt the most. For a while they found some gold, but after it ran out they decided to stay. There was nothing to go back for. Most of them were ex-convicts, escaped convicts, failed colonists, general scum—even a travelling actor tired of doing bad shows for stupid colonists. Why go back to the city? It would be just more poverty, misery or servitude. One of the escaped convicts by the name of Simpson kept the notebook. Some of it is his information, but the rest of the notebook is his obsession with his dreams. He dreamed he should found his own town, independent of the rest of mankind, so he tried to. And what material did he have? Criminals, retards, the lost, the desperate—if they hadn't been that they would have returned to civilisation. (*Smiling*) So what we have before us is the true Australian culture.

ROSS: What about the way they talk?

WILLIAM: Simpson, like his sister, had a cleft palate. Their language is a word salad made up of Cockney, Scottish, Irish, East Anglia dialect and learnt from people who couldn't speak properly. There must have been a genetic thread of retardation running through the original group because some of them just didn't learn to speak.

FRANCIS: Perhaps they didn't feel the necessity of speaking?

WILLIAM: (*amused by the notion*) Of the younger ones, only Betsheb can talk. Ayre forces her to. Once Ayre dies, Betsheb will be the last repository of their culture. Stef is Angel's son; he's the final genetic mockery. Betsheb's brother died recently.

FRANCIS: The corpse?

WILLIAM: Yes. And Mac will never be able to have children because his genitals are malformed. You can see the degeneration in even their names: Betsheb, Bethsheba. Stef, Stephen. Ayre, probably Clare. Queenie Ayre is a woman I admire more each day. It would have taken a lot of courage to come back to the world of 'rack 'n' cat'. Back to the world she had only heard about, a world of racks, whips, prison, hatred of the poor. Upper classes, lower classes, poverty, torture. She knows they have no future in the wilderness. Inside her head she has kept everything she deems important. Dreams, memories, snatches of songs, folklore, Bible stories...it's had to be passed on by word of mouth. After Simpson died and his sister, my guess is that everyone was illiterate.

> (*Silence. The three look curiously vulnerable and are embarrassed as everyone stares at them; that is, all except* STEF, *who stares at the sky.*)

FRANCIS: What's going to happen to them? There's been nothing in the papers.

WILLIAM: We decided not to let the public know until we knew a little more about them. We plan to release the information on Tuesday. (*To* ROSS) That's why you're down here? (ROSS *nods.*)
So, ladies and gentlemen, the children of our past.

> (AYRE *points to* ELIZABETH.)

ELIZABETH: What is it, Ayre?

AYRE: (*motioning to* ELIZABETH'S *neck*) Shiny, shiny.

ELIZABETH: (*giving her the necklace*) For tonight.

> (*She puts it around* AYRE'S *neck.* AYRE *is very pleased.* PETER *sits down to have a drink.* WILLIAM *pours one for* ROSS. FRANCIS *approaches* BETSHEB.)

FRANCIS: You wear your dress with more ease than I wear this monkey suit. It's Peter's.

BETSHEB: I look fer thee, dawnytime, day fer day.

FRANCIS: (*not understanding*) I'm sorry...

> (WILLIAM, *who has been watching them, translates.*)

WILLIAM: I looked for you every morning, day after day.

> (FRANCIS *looks to* WILLIAM *as if to say, 'Are you translating?'* WILLIAM *nods.*)

BETSHEB: I nowt more afeard.

WILLIAM: I'm not afraid any more. (*A broad smile as she remembers something.*)

BETSHEB: I see car—

WILLIAM: I was in a car.

BETSHEB: Windwhistlin'.

WILLIAM: It went quickly.

BETSHEB: 'ome, country groan 'n' moan 'n' run.

WILLIAM: Factories and houses make noises and the landscape from the car makes it look like it's running.

BETSHEB: Voice in a stick.

WILLIAM: Telephone. She loves hearing people speak on the telephone.

BETSHEB: I laugh. Let go.

> (*She demonstrates listening on the telephone.*)
> Demon or 'eaven?

WILLIAM: The voices, are they from heaven or hell?

> (STEF, *who has been stalking* ROSS *for some time, pounces on him and starts to chew at his ankle, growling.*)

WILLIAM: Pay no attention.

ROSS: (*thin-lipped*) I'll try.

ELIZABETH: Shall we sit? Francis, you escort Betsheb.

(ROSS *pretends not to notice* STEF *clinging to his trousers by the teeth as he makes his awkward way to the table.* BETSHEB *is highly excited at meeting* FRANCIS *again.* WILLIAM *pulls* STEF *free of* ROSS' *trousers.*)

ROSS: Much appreciated, Dr Archer.

(WILLIAM *sits* STEF *at the table.* BETSHEB *suddenly cries out like a magpie. Everyone looks at her. Now that she has their attention she is going to show off. She remembers how* FRANCIS *enjoyed her perform-ance down by the river, so she steps away and begins to promenade like a grande dame.*)

BETSHEB: Rack 'n' cat, rack 'n' cat, rack 'n' cat . . .

(*After this she turns around for her return walk.* FRANCIS *realises what will come next.*)

FRANCIS: (*horrified*) Betsheb!

(*But* BETSHEB *doesn't hear him. She farts loudly, much to* AYRE'S *amusement, and pretends discreetly to wave the smell away. She notices that no one else is laughing.*)

ELIZABETH: (*to* WILLIAM) You couldn't get anything more Australian than that! (*To a worried* BETSHEB) Bravo, Betsheb! (*Applauding*) Bravo, Bet-sheb! (*Applauding*) Bravo!

(*The others applaud.* BETSHEB *is pleased.* STEF *is fascinated by the candles, especially the one near him. He blows it out.*)

(*To* WILLIAM) Where's Mary? She's got the matches.

ROSS: Allow me, Mrs Archer.

(ROSS *takes out his matches and relights the candle.* STEF *blows it out again: he is enjoying this game.*)

ELIZABETH: I think, Mr Ross, that shifting the candle might save an enormous match bill.

ROSS: I think you may be right, Mrs Archer.

(ROSS *shifts the candle.* STEF *is very annoyed and lunges across the table at it, scattering plates and glasses everywhere. He grabs the candle and sinks back in his chair, holding it inches from his face. He stares at its flame as if mesmerised by it.* ROSS *goes to take the candle from* STEF *but the boy growls at him.*)

ELIZABETH: For your own safety, Minister, I suggest you let Stef keep it.

(ROSS *does so.*)

(WILLIAM *pours the champagne.*)

WILLIAM: I thought we might make a toast to our visitors.

(BETSHEB *goes to drink her champagne.*)

FRANCIS: Betsheb . . . not yet.

(AYRE *has got hers and gulps it down.* BETSHEB *sees her and follows suit.*)

ELIZABETH: I suppose a Queen is entitled to invent her own table manners.

(*She indicates to* WILLIAM *that he should pour more champagne for the women.*)

  William, short and sweet before it's too late.

(WILLIAM *raises his glass and the others, except for* STEF, *do likewise.* AYRE *and* BETSHEB *raise their glasses, curious as to the meaning of this ritual.*)

WILLIAM: To our five aliens who have landed on this strange planet, no longer called Van Dieman's Land but Tasmania. And, to their Queen, Queenie Ayre.

ALL: Queenie Ayre.

(STEF *is staring at the candle.* AYRE *downs her glass quickly. The others sip theirs.* BETSHEB *carefully imitating* FRANCIS.)

(1985)

Thomas Shapcott
from THE WHITE STAG OF EXILE

1899. June. Brisbane

KÁROLY PULSZKY IN GEORGE STREET

I seem in a mood for the unreal: even a street of shopkeepers is not real in a certain light. The light, here, is certain only of its memory of eucalyptus bark, shade-tree darkness with mosquitoes, tiers of hoop-pines, their particular stiffness.

Or the flash across water to the mangrove beds as a white heron arches. Yesterday, two pelicans.

Against the reality of birds in flight, or birds crushing waters into reflections and loops, these houses have no substance. The timber walls have forgotten wood, tin squinting all angles has surely forgotten earth and the underground storehouses of geology that were their origin.

HABERDASHERY   GREENGROCER   REAL ESTATE
THE BANK OF AUSTRALASIA

Men wear the garments of London or Vienna. Unreal, the burden of garments on men here. Gloves. The determination of hats. My mother would have defined all this with some presence. I find it hard, now, to be amused or amusing.

Is the business of selling, buying, spreading the rank butter of profit any more real than the business of sitting, looking, being amused or not amused?

My business was seeing. My reality was the clear world of vision, and it seemed specific. It was an ordering and serving, it was spread by fine artisans, strong with their hands.

In this climate the hands sweat in their gloves: this is called 'Winter'.

Brown ink, black ink, paper. What is *insurance*?

Yesterday someone before me in the bank brought in a bag of stone: gold. He exchanged it for paper. He will trade that paper for title deeds as if he were to become the possessor of land. Wild grasses carry seeds that clamber into wool and would burrow like worms into flesh. They will not be purchased. They will be owners forever or as long as forever matters.

Pods rattle among stained and torn leaves, grotesque. More than beautiful. Insects croak out, birds yelp, *beautiful, beautiful*.

At noon even horse-and-cart noise becomes apologetic, the noise of humans separates like glass splintering. I am lost in the mood of these times. How can only the grasslands be real? Europe has never seemed further. I have never felt more invisible.

1899. June 4th. Brisbane

KÁROLY PULSZKY REMEMBERS JOKES

You heard the one about Diogenes, who went from place to place with a lamp in search of an honest man? When he reached Hungary he did not have to ask. He took one look then said: 'Here, take my lamp.'

It is not that the search is improbable.

Bitterness stings in the eye like oily smoke.

In my pocket, a linen handkerchief defines me: folded, precise, not to be used except as a measure of hiding secret evidence of process and decay. Two months, and each morning I still pursue old rituals. I am dried out, but still the habit instructs me: grooming, cuff links, trimming of the new beard, how else begin the routine of each day? Every act is a disguise.

I am surprised each time at the fluids within, at the fluids which surface.

We imagine ancestors to have acted like us. Aquincum, the capital of Pannonia Inferior (now Budapest) revealed, in my days as student archaeologist, habits that were not inferior to the most elegant taste, to the most colonial assiduity. In colonial centres the forms are notoriously important.

It is not that the capitals, the centres change, but that the outposts must grip tight for fear of being spun off. There is no flexibility in Aquincum or in Brisbane. But there are salons here where the newest German philosophers are entertained (by proxy). Import and indent booksellers make a killing. Diogenes would have liked this point. Why did I never think of Budapest as an outpost? It was my centre.

Yet even houses can become ineffably strange; like my mother's descriptions of the American South, with 'open galleries on columns'. She wrote, also, about the burden of the heat, a winter clear as alpine air but curiously heavy, gripping the rim of the edge, the disc, the circle.

Here, also, the houses themselves are on stilts and pillars. The witch house on chicken legs, Baba Yaga.

Baba—Baby—why do I think of the Comtesse de Chevigné?

We love where we can.

It was not love. Appetite discards handkerchiefs, it has no time.

You heard the one about Diogenes with his lamp? He traded it in Plato's cave. In Plato's cave was Baba Yaga. A child was screaming, eyes stung by vision and by loss of vision and by shadows on the wall, firelit shadows that were the closest we come to explaining anything. But the child screamed only anger at the indifference of those who would not look even at shadows. I was that child.

The Comtesse de Chevigné is further away than Aquincum, where my studies began. They end in a place where even men are shadows. Sometimes, in this strong energy of sunlight I feel there is nothing, nobody here at all. Yet I am surrounded.

(1984)

Randolph Stow
from VISITANTS

CAWDOR

The church at Wayouyo plays a rather mysterious role in the life of the community. The Methodist Mission on Osiwa Island was established in 1870, and at some time during that decade missionaries visited Kailuana and supervised the building of a church on the site of the present structure. It has been enlarged and rebuilt several times. For about twenty years a Polynesian or Osiwan catechist was in residence. Mr MacDonnell, when he arrived in 1908, immediately established hostile relations with the white missionaries on Osiwa, and his views seem to have spread to the Kailuana villages. The life of the native catechists became increasingly difficult, and after the 1914–18 War no more were sent to the island.

In the years since, however, singing and some form of worship has taken place in the building, often under the direction of someone who could be called, in a general way, a religious leader. BOITOKU, who is the garden-magician of a section of Wayouyo, has recently played this part. So, at some time or other, has DIPAPA. What they do during these ceremonies, apart from singing an eerie local version of 'Daisy, Daisy', I have not been able to discover. It probably contains an element of Christianity, but certainly they acknowledge no debt to the Bible. There may be a clue in the fact that they claim 'Daisy, Daisy' as an invention of their ancestors.

But the church was not the focus of this outbreak. As was known to the main actors in the cult, the 'painted men', the centre of activities was the group of stone called Ukula'osi. It is only through the stones that one can explain the suddenness of the hysteria which took hold of the 'painted men'.

On October 29th a rumour went through the villages that a space-ship had taken away three men living on the island of Budibudi, where they guarded DIPAPA's betelnut plantation. This seems to have been interpreted (by DIPAPA first, I should say, and by METUSELA and BOITOKU) as a hopeful sign, a sign that the visitants needed more information about Wayouyo and had taken the men aboard as guides.

When asked why they should connect the stones with the space-ship, all the men implicated said that they had heard of the connection from BENONI, who had heard it from me. I shall have to return to this, obviously.

On October 30th BOITOKU (acting for DIPAPA, I suspect) spread the 'talk' through the group which became the hard core of the 'painted men'. There were perhaps twenty, perhaps forty of these, all men over 35, and all unfriendly to BENONI. Every one of them would have been familiar with the tradition attached to the stones: that if they were moved, a great wind would destroy the villages, that there would be famine, and that all the people would go mad.

Under the direction of METUSELA (I believe), these men went to the stones at Ukula'osi and moved them.

I consider this sufficient to explain the hysteria. They had expected to be destroyed instantly by a wind, and were not. They had expected to go mad, and in a sense did. They had accepted the possibility of a famine and were easily persuaded to set about creating one.

The stones, which formed a roughly oval pattern, were rearranged in a circle. The ground inside the circle was picked clean of weeds and pebbles, and swept ritually by a magician (presumably BOITOKU), in preparation for the space-craft which was to use it as a landmark.

Later they set about constructing a shed or warehouse for the cargo from the craft. Work continued on this throughout the next three days and nights.

When the violence began on the night of October 31st, it was the 'painted men', in their almost intoxicated state, who spearheaded it. But they were very quickly joined by the majority of males in all three villages of Kailuana. I do not believe that this reaction had, at that stage, anything in particular to do with the 'star-machine'. I believe that myths and traditions of the 'cargo' type are part of their experience, of their memory. But I may be wrong. I admit that I have good reason to doubt my own judgement on a number of matters.

After the burning of Obomatu, all returned to Wayouyo, where preparations had been made in and around the church for the next revelation. From this moment it becomes clear that the mind behind the destrucion was that of the old chief, DIPAPA.

BENONI

In the clearing they had lighted a fire. It was the children who were feeding it at first, the small boys, running in out of the dark with bundles of wood and throwing them at the flames so that the sparks puffed upwards. Then they cheered and pushed each other about, full of excitement, but not knowing why or what to do.

All the time men and women were passing them by, going to join the crowd that pressed about the church. They were packed in front of it so thick that you could not see in, and at the sides the walls were bending under the weight of the taller men, who jostled each other to get a sight, over the top of the walls, of the things and the people inside. Their shoulders shone with the firelight and their faces shone with the torches they were staring towards. They would turn back and call and beckon to one another, their faces hot and moved like boys watching a fight.

Through the bodies came a quick, loud, confusing music, that was made, you knew, by people not listening to one another, but hearing only themselves; their own finger-drums, their own panpipes, or moaning to themselves the very old songs whose words nobody understands. It was a sound like I had never heard before, of very hungry, very lonely people. Now and again there was the sound of a conch, hollow and low.

I left Saliba to push my way through the men by the walls, to look in over their shoulders. In front of me, in the middle of the church, my uncle was sitting on a carved stool. The side of his head was towards me, the side with the tattered ear-lobe. He stared over the heads of the crowd at the glow of the fire, making munching movements sometimes with his lips, and twisting his fingers together round the top of an ebony walking-stick carved with the leaves and tendrils of yam-vines.

At each side of him, in two lines, the painted men sat cross-legged on the floor. They had driven their torches into the soft ground and the flames swayed in front of their faces. They were my uncle's men, all of them, none of them young and none of them friends of mine. Like him, they stared ahead of them, drumming or piping or droning their songs, each one quiet, but together loud and vague like the sea.

Near the back of the church the pilot was hanging from his rope, nailed to his aeroplane, which trembled. Because of the flickering of the light and the twisting of the rope his white eyes seemed to move and shine. Past him, against the back wall, someone had built a little hut of matting, round and pointed like a shell. Out of the hut, in the small silence between the other nosies, came cries and moans, growing louder and faster: *Aï! A'i! A'a'i!* Then fading away: *A! A'o! A-a-a!*

SALIBA

Dipapa clenched his hands about his stick. He lifted himself to his feet, and stood looking at the people.

All the sounds stopped. Everything but the cries in the little house, which grew and grew.

'You hear,' Dipapa called, in his tired, wandering old man's voice. 'A man will appear. A man will speak.'

Then a great shout pierced through the hut of matting, deep like a conch, and as Dipapa turned back to it a man burst out, pushing away the flaps that were its doors, and stumbled, reeling, between the torches, to the front of the church. His head was lifted very high, towards the stars, and his eyes were nearly closed. Only a little white showed between the lids. In his two hands, lifted to the sky, he held the old sword of the King of France. All his body was trembling, and he clung to the sword as if he was afraid of what was happening to him and only had trust in that.

Nobody said: It is Metusela. It was Metusela, and yet it was not.

Our bones were tight with fear. We did not seem to breathe.

'What man are you?' called Dipapa across the church. 'Speak tell us. What is your name?'

And then we heard the voice. Not Metusela's voice. Metusela's little body was shaking, the sweat made stripes on his face. But the voice that came out of his mouth was huge and deep and calm.

'I am Taudoga,' it said. 'A man of the stars.'

Behind Metusela, over his head, the pilot looked down on us. The voice seemed to come from him, not from the frightened little man in the torn Dimdim shorts.

'Today I will speak to you,' it said. 'I will tell you of your ancestors and the ancestors of Dimdim.

'Two brothers came from the stars and crashed at Odakuna. The older brother was Kulua'ibu. The younger brother was Dovana.

'The older brother said: "I will make a net and go fishing. You open the box, and build us a house here at Odakuna."

'The older brother went away to fish. The younger brother opened their box of tools. In the box were nails, a hammer, a saw. He built a house and began to roof it, nailing down the corrugated iron.

'Later the older brother came back from fishing. He looked for his younger brother and could not find him. But he just thought: "He is hiding from me," and went away into the bush to gather vines.

'But soon he began to grow suspicious, he began to grow angry, his belly was hot. He shouted: "While I was away, fishing for all of us, my brother was sleeping with my wife."

'When the younger brother heard that, he was mad with rage. He said: "Tomorrow I will pack up our belongings and go. If you take back what you said, I will give you the toolbox." But the older brother was too angry, he would not take back what he said.

'So one day the younger brother, Dovana, and his mother and his sister, packed up the belongings and went away to Dimdim.

'And the older brother stayed. With vines alone he lashed together his house and his canoe. He went foraging in the forest and found nothing but vines.

'Because the younger brother had taken away the iron, the saw, the nails, the hammer, everything. He had taken them all away to Dimdim.

'That is why you have nothing. Your ancestor was foolish and angry, he let his younger brother take the things that belonged to him. The ancestor of the Dimdims was clever and a thief.

'And when other star-machines came, with bully-beef and knives and axes and trousers and all those somethings for your ancestor, Dovana's people tricked them into landing in Dimdim. They promised they would send those things to your people, but they stole them instead. So the Dimdims have everything, you have nothing.

'They will steal even what you have. Misa Makadoneli lives on your land. He gives you orders. Misa Kodo gives you orders. If you have money, Misa Kodo is going to take it for the Governemt. He will take your shillings and give you instead a piece of paper, with writing on it, saying to himself: You fools.

'But the people in the stars have found out what happened to the cargo they meant for Kailuana. We know that the Dimdims stole it. We are very angry.

'That is why we have told you to burn Olumata and Obomatu. You do not need those houses. You will have houses with roofs of iron. You do not need yams or banana-palms or betelnut. You will have bully-beef and tinned peaches and rum. Burn your houses. Burn your food. Burn your skirts and yavis and ramis. Go hungry till we come. Go naked till we come. Dance, sing, make love. We are very near. We may come tomorrow. We are coming with trucks and shotguns and bombs. We are bringing the children of Kulua'ibu their cargo.'

(1979)

Section F

THE VISION SPLENDID

AUSTRALIA FACES THE DAWN: 2nd JANUARY, 1901.

As the preceding Sections have demonstrated, Australia has been represented in literary form in a variety of ways by different groups at different
periods. It is apparent in so much of that writing that the representation of
Australia is of central cultural concern: to describe Australia most convin-
cingly is to earn a role as one of the custodians of a particular piece of
cultural property. It also becomes apparent that this image-making is
polemical, a matter of debate, argument and contest. Each of the images
provides a means by which we are taught to identify Australian-ness and is
hence a way of characterising a specific version of Australian culture. All
are ways of giving form to particular versions of 'the national experience'
or 'the national identity'.

This Section exemplifies, in part, that version of 'the national experience' which is commonly felt to be the most characteristic, that which articulates what is often called 'the Australian legend' or 'the national myth'. But it also provides the evidence to demonstrate that what is 'characteristic' only seems to be so because it has been characterised. It is a process by which certain conventions of description, selection and language become sufficiently familiar to seem 'natural', whether or not they are 'true'.

This Section also exemplifies, however, the alternative proposition that these conventions, precisely because they have an ideological function, are contentious and therefore subject to revision or subversion. So we have included not only some of the 'classic' pieces of the writing of 'the Australian legend', such as 'The Wild Colonial Boy', but also some careful rewritings of it, such as Moya Costello's 'An Imaginary Conversation with Brian "Squizzy" Taylor'. Similarly, Bruce Dawe's 'Homecoming' might be seen (in part) as a revision of the Anzac tradition which has one of *its* classic re-presentations (though not without some subtle ambivalence) in the preceding extract, from Davison's *The Wells of Beersheba*. What is sometimes even more interesting is that the so-called 'classic' texts of 'the Australian legend' often begin to unravel from within, to display ambivalence, to present some evidence for a view contrary to the one they overtly present. This is the case in the delightfully polyphonic extract from Kingsley's *The Recollections of Geoffry Hamlyn*, a text commonly read as immigrant propaganda and pastoral promotion.

The 'standard' version of the Australian 'myth' has been written about exhaustively and exhaustingly. It has indeed become a 'standard', a measure by which both art and life are often judged. It has certain features that can readily be identified. It prefers bush (usually 'Bush') settings because, as the argument goes, that is where the distinctive, unique, true Australian experience is to be found in contrast to the cities, where 'life is much the same as anywhere else'. Of the many potential varieties of Australian bush scenery, it generally prefers those which *it* can describe as 'harsh', 'rugged', 'hostile' and 'inhospitable'; expectations of civilised life and culture, economic success or personal triumph are thus diminished—and those things become correspondingly suspect. The social relations depicted are often transitory and almost exclusively male: mateship is the valorised model. The characteristic narrative is that of survival rather than triumph, though optimism for the future is frequently asserted, since the struggle must be seen as worthwhile. The 'standard' literary style and presentation are said to be (reflecting the land and its putative ethos) sparse, unadorned, laconic. The preferred mode is irony.

This set of values became an article of faith with those social and literary critics grouped together under the loose title of 'radical nationalists'. The most famous statement of the myth is in Russel Ward's *The Australian Legend* (1958), a book that indicates its appropriation of monolithic orthodoxy in its very title:

the 'typical Australian' is a practical man, rough and ready in his manners and quick to decry any appearance of affectation in others. He is a great improviser, ever willing to 'have a go' at anything, but willing too to be content with a task done in a way that is 'near enough'. Though capable of great exertion in an emergency, he normally feels no impulse to work hard without good cause. He swears hard and consistently, gambles heavily and often, and drinks deeply on occasion. Though he is 'the world's best confidence man', he is usually taciturn rather than talkative, one who endures stoically rather than one who acts busily. He is a 'hard case', sceptical about the value of religion and cultural pursuits generally. He believes that Jack is not only as good as his master but, at least in principle, probably a good deal better and so he is a great 'knocker' of eminent people unless, as in the case of his sporting heroes, they are distinguished by physical prowess. He is a fiercely independent person who hates officiousness and authority, especially when these qualities are embodied in military officers and policemen. Yet he is very hospitable and, above all, will stick to his mates through thick and thin, even if he thinks they may be in the wrong...He tends to be a rolling stone, highly suspect if he should chance to gather much moss.

The first item in this Section, Douglas Stewart's 'Terra Australis', in its very form and subject provides evidence for the point made earlier about discursive contention. Australia is a subject for debate and the positions taken are markedly contrasting ones. Judith Wright, in her famous essay, 'Australia's Double Aspect' (printed later in the Cultural Politics Section) argues that the two most common opposing representations of Australia have been what she calls 'the reality of exile' (unfamiliarity, disappointment) and 'the sense of liberty, of a new chance'. In 'Terra Australis' both positions are subject to scrutiny. The poem, an example of the sub-genre of 'voyager poems' which take exploration as their subject and theme, is based on an imaginary mid-Pacific meeting between the Portuguese navigator Captain Pedro Ferdinand de Quiros (1563–1614), who sought the Great South Land as an opportunity to establish a new, pure spiritual community, and the equally Utopian William Lane (1861–1917), who left Australia in 1893 aboard the *Royal Tar* to found the Utopian-socialist New Australia Settlement in Paraguay. Neither Lane nor de Quiros fulfilled his dreams. Lane left Australia after the failure of the strikes of 1891 to produce the radical reorientation of Australia he desired. That period represented for many the end of the hope that Australia would be the world's 'social laboratory', the last opportunity for European society to find a new and juster expression. Austrialia del Espiritu Santo was the name de Quiros gave Vanuatu (named the New Hebrides by Cook) in the mistaken belief that he had found the desired Great South Land.

R. D. FitzGerald's 'Quayside Meditation' juxtaposes images of Sydney Harbour from the past and the present to reflect on the process by which the historical past is used to explain and determine the present.

'Botany Bay' offers a version of the convict period considerably different from those common later. As the Introduction to Convictism notes, the later versions often adopt the Gothic mode, and maintain a peculiar tension between the melodramatic and the documentary. This text of the widely-known song seems to have been used in a London stageplay in 1885; another earlier form derives from an English street ballad. Both forms could be used to illustrate the important point that some of the most persistent ideas about Australia originated outside it. Cavalier humour in the face of adversity is a feature found in much later popular literature as well, and is one of the components of the myth of the hard-bitten Australian.

The Australian littoral has spawned a more modern myth and in 'Sydney Surfing', Jean Curlewis can be seen in mythopeic mode, deliberately and stylishly setting about giving mythic status to the customs of the beach. Her description culminates in the apotheosis of the surfer as 'young Greek god', a curious climax in an argument that has stressed distinctive Australianness. But that is a feature of much of the writing that seeks to construct Australian myths: the only available cultural references seem to be those of European antiquity.

For Moya Costello the range of cultural reference is more varied, but the desire to mythologize the subject equally apparent in the vernacular stylishness of the self-conscious rendering of a contemporary argot. Just as Curlewis' piece rests on an awareness of the cultural referentiality of the Greek god, so Costello's in its turn rests on an awareness of the very myth Curlewis was creating—that of the surfer. Like Curlewis (though parodically) Costello is then able to play the Australian 'ingenuity' and uniqueness off against the imported culture—in this case, European punk. Even the final element of Curlewis' account is set up for revision in Costello's: the intellectuality of beach culture. The concern with vernacular is also a traditional Australian literary one.

In a sense, Costello's Brian 'Squizzy' Taylor is a modern 'Wild Colonial Boy'. The name is based on that of Leslie 'Squizzy' Taylor, who operated protection and prostitution rackets and planned robberies in Melbourne just after the 1914–18 war. He and another criminal shot each other dead in 1927. The 'Wild Colonial Boy' of the ballad partakes solidly of the characteristics of the legend as Russel Ward describes it, but it is apparent that it also draws on older, British, myths as well.

Although perhaps embarrassing to modern readers, Farrell's 'Australia' is an extraordinarily comprehensive repository of the tropes in which the literary construction of the nation has been embodied. It is also one of a huge number of poems which 'take' Australia (or Terra Australis) as their title: others by Wentworth (1823), O'Dowd (1900), Hope (1939), McAuley (1942) and Walwicz (1981) are in the following Section. Among the tropes—figures of speech around which significant ideas become clustered—that Farrell's poem exemplifies are future orientation and optimism ('promise boundless'); organic growth from youth to maturity ('like some sweet child'); and the powerful presumption of innocence, that contrasts with the corruption or exhaustion of Europe. In this latter respect, one might compare it with Hope's 'Australia' or, more ironically, Walwicz's. The assumption that underpins each of these tropes is the notion of *tabula rasa* (blank page) or *terra nullius* (empty land). The symbolic narrative of the Vision Splendid is presented in classic form here: the empty land, figured as an absence and as deficient ('fruitless, scentless, soundless') but also as undefiled and unwritten, awaits the masterful filling of that emptiness by the English 'seekers' whose sacred task, represented here by the enterprise of the poet, is to write on the blank page, to give tongue to the silent land, and to put into history the land that has thus far been outside history. Characteristically, too, therefore, it represents the paradox that fascinates A. D. Hope as well: that this is the youngest and oldest of lands. By conjoining its *geological* antiquity and the brevity of its 'human history', the claim to the land of the Aboriginal inhabitants is erased.

That conjunction is confronted in one of the classic texts of mid-nineteenth-century Anglo-Australian settlement literature, Henry Kingsley's *The Recollections of Geoffry Hamlyn*, which records one of the narratives of post-convict immigration: Australia as an Arcadian site for the restoration of English fortunes. Most of the characters in the novel fall on hard times at 'home', journey to Australia, and are rewarded to the extent that most are enabled to return 'home' to buy back the family estate. In this extract the conversation between Major Buckley, the patriarch, and Doctor Mulhaus, the one non-Anglo-Saxon in the novel, takes place on a site that emphasises the antiquity of the land and the newness of human enterprise. The parenthetical dissident interventions of the Doctor into the Major's 'vision splendid' are an interesting and very early example of the way in which the imperial assumptions of the pastoral romance can be exposed. The extract does this by making the text speak not with one voice but with two.

In the pieces that follow, the pastoral ideal is transmuted into the later-nineteenth-century form with which we are more familiar. Mary Hannay Foott's 'Where the Pelican Builds' shows the transition to the dark underside of the idyll, while Gordon's 'The Sick Stockrider' catches the ambivalence of the tradition (and of the elegy generally) as it celebrates the mateship, adventure and even the literary energy ('the yarns Jack Hall invented, and the songs Jem Roper sung') while mourning the passing of a golden age. Lawson's poem about the bush school reminds us just how often nostalgia for a receding past is a feature of the vision. Like Paterson's poem that follows, it also exemplifies another trope: the contrast between culturally transmitted knowledge and local experience.

Paterson's famous line which has become emblematic of the optimistic vision of the boundless opportunities of the outback: 'And he sees the vision splendid of the sunlit plains extended', contains a quotation from Wordsworth's ode, 'Intimations of Immortality from Recollections of Early Childhood', itself a poem of retrospect and prospect. But it is also notable that 'Clancy of the Overflow' sustains a tension between different modes of discourse. The memorable image of the 'thumbnail dipped in tar' is juxtaposed with the legalism 'verbatim' which in turn is followed by the ungrammatical 'we don't know where he are'. Finally, the poem articulates one of the major items of faith in the Australian legend: the moral superiority of the Bush over the City.

The wit, and the quickness of wit of the colonial confidence trickster is one of the many appeals of Norman Lindsay's extraordinarily popular *Magic Pudding*, about an enduring pudding which must constantly be protected from the unscrupulous. This, and the following items, show how readily the legend turns into the yarn and the tall tale. Australia, as an exotic site for the European imagination, has always presumed the power to extend credulity, and in the work of Lower and Hardy the yarn/tall tale can be seen as a well-developed literary (and certainly popular) genre.

Just as 'Clancy' juxtaposed bush knowledge and literary style, so Gibson's 'On the Prevalence of "Bill" in Australian Literature' assumes a tension between the 'real' and the 'literary', a trope taken up in a variety of ways in a later Section, Realism and Romance. The same tension is represented in Henry Lawson's 'Some Popular Australian Literary Mistakes'; and Barbara Baynton once satirised the phenomenon Gibson complains of by calling one of her characters 'Billjim'.

If Farrell's 'Australia' was a repository of the tropes that go to make up 'the vision splendid', then Mudie's 'They'll Tell You About Me' is an equally comprehensive gathering of the components of legend-making. As well as providing an amazing catalogue of the historical, proverbial, legendary and mythical, it also reflects on the process by which identity (the poem is, after all, spoken by a representative 'I') and national unity are achieved. Most of the references can be found in Wilkes' *Dictionary of Australian Colloquialisms*, Wilde, Hooton and Andrews' *Oxford Companion to Australian Literature* or Wannan's *Australian Folklore*.

As has been apparent in so many of these pieces, a central feature of the Australia being constructed is its emptiness, its unknownness and *thus* its promise. It is not surprising then to discover that the stories of explorers provide a crucial narrative paradigm. Webb's 'Eyre All Alone' is one of the major reflections on this particular model of the usable past. In contrast, the next item presents a contemporary report of the eyewitness account of one of the normally silent partners of exploration, the Aboriginal Jackey Jackey, indispensable to Kennedy as a guide.

Like Webb, Randolph Stow considers how the history of exploration is transformed into literary experience. Adam Lindsay Gordon committed suicide the day after his final volume of verse was published in 1870, and Barcroft Boake even more melodramatically in 1892.

The transformation of history is also apparent in the way in which the Eureka Stockade has been represented as the one act of heroic defiance of imperial authority in Australia. Richardson's account in *The Fortunes of Richard Mahony* is one of a surprisingly small number of major literary treatments of the 'Diggers' Rebellion' of 1854.

As Thea Astley powerfully reminds us in *A Kindness Cup*, imperial authority was given military expression in Australia in other ways. Her novel records the response of a country-town schoolteacher to the appalling treatment of local Aborigines that culminates in a massacre; it is based on events that occurred near Mackay in Queensland.

Ray Lawler's *Summer of the Seventeenth Doll* has been read as a classic celebration of mateship and the Bush ideal, but the play in fact shows the ideal coming apart. Even in this opening scene the annual ritual of the two cane-cutting mates, the taciturn, rugged Roo and the gregarious Barney, who are travelling to Melbourne for the lay-off season, threatens ominously to break down even as some of the characteristic 'virtues' of the Australian legendary character are celebrated.

One of the most persistent and sustaining elements of the Australian legend has been the 'digger'. Davison's *The Wells of Beersheba* gives it one of its more romantic-heroic expressions in a description of one of the last cavalry charges (in Palestine, 1917), while Bruce Dawe's 'Homecoming', in responding to the televised bagging of bodies during the Vietnam War, records the moment when that expression became forever impossible.

If The Vision Splendid is to be read in full, it needs to be placed alongside some of the material in Living in Aboriginal Australia and The Migrant Experience, which present contrary, or certainly other visions. In posing the problem of literary representation it also relates closely to the argument of Realism and Romance, and in subject matter it is amplified by Place and People.

Alan Lawson/Ken Goodwin

Douglas Stewart
TERRA AUSTRALIS

1

Captain Quiros and Mr William Lane,
Sailing some highway shunned by trading traffic
Where in the world's skull like a moonlit brain
Flashing and crinkling rolls the vast Pacific,

Approached each other zigzag, in confusion,   5
Lane from the west, the Spaniard from the east,
Their flickering canvas breaking the horizon
That shuts the dead off in a wall of mist.

'Three hundred years since I set out from Lima
And off Espiritu Santo lay down and wept   10
Because no faith in men, no truth in islands –
And still unfound the shining continent slept;

'And swore upon the Cross to come again
Though fever, thirst and mutiny stalked the seas
And poison spiders spun their webs in Spain,   15
And did return, and sailed three centuries,

'Staring to see the golden headlands wade
And saw no sun, no land, but this wide circle
Where moonlight clots the waves with coils of weed
And hangs like silver moss no sail and tackle,   20

'Until I thought to trudge till time was done
With all except my purpose run to waste;
And now upon this ocean of the moon,
A shape, a shade, a ship, and from the west!'

2

'What ship?' 'The *Royal Tar*!' 'And whither bent?'   25
'I seek the new Australia.' 'I, too, stranger;
Terra Australis, the great continent
That I have sought three centuries and longer;

'And westward still it lies, God knows how far,
Like a great golden cloud, unknown, untouched,   30
Where men shall walk at last like spirits of fire
No more by oppression chained, by sin besmirched.'

'Westward there lies a desert where the crow
Feeds upon poor men's hearts and picks their eyes;
Eastward we flee from all that wrath and woe   35
And Paraguay shall yet be Paradise.'

'Eastward,' said Quiros, as *San Pedro* rolled,
High-pooped and round in the belly like a barrel,
'Men tear each other's entrails out for gold;
And even here I find that men will quarrel.'   *40*

'If you are Captain Quiros you are dead.'
'The report has reached me; so is William Lane.'
The dark ships rocked together in the weed
And Quiros stroked the beard upon his chin:

'We two have run this ocean through a sieve   *45*
And though our death is scarce to be believed
Seagulls and flying-fish were all it gave
And it may be we both have been deceived.'

3

'Alas, alas, I do remember now;
In Paradise I built a house of mud   *50*
And there were fools who could not milk a cow
And idle men who would not though they could.

'There were two hundred brothers sailed this ocean
To build a New Australia in the east
And trifles of money caused the first commotion   *55*
And one small cask of liquor caused the last.

'Some had strange insects bite them, some had lust,
For wifeless men will turn to native women,
Yet who could think a world would fall in dust
And old age dream of smoke and blood and cannon   *60*

'Because three men got drunk?' 'With Indian blood
And Spanish hate that jungle reeked to Heaven;
And yet I too came once, or thought I did,
To Terra Australis, my dear western haven,

'And broke my gallows up in scorn of violence,   *65*
Gave land and honours, each man had his wish,
Flew saints upon the rigging, played the clarions:
Yet many there were poisoned by a fish

'And more by doubt; and so deserted Torres
And sailed, my seamen's prisoner, back to Spain.'   *70*
There was a certain likeness in the stories
And Captain Quiros stared at William Lane.

4

Then 'Hoist the mainsail!' both the voyagers cried,
Recoiling each from each as from the devil;
'How do we know that we are truly dead   *75*
Or that the tales we tell may not be fable?

'Surely I only dreamed that one small bottle
Could blow up New Australia like a bomb?
A mutinous pilot I forebore to throttle
From Terra Australis send me demented home?   *80*

'The devil throws me up this Captain Quiros,
This William Lane, a phantom not yet born,
This Captain Quiros dead three hundred years,
To tempt me to disaster for his scorn—

'As if a blast of bony breath could wither   *85*
The trees and fountains shining in my mind,
Some traveller's tale, puffed out in moonlit weather,
Divert me from the land that I must find!

'Somewhere on earth that land of love and faith
In Labour's hands—the Virgin's—must exist,   *90*
And cannot lie behind, for there is death,
So where but in the west—but in the east?'

At that the sea of light began to dance
And plunged in sparkling brine each giddy brain;
The wind from Heaven blew both ways at once   *95*
And west went Captain Quiros, east went Lane.

                                                        (1949)

R. D. FitzGerald
QUAYSIDE MEDITATION

This concrete city with glass, towering walls
grows newly up and does not share the years,
nearly two hundred now, which stone recalls

or harbour noise; and in this haunted time
I turn my back on it where in my ears   *5*
voices and ship-names from an older earth

echo out well beyond what I might claim
myself as yesterdays. . .though mine have known
(and longer gone than *Lawhill* from her berth,

that lone intruder upon steam and steel)   *10*
the masted ships (*Helen B. Stirling* one)
anchored in Birchgrove, five or six together.

For war brought back vessels of square-rigged sail;
but earlier still *Sobraon* off Cockatoo
tugged at fast moorings; and I see my father   *15*

pointing me out her rows of dummy ports
right to the waterline, which once would do
duty for cannon, make her seem, by bluff,

a bristling frigate. So in fabled parts,
the dangerous China seas, that skin-thin paint   20
had tricked Malayan pirates, scared them off.

And when you think of it this links my life
of not yet sixty years with what seems faint
in legendary lore and wholly lost,

namely the wooden ships of war. In brief   25
time is so shortened, since the day's brought near
of Nelson and Trafalagar and the rest,

that what's-to-come no longer looms a place
separate from all being but, joining here
the world we have walked thus far, is even our own.   30

Saying which, I can turn about and face
concrete and glass as things familiar—known
like brick, shell-mortar, and grey Hawkesbury stone.

(1960)

Anonymous
BOTANY BAY

Farewell to old England for ever,
Farewell to my rum culls as well,
Farewell to the well-known Old Bailey,
Where I used for to cut such a swell.

Chorus Singing, too-ral, li-ooral, li-addity,   5
         Singing, too-ral, li-ooral, li-ay.
         Singing, too-ral, li-ooral, li-addity,
         Singing, too-ral, li-ooral, li-ay.

There's the captain as is our commander,
There's the bo'sun and all the ship's crew,   10
There's the first- and the second-class passengers,
Knows what we poor convicts goes through.

'Tain't leaving old England we care about,
'Tain't cos we misspells wot we knows,
But because all we light-fingered gentry   15
Hops round with a log on our toes.

For fourteen long years I have ser-vi-ed,
And for fourteen long years and a day,
For meeting a bloke in the area,
And sneaking his ticker away.   20

Oh had I the wings of a turtle-dove,
I'd soar on my pinions so high,
Slap bang to the arms of my Polly love,
And in her sweet presence I'd die.

Now, all my young Dook-ies and Duch-ess-es,   25
Take warning from what I've to say—
Mind all is your own as you touch-es-es,
Or you'll meet us in Botany Bay.

(1886)

Jean Curlewis
from SYDNEY SURFING

We don't realise it of course. The phenomenon of our surfing beaches. We
are not a modest race and in most cases we are more apt to exaggerate,
rather than underestimate our country's attractions. But we don't realise
surfing.

We have grown up with it and to us it seems quite natural. But it
staggers tourists—yes, even Americans. America, Holland, Norway,
Sweden and South Africa have all written to the Australian Surf Life-
Saving Association for handbooks of our methods as the first step towards
emulating us.

Our surfing beaches. Our long coast scalloped as neatly as a guest towel.
In each scallop, a mile or so of beach sprinkled as thickly with multi-
coloured bathers as a birthday cake with sugar hundreds-and-thousands.
Behind each beach, a village like a vaudeville—a fantastic revue of merry-
go-rounds, soda fountains, picture shows, bandstands. Piles of white flats,
airy as houses built of playing cards. Behind the villages, hills hollowed
like amphitheatres. Tier upon tier of houses, all the way up, like boxes at
an opera. From each balcony, pink and yellow bathing suits and blue and
red towels hung out to dry like flags.

In the steep garden husbands and wives garden domestically in their
bathing suits. Butcher boys dash on their rounds with towels round their
necks. Babies come home from kindergarten, flick their diminutive bathers
from the clothes line, and nonchalantly depart again for a surf, quite on
their own. Business men come home from the office and go for a dip
before dinner as inevitably as men in other cities wash their hands. In the
kitchenettes, saucepans cook unattended on the gas rings. For in a surfing
city recipes always read 'Simmer forty minutes while you have your surf.'

That is on a week-day. On Sundays three surfs are considered reasonable. The first lasts from waking until breakfast, the second from breakfast
until lunch, the third from lunch until dinner. Of course, if it is really hot
and you do not mind sharks you can go in again from dinner until
midnight. At Clovelly one recent heatwave night a rank of cars one mile
long drew up along the beach. At Bondi, bathing suits and full evening
dresses walked together along the lighted promenade. People came from
the theatres at half-time and finished the evening in the water. Mothers put
their babies to sleep on the sand—entire families camped out all night.

Twenty-seven short years ago surfing did not exist. Bathing on open
beaches was forbidden. It was considered improper. Not until 1902 were
the restrictions lifted. We shall not state on which beach was shot the first
shoot. That is a question which still shakes councils and surf clubs to their
foundations.

Other games are confined to the young and strong. Here on the beach an elderly lady placidly parks her spectacles with her towel and wades happily into the fray. A father takes a baby a few months old from its mother and holds it so that the foam brushes its bare feet. The baby goes on sucking its comforter quite unperturbed.

But the actual surfing is only half of it. One does not go for just a dip. One goes for 'a dip and a bake'. To visitors from overseas the sunbaking is just as surprising as the bathing. They come to the beach wall and lean over—and their first impression is of a battlefield. For acres the beach is covered with smooth brown bodies that seem sun-slain. Some are flung face downwards—others lie face up, eyes closed, the sun beating on their faces. All are immobile as marble. They do not stir and sigh as sleepers do—no sleeper was ever so passionately abandoned to sleep as these bodies are to the sun.

An English visitor once stared down at the tranced figures. He was a thin highly intelligent University man and he peered through his *pince-nez* for some time very curiously. Then he turned suddenly: 'What,' he asked, 'are they all thinking about?'

What are they all thinking about? What do they see in the gold-brown mesmeric dusk behind their closed lids while the heat soaks out of the sand into every pore of their skins? That Englishman has been ten years in Australia by now. Does he still wonder what they think about? Did he spend too many years at his University learning how to think, for him ever to master the trick of how to fling himself on the hot sand, stop his mind like a clock, and *not think at all*?

What is it doing to the race, physically and mentally, these hours, days, years, of mixing with sea and sun? For an answer to the physical question, one has only to glance at the ranks of the surf clubs. The tourist or journalist who could write a description of them without employing the phrase 'young Greek gods' or 'statues of bronze', has not yet been born. It simply cannot be done.

For the surf is a sculptor. Those tons of breakers fall like mallet blows and swimmers are chiselled slim and straight. The foam, fizzing and stinging like iced champagne, restores to slack fibres the priceless quality that doctors call 'tone'. The sun polishes the skin to an incredible smoothness. Until the Australian surfer looks like—I cannot help it—a young Greek god.

The extraordinary glow of well-being after a surf! A philosopher once laid down the maxim that one should never commit suicide until one had had a good dinner. He should have said 'Until one had had a good surf'.

(1929)

Moya Costello
AN IMAGINARY CONVERSATION ABOUT BRIAN 'SQUIZZY' TAYLOR

Hey, I must tell you what happened the other day. You know how we went up the coast, um, with this young guy? He was like, ah, a self-styled punk. Yeah. Only about 14. Well, he got involved in London, he was staying there for a while, with these working-class kids; you know, like REAL punks. They wrecked football trains and he got hooked on cough mixture and god knows what, dog pills, gaad. Well he came up the coast with us, to dry out, and its just RIFE with hippies, you know blonde hair, Balinese gear, God. They went CRAZY over Richard Clapton, he had a concert there, when he sang 'I've got those blue bay blues', you know, about Byron Bay? I mean, that song must have been written ten years ago.

Well, O God, he wore a heavy German overcoat, like a military one and hobnailed boots, like these great clumping things, and he had black pants, and short spiky hair dyed red, you know. And he walked onto the sand; I mean this is the middle of summer, the proverbial burning deserts. And I thought, WHAT IS THIS GUY GOING TO DO? And then I thought, I mean, what do punks do in summer? No, really. What do you do in black plastic? I mean it's non-absorbent, right? Surely you have to consider these things. Unless, I dunno, punks go in for endurance tests. I mean it's just downright uncomfortable. And black. All that black, it just absorbs the heat. And try to keep looking pasty-faced. They probably raid the chemists for Block-Out. I mean how'yr gunna avoid a tan? Well, you just couldn't go out, could you?

I mean punks are REALLY OUT OF PLACE IN AUSTRALIA, AREN'T THEY? WINTER IS THE SEASON OF THE PUNK. They must have a REALLY HARD TIME IN AUSTRALIA.

Well you'll never guess. I was just looking at the paper the other day, and what do you think? I saw this piece about this Brian 'Squizzy' Taylor, or something, and he's a PUNK SURFIE. Can you imagine that? I mean, it's taken an Australian to do it? Are Australians known for their ingenuity or something? 'Cause this guy's got it. He's won some surfing award or something, you know, like riding a board? He's got these black wraparound sun-glasses and tight pants and sand-shoes, and he walks onto the beach like that, I mean ISN'T THAT AMAZING?

It's like, well I think it was an art book, yeah, on Van Gogh, and in it his letters to his brother were quoted, and I remember looking up the references and finding they hadn't been published in English, then, I don't know, a few weeks later a book of his letters came out, in hardback. It's one of the few hardbacks I've bought, I've bought another one I think it was Blood Red Sister Rose, you know, by the Australian guy, um, Thomas Keneally, that's right; or another time I'd seen a programme on Che Guevara and Tanya, his last girlfriend, and then I was just looking at some poetry, in a bookshop and I saw a poem about Tanya by William Carlos Williams, or one of the American women poets, um, Ann Sexton or someone. Yeah, and then I was thinking about how punks manage in Australia and here's this guy in the paper, ISN'T THAT INCREDIBLE?

(1982)

Anonymous
THE WILD COLONIAL BOY

There was a wild colonial boy, Jack Donahoe by name,
Of poor but honest parents he was born in Castlemaine.
He was his father's dearest hope, his mother's pride and joy.
O, fondly did his parents love their Wild Colonial Boy.

Chorus:
   So ride with me, my hearties, we'll cross the mountains high.   5
   Together we will plunder, together we will die.
   We'll wander through the valleys and gallop o'er the plains,
   For we scorn to live in slavery, bound down with iron chains!

He was scarcely sixteen years of age when he left his father's home,
A convict to Australia, across the seas to roam.   10
They put him in the Iron Gang in the Government employ,
But ne'er an iron on earth could hold the Wild Colonial Boy.

And when they sentenced him to hang to end his wild career,
With a loud shout of defiance bold Donahoe broke clear.
He robbed those wealthy squatters, their stock he did destroy,   15
But never a trap in the land could catch the Wild Colonial Boy.

Then one day when he was cruising near the broad Nepean's side,
From out the thick Bringelly bush the horse police did ride.
'Die or resign, Jack Donahoe!' they shouted in their joy.
'I'll fight this night with all my might!' cried the Wild Colonial Boy.   20

He fought six rounds with the horse police before the fatal ball,
Which pierced his heart with cruel smart, caused Donohoe to fall.
And then he closed his mournful eyes, his pistol an empty toy,
Crying: 'Parents dear, O say a prayer for the wild Colonial Boy.'

(1860s)

John Farrell
from AUSTRALIA

O Land of widest hope, of promise boundless,
   Why wert thou hidden in a dark, strange sea
To wait through ages, fruitless, scentless, soundless,
   Till from thy slumber men should waken thee?—
Why did'st thou lie, with ear that never hearkened   5
   The sounds without, the cries of strife and play,
Like some sweet child within a chamber darkened
   Left sleeping far into a troubled day?—

What opiate sealed thine eyes while all the others
   Grew tired and faint in East and West and North;   10
Why did'st thou dream until thy joyful brothers
   Found where thou wast, and led thee smiling forth?—

Why did'st thou mask the happy face thou wearest?
  Why wert thou veiled from all the eager eyes?
Why left so long, O first of lands and fairest,   15
  Beneath the tent of unconjectured skies?

Then, sweet Australia, fell a benediction
  Of sleep upon thee, where no wandering breath
Might come to tell thee of the loud affliction
  Of cursing tongues and clamouring hosts of death;   20
And with the peace of His great love around thee,
  And rest that clashing ages could not break,
Strong-sighted eyes of English seekers found thee,
  Strong English voices cried to thee 'Awake!'

Here were no dreadful vestiges imprinted   25
  With evil messages and brands of Cain,
No mounds of death or walls of refuge dinted
  With signs that Christ had lived and died in vain;
No chill memorials here proclaimed the story
  Of kingships stricken for and murders done;   30
Here was a marvel and a separate glory,
  One land whose history had not begun!

One unsown garden, fenced by sea-crags sterile,
  Whose iron breasts flung back the thundering waves,
From all the years of fierce unrest and peril,   35
  And slaves, and lords, and broken blades, and graves;
One gracious freehold for the free, where only
  Soft dusky feet fell, reaching not thy sleep;
One field inviolate, untroubled, lonely,
  Across the dread of the uncharted deep!   40

O dear and fair! awakened from thy sleeping
  So late! The world is breaking into noon;
The eyes that all the morn were dim with weeping
  Smile through the tears that will cease dropping soon!
Thine have no tears in them for olden sorrow,   45
  Thou hast no heartache for a ruined past;
From bright to-day to many a bright to-morrow
  Shall be thy way, O first of lands and last!

                                        (1886)

Henry Kingsley
THE RECOLLECTIONS OF
GEOFFRY HAMLYN

from CHAPTER 36

In front of the Brentwoods' house the plains stretched away for a dozen miles or so, a bare sheet of grass with no timber, grey in summer, green in winter. About five miles off it began to roll into great waves, and then heaved up into a high bald hill, a lofty down, capped with black rocks, bearing in its side a vast round hollow, at the bottom of which was a little swamp, perfectly circular, fringed with a ring of white gum-trees, standing in such an exact circle that it was hard to persuade oneself that they were not planted by the hand of man. This was the crater of the old volcano. Had you stood in it you would have remarked that one side was a shelving steep bank of short grass, while the other reared up some five hundred feet, a precipice of fire-eaten rock. At one end the lip had broken down, pouring a torrent of lava, now fertile grass-land, over the surrounding country, which little gap gave one a delicious bit of blue distance. All else, as I said, was a circular wall of grass, rock, and tumbled slag.

This was Mirngish. And the day after the earthquake there was a fresh eruption in the crater. An eruption of horsemen and horse-women. An eruption of talk, laughter, pink-bonnets, knives and forks, and champagne. Many a pleasant echo came ringing back from the old volcano walls overhead, only used for so many ages to hear the wild rattle of the thunder and the scream of the hungry eagle.

Was ever a poor old worn-out grass-grown volcano used so badly? Here into the very pit of Tophet had the audacious Captain that very morning sent on a spring-cart of all eatables and drinkables, and then had followd himself with a dozen of his friends, to eat and drink, and talk and laugh, just in the very spot where of old roared and seethed the fire and brimstone of Erebus.

Yet the good old mountain was civil, for we were not blown into the air, to be a warning to all people picnicing in high places; but when we had eaten and drunk, and all the ladies had separately and collectively declared that they were *so* fond of the smell of tobacco in the open air, we followed the Doctor, who led the way to the summit of the hill.

I arrived last, having dragged dear fat old Mrs Mayford up the slippery steep. The Doctor had perched himself on the highest flame-worn crag, and when we all had grouped ourselves below him, and while the wind swept pleasantly through the grass, and rushed humming through the ancient rocks, he in a clear melodious voice thus began:—

'Of old the great sea heaved and foamed above the ground on which we stand; aye, above this, and above yon farthest snowy peak, which the westering sun begins to tinge with crimson.

'But in the lapse of ten thousand changing centuries, the lower deeps, acted on by some Plutonic agency, began to grow shallow; and the imprisoned tides began to foam and roar as they stuggled to follow the moon, their leader, angry to find that the stillness of their ancient domain was year by year invaded by the ever-rising land.

'At that time, had man been on the earth to see it, those towering Alps were a cluster of lofty islands, each mountain pass which divides them was a tide-swept fiord, in and out of which, twice in the day, age after age, rushed the sea, bringing down those vast piles of water-worn gravel which you see accumulated, and now covered with dense vegetation, at the mouth of each great valley.

'So twenty thousand years went on, and all this fair champagne country which we overlook became, first a sand-bank, then a dreary stretch of salt-saturated desert, and then, as the roar of the retiring ocean grew fainter and fainter, began to sustain such vegetation as the Lord thought fit.

'A thousand years are but as yesterday to Him, and I can give you no notion as to how many hundred thousand years it took to do all this; or what productions covered the face of the country. It must have been a miserably poor region: nothing but the débris of granite, sandstone, and slate; perhaps here and there partially fertilized by rotting sea-weed, dead fish and shells; things which would, we may assume, have appeared and flourished as the water grew shallower.

'New elements were wanting to make the country available for man, so soon to appear in his majesty; and new elements were forthcoming. The internal fires so long imprisoned beneath the weight of the incumbent earth, having done their duty in raising the continent, began to find vent in every weak spot caused by its elevation.

'Here, where we stand, in this great crack between the granite and the sandstone, they broke out with all their wildest fury; hurling stones high in the air, making mid-day dark with clouds of ashes, and pouring streams of lava far and wide.

'So the country was desolated by volcanoes, but only desolated that it might grow greener and richer than ever, with a new and hitherto un-known fertility; for, as the surface of the lava disintegrated, a new soil was found, containing all the elements of the old one, and many more. These are your black clay, and your red burnt soil, which, I take it, are some of the richest in the world.

'Then our old volcano, our familiar Mirngish, in whose crater we have been feasting, grew still for a time, for many ages probably; but after that I see the traces of another eruption; the worst, perhaps, that he ever accomplished.

'He had exhausted himself, and gradually subsided, leaving a perfect cup or crater, the accumulation of the ashes of a hundred eruptions; nay, even this may have been filled with water, as is Mount Gambier, which you have not seen, forming a lake without a visible outlet; the water draining off at that level where the looser scoriae begin.

'But he burst out again, filling this great hollow with lava, till the accumulation of the molten matter broke through the weaker part of the wall, and rolled away there, out of that gap to the northward, and forming what you now call the 'stony rises,' —turning yon creek into steam, which by its explosive force formed that fantastic cap of rocks, and swelling into great bubbles under the hot lava, made those long underground hollows which we now know as the caves of Bar-ca-nah.

'Is he asleep for ever? I know not. He may arise again in his wrath and fill the land with desolation; for that earthquake we felt yesterday was but a wild throe of the giant struggling to be free.

'Let us hope that he may not break his chains, for as I stand here gazing on those crimson Alps, the spirit of prophecy is upon me, and I can see far into the future, and all the desolate landscape becomes peopled with busy figures.

'I see the sunny slopes below me yellow with trellissed vines. They have gathered the vintage, and I hear them singing at the wine-press. They sing that the exhausted vineyards of the old world yield no wine so rare, so rich, as the fresh volcanic slopes of the southern continent, and that the princes of the earth send their wealth that their hearts may get glad from the juice of the Australian grapes.

'Beyond I see fat black ridges grow yellow with a thousand cornfields. I see a hundred happy homesteads, half-hidden by clustering wheatstacks. What do they want with all that corn? say you; where is their market!

'There is their market! Away there on the barren forest ranges. See, the timber is gone, and a city stands there instead. What is that on the crest of the hill? A steam-engine: nay, see, there are five of them, working night and day, fast and busy. Their cranks gleam and flash under the same moon that grew red and lurid when old Mirngish vomited fire and smoke twenty thousand years ago. As I listen I can hear the grinding of the busy quartz-mill. What are they doing? you ask. They are gold-mining.

'They have found gold here, and gold in abundance, and hither have come, by ship and steamship, all the unfortunate of the earth. The English factory labourer and the farmer-ridden peasant; the Irish pauper; the starved Scotch Highlander. I hear a grand swelling chorus rising above the murmur of the evening breeze; that is sung by German peasants revelling in such plenty as they never knew before, yet still regretting fatherland, and then I hear a burst of Italian melody replying. Hungarians are not wanting, for all the oppressed of the earth have taken refuge here, glorying to live under the free government of Britain; for she, warned by American experience, has granted to all her colonies such rights as the British boast of possessing.'

I did not understand him then. But, since I have seen the living wonder of Ballarat, I understand him well enough.

He ceased. But the Major cried out, 'Go on, Doctor, go on. Look farther yet, and tell us what you see. Give us a bit more poetry while your hand is in.'

He faced round, and I fancied I could detect a latent smile about his mouth.

'I see,' said he, 'a vision of a nation, the colony of the greatest race on the earth, who began their career with more advantages than ever fell to the lot of a young nation yet. War never looked on them. Not theirs was the lot to fight, like the Americans, through bankruptcy and inexperience towards freedom and honour. No. Freedom came to them, Heaven-sent, red-tape-bound, straight from Downing-street. Millions of fertile acres, gold in bushels were theirs, and yet—'

'Go on,' said the Major.

'I see a vision of broken railway arches and ruined farms. I see a vision of a people surfeited with prosperity and freedom grown factious, so that now one party must command a strong majority ere they can pass a law the goodness of which no one denies. I see a bankrupt exchequer, a drunken Governor, an Irish ministry, a —'

'Come down out of that,' roared the Major, 'before I pull you down. You're a pretty fellow to come out for a day's pleasure! Jeremiah was a saint to him,' he added, turning appealingly to the rest of us. 'Hear my opinion, "per contra", Doctor. I'll be as near right as you.'

'Go on, then,' said the Doctor.

'I see,' began the Major, 'the Anglo-Saxon race—'

'Don't forget the Irish, Jews, Germans, Chinese, and other barbarians,' interrupted the Doctor.

'Asserting', continued the Major, scornfully, 'as they always do, their right to all the unoccupied territories of the earth—'

('Blackfellow's claims being ignored,' interpolated the Doctor.)

'And filling all the harbours of this magnificent country—'

('Want to see them.')

'With their steamships and their sailing vessels. Say there be gold here, as I believe there is, the time must come when the mines will be exhausted. What then? With our coals we shall supply—'

('Newcastle,' said the Doctor, again.)

'The British fleets in the East Indies—'

'And compete with Borneo,' said the Doctor, quietly, 'which contains more coal than ever India will burn, at one-tenth the distance from her that we are. If that is a specimen of your prophecies, Major, you are but a Micaiah after all.'

'Well,' said the Major, laughing, 'I cannot reel it off quite so quick as you; but think we shall hardly have time for any more prophesying; the sun is getting very low.'

(1859)

Mary Hannay Foott
WHERE THE PELICAN BUILDS

[The unexplored parts of Australia are sometimes spoken of by the bushmen of Western Queensland as the home of the pelican, a bird whose nesting place, so far as the writer knows, is seldom, if ever found.]

The horses were ready, the rails were down,
　　But the riders lingered still,—
　　　One had a parting word to say,
　　And one had his pipe to fill.
Then they mounted, one with a granted prayer,   5
　　And one with a grief unguessed.
　　　'We are going' they said, as they rode away—
　　'Where the pelican builds her nest!'

They had told us of pastures wide and green,
    To be sought past the sunset's glow;   10
      Of rifts in the ranges by opal lit;
    And gold 'neath the river's flow.
And thirst and hunger were banished words
    When they spoke of that unknown West;
      No drought they dreaded, no flood they feared,   15
    Where the pelican builds her nest!

The creek at the ford was but fetlock deep
    When we watched them crossing there;
      The rains have replenished it thrice since then
    And thrice has the rock lain bare.   20
But the waters of Hope have flowed and fled,
    And never from blue hill's breast
      Come back—by the sun and the sand devoured—
    Where the pelican builds her nest!

                                  (5 March 1881)

Adam Lindsay Gordon
THE SICK STOCKRIDER

Hold hard, Ned! Lift me down once more, and lay me
    in the shade.
    Old man, you've had your work cut out to guide
Both horses, and to hold me in the saddle when I sway'd
    All through the hot, slow, sleepy, silent ride.
The dawn at 'Moorabinda' was a mist rack dull and dense,   5
    The sunrise was a sullen, sluggish lamp;
I was dozing in the gateway at Arbuthnot's bound'ry fence,
    I was dreaming on the Limestone cattle camp.
We crossed the creek at Carricksford, and sharply through the haze,
    And suddenly the sun shot flaming forth;   10
To southward lay 'Katâwa', with the sandpeaks all ablaze,
    And the flush'd fields of Glen Lomond lay to north.
Now westward winds the bridle path that leads to Lindisfarm,
    And yonder looms the double-headed Bluff;
From the far side of the first hill, when the skies are clear and calm,   15
    You can see Sylvester's woolshed fair enough.
Five miles we used to call it from our homestead to the place
    Where the big tree spans the roadway like an arch;
'Twas here we ran the dingo down that gave us such a chase
    Eight years ago—or was it nine?—last March.   20
'Twas merry in the glowing morn, among the gleaming grass,
    To wander as we've wandered many a mile,
And blow the cool tobacco cloud, and watch the white wreaths pass,

Sitting loosely in the saddle all the while.
'Twas merry 'mid the blackwoods when we spied the station roofs,   25
   To wheel the wild scrub cattle at the yard,
With a running fire of stockwhips and a fiery run of hoofs;
   Oh! the hardest day was never then too hard!

Aye! we had a glorious gallop after 'Starlight' and his gang,
   When they bolted from Sylvester's on the flat;   30
How the sun dried reed-beds crackled, how the flint-strewn ranges
      rang
   To the strokes of 'Mountaineer' and 'Acrobat'.
Hard behind them in the timber, harder still across the heath,
   Close beside them through the tea-tree scrub we dash'd;
And the golden-tinted fern leaves, how they rustled underneath!   35
   And the honeysuckle osiers, how they crash'd!

We led the hunt throughout, Ned, on the chestnut and the grey,
   And the troopers were three hundred yards behind,
While we emptied our six-shooters on the bush-rangers at bay,
   In the creek with stunted box-tree for a blind!   40

There you grappled with the leader, man to man and horse to horse,
   And you roll'd together when the chestnut rear'd;
He blazed away and missed you in that shallow watercourse—
   A narrow shave—his powder singed your beard!

In these hours when life is ebbing, how those days when life
      was young   45
   Come back to us; how clearly I recall
Even the yarns Jack Hall invented, and the songs Jem Roper sung!
   And where are now Jem Roper and Jack Hall?

Aye! nearly all our comrades of the old colonial school,
   Our ancient boon companions, Ned, are gone;   50
Hard livers for the most part, somewhat reckless as a rule,
   It seems that you and I are left alone.

There was Hughes, who got in trouble through that business
      with the cards,
   It matters little what became of him;
But a steer ripp'd up MacPherson in the Cooraminta yards,   55
   And Sullivan was drown'd at Sink-or-swim;
And Mostyn—poor Frank Mostyn—died at last a fearful wreck,
   In 'the horrors,' at the Upper Wandinong,
And Carisbrooke, the rider, at the Horsefall broke his neck,
   Faith! the wonder was he saved his neck so long!   60

Ah! those days and nights we squandered at the Logans'
      in the glen—
   The Logans, man and wife, have long been dead.
Elsie's tallest girl seems taller than your little Elsie then;
   And Ethel is a woman grown and wed.

I've had my share of pastime, and I've done my share of toil,   65
   And life is short—the longest life a span;

I care not now to tarry for the corn or for the oil,
  Or for the wine that maketh glad the heart of man.
For good undone and gifts misspent and resolutions vain,
  'Tis somewhat late to trouble. This I know—   70
I should live the same life over, if I had to live again;
  And the chances are I go where most men go.

The deep blue skies wax dusky, and the tall green trees grow dim,
  The sward beneath me seems to heave and fall;
And sickly, smoky shadows through the sleepy sunlight swim,   75
  And on the very sun's face weave their pall.
Let me slumber in the hollow where the wattle blossoms wave,
  With never stone or rail to fence my bed;
Should the sturdy station children pull the bush flowers on my grave,
  I may chance to hear them romping overhead.   80

(1869)

Henry Lawson
THE OLD BARK SCHOOL

It was built of bark and poles, and the floor was full of holes
  Where each leak in rainy weather made a pool;
And the walls were mostly cracks lined with calico and sacks—
  There was little need for windows in the school.

Then we rode to school and back by the rugged gully track,   5
  On the old grey horse that carried three or four;
And he looked so very wise that he lit the master's eyes
  Every time he put his head in at the door.

He had run with Cobb and Co.—'that grey leader, let him go!'
  There were men 'as knowed the brand upon his hide',   10
And as knowed it on the course'. Funeral service: 'Good old horse!'
  When we burnt him in the gully where he died.

And the master thought the same. 'Twas from Ireland that he came,
  Where the tanks are full all summer, and the feed is simply grand;
And the joker then in vogue said his lessons wid a brogue—   15
  'Twas unconscious imitation, let the reader understand.

And we learnt the world in scraps from some ancient dingy maps
  Long discarded by the public-schools in town;
And as nearly every book dated back to Captain Cook
  Our geography was somewhat upside-down.   20

It was 'in the book' and so—well, at that we'd let it go,
  For we never would believe that print could lie;
And we all learnt pretty soon that when we came out at noon
  'The sun is in the south part of the sky.'

And Ireland! *that* was known from the coast line to Athlone: 25
  We got little information *re* the land that gave us birth;

Save that Captain Cook was killed (and was very likely grilled)
   And 'the natives of New Holland are the lowest race on earth'.

And a woodcut, in its place, of the same degraded race
   Seemed a lot more like a camel than the black-fellows we knew;   30
Jimmy Bullock, with the rest, scratched his head and gave it best;
   But his faith was sadly shaken by a bobtailed kangaroo.

But the old bark-school is gone, and the spot it stood upon
   Is a cattle-camp in winter where the curlew's cry is heard;
There's a brick-school on the flat, but a schoolmate teaches that,   35
   For, about the time they built it, our old master was 'transferred'.

But the bark-school comes again with exchanges 'cross the plain—
   With the *Out-Back Advertiser*; and my fancy roams at large
When I read of passing stock, of a western mob or flock,
   With 'James Bullock', 'Grey', or 'Henry Dale' in charge.   40

And I think how Jimmy went from the old bark school content,
   With his 'eddication' finished, with his pack-horse after him;
And perhaps if I were back I would take the self-same track,
   For I wish my learning ended when the Master 'finished' Jim.

                                (1897)

A. B. ('Banjo') Paterson
CLANCY OF THE OVERFLOW

I had written him a letter which I had, for want of better
   Knowledge, sent to where I met him down the Lachlan, years ago,
He was shearing when I knew him, so I sent the letter to him,
   Just 'on spec', addressed as follows, 'Clancy, of The Overflow'.

And an answer came directed in a writing unexpected,   5
   (And I think the same was written with a thumb-nail dipped in tar)
'Twas his shearing mate who wrote it, and *verbatim* I will quote it:
   'Clancy's gone to Queensland droving, and we don't know where
      he are.'

                *

In my wild erratic fancy visions come to me of Clancy
   Gone a-droving 'down the Cooper' where the Western drovers go;   10
As the stock are slowly stringing, Clancy rides behind them singing,
   For the drover's life has pleasures that the townsfolk never know.

And the bush hath friends to meet him, and their kindly voices
      greet him
   In the murmur of the breezes and the river on its bars,
And he sees the vision splendid of the sunlit plains extended,   15
   And at night the wond'rous glory of the everlasting stars.

                *

I am sitting in my dingy little office, where a stingy
   Ray of sunlight struggles feebly down between the houses tall,
And the foetid air and gritty of the dusty, dirty city
   Through the open window floating, spreads its foulness over all.   20

And in place of lowing cattle, I can hear the fiendish rattle
  Of the tramways and the 'buses making hurry down the street,
And the language uninviting of the gutter children fighting,
  Comes fitfully and faintly through the ceaseless tramp of feet.

And the hurrying people daunt me, and their pallid faces haunt me   25
  As they shoulder one another in their rush and nervous haste,
With their eager eyes and greedy, and their stunted forms and weedy,
  For townsfolk have no time to grow, they have no time to waste.

And I somehow rather fancy that I'd like to change with Clancy,
  Like to take a turn at droving where the seasons come and go,   30
While he faced the round eternal of the cash-book and the journal—
  But I doubt he'd suit the office, Clancy, of 'The Overflow'.

                                                    (1890)

Norman Lindsay
from THE MAGIC PUDDING

'One of the great advantages of being a professional puddin'-owner,' said
Sam Sawnoff, 'is that songs at breakfast are always encouraged. None of
the ordinary breakfast rules, such as scowling while eating, and saying the
porridge is as stiff as glue and the eggs are as tough as leather, are
observed. Instead, songs, roars of laughter, and boisterous jests are the
order of the day. For example, this sort of thing,' added Sam, doing a
rapid back-flap and landing with a thump on Bill's head. As Bill was
unprepared for this act of boisterous humour, his face was pushed into the
Puddin' with great violence, and the gravy was splashed in his eye.

'What d'yer mean, playin' such bungfoodlin' tricks on a man at breakfast?' roared Bill.

'What d'yer mean,' shouted the Puddin', 'playing such foodbungling
tricks on a Puddin' being breakfasted at?'

'Breakfast humour, Bill, merely breakfast humour,' said Sam, hastily.

'Humour's humour,' shouted Bill, 'but puddin' in the whiskers is no
joke.'

'Whiskers in the Puddin' is worse than puddin' in the whiskers,' shouted
the Puddin', standing up in his basin.

'Observe the rules, Bill,' said Sam hurriedly. 'Boisterous humour at the
breakfast table must be greeted with roars of laughter.'

'To Jeredelum with the rules,' shouted Bill. 'Pushing a man's face into
his own breakfast is beyond rules or reason, and deserves a punch in the
gizzard.'

Seeing matters arriving at this unpromising situation, Bunyip Bluegum
interposed by saying, 'Rather than allow this happy occasion to be marred
by unseemly recriminations, let us, while admitting that our admirable
friend, Sam, may have unwittingly disturbed the composure of our admirable friend, Bill, at the expense of our admirable Puddin's gravy, let us, I
say, by the simple act of extending the hand of friendship, dispel in an

instant these gathering clouds of disruption. In the words of the poem—

> 'Then let the fist of Friendship
> Be kept for Friendship's foes.
> Ne'er let that hand in anger land
> On Friendship's holy nose.'

These fine sentiments at once dispelled Bill's anger. He shook hands warmly with Sam, wiped the gravy from his face, and resumed breakfast with every appearance of hearty good humour.

The meal over, the breakfast things were put away in the bag, Sam and Bill took Puddin' between them, and all set off along the road, enlivening the way with song and story. Bill regaled them with portions of the 'Ballad of the *Salt Junk Sarah*', which is one of those songs that go on for ever. Its great advantage, as Bill remarked, was that as it hadn't got an ending it didn't need a beginning, so you could start it anywhere.

'As for instance,' said Bill, and he roared out—

> 'Ho, aboard the *Salt Junk Sarah*,
> Rollin' home across the line,
> The Bo'sun collared the Captain's hat
> And threw it in the brine.
> Rollin' home, rollin' home,
> Rollin' home across the foam,
> The Captain sat without a hat
> The whole way rollin' home.'

Entertaining themselves in this way as they strolled along, they were presently arrested by shouts of 'Fire! Fire!' and a Fireman in a large helmet came bolting down the road, pulling a fire hose behind him.

'Aha!' said Bill. 'Now we shall have the awe-inspirin' spectacle of a fire to entertain us,' and, accosting the Fireman, he demanded to know where the fire was.

'The fact is,' said the Fireman, 'that owing to the size of this helmet I can't see where it is; but if you will kindly glance at the surrounding district, you'll see it about somewhere.'

They glanced about and, sure enough, there was a fire burning in the next field. It was only a cowshed, certainly, but it was blazing very nicely, and well worth looking at.

'Fire,' said Bill, 'in the form of a common cowshed, is burnin' about nor'-nor'-east as the crow flies.'

'In that case,' said the Fireman, 'I invite all present to bravely assist in putting it out. But,' he added impressively, 'if you'll take my advice, you'll shove that Puddin' in this hollow log and roll a stone agen the end to keep him in, for if he gets too near the flames he'll be cooked again and have his flavour ruined.'

'This is a very sensible feller,' said Bill, and though Puddin' objected strongly, he was at once pushed into a log and securely fastened in with a large stone.

'How'd you like to be shoved in a blooming log,' he shouted at Bill, 'when you was burning with anxiety to see the fire?' but Bill said severely,

'Be sensible, Albert, fires is too dangerous to Puddins' flavours.'

No more time was lost in seizing the hose and they set off with the greatest enthusiasm. For, as everyone knows, running with the reel is one of the grand joys of being a fireman. They had the hose fixed to a garden tap in no time, and soon were all hard at work, putting out the fire.

Of course there was a great deal of smoke and shouting, and getting tripped up by the hose, and it was by the merest chance Bunyip Bluegum glanced back in time to see the Wombat in the act of stealing the Puddin' from the hollow log.

'Treachery is at work,' he shouted.

'Treachery,' roared Bill, and with one blow on the snout knocked the Fireman endways on into the burning cinders, where his helmet fell off, and exposed the countenance of that snooting, snouting soundrel, the Possum.

The Possum, of course, hadn't expected to have his disguise pierced so swiftly, and, though he managed to scramble out of the fire in time to save his bacon, he was considerably singed down the back.

'What a murderous attack!' he exclaimed. 'O, what a brutal attempt to burn a man alive!' and as some hot cinders had got down his back he gave a sharp yell and ran off, singeing and smoking. Bill, distracted with rage, ran after the Possum, then changed his mind and ran after the Wombat, so that, what with running first after one and then after the other, they both had time to get clean away, and disappeared over the skyline.

'I see it all,' shouted Bill, casting himself down in despair. 'Them low puddin'-thieves has borrowed a fireman's helmet, collared a hose, an' set fire to a cowshed in order to lure us away from the Puddin'.'

'The whole thing's a low put-up job on our noble credulity,' said Sam, casting himself down beside Bill.

'It's one of the most frightful things that's ever happened,' said Bill.

'It's worse than treading on tacks with bare feet,' said Sam.

'It's worse than bein' caught stealin' fowls,' said Bill.

'It's worse than bein' stood on by cows,' said Sam.

'It's almost as bad as havin' an uncle called Aldobrantifoscofornio,' said Bill, and they both sang loudly—

> 'It's worse than weevils, worse than warts,
> It's worse than corns to bear.
> It's worse than havin' several quarts
> Of treacle in your hair.
>
> It's worse than beetles in the soup,
> It's worse than crows to eat.
> It's worse than wearin' small-sized boots
> Upon your large-sized feet.
>
> It's worse than kerosene to boose,
> It's worse than ginger hair.
> It's worse than anythin' to lose
> A Puddin' rich and rare.'

(1918)

Lennie Lower
WHERE THE COOLER BARS GROW

I'm only a city boy. Until a short time ago I'd never seen a sheep all in one piece or with its fur on. That's why, when people said to me, 'Go west, young man, or east, if you like, but go,' I went.

Truth to tell, I thought it would be safer. I had a shotgun and a rifle, and a bag of flour, and two sealed kerosene tins of fresh water in the luggage van. I thought of taking some coloured beads for the natives, but decided it was too expensive.

I forget now where it was I went to. Anyhow, it was full of wheat silos and flies, and there was a horse standing on three legs under a tree. There were no other signs of life except a faint curl of smoke coming from the hotel chimney.

When I walked into the bar there was nobody there, so I walked out the back to the kitchen and there was nobody there. I went out to the front veranda again, and saw a little old man picking burrs off his socks.

'Good-day!' I said.

'Day!' he replied.

'Where's everybody?' I asked.

'Never heard of him. Unless you mean old Smith. He's down by the crick. You're a stranger, aren't you?'

'Just got off the train. Where's the publican?'

'Do you want a drink?'

'Yes.'

'Orright!'

So we went into the bar and had a drink.

'I want to book a room here,' I told him.

'Don't be silly!' he replied. 'Sleep out on the veranda with the rest of us if you've got blankets. They're decoratin' the School of Arts with the sheets. You going to the dance?'

'I can't dance!'

'Strike me pink, who wants to! We leave that to the women. There ought to be some good fights at this one. When I was younger there wasn't a man could stand up to me on the dance floor. Here comes somebody now.'

'Day.'

'Day. Don't you bring that horse into the bar! Hang it all, you've been told about that before.'

'He's quiet. I broke him in yesterday. Hear about Snowy? Got his arm caught in the circular saw up at the timber mill.'

'That's bad.'

'Too right it is! They've got to get a new saw. Whoa there!'

'Take him out into the kitchen. The flies are worryin' him.'

'Goodo. Pour me out a beer.'

'Pour it out yourself.'

'Go to bed, you old mummified ox!'

'I'll give you a belt in the ear, you red-headed son of a convict!'

'Give it to your uncle. Giddap!'

'One of me best friends,' said the old man, as the horse was led into the kitchen.

'I suppose,' said the red-headed one, returning, 'it'll be all right if he eats that cake on the kitchen table? Won't do him any harm, will it?'

'That's for supper at the dance!'

'Well, I'll go and take it off him. There's a good bit of it left.'

Outside on the veranda voices were heard.

'I wouldn't sell that dog for a thousand pounds.'

'I wouldn't give you two bob for 'im.'

'You never had two bob in your life! You ever seen a sheep dog trial? That dog has won me more prizes at the Show than ten other dogs.

'Why,' he continued, 'you could hang up a fly-veil, point out one particular hole in it and that dog could cut a fly out of a bunch and work him through that hole.'

'Good-day!'

'Day!'

'No sign of rain yet.'

'No. I heard of a swaggie who had to walk eighty miles to get water to boil his billy, and when he got there he found he'd forgotten his cup and saucer, and by the time he'd walked back for his cup and saucer there was a bushfire started in the waterhole, it was that dry.'

'Don't bring your horses into the bar!'

'Don't take any notice of the old crank. Why don't you put this beer out in the sun to get cool? If it was any flatter you'd have to serve it in a plate. Going to the Show this year?'

'Of course I am. Why don't you teach that horse manners?'

'Good-day, Mrs Smith.'

'Who put that horse in my kitchen?'

'Is he in the kitchen? Well, what do you think of that!'

'Fancy him being in the kitchen!'

'In the kitchen, of all places!'

'Who could have let him in?'

'Never mind about that. Get him out at once, Jack! Wipe up that counter. I told you to cut some wood this morning. And put that dog outside and get the broom and sweep up the bar. Wash those glasses first.'

By this time we were all out on the veranda.

'She hasn't found out about the horse eating the cake,' said somebody. 'Better go for a walk somewhere, eh?'

But that was years ago. They've got radios and refrigerators in the bush now, and that's why you see me mournfully wandering about the cattle stalls at Show time. I'm thinking of the good old days before the squatters took up polo, and started knitting their own berets. When men were men, and women were useful about the farm when the plough horse took sick.

> *Wrap me up in my stockwhip and blanket*
> *And bury me deep down below*
> *Where the farm implement salesmen won't molest me,*
> *In the shades where the cooler bars grow.*

Ah, me!

(?1930s)

G.H. Gibson ('Ironbark')
ON THE PREVALENCE OF 'BILL' IN AUSTRALIAN LITERATURE

How we wish the clever writers
   Of our prose and of our verse
For their characters would take a wider range!
There are some which keep recurring
   Like a decimal—we curse   5
Their recurrence, and we're aching for a change.

We are weary of the legend
   Where the sergeant of police
Loves the fascinating sister of a 'crook',
And condones a lot of felonies   10
   And breaches of the peace.
And won't prosecute when cattle have been 'shook'.

People say, 'It's so Australian!'
   And some similar event
May have happened long ago as in the tale,   15
But police are not romantic
   Now—at least to that extent—
And the 'crooks' they cop are handed to the gaol.

There's the big gum-booted digger
   Crimson-shirted, with the sash   20
Which he wore when Ballarat first played the game
And he's nearly always doing
   Something venturesome and rash
When he isn't 'slinging mullock' in his claim.

All the writers since the 'fifties'   25
   Have delighted in this type,
Who is always big and masterful and flash.
And, whatever he is doin'—
   Diggin'—dancin'—stewin' tripe—
Why, he always wears the shirt and boots and sash.   30

There's the beautiful bush maiden—
   Though her father keeps a pub,
In the local estimation she is IT!—
And she rides unbroken 'brumbies'
   Through impenetrable scrub—   35
An exasperating female, you'll admit.

She is cultured and accomplished,
   And with virtue she's supplied
In accordance with a lavish kind of scale.
So, when tempted by the squatter,   40
   She prefers to be the bride
Of a humble chap who runs the local mail.

Ah! these types are too familiar,
  They disturb our peace of mind;
But the one which makes us actually ill,   45
Is that weird, elusive bushman—
  He's in every tale, you'll find—
And he bears the simple sobriquet of 'Bill'.

This great prevalence of William
  Makes our indignation boil—   50
Every reader of Australian fiction knows
How he prances through the poems
  Which are 'racy of the soil',
While he positively permeates our prose.

He's a shepherd, he's a shearer,   55
  He's a breaker-in of nags,
And he always swims some river in a flood.
But he wrecks our nervous system,
  And reduces it to rags,
'Till we really feel we want to have his blood.   60

He's a stockman, he's a drover—
  He's on any kind of 'lay'
Which may chance to suit the man who slings the ink—
But he always plays the hero
  In an offhand kind of way—
That's enough to make a reader take to drink.

There is game and there is glory
  To be gathered by the bard,
Or the fiction-manufacturer who will
Write a stirring backblock story   70
  (Oh! we know it will be hard!)
Or a poem that is innocent of Bill.

                                              (?1900)

Frank Hardy
THE GREAT AUSTRALIAN LARRIKIN
(*as told by Billy Borker in the Albion Hotel,
Parramatta*)

What would be the best Australian story you ever heard, Billy?

The Great Australian Larrikin, as my father called it, is one of the best,
I'd reckon, Jerome.

Have another drink and tell me about him.

Don't mind if I do. This fella's name was Dooley Franks. A real
knockabout man. Lived here in Parramatta. Ran a double, did a bit of
urging at the races, sold smuggled transistors. One night he went to
Tommo's two-up school and won five hundred quid backing the tail. So he
decided to join the Tattersall's Club. Up he choofs to the uniformed

flunkey at the club door, wearing a polo neck jumper, suede shoes, and one of them small brimmed hats with a yellow feather in it. 'Here, fill in this form,' the flunkey says dubiously; 'the committee will consider your application and let you know in due course.' When the committee meets, the secretary says: 'This Dooley Franks is an urger. We can't have him in the club.' The committee members could not have agreed more: most of them *used* to be urgers, see. 'Dooley Franks hasn't got two pennies to clink together. Just tell him the joining fee—a hundred pounds—and that'll be the end of it.'

So they write Dooley a letter and he bounces back and slams a bundle of tenners on the counter in front of the flunkey. Well, the committee got really worried. The secretary says: 'Tell him he has to have three sponsors, famous people, not Australians. The furthest he's ever been from Parramatta is to the Kembla Grange racecourse.' They think they've got old Dooley Franks beat, see. So the flunkey tells him: 'Three famous people, not Australians.' 'Why didn't you say so in the first place?' Dooley says, 'would have saved time and trouble. Eisenhower (he was President at that time), Khrushchev and the Pope. Just tell 'em Dooley Franks from Parramatta wants a reference.'

He was joking, of course?

Wait till I tell yer. Don't spoil the story, mate, one of the best Australian stories ever told. Well, the committee got a shock, needless to say. Now, the secretary was a hard case, so he says: 'Listen, this here Dooley Franks couldn't know Eisenhower, Khrushchev or the Pope. Tell you what we'll do. We'll offer to take him over to Washington, Moscow and Rome, in person. Then we'll hear no more about it.' They write to Dooley Franks and he says: 'All right with me. Air letters would be cheaper, but if you insist.' The secretary says: 'We're stuck with it now. We'll put in a hundred quid each and I'll go with him. It'll be the joke of the century.' Away they go by air to Washington, up the steps to the White House. They wait around in corridors for about three days and eventually they get an appointment with one of Eisenhower's side-kicks. 'I'm from Tattersall's Club, Sydney,' the secretary says. The Yank is puzzled. 'Sydney?' he asks, 'where's that?' 'Australia,' the secretary tells him. 'Ah, yeah,' the Yank replies. 'That's where we sell all our old films to the television stations.' 'We want to see President Eisenhower,' the secretary says. 'You can't just come here and see the President. You have to have an appointment.' Well, Dooley Franks is getting a bit impatient, see, so he says: 'Listen, just tell Ike Dooley Franks wants to see him. The bloke who pinched six tins of petrol for him when his car ran out on the road to Paris. Dooley Franks from Parramatta.' Well, the Yank goes away and comes back. 'Mister Franks,' he says, 'why didn't you say so in the first place? President Eisenhower will see you right away.' 'Can I come too?' the secretary says. 'No, the President wants to have a private chat with Mister Franks.'

Surely he didn't actually know Eisenhower?

Well, he came back six hours later high as a kite. 'Sorry to keep you waiting,' he tells the secretary. 'Me and Ike got talking old times over a few drinks and lost track of time.' So they head off for Moscow.

Ah, don't tell me...

Up to the Kremlin gates with an interpreter they go. Freezing cold night, thirty-eight below. The secretary puts over a spiel about the Tattersall's

Club and Dooley tells the bloke on the gate: 'Just tell Nikita that Dooley Franks from Parramatta wants to see him. Was treasurer of the Sheepskins For Russia appeal during the war, sailed on the North Sea convoys and sold Russian magazines on the Sydney waterfront.' Well, to make a long story short, the same thing happens: Khrushchev wants to see Comrade Franks, and the secretary of the Tattersall's Club is left freezing in the Red Square. Dooley comes out eventually, and next day they head for Rome. And the secretary is thinking: What will I tell the committee when I get back? They'll never believe me. If he gets in to see the Pope, I'm going with him.

And did he?

Well, they see a cardinal, but he says you have to make an appointment for an audience with the Pope. So Dooley tells him: 'Just say Dooley Franks from Parramatta; was an altar boy at St Patrick's Cathedral, got a brother a priest and a sister a nun.' The cardinal comes back—if you don't believe me you can ask old Dooley himself—he says the Pope will grant a private audience to Mister Franks. The secretary begs to be let in. 'I must see them together,' he says. 'His Holiness wishes to see only Mister Franks. But if you want to see them together you can stand down in the square. His Holiness will appear on the balcony at one o'clock and I'll arrange for Mister Franks to stand with him.' Well, the secretary is desperate: what's he going to tell the committee? He goes away and comes back at one o'clock. The square is packed with fifty thousand people. The secretary is so far away he can't even see the balcony. The crowd cheers. There's a Yankee tourist standing near by with a pair of field-glasses. The secretary begs him: 'Lend me your field-glasses.' The Yank says: 'They're not field-glasses, they're binoculars. And you can't borrow them. I've come ten thousand miles to see the Vatican....' The secretary says: 'Well, what can you see?' 'Two men standing on the balcony,' the Yank tells him. The secretary tugs his arm. 'Can you recognise them? Who are they?' The Yank takes a good look through his binoculars: 'Well, I can't place the guy in the funny hat but the other guy is definitely Dooley Franks from Parramatta.'

Now I've heard everything.

(1964)

Ian Mudie
THEY'LL TELL YOU ABOUT ME

Me, I'm the man that dug the Murray for Sturt to sail down,
I am the one that rode beside the man from Snowy River,
and I'm Ned Kelly's surviving brother (or did I marry his sister?
I forget which), and it was my thumbnail that wrote that Clancy
had gone a-droving, and when wood was scarce I set the grass on fire   5
and ran with it three miles to boil my billy, only to find
I'd left the tea and sugar back with my tucker-bag,
and it was me, and only me, that shot through with the padre's
    daughter,
shot through with her on the original Bondi tram.

But it's a lie that I died hanging from a parrot's nest   10
with my arm in the hollow limb when my horse moved from
    under me;
I never die, I'm like the Leichhardt survivor I discovered
fifty years after the party had disappeared; I never die,
I'm Lasseter and Leichhardt both: I joined the wires of the OT
so that Todd could send the first message from Adelaide to Darwin;   15
I settled everywhere long before the explorers arrived;
my tracks criss-cross the Simpson Desert like city streets,
and I've hung my hat on Poeppel's Peg a thousand times.
It was me who boiled my billy under the coolabah,
told the bloke in the flash car to open his own flamin' gates,   20
put the goldfields pipe-line through where the experts said nobody
    could,
wanted to know 'Who's robbing this coach, you or Ned Kelly?',
had the dog sit on my tucker-box outside of Gundagai,
yarned with Tom Collins while we fished for a cod someone'd
    caught years before,
and gave Henry Lawson the plots to make his stories from.   25
Me, I've found a hundred wrecked galleons on the Queensland coast,
dripping with doubloons, moidores and golden Inca swords,
and dug a dozen piles of guilders from a Westralian beach;
I was the one that invented the hollow wood-heap,
and I built the Transcontinental, despite heat, dust, death, thirst,
    and flies.   30
I led the ragged thirteen; I fought at Eureka and Gallipoli and Lae;
and I was a day too early (or was it too late?) to discover Coolgardie,
lost my original Broken Hill share in a hand of euchre,
had the old man kangaroo pinch my coat and wallet,
threw fifty heads in a row in the big game at Kal,   35
took a paddle-steamer seventy miles out of the Darling on a heavy dew,
then tamed a Gippsland bunyip and sooled him on
to capture the Tantanoola Tiger and Fisher's Ghost
and became Billy Hughes's secretary for a couple of weeks.
Me, I outshore Jacky Howe, gave Buckley his chance,   40
and have had more lonely drinks than Jimmy Woods;
I jumped across Govett's Leap and wore an overcoat in Marble Bar,
seem to remember riding the white bull through the streets of Wagga,
sailed a cutter down the Kindur to the Inland Sea,
and never travelled until I went to Moonta.   45
Me, I was the first man ever to climb to the top of Ayers Rock,
pinched one of the Devil's Marbles for the kids to play with,
drained the mud from the Yarra, sold the Coathanger for a gold brick,
and asked for beer off the ice at Innamincka.
Me, yesterday I was rumour,   50
today I am legend,
tomorrow, history.
If you'd like to know more of me
inquire at the pub at Tennant Creek
or at any drover's camp   55
or shearing-shed,
or shout any bloke in any bar a drink,

or yarn to any bloke asleep on any beach;
they'll tell you about me,
they'll tell you more than I know myself.   60
After all, they were the ones that created me,
even though I'm bigger than any of them now
—in fact, I'm all of them rolled into one.

For anyone to kill me he'd have to kill
every single Australian,   65
every single one of them,
every single one.

(1952)

Francis Webb
from EYRE ALL ALONE

1. SOUTH AUSTRALIAN SETTLER

East to west. Our little township is a lesion
On the plump hinder parts of nothing. Scratching, scratching,
The moody nails of the sun. Or say, our stony
Brain and gullet wobble corroboree
With London, tall lady Exeter, Broad Devon,   5
And other tender ghosts swaying towards the palate:
Comes always that militant toothpick of such good weather.
We are isolated. Is man man?
He shrugs among guffaws, transports of old jailbird dayshine
Riotous in the stocks, and drooling.   10
Listen, man, watch for the seamstress, the yawning mildewed whaler
Unwinding east to west a slack cotton of news:
Man to man: brave golden organic thread
Nibbled to nothing between teeth of mother sea.

So we dream of the stock-route, east to homely west,   15
To Perth, and the Sound, and the river of elder swans:
Now a huge cable of winged sheep and bullocks
Whirls through vast fords, milky ways, lies coiled
Upon fat pastures. Man to man. Which is sometimes
God to man, under all seven stars, westward.   20

Walk, walk. From dubious footfall one
At Fowler's Bay the chosen must push on
Towards promised fondlings, dancings of the Sound.
Fourth plague, of flies, harries this bloodless ground.
Cliff and salt balance-wheel of heathen planet   25
Tick, twinkle in concert to devise our minute.
But something on foot, and burning, nudges us
Past bitter waters, sands of Exodus.

5. WYLIE

Wylie, the huddled works
Of my soul, in motion:
Three pampered patriarchs   30
In glib collusion.
Hurrah for the catlike mile,
The gin of your vision,
And your boomerang-shaped smile.
Sons and daughters germinate in your eyes,   35
Through their territory I grovel on hands and knees.

Mistrust, and hate, and a dark gargantuan sorrow
Are Wylie who will walk with me tomorrow.

Wylie, I lie awake.
Your muddy vital river   40
Flows, dawdles for my sake.
Lie still—no, turn over.
We evolve our own flies and flames
In the never-never,
Says that rugged fisherman James.   45
My lapdog will has run wild, fathered, and found me.
My agents listen and finger their weapons round me.

.

.

.

8. ABORIGINALS

All my days and all my nights
You haunt me.
Once came a yell or shriek at eleven exactly.   50
Joy, or welcome? Cowering, I peeped at the rifle
That will not fire. Once in the hungry scrub
Leaves and branches came together as a shadow,
Make a sleekness rippling, running about out of earshot.   55
Innumerable times the great Expedition of my thought
Has gone to pieces,
Frightened horses galloping in all directions.

You are everywhere at once.

My instinct is to shudder away from you.   60
Love? It is for dry bread like a stone in my mouth,
For petty concentric days stemming from me,
For stars all white abroad in my fame,
For sleep crawling solicitously towards me,
For myself at all ages since I began walking.   65

These days I hardly say a word to Wylie.

You are beyond me—and so often
Dangerously close, it seems. I do not look for
Truce, rule of life; but gratefully follow your footprints
To water, water on the fifth day.   70

10. BANKSIA

History, wasted and decadent pack-horse
Munching a handful of chaff, dry old national motives,
Shambles skinny and bony into the final push,
Picking up, putting down his heavy tuneless hooves
Girt with rusted iron, so tenderly.   75

Baxter is dead. Wylie, can you hear the Sound?

I hear large agnostic ribaldries of an ocean.

Evening in muffler creeps towards epic adventure,
To lull the blazing colossi of a blindness.
But suns will rock in my sleep, maul the moth-eaten pockets   80
Of memory for a few counterfeit coppers
To thump on the counters of stalls in a looted market.

Wylie, what can you see?
                                    I see a flower.

Turn the horses loose. Out of earth a power:
Banksia, honeysuckle, forked-lightning-fruit of pain.
Motive pierces the cloud-scrub once again.

Swimming oversea, underfoot, the brawny light
Sings savour of this unique approaching night.
Stolid elation of a single star.
Banksia, carry fire, like the thurifer   90
Over my sandy tongue-tied barren ground.

Wylie, what do you hear?
                                    I hear the Sound.

14. THE SOUND

The final days, with grey straight lines of rain,
A geometry ruling without angle or curve
The scourged eyeball. But these outlines of mountains,   95
Shape of the breast, of the ranges back of the Sound:
These would pick expedient pockets of eyeball and soul.
So look hard at horses, goods, firearms, spare a glance
To the honest countryside under your foot and about you
—Snug wet sands and the petty bloodless tree.   100
Adelaide, my great expedition; Baxter, I am calling.
And another night of the grey unrelenting straight lines.

We struggle through the last ditch of the King's River.

Outside Albany a swarm of Wylie's tribesmen
Gather him up; he is taken back to earth,   105
He is growth, he is a gallant tree in flower,
He is unbound geometries of the good soil.

Looking down, or up, at the town from the brow of this hill
I am truly alone. And hardly visible now
The straight grey lines. I am coming, I am rainfall,   *110*
And all doors are closed and stilled the merrymaking.
One year on the march, an epoch, all of my life.

But their faces will be golden when the doors open,
Their dress shining. My torn stinking shirt, my boots,
And hair a tangle of scrub; the long knotted absurd beard   *115*
That is my conscience grown in the desert country.
How shall I face their golden faces, pure voices?
O my expedition: Baxter, Wylie!

But the rain has stopped. On the main road Someone moves.

(1961)

Jackey Jackey
THE DEATH OF KENNEDY

from SYDNEY MORNING HERALD

I told Mr Kennedy that very likely those blackfellows would follow us,
and he said, 'No, Jackey, those blacks are very friendly;' I said to him 'I
know those blackfellows well, they too much speak;' we went on some
two or three miles and camped; I and Mr Kennedy watched them that
night, taking it in turns every hour all night; by-and-bye I saw the blackfellows; it was a moonlight night; and I waked up to Mr Kennedy; and said
to him there is plenty of blackfellows now; this was in the middle of the
night; Mr Kennedy told me to get my gun ready; the blacks did not know
where we slept, as we did not make a fire; we both sat up all night; after
this daylight came, and I fetched the horses and saddled them; then we
went on a good way up the river, and then we sat down a little while, and
we saw three blackfellows coming along our track and they saw us, and
one fellow ran back as hard as he could run, and fetched up plenty more
like a flock of sheep almost; I told Mr Kennedy to put the saddles on the
two horses and go on, and the blacks came up and they followed us all the
day; all along it was raining, and I now told him to leave the horses and
come on without them, that the horses make too much track. Mr Kennedy
was too weak, and would not leave the horses. We went on this day till
towards evening, raining hard and the blacks followed us all the day, some
behind, some planted before; in fact, blacks all around following us. Now
we went into a little bit of a scrub, and I told Mr Kennedy to look behind
always; sometimes he would do so, and sometimes he would not look
behind to look out for the blacks. Then a good many blackfellows came
behind in the scrub, and threw plenty of spears, and hit Mr Kennedy in the
back first. Mr Kennedy said to me 'Oh! Jackey, Jackey! shoot 'em, shoot
'em.' Then I pulled out my gun and fired, and hit one fellow all over the
face with buck shot; he tumbled down, and got up again and again, and
wheeled right round, and two blackfellows picked him up and carried him
away. They went away then a little way, and came back again, throwing

spears all around more than they did before: very large spears. I pulled out
the spear at once from Mr Kennedy's back, and cut out the jag with Mr
Kennedy's knife: then Mr Kennedy got his gun and snapped, but the gun
would not go off. The blacks sneaked all along by the trees, and speared
Mr Kennedy again in the right leg above the knee a little, and I got speared
over the eye, and the blacks were now throwing their spears all ways,
never giving over, and shortly again speared Mr Kennedy in the right side;
there were large jags to the spears, and I cut them out and put them into
my pocket. At the same time we got speared, the horses got speared too,
and jumped and bucked all about, and got into the swamp. I now told Mr
Kennedy to sit down, while I looked after the saddle bags, which I did;
and when I came back again, I saw blacks along with Mr Kennedy; I then
asked him if he saw the blacks with him, he was stupid with the spear
wounds, and said, No; then I asked him where was his watch; I saw the
blacks taking away watch and hat as I was returning to Mr Kennedy; then
I carried Mr Kennedy into the scrub, he said, 'Don't carry me a good way;'
then Mr Kennedy looked this way very bad (Jackey rolling his eyes) I said
to him, 'Don't look far away,' as I thought he would be frightened; I asked
him often, 'Are you well now?' and he said 'I don't care for the spear
wound in my leg, Jackey, but for the other two spear wounds in my side
and back,' and said, 'I am bad inside, Jackey.' I told him blackfellows
always die when he got spear in there (the back); he said, 'I am out of
wind, Jackey;' I asked him, 'Mr Kennedy, are you going to leave me?' and
he said, 'Yes, my boy, I am going to leave you,' he said, 'I am very bad,
Jackey; you take the books, Jackey, to the captain, but not the big ones,
the Governor will give anything for them;' I then tied up the papers, he
then said, 'Jackey, give me paper, and I will write;' I gave him paper and
pencil, and he tried to write, and he then fell back and died, and I caught
him as he fell back and held him, and I then turned round myself and
cried.

(6 March 1849)

Randolph Stow
THE SINGING BONES

'Out where the dead men lie.'
Barcroft Boake

Out there, beyond the boundary fence, beyond
the scrub-dark flat horizon that the crows
returned from, evenings, days of rusty wind
raised from the bones a stiff lament, whose sound
netted my childhood round, and even here still blows.   5

My country's heart is ash in the market-place,
is aftermath of martyrdom. Out there
its sand-enshrined lay saints lie piece by piece,
Leichhardt by Gibson, stealing the wind's voice,
and Lawson's tramps, by choice made mummia and air.   10

No pilgrims leave, no holy-days are kept
for these who died of landscape. Who can find,
even, the camp-sites where the saints last slept?
Out there their place is, where the charts are gapped,
unreachable, unmapped, and mainly in the mind.   15

They were all poets, so the poets said,
who kept their end in mind in all they wrote
and hymned their bones, and joined them. Gordon died
happy, one surf-loud dawn, shot through the head,
and Boake astonished, dead, his stockwhip round his throat.   20

Time, time and time again, when the inland wind
beats over myall from the dunes, I hear
the singing bones, their glum Victorian strain.
A ritual manliness, embracing pain
to know; to taste terrain their heirs need not draw near.   25

(1968)

'Henry Handel Richardson'
(Ethel Florence Robertson)
from THE FORTUNES OF RICHARD MAHONY

VOLUME 1, PART 2

CHAPTER I

Over the fathomless grey seas that tossed between, dissevering the ancient
and gigantic continent from the tiny motherland, unsettling rumours ran.
After close on forty years' fat peace, England had armed for hostilities
again, her fleet set sail for a foreign sea. Such was the news the sturdy
clipper-ships brought out, in tantalising fragments; and those who, like
Richard Mahony, were mere birds-of-passage in the colony, and had
friends and relatives going to the front, caught hungrily at every detail. But
to the majority of the colonists what England had done, or left undone, in
preparation for war, was of small account. To them the vital question was:
will the wily Russian Bear take its revenge by sending men-of-war to
annihilate us and plunder the gold in our banks—us, months removed
from English aid? And the opinion was openly expressed that in casting off
her allegiance to Great Britain, and becoming a neutral state, lay young
Australia's best hope of safety.

But, even while they made it, the proposers of this scheme were knee-
deep in petty, local affairs again. All Europe was depressed under the
cloud of war; but they went on belabouring hackneyed themes—the
unlocking of the lands, iniquitous licence-fees, official corruption. Mahony
could not stand it. His heart was in England, went up and down with
England's hopes and fears. He smarted under the tales told of the in-
efficiency of the British troops and the paucity of their numbers; under the

painful disclosures made by journalists, injudiciously allowed to travel to the seat of war; he questioned, like many another of his class in the old country, the wisdom of the Duke of Newcastle's orders to lay siege to the port of Sebastopol. And of an evening, when the store was closed, he sat over stale English newspapers and a map of the Crimea, and meticulously followed the movements of the Allies.

But in this retirement he was rudely disturbed, by feeling himself touched on a vulnerable spot—that of his pocket. Before the end of the year trade had come to a standstill, and the very town he lived in was under martial law.

On both Ballarat and the Bendigo the agitation for the repeal of the licence-tax had grown more and more vehement; and spring's arrival found the digging-community worked up to a white heat. The new Governor's tour of inspection, on which great hopes had been built, served only to aggravate the trouble. Misled by the golden treasures with which the diggers, anxious as children to please, dazzled his eyes, the Governor decided that the tax was not an outrageous one; and ordered licence-raids to be undertaken twice as often as before. This defeat of the diggers' hopes, together with the murder of a comrade and the acquittal of the murderer by a corrupt magistrate, goaded even the least sensitive spirits to rebellion: the guilty man's house was fired, the police were stoned, and then, for a month or more, deputations and petitions ran to and fro between Ballarat and Melbourne. In vain: the demands of the voteless diggers went unheard. The consequence was that one day at the beginning of summer all the troops that could be spared from the capital, along with several pieces of artillery, were raising the dust on the road to Ballarat.

On the last afternoon in November work was suspended throughout the diggings, and the more cautious among the shop-keepers began to think of closing their doors. In front of the 'Diggers' Emporium', hard as a burnt crust, a little knot of people stood shading their eyes from the sun. Opposite, on Bakery Hill, a monster meeting had been held and the 'Southern Cross' hoisted—a blue bunting that bore the silver stars of the constellation after which it was named. Having sworn allegiance to it with outstretched hands, the rebels were lining up to march off to drill.

Mahony watched the thin procession through narrowed lids. In theory he condemned equally the blind obstinacy of the authorities, who went on tightening the screw, and the foolhardiness of the men. But—well, he could not get his eye to shirk one of the screaming banners and placards: 'Down with Depotism!' 'Who so base as be a Slave!' by means of which the diggers sought to inflame popular indignation. 'If only honest rebels could get on without melodramatic exaggeration! As it is, those good fellows yonder are rendering a just cause ridiculous.'

Polly tightened her clasp of his arm. She had known no peace since the evening before, when a rough-looking man had come into the store and, with revolver at full cock, had commanded Hempel to hand over all the arms and ammunition it contained. Hempel, much to Richard's wrath, had meekly complied; but it might have been Richard himself; he would for certain have refused; and then. . .Polly had hardly slept for thinking of it. She now listened in deferential silence to the men's talk; but when old Ocock—he never had a good word to say for the riotous diggers—took his pipe out of his mouth to remark: 'A pack o' Tipperary boys spoilin' for a fight—that's what I say. An' yet, blow me if I wouldn't 'a bin glad if one o' my two 'ad 'ad spunk enough to join 'em,'—at this Polly could not refrain from saying pitifully: 'Oh, Mr Ocock, do you really *mean* that?' For both Purdy and brother Ned were in the rebel band, and Polly's heart was heavy because of them.

'Can't you see my brother anywhere?' she asked Hempel, who held an old spyglass to his eyes.

'No, ma'am, sorry to say I can't,' replied Hempel. He would willingly have conjured up a dozen brothers to comfort Polly; but he could not swerve from the truth, even for her.

'Give me the glass,' said Mahony, and swept the line.—'No, no sign of either of them. Perhaps they thought better of it after all.—Listen! now they're singing—can you hear them? The *Marseillaise* as I'm alive.—Poor fools! Many of them are armed with nothing more deadly than picks and shovels.'

'And pikes,' corrected Hempel. 'Several carry pikes, sir.'

'Ay, that's so, they've bin 'ammerin' out bits of old iron all the mornin',' agreed Ocock. 'It's said they 'aven't a quarter of a firearm apiece. And the drillin'! Lord love yer! 'Alf of 'em don't know their right 'and from their left. The troops 'ull make mincemeat of 'em, if they come to close quarters.'

'Oh, I hope not!' said Polly. 'Oh, I do hope they won't get hurt.'

Patting her hand, Mahony advised his wife to go indoors and resume her household tasks. And since his lightest wish was a command, little Polly docilely withdrew her arm and returned to her dishwashing. But though she rubbed and scoured with her usual precision, her heart was not in her work. Both on this day and the next she seemed to exist solely in her two ears. The one strained to catch any scrap of news about 'poor Ned'; the other listened, with an even sharper anxiety, to what went on in the store. Several further attempts were made to get arms and provisions from Richard; and each time an angry scene ensued. Close up beside the thin partition, her hands locked under her cooking-apron, Polly sat and trembled for her husband. He had already got himself talked about by refusing to back a Reform League; and now she heard him openly declare to some one that he disapproved of the terms of this League, from A to Z. Oh dear! If only he wouldn't. But she was careful not to add to his worries by speaking of her fears. As it was, he came to tea with a moody face.

The behaviour of the foraging parties growing more and more threatening, Mahony thought it prudent to follow the general example and put up his shutters. Wildly conflicting rumours were in the air. One report said a contingent of Creswick dare-devils had arrived to join forces with the insurgents; another that the Creswickers, disgusted at finding neither firearms nor quarters provided for them, had straightway turned and marched the twelve miles home again. For a time it was asserted that Lalor, the Irish leader, had been bought over by the government; then, just as definitely, that his influence alone held the rebel faction together. Towards evening Long Jim was dispatched to find out how matters really stood. He brought back word that the diggers had entrenched themselves on a piece of rising ground near the Eureka lead, behind a flimsy barricade of logs, slabs, ropes and overturned carts. The Camp, for its part, was screened by a breast-work of firewood, trusses of hay and bags of corn;

while the mounted police stood or lay fully armed by their horses, which were saddled ready for action at a moment's notice.

Neither Ned nor Purdy put in an appearance, and the night passed without news of them. Just before dawn, however, Mahony was wakened by a tapping at the window. Thrusting out his head he recognised young Tommy Ocock, who had been sent by his father to tell 'doctor' that the soldiers were astir. Lights could be seen moving about the Camp, a horse had neighed—father thought spies might have given them the hint that at least half the diggers from the Stockade had come down to Main Street last night, and got drunk, and never gone back. With a concerned glance at Polly Mahony struggled into his clothes. He must make another effort to reach the boys—especially Ned, for Polly's sake. When Ned had first announced his intention of siding with the insurgents, he had merely shrugged his shoulders, believing that the young vapourer would soon have had enough of it. Now he felt responsible to his wife for Ned's safety: Ned, whose chief reason for turning rebel, he suspected, was that a facetious trooper had once dubbed him 'Eytalian organ-grinder', and asked him where he kept his monkey.

But Mahony's designs of a friendly interference came too late. The troops had got away, creeping stealthily through the morning dusk; and he was still panting up Specimen Hill when he heard the crack of a rifle. Confused shouts and cries followed. Then a bugle blared, and the next instant the rattle and bang of musketry split the air.

Together with a knot of others, who like himself had run forth half dressed, Mahony stopped and waited, in extreme anxiety; and, while he stood, the stars went out, one by one, as though a finger-tip touched them. The diggers' response to the volley of the attacking-party was easily distinguished: it was a dropping fire, and sounded like a thin hail-shower after a peal of thunder. Within half an hour all was over: the barricade had fallen, to cheers and laughter from the military; the rebel flag was torn down; huts and tents inside the enclosure were going up in flames.

Towards six o'clock, just as the December sun, huge and fiery, thrust the edge of its globe above the horizon, a number of onlookers ran up the slope to all that was left of the ill-fated stockade. On the dust, blood-stains, now set hard as scabs, traced the route by which a wretched procession of prisoners had been marched to the Camp gaol. Behind the demolished barrier huts smouldered as heaps of blackened embers; and the ground was strewn with stark forms, which lay about—some twenty or thirty of them—in grotesque attitudes. Some sprawled with outstretched arms, their sightless eyes seeming to fix the pale azure of the sky; others were hunched and huddled in a last convulsion. And in the course of his fruitless search for friend and brother, an old instinct reasserted itself in Mahony: kneeling down he began swiftly and dexterously to examine the prostrate bodies. Two or three still heaved, the blood gurgling from throat and breast like water from the neck of a bottle. Here, one had a mouth plugged with shot, and a beard as stiff as though it were made of rope. Another that he turned over was a German he had once heard speak at a diggers' meeting—a windy braggart of a man, with a quaint impediment in his speech. Well, poor soul! he would never mouth invectives or tickle the ribs of an audience again. His body was a very colander for wounds. Some had not bled either. It looked as though the soldiers had viciously gone on prodding and stabbing the fallen.

Stripping a corpse of its shirt, he tore off a piece of stuff to make a bandage for a shattered leg. While he was binding the limb to a board, young Tom ran up to say that the military, returning with carts, were arresting every one they met in the vicinity. With others who had been covering up and carrying away their friends, Mahony hastened down the back of the hill towards the bush. Here was plain evidence of a stampede. More bloodstains pointed the track, and a number of odd and clumsy weapons had been dropped or thrown away by the diggers in their flight.

He went home with the relatively good tidings that neither Ned nor Purdy was to be found. Polly was up and dressed. She had also lighted the fire and set water on to boil, 'just in case'. 'Was there ever such a sensible little woman?' said her husband with a kiss.

The day dragged by, flat and stale after the excitement of the morning. No one ventured far from cover; for the military remained under arms, and detachments of mounted troopers patrolled the streets. At the Camp the hundred odd prisoners were being sorted out, and the maimed and wounded doctored in the rude little temporary hospital. Down in Main Street the noise of hammering went on hour after hour. The dead could not be kept, in the summer heat, must be got underground before dark.

Mahony had just secured his premises for the night, when there came a rapping at the back door. In the yard stood a stranger who, when the dog Pompey had been chidden and soothed, made mysterious signs to Mahony and murmured a well-known name. Admitted to the sitting-room he fished a scrap of dirty paper from his boot. Mahony put the candle on the table and straightened out the missive. Sure enough, it was in Purdy's hand—though sadly scrawled.

Have been hit in the pin. Come if possible and bring your tools. The bearer is square.

Polly could hear the two of them talking in low, urgent tones. But her relief that the visitor brought no bad news of her brother was dashed when she learned that Richard had to ride out into the bush, to visit a sick man. However she buttoned her bodice, and with her hair hanging down her back went into the sitting-room to help her husband; for he was turning the place upside down. He had a pair of probe-scissors somewhere, he felt sure, if he could only lay hands on them. And while he ransacked drawers and cupboards for one or other of the few poor instruments left him, his thoughts went back, inopportunely enough, to the time when he had been surgeon's dresser in the Edinburgh Royal Infirmary. *O tempora, O mores!* He wondered what old Syme, that prince of surgeons, would say, could he see his whilom student raking out a probe from among the ladles and kitchen spoons, a roll of lint from behind the saucepans.

Bag in hand, he followed his guide to where the latter had left a horse in safe-keeping; and having lengthened the stirrups and received instructions about the road, he set off for the hut in the ranges which Purdy had contrived to reach. He had an awkward cross-country ride of some four miles before him; but this did not trouble him. The chance-touched spring had opened the gates to a flood of memories; and, as he jogged along, he re-lived in thought the happy days spent as a student under the shadow of Arthur's Seat, round the College, the Infirmary and old Surgeons' Square.

Once more he sat in the theatre, the breathless spectator of famous surgical operations; or as house-surgeon to the Lying-in Hospital himself assisted in daring attempts to lessen suffering and save life. It was, of course, too late now to bemoan the fact that he had broken with his profession. Yet only that very day envy had beset him. The rest of the fraternity had run to and from the tents where the wounded were housed, while he, behung with his shopman's apron, pottered about among barrels and crates. No one thought of enlisting his services; another, not he, would set (or bungle) the fracture he had temporarily splinted.

The hut—it had four slab walls and an earthen floor—was in darkness on his arrival, for Purdy had not dared to make a light. He lay tossing restlessly on a dirty old straw palliasse, and was in great pain; but greeted his friend with a dash of the old brio.

Hanging his coat over the chinks in the door, and turning back his sleeves, Mahony took up the lantern and stooped to examine the injured leg. A bullet had struck the right ankle, causing an ugly wound. He washed it out, dressed and bandaged it. He also bathed the patient's sweat-soaked head and shoulders; then sat down to await the owner of the hut's return.

As soon as the latter appeared he took his leave, promising to ride out again the night after next. In spite of the circumstances under which they met, he and Purdy parted with a slight coolness. Mahony had loudly voiced his surprise at the nature of the wound caused by the bullet: it was incredible that any of the military could have borne a weapon of this calibre. Pressed, Purdy admitted that his hurt was a piece of gross ill-luck: he had been accidentally shot by a clumsy fool of a digger, from an ancient holster-pistol.

To Mahony this seemed to cap the climax; and he did not mask his sentiments. The pitiful little forcible-feeble rebellion, all along but a futile attempt to cast straws against the wind, was now completely over and done with, and would never be heard of again. Or such at least, he added, was the earnest hope of the law-abiding community. This irritated Purdy, who was spumy with the self-importance of one who has stood in the thick of the fray. He answered hotly, and ended by rapping out with a contemptuous click of the tongue: 'Upon my word, Dick, you look at the whole thing like the tradesman you are!'

These words rankled in Mahony all the way home.—Trust Purdy for not, in anger, being able to resist giving him a flick on the raw. It made him feel thankful he was no longer so dependent on this friendship as of old. Since then he had tasted better things. Now, a woman's heart beat in sympathetic understanding; there met his, two lips which had never said an unkind word. He pushed on with a new zest, reaching home about dawn. And over his young wife's joy at his safe return, he forgot the shifting moods of his night-journey.

It had, however, this result. Next day Polly found him with his head in one of the great old shabby black books which, to her mind, spoilt the neat appearance of the bookshelves. He stood to read, the volume lying open before him on the top of the cold stove, and was so deeply engrossed that the store-bell rang twice without his hearing it. When, reminded that Hempel was absent, he whipped out to answer it, he carried the volume with him.

(1917; revised 1930)

Thea Astley
A KINDNESS CUP

from CHAPTER 1

'Boys,' Mr Dorahy said, 'let us recapitulate...

'I cannot believe,' he continued musingly, his finger poised at a certain section of the Gallic Wars, 'that men are rational beings when I observe their militaristic antics. I mean the drill protocol claptrap, of course, quite apart from the specifics of learning how to kill.' His thin and rather sour face was extremely gentle. He smiled with the terrible snaggle teeth that all who had grown to love failed now to notice. 'What do you think, Jenner?'

'Are you serious, sir?'

'Of course.'

'But we have our own sort of drill, sir. I mean terms and classroom behaviour and...'

'When,' Mr Dorahy interrupted, but still gently, 'have I ever required a clicking to, a standing to, a goose-stepping hop to it?'

Jenner's round sixteen-year-old face began a small grin. 'We just do it, sir.'

'You miss my point, boy. You miss it.' Dorahy sighed and stared bleakly past the eight faces to the school paddock, still being fenced, at workmen whacking on wood for the new school block beyond the pepper-trees.

'Close your Livy,' he said tiredly. 'If you'll give me all that keen attention of yours, I'll try to draw a parallel.'

'Parable, sir?' a shaggy lad next to Jenner inquired with a smirk.

'If you like,' Mr Dorahy said. He could feel reluctance lumping his tongue. '*If* you like. Tarquinius Sextus, as you will recall, was a bastard par excellence.' The boys began to laugh quietly. 'His bastardry,' continued Mr Dorahy without a muscle-twitch of amusement, 'entered the fields of male folly which ruined not only himself, I mean his soul, but a family line!'

He began to quote but no one understood, so he dragged himself from his chair and scribbled the Latin on the board. 'Buckmaster,' he said, 'translate.'

The clock hands were staggering. Time passed slowly in that cube of heat and flies. Clause gobbets. Literal patches of historic infinitive. Torture, Dorahy decided. Sheer mindless torture. He said, 'Take over, Jenner.'

Jenner bumbled for a while, testing words with his incompetent tongue. He crashed over the last sentence—'...and there to her surprise Tarquinius found her lying unclad.'

Dorahy coughed. He coughed out this dust and the dust became the expectations of three failed years.

'A little more delicately, I think: "And there surprised Lucretia lying naked." It was Tarquin who did the surprising in the literal sense of the word, boys. Not the unfortunate lady. Though doubtless she, too, was surprised in your sense. I'll read it to you again. "And there the Tarquin, black and forceful, surprised Lucretia lying naked."' He repeated the last two words softly and a terrible adolescent excitement charged the room. The angle of his vowel, that first vowel, lecherously over-toned plus the quiet refinement of the soured mouth and face made for frightful antithesis.

Outside a world of trees and umber. Flies inside drumming window-heat, taking glass for air.

'The militaristic claptrap and the insolvency of the rapist are equally sub-human—is what I mean. Is very much what I mean.'

Buckmaster didn't quite scowl. He was later to sire three half-castes. 'Women!' he whispered hissingly along the row. 'Gins!' he whispered. And he scrawled furtively a set of parted legs on the margin of his Livy.

'If your thinking, Buckmaster,' Mr Dorahy proceeded gently, 'lies only in the force of your genitals, God help the world.'

Buckmaster senior later said, leaning on his silver-topped riding crop, 'You cannot speak to the boys like this. There are certain matters. Things such as. . .Decencies must. . .'

'In this noisome little colony,' Mr Dorahy replied mildly with more sweat than usual running down the edges of his weary hair, 'where masculinity is top dog, it seems to me that some occasional thought should be given, chivalrously you understand—*do* you understand?—to the sex that endures most of our nastiness.'

'You're mad,' Buckmaster said.

'You become that which you do.'

Mr Buckmaster allowed himself a tiny bleached smile. 'Any bloody teacher in this place would have to be mad.'

'I meant you,' Mr Dorahy said. The small scar of some long-forgotten protest whitened on his cheek. 'Would you want your son to become one of the mindless, insensitive, money-grubbing bulls you see around this town and that he gives every indication of aping?'

'I'll have you sacked, by Christ!' Pulling at his crotch. His cutaway donned for the occasion—running the bejesus out of a back-town schoolie—stank in the heat. Summer was crouching all over the town.

'Please do,' Mr Dorahy said. 'I am so tired.'

But it did not could not happen. Who else was there for a pittance in a provisional school slapped hard in the sweating sugar-grass north of the tropic?

I am single, Mr Dorahy told himself proceeding through the drudgeries of instruction. I am single and thirty-seven and in love with landscape. Even this. Other faces cut close to the heart. His assistants, say, who took the junior forms. Married and widowed Mrs Wylie gathering in the chickens for a spot of rote tables or spelling, beating it out in an unfinished shack at the boundary fence. Or Tom Willard with his combined primary forms and his brimstone lay-preaching on the Sabbath. Or himself as a gesture to culture, keeping on the bigger boys of his parish, for he was priestly enough to use that word, for a bit of elementary classics and a purging of Wordsworth. It all seemed useless, as foolish as trying to put Tintern Abbey into iambic hexameters. He had come with a zealot's earnestness, believing a place such as this might need him. And there was, after all, only loneliness: he was cut off from the pulse of the town, although, he insisted to himself rationalising furiously, he had been regularly to meetings of the Separation League and had blown only occasional cold air on their hot. He had drunk with the right men. He had kept his mouth closed. He had assumed nothing. And yet other faces, the wrong sort because they were black, had their own especial tug, the sad black flattened faces of the men working with long knives in the cane and their scabby children making games in the dust at the entrances and exits of towns. The entrances. The exits. Observe that, he cautioned himself.

He was friendly with them, as friendly perhaps as Charlie Lunt on his hopeless block of land west of the township; friendly even when they robbed his accessible larder, noting the small fires they made at the boundary fences of his shack; or when he caught Kowaha, shinily young, pilfering sugar and flour, eyes rolling like humbugs with the lie of it while he did a bishop's candlesticks—'But I gave them to you'—confusing her entirely. Bastardry not intended, he told his ironic self. Yet she asked next time, and the next, always at half-light so that the scurrilous tongues of settlers along the road were never sure of shadow or concretion.

Nort, Mr Dorahy inscribed meticulously on Buckmaster's ill-spelled prose.

(1974)

Ray Lawler
SUMMER OF THE SEVENTEENTH DOLL

from ACT 1, SCENE 1

BARNEY: No? Well, now I'll tell you something. You've got a bit of a battle ahead of you, too.
> (*She looks questioningly at him. He speaks on a quieter note.*)
> You heard what Emma said, 'bout if it hadn't been for her we wouldn't be here? 'S true.

OLIVE: (*disbelieving*) Aah...

BARNEY: I'm telling yer, when you weren't down at the terminal, for a minute or two Roo was talkin' about tryin' to get in some joint he knows at North Melbourne—

OLIVE: (*staring*) Lots of times I haven't been down to meet yez. Saturdays...

BARNEY: He wasn't mad at yer not being there. It's nothing like that.

OLIVE: What then?

BARNEY: (*hesitating*) He's broke.

OLIVE: Roo?

BARNEY: I had to buy his ticket down.

OLIVE: (*incredulous*) But how can he be broke? Before he even gets here?

BARNEY: (*sighing*) You dunno what a bloody awful season it's been, everythin' went wrong. Worst we've ever had, I reckon.

OLIVE: Couldn't you get work?

BARNEY: (*scornfully*) Oh it wasn't that, the work was there, any amount of it. It was just plain bad luck.
> (*She makes a move towards the archway.*)
> Now don't go runnin' up to him, he's chockablock, you'd better hear it from me.
> (*She hesitates, then returns.*)

OLIVE: (*flatly*) What happened?

BARNEY: Well, first set off, Roo, the silly cow, strains his back—There's no need to throw a fit, nothin' serious, nearly better. But it slowed him down all through the season, see. (*Frankly putting his cards on the table*) Roo's a pretty hard man, y'know, on the job. Got no use for anyone can't pull their weight; and bein' able to pick and choose almost, 'coz everyone knows he's one of the best gangers there is, gen'rally he gets a champion bunch together. But he's gotta be hard doin' it sometimes. (*Facing her*) This year he got the boys to turn off Tony Moreno. You must've heard us talk of Tony, real character, everyone likes him, but anyway Roo thought he was gettin' too slow. Instead he takes on a big young bloke we'd heard a lot about, name of Johnnie Dowd. Cracked up to be as fast as lightnin'.

OLIVE: Was he?

BARNEY: Yeah. Not as good as Roo, when he's fit, mind yer, but he could run rings round the best of us. And this time he even made Roo look a bit sick.

OLIVE: Did Roo know?

BARNEY: Well, that's the point. He's fast at both loadin' and cuttin', this Dowdie, and got a head on him, just the same as Roo, and it's not often you get fellers like that. The boys noticed it and they started pickin', telling Roo he'd have to watch out or they'd have a new ganger. Didn't mean nothin' by it, just jokin', but Roo takes it up the wrong way. Instead of pointin' out that he had a bad back, he puts himself to work by this Dowd—gunna show him up, see. Well, that's just what he shouldna done, the kid towelled him up proper. I never seen Roo git so mad, in no time at all he'd made it a running fight between 'em....

OLIVE: The damned fool!

BARNEY: That's what I told him. Calm down, I says, what's it matter...

OLIVE: (*exasperated*) And with a busted back, how the hell could he win?

BARNEY: (*shrugging*) I dunno. Reckons he's twice as good as everyone else, I s'pose. Anyway, 'bout two months ago, flamin' hot day it was, gettin' near knock-off time, they had a blue.

OLIVE: Bad?

BARNEY: Pretty bad. I was right on the spot when it happened. Started off over nothing. They was workin' side by side, and when Dowdie finishes the strip he looks back to see how far behind Roo was. Well, right at that moment Roo's knees went. Never seen anythin' like it, they just buckled under him and there he was, down on the ground. This strikes Dowd as bein' funny, see, and he starts to laugh. Well, that did it. Roo went him and it was on, cane knives and the lot. Took six of us to separate 'em, could've been murder, I reckon. Course the boys all blamed Roo for it, so he did his block again, packed up his gear and walked off. (*After an uncomfortable pause*) I didn't see him after that till I picked him up at Brisbane a week ago.

OLIVE: You didn't go with him?

BARNEY: No.

OLIVE: Why not?

BARNEY: (*disturbed*) I dunno. It was all messed up. You know what Roo's always been to me, a sort of little tin god. I've never seen him in the wrong before.

OLIVE: He's been wrong plenty of times.

BARNEY: (*Strongly*) Not to me he hasn't. Not even in the—War.

OLIVE: Well, go on. What happened?

BARNEY: Nothin'. He went off and I stayed. Then, like I said, I picked him up in Brisbane a week ago. By then he hardly had a razoo.

OLIVE: What was it—booze?

BARNEY: Yeah. Been hitting it pretty heavy. We didn't talk much about it, I think he's got a spite on me for not walkin' out with him. But honest, the way I felt at the time, I just couldn't—

> (*She is staring accusingly at him, and he escapes her eyes with a twisted shrug.*)

Apart from that, I needed the money. And of course I had to put me foot in it all over again by tellin' him how they made Dowdie ganger in his place, and what a bottling job he done.

> (*Unperceived by either of them,* ROO *moves downstairs to stand in the entrance.*)

Well, you gotta give him credit, for a kid he made a very smart fist of it...

ROO: (*crudely*) Yeah. And have you told her 'bout the big booze-up he threw when yez all got back to Cairns?

> (BARNEY *looks at him and then turns away, ashamed.*)

BARNEY: Bein' sarcastic won't get you anywhere.

ROO: Blabber-gutsing doesn't take you far, either.

OLIVE: It's not his fault. I asked him (*Addressing* BARNEY) Better take your cases up.

> (*He moves toward the arch and she adds hastily, remembering.*)

Oh, you're in the little back room for tonight.

> (BARNEY *grins wryly, with a flash of his former spirits.*)

BARNEY: Is it as bad as that?

> (*She nods and he carries on to pick up his bag and exit upstairs. There is an embarrassed pause.*)

ROO: If I know him when he opens his big trap, I don't s'pose he's left much to tell.

OLIVE: (*on edge*) One or two things. Where you was thinkin' of going in North Melbourne, for instance?

ROO: (*shrugging irritably*) Aah, who the hell cares about that?

OLIVE: Me, for one. I'd like to know what's around there you can't get here.

ROO: (*sulkily*) I got a kind of cousin, used to keep a grocery shop. Bloke named Wallace.

OLIVE: Well, that's lovely, that is. After seventeen years, the first time there's trouble, that's who you go to, bloke named Wallace in a grocery shop.

ROO: (*turning on her angrily*) Olive, I'm broke. D'yer understand? Flat, stoney, stinkin' broke!

OLIVE: (*shrilly*) Yeah, and I'd care a lot for that, wouldn't I? That's how I've always met you, standin' on the front verandah with a cash register, looking like a—like a bloody—

> (*She breaks off, overcome by sudden gasping tears, gropes for a handkerchief.* ROO *is troubled and comes from behind to take her in his arms, drawing her to him with the gentle ease of long familiarity.*)

Roo: (*humbly*) Olive, I wasn't thinkin'. Aw, c'mon, hon, you know I didn't mean that.

Olive: (*muffled*) Fellers like you—yer ought to be kicked.

Roo: I was lookin' for something to make it easy.

Olive: (*twisting in his arms to face him*) What's wrong with me? I'm workin', ain't I?

Roo: (*stubbornly*) I won't bludge on you.

Olive: (*tearfully*) You can lay off here just as you always have, and—and I can—

Roo: (*finally*) I won't bludge. I'll get a job or somethin'.

Olive: A job?

Roo: Well, something or other, we'll think about it tomorrow. Now stop your crying and let's forget it. It'll work out all right. You pleased to see me?

Olive: (*hoarsely*) If you hadna come I would have gone looking for you with a razor.

(*They hold each other in a long kiss.*)

Roo: You know what we both need, don't yer? A nice long beer to cool us down...

(*Olive draws away from him, giggling, her spirits already swinging back on the upsurge.*)

Olive: I've already had some. Me and Pearl was in the middle of cracking a bottle when you got here. (*Fishing it out from under the table and holding it aloft*) Look, we hid it so you wouldn't know.

Roo: Well, what a pair of clowns you are!

(*Suddenly it seems very funny, and they roar with laughter. She rushes up to the arch. He crosses to the sideboard, turns on the radio, which presently plays gay infectious music.*)

C'mon, my tongue's hanging out after that long plane trip.

Olive: (*calling upstairs*) Up there, Cazaly—come on down—the party's on—

Roo: Get 'em all in...

Olive: (*calling towards the kitchen*) Pearl, don't be all night with that salad. I told him...

Pearl: (*off*) Be right with you.

(*Barney comes downstairs with an armful of presents, among them the seventeenth doll. He sneaks past Olive to enter the room and hands the doll to Roo, who quickly hides it behind his back.*)

Olive: Come on, Emma, Roo's poured you a beer.

Emma: (*off, her voice raised in mechanical fury*) Wouldn't soil me lips.

(*Laughing, Olive comes back from the kitchen entrance. Pearl enters bearing a large bowl of salad, followed by Emma. When Olive is at archway Roo holds high the gift.*)

Roo: Here you are—the seventeenth doll!

(*She gives a cry of sheer happiness and rushes down into his encircling arms. Barney is standing by, watching with a grin. Music reaches a peak. Blackout.*)

(1955)

Frank Dalby Davison
from THE WELLS OF BEERSHEBA:
A LIGHT HORSE LEGEND

The men of the 4th and 12th Regiments mounted. They were learned in desert warfare. They knew what had been given them to do, and why. Twelve thousand horses who had done all that could be asked of them had need to drink—or a battle into which an army had been thrown would be lost. They knew, also, what they were about to face. Two years of fighting had taught them that.

In such a moment the minds and hearts of men rise to a condition in which mean things cannot touch them. A condition such as is known to attacking infantry when the moment comes to leave their trenches. Circumstance has dedicated them to grand adventure. They are buoyed up by a heroism in which all share. Consequences no longer matter. Death is an incident. Fear falls from them, and they become more than men.

A wave of such subtle excitement as swept through the mounted ranks communicated itself to the beasts they rode. Saddle-worn, parched, and over-loaded, weight seemed to fall from their burdened bodies; they tossed their heads and fidgeted from hoof to hoof as if they were fresh from their home paddocks. There was a pressing and jostling among their ranks as the regiments, squadron by squadron, rode out from cover and wheeled.

They wheeled prettily, like men and horses at drill. The pivot men bore on their reins and the flank came round at a smart canter. They looked almost gay. Brownish ranks of horses with a sprinkle of roan, chestnut, and grey. Tails were flying; heads reefing at the bits. The ray of the setting sun was on their fronts; a coppery glow, diffused through the dry mist of the battlefield. They advanced.

The pace, at first, was a smart trot, with an eye to the careful alignment of the ranks. The sound of their hooves and the rise and fall of the men in the saddles were in brisk staccato.

The pace quickened to a canter, then to a gallop. The men sat still in their seats. Sound and movement were in swinging rhythm.

Some of the men rode with rifle and fixed bayonet balanced across the thigh. Others with rifle slung across the back; the bare bayonet gripped in the hand.

The Turk had seen them, and laid his guns. His shells began to burst among them. Each deafening crash, drowned for a moment, the roar of hooves, and seemed to defy them; but they rode on, line after line, resolute and unfaltering. Spurts of flame and soil shot up, gapping their ranks. A long-striding bay was the first to go down. He blundered, as if the hounds of death had laid him by the heels. His was a long, lurching, staggering fall; for the will to race on died hard in him. The weaving hooves of his mates swept by him and over him. A sheet of flame leaped up, and before it a chestnut reared with a torn chest and fell backwards, throwing his rider.

The shelling increased in intensity. Crash after crash resounded among them. The ranks were thinning. Where men had ridden knee to knee they rode now with a space beside them. Men dropped from the saddles and riderless horses galloped on shoulder to shoulder with the rest.

A wide track was littered with the fallen but the living still rode on. The pace quickened as horse laboured to gain the lead, and horse laboured to keep stride by stride with his neighbour. Nostrils reddened, eyes widened, jaws gaped, and tossing heads sent the spume flying. They shook the ground as they thundered across it. The beating of their hooves was like a roll of many drums, *accelerando*. It rose and swelled and stayed, filling the space between earth and sky.

Not one of the horses, alone, could have stood the pace and the weight for half the distance; but each was possessed of something not of himself, but of all. Beat after beat their hooves smote the ground. Stride after stride they swept across it. The fallen were leaped, scarcely seen.

Among the men there was a sudden gasp of amazement and derision. The shells no longer fell among them. They were falling on the ground behind. The enemy gunners could not keep their guns on the fast moving target!

The distance was drawing short, now. They would soon be in the zone of rifle and machine-gun fire.

A whistling passed between their ranks. A rider, sitting erect, went limp, then toppled from the saddle as if he had fallen asleep. Another and another disappeared among the welter of hooves. Horses were dropping. Bullets richochetted and flew snarling across the ranks.

The troopers could now see the men who were firing at them—heads and shoulders above the trenches, the right elbows pumping cartridges into the rifles. Red flame jetting from a traversing machine-gun.

Again that sudden, surprised emergence into a deathless zone. The nerves of the enemy riflemen had failed them. They had forgotten to lower their sights! The bullets were whistling harmlessly overhead.

In the last hundred yards it seemed to the riders not that they raced to the trenches, but that the trenches were drawn to them.

There were brown-clad figures that leaped from cover and ran toward the town, their arms abandoned. There were men in clumsy grey cloth who wrestled frantically with a jammed machine-gun until the hooves were on them.

The trenches yawned abruptly; almost before the horses saw them. There was a blundering fall or two, a wrenched and sudden leaping. For the riders, looking down, there was a swift vision of men crouched fearfully in the trench bottom and of others stabbing upward with the bayonet. Then came the staggering scramble across the parados and the race for the next trench line.

As the charging lines massed within the redoubt there was a minute of seeming confusion. Unable to progress, men leaped to the ground and jumped into the trenches. There were shouts in strange tongues and the clash of hand-to-hand fighting. Horses, abandoned, stood blown and sweating or ran to and fro in alarm. Then out of chaos came order.

The centre had gone clear across the redoubt. Men and horses were streaming in a packed wedge across the open ground.

From within the town sounded heavy explosions as the enemy fired his dumps.

On a hilltop stood a group of men with red-tabbed shoulders and glossy field-boots. They all were quite motionless. Each had field-glasses trained on the distant scene. The sun was gone; but the failing light was sufficient to reveal the last moments of the great charge. Distantly, they saw men and horses gallop up to the buildings of the town and disappear between them.

An officer lowered his glasses.

'The battle is ours, sir!' he said. His voice was vibrant with the mirth and emotion of a man who has stood with Jove and watched men and horses perform a miracle.

The general lowered his glasses but did not speak. His eyes turned toward the plain. The empurpled twilight was filled with a muttering of hooves and a rumbling of wheels as brigades and batteries galloped to fill the widening gap. He would rest his horses to-night, but to-morrow they must press forward to get behind Gaza and grip the enemy in his hinderparts. Waterless country must be crossed. He had need to plan anew. There was little time for jubilation in the mind that must be ever thinking forwardly. But his spirit fed on the bread of satisfaction. He knew now that Turkish nerves were not proof against resolute horsemen. In prophetic vision he saw the battles to come and the entry of his cavalry into the cities of Palestine.

The day was gone. The moon looked down on the still and silent field. In the town, men laboured. The smell of water, cold and sweet, was released on the dusty air. Standing, weary and patient, out among the ridges, the horses smelled it, and a whinny ran from line to line.

Throughout the night the streets of the town were loud with the clatter of hooves walking. Brigade after brigade, the horses were led in, light horse and gunner, to drink with slackened girths and bitless mouths at the wells of Beersheba.

(1933)

Bruce Dawe
HOMECOMING

All day, day after day, they're bringing them home,
they're picking them up, those they can find, and bringing them
                                        home,
they're bringing them in, piled on the hulls of Grants, in trucks, in
                                        convoys,
they're zipping them up in green plastic bags,
they're tagging them now in Saigon, in the mortuary coolness   5
they're giving them names, they're rolling them out of
the deep-freeze lockers—on the tarmac at Tan Son Nhut
the noble jets are whining like hounds,
they are bringing them home
—curly-heads, kinky-hairs, crew-cuts, balding non-coms   10
—they're high, now, high and higher, over the land, the steaming
                                        chow mein
their shadows are tracing the blue curve of the Pacific
with sorrowful quick fingers, heading south, heading east,
home, home, home—and the coasts swing upward, the old
                                        ridiculous curvatures
of earth, the knuckled hills, the mangrove-swamps, the desert
                                        emptiness...   15
in their sterile housing they tilt towards these like skiers
—taxiing in, on the long runways, the howl of their homecoming
                                        rises
surrounding them like their last moments (the mash, the splendour)
then fading at length as they move
on to small towns where dogs in the frozen sunset   20
raise muzzles in mute salute,
and on to cities in whose wide web of suburbs
telegrams tremble like leaves from a wintering tree
and the spider grief swings in his bitter geometry
—they're bringing them home, now, too late, too early.   25

                                        (1968)

Section G

MAPPING AND NAMING

One of the most persistent beliefs about that part of the world colonised by Europeans since the sixteenth century is expressed in the name most commonly given to it: the New World. As several of the items in the previous Section exemplified, one of the key images of that 'newness' was its silence, its emptiness of language. And, as the Introduction to that Section, together with the remarks of Dr Mulhaus in the extract there from *The Recollections of Geoffry Hamlyn*, suggested, it was a crucial part of the imperial enterprise to overlook the 'oldness' of the existing inhabitants and the validity of their naming of the place. Naming is a potent and contentious strategy because it confers ownership. And, as John Dunmore Lang pointedly observes in 'Colonial Nomenclature', as early as 1823, it is ideologically loaded as well. Lang, who wrote this poem in the year of his arrival in the colony as its first Presbyterian minister, was to have a long and controversial career as a radical reformer: for him, to name the land was to invest it with political significance. As a republican he preferred the names of democrats (like Hampden) and Aboriginal names (stanza 2) to those of Governors (like Macquarie) and imperial officials (like Goulburn).

In the early myths of the New World, especially those projected on to the United States and taken up there by writers and literary critics until well into the 1950s, one of the most potent images of the writer was that of 'the New Adam', the divinely-licensed namer of the new world that has been put at his disposal in the 'New Eden'. In other situations, the fissure between the 'new' place and the European languages and systems of knowledge and meaning that were trying to comprehend it seemed to necessitate conceptualising the land as strange, even as being outside discourse, language and meaning. Naming, then, is an attempt to bring the 'strange' land into familiar discourse. But the strangeness of the land is not always to be overcome. As several items here and in The Vision Splendid show, the image of the land as strange, exotic and harsh is a persistent one; it may be a device for retaining the power of the familiar culture to designate what is strange and what is familiar.

In countries like Australia, New Zealand, Canada, the United States, South Africa, Mexico, Argentina, Brazil, the West Indies and Paraguay, where a transported European society displaced, both physically and culturally, a pre-existing native one, the issue of naming the land is doubly contentious because the 'new', white, population is both colonising and colonised. As has already been observed, the naming of a 'new' country by 'settlers' is part of a contest which the 'settler' culture wages against the native one. But there is, sooner or later, also another contest which the 'settler' culture wages against the imperial centre, a struggle to name in a way that implies some sense of a *local* version of the metropolitan language (Australian-English, Argentinian-Spanish), and therefore a distinctive local experience and identity. It is part of the colonising culture's attempt to throw off the feeling of being colonised, of being the colonial subject of the imperial power (Britain, Spain, Portugal). (This part of the argument is pursued more directly in Cultural Politics.) It is also an attempt to name the country in a way that figures some sense of belonging rather than mere ownership. In this project, native terms, characters, and experience are often appropriated to indicate that an affinity with the land has been attained. So, the issue remains an ambiguous one: European naming suppresses 'native' names but must eventually acknowledge their potency in order to assert 'true' belonging. Naming, as Les Murray points out in 'Second Essay on Interest', is actually 'renaming'.

If (white) history is felt to be short, the maps unfilled, and the national imaginary (or repository of significant images) relatively meagre, it is assumed to be the duty of writers to supply the lack, to provide images of the land and its experience that will sustain. And while many of the writers in this Section take that metaphysical national duty seriously, most seem conscious of it as a discursive process, one by which cultural meaning is attached to images of the physical environment. James McAuley's 'Terra Australis' makes the point well. The poem insists upon Australia as a place in myth, as having its existence in imagined constructions, a 'country of the mind', to borrow a much-quoted phrase from the end of White's *Voss*. But 'Terra Australis' also makes clear that the nature of that country may vary according to the ideological predisposition of the writer. So, it may be a land which reflects the egalitarian Australian legend (stanza 2), one which is modelled on a gloomy metaphysical conviction of alienation and exile (stanza 3), or one which is the natural site for the isolated Romantic hero (stanza 4). In each case, the land (topographical and intellectual) seems to make available an appropriate metaphor for the preferred ideology.

Though thirty years, a generation, and poetic style separate 'Terra Australis' from the poem that follows it, Michael Dransfield's 'Geography', there is a remarkable similarity in the images they use. 'Geography' also shares some basic preoccupations with A. D. Hope's 'Australia', another poem markedly different from it in other ways. Like 'Australia', 'Geography' expresses a romantic desire for the spiritual purity of desert landscapes where Hope locates 'some spirit which escapes/ The learned doubt' and where Dransfield locates 'chapels of pure vision'. While Hope (recalling even Dampier) defines 'his' Australia in terms of what it does not have ('without songs, architecture, history'), he attempts to recuperate these deficiencies and see them as offering a distinctive site for a somehow purer human experience. All three exemplify the basic drive of these mapping and naming texts to locate in the landscape the naturalising source of a preferred vision of culture, nation or spiritual belief. Hope's opening two stanzas, frequently quoted, exemplify this perfectly: the very map of the country becomes a visual metaphor for that vision. It is, instructively, also one of a very large number of texts in which the land is designated as female, a strange, passive place to be entered, written on and subordinated to the (usually male) power of the explorer, settler or poet.

The same concern to find the appropriate relationship between land and meaning invests O'Dowd's 'Australia'. On the eve of Federation, and at the end of one century and the beginning of the next, O'Dowd sees Australia itself poised on the verge of a choice of futures, and as in several of the items in The Vision Splendid that tension derives from the perception of Australia itself as a paradox, the youngest and oldest of lands, a land of omens and auguries, a prison or a social laboratory. O'Dowd's uncertainty about Australia's future seems to demand an answer, a choice to be made between Australia as a replica of the corruption of the Old World or the birthplace of the New Eden.

The opening essay in this Section, Malouf's 'A First Place: A Mapping of the World', bespeaks a less urgent, more confident sense of place. Malouf is concerned with two issues: 'how we might begin to speak accurately of where and what we are' and the influence of place upon social habits, sensibility and literary forms. His text accepts the proposition made by so many items here, that geography is destiny, but asks that we be more precise about it. Unlike many others, Malouf's argument stresses difference, not unity; it asks us, for instance, 'how many different sorts of Australian writing there may be'. It seeks to describe how the way one writes might be influenced by the particular kind of space (locality, house) in which one grew up: it is not simply a matter of preferred images (palms rather than snow gums) but preferred forms, modes and styles of writing.

While difference is something Malouf would want to celebrate, it was something for Dampier to despise. The persistence of Dampier's view of Australia (the first written in English) is demonstrated in Lawson's 'The Old Bark School' in the previous Section: there Lawson recalls being taught (two hundred years later) Dampier's opinion of Australian Aboriginals: 'the miserablest People in the world'. Not only are the human inhabitants miserable; so, to Dampier's eyes, was almost every aspect of the physical environment. Dampier's view was instrumental in discouraging further British interest in what was then known as New Holland; it also gave rise to a long-lasting set of visual images that were hard to displace. Notice how often Dampier's descriptions are expressed as negatives, how often he inscribes deficiency upon the new land: 'no sort of Animal', 'no sort of Cloaths', 'destitute of water', 'Neither is the Sea very plentifully stored with Fish'. Despite this, Dampier did return to Australia (in 1699, with Admiralty support) and explored a great deal of the West and North coasts of Australia.

Almost three hundred years later, the voice of another new arrival is raised in anger at the physical and social environment of its inhabitants and their customs. Like Dampier, the speaker of Ania Walwicz's prose poem inscribes deficiency and articulates her mapping of the country in negative terms. But there is a difference: Dampier was not afraid of being rejected by the 'natives of New Holland', not disturbed by their indifference to him: Walwicz speaks *to* Australians rather than about them.

Like the explorer of earlier centuries, the tourist, the traveller and the expatriate have been significant transmitters of cultural knowledge, impressions, and facts: they have also been, for many writers, convenient (even autobiographical) vehicles for registering intercultural perceptions. They continue a tradition of travel-writing that goes back to the medieval period. Almost always the interest is fairly much divided between the culture being observed and the way that the reactions of the observer exhibit something of his or her familiar culture and its preoccupations. In Australian Literature, the traveller is especially important—Richardson's *The Fortunes of Richard Mahony*, White's *The Aunt's Story* and *The Twyborn Affair*, Stead's *For Love Alone*, most of the novels of Martin Boyd and Moorhead's *Remember the Tarantella*, Bail's *Homesickness* and Moorhouse's *Room Service* are just a few. Like many texts that use the device of the traveller or expatriate, Anna Couani's 'Remember to Forget' gradually becomes an anatomy of the Australian characater. Although its expression is more subtle, and the intercultural analysis much more complex, Couani's speaker also finds herself drawing attention to lack, to absence: 'the *real* Australian attitude is never expressed', 'an absence of character', 'their lack of aspirations'. And there are particular things that 'women should talk about' that you have to forget in Australia.

In 1823, William Charles Wentworth, having already gained one kind of fame as one of the first party of Europeans to cross the Great Dividing Range (in 1813), and on his way to greater repute as a colonial politician, influential in the achievement of representative government by New South Wales (in 1842), won second place in the Cambridge University Chancellor's prize for poetry. The set subject for the year was Australasia. Though written in England, Wentworth's poem was nevertheless the first major Australian poem in English which could rightfully begin as it does, 'Land of my birth'. Since the subject seemed to call for an ode, and perhaps because of his own idealism, Wentworth inscribes Australia in the most heroic terms. There are no deficiencies in his Australia: it is 'the new-born glory of the southern skies'. And that early image is really the key to Wentworth's naming of Australia. His description emphasises the *familiarity* of the physical scenes, its hospitability, its gentleness: it resembles an English park. It is, in fact, as he finally admits, 'a new Britannia in another world', a chance for England to revive itself in the south, a replica of all that is best about 'home'. In proof of this he expresses his optimism that it will (someday) produce an 'Austral Shakespeare'. While such an idea might seem merely amusing now, it was remarkably durable in some circles. As late as the 1950s, A. D. Hope, for instance, was arguing that Australian literature would prove its maturity by producing a masterpiece; the *Times Literary Supplement* even later continued to see the Commonwealth as the place where the faded energy of English culture and language could be revived. While the newness of the land is mostly emphasised, Wentworth's language changes significantly when he begins to discuss the Aboriginal inhabitants; they, the 'lords of this old domain', have an 'ancient lineage'. At this point in Australian history the pressure of pastoral expansion (which his crossing of the Mountains did more to bring about than any other act) was so limited that the Aborigines were yet to be considered a major threat to prosperity: it fits his democratic vision of the new land to speak of them in the language of the noble savage ('pure native sons of savage liberty'), with 'savage' meaning 'not civilised' rather than violent or cruel.

As Frederick Sinnett observes in the extract that opens Realism and Romance (see also the Introduction to that Section) the lack of antiquity in Australia (ruins, ghosts, etc.) inhibits certain kinds of writing. Barron Field's solution to the problem, and one adopted by many writers and politicians over the next century or so, was to replace a concern with history with a belief in the future. In the light of this belief, the ship is an appropriate metaphor for poetry in Australia since it figures prophecy, anticipation and contact with culture, spirituality and home, to which he hopes it will soon return him. In the controversy between Lord Byron and Bowles over the value of Alexander Pope's poetry, Byron took the view that poetry need not follow conventional poetic diction, that plain sense required plain language. The significance of the controversy here is that it reminds Field of an active literary culture from which he feels exiled.

Peter Porter, an Australian expatriate in England, also finds in another poetic text, George Chapman's 1618 translation of the ancient Greek poet, Hesiod, the provocation to reflect upon *his* native land. This poem was the beginning of a celebrated debate between Porter and his friend (but poetic antagonist), Les Murray, about the two strains of Australian poetry that Porter had called the Attic and the Boeotian: roughly the civilised or genteel and the rural or rough. Porter finds in the ancient Greek poem a series of emblems for *his* vision of the Australian experience. They are the names that he templates onto the Australian landscape. Like O'Dowd and Judith Wright, he finds two strands of feeling: 'Some of us feel at home nowhere,/ Others in one generation fuse with the land.' Hesiod, said to be the founder of didactic poetry in the Western world, lived near Ascra, close to Mount Helicon, the sacred home of the muses; like the poet addressed in Porter's poem (whom it is tempting to identify as Les Murray, 'the Taree smallholder'), he travelled little and received his inspiration from his humble rural pursuits. The title of the poem echoes Keats' 'On First Looking into Chapman's Homer': the 'view from Darien' (line 9) alludes to that poem. *The Works and Days*, Hesiod's major extant work, celebrates the rural life of Boeotia. It was translated by Chapman under the name of *The Georgics*.

In a number of the poems in this Section, the relation between time and space, between history and place, has been important. In Harpur's long poem, 'The Creek of the Four Graves' (abridged here in some places), the name derives from actual 'colonial' experience in the place. It is a classic poem of naming. In line 19 we are introduced to 'a nameless Creek', but we already know from the title that the creek has a name. The anticipation is produced, then, that we will learn 'how the Creek got its name'. The narrative of westward, pastoral expansion inevitably produces conflict with the native inhabitants: it is out of this conflict that the Creek 'earns' its name. In terms of the relation between history and place it is notable that the poem extends the sense of historicity: 'I verse a Settler's tale of olden times', the use of the archaic name, Egremont, and terms such as 'wolds' are attempts to stretch the sense of the past, to give the story the status of antiquity.

Time, and the opportunity provided by natural phenomena to reflect on it, is one of Judith Wright's abiding concerns. 'Cycads' is based on a notable specimen (said to be possibly two thousand years old) that grew near Wright's home at Mt Tamborine, in south-east Queensland: it was later destroyed by vandals. Cycads are 'primitive', ancient, and slow-growing plants, for Wright an ideal object of contemplation, an image discovered in the land rather than one imposed on it.

For John Shaw Neilson, too, the naming is in the interests of securing a closer emotional relationship to the country, one already named 'poor'. The process by which he seeks to do that is to produce an inventory of its features, to survey its flora and fauna in order to recuperate the land from the limiting designation of 'poverty', to revise its ideological place. 'The Poor, Poor Country' was written during drought and rural recession.

Similarly, for Eve Langley the dead kangaroo in 'Native-Born' provokes a different, more personal mapping and naming. Prodded by the death of the kangaroo, and the culturally-confident young Italian ploughman, the speaker seeks an identity with the land, the kangaroo as representative of it, and the emotional intensity implied in 'young Camelli's' song. She invokes image after image of the land, its climate and its predators, aching towards an adequate response.

Each of the final three poems reverts to the enterprise of finding the land to be a metaphor. Murray's 'The Quality of Sprawl' finds in the landscape the metaphor for a whole set of social customs, styles and beliefs that are privileged by that association. Bea Miles (line 40) was a famous Sydney eccentric, known, among many other things, for her love of riding in taxis. Sprawl is also one of the features that James McAuley discovers to be inherent in the place that he names. His 'Envoi' needs to be read alongside his slightly later 'Terra Australis' and Hope's 'Australia', with which it shares extraordinary similarities.

In Mapping and Naming the country, all the texts presented bring it under the control of a particular set of metaphors and place it in a particular ideology, a particular way of seeing Australia, together with a set of beliefs about its appropriate future. Some are dogmatic and mono-lithic in their vision; some, consciously or unconsciously, transport their vision from elsewhere and seek to impose it; some are pluralist and prepared to allow for contradictory demands. But all rely on Australia as a source of metaphor.

Alan Lawson/Ken Goodwin

David Malouf
A FIRST PLACE: THE MAPPING OF A WORLD

My purpose tonight is to look at the only place in Australia that I know well, the only place I know from inside, from my body outwards, and to offer my understanding of it as an example of how we might begin to speak accurately of where and what we are. What I will be after is not facts—or not only facts, but a description of how the elements of a place and our inner lives cross and illuminate one another, how we interpret space, and in so doing make our first maps of reality, how we mythologize spaces and through that mythology (a good deal of it inherited) find our way into a culture. You will see, I hope, how a writer might be particularly engaged by all this, and especially a writer of fiction; and you will see too why any one man might have only a single place he can speak of, the place of his earliest experience. For me that was Brisbane. It has always seemed to me to be a fortunate choice—except that I didn't make it. But then the place you get is always, in the real sense of the word, fortunate, in that it constitutes your fortune, your fate, and is your only entry into the world. I am not suggesting that Brisbane is unique in offering the sort of reading I mean to make. The city is unique, as all places are, but the reading, the method I hope, is not.

To begin then with topography.

The first thing you notice about this city is the unevenness of the ground. Brisbane is hilly. Walk two hundred metres in almost any direction outside the central city (which has been levelled) and you get a view—a new view. It is all gullies and sudden vistas. Not long views down a street to the horizon—and I am thinking now of cities like Melbourne and Adelaide, or Manchester or Milan, those great flat cities where you look away down endless vistas and the mind is drawn to distance. Wherever the eye turns here it learns restlessness, and variety and possibility, as the body learns effort. Brisbane is a city that tires the legs and demands a certain sort of breath. It is not a city, I would want to say, that provokes contemplation, in which the mind moves out and loses itself in space. What it might provoke is drama, and a kind of intellectual play that delights in new and shifting views, and this because each new vista as it presents itself here is so intensely colourful.

The key colour is green, and of a particular density: the green of mangroves along the riverbanks, of Moreton Bay figs, of the big trees that are natives of this corner of Queensland, the shapely hoop-pines and bunyas that still dominate the skyline along every ridge. The Australian landscape here is not blue-grey, or grey-green or buff, as in so much of southern Australia; and the light isn't blond or even blue. It is a rich golden pink, and in the late afternoon the western hills and the great flat expanse of water that is the Bay create an effect I have seen in other places only before or after a storm. Everything glows from within. The greens become darkly luminous. The sky produces effects of light and cloud that are, to more sober eyes, almost vulgarly picturesque. But then, these are the sub-tropics. You are soon made aware here of a kind of moisture in the air that makes nature a force that isn't easily domesticated—everything grows too fast, too tall, it gets quickly out of control. Vegetation doesn't complement the man-made, it fiercely competes with it; gardens are always on the point of turning themselves into wilderness, hauling down fences, pushing sheds and outhouses over, making things look ramshackle and halfway to ruin. The weather, harsh sunlight, hard rain, adds to the process, stripping houses of their paint, rotting timber, making the dwellings altogether less solid and substantial, on their high stumps, than the great native trees that surround them.

I'll come back to those houses in a moment. It is no accident that they should have invaded a paragraph that is devoted to nature, since they are, in this place, so utterly of it, both in form and substance. Open wooden affairs, they seem often like elaborated tree-houses, great grown-up cubby-houses hanging precariously above ground.

Now what you abstract from such a landscape, from its greenness, its fierce and damply sinister growth, its power compared with the flimsiness of the domestic architecture, its grandeur of colour and effect, its openness upwards to the sky—another consequence of all those hills—is something other, I would suggest, than what is abstracted from the wide, dry landscapes of Southern Australia that we sometimes think of as 'typical'. It offers a different notion of what the land might be, and relates it to all the daily business of life in a quite different way. It shapes in those who grow up there a different sensibility, a different cast of mind, creates a different sort of Australian.

So much then for the lay of the land; now for that other distinctive feature of the city, its river. Winding back and forth across Brisbane in a classic meander, making pockets and elbows with high cliffs on one side and mud-flats on the other, the River is inescapable. It cuts in and out of every suburb, can be seen from every hill. It also keeps the Bay in mind, since that, clearly, is where all its windings, its odd turns and evasions, lead. But this river does not have the same uses for the citizen as the rivers that flow through other towns.

We think of the Thames, or the Seine or the Tiber or the Arno, and it is clear how they are related to the cities they have growing up on their banks. They divide them, north and south. They offer themselves as a means of orientation. But the river in Brisbane is a disorienting factor. Impossible to know which side of it you are on, north or south, or to use it for settling in your mind how any place or suburb is related to any other.

So the topography of Brisbane, broken up as it is by hills and by the endless switching back and forth upon itself of the river, offers no clear map for the mind to move in, and this really is unusual—I know of no other city like it. Only one thing saves you here from being completely mapless, and that is the net—the purely conceptual net—that was laid down over the city with the tramline system. Ideally it is a great wheel, with the business centre as the hub and a set of radial spokes that push out into the suburbs. The city is conceived of in the minds of its citizens in terms of radial opposites that allow them to establish limits, and these are the old tram termini: Ascot/Balmoral, Clayfield/Salisbury, Toowong/the Grange, West End/New Farm Park, to mention only a few; and this sense of radial opposites has persisted, and continues to be worked with, though the actual tramlines have long since been replaced with 'invisible' (as it were) bus routes. The old tramline system is now the invisible principle that holds the city together and gives it a shape in people's minds.

But that wheels-shape, as I said at the beginning, was ideal—not actual. I lived at Ascot. I have always thought of Balmoral as being at the other end of the city geographically—say, an hour's tram journey or twelve to fifteen miles away. But when I looked at a map recently I discovered that it is, in fact, only half a mile away on the opposite side of the river. Space, in this city, is unreadable. Geography and its features offer no help in the making of a mental map. What you have to do here is create a conceptual one. I ask myself again what habits of mind such a city may encourage in its citizens, and how, though taken for granted in this place, they may differ from the habits of places where geography declares itself at every point as helpful, reliable, being itself a map.

I have already referred briefly to the Brisbane house, setting its insubstantiality for a moment against the solidity of the big local trees, evoking the oddness with which it places itself, reared high on tree-stumps, on the side of its hill.

The houses are of timber, that is the essence of the thing, and to live with timber is to live with a material that yields at every step. The house is a living presence as a stone house never can be, responding to temperature in all its joists and floorboards, creaking, allowing you to follow every step sometimes, in every room. Imagine an old staircase and magnify its physical presence till it becomes a whole dwelling.

Children discover, among their first sensual experiences in the world of touch, the feel of tongue-and-groove boards, the soft places where they have rotted, the way paint flakes and the wood underneath will release sometimes, if you press it, a trickle of spicy reddish dust. In earlier days they often made themselves sick by licking those walls and poisoning themselves with lead.

You learn in such houses to listen. You build up a map of the house in sound, that allows you to know exactly where everyone is and to predict approaches. You also learn what *not* to hear, what is not-to-be-heard, because it is a condition of such houses that everything *can* be heard. Strict conventions exist about what should be listened to and these soon become habits of not-listening, not-hearing. So too, habits grow up of not-seeing.

Wooden houses in Brisbane are open. That is, they often have no doors, and one of the conventions of the place (how it came about might be a study in itself) is that doors, for the most part, are not closed. Maybe it is a result of the weather. Maybe it has something to do with the insistence that life as it is lived up here has no secrets—or should have none. Though it does of course.

Whatever the reason, bedroom doors in a Brisbane house are kept open—you get used to that. Even bathroom doors have no locks and are seldom closed. The proximities are dealt with, and privacy maintained, by just those subtle habits of not-seeing, not-hearing that growing up in such a house creates in you as a kind of second nature. There is something almost Indian about all this. How different from life as it is lived in solid brick houses, with solid walls and solid doors and the need to keep them sealed against the air. Brisbane houses are unsealable. Openness to the air, to the elements, is one of the conditions of their being—and you get used to that too.

So there it is, this odd timber structure, often decorated with wooden fretwork and scrolls of great fantasy, raised on tree-stumps to leaf level and still having about it some quality of the tree—a kind of tree-house expanded. At the centre a nest of rooms, all opening on to a hallway that as often as not runs straight through from front to back, so that when you step up to the front door of the house you can see right through it to trees or sky. Around the nest of rooms, verandahs, mostly with crossed open-work below and lattice or rolled venetians above; an intermediary space between the house proper, which is itself only half closed in, and the world outside—garden, street, weather.

Verandahs have their own life, their own conventions, but serve, for the most part, to make the too-open interior seem closed, therefore safe and protected. Weather beats in on the verandah and the house stays dry. Hawkers and other callers may be allowed up the front steps on to the verandah, but the house, utterly visible and open right through, remains inviolate. There are conventions about this too. You develop a keen sense, from early on, if you grow up in such a house, of what is inside and safe and what is out there at the edge, a boundary area, domestic but exposed.

Inside and out—that is one aspect of the thing: the nest of rooms at the centre and the open verandah. But there is also upstairs and down, and this doesn't at all mean the same thing here as in the two-storeyed terrace, where upstairs means sleeping and downstairs is public life. Upstairs in the Brisbane house is everything: the division between night and day might at the very least be established as one side or the other of a hall. Downstairs here means under-the-house, and that is in many ways the most interesting place of all.

It comes into existence as a space because of the need to get those houses up on stumps, to get them level on the hills it might be, or to keep them cool by providing a buffer of cool air underneath. There are several explanations, no one of them definitive.

So the space down there may be a cube, but is more often a wedge of deepening dark as the high house-stumps at the back diminish till they are as little at the front as a metre or half-a-metre high.

The stumps are capped with tin and painted with creosote against termites. The space they form is closed in with lattice, sometimes all the way to the ground, sometimes to make a fringe a half-metre or so below floor level. The earth is bare, but flooring boards being what they are, a good deal of detritus falls down there from the house above: rusty pins and needles, nails, tacks, occasionally a peachstone or some other rubbish where a child has found a crack big enough to push it through. And a good deal of what the house rejects in other ways also finds its way down there: old sinks or cisterns or bits of plumbing, bed-frames, broken chairs, a superannuated ice-box or meat safe, old toys.

It's a kind of archaeological site down there, and does in fact develop a time dimension of its own that makes that process of falling below, or sending below, or storing below, a passage out of the present into limbo, where things go on visibly existing as a past that can be re-entered, a time-capsule underworld. Visiting it is a way of leaving the house, and the present and daylight and getting back to the underside of things.

It's a sinister place and dangerous, but you are also liberated down there from the conventions. It's where children go to sulk. It's where cats have their kittens and sick dogs go. It's a place to hide things. It is also, as children discover, a place to explore; either by climbing up, usually on a dare, to the dark place under the front steps—exploring the dimensions of your own courage, this is, or your own fear—or by exploring, in the freedom down there, your own and other people's bodies. There can be few Brisbane children who do not associate under-the-house, guiltily or as a great break-out of themselves, with their first touch or taste of sex.

A landscape and its houses, also a way of life; but more deeply, a way of experiencing and mapping the world. One of our intellectual habits, it seems to me, is the visualizing, in terms drawn from the life about us, of what is not visible but which we may need to see. One such entity is what we call mind or psyche. One observes in Freud's description of how the mind works how essential architectural features are, trapdoors, cellars, attics, etc. What I mean to ask here is how far growing up in the kind of house I have been describing may determine, in a very particular way, not only habits of life or habits of mind but the very shape of the psyche as Brisbane people conceive it, may determine, that is, how they visualize and embody such concepts as consciousness and the unconscious, public and private areas of experience, controlled areas and those that are pressingly uncontrollable or just within control—and to speak now of my own particular interest, how far these precise and local actualizations may be available to the writer in dealing with the inner lives of people. What I mean to suggest, as least problematically, is ways in which thinking and feeling may be intensely local—though that does not necessarily make them incomprehensible to outsiders, and it is the writer's job, of course, so long as we are in the world of his fiction, to make insiders of all of us.

We have tended, when thinking as 'Australians', to turn away from difference, even to assume that difference does not exist, and fix our attention on what is common to us; to assume that some general quality of Australianness exists, a national identity that derives from our history in the place and from the place itself. But Australians have had different histories. The states have produced, I would want to claim, very different social forms, different political forms as well, and so far as landscape and climate are concerned, Australia is not one place. It might be time to forget likeness and look closely at the many varieties of difference we now exhibit, to let notions of what is typically Australian lapse for a time while we investigate the different sorts of landscape the country presents us with, the different styles, social, political, educational of the states, the different styles of our cities, and even of suburbs within cities, and for those of us who are concerned with literature, for example, to ask ourselves how many different sorts of Australian writing there may be and how much the differences between them may be determined by the particular social habits and physical features of *place*. Is there, to come back to the present occasion, a Brisbane way of experiencing things that we could isolate in the works of writers who, even if they have not spent their writing life in the city, grew up there, and were in their first experience of the world shaped by it: in Peter Porter, Gwen Harwood, John Blight, for example, and in a slightly later generation Judith Rodriguez, Rodney Hall (though he came there as a child), Humphrey McQueen, Gerard Lee, Rhyll McMaster, myself? Is there something in the style of mind of these writers, even in their use of language a restlessness, a delight in variety and colour and baroque effects, in what I called earlier 'drama' and 'shifting views' that we might trace back to the topography of the place and the physical conditions it imposes on the body, to ways of seeing it imposes on the eye, and at some less conscious level, to embodiments of mind and psyche that belong to the first experience and first mapping, of a house.

These are open questions, I know; but I think I know some of the answers from my own experience—and it is, of course, from my own experience that I have been speaking. In outlining the contours of a sensibility, and tracing them back to place, I have largely been speaking of myself, though I have not wanted here to put everything in merely personal terms—I believe they are not merely personal—or to indulge too closely in autobiography. The question I raise is a general one. It may be the right time to ask it.

(1984)

William Dampier
from A NEW VOYAGE ROUND
THE WORLD: 1688

New Holland is a very large Tract of Land. It is not yet determined whether it is an Island or a main Continent; but I am certain that it joyns neither to Asia, Africa, nor America. This part of it that we saw is all low even Land, with Sandy Banks against the Sea, only the Points are rocky, and so are some of the Islands in this Bay.

The Land is of a dry sandy Soil, destitute of Water, except you make Wells; yet producing divers sorts of Trees; but the Woods are not thick, nor the Trees very big. Most of the Trees that we saw are Dragon-trees [*Drœcena Draco*], as we supposed; and these too are the largest Trees of any there. They are about the bigness of our large Appletrees, and about the same heighth: and the Rind is blackish, and somewhat rough. The Leaves are of a dark colour; the Gum distils out of the Knots or Cracks that are in the Bodies of the Trees. We compared it with some Gum Dragon, or Dragon's Blood, that was aboard, and it was of the same colour and taste. The other sorts of Trees were not known by any of us. There was pretty long Grass growing under the Trees; but it was very thin. We saw no Trees that bore Fruit or Berries.

We saw no sort of Animal, nor any Track of Beast, but once; and that seemed to be the Tread of a Beast as big as a great Mastiff-Dog. Here are a few small Landbirds, but none bigger than a Blackbird; and but few Seafowls. Neither is the Sea very plentifully stored with Fish, unless you reckon the Manatee and Turtle as such. Of these Creatures there is plenty; but they are extraordinary shy; though the Inhabitants cannot trouble them much, having neither Boats nor Iron.

The Inhabitants of this Country are the miserablest People in the world. The Hodmadods of Monomatapa, though a nasty People, yet for Wealth are Gentlemen to these; who have no Houses and skin Garments, Sheep, Poultry, and Fruits of the Earth, Ostrich Eggs, &c. as the Hodmadods have: And setting aside their Humane Shape, they differ but little from Brutes. They are tall, strait-bodied, and thin, with small long Limbs. They have great Heads, round Foreheads, and great Brows. Their Eye-lids are always half closed, to keep the Flies out of their Eyes; they being so troublesome here, that no Fanning will keep them from coming to ones Face; and without the assistance of both Hands to keep them off, they will creep into ones Nostrils, and Mouth too, if the Lips are not shut very close: so that from their Infancy being thus annoyed with these Insects, they do never open their Eyes as other People: And therefore they cannot see far, unless they hold up their Heads, as if they were looking at somewhat over them.

They have great Bottle Noses, pretty full Lips, and wide Mouths. The two Fore-teeth of their Upper jaw are wanting in all of them, Men and Women, Old and Young; whether they draw them out, I know not: Neither have they any Beards. They are long visaged, and of a very unpleasing Aspect, having no one graceful Feature in their Faces. Their Hair is black, short and curl'd, like that of the Negroes; and not long and lank like the common Indians. The colour of their Skins, both of their Faces and the rest of their Body, is coal black, like that of the Negroes of Guinea.

They have no sort of Cloaths, but a piece of the Rind of a Tree ty'd like a Girdle about their Waists, and a handful of long Grass, or 3 or 4 small green Boughs full of Leaves, thrust under their Girdle, to cover their Nakedness.

They have no Houses, but lie in the open Air, without any covering; the Earth being their Bed, and the Heaven their Canopy. Whether they cohabit one Man to one Woman, or promiscuously, I know not: but they do live in Companies, 20 or 30 Men, Women, and Children together. Their only Food is a small sort of Fish, which they get by making Wares [weirs] of Stone across little Coves or Branches of the Sea; every Tide bringing in the small Fish, and there leaving them for a Prey to these People, who constantly attend there to search for them at Low-water. This small Fry I take to be the top of their Fishery: They have no Instruments to catch great Fish, should they come; and such seldom stay to be left behind at Low-water: Nor could we catch any Fish with our Hooks and Lines all the while we lay there. In other Places at Low-water they seek for Cockles, Muscles, and Periwincles: Of these Shell-fish there are fewer still: so that their chiefest dependance is upon what the Sea leaves in their Wares; which, be it much or little they gather up, and march to the Places of their abode. There the old People that are not able to stir abroad by reason of their Age, and the tender Infants, wait their return; and what Providence has bestowed on them, they presently broil on the Coals, and eat it in common. Sometimes they get as many Fish as makes them a plentiful Banquet; and at other times they scarce get every one a taste: But be it little or much that they get, every one has his part, as well the young and tender, the old and feeble, who are not able to go abroad, as the strong and lusty. When they have eaten they lie down till the next Low-water, and then all that are able march out, be it Night or Day, rain or shine, 'tis all one; they must attend the Wares, or else they must fast: For the Earth affords them no Food at all. There is neither Herb, Root, Pulse nor any sort of Grain for them to eat, that we saw; nor any sort of Bird or Beast that they can catch, having no Instruments wherewithal to do so.

I did not perceive that they did worship any thing. These poor Creatures have a sort of Weapon to defend their Ware, or fight with their Enemies, if they have any that will interfere with their poor Fishery. They did at first endeavour with their Weapons to frighten us, who lying ashore deterr'd them from one of their Fishing-places. Some of them had wooden Swords, others had a sort of Lances. The Sword is a piece of Wood shaped somewhat like a Cutlass. The Lance is a long strait Pole sharp at one end, and hardened afterwards by heat. I saw no Iron, nor any other sort of Metal; therefore it is probable they use Stone-Hatchets, as some Indians in America do, described in Chap. IV.

How they get their Fire I know not; but, probably, as Indians do, out of Wood. I have seen the Indians of Bon-Airy do it, and have my self tryed the Experiment: They take a flat piece of Wood that is pretty soft, and make a small dent in one side of it, then they take another hard round Stick, about the bigness of ones little Finger, and sharpening it at one end like a Pencil, they put that sharp end in the hole or dent of the flat soft piece, and then rubbing or twirling the hard piece between the Palms of their Hands, they drill the soft piece till it smoaks, and at last takes fire.

These People speak somewhat thro' the Throat; but we could not understand one word that they said. We anchored, as I said before, January the 5th, and seeing Men walking on the Shore, we presently sent a Canoa to get some Acquaintance with them: for we were in hopes to get some Provision among them. But the Inhabitants, seeing our Boat coming, run away and hid themselves. We searched afterwards 3 Days in hopes to find their Houses; but found none: yet we saw many places where they had made Fires. At last, being out of hopes to find their Habitations, we searched no farther; but left a great many Toys ashore, in such places where we thought that they would come. In all our search we found no Water, but old Wells on the sandy Bays.

(1697)

Ania Walwicz
AUSTRALIA

You big ugly. You too empty. You desert with your nothing nothing nothing. You scorched suntanned. Old too quickly. Acres of suburbs watching the telly. You bore me. Freckle silly children. You nothing much. With your big sea. Beach beach beach. I've seen enough already. You dumb dirty city with bar stools. You're ugly. You silly shoppingtown. You copy. You too far everywhere. You laugh at me. When I came this woman gave me a box of biscuits. You try to be friendly but you're not very friendly. You never ask me to your house. You insult me. You don't know how to be with me. Road road tree tree. I came from crowded and many. I came from rich. You have nothing to offer. You're poor and spread thin. You big. So what. I'm small. It's what's in. You silent on Sunday. Nobody on your streets. You dead at night. You go to sleep too early. You don't excite me. You scare me with your hopeless. Asleep when you walk. Too hot to think. You big awful. You don't match me. You burnt out. You too big sky. You make me a dot in the nowhere. You laugh with your big healthy. You want everyone to be the same. You're dumb. You do like anybody else. You engaged Doreen. You big cow. You average average. Cold day at school playing around at lunchtime. Running around for nothing. You never accept me. For your own. You always ask me where I'm from. You always ask me. You tell me I look strange. Different. You don't adopt me. You laugh at the way I speak. You think you're better than me. You don't like me. You don't have any interest in another country. Idiot centre of your own self. You think the rest of the world walks around without shoes or electric light. You don't go anywhere. You stay at home. You like one another. You go crazy on Saturday night. You get drunk. You don't like me and you don't like women. You put your arm around men in bars. You're rough. I can't speak to you. You burly burly. You're just silly to me. You big man. Poor with all your money. You ugly furniture. You ugly house. Relaxed in your summer stupor. All year. Never fully awake. Dull at school. Wait for other people to tell you what to do. Follow the leader. Can't imagine. Work horse. Thick legs. You go to work in the morning. You shiver on a tram.

(1981)

Anna Couani
REMEMBER TO FORGET

The wind comes up in a strengthening way. The cold is never a biting cold. The salty air is always invigorating.
—Unhappiness is something to sing songs about and sing them from the cliffs around the bay where no one hears you. Or not.
Sing them to me.
The wind refreshes.
—And then, we rest.

—Have you ever had that experience of looking across at the person with you and suddenly realizing that this is the person, the person you'll stay with?

Night after night after night in the bars of Amsterdam we talked about the ways different countries differed.
—You know I've travelled all over the world don't you—any place you can name. Well, I'll tell you this—Australia's great for a holiday but I wouldn't live there. It's unique I'll say that. Anyone can feel at home there because it has a strange character or atmosphere which is like an absence of character, a kind of neutrality. I think it's very tolerant or maybe just very anonymous. No really, I do *like* Australia. When I lived there I liked it. But I realize coming away again that there's some strange pressure there. It's subliminal, very subtle. I don't think I could describe it exactly because it's an abstract quality which pervades everything there, the work situation, the politics, the social life. It's a place that gets you down. The amount of drinking the people do is phenomenal. And it's as though

everyone's bitten by the same bug—some kind of desperation or hysteria which is never expressed. They're stoics, the Aussies. The most cynical people in the world. Beyond morality—like the English but more sophisticated because they never say *anything*. The English talk and talk and talk, endlessly trying to reason things out, playing with words really but they're expressing attitudes. The *real* Australian attitude is never expressed. If you talk to an Australian about being Australian, they just say, 'What's it to you,' or 'Why don't you go back to Ponseville, mate, where you belong,' or 'Want a match? Your face and my arse. Christ all this talking's given me a thirst.' They're always on the defensive. To get an opinion out of them is like getting blood from a stone. They think conversation on a serious level is a joke. Not that they're so wrong. I'm sure they know they have opinions and that you might differ in opinion but that seems irrelevant to them. They just laugh and say, 'Don't get your tits in a tangle, come and have a beer.' They make friends with the people they happen to be thrown together with, nor necessarily the people they like.

Everything's said in what's *not* said. Everything's strangely inverse not quite perverse. They've got a strong ethical code but they probably couldn't or wouldn't tell you what it is. I think it's a bit Japanese, Zen you know but without tradition or maybe just a tradition which has never been articulated. A conspiracy of silence. They present this strange face to the world—of boomerangs, kangaroos, country life, the out-of-doors. It's a fantasy tradition and you get the feeling that they like that because it means they have protection. No one gets to what they really are, what the Australian character is, particularly the good side of it.

I can think of one really tragic thing about Australians though and that's their lack of aspirations. Ambition is considered very bad, unethical. They say, 'Why do you want to crawl to top of the shit heap, hey, got some kind of problem?' Their taboos aren't like the taboos of other countries. I expected them to be like the English or Americans, they're not.

I was in one of the pubs in the city once and the people who were drinking were the most 'Australian' men I'd seen. They were screaming and punching each other in the shoulder and speaking the broadest Australian dialect. I asked the barman about these people. He said they weren't celebrating any special occasion, that this particular group were always like this. Then he told me they were mostly important people—some were rich, some were public figures, some were artists and writers—you know the kind of group I mean. So in Australia, the people who are least Australian, the ones who know about international affairs, who travel etc. are the ones who take up the Australian stereotype most strongly for fear of looking un-Australian.

—Choose a country or a city or a town. Which country is it? Don't tell me. Now close your eyes and tell me what you see and I'll guess where it is. When you remember something as a visitor it's always typical.
—I remember the island and every time I think of it it's the same picture again and again of the main street and then close up, the kiosks, then closer, the racks of postcards on the metal tree, like a pine tree and the worry beads. It's night, the kiosks are yellow, the light inside them is yellow. There are other pictures I can think of also. The beautiful village

with the strange little harbour, the silence. And another—on top of the hill I suddenly see the big concrete cross. It was always there but I only noticed it once. The sunshine, the sunshine, the sunshine, the song—'Good-morning Sun'.
The misty islands, the coast of Turkey.
—Now we're treading on unfamiliar ground again. The cross—why do you think of the cross.
—When I was a child in the mountains there was a cross on the top of a mountain at the cliff's edge. A young kid fell from the place the cross stands and died. Everything you see reminds you of something significant. If it doesn't you don't notice it.
—There's something about the physical appearance of things sometimes which embodies an idea. Sometimes I can recall something exactly, some feeling of a place but it's a picture, and it's difficult to say what this is. Like in Amsterdam I remember a picture which has many of the canals, and many of the buildings at both day and night. Something I never could've seen—there's much more in the picture than I could see at any moment I was there.
It's like lots of simultaneous pictures—you couldn't make it.
—Yes. And how could you make a picture which showed that you felt you'd seen this before. Or one where a row of buildings also means for you a time when you worked too hard for 2 weeks.
—A really bleached-out glarey day always reminds me of being hung over. You know how your eyes are more sensitive to light.
—Sunny early mornings—they're beautiful but can seem sinister if you have to set out early to do something difficult. And all the years of going to work in the early morning. But then there are trips to the sea at dawn or watching the sunrise over the city after staying up all night.
—That's Australia—sunrise at the beach, sunrise over the city.

Here is a beautiful painting of an old-fashioned steamship on the sea. It is night and everything is lit up by the full moon.
—This is a painting for the full moon. Do you see this ship. Inside the hull are all the hidden thoughts which lie between us.
—What are they?
—We don't know, we can't. Forget it. It's just a painting.

—I remember the night we slept at the orchard just before the full moon. Remember the first night? I was walking on the broken glass. I just remember that now. It was okay, it didn't hurt me. But that was strange. We were both walking on the broken glass beside the bed.

Now the moon wanes, another month finishes. Everything was filled up and now it's draining out. Preparing for another ascent.
—You're tied to the moon.
—Every woman's tied to the moon. Women have lunar cycles.
—But you're completely up when the moon's full and afterwards, you come down as the moon does. In the evening you rise when the moon rises and you're tired as the moon fades in the morning.
—Some people aren't only influenced by the moon but subject to it, dominated by it. It gives them their strength and it takes their strength

away. The full moon can be a strange time for people ruled by the moon because they're strongest at this time but strong in a lunar way—that's a passive receptive way. Everything depends on what's being received. You're like a boat tossed about on the waves. The stronger the impulses around you are, the more rocked by them you are. Lunar people are often overwhelmed at this time. But when it breaks, you surface again. It's just a couple of days. Women should talk about it more and help each other through these times because it's possible to become quite unhinged.
—And in Australia?
—Forget it. There, you'd think the moon didn't exist. It's one of the secrets. It comes dangerously close to a direct hit at one of the taboo subjects. Remember?
—I want to feel, I want to think, I want to live and love.
—Don't go to Australia.
—There's no love there.
—There is love. It's love which binds us together. But in Australia it's been stretched like a very thin high-tensile wire. Sometimes visible but mostly invisible. In Australia you can't *want* to love, you either do or you don't and you don't tell anyone about it. Not even the people you love. You can't want to *be* loved either. You realize you *are* loved.
—Afterwards.
—After what?
—After you've felt you weren't loved. When you get used to the idea of not being loved. These secret things take years to understand. I think maybe some people don't ever understand. But now it's changing a bit at last. They're starting to come in from the cold like the old stockman returning to the bright lights of the station after 2 weeks riding the fences in the cold and the dust. While he's away he has to remember the warmth and light of his home but when he comes back he can forget it.
—He says, And then I get home and wouldn't you know—the wife started her period today. Forget it.
—I think you're starting to understand.

(1982)

James McAuley
TERRA AUSTRALIS

Voyage within you, on the fabled ocean,
And you will find that Southern Continent,
Quiros' vision—his hidalgo heart
And mythical Australia, where reside
All things in their imagined counterpart.   5

It is your land of similes: the wattle
Scatters its pollen on the doubting heart;
The flowers are wide-awake; the air gives ease.
There you come home; the magpies call you Jack
And whistle like larrikins at you from the trees.   10

There too the angophora preaches on the hillsides
With the gestures of Moses; and the white cockatoo,
Perched on his limbs, screams with demoniac pain;
And who shall say on what errand the insolent emu
Walks between morning and night on the edge of the plain?   15

But northward in valleys of the fiery Goat
Where the sun like a centaur vertically shoots
His raging arrows with unerring aim,
Stand the ecstatic solitary pyres
Of unknown lovers, featureless with flame.   20

(1942)

Michael Dransfield
from GEOGRAPHY

III

in the forest, in unexplored
valleys of the sky, are chapels of pure
vision. there even the desolation of space cannot
sorrow you or imprison. i dream of the lucidity of the vacuum,
orders of saints consisting of parts of a rainbow,   5
identities of wild things / of
what the stars are saying to each other, up there
above the concrete and minimal existences, above
idols and wars and caring. tomorrow
we shall go there, you and your music and the   10
wind and i, leaving from very strange
stations of the cross, leaving from
high windows and from release,
from clearings
in the forest, the uncharted   15
uplands of the spirit

(1972)

Bernard O'Dowd
AUSTRALIA

Last sea-thing dredged by sailor Time from Space,
Are you a drift Sargasso, where the West
In halcyon calm rebuilds her fatal nest?
Or Delos of a coming Sun-God's race?
Are you for Light, and trimmed, with oil in place,   5
Or but a Will o' Wisp on marshy quest?
A new demesne for Mammon to infest?
Or lurks millennial Eden 'neath your face?

The cenotaphs of species dead elsewhere
That in your limits leap and swim and fly,   10
Or trail uncanny harp-strings from your trees,
Mix omens with the anguries that dare
To plant the Cross upon your forehead sky,
A virgin helpmate Ocean at your knees.

                                                        (1900)

A. D. Hope
AUSTRALIA

A Nation of trees, drab green and desolate grey
In the field uniform of modern wars,
Darkens her hills, those endless, outstretched paws
Of Sphinx demolished or stone lion worn away.

They call her a young country, but they lie: 5
She is the last of lands, the emptiest,
A woman beyond her change of life, a breast
Still tender but within the womb is dry.

Without songs, architecture, history:
The emotions and superstitions of younger lands,   10
Her rivers of water drown among inland sands,
The river of her immense stupidity

Floods her monotonous tribes from Cairns to Perth.
In them at last the ultimate men arrive
Whose boast is not: 'we live' but 'we survive',   15
A type who will inhabit the dying earth.

And her five cities, like five teeming sores,
Each drains her: a vast parasite robber-state
Where second-hand Europeans pullulate
Timidly on the edge of alien shores.   20

Yet there are some like me turn gladly home
From the lush jungle of modern thought, to find
The Arabian desert of the human mind,
Hoping, if still from the deserts the prophets come,

Such savage and scarlet as no green hills dare   25
Springs in that waste, some spirit which escapes
The learned doubt, the chatter of cultured apes
Which is called civilization over there.

                                                        (1939)

W. C. Wentworth
from AUSTRALASIA

Land of my birth! tho' now, alas! no more
Musing I wander on thy sea-girt shore,
Or climb with eager haste thy barrier cliff,
To catch a glimmer of the distant skiff,
That ever and anon breaks into light,   5
And then again eludes the aching sight,
Till nearer seen she bends her foaming way
Majestic onward to yon placid bay,
Where Sydney's infant turrets proudly rise,
The new-born glory of the southern skies;—   10
Dear Australasia, can I e'er forget
Thee, Mother Earth? Ah no, my heart e'en yet
With filial fondness loves to call to view
Scenes, which though oft remember'd, still are new;
Scenes, where my playful childhood's thoughtless years   15
Flew swift away, despite of childhood's tears;
Where later too, in manhood's op'ning bloom,
The tangled brake, th' eternal forest's gloom,
The wonted brook, where with some truant mate
I lov'd to plunge, or ply the treach'rous bait;   20
The spacious harbour with its hundred coves,
And fairy islets—seats of savage loves,
Again beheld—restampt with deeper die
The fading visions of my infancy.

  Ye primal tribes, lords of this old domain,   25
Swift-footed hunters of the pathless plain,
Unshackled wanderers, enthusiasts free,
Pure native sons of savage liberty,
Who hold all things in common, earth, sea, air,
Or only occupy the nightly lair,   30
Whereon each sleeps; who own no chieftain's pow'r,
Save his, that's mightiest of the passing hour;
Say—whence your ancient lineage, what your name
And from what shores your rough forefathers came?
Untutor'd children, fresh from Nature's mould,   35
No songs have ye to trace the time of old:—
No hidden themes, like these, employ your care,
For you enough the knowledge that ye are:—
Let Learning's sons, who would this secret scan,
Unlock its mystic casket if they can,—   40
To your unletter'd tastes are sweeter far
The dance of battle, and the song of war,
'Mid hostile ranks the deadly spear to throw,
Or see the foeman stagg'ring 'neath your blow:—
To you, ye sable hunters, sweeter too   45
To spy the track of bounding kangaroo,

Or long neck'd Emu:—quick with eagle gaze
Her path you follow thro' the tangled maze,
O'er boundless wilds your panting game pursue,
And come, like trusty hounds, at last in view;   50
Then creeping round her, soon the forest's pride
Is hemm'd with bristly spears that pierce her side.
And now, the labours of the chase being o'er,
And Nature's keen suggestions heard no more,
In uncouth numbers seated in a ring   55
Your ancient fathers' warlike feats ye sing,
Or striking each his shield, with clatt'ring lance,
The early night exhaust in Pyrrhic dance.

Celestial poesy! whose genial sway
Earth's furthest habitable shores obey;
Whose inspirations shed their sacred light.
Far as the regions of the Arctic night,
And to the Laplander his Boreal gleam
Endear not less, than Phoebus' brighter beam—
Descend thou also on my native land,   65
And on some mountain-summit take thy stand;
Thence issuing soon a purer fount be seen,
Than charm'd Castalia or fam'd Hippocrene;
And there a richer, nobler fane arise,
Than on Parnassus met th' adoring eyes.   70
And tho', bright Goddess, on those far blue hills,
That pour their thousand swift pellucid rills,
Where Warragumba's rage has rent in twain
Opposing mountains,—thund'ring to the plain,
No child of song has yet invok'd thy aid,   75
'Neath their primeval solitary shade,—
Still, gracious pow'r, some kindling soul inspire,
To wake to life my country's unknown lyre,
That from creation's date has slumb'ring lain,
Or only breath'd some savage uncouth strain;—   80
And grant that yet an Austral Milton's song
Pactolus-like flow deep and rich along;—
An Austral Shakspeare rise, whose living page
To Nature true may charm in ev'ry age;—
And that an Austral Pindar daring soar,   85
Where not the Theban Eagle reach'd before.

And, oh Britannia! shouldst thou cease to ride
Despotic Empress of old Ocean's tide;—
Should thy tam'd Lion—spent his former might,—
No longer roar the terror of the fight;—   90
Should e'er arrive that dark disastrous hour,
When bow'd by luxury, thou yield'st to pow'r;—
When thou, no longer freest of the free
To some proud victor bend'st the vanquish'd knee;—

May all thy glories in another sphere   95
Relume, and shine more brightly still than here;
May this, thy last-born infant,—then arise,
To glad thy heart, and greet thy parent eyes;
And Australasia float, with flag unfurl'd,
A new Britannia in another world.   100

(1823)

Barron Field
ON READING THE CONTROVERSY
BETWEEN LORD BYRON AND MR BOWLES

Anticipation is to a young country what antiquity is to an old.

Whether a ship's poetic?—Bowles would own,
If here he dwelt, where Nature is prosaic,
Unpicturesque, unmusical, and where
Nature reflecting Art is not yet born;—
A land without antiquities, with one,   5
And only one, poor spot of classic ground,
(That on which Cook first landed)—where, instead
Of heart-communings with ancestral relics,
Which purge the pride while they exalt the mind,
We've nothing left us but anticipation,   10
Better (I grant) than utter selfishness,
Yet too o'erweening—too American;
Where's no past tense; the ign'rant present's all;
Or only great by the *All hail hereafter!*
One foot of future's glass should rest on past;   15
Where hist'ry is not, prophecy is guess—
If here he dwelt, Bowles (I repeat) would own,
Except the native maidens and the flowers,
The sky that bends o'er all, and southern stars,
A ship's the only poetry we see.   20
For, first, she brings us 'news of human kind',
Of friends and kindred, whom perchance she held
As visitors, that she might be a link,
Connecting the fond fancy of far friendship,
A few short months before, and whom she may   25
In a few more, perhaps, receive again.
Next is a ship poetic, forasmuch
As in this spireless city and profane,
She is to my home-wand'ring phantasy,
With her tall anchor'd masts, a three-spir'd minster,   30
Vane-crown'd; her bell our only half-hour chimes.
Lastly, a ship is poetry to me,
Since piously I trust, in no long space,
Her wings will bear me from this prose-dull land.

(1823)

Peter Porter
ON FIRST LOOKING INTO CHAPMAN'S HESIOD

For 5p at a village fête I bought
Old Homer-Lucan who popped Keats's eyes,
Print smaller than the Book of Common Prayer
But Swinburne at the front, whose judgement is
Always immaculate. I'll never read a tenth   5
Of it in what life I have left to me
But I did look at *The Georgics*, as he calls
The Works and Days, and there I saw, not quite
The view from Darien but something strange
And balking—Australia, my own country   10
And its edgy managers—in the picture of
Euboeaen husbandry, terse family feuds
And the minds of gods tangential to the earth.

Like a Taree smallholder splitting logs
And philosophizing on his dangling billies,   15
The poet mixes hard agrarian instances
With sour sucks to his brother. Chapman, too,
That perpetual motion poetry machine,
Grinds up the classics like bone meal from
The abattoirs. And the same blunt patriotism,   20
A long-winded, emphatic, kelpie yapping
About our land, our time, our fate, our strange
And singular way of moons and showers, lakes
Filling oddly—yes, Australians are Boeotians,
Hard as headlands, and, to be fair, with days   25
As robust as the Scythian wind on stone.

To teach your grandmother to suck eggs
Is a textbook possibility in New South Wales
Or outside Ascra. And such a genealogy too!
The Age of Iron is here, but oh the memories   30
Of Gold—pioneers preaching to the stringybarks,
Boring the land to death with verses and with
Mental Homes. 'Care-flying ease' and 'Gift-
Devouring kings' become the Sonata of the Shotgun
And Europe's Entropy; for 'the axle-tree, the quern,   35
The hard, fate-fostered man' you choose among
The hand castrator, kerosene in honey tins
And mystic cattlemen: the Land of City States
Greets Australia in a farmer's gods.

Hesiod's father, caught in a miserable village,   40
Not helped by magic names like Helicon,
Sailed to improve his fortunes, and so did
All our fathers—in turn, their descendants
Lacked initiative, other than the doctors' daughters
Who tripped to England. Rough-nosed Hesiod   45

Was sure of his property to a slip-rail—
Had there been grants, he'd have farmed all
Summer and spent winter in Corinth
At the Creative Writing Class. Chapman, too,
Would vie with Steiner for the Pentecostal   50
Silver Tongue. Some of us feel at home nowhere,
Others in one generation fuse with the land.

I salute him then, the blunt old Greek whose way
Of life was as cunning as organic. His poet
Followers still make me feel déraciné   55
Within myself. One day they're on the campus,
The next in wide hats at a branding or
Sheep drenching, not actually performing
But looking the part and getting instances
For odes that bruise the blood. And history,   60
So interior a science it almost seems
Like true religion—who would have thought
Australia was the point of all that craft
Of politics in Europe? The apogee, it seems,
Is where your audience and its aspirations are.   65

'The colt, and mule, and horn-retorted steer'—
A good iambic line to paraphrase.
Long storms have blanched the million bones
Of the Aegean, and as many hurricanes
Will abrade the headstones of my native land: 70
Sparrows acclimatize but I still seek
The permanently upright city where
Speech is nature and plants conceive in pots,
Where one escapes from what one is and who
One was, where home is just a postmark   75
And country wisdom clings to calendars,
The opposite of a sunburned truth-teller's
World, haunted by precepts and the Pleiades.

                                                      (1975)

John Dunmore Lang
COLONIAL NOMENCLATURE

'Twas said of Greece two thousand years ago,
    That every stone i' the land had got a name.
Of New South Wales too, men will soon say so too;
    But every stone there seems to get the same.
'Macquarie' for a name is all *the go*:   5
    The old Scotch Governor was fond of fame,
Macquarie Street, Place, Port, Fort, Town, Lake, River:
'Lachlan Macquarie, Esquire, Governor', for ever!

I like the native names, as Parramatta,
   And Illawarra, and Woolloomoolloo;   10
Nandowra, Woogarora, Bulkomatta,
   Tomah, Toongabbie, Mittagong, Meroo;
Buckobble, Cumleroy, and Coolingatta,
   The Warragumby, Bargo, Burradoo;
Cookbundoon, Carrabaiga, Wingecarribbee,   15
The Wollondilly, Yurumbon, Bungarribbee.

I hate your Goulburn Downs and Goulburn Plains,
   And Goulburn River and the Goulburn Range,
And Mount Goulburn and Goulburn Vale! One's brains
   Are turned with Goulburns! Vile scorbutic mange   20
For immortality! Had I the reins
   Of Government a fortnight, I would change
These Downing Street appellatives, and give
The country names that should deserve to live.

I'd have Mount Hampden and Mount Marvell, and   25
   Mount Wallace and Mount Bruce at the old Bay.
I'd have them all the highest in the land,
   That men might see them twenty leagues away.
I'd have the Plains of Marathon beyond
   Some mountain pass yclept Thermopylæ.   30
Such are th' immortal names that should be written
On all thy new discoveries, Great Britain!

(1823)

A.D. Hope
COUNTRY PLACES

Hell, Hay and Booligal!

I glean them from signposts in these country places,
Weird names, some beautiful, more that make me laugh.
Driving to fat-lamb sales or to picnic races,
I pass their worshippers of the golden calf
And, in the dust of their Cadillacs, a latter-day Habbakuk   5
Rises in me to preach comic sermons of doom,
Crying: 'Woe unto Tocumwal, Teddywaddy, Tooleybuc!'
And: 'Wicked Wallumburrawang, your hour has come!'

But when the Four Horsemen ride their final muster
And my sinful country sinks in the fiery rain   10
One name shall survive the doom and the disaster
That fell on the foolish cities of the plain.
Like the three holy children or the salamander
One place shall sing and flourish in the fire:
It is Sweet Water Creek at Mullengandra   15
And there at the Last Day I shall retire.

When Numbugga shrieks to Burrumbuttock:
'The curse of Sodom comes upon us all!'
When Tumbarumba calls for spade and mattock
And they bury Hell and Hay in Booligal;   20
When the wrath of God is loosed upon Gilgandra
And Gulargambone burns red against the west,
To Sweet Water Creek at Mullengandra
I shall rise and flee away and be at rest.

When from Goonoo Goonoo, Underbool and Grong Grong   25
And Suggan Buggan there goes up the cry,
From Tittybong, Drik Drik and Drung Drung,
'Help, Lord, help us, or we die!'
I shall lie beside a willow-cool meander, or
Cut myself a fly-whisk in the shade,   30
And from Sweet Water Creek at Mullengandra
Fill my cup and whet my whistle unafraid.

When Boinka lies in ruins (more's the pity!),
And a heavenly trump proclaims the End of Grace,
With: 'Wombat is fallen, is fallen, that great city!'   35
Adding: 'Bunyip is in little better case;'
When from Puckapunyal and from Yackandandah
The cry goes up: 'How long, O Lord, how long?'
I shall hear the she-oaks sough at Mullengandra
And the Sweet Waters ripple into song: 40

Oh, there's little to be hoped for Grabben Gullen
And Tumbulgum shrinks and shudders at its fate;
Folks at Wantabadgery and Cullen Bullen
Have Buckley's chance of reaching Heaven's gate;
It's all up with Cootamundra and Kiandra   45
And at Collarenebri they know they're through;
But at Sweet Water Creek at Mullengandra
You may pitch your camp and sleep the whole night through.

God shall punish Cargelligo, Come-by-Chance, Chinkapook;
They shall dance no more at Merrijig nor drink at Gentleman's Halt; 50
The sin of Moombooldool He shall in no wise overlook;
Wee Jasper and Little Jillaby, He shall not condone their fault;
But though I preach down Nap Nap and annihilate Narrandera,
One place shall yet be saved, this I declare:
Sweet Water Creek at Mullengandra   55
For its name and for my sake the Lord shall spare.

Coda
Alas! my beautiful, my prosperous, my careless country,
She destroys herself: the Lord will come too late!
They have cut down even their only tree at One Tree;
Dust has choked Honey Bugle and drifts over Creeper Gate;   60
The fires we lit ourselves on Mount Boothegandra
Have made more ruin than Heaven's consuming flame;
Even Sweet Water Creek at Mullengandra,
If I went there now, would it live up to its name?

                                                    (1973)

Charles Harpur
from THE CREEK OF THE FOUR GRAVES

PART I

I verse a Settler's tale of olden times—
One told me by our sage friend, Egremont,
Who then went forth, meetly equipt, with four
Of his most trusty and adventurous men
Into the wilderness,—went forth to seek   5
New streams and wider pastures for his fast
Augmenting flocks and herds. On foot were all,
For horses then were beasts of too great price
To be much ventured upon mountain routes,
And over wild wolds clouded up with brush,   10
Or cut with marshes, perilously pathless.

　　So went they forth at dawn: and now the sun
That rose behind them as they journeyed out,
Was firing with his nether rim a range
Of unknown mountains that, like rampires, towered   15
Full in their front; and his last glances fell
Into the gloomy forest's eastern glades
In golden masses, transiently, or flashed
Down on the windings of a nameless Creek,
That noiseless ran betwixt the pioneers   20
And those new Apennines;—ran, shaded up
With boughs of the wild willow, hanging mixed
From either bank, or duskily befringed
With upward tapering feathery swamp-oaks—
The sylvan eyelash always of remote   25
Australian waters, whether gleaming still
In lake or pool, or bickering along
Between the marges of some eager stream.

　　Before them, thus extended, wilder grew
The scene each moment—and more wilder.   30
For when the sun was all but sunk below
Those barrier mountains,—in the breeze that o'er
Their rough enormous backs deep fleeced with wood
Came whispering down, the wide upslanting sea
Of fanning leaves in the descending rays   35
Danced interdazzlingly, as if the trees
That bore them, were all thrilling,—tingling all
Even to the roots for very happiness;
So prompted from within, so sentient, seemed
The bright quick motion—wildly beautiful.   40

　　But when the sun had wholly disappeared
Behind those mountains—O what words, what hues
Might paint the wild magnificence of view
That opened westward! Out extending, lo,
The heights rose crowding, with their summits all   45

Dissolving, as it seemed, and partly lost
In the exceeding radiancy aloft;
And, thus transfigured, for awhile they stood
Like a great company of Archaeons, crowned
With burning diadems, and tented o'er   50
With canopies of purple and of gold!

Here halting wearied, now the sun was set,
Our travellers kindled for their first night's camp
The brisk and crackling fire, which also looked
A wilder creature than 'twas elsewhere wont,   55
Because of the surrounding savageness.
And soon in cannikins the tea was made
Fragant and strong; long fresh-sliced rashers then
Impaled on whittled skewers, were deftly broiled
On the live embers, and, when done, transferred   60
To quadrants from an ample damper cut,
Their only trenchers,—soon to be dispatched
With all the savoury morsels they sustained,
By the keen tooth of healthful appetite.

The silent business of their supper done,   65
The Echoes of the solitary place,
Came as in sylvan wonder wide about
To hear, and imitate tentatively,
Strange voices moulding a strange speech, as then
Within the pleasant purlieus of the fire   70
Lifted in glee—but to be hushed ere long,
As with the night in kindred darkness came
O'er the adventurers, each and all, some sense—
Some vague-felt intimation from without
Of danger, lurking in its forest lairs.   75

But nerved by habit, and all settled soon
About the well-built fire, whose nimble tongues
Sent up continually a strenuous roar
Of fierce delight, and from their fuming pipes
Full charged and fragrant with the Indian weed,   80
Drawing rude comfort,—typed without, as 'twere,
By tiny clouds over their several heads
Quietly curling upward;—thus disposed
Within the pleasant firelight, grave discourse
Of their peculiar business brought to each   85
A steadier mood, that reached into the night.

The simple subject to their minds at length
Fully discussed, their couches they prepared
Of rushes, and the long green tresses pulled
Down from the boughs of the wild willows near.   90
Then four, as pre-arranged, stretched out their limbs
Under the dark arms of the forest trees.

PART II

Meanwhile the cloudless eastern heaven had grown
More and more luminous—and now the Moon
Up from behind a giant hill was seen   *95*
Conglobing, till—a mighty mass—she brought
Her under border level with its cone,
As thereon it were resting: when, behold
A wonder! Instantly that cone's whole bulk,
Erewhile so dark, seemed inwardly a-glow   *100*
With her instilled irradiance; while the trees
That fringed its outline, their huge statures dwarfed
By distance into brambles, and yet all
Clearly defined against her ample orb,—
Out of its very disc appeared to swell   *105*
In shadowy relief, as they had been
All sculptured from its substance as she rose.

    There standing in his lone watch, Egremont
On all this solemn beauty of the world
Looked out, yet wakeful; for sweet thoughts of home   *110*
And all the sacred charities it held,
Ingathered to his heart, as by some nice
And subtle interfusion that connects
The loved and cherished (then the most, perhaps,
when absent, or when passed, or even when *lost*)   *115*
With all serene and beautiful and bright
And lasting things of Nature. So then thought
The musing Egremont: when sudden—hark!
A bough crackt loudly in a neighbouring brake,
And drew at once, as with a 'larum, all   *120*
His spirits thitherward in wild surmise.

    But summoning caution, and back stepping close
Against the shade-side of a bending gum,
With a strange horror gathering to his heart,
As if his blood were charged with insect life   *125*
And writhed along in clots, he stilled himself,
Listening long and heedfully, with head
Bent forward sideways, till his held breath grew
A pang, and his ears rang. But Silence there
Had recomposed her ruffled wings, and now   *130*
Brooded it seemed even stiller than before
Deep nested in the darkness: so that he,
Unmasking from the cold shade, grew ere long
More reassured from wishing to be so,

And to muse, Memory's suspended mood,   *135*
Though with an effort, quietly recurred.

But there again—crack upon crack! And hark!
O Heaven! have Hell's worst fiends burst howling up
Into the death-doom'd world? Or whence, if not
From diabolic rage, could surge a yell   *140*
So horrible as that which now affrights
The shuddering dark? Ah, Beings as fell are near!
Yea, Beings, in their dread inherited hate
And deadly enmity, as vengeful, come
In vengeance! For behold, from the long grass   *145*
And nearer brakes, a semi-belt of stript
And painted Savages divulge at once
Their bounding forms!—full in the flaring light
Thrown outward by the fire, that roused and lapped
The rounding darkness with its ruddy tongues   *150*
More fiercely than before,—as though even *it*
Had felt the sudden shock the air received
From their dire cries, so terrible to hear!

A moment in wild agitation seen
Thus, as they bounded up, on then they came   *155*
Closing, with weapons brandished high, and so
Rushed in upon the sleepers! three of whom
But started, and then weltered prone beneath
The first fell blow dealt down on each, by three
Of the most stalwart of their pitiless foes!   *160*
But one again, and yet again, heaved up—
Up to his knees, under the crushing strokes
Of huge-clubbed nulla-nullas, till his own
Warm blood was blinding him! For he was one
Who had with Misery nearly all his days   *165*
Lived lonely, and who therefore, in his soul,
Did hunger after hope, and thirst for what
Hope still had promised him,—some taste at least
Of human good however long deferred,
And now he could not, even in dying, loose   *170*
His hold on life's poor chances of to-morrow—
Could not but so dispute the terrible fact
Of death, even in Death's presence! Strange it is:
Yet oft 'tis seen that Fortune's pampered child
Consents to his untimely power with less   *175*
Reluctance, less despair, than does the wretch
Who hath been ever blown about the world
The straw-like sport of Fate's most bitter blasts,
Vagrant and tieless.

Struck through with a cold horror, Egremont,   *180*

Standing apart,—yea, standing as it were
In marble effigy, saw this, saw all!
And when out thawing from his frozen heart
His blood again rushed tingling,—with a leap
Awaking from the ghastly trance which there   185
Had bound him, as with chill petrific bonds,
He raised from instinct more than conscious thought
His death-charged tube, and at that murderous crew
Firing! saw one fall ox-like to the earth;—
Then turned and fled! Fast fled he, but as fast   190
His deadly foes went thronging on his track!
Fast! for in full pursuit, behind him yelled
Wild men whose wild speech hath no word for *mercy*!
And as he fled, the forest beasts as well,
In general terror, through the brakes a-head   195
Crashed scattering, or with maddening speed athwart
His course came frequent. On—still on he flies—
Flies for dear life! and still behind him hears,
Nearer and nearer, the so rapid dig
Of many feet,—nearer and nearer still!   200

PART III

So went the chase! And now what should he do!
Abruptly turning, the wild Creek lay right
Before him! But no time was there for thought:
So on he kept, and from a bulging rock
That beaked the bank like a bare promontory,   205
Plunging right forth and shooting feet-first down,
Sunk to his middle in the flashing stream—
In which the imaged stars seemed all at once
To burst like rockets into one wild blaze
Of interwrithing light. Then wading through   210
The ruffled waters, forth he sprang and seized
A snake-like root that from the opponent bank
Protruded, and round which his earnest fear
Did clench his cold hand like a clamp of steel,
A moment,—till as swiftly thence he swung   215
His dripping form aloft, and up the dark
O'erjutting ledge went clambering in the blind
And breathless haste of one who flies for life:
When in its face—O verily our God
Hath those in his peculiar care for whom   220
The daily prayers of spotless Womanhood
And helpless Infancy are offered up!—
When in its face a cavity he felt,
The upper earth of which in one rude mass
Was held fast bound by the enwoven roots   225
Of two old trees,—and which, beneath the mould,
Just o'er the clammy vacancy below,
Twisted and lapped like knotted snakes, and made

A natural loft-work. Under this he crept,
Just as the dark forms of his hunters thronged　　230
The bulging rock whence he before had plunged.

　　Duskily visible, thereon a space
They paused to mark what bent his course might take
Over the farther bank, thereby intent
To hold upon the chase, which way soe'er　　235
It might incline, more surely. But no form
Amongst the moveless fringe of fern was seen
To shoot up from its outline,—up and forth
Into the moonlight that lay bright beyond,
In torn and shapeless blocks, amid the boles　　240
And mixing shadows of the taller trees,
All standing now in the keen radiance there
So ghostly still, as in a solemn trance.
But nothing in the silent prospect stirred—
No fugitive apparition of the view　　245
Rose, as they stared, in fierce expectancy:
Wherefore they augured that their prey was yet
Somewhere between,—and the whole group with that
Plunged forward, till the fretted current boiled
Amongst their crowding trunks from bank to bank;　　250
And searching thus the stream across, and then
Lengthwise, along the ledges,—combing down
Still, as they went, with dripping fingers, cold
And cruel as inquisitive, each clump
Of long-flagged swamp-grass where it flourished high,—　　255
The whole dark line passed slowly, man by man,
Athwart the cavity—so fearfully near,
That as they waded by the Fugitive
Felt the strong odor of their wetted skins
Pass with them, trailing as their bodies moved　　260
Stealthily on,—coming with each, and going.

　　But their keen search was keen in vain. And now
Those wild men marvelled,—till, in consultation,
There grouped in dark knots standing in the stream
That glimmered past them, moaning as it went,　　265
His vanishment, so passing strange it seemed,
They coupled with the mystery of some crude
Old fable of their race; and fear-struck all,
And silent, then withdrew. And when the sound
Of their receding steps had from his ear　　270
Died off, as back to the stormed Camp again
They hurried to despoil the yet warm dead,
Our Friend slid forth, and springing up the bank,
Renewed his flight, nor rested from it, till
He gained the welcoming shelter of his Home.　　275

　　Return we for a moment to the scene
Of recent death. There the late flaring fire

Now smouldered, for its brands were strown about,
And four stark corses, plundered to the skin
And brutally mutilated, seemed to stare   280
With frozen eyeballs up into the pale
Round visage of the Moon, who, high in heaven,
With all her stars, in golden bevies, gazed
As peacefully down as on a bridal there
Of the warm Living—not, alas! on them   285
who kept in ghastly silence through the night
Untimely spousals with a desert death.

   Afterwards there, for many changeful years,
Within a glade that sloped into the bank
Of that wild mountain Creek—midway within,   290
In partial record of a terrible hour
Of human agony and loss extreme,
Four grassy mounds stretched lengthwise side by side,
Startled the wanderer;—four long grassy mounds
Bestrewn with leaves, and withered spraylets, stript   295
By the loud wintry wingéd gales that roamed
Those solitudes, from the old trees which there
Moaned the same leafy dirges that had caught
The heed of dying Ages: these were all;
And thence the place was long by travellers called   300
The Creek of the Four Graves. Such was the tale
Egremont told us of the wild old times.

                            (1845; revised 1867)

Judith Wright
THE CYCADS

Their smooth dark flames flicker at time's own root.
Round them the rising forests of the years
alter the climates of forgotten earth
and silt with leaves the strata of first birth.

Only the antique cycads sullenly   5
keep the old bargain life has long since broken;
and, cursed by age, through each chill century
they watch the shrunken moon, but never die,

for time forgets the promise he once made,
and change forgets that they are left alone.   10
Among the complicated birds and flowers
they seem a generation carved in stone.

Leaning together, down those gulfs they stare
over whose darkness dance the brilliant birds
that cry in air one moment, and are gone;   15
and with their countless suns the years spin on.

Take their cold seed and set it in the mind,
and its slow root will lengthen deep and deep
till, following, you cling on the last ledge
over the unthinkable, unfathomed edge   20
beyond which man remembers only sleep.

(1947)

John Shaw Neilson
THE POOR, POOR COUNTRY

Oh 'twas a poor country, in Autumn it was bare,
The only green was the cutting grass and the sheep found little there.
Oh, the thin wheat and the brown oats were never two foot high,
But down in the poor country no pauper was I.

My wealth it was the glow that lives forever in the young,   5
'Twas on the brown water, in the green leaves it hung.
The blue cranes fed their young all day—how far in a tall tree!
And the poor, poor country made no pauper of me.

I waded out to the swan's nest,—at night I heard them sing,
I stood amazed at the Pelican, and crowned him for a king;   10
I saw the black duck in the reeds, and the spoonbill on the sky,
And in that poor country no pauper was I.

The mountain-ducks down in the dark made many a hollow sound,
I saw in sleep the Bunyip creep from the waters underground.
I found the plovers' island home, and they fought right valiantly, 15
Poor was the country, but it made no pauper of me.

My riches all went into dreams that never yet came home,
They touched upon the wild cherries and the slabs of honey-comb,
They were not of the desolate brood that men can sell or buy,
Down in that poor country no pauper was I.   20

*   *   *   *   *

The New Year came with heat and thirst and the little lakes were low,
The blue cranes were my nearest friends and I mourned to see them go;
I watched their wings so long until I only saw the sky,
Down in that poor country no pauper was I.

(1927)

Eve Langley
NATIVE-BORN

In a white gully among fungus red
  Where serpent logs lay hissing at the air,
I found a kangaroo. Tall, dewy, dead,
  So like a woman, she lay silent there.

Her ivory hands, black-nailed, crossed on her breast,   5
  Her skin of sun and moon hues, fallen cold.
Her brown eyes lay like rivers come to rest
  And death had made her black mouth harsh and old.
Beside her in the ashes I sat deep
  And mourned for her, but had no native song   10
To flatter death, while down the ploughlands steep
  Dark young Camelli whistled loud and long,
'Love, liberty, and Italy are all.'
  Broad golden was his breast against the sun.
I saw his wattle whip rise high and fall   15
  Across the slim mare's flanks, and one by one
She drew the furrows after her as he
  Flapped like a gull behind her, climbing high,
Chanting his oaths and lashing soundingly,
  While from the mare came once a blowing sigh.   20
The dew upon the kangaroo's white side
  Had melted. Time was whirling high around,
Like the thin wommera, and from heaven wide
  He, the bull-roarer, made continuous sound.
Incarnate lay my country by my hand: 25
  Her long hot days, bushfires, and speaking rains,
Her mornings of opal and the copper band
  Of smoke around the sunlight on the plains.
Globed in fire-bodies the meat-ants ran
  To taste her flesh and linked us as we lay,   30
For ever Australian, listening to a man
  From careless Italy, swearing at our day.
When, golden-lipped, the eagle-hawks came down
  Hissing and whistling to eat of lovely her,
And the blowflies with their shields of purple brown   35
  Plied hatching to and fro across her fur,
I burnt her with the logs, and stood all day
  Among the ashes, pressing home the flame
Till woman, logs, and dreams were scorched away,
  And native with night, that land from whence they came.   40

(1941)

Les A. Murray
SECOND ESSAY ON INTEREST: THE EMU

Weathered blond as a grass tree, a huge Beatles haircut
raises an alert periscope and stares out
over scrub. Her large olivine eggs click
oilily together; her lips of noble plastic
clamped in their expression, her head-fluff a stripe   5
worn mohawk style, she bubbles her pale-blue windpipe:

the emu, *Dromaius novaehollandiae*,
whose stand-in on most continents is an antelope,
looks us in both eyes with her one eye
and her other eye, dignified courageous hump,   *10*
feather-swaying condensed camel, Swift Courser of New Holland.

Knees backward in toothed three-way boots, you stand,
Dinewan, proud emu, common as the dust
in your sleeveless cloak, returning our interest.
Your shield of fashion's wobbly: you're Quaint, you're Native,   *15*
even somewhat Bygone. You may be let live
but beware: the blank zones of Serious disdain
are often carte blanche to the darkly human.
Europe's boats on their first strange shore looked humble
but, Mass over, men started renaming the creatures.   *20*
Worship turned to interest and had new features.
Now only life survives, if it's made remarkable.

Heraldic bird, our protection is a fable
made of space and neglect. We're remarkable and not;
we're the ordinary discovered on a strange planet.   *25*
Are you Early or Late, in the history of birds
which doesn't exist, and is deeply ancient?
My kinships, too, are immemorial and recent,
like my country, which abstracts yours in words.
This distillate of mountains is finely branched, this plain   *30*
expanse of dour delicate lives, where the rain,
shrouded slab on the west horizon, is a corrugated revenant
settling its long clay-tipped plumage in a hatching descent.

Rubberneck, stepped sister, I see your eye on our jeep's load.
I think your story is, when you were offered   *35*
the hand of evolution, you gulped it. Forefinger and thumb
project from your face, but the weighing palm is inside you
collecting the bottletops, nails, wet cement that you famously swallow,
your passing muffled show, your serially private museum.
Some truths are now called *trivial*, though. Only God approves them. *40*
Some humans who disdain them make a kind of weather
which, when it grows overt and widespread, we call *war*.
There we make death trivial and awesome, by rapid turns about,
we conscript it to bless us, force-feed it to squeeze the drama out;
indeed we imprison and torture death—this part is called *peace*— *45*
we offer it murder like mendicants, begging for significance.
You rustle dreams of pardon, not fleeing in your hovercraft style,
not gliding fast with zinc-flaked legs dangling, feet making high-tensile
seesawing impacts. Wasteland parent, barely edible dignitary,
the disinterested spotlight of the lords of interest   *50*
and gowned nobles of ennui is a torch of vivid arrest
and blinding after-darkness. But you hint it's a brigand sovereignty
after the steady extents of God's common immortality
whose image is daylight detail, aggregate, in process yet plumb
to the everywhere focus of one devoid of boredom.   *55*

                                                                (1982)

Les A. Murray
THE QUALITY OF SPRAWL

Sprawl is the quality
of the man who cut down his Rolls-Royce
into a farm utility truck, and sprawl
is what the company lacked when it made repeated efforts
to buy the vehicle back and repair its image.   5

Sprawl is doing your farming by aeroplane, roughly,
or driving a hitchhiker that extra hundred miles home.
It is the rococo of being your own still centre.
It is never lighting cigars with ten-dollar notes:
that's idiot ostentation and murder of starving people.   10
Nor can it be bought with the ash of million-dollar deeds.

Sprawl lengthens the legs; it trains greyhounds on liver and beer.
Sprawl almost never says Why not? with palms comically raised
nor can it be dressed for, not even in running shoes worn
with mink and a nose ring. That is Society. That's Style.   15
Sprawl is more like the thirteenth banana in a dozen
or anyway the fourteenth.

Sprawl is Hank Stamper in Never Give an Inch
bisecting an obstructive official's desk with a chain saw.
Not harming the official. Sprawl is never brutal   20
though it's often intransigent. Sprawl is never Simon de Montfort
at a town-storming: Kill them all! God will know his own.
Knowing the man's name this was said to might be sprawl.

Sprawl occurs in art. The fifteenth to twenty-first
lines in a sonnet, for example. And in certain paintings;   25
I have sprawl enough to have forgotten which paintings.
Turner's glorious Burning of the Houses of Parliament
comes to mind, a doubling bannered triumph of sprawl—
except, he didn't fire them.

Sprawl gets up the nose of many kinds of people   30
(every kind that comes in kinds) whose futures don't include it.
Some decry it as criminal presumption, silken-robed Pope Alexander
dividing the new world between Spain and Portugal.
If he smiled *in petto* afterwards, perhaps the thing did have sprawl.

Sprawl is really classless, though. It's John Christopher Frederick Murray   35
asleep in his neighbours' best bed in spurs and oilskins
but not having thrown up:
sprawl is never Calum who, in the loud hallway of our house,
reinvented the Festoon. Rather
it's Beatrice Miles going twelve hundred ditto in a taxi,   40
No Lewd Advances, No Hitting Animals, No Speeding,
on the proceeds of her two-bob-a-sonnet Shakespeare readings.
An image of my country. And would that it were more so.

No, sprawl is full-gloss murals on a council-house wall.
Sprawl leans on things. It is loose-limbed in its mind.   45
Reprimanded and dismissed
it listens with a grin and one boot up on the rail
of possibility. It may have to leave the Earth.
Being roughly Christian, it scratches the other cheek
and thinks it unlikely. Though people have been shot for sprawl.   50

(1983)

James McAuley
ENVOI

There the blue-green gums are a fringe of remote disorder
And the brown sheep poke at my dreams along the hillsides;
And there in the soil, in the season, in the shifting airs,
Comes the faint sterility that disheartens and derides.

Where once was a sea is now a salty sunken desert,   5
A futile heart within a fair periphery;
The people are hard-eyed, kindly, with nothing inside them,
The men are independent but you could not call them free.

And I am fitted to that land as the soul is to the body,
I know its contractions, waste, and sprawling indolence;   10
They are in me and its triumphs are my own,
Hard-won in the thin and bitter years without pretence.

Beauty is order and good chance in the artesian heart
And does not wholly fail, though we impede;
Though the reluctant and uneasy land resent   15
The gush of waters, the lean plough, the fretful seed.

(1936-38)

Section H

CULTURAL POLITICS

Part of the argument of many of these Sections has been that texts can often be seen as participating in debates about the culture and its appropriate definition and practices: that literary texts do cultural work. The items chosen here engage explicitly in these debates. In many cases the writers see themselves as directly and appropriately concerned with contemporary issues in a polemical way. Others see these contemporary issues as impinging on their interests as writers, or concern themselves with the social relations and economic and personal circumstances of writers. In all cases they regard the writer's function as having effect in the world, not as separate from it. The issues considered in literary and cultural discussions are continuous with those addressed in the fiction and poetry collected in other Sections of this Anthology *and* with issues taken up in public debate about more overtly political and social questions. The items collected here also serve to dispel the belief that there has been no literary culture in Australia. They demonstrate a lively engagement by writers with a range of continuing debates, a close knowledge of and involvement with the works of other writers and a continuing sense of a valued literary community. This is just as evident in 'Banjo' Paterson's account of literary life in the 1880s as in Drusilla Modjeska's of the 1980s.

This, then, is one of several places in this Anthology in which 'literature' is conceived of as extending far beyond the bounds of Poetry-Fiction-Drama. Elsewhere there have been navigators', explorers', and settlers' journals, newspaper reports, journalism, personal reminiscence and trans-criptions of oral poetry and autobiography. Here also are extracts from diaries, a radio talk, a private letter, an autobiographical essay and an editorial from a new journal. Cultural Politics are also taken up by items placed in other Sections: Robin Boyd's 'Pioneers and Aboraphobes' (Sec-tion A); 'An Anti-Chinese Public Meeting' (D); Rex Ingamells' 'The Word "Jindyworobak"' (E); and 'Ironbark' Gibson's 'On the Prevalence of "Bill" in Australian Literature' (F).

Partly to demonstrate the diversity of the forms of Australian writing, but also to show that literary commentary is not separable from other forms of cultural intervention, we have included here a few pieces of literary criticism. They range over a nineteenth-century newspaper review; introductions to volumes of poems and an anthology; an influential article on Australian poetry; and a paper delivered at a 1987 literary festival. Literary criticism is itself concerned to influence notions of what consti-tutes a particular reality; it may, as in the examples here, be concerned with the appropriate language or subject matter of Australian poetry (and hence with the characteristics of Australian life) or with the place in Australian culture of women and their literary production. Readers may also like to turn to the extract from the first extended piece of Australian literary criticism, Frederick Sinnett's 'The Fiction Fields of Australia' in-cluded in Section J, and to David Malouf's 'A First Place: A Mapping of the World' in Section G (like White's 'The Prodigal Son' printed in this Section, a combination of literary commentary and personal apologia).

Marcus Clarke's *The Future Australian Race* was printed in Melbourne in 1877 when Clarke was working as a sub-librarian, a newspaper essayist and columnist and continuing to write novels and plays. He wrote for numerous newspapers and was constantly involved in the issues of the day. While Clarke's career was short—he died at thirty-five—it was extremely prolific, typical of that of many Australian working writers of both centur-ies, and in the twentieth century, writing for radio, television and film was added to the repertoire of the professional writer. *The Future Australian Race* is an example of the pamphlet, a form of publication not often seen today, but one which remained popular until the 1930s. It consisted of twenty-two pages, and was issued in soft wrappers. In it Clarke, writing in the mock-serious tone he often affected, makes great play with some of the ideas of romantic nationalism then current in Britain, France, Germany and the United States. Clarke has quite a deal of fun with the basic proposition that culture is dependent on climate or, as the Introduction to

Mapping and Naming puts it, that geography is destiny. The English historian, Henry Thomas Buckle, may have provided the stimulus for this essay. Buckle's *History of Civilisation in England* (1857, 1861) argued that the intellectual character of nations was determined by their environment: that climate influenced social organisation, size of population and the production and distribution of ideas. In more sophisticated form, the assumption that culture derives from the distinctive features of the nation, determined by—as the French literary historian, Hippolyte Taine put it in 1863—race, environment (geographical, social, political) and historical moment, has been an underpinning assumption of most national literary history in Australia, as elsewhere.

This assumption certainly underpins P. R. ('Inky') Stephensen's *The Foundations of Culture in Australia*. Stephensen firmly believed, as he writes elsewhere in the essay, that 'Art and Literature are at first nationally created, but become internationally appreciated'. It followed then that the national elements were to be foregrounded in any analysis of the production of literature and literary meaning; and that literary culture contributed significantly to national self-definition. This pair of assumptions perhaps explain why so much polemical energy has been expended on discussions of literature: in discussing literature one might affect that sense of national self-definition. Certainly, this is what Stephensen himself set out to do. He objected, for instance, to writing about the convict period since this confirmed British prejudices about Australia's colonial origins and, as is clear from this brief section from the first part of his long essay, he wished that cultural baggage to be expelled from Australian culture in its progress towards autonomy. Stephensen was involved in public controversy throughout his erratic career. He was, in turn, a Communist, publisher of D. H. Lawrence and Xavier Herbert, translator of Nietzsche, and later founding member of the Australia First Movement, which in its strident isolationist nationalism, anti-Semitism and anti-Communism was sympathetic to the Nazi government of Germany. He was interned from 1942–5 because of his membership of Australia First. *The Foundations of Culture in Australia* influenced the Jindyworobak movement as well as many of those writers loosely grouped as radical nationalists. Some of its intellectual associations may be seen here in A.A. Phillips's 'The Cultural Cringe', Brian Penton's *Think—Or Be Damned*, and in a curious form in Lawson's Letter to Lord Beauchamp; it finds a precursor in Kendall's astute survey, 'Brunton Stephens' Poetry'.

Like Clarke, Brian Penton was a working journalist (eventually editor of the Sydney *Telegraph*, 1941–51) as well as a novelist and polemicist. His two novels, *Landtakers* (1934) and *Inheritors* (1936), are powerful revisions of the stock characteristics of Australian historical fiction. In most of his work, Penton was an iconoclast, 'concerned to establish a fact which is out of line with legend'. In this extract from *Think—Or Be Damned* (a kind of extended pamphlet of over ninety pages), he seeks to subvert some of the myths upon which a version of Australian society that he opposed was founded—'the national falsehood' upon which 'the national character' is based. The Vision Splendid takes a bit of a beating at Penton's hands. (The Mitchell Library referred to is part of the State Library of New South Wales in Sydney and contains the largest collection of Australian literary and historical material.)

His assertion that Australians think or do nothing new sits uneasily with Sir Walter Murdoch's rhetorical discovery of newness in the poetry of Bernard O'Dowd. Murdoch seems intent on finding in O'Dowd not merely poetic craft to admire but forms and styles of poetry somehow fitted to the landscape ('a lean athletic kind of beauty'). Like, in their various ways, Sinnett, Kendall, Phillips, Stephensen and White, he warns against the Scylla of excessive Australianism ('We were terribly tired of the race-course in Australian poetry') and the Charybdis of 'second-hand poetic ornaments made in England'. They have, in many guises, been consistent anxieties in the discussion of Australian writing.

Henry Kendall took the opportunity provided by his review of James Brunton Stephens' poetry to produce a survey of the major achievements and features of Australian poetry since 1788. He celebrates the achievements of Caucasian energy in a land that was once (recalling Farrell's 'Australia' in Section F, The Vision Splendid) 'wholly the site of a large dark majesty'. In familiar fashion he figures Australia as the country of the future and, in a trope that is common in 'new' nations, one in which the demands of pioneering life have driven out the materials and the opportunity for the making of great literature. In such a cultural model, it is not at all uncommon for the writer to proclaim a beginning, fulfilling the desire for origins. So Kendall announces the 'pale dawn' of a national literature. Mr Dalley was William Bede Dalley (1831–88), son of convict parents and first Australian member of the Privy Council; Harpur's 'The Creek of the Four Graves' is in Section G, Mapping and Naming; the author of The Man in the Iron Mask was George Gordon McCrae, a Scottish immigrant influential in literary circles.

If Kendall concluded with the call to go past the work of those for whom Australia was not truly home, Arthur Patchett Martin, writing in the centenary year of white settlement, discovers Australia to have become newsworthy to the world. Martin's essay formed an Introduction to one of the three anthologies of Australian poetry that the imperial entrepreneur Douglas Sladen produced for the English market during 1888. That the work was directed to English readers is demonstrated by the jokes about the exotic nature of Australia in the second paragraph (the laughing jackass in the gum-tree); the Mr Froude mentioned there is the English historian J.A. Froude, who visited Australia in 1885; Martin himself left Australia in 1882 at the age of thirty-one and, like Sladen (whose Australian experience amounted to a one-year spell as Lecturer in History at Sydney University) acquired the status of an Australian expert in England. While Martin also desires a balance between local and international influences (which he topically calls 'Imperial' and 'Home Rule'), his position is finally an internationalist one: Australia is merely part of English culture. Nevertheless, his call for 'an Australian school of criticism' is an important and frequently repeated one, reminding us that arguments about Australian Literature are (often concealed) arguments about appropriate critical practice.

A.A. Phillips' term, 'the cultural cringe', has long since entered the Australian vocabulary and been exported to other post-colonial societies to which it is equally appropriate. This essay, in many ways, epitomises those which precede it in this Section. It is polemical, concerned with Australian culture as a species of national self-definition and as a phenomenon that functions in antagonistic relation to British culture, and seeks forms of developing cultural maturity. It also manifests that witty rhetorical mockery which has been a notable feature of several of these pieces: 'the problems of colonialism...sit as heavily on the Australian reader as the plum-pudding of an Australian Christmas', the 'Public School Englishman with his detection of a bad smell permanently engraved on his features'. His rejection of the gravity of English judgment is enunciated in the attitude to the language. One of the most influential mid-twentieth-century critics, especially through his book *The Australian Tradition* from which this essay is taken, Phillips' critical work emphasised the 'democratic' strand of Australian writing, later designated 'radical nationalist'.

Judith Wright was also one of the most influential of critics in the 1950s and 1960s. 'Australia's Double Aspect' was the Introduction to her *Preoccupations in Australian Poetry*, long regarded as the most important book on Australian poetry. Her formulation of the doubleness of the experience of Australia has not only been a durable one—the 'two strains of feeling...the sense of exile,...the sense of liberty' have been widely quoted—but it is also one with a long lineage. Several items in this Section, for instance, adopt a fundamentally dichotomous model of Australian culture, and this dichotomous habit of mind is to be found as well in Wright's poetry. For her, the way in which poets respond in language to the landscape is of central concern. She edited an anthology, *New Land, New Language*, and the adaptation model implied in that title can be seen clearly in the essay printed here. It ends, much as Kendall's piece does eighty-four years earlier, with the annunciation of a beginning; and the terms of the apotheosis almost echo Kendall's: 'we are beginning to write, no longer as transplanted Europeans...but as men [sic] with a present to be lived in and a past to nourish us.'

There was something more secure in the announcement of a new beginning made by Louisa Lawson. 'About Ourselves' is the editorial from the first issue of *The Dawn* in May 1888. *The Dawn*, Australia's first feminist journal, ran until 1905, making it one of the most durable of nineteenth-century Australian periodicals. Appearing monthly, and containing poetry and fiction and news on women's issues, it used exclusively female writers, editors and printers (with rare exceptions). Louisa Lawson, who wrote much of the material for the magazine (often, as here, pseudonymously) as well as editing it, also published the first book of her son, Henry. The note of diversity which Louisa Lawson wished to sound in *The Dawn* continues as a theme in Drusilla Modjeska's paper on more recent women's writing. Lawson's effort was not the liberal feminist one of equal opportunity but the more radical position of difference (which oddly betrays its position, from the perspective of late twentieth-century feminist thinking, in noting that 'no slattern ever won the respect of any man worth loving'). But even in that Lawson wishes to stress the diversity of women's experience and values.

That there was, by 1987, a community of women's writing is amply demonstrated in the very form of Drusilla Modjeska's paper. Delivered as a contribution to a panel at the Festival of Sydney Writers' Week in 1987, it often addresses other writers who are present or whose work is an active presence for Modjeska's audience. The other panel members were Jan McKemmish, Jean Bedford and Kate Grenville. But what Modjeska enunciates through the fragmented form of her paper, with its abrupt transitions, numerous quotations and addresses to writers is the diversity of women's writing. In doing so she avoids speaking of women's writing as though it were homogeneous, denies that women can be spoken of generically and permits women to speak with their own voices.

Although forty-two years separate the two occasions, Nettie Palmer's account of her meeting with Henry Handel Richardson also celebrates female community and companionship and, under different social conditions, women's writing. Richardson's explanation of her choice of pseudonym is interesting and a subject which has been discussed in a confused manner. In both Modjeska's and Palmer's texts, the reception of women's literary work is a major issue, as it has been in much feminist scholarship.

To exemplify a sense of writerly community, Nettie Palmer is perhaps the most appropriate of all Australian writers. An indefatigable correspondent, reviewer, broadcaster, lecturer and host, Nettie rather than her perhaps more prominent husband Vance was the linchpin of much interaction between Australian writers from the 1920s until her death in 1964. She constantly asserted the need for writers to work for the continuity of the community of letters. The second short extract from her journal gives some sense of that community. AGS, to whom Neilson refers, was A.G. Stephens, literary editor of the *Bulletin*, 1896–1906, and Neilson's editor and literary adviser.

Paterson's reminiscence of Sydney in the early days of the *Bulletin*, the 1880s and 1890s, also captures that sense of literary community. Like Lawson's mendicant Letter to Lord Beauchamp that follows, it manifests the financial anxiety that characterised Lawson's dealings with people. The social and economic relations of writers as semi-autonomous professionals dependent on selling their work is a natural concern. Beauchamp was Governor of New South Wales; Lawson, with his family, left for England in April 1900 and returned in 1902. In the letter Lawson refers to several matters which have remained consistent problems in Australian cultural politics: the syndication of foreign literary material in Australian periodicals (the subject of a tariff enquiry in the 1940s), the small size of the Australian market, and the dominance of it by English publishers. Despite the final sentence, this was not the last begging letter Lawson wrote; nor was it the first. Lawson was helped on this occasion by Beauchamp, by David Scott Mitchell (a noted book collector whose collection founded the Mitchell Library), and by his publisher, George Robertson.

If Lawson gives the writer's reasons for leaving Australia, Patrick White gives his reasons for coming back. Like Malouf's 'A First Place: The Mapping of the World', 'The Prodigal Son' addresses itself to questions of cultural politics while offering a personal vision of the writer's own place in the world. Written for the magazine *Australian Letters* in 1958, shortly after the reception of *The Tree of Man* (1956) and *Voss* (1957) had brought him to prominence, it participates in an argument about expatriatism that had persisted in Australia since before Lawson's time and which was to flourish particularly in the 1960s. White's intervention was provoked by an essay extolling expatriatism in the previous issue by Alister Kershaw, a well-known Australian broadcaster and minor poet, living in Paris. Influential and widely-quoted, White's article subscribed to and popularised the pseudo-historical view that 'the Australian novel...[was] the dreary dun-coloured offspring of journalistic realism'. Like Nettie Palmer's reminiscence of Henry Handel Richardson, it also gives fascinating information about a writer's working practices and the genesis of major works and explores anxieties about reception, though the assertion that Australian reviews were hostile is founded on a small selection. It also develops the argument that has flourished throughout this Section about the necessary post-colonial antagonism between Australian culture and English culture from which it must, to some extent, free itself. This it accomplishes by articulating a powerful engagement with, and commitment to, the culture of the writer's own place.

Alan Lawson/Ken Goodwin

Marcus Clarke
from THE FUTURE AUSTRALIAN RACE

The quality of a race of beings is determined by two things: food and climate. The measure of that quality is the measure of the success in the race's incessant struggle to wrest nature to its own advantage. The history of a nation is the history of the influence of nature modified by man, and of man modified by the influence of nature. The highest practical civilisations have been those in which man came off victor in the contest, and employed the wind to drive his ships, the heat to work his engines, the cataract to turn his mills. The lowest, those in which nature reduced men to the condition of brutes—eating, drinking and feeding. Given the price of the cheapest food in the country, and the average registration of the thermometer, and it is easy to return a fair general estimate of the national characteristics. I say a general estimate, because other causes—the height of mountains, the width of rivers, the vicinity of volcanoes, etc., induce particular results. But the intelligent mind, possessed of information on the two points of food and climate can confidently sum up, first, the bodily vigour; second, the mental vigour; third, the religion; fourth, the political constitution of a nation.

Before speculating on future events, let us apply our test to history. The climate of Egypt is hot and moist, the inundation of the Nile renders the soil wonderfully fertile, and food is extremely cheap and easily obtained. The climate of India is hot, and the inhabitants live for the most part on rice, which is cheap and usually obtained in abundance. The climate of Mexico is hot. Indian corn, which forms the staple of the food of the inhabitants, is astonishingly prolific and consequently cheap. Now cheap food means in all cases cheap marriage, or in other words rapid reproduction of the species. A hot climate means small expense in house-building, clothing or furniture. A man sells his labour to meet his requirements, and in a hot country his requirements are few. In a hot country, therefore, wages are low, and the rapid increase of population renders human life of little value. The difference between the labourer and the employer of labour, then, is great, and from this difference comes tyranny on the one side and slavery on the other. The rich grow richer and the poor poorer. Wealth means leisure, and leisure means luxury and learning. Consequently we should expect to find that a nation living under these conditions would present the following characteristics:—A poor and enslaved peasantry, a rich and luxurious aristocracy, who cultivate great learning and some taste for art.

Now, this condition answers precisely to the condition in which Anthony found Egypt, Warren Hastings found India, and Cortez found Mexico. In each place the nobles lived in incredible luxury and the poor in incredible misery. The learning of each nation was the marvel of its successors. The expenditure of human life in each was terrible. Human beings were not only sacrificed in thousands for the building of the gigantic temples common to each country, but absolutely slaughtered like sheep to celebrate the triumphs of a conqueror, or appease the anger of a god. It is remarkable that the religion of each nation was bloodthirsty and full of terror. Siva the destroyer, Typhon the Betrayer, Kitzpolchi, God of the Smoking Hearts, alike demanded offerings of blood and tears. It is quite easy to account for this. Each nation grew up among scenes of natural grandeur, and a witness to the almost daily performance of the most majestic operations of nature. The hurricane, the storm, the simoom, the flood, the earthquake—all were familiar to their minds, and poets were created by the influence of the scenery which they described. Men having, by the expenditure of their own blood, modified nature with aqueducts, canals and roads, nature modified their struggles for freedom by the imposition of a terrible superstition which darkened all their days.

It is an absolute fact that religion is, in all cases, a matter of diet and climate. The Greek, with pure air, light soil, and placid scenery, invented an exquisite anthropomorphism, in which he deified all his own attributes. The Egyptian, the Mexican, and the dweller by the Ganges invented a cruel and monstrous creed of torture and death. The influence of climate was so strong upon the ancient Jews that they were perpetually relapsing from Theism into the congenial cruelties of Moloch and Astarte. Remove them into another country, and history has no record of a people—save, perhaps, the modern Pagans of our Universities—more devotedly attached to the purest form of intelligent adoration of the Almighty. The Christian faith, transported to the Libyan deserts, or the rocks of Spain, became burdened with horrors, and oppressed with saint-worship. The ferocious African's Mumbo Jumbo, the West Indian's Debbel-debbel, are merely the products of climate and the result of a dietary scale. Cabanis says that religious emotion is secreted by the smaller intestines. Men 'think they are pious when they are only bilious'. Men who habitually eat non-nitrogenous substances and pay little attention to the state of their bowels are always prone to gloomy piety. This is the reason why Scotchmen and women are usually inclined to religion.

Now let us consider what climate and food will do for Australians.

In the first place, we must remember that the Australasian nation will have an empire of many climates, for it will range from Singapore and Malacca in the north, to New Zealand in the south. All varieties of temperature will be traversed by the railroad traveller of 1977. The enormous area of Australia, that circle whose circumference is the sea, and whose centre is a desert, is a strong reason against federation. It is more than likely that what should be the Australian Empire will be cut in half by a line drawn through the centre of the continent. All above this line—Queensland and the Malaccas, New Guinea, and the parts adjacent—will evolve a luxurious and stupendous civilisation only removed from that of Egypt and Mexico by the measure of the remembrance of European democracy. All beneath this line will be a Republic, having the mean climate, and, in consequence, the development of Greece. The intellectual capital of this Republic will be Victoria. The fashionable and luxurious capital on the shore of Sydney Harbour. The governing capital in New Zealand.

The inhabitants of this Republic are easily described. The soil is for the most part deficient in lime, hence the bones of the autochthones will be long and soft. The boys will be tall and slender like cornstalks. It will be rare to find girls with white and sound teeth. A small pelvis is the natural result of small bones, and a small pelvis means a sickly mother and stunted children. Bad teeth mean bad digestion, and bad digestion means melancholy. The Australians will be a fretful, clever, perverse, irritable race. The climate breeds a desire for out-of-door exercise. Men will transact their business under verandahs, and make appointments at the corners of streets. The evening stroll will be an institution. Fashion and wealth will seek to display themselves out of doors. Hence domesticity will be put away. The 'hearth' of the Northerner, the 'fireside' of Burns' Cottar, will be unknown. The boys, brought up outside their homes' four walls, will easily learn to roam, and as they conquer difficulties for themselves will learn to care little for their parents. The Australasians will be selfish, self-reliant, ready in resource, prone to wander, caring little for home ties. Mercenary marriage will be frequent, and the hotel system of America will be much favoured. The Australasians will be large meat-eaters, and meat-eaters require more stimulants than vegetarians. The present custom of drinking alcohol to excess—favoured alike by dietary scale and by carnivorous practices—will continue. All carnivora are rash, gloomy, given to violences. Vegetarians live at a lower level of health, but are calmer and happier. Red radicals are for the most part meat-eaters. A vegetarian— Shelley *exceptio quæ probat regulam*—is a Conservative. Fish eaters are invariably moderate Whigs. The Australians will be content with nothing short of a turbulent democracy.

There is plenty of oxygen in Australian air, and our Australasians will have capacious chests also—*cœteris paribus*, large nostrils. The climate is unfavourable to the development of a strumous diathesis; therefore, we cannot expect men of genius unless we beget them by frequent intermarriage. Genius is to the physiologist but another form of scrofula, and to call a man a poet is to physiologically insult the mother who bore him. When Mr Edmund Yates termed one of his acquaintances a 'scrofulous Scotch poet', he intended to be personal. He was merely tautological. It may be accepted as an axiom that there has never existed a man of genius who was not strumous. Take the list from Julius Cæsar to Napoleon, or from Job to Keats, and point out one great *mind* that existed in a non-strumous body. The Australasians will be freed from the highest burden of intellectual development.

For their faces. The sun beating on the face closes the eyes, puckers the cheeks, and contracts the muscles of the orbit. Our children will have deep-set eyes with overhanging brows; the lower eyelid will not melt into the cheek, but will stand out *en profile*, clear and well-defined. This, though it may add to characater, takes away from beauty. There will be necessarily a strong development of the line leading from nostril to mouth. The curve between the centre of the upper lip and the angle of the mouth will be intensified; hence, the upper lip will be shortened, and the whole mouth made fleshy and sensual. The custom of meat-eating will square the jaw, and render the hair coarse but plentiful. The Australasian will be a square-headed, masterful man, with full temples, plenty of beard, a keen eye, a stern and yet sensual mouth. His teeth will be bad, and his lungs good. He will suffer from liver disease, and become prematurely bald— average duration of life in the unmarried, fifty-nine; in the married, sixty-five and a decimal.

The conclusion of all this is, therefore, that in another hundred years the average Australasian will be a tall, coarse, strong-jawed, greedy, pushing, talented man, excelling in swimming and horsemanship. His religion will be a form of Presbyterianism; his national policy a democracy tempered by the rate of exchange. His wife will be a thin, narrow woman, very fond of dress and idleness, caring little for her children, but without sufficient brain-power to sin with zest. In five hundred years, unless recruited from foreign nations, the breed will be wholly extinct; but in that five hundred years it will have changed the face of Nature, and swallowed up all our contemporary civilisation. It is, however—perhaps, fortunately— impossible that we shall live to see this stupendous climax.

(1877)

P.R. Stephensen
from THE FOUNDATIONS OF CULTURE IN AUSTRALIA

COLONY OR NATION

What then of culture in Australia? Here is not a mere vicinity, but a whole continent, unique in its natural features, and unique in the fact of its continental homogeneity of race and language. Australia is the only continent on the earth inhabited by one race, under one government, speaking one language. The population at present is not much greater than was that of Britain in Shakespeare's time, but by the end of the twentieth century we may expect that the population will expand to at least twenty millions, remaining of European parent-stock, but with locally-developed characteristics, and with a locally-created culture. Australia will then become indubitably recognised as a nation, and will lose all trace of colonial status.

As a colony, we exported raw material and imported manufactured goods and loans. The trade traffic was two-ways. *We imported also the imponderables, culture, by a system of one-way traffic.* As a nation we shall continue to import culture,' but we shall export it also, as our contribution to world-ideas—there will then be a two-ways traffic in the imponderables.

As this present time (1935) we are no longer a colony pure and simple, nor yet are we a Nation fully-fledged. We are something betwixt and between a colony and a nation, something vaguely called a 'Dominion', or a 'Commonwealth' with 'Dominion status'. We are loosely tied to other Dominions in the British Empire by law, strongly tied by sentiment and an idea of mutual protection. Inasmuch as we are politically autonomous, we have entered into virtual alliances (political, military, commercial, and sentimental) with other Dominions or Colonies in the Empire, including Canada, the Irish Free State, South Africa, New Zealand, Great Britain, and Jamaica. Where it will all lead to we do not know; but the virtual alliance gives us a sense of security in international affairs for the time being. The political and legal ties that bind us to the other 'Dominions' are loose enough, but the sentimental and financial tie is strong, particularly with the 'Dominion' called Great Britain. And the cultural tie is strong.

Is it sedition or blasphemy to the idea of the British Empire to suggest that each Dominion in this loose alliance will tend to become autonomous politically, commercially, and *culturally*? A military alliance between the various component 'nations' of the Empire may perhaps survive long after the other ties have, in fact, been weakened—though this would be contrary to the lessons of history. Such a prognostication has nothing to do with æsthetics. What matters for present purposes is that Australia has nowadays an acknowledged right to become one of the nations of the world. Australian nationalism, with or without the idea of the British Empire, has a right to exist; and there can be no nation without a national place-idea; a national culture.

(1936)

Brian Penton
from THINK—OR BE DAMNED

Not all forms of national falsehood are, however, to be checked against the kind of facts codified by statisticians. There are others, as dangerous as lies about education, the tariff system, and the standard of living, not so easy to uncover. Such, for example, as define the national character to us. Here you move in Cloud Cuckoo Land, where Germans despise Frenchmen and Frenchmen despise Germans and Anglo-Saxons despise both—all on the grounds that God is made in their own special image. In this field we have not perpetrated more hocus-pocus than others, perhaps not as much: our pretensions are fed by only a short history and that unromantically lacking in blood and battle. But we do look down on our neighbours—the Chinks and the Japs—and on Dagoes and Pommies.

It is toward the Pommy that our national bosom is thumped most vigorously. We contemn this apple-cheeked migrant as a man of small valour, resourcefulness, and independence; for we, as every one knows, are the most resourceful and independent people in the world, a devil-may-care race, proud of our reluctance to kowtow to social superiors, to salute officers, to say 'Sir', as the weak-kneed, home-grown Anglo-Saxon does, bronzed and sinewed by the Wide Open Spaces in contrast to the anaemic, city-bred English—untamed, unfettered by conventions and outworn traditions. This is the picture of the Dinkum Aussie every Dinkum Aussie likes to get from his newspapers and poets.

To check the authenticity of this rugged hero, and the theory that he derives from hard-drinking, hard-riding pioneer ancestors who came out to escape the monstrous injustices and social inequalities of the Old Land and found a nation of free and equal brothers, you will move your semantic laboratory to the Mitchell Library. There you will soon learn that our forebears, in so far as they had any choice in coming (and for the most footloose that choice was often limited to starving at home or taking passage to the Land of Sin, Sweat, and Sorrow, a prospect so uninviting to contemporary imagination that some criminals begged to be hanged rather than transported), were consumed on arrival with no zeal for erecting a classless Utopia but wholly and solely with making enough money to get back to the injustices and social inequalities of the Old Land, and, while they were in the process, with maintaining those injustices and class distinctions in an environment even more admirably suited for doing so than aristocratic eighteenth century England—namely, his Majesty's penal settlement of New South Wales.

Here the nuances of social distinction were far more subtle than the difference between squire and forelock-pulling hind. There were great crooks and little crooks, murderers and handkerchief snatchers, absconding bankrupts and petty larcenists, ticket-of-leave men and time expired men, soldiers and officers, freemen with a record and lilywhite freemen—a set-up for complicated snobbery. The convict had to raise his hat to a freeman. When he left clink he made up for it by refusing to raise his hat to any one under any circumstances. Was this, perhaps, you will wonder, the origin of our reluctance to salute and say 'Sir'?

A brief survey of our early history will thus quickly dispose of the fond national shibboleth that our country was established by earnest democrats, and will convince you that, left to our first forefathers, Australia Felix would have developed not towards a democracy of free and equal brothers but would have perpetuated all the social extremes of eighteenth century England, with the retired military officer or freeman on his land grant and the convict peasant in his cottage. Some such idea was in the mind of Macarthur and other early Australian nation builders.

But the plans of man count less in history than the microscopic activities of bacteria in the soil or the geological accidents of a million years ago. An accident of this kind spread a layer of gold-bearing rock across the southeastern corner of the continent and this, assisted by certain social and economic ferments in the Old World, twisted our destiny into a new pattern by tapping the stream of migrants from Europe to the much more attractive, because nearer and richer and better known empty spaces of the American continent.

Again, these gold-diggers did not come to Australia at the beck of any social idea. They came to get gold and take it back to the Old World to spend. Some of them did. But as there is always less of a good thing than there is reputed to be, most of them did not. And here the little dynasty-creating, history-making microbes played their part, for if the micro-organisms, without which pasture and crops do not grow, had been more active on our parched western plains, disappointed diggers would have settled down as contented small freehold farmers instead of having to go and dig gold for the big gold companies that alone could afford the machinery to get it out, or to live in pigsty huts on convict rations shearing the wool of the rich squatter who had got his clutches on the land first. Out of disappointment and resulting discontent came the trade unions, the big, abortive strikes of the nineties, the Parliamentary Labour Party, and what we now have of that undefinable essence called democracy.

You will decide that, though somewhat oversimplified, this picture is a fair enough representation of our history. It will drive home the point, against popular legend, that our democracy is not the creation of hardy individualists but of men so weak and frustrated that they had to unite to achieve elementary rights against powerful vested interests.

The legend of the independent Australian has long puzzled thoughtful observers, who see on every hand evidence of spineless timidity in the face of authority. That we should have failed to produce any kind of distinctive national art, and in this area be always utterly supine in goggling admiration of any third-rate product handed in from abroad and neglectful of any singer, writer, or painter bred in the country until foreign lands have stamped approval on him, is not surprising, since our people have only just emerged from the arduous era of pioneering; but that we should bow in humble acquiescence to politicians who take from us the right to drink a pot of beer after six o'clock or to place a bet on a racehorse off the course—two activities which provide the main solace and entertainment of a large proportion of the population—argues an extraordinary lack of spunk.[...]

Independence is an intellectual and spiritual quality which fruits only at an advanced stage of cultural development. It is not observed, for example, in taboo-haunted savages, where the will of the tribe has a mystic power. Nor is it observed in pioneering peoples, who naturally huddle together in a self-protective mob against the strangeness and dangers of a new country. There are plenty of reasons and excuses. We are not concerned with these, since this is not a work on morals. We are only concerned to establish a fact which is out of line with legend. And the fact is that this devil-may-care people, in its mental processes, is timid, respectable and generally conservative. Its normal reaction to a really independent mind, to a new idea, or a new phase of thought is moral horror or outrage, or at least ridicule or contempt and indifference. To understand this is useful, because only by understanding that we are not an alert and brave new world but a respectable old one will we ever break down the barriers which at present isolate us from the world's restless innovating thought.

The theory that we are the world's newest people collapses, of course, as soon as we observe the outside world at first-hand and find that we are still struggling with intellectual and spiritual problems which Europe and America disposed of fifty years ago. The radicalism of our radicals and the modernity of our young moderns is *vieux jeu* in other lands. D.H. Lawrence, an acute observer, propounded the theory after a visit to Australia that every offshoot or colonizing people remains at the stage of mental and spiritual development which was current in the homeland when the pioneers set off adventuring. This is the national counterpart of the Oedipus Complex.

(1941)

Walter Murdoch
from INTRODUCTION TO THE POEMS OF BERNARD O'DOWD

We were terribly tired of the race-course in Australian poetry. Like Tennyson's lotus-eaters, we had had enough of action. We were listening for another voice. And here, in certain poems written in the simplest form known to English verse—the four-lined stanza of the old ballads and of such things as Wordsworth's 'We are Seven'—was the new voice speaking to us. These poems struck a note not heard before in the Australian chorus. This was the poetry not of action but of impassioned thought. There was nothing about horses in it, but a great deal about Australia—

her character, her destiny, what she was trying to be and do, her hopes, her fears, her democratic faith...

It was not only the race-course that had begun to pall on us; we were also weary of the jingle, so long the bane of Australian verse; weary, too, of secondhand poetic ornaments made in England. The new poet wrote no jingles; and he seemed to despise ornament. His verse had an austere simplicity of form, a classical severity, a lean athletic kind of beauty new to our country's literature. This plain bare style of his was no accident, but the deliberate choice of a poet who had pondered long on the question, what form was best suited to be the vehicle of the message he had to deliver. In this volume you will find his one piece of verse, 'The Poet', in which his thought wears the dress of the popular jingle; and that he had misgivings about it is clear from a letter he wrote to a friend who had praised it. 'Your kind words about "The Poet" I read with mixed feelings. The thought is all right, but the form in which I put it?...It's as subtle a temptation as I've ever got, for, while I think I could reel off that sort of thing by the yard, I have persistently denied myself the pleasure of doing so for years because I have thought that the real Muse didn't like it, and that there was altogether too much of it locally. I felt I could trust myself in this instance, because I wanted to say it and to say it simply, and as nearly logically as possible, to an argumentative circle of run-as-you-read readers. In the result, I happened to *like* the verse myself, and for that reason am really glad that you do. But I felt the experiment was a dangerous one.'

(1941)

Henry Kendall
BRUNTON STEPHENS' POETRY

Ninety-two years have passed away since Arthur Phillip stood by the beautiful waters of Sydney Cove, on the bank of a 'small stream stealing silently through the thick woods'. The marvellous march of civilization in Australia, in the comparatively short space between that date and the present moment is so well known — so emphasized on the features of things—that there is no need to dwell upon it here. The land that less than a century ago was wholly the site of a large dark majesty of unexplored wilderness is now radiant with shining manifestations of Caucasian life and glorious with magnificent issues, of Caucasian energy. Noble cities— in no qualified sense of the term—beam on its shores; the great gladdening shout of the iron horse breaks across its lordly hills and broad stately plains; and mighty ships from all parts of the peopled world ride upon its harbours. Its amazing natural wealth is being developed; and the issues of its mines, its soil, and its vast forests have secured for it a reputation of the highest commercial value. The beauty of its daughters has been more than once 'noised abroad'; and in the domain of physical achievements, its sons are yearly adding to their high reputation. The Universities here have already sent forth young men whose brilliant natural ability, wedded to scholarship, has made them eminent in the pulpit, at the bar, and under the dome of the senate-house. The country has given birth to statesmen, orators, lawyers, and men of science whose names would grace any community in the cultured world. But has it produced, through all the years that have come and gone since the grand old day when Phillip paused by its wonderful waters, *one* genius of the purely literary order? Has it ever been represented in the splendid province of the world's *belles-lettres*? I venture to say, it *has*. Notwithstanding the fact that it is a new country, not mossed, as England is, with beautiful traditions—that it has all its traditions to form—that it has no great Past for its sons to fall back upon, I fearlessly assert that enough has been done to show that the dawn of a national literature is breaking upon it, and that two or three Australians have helped to create this dawn. It may be said with some degree of force that its beginnings are pale; but then it must be remembered that the grander beamings and pulses of genius that we meet with in the writings of men like Byron or Shelley are not to be found in the works of the English fathers who preceded Chaucer. It also must be borne in mind that society here is, as yet, novel, and so restless that it is difficult to mirror its characteristics either in prose or verse. Here almost everybody is necessarily on the move; for a young nation cannot very well be quiescent. Hurry and bustle must exist in a country where there is so much to gain by commercial and manual industry; and hence our people are too mobile for the purposes of Art. Apart from this, there is no adequate audience here for literary genius. A community that is often in motion sixteen hours out of the twenty-four is rarely in the mood for books of a high and exacting character. It is, as a rule, content with the text of the newspaper, and the lighter novels of the day. Certainly, we have a leisured class; but then it is a small one, and its members are not all lettered. The results of circumstances like these must be obvious.

Nevertheless, in face of all these depressing conditions, the features of Australian life and peculiarities of Australian scenery have been more than once faithfully mirrored in characteristic prose and verse. Forty years ago a young bushman—a native of New South Wales—one whose sponsors were the mountains, and whose mates were torrent and tree, commenced singing of the *flora* and *fauna* of his country in a language of unmistakable novelty and beauty. This was the lamented Charles Harpur. He never did anything very astonishing in the fragments he has left; we find none of those magnificent qualities which surprise and excite, like the sudden noise of multitudes, the glitter of armies, or the glorious strains of cathedral music. His genius was purely pastoral, and his command over verbal resources was never remarkable; but he wrote at least three poems which, some one of these days, will be taken from their nearly forgotten shelf and placed amongst the most precious of our literary possessions. The 'Creek of the Four Graves'—the best of the writings referred to—is as full of leaf and bird and the sound of singing waters as is an Illawarra mountain glen. Back there, in a forsaken grave near Bathurst, lie the remains of Daniel Henry Deniehy, another Australian whose achievements in the field of purely aesthetical letters must cause him to be instanced. Brilliant orator, acute critic, and exalted lover of the True and Beautiful, he shone before us during a few memorable years, and then that fine spirit of his flickered out in the shadow unspeakable and the agony that is not to be named. Among mighty and monumental men there is no place for him—no throne for Harpur; but the glorious Australian sunshine is not absent from their graves. Over the last home of Harpur the wild oak—that elfin harp of the solitudes—iterates its mysterious music year after year. The air is full of the sounds that passed into his life. The hushed voices of far torrents, the low thunder of heavy remote waves, the seaward-travelling song of high mountain winds, the dialogue of leaf and bird, and the inarticulate melodies of running waters are all there. He sleeps in the arms of the beautiful Mother of all; and his touching epitaph is a poem traced in letters of the bright, soft, gracious woodland mosses.

Other natives of the soil might be mentioned; but not one of them, to my thinking, has caught the colour and tone of Australian scenery and life as Harpur did. From time to time Mr Dalley (a man of unquestionable genius) has given us exquisite work; but he is not one of us. In the 'sweet session of silent thought', this highly endowed scholar sits with the laurelled fathers of the great Past, and his voice seems far away from us. He was born amongst us; but he lives beside us. Turning from him to certain Australians who have written verse and prose, I may say of them that they have, as a rule, looked at Nature through the spectacles of books. Many of their productions are admirable; but, after all, their best prose shines with borrowed light, and their best verse is merely the mummy of the old world canticle floating under an antipodal sky. There have been, and there are still brilliant writers here who are not natives; but the flowers that all but two of them have presented us are wholly exotic. They merely work in an exquisite English garden fenced in from our strange vast new-world wilderness. The chief of these are Marcus Clarke, and the author of that stately poem, 'The Man in the Iron Mask'. They certainly paint colonial life and scenery; but they use a northern brush, and it is dipped in northern colours.

(1880)

Arthur Patchett Martin
from CONCERNING AUSTRALIAN POETS

Once it was thought no good could come out of the colonies, now nothing *but* good. The tone of English criticism on everything colonial seems just now exclusively flattering, and we are in danger of being spoiled, strutting about in honours too easily won.

Our colonial members of parliament, excellent fellows some of them in their way, come 'home' and are forthwith translated into 'statesmen,' and wear from that out a Baconian brow. Now, owing to Douglas Sladen's introduction, the poets are to have a turn. But lest this genial kindliness be mistaken for stern criticism, I would fain give another illustration of English opinion, on matters colonial, even though it sadly wounds my *amour propre*.

Among the odd efforts of my idle fancy in the Australian Bush, near Fernshawe, was the composition of a set of verses on a Laughing Jackass, the curious bird which so fascinated Mr Froude. I fantastically styled these verses 'The Cynic of the Woods', and in the middle of my discourse addressed him bluntly as 'Jackass'. The matter is plain enough to a colonial reader, but a volume containing it fell into the hands of an English friend who I had judged to be of a sombre turn of mind, a statistician and political economist, one who like Cardinal Manning had given his early prime to the study of Ricardo. He expressed himself as delighted with my ballad of the Jackass; and wrote to say that it was admirable. Nothing, he said, had so much amused him as this idea of the Jackass laughing at the poet; but he thought I had strained a point in putting the animal up in the boughs, as he had never heard even of a wild ass sufficiently agile to climb a gum-tree.

The moral, perhaps, is that Australian literature will only be in a fair way of development when there is side by side with it an Australian school of criticism. For, after all, one should be judged by one's own people. This is the 'Home-rule' side of the question; there is also the 'Imperial' view, which is based on our greatest common heritage—language. Douglas Sladen told us in verse that we Australians are only a new variety of the original English stock. This is perfectly true. Literature, too, has ceased to be tribal, and the only barrier that prevents a supreme poet like Tennyson from speaking to the whole world at once, is that of language. It is also the link that binds America and Australia, whether they will or no, to the mother-country. Nor in our petty endeavour to establish an 'Australian literature', should we forget that we share in the greatest heritage of England. We, too, if our voices are clear enough, can speak from our remote weird Bush, and our new flourishing cities, to three Continents— only there are so many talking at the same time, that we do not always get a good hearing.

(1888)

A. A. Phillips
from THE CULTURAL CRINGE

Once upon a time (and not very long ago), the Australian Broadcasting Commission used to present a Sunday programme, designed to cajole a mild Sabbatarian bestirment of the wits. Paired musical performances were broadcast, one by an Australian, one by an oversea executant, but with the names and nationalities withheld until the end of the programme. The listener was supposed to guess which was the Australian and which the alien performer. The idea was that quite often he guessed wrong, or gave it up, because, strange to say, the local lad proved no worse than the foreigner. This unexpected discovery was intended to inspire a nice glow of patriotic satisfaction.

I am not jeering at the ABC for its quaint idea. The programme's designer had rightly diagnosed a disease of the Australian mind, and was applying a sensible curative treatment. The dismaying circumstance is that such a treatment should be necessary, or even possible; that, in any nation, there should be an assumption that the domestic cultural product will be worse than the imported article.

The devil of it is that the assumption will often be correct. The numbers are against us, and an inevitable quantitative inferiority easily looks like a qualitative weakness, under the most favourable circumstances—and our circumstances are not favourable. We cannot shelter from invidious comparisons behind the barrier of a separate language; we have no long-established or interestingly different cultural tradition to give security and distinction to its interpreters; and the centrifugal pull of the great cultural metropolises works against us. Above our writers—and other artists— looms the intimidating mass of Anglo-Saxon achievement. Such a situation almost inevitably produces the characteristic Australian Cultural Cringe— appearing either as the Cringe Direct, or as the Cringe Inverted, in the attitude of the Blatant Blatherskite, the God's-Own-country-and-I'm-a-better-man-than-you-are Australian Bore.

The Cringe mainly appears in a tendency to make needless comparisons. The Australian reader, more or less consciously, hedges and hesitates, asking himself, 'Yes, but what would a cultivated Englishman think of this?' No writer can communicate confidently to a reader with the 'Yes, but' habit; and this particular demand is curiously crippling to critical judgment. Confronted by Furphy, we grow uncertain. We fail to recognise the extraordinarily original structure of his novel because we are wondering whether an Englishman would not find it too complex and self-conscious. No one worries about the structural deficiencies of *Moby Dick*. We do not fully savour the meaty individualism of Furphy's style because we are wondering whether perhaps his egoistic verbosity is not too Australianly crude; but we accept the egoistic verbosity of Borrow as part of his quality.

The Australian writer normally frames his communication for the Australian reader. He assumes certain mutual pre-knowledge, a responsiveness to certain symbols, even the ability to hear the cadence of a phrase in a certain way. Once the reader's mind begins to be nagged by the thought of how an Englishman might think about this, he loses the fine edge of his Australian responsiveness. It is absurd to feel apologetic about *Such is Life* or *Coonardoo* or *Melbourne Odes* because they would not seem quite right to an English reader; it is part of their distinctive virtue that no Englishman can fully understand them.

I once read a criticism which began from the question, 'What would a French classicist think of *Macbeth*?' The analysis was discerningly conducted and had a certain paradoxical interest; but it could not escape an effect of comic irrelevance.

A second effect of the Cringe has been the estrangement of the Australian intellectual. Australian life, let us agree, has an atmosphere of often dismaying crudity. I do not know if our cultural crust is proportionately thinner than that of any other Anglo-Saxon community—such evidence as the number of books we buy and the proportion of subscribers commanded by our more intelligent papers, would suggest that in fact our cultural attainments are rather above the average Anglo-Saxon level. To the intellectual, however, the crust *feels* thinner, because, in a small community, there is not enough of it to provide the individual with a protective insulation. Hence, more than most intellectuals, he feels a sense of exposure. This is made much worse by that deadly habit of English comparison. There is a certain type of Australian intellectual who is forever sidling up to the cultivated Englishman, insinuating 'I, of course, am not like these other crude Australians. I understand how you must feel about them; I should be more at home in Oxford or Bloomsbury' (the use of Bloomsbury as a symbol of intellectuality is badly out of date; but, then, so as a rule is the Australian Cringer).

This tendency is deepened by the nature of the Englishman—at least of the upper-class Englishman. It is not simply that he is so sure of his superiority. The Frenchman and the German are no less firmly convinced that they are the crowning achievements of history. The trouble is that the Englishman is so quietly convincing about his superiority. The beautiful sheen of his self-assurance exercises an hypnotic influence on its victims. [...]

The critical attitude of the [Australian] intellectual towards the community is, of course, not in itself harmful; on the contrary, it could be a healthy, even a creative influence, if the criticism were felt to come from within, if the critic had a sense of identification with his subject, if his irritation came from a sense of shared shame rather than from a disdainful separation. It is his refusal to participate, the arch of his indifferent eyebrows, which exerts the chilling and stultifying influence.

Thinking of this type of Australian intellectual, I am a little uneasy about my phrase 'cultural cringe'; it is so much the kind of missile which he delights to throw at the Australian mob. I hope I have made it clear that my use of the phrase is not essentially unsympathetic, and that I regard the denaturalised intellectual as the Cringe's unhappiest victim. If any of the breed use my phrase for his own contemptuous purposes, my curse be upon him. May crudely-Dinkum Aussies spit in his beer, and gremlins split his ever-to-be-precisely-agglutinated infinitives.

The Australian writer is affected by the Cringe, because it mists the responsiveness of his audience, and because its influence on the intellectual deprives him of a sympathetically critical audience. Nor can he entirely escape its direct impact. The core of the difficulty is the fact that, in the back of the Australian mind, there sits a minatory Englishman. He is not even the most suitable type of Englishman—not the rare pukka sahib with his deep still pool of imaginativeness, and his fine urbanity; not the common man with his blending of solidity and tenderness: but that Public School Englishman with his detection of a bad smell permanently engraved on his features, who has left a trail of exasperation through Europe and of smouldering hatred through the East, and whose indifference to the Commonwealth is not even studied.

Subconsciously the educated Australian feels a guilty need to placate this shadowy figure (Freud has a name for it). His ghost sits in on the tête-à-tête between Australian reader and writer, interrupting in the wrong accent.

It may be said—it often is—that this is a healthy influence, ensuring that we shall measure our cultural achievements by universal standards, protecting us from the dangers of parochialism. This is only a little of the truth. Finely responsive reading is primarily an act of surrender, only secondarily an act of judgment. That minatory ghost prevents the unqualified readiness to meet the writer on his own terms which should precede a critical appraisement. The Australian writer has almost conquered the problems of colonialism; they still sit as heavily on the Australian reader as the plum-pudding of an Australian Christmas.

What is the cure for our disease? There is no short-cut to circumvent the gradual processes of national growth—which are already having their effect. As I have already suggested, the most important development made in Australian writing over the last twenty years has been the progress in the art of being unself-consciously ourselves. In the same period there has also been a similar, though slower, development in the response of the Australian reader. That response will develop more rapidly in discrimination and maturity of judgment, as the present increasing interest in Australian studies within the universities takes its effect. Meanwhile the pace of those developments can be quickened if we articulately recognise two facts: that the Cringe is a worse enemy to our cultural development than our isolation, and that the opposite of the Cringe is not the Strut, but a relaxed erectness of carriage.

(1950)

Judith Wright
AUSTRALIA'S DOUBLE ASPECT

It is only necessary to look at Australia's literature, in order to see that for very many of her writers she has presented herself as the most difficult of technical problems. Before one's country can become an accepted background against which the poet's and novelist's imagination can move unhindered, it must first be observed, understood, described, and as it were absorbed. The writer must be at peace with his landscape before he can turn confidently to its human figures.

But in Australian writing the landscape has, it almost seems, its own life, hostile to its human inhabitants; it forces its way into the foreground, it takes up an immense amount of room, or sometimes it is so firmly pushed away that its obvious absence haunts us as much as its presence could do. Thus it haunts us in the novels of Henry Handel Richardson (where it is the ever-present, inexorably shabby and ugly background for the downfall of a man who is alien to it until his death) as it does in the passionate and over-coloured descriptions of Eve Langley in *The Pea Pickers*; and its influence is present by implication as much in Brennan's poetry, where landscape is deliberately universalized, as in the most aboriginal of Jindy jingle.

This is because Australia has from the beginning of its short history meant something more to its new inhabitants than mere environment and mere land to be occupied, ploughed and brought into subjection. It has been the outer equivalent of an inner reality; first, and persistently, the reality of exile; second, though perhaps we now tend to forget this, the reality of newness and freedom.

Since Harpur, the free-born descendant of transported convicts, chose to be the first poet of his country—

Lo! 'tis the land of the grave of thy father!
'Tis the cradle of Liberty...

and dedicated himself to dreams of a time when

> all men shall stand
> proudly beneath the fair wide roof of heaven
> as God-created equals...

the two strains of feeling (for the conservative, the sense of exile, and for the radical, the sense of liberty, of a new chance) have, at least until very recently, been recognizable in all that was written here.

This double aspect of the inner Australia, as we might call it, has been matched and reinforced by the outer physical reality of the country itself. As a land of exile, it could scarcely have been more alien to all European ideas either of natural beauty or of physical amenity; its unknown plants and animals, its odd reversals of all that British invaders knew and understood of their own country (in the habits of the eucalypts, almost incredulously noted by early botanists, of shedding their bark seasonally and retaining their leaves; the alternations of drought and flood; the difficulties of soil and climate that made nonsense of the early efforts of farmers unaccustomed to any but English conditions; the transposition of the seasons, the unfamiliarity of the night sky). But from the beginning of settlement there were rebels who hoped to make here a country that would lead the world towards new concepts of human freedom—men like Harpur and like many others articulate or inarticulate, who saw Australia as a great opportunity to establish Utopia, 'meet cradle for the birth sublime of just Equality', as Harpur put it—and to such men these differences scarcely counted. What did matter was the size and the silence of this country, in which the law and civilization were soon outdistanced by any traveller beyond the coastal settlements.

So from the first Australia, as a condition of life, loomed large in the consciousness of her white invaders. She seemed either a prison, a land to be escaped from as soon as possible or to be endured till death, or to the few who saw Utopia in her, a new country, a country of hope and faith. At first, at any rate, there was little notion of her as a possible source of wealth and easy living. The disciplines she imposed were too hard; the conditions she made were too grinding; she had too little immediate wealth to offer. There were in Australia no sources of easy money, until the gold-rushes began; America's obvious abundance in furs, forests, pastures and minerals had made her early settlers predict and boast of her future as a great nation, but in Australia little or none of such faith was possible. A distant dependency of England, she had little to offer except hard work, loneliness and dreadful isolation; and probably this loneliness caused her early inhabitants to exaggerate her strangeness—the lost and ancient quality that Lawrence later felt.

So Marcus Clarke wrote in all seriousness [in the preface to *Poems of the Late Adam Lindsay Gordon*, Melbourne: Massina, 1880]:

What is the dominant note of Australian scenery? That which is the dominant note of Poe's poetry—Weird Melancholy...The Australian mountain forests are funereal, secret, stern. Their solitude is desolation. They seem to stifle in their black gorges a story of sullen despair. No tender sentiment is nourished in their shade. In other lands the dying year is mourned, the falling leaves drop lightly on the bier. In the Australian forests no leaves fall...The very animal life of these frowning hills is either grotesque or ghostly. Great grey kangaroos hop noiselessly over the coarse grass. Flights of white cockatoos stream out shrieking like evil souls. The sun suddenly sinks, the mopokes burst out into horrible peals of semi-human laughter. The natives aver that, when night comes, from out the bottomless depths of some lagoon the Bunyip rises, and, in form like a monstrous sea-calf, drags his loathsome length from out the ooze. From a corner of the silent forest rises a dismal chant, and around a fire dance natives painted like skeletons. All is fear-inspiring and gloomy...Hopeless explorers have named (the mountains) out of their suffering—Mount Misery, Mount Dreadful, Mount Despair...The soul, placed before the frightful grandeur of these barren hills, drinks in their sentiment of defiant ferocity, and is steeped in bitterness.

So much for Australia's mountains. Her plains Clarke called 'shelterless and silent', her trees and flowers, in which Banks had delighted, Clarke called 'grotesque and weird', 'the strange scribblings of Nature learning how to write'. So far Clarke speaks as an alien—as one of those for whom Australia was a land of exile and terror. But he saw, too, the other side of the picture; the side seen by Australia's first lovers, the rebels against civilization; for he goes on:

Some see no beauty in our trees without shade, our flowers without perfume, our birds who cannot fly, and our beasts who have not yet learned to walk on all fours. But the dweller in the wilderness...becomes familiar with the beauty of loneliness...learns the language of the barren and uncouth, and can read the hieroglyphs of haggard gumtrees, blown into odd shapes, distorted with fierce hot winds, or cramped with cold nights, when the Southern Cross freezes in a cloudless sky of icy blue...and the Poet of our desolation begins to comprehend why free Esau loved his heritage of desert sand, better than all the bountiful richness of Egypt.

The violent reaction of the European consciousness against what it saw in this new country, and the conditions that had to be endured here, has persisted until our own day. Its modern reflection can be found in the novels of Martin Boyd, for instance, with their uneasy movement from Australia to England and back to Australia again. In them, not only the characters but the writing itself seems never at home in either country—nostalgic for both, yet settled in neither. Boyd is no 'free Esau'—for him the country stations that supported his families' fortunes were 'all in remote burning plains, blasted by the January sun...they were all built of corrugated iron and they all smelt of sheep'. Civilization, for the people of Boyd's novels, in so far as it exists here at all, is embodied precariously in a certain group of people in Melbourne. Only the very youngest of his characters, in a family Australian-born for generations, begins to come to terms with the country through the medium of art. And though this strain in our writing may seem to us now outdated, outgrown, we should be honest enough to recognize that it was and remains real enough to influence our feeling still in many ways.

This contradiction, this inner argument between the transplanted European and his new country, takes many forms, but in one way or another it is to be seen in almost every Australian writer. In Christina Stead's *Seven Poor Men of Sydney*:

> Blount stirred himself and said: 'Why are we here? Nothing floats down here, this far south, but is worn out with wind, tempest and weather; all is flotsam and jetsam. They leave their rags and tatters here; why do we have to be dressed? The sun is hot enough, why can't we run naked in our own country, in our own land, to work out our own destiny?...This land was last discovered: Why? A ghost land, a continent of mystery; the very pole disconcerted the magnetic needle so that ships went astray, ice and fog and storm bound the seas, a horrid destiny in the Abrolhos, in the Philippines, in the Tasman seas, in the Southern Ocean, all protected the malign and bitter genius of this waste land. Its heart is made of salt: it suddenly oozes from its burning pores, gold which will destroy men in greed, but not water to give them drink. Jealous land! Ravishers over-bold! And lost legion! Our land should never have been won.'

That is, essentially, the cry of the exiled European; and it is in Henry Handel Richardson's great trilogy of novels that the story of the exiled European is most clearly set out. That is the story of Richard Mahony, for whom Australia was precisely the Antipodes; who, when he made money, promptly returned to England to spend it. Yet, like the families in Boyd's novels, he was no longer able to merge with his English background, and returned at last to Australia, to die there broken and deranged. Richardson is sparing with her descriptions of the Australian landscape; it is for most of the immensely long novel sketched in only as a background to Mahony's gradual and inevitable downfall. But the last book ends, not on a human note, but a natural:

> Amid these wavy downs Mahony was laid to rest...A quarter of a mile off, behind a ridge of dunes, the surf driving in from the Bight, breaks and booms eternally on the barren shore. Thence, too, come the fierce winds which, in stormy weather, hurl themselves over the land, where not a tree, not a bush, nor even a fence stands to break their force.—Or to limit the outlook. On all sides the eye can range, unhindered, to where the vast earth meets the infinitely vaster sky. And, under blazing summer suns, or when a full moon floods the night, no shadow falls on the sun-baked or moon-blanched plains, but those cast by the few little stones set up in human remembrance.
> ...But, those who had known and loved him passing, scattering, forgetting, rude weeds choked the flowers, the cross toppled over, fell to pieces and was removed, the ivy that entwined it uprooted. And, thereafter, his resting-place was indistinguishable from the common ground. The rich and kindly earth of his adopted country absorbed his perishable body, as the country itself had never contrived to make its own, his wayward, vagrant spirit.

From one viewpoint one might look at Richardson's novel-sequence as a kind of attempt, on the part of the exile-consciousness, to understand and reconcile itself with the alien country that is gradually overcoming and changing it and with which in the end it must be merged. The novels make a kind of bridge between Europeanism and the unknown thing that is to be made of Europeans by Australia, and in them, perhaps, Richardson, herself doubly an exile, reconciled herself not only with her own hard childhood and the loss of her sensitive rebellious father, but with the Australia from which, though she was born there, she had herself turned away. That final image of the body of Mahony absorbed and annihilated by the country in which he had suffered as a stranger, is transformed from bitterness into peace by those two significant words—'rich' and 'kindly'. In them, it seems, Richardson forgives all the barren grimness, rawness and cruelty of the little town on the plains where Richard had suffered the last stages of his martyrdom—of the country that had seemed to Mary, as she travelled through it, 'the flattest, barest, ugliest country she had ever had the misfortune to see...the last word in loneliness and desolation'.

The unifying image—the image that brings peace for the first time since Mahony's bitter story began—is Mahony's grave. Just so, Harpur, taking on himself the task of becoming Australia's first poet, had cried—

See, 'tis the land of the grave of thy father...

It is curious—or perhaps not so curious—that this theme, of the European mind in contact with a raw, bleak and alien life and landscape, struggling with it in a suffering whose only consummation and reconciliation is found in death, is taken up again in Patrick White's *Voss*. 'You see,' says Judd, the deserter and murderer, at the end of the book, 'if you live and suffer long enough in a place, you do not leave it altogether. Your spirit is still there.' And so, as Laura sums up the story, Voss through his death 'is still there in the country and always will be. His legend will be written down, eventually, by those who have been troubled by it.'

This, then, both Richardson and White, our two greatest novelists, have told us, is one way of reconciliation: where man has suffered, whether he is suffering, like Mahony, as an unwilling exile, or like Voss, as a dedicated seeker, the conflict of spirit and country ends in some kind of unity. By virtue of such suffering and struggle, the country becomes less alien to us: the vicarious sacrifice of Voss means to Laura, and to little Topp, the disappointed music-master, and to others, the possibility of understanding, loving and interpreting the 'sour colonial soil' on which they find themselves. 'Knowledge,' says Laura, 'was never a matter of geography. Quite the reverse, it overflows all maps that exist. Perhaps true knowledge only comes of death by torture in the country of the mind.'

'Death by torture in the country of the mind'—it is perhaps too melodramatic a way of putting it, for any lesser man than White's particular explorer-Christ. Nevertheless, there is certainly a sense in which Laura's words are true for all white Australians; a certain kind of death is indeed what Australia has demanded of us, a death of some things in us, to make room, perhaps, for others. Change itself is a kind of death, and Australia has changed us.

Lawrence, whose insight both into people and places was often so sharply illuminating, saw in us the sign of this death; a kind of apathy, and emptiness, a void. He saw that something had gone out of the European consciousness, in this country, and that as yet nothing had taken its place. And he related this emptiness to the country itself, that country of 'the previous world—the world of the coal age! The lonely, lonely world that had waited, it seemed, since the coal age... What was the good of trying to be an alert, conscious man here? You couldn't.'

Those words strike farther home into the central relationship of the white Australian and his country, perhaps, than any written by the native-born. Lawrence saw what lies deeper in us than we know—the scar left by the struggle to conquer and waken, for our own purposes, a landscape that had survived on its own terms until the world's late days. Its only human inhabitants had been the Aborigines whom we dispossessed—who were bound to the land we took from them, by the indissoluble link of religion and totemic kinship, so that our intrusion on the land itself became a kind of bloodless murder, even where no actual murder took place.

Our conflict both with land and people went deeper, perhaps, because there was in it so little of the heroic, so that we could not bolster up our self-esteem by boasting of our conquests; and because there was in it, too, so much of compromise. The country allowed us in easily enough; no battles were fought for it. The real battle was of a different order, not so much for conquest as for survival, and in surviving we found ourselves, for many years, living on Australia's terms rather than our own.

The weapons of the country were its emptiness, its sameness, its distances, its extremes of climate; the weapons of its settlers were endurance, persistence, a home-made ingenuity, and a sardonic attitude to the failures and reverses that they soon learned to expect. The struggle that developed these qualities necessarily took away, at the same time, the more specifically European virtue that Lawrence calls 'alert consciousness', and much else went with it also. So, in recent years, James McAuley writes of his countrymen—

The people are hard-eyed, kindly, with nothing inside them;
The men are independent, but you could not call them free.

The alteration that Lawrence sensed in us was not something superficial; it was not simply that the external customs and habits of life in civilized Europe had rubbed off in the struggle. Something had left us, had 'died by torture in the country of the mind'. White tells us that this is one way, at least, to true knowledge—to die is also to be reborn. But both Lawrence and McAuley would have it that, as yet, the emptiness remains. We have not yet, perhaps, reached that point of equilibrium at which we can feel that this country is truly ours by right of understanding and acceptance, and from which we can begin to grow again.

Perhaps this is why we tend still—in fact, increasingly—to crowd into cities in order to keep ourselves warm. We have not yet a culture in which both city and country have their proper place, each complementing the other; we have not assimilated the two ways of living to each other. The European never lived by bread alone; he had something else to sustain him, the sense of belonging to a tradition, of sharing in a long inheritance of achievement both of mind and heart which is symbolized in the names of countries—England, France, Italy, Greece—and which formed for him a kind of interpretation and framework for his own life and himself, his landscape and his cities. He shared, however vicariously and unconsciously, in an art, a literature and a culture that stretched far into the past.

But when he came to Australia—as Europeans are still coming—the older culture which had given his life a meaning beyond the personal, by linking him with the past, began to lose its power over him. It had authority still, but his real share in it dribbled away; for the true function of an art and a culture is to interpret us to ourselves, and to relate us to the country and the society in which we live.

So the new Australian (and all of us, to some extent, are new Australians) has in truth died a little. This is what our 'literature of exile' recognizes in us, and here it has the real importance of true literature. For if we reject outright the literature of nostalgia, we fail to understand something important about ourselves, and will not be able to set about making Australia into our real spiritual home. In the same way, if we accept it too whole-heartedly, and take too seriously the notion that ours is a transplanted community, we deny the second aspect of our situation as Australians—the opportunity that is given us to make our loss into a gain, to turn Australia into a reality, to become something new in the world; to be not, as Hope puts it, 'second-hand Europeans' timidly pullulating on alien shores, but a people who have seized the chance to make a new kind of consciousness out of our new conditions.

The 'literature of exile' points to something in us of lingering dependence and uncertainty, to a habit of mind (which shows itself particularly in conservative politicians today) that distrusts its own judgment and prefers 'second-hand Europeanism' to insecurely based Australianism. We have made much of our so-called newly emerging national consciousness, of our 'Australian legend'. But just what does the Australian legend, so far, consist in? We ought to look as closely as we can, for the past holds the clue to the present, and we ourselves are the present. So far as Australia is not yet wholly our country of the mind, it is because we have not yet understood and interpreted our relation to her.

The easy way of making a national legend was not for us. Australia presented a blank and negative front to our efforts at self-aggrandizement, either through easy wealth or heroic conquest. It seems possible that this fact has had something to do with the persistence, even up to the present time, of that 'exile-consciousness' I have pointed to in the work of various of our writers.

But what was in its time, new, is the second strain of feeling for Australia running through our literature, of a wholly opposite kind—the strain of feeling that begins most clearly, from a literary point of view, in the work of Harpur. This is the attitude that has arisen from the sense that here something new could be made, some kind of new relationship between men was mistily becoming possible. This second side of our consciousness forms a current that has found expression in the work of such writers as Tom Collins, Henry Lawson, O'Dowd, Eleanor Dark, and others; it is the attitude that Russel Ward has documented in his recent book, *The Australian Legend*; it is, of course, what we mean, or what we ought to mean, when we talk of the importance of the work of the balladists and the '*Bulletin* writers' of the 'nineties and after.

To begin with, of course, it is significant that the feeling of being Australian—of belonging to this country and no other—should have taken its rise so evidently in a radical and political approach, and in writers who have regarded human relations as the starting-point of literature, human relations of a purely social and general kind. These writers are concerned much less with landscape or with the European past, with the subtler questions of human motive, than with the future. What gave them their particular brand of optimistic reformism was just that fact against which the 'exile-consciousness', the European consciousness, rebelled—the fact that, faced with unpredictable and uncompromising new conditions, the European culture to which the upper strata of our society clung has had to change, and has made way in important respects for something new.

Price Warung's famous version of the Convict Oath, which, as Ward points out, may well have been authentic, ought I think to be taken as a starting-point when we think of the development of this attitude. It runs;

> Hand to hand
> On Earth, in Hell,
> Sick or well,
> On Sea, on Land,
> On the square, ever...
>
> Stiff or in Breath,
> Lag or Free,
> You and Me,
> In Life, in Death,
> On the Cross, never.

And though similar oaths may well have been current in other and older countries, among convicts and men otherwise at cross-purposes with vested authority, this oath or the attitude it represents is for Australia the germ of the 'something new' that we now feel to be in some sense our own, and that passed into our literature in the work, especially, of Lawson and Furphy. It epitomizes the basic attitude between man and man that enabled the bush workers to survive as they travelled their hard tracks from job to job, and that helped the early settlers to face their hardships.

But more than that, it represents the bare bones of human relations; that which has made it possible for man himself to survive in the world and build his societies. It is, one might say, the basic oath of all men, in society; since no man can survive alone, but everyone is dependent on his neighbour in a mutual bargain of trust. The difference, in what was best in the Australian interpretation of it, is that mutual trust implies for us equality between man and man, equality of a kind that transcends the necessary difference of circumstances and work and intelligence and income. As Harpur put it, so at our best we think of ourselves, standing as 'God-created equals'.

Now this *is* a new thing, this sense in the best of us that we are equals; and Furphy and Lawson were supremely right in seizing on it as their deepest theme. The danger today is that, in our present reaction against the often over-sentimentalized emphasis on 'mateship' and the 'Australian legend', we may forget the truth that lies behind it and thereby lose the strength it gave us. For it did, in fact, form the basis of such real Australianity as we have.

Of course, it has been used both falsely and shallowly. Also, the radical writers who took the equality of man as their theme have shared a kind of optimism about the nature of man—Australian man, at any rate—that seems nowadays to leave out a good deal. This particular kind of optimism was always a necessary ingredient in the radical reformism that put its faith in the perfectibility of man, from Godwin and the Encyclopaedists onward; the notion of original sin was as old-fashioned, to such reformism, as the notion of human perfectibility begins to look to us today. But we ought not to dismiss that notion until we are sure we have understood just where its bearing lies. It is worthwhile trying to separate, in the work of these writers, what is sentimental and temporary from what is basic and true for us as well as for them: to free them, that is, from the limitations of their time and to see them in proper perspective.

In their work we find the chief difference between, say, the Australian and American dreams. Where the American dream made use of the competitive individualistic element in life, the freedom of any man to become richer and better than his fellows by hard work and emulation, the Australian dream emphasizes man's duty to his brother, and man's basic equality, the mutual trust which is the force that makes society cohere.

If it is universalized, it holds the key not only to our proper nationhood, but to the unifying of Australia's double aspect, firstly as a society of transplanted Europeans, and secondly as a new country with a separate contribution to make in the world.

Certainly we have lost something in our struggle in the country of the mind, but it is possible now to see that we have gained something too, even if we are not yet conscious of what it is. We are becoming identified with this country; we are beginning to know ourselves no longer exiles, but at home here in a proper sense of the term. We are beginning to write, no longer as transplanted Europeans, nor as rootless men who reject the past and put their hopes only in the future, but as men with a present to be lived in and a past to nourish us.

(1964)

Louisa Lawson ('Dora Falconer')
ABOUT OURSELVES

from THE DAWN (*Editorial*)

'Woman is not uncompleted man, but diverse.' Says Tennyson, and being diverse why should she not have her journal in which her divergent hopes, aims, and opinions may have representation. Every eccentricity of belief, and every variety of bias in mankind allies itself with a printing-machine, and gets its singularities bruited about in type, but where is the printing-ink champion of mankind's better half? There has hitherto been no trumpet through which the concentrated voice of womankind could publish their grievances and their opinions. Men legislate on divorce, on hours of labour, and many another question intimately affecting women, but neither ask nor know the wishes of those whose lives and happiness are most concerned. Many a tale might be told by women, and many a useful hint given, even to the omniscient male, which would materially strengthen and guide the hands of law-makers and benefactors aspiring to be just and generous to weak and unrepresented womankind.

Here then is DAWN, the Australian Woman's Journal and mouthpiece —phonograph to wind out audibly the whispers, pleadings, and demands of the sisterhood.

Here we will give publicity to women's wrongs, will fight their battles, assist to repair what evils we can, and give advice to the best of our ability.

Half of Australian women's lives are unhappy, but there are paths out of most labyrinths, and we will set up finger posts. For those who are happy—God bless them! have we not laid on the Storyteller, the Poet, the Humourist, and the Fashion-monger?

We wear no ready made suit of opinions, nor stand on any platform of woman's rights which we have as yet seen erected. Dress we shall not neglect, for no slattern ever yet won the respect of any man worth loving. If you want 'rings on your fingers and bells on your toes' we will tell you where they can best be bought, as well as sundry other articles of woman's garniture.

We shall welcome contributions and correspondence from women, for nothing concerning woman's life and interest lies outside our scope.

It is not a new thing to say that there is no power in the world like that of women, for in their hands lie the plastic unformed characters of the coming generation to be moulded beyond alteration into what form they will. This most potent constituency we seek to represent, and for their suffrages we sue.

(1888)

Drusilla Modjeska
THE EMERGENCE OF WOMEN WRITERS SINCE 1975

The following talk was given at a forum on the above topic at the Festival of Sydney Writers' Week in January 1987.

Open any book page in any major daily or literary journal these days and more likely than not you will see some reference to the ascendancy of contemporary women writers, comments that are often startled, occasionally generous, sometimes defensive and now and then just plain nasty. And I think it is to this sudden visibility of women writers that seems to bewilder so many people (or at least certain sorts of people) that we are meant to address ourselves this afternoon. But in fact I don't think any of us are going to, at least not in any direct way, and the reasons are simple. First of all what is this category 'woman writer' anyway? How can one say anything sensible about, say, Elizabeth Jolley, Blanche d'Alpuget and Finola Moorhead in the same sentence? Or even Jan McKemmish, Jean Bedford and Kate Grenville. There are many ways of talking about writers, and writing and gender is an important one, but still only one among many. Second, why is it so easily and repeatedly passed over that women have in any case always been among the most successful and widely read of Australian writers? This isn't such a peculiar situation. Women's visibility as writers has always moved with the shifts in the publishing industry, with feminism and public awareness of the politics of gender, and these are factors that have intersected in different ways at different times. So, what's *emerging*?

What is invidious about some of the comments on the current position of women writers is the implication (and that isn't new either) that a lot of contemporary women writers are mediocre and are only where they are because they are supported by a defensive wall of feminist critics and what one reviewer calls solidarity buying by women readers. The only possible response to this, and it's important enough to bother, is to point out the assumptions it is based on: that the universal term 'writer' is masculine and that for women to write is still a matter for comment; that there are universal standards of what consitutes good writing which women tend to contravene, or some women (as buyers, it seems, as well as writers); and that how well a book does is a matter of negotiation or conspiracy between writers and readers with a little bit of help from the critics, and that some books doing too well means others do too badly.

In other words it is a matter of the assumptions about standards and economics that are built into this discourse. It is to these issues I want to address myself and in doing so I'm going to change tack and go back to 1975, and I'm going to tell a story, a story of sorts, about women and writing way back then, a rather fragmented and discontinuous story, but that's part of the story, and the point is not about then, but about now.

1975. Frank Moorhouse was going strong. He was about to publish *Conference-ville*, his fourth book of fiction. He'd co-founded *Tabloid Story* in 1972 as a forum for contemporary short fiction which then meant urban, outspoken, at least a bit experimental and predominantly male.

1975. Even Michael Wilding was going strong, though I wish for rhetorical reasons I could say that *The Phallic Forest* was published that year. But it wasn't. It came out in 1978.

1975. Women were writing away, of course, Jessica Anderson, Thea Astley, Barbara Hanrahan, Nancy Cato, mostly quietly. But there were rumbles. Dorothy Hewett is rarely quiet and *The Chapel Perilous* was produced in 1972. Elizabeth Riley's under-rated *All That False Instruction* should have raised more interest—or alarm—than it did in 1975. But that same year the murmurs grew louder with Kate Jennings' anthology of poetry *Mother I'm Rooted*, and a volume of her own poems. Included among her own poems in *Come To Me My Melancholy Baby* was her front lawn speech of 1970 addressed to the male New Left during the Vietnam War Moratorium, but as poetry it was addressed to the sort of men who were writing in *Tabloid Story*. 'I would like to speak,' she said. 'I would like to give a tubthumping tablebanging emotional rap AND be listened to, not laughed at.' Terrific stuff. You can't do that these days. We are listened to all too deferentially, no one dares to laugh, but I wonder sometimes if we are heard—because if we were we wouldn't be paraded up here today, that odd spectacle, a bevy of women writers.

'I'm no sweet virgin sock washer either.' That's Vicki Viidikas around the same time.

'All I know about poetry is that it has something to do with sex, something very close to sex.' That's Sylvia Kantarizis in *Mother I'm Rooted*. 'Some poems fall anyhow/all of a heap anywhere, dishevelled/legs apart in loneliness/and desperation,/and you talk about standards. And you talk about standards,' Kate Jennings yelled, and it became a catchcry. 'It was years,' she said recently, 'before we learned that rage and a well developed sense of indignation doesn't make good writing.' But in fact in re-reading *Mother I'm Rooted*, a lot of it stands up really well as poetry, it's not just rage and polemics; and one of the reasons, it seems to me, is that so many of the contributors understood from the start that poetry is about language and power in its many guises and that gender has to do with both, and with the meanings we can make and take, for ourselves and for the future. 'he may be brilliant/at writing/the southern end/of sentences./he cannot calculate/the yarrow straws/or understand/the read-out.' That's Pamela Cocabola Brown twelve years ago now. And Vicki Viidikas again, at the same time: 'So many words, she/threads them, carefully/like jewels.'

But still no-one was too worried in the Book Pages, though there were more signs of things to come. In 1976 Elizabeth Jolley's first volume of short stories. Already three novels by Barbara Hanrahan. And then in 1977 another dissonant voice, Helen Garner's *Monkey Grip*. It's strange now to think of her voice as dissonant, but then it was. The reviews weren't good. In fact some were awful. But people bought it anyway— people, I don't know what sort, male or female, perhaps this was the beginning of that nasty feminine habit of solidarity buying, who knows? But whatever, whoever, readers voted with their feet or their pockets and this was noticed by those who stand to make money from books (and writers were by no means in the front row of those). The following year *Monkey Grip* won the National Book Council Award, and Helen Garner was on the map. That strange creature women's writing was suddenly visible and talked about as if it were a new event. What was meant, I suppose, was that with *Monkey Grip* the overt intersection of feminism and writing heralded by Dorothy Hewett, Elizabeth Riley and *Mother I'm Rooted* couldn't be ignored. Here was writing straight out of an inner city feminist subculture. 'The sink's blocked in Darlinghurst./I never could eat spaghetti effectively/too unmarried or something.' That's Gig Ryan now, ten years later in *The Penguin Book of Australian Women Poets*. Most significantly of all, McPhee Gribble was on the map. A then-small publishing company run by two women, *Monkey Grip* was their second novel. Their first was Glen Tomasetti's lovely *Thoroughly Decent People*. Now McPhee Gribble is one of the premier fiction publishers of both women and men (I hasten to add), along with Penguin and University of Queensland Press. But neither of the latter were touching feminist fiction then, though feminist history and sociology were doing rather better.

Now in 1987 Penguin has an impressive stable of writers who are women, as do all the mainstream and small press fiction publishers in this country. The economics of publishing have changed hugely in ten years and a factor in these changes, though probably overall only a minor one, has been the effect of feminism on the market. So where writing that was conscious of itself as feminist (and I use the term loosely and widely) ten years ago was causing a bit of a stir on the sidelines, in some forms it is now central, in others still on the margins, but even there it has settled in.

So the question should be asked whether the worries of those who feel displaced by this turn of events should be sheeted home to the solidarity buyers and to biased critics, or to the marketing strategies of Penguin and the large publishers. Publishing is big business and while few writers make any money worth mentioning, yes, some do make more than others and some books do sell better than others. Some titles get much better marketing and promotion than others and it does make a difference. And mainstream publishers take and favour particular sorts of books, small presses take others for different reasons, and they work on each other; there are no clear boundaries, the arguments around gender and writing broaden and intersect with a complex of arguments around the nature of writing and the contemporary and the commercial. It gets harder and harder to talk about women's writing as a category.

'Sometimes I wake up in the middle of the night and feel as if I'm at the bottom of a pit. Maybe it's lack of oxygen. Maybe I've fallen into a hole between the past and the kind of future we want. Maybe it's just a cloud passing over the moon.' (Barbara Brooks in *Writers In The Park: The Book*.)

And, yes, I think there is a readership out there which knows what it is to wake in the night and which knows what it wants to read and what it doesn't want to read, and why. We are formed as readers by the same world and the same climate as writers. There are lots of good readers around as well as writers, and there's something else for those who feel displaced to think about.

'Better to be a man, I thought/but men no doubt, get trapped because they fit.' (Kerryn Higgs in *Mother I'm Rooted*.) 'Certain types of costumes immobilise the wearer.' (Susan Hampton in *The Penguin Book of Australian Women Poets*.)

One irony is that the visibility or success of many women as writers right now is the result of both that certainty of ten years ago and the inevitability of paradox and ambiguity that was to follow. What was certain then was that we didn't fit, at least not comfortably, and that the costumes we had worn were immobilising. But then what? It is much easier to confront and to discard than to construct: 'I found it a great relief/to sit down by this river/and invent my sanity.' That's Kerryn Higgs optimistic in *Mother I'm Rooted*. And Finola Moorhead ten years later in *Difference*: 'As for women making up a language of their own and consigning themselves to dreaded "marginality", be reasonable.'

It may be that one of the reasons *Monkey Grip* was poorly reviewed but widely read was not only because it was about junkies and communal houses and feminism and dope and sex and rock and roll but because it didn't follow the old-fashioned narrative shape of conflict and climax and resolution, but sloped along following the rise and fall of tension and desire, with patterns of repetition but no single moment of illumination, no inevitable succession of victory or defeat, but a rhythm of lapse and surge and change that could only ever be partial, in both senses of the word. You might well say that such narrative experiments were hardly remarkable in the mid-seventies, even in Australia. After all, there were all those fellows flashing about with their discontinuous narratives and tabloid anti-stories.

But thinking about things like the shape of narrative and the shape of our lives makes a difference to how one writes and does unsettle expectations and comfortable reading habits. So does thinking about ways of representing rape and all the violent and ghastly things that happen to women, without making women the victims and men the spectators; and how to write about the sorrows of love without adding to that awful lament that echoes through the generations, 'Oh never leave me, oh don't deceive me.' And how to write in ways which take account of the rhythms of the body and of the unconscious, and of desires that are barely known.

In thinking about these things, of course, no-one was starting from scratch. Our inheritance was, and is, long and strong and even if each generation has to find them for themselves, there are Dorothy Richardson, Marguerite Duras, Djuna Barnes, Christina Stead and of course Virginia Woolf and Doris Lessing. Most important of all, these writers had already radically undermined the notion of that seamlessly unified self that lies at the heart of so much (dare I say it) patriarchal fiction, confidently dealing with contradictions and ambiguity, resolving conflict, answering questions:

'I can't write autobiography because there is no me/Me is not a stable reality/the collective/me in the changing world no propped up statue/in the square for pigeons to shit on turning green.' That's Dorothy Hewett's poem 'Creeley in Sydney'.

Another irony is that this visibility of women who are writing, and which is often represented as some sort of unified onslaught when it is in fact quite the opposite, comes at a time when feminism in general is marked much more by a sense of dispersal and loss than it is by any sense of unity or certainty.

And we should be listened to, as writers and as critics, when we say it is time to dispense with the false unities we carry from before, which act with the power of cliché and tie us to nostalgia for a past that was never quite like that; and to acknowledge the strengths that exist *because of* the differences in women's writing, its capacity for ambiguity and fluidity, its ability to speak in the gaps and fissures, in the lacunae of our many selves; and to accept the ways in which this joins us to all sorts of other writings and other possibilities, and other difficulties. 'Her skill is paradoxical.' Vicki Viidikas knew that way back then in *Mother I'm Rooted*.

So we can begin to put unlikely names into the same sentence once we give up talking in terms of redressing balances (as if there were an equilibrium that could be reached) and start talking about textual strategies. We could consider things like the shift of emphasis in narrative from spectatorship to curiosity, so that women are not looked at voyeuristically, but circled around, thought about, mapped; consider the possibilities of transgressive narratives with do not restore order, settle conflict, answer questions; consider narratives which act out the desire to know through the feminine as investigative, and at those forms of narrative which question their own discourse: 'I can remember so much, the mood, the weather, the way light comes into the room. A fly crawling up the wall. But the words escape me.' Barbara Brooks again, this time in *Frictions*.

I am stressing these shifts within narrative (which do not, anything like, only occur in writing by women) not because I see them as paramount, and certainly not as universal, but because I want to end by saying that we should take care with the stories we tell, they become part of our lives, part of our history. What we say about the last ten years is part of the way in which we can go forward. The danger of looking for unities where there are none is that we risk being hobbled: 'There are no smoking signs in the waiting area but everyone is smoking. Despite this I wait for an hour or so before I roll a cigarette.' Pamela Brown in *Frictions*.

The danger of taking an equal opportunities line is that it assumes that if the moral imperatives of discrimination could be satisfied, we could all settle down in a comfortable place. But we should remember what happens to those who fit too well and the disabling ease with which such expectations fail. And that's the rub, for it is not a destination that we are bound for. There is no happy end to the story, there is no rose covered cottage, no writers' utopia at the end of the track, although we *have* embarked on what Christina Stead, who could get away with such flourishes, called 'a grand and perilous journey'. We know it as rather more modest, but absorbing nonetheless, and worth putting ourselves on the line for.

(1987)

Nettie Palmer
from FOURTEEN YEARS: EXTRACTS FROM A PRIVATE JOURNAL 1925–39

July 26th, 1935 Yesterday and to-day I was at 'Green Ridges'; my first time of meeting with Henry Handel Richardson, except by telephone a month ago (a firm voice, recognizably Australian still) and by letters for the past ten years. And by her books.

All was accurately arranged. Miss Olga Roncoroni ('my friend and secretary') drove me out from Hastings along the high road; we passed through a tight little village, then along the road to this lane near Fairlight. Miss R. sounded the horn as we drew up near the gate. As we entered the front door, the staircase was on the left; HHR was standing on the bottom step to receive. Formal, yet making her own rules; a slight and perhaps— as the press says—'diminutive' figure, yet commanding. She wore a velvet house coat and dark slacks, wore her clothes as if she meant them.

Tea in the big room downstairs: grand piano: Böcklin prints—*Maurice Guest* period. The french window opened on the rather formal garden; beyond that, there were miles of empty green ridges to the Channel cliffs. (Hastings was further to the right.) Summer haze; timeless summertime, 'all the long, blest, eventless day'.

Long talk with HHR after dinner in her study upstairs. Here was another piano, a radio ('it's the only way you can hear modern music without making the journey to London'), a stylized bust of HHR by the Roumanian, Sava Botzaris. The huge windows gave a wide view over the ridges, the bay, the Channel. But I sat with my back to the window, by some shelves nearly filled with books by Australians. HHR on another sofa across the room.

The talk wandered like a quiet river around themes raised in our letters during the years. HHR said she was glad I had never hesitated in the use of her pen-name, her name. There was that time in 1929 when the press at home had sudden headlines about *Ultima Thule*: 'Australian Woman

Writer Leaps to Fame.' (Leap in slow motion; it was 21 years since *Maurice Guest* had first appeared.) Two editors, knowing I had written about her books for years, now wired me: 'Who is Henry Handel Richardson?' I said she was HHR and a great writer: I gave literary particulars. It wasn't my fault that, after all, sundry relatives and friends had come to light with personal information the editors wanted; her looks, her likings and that she was Mrs. J.G. Robertson, her husband being Professor of German Language and Literature and director of Scandinavian Studies at University College, London.

'But I've worked more than twenty years to establish my own name,' she said. 'Why shouldn't I have it? After all, Richardson was the name I was born with—and perhaps I place an almost oriental valuation on a personal name; any way, why should a woman lose her name on marriage? As for Henry, well, *Maurice Guest* appeared at the time of feminist agitation, and I wanted the book to be a test. No one, positively no reviewer, spotted it as "just a woman's work". Handel—an uncle in Ireland, rather musical, adopted it, and I took it over. My husband rejoiced that I wasn't merely Mrs. J.G. Robertson.

'Those who begrude me my HHR are all of a piece with the journalists and librarians greedy for identifications. I insist that *Maurice Guest* and *Mahony* are works of fiction, not just essays in autobiography. There's that German baron, botanist and musician, in *Ultima Thule*. Of course I had Baron von Müller somewhat in mind; but all I knew of him was gathered from an old photograph, found in a family album. The rest was imaginary. I believe my father knew the Baron in earlier life, and his botanical studies were common property, of course. As for the music, well, all Germans of that date had it in them. His face, with its brown beard, might have been that of my counterpoint teacher in Leipzig...So much you see' (she spoke very firmly), 'for the "facts" in *Richard Mahony*.'

Some time during the long evening the blinds were drawn, the lingering light shut out. All I remember is that HHR's face across the room was first shadowed, though still firm, then clear again. Her alert talk is what stays in the mind, its vigorous questions, its firm outlines.

I didn't expect to see her this morning, as she usually sits down at her study-desk at 9.30, takes up a well-sharpened pencil from a dozen on her tray, and works till lunchtime, when she hands the result, whether pages or sentences, to Miss R. for typing out. To-day, though, there was a walk for three, further up Tilekiln Lane and out of it, climbing to the old Coastguard station on the rise, and looking over towards Romney Marsh and, again, the sea. HHR walks lightly and strongly. It's hard to remember how uncertain her health is: easier to grasp that lately she played tennis nearly every afternoon; that was, I think, till her husband died two years ago. Then she left their house in Regent's Park, placed her husband's collection of books in the University as he wished, found this house and made a few alterations, and built up a way of life here—so that she could write steadily, as before.

Here is her house, alone and self-contained, with Miss R. to keep visitors and inquirers away, in person or on the telephone. Visitors, if they must come, can be received in the drawing-room, which looks intimate and hospitable enough, being within the shell that HHR keeps round her. But the drawing-room, for her, is almost a public room, and on the ground floor. She needs to retreat and retreat into perfect solitude for work. It's only by passing through her bedroom, and then through a muffled baize-door beside her bed, that you reach her own study.

People call this secretiveness, but it's rather economy of effort, all for the sake of her writing; she finds it exhausting to meet more than one or two people at the same time, and she can't afford exhaustion, so she keeps withdrawn. She knows where she's going; she has known it ever since she was a child. When they flattered her about her music, and sat her at the piano, a child of eight or so, to play at country concerts, she wanted to play with her pencil, too; wanted to write poetry. When she went to study music at Leipzig, she worked at it hard enough—six hours' practice a day—but while she practised her scales she'd prop a book before her, one of the classic novels of Europe. At last her ambitious, energetic mother gave in and admitted that, for all her marked inborn talent, her training had come too late to make her a concert performer, and HHR was overjoyed; it left her free to write. Married and in London, she settled down to write; her husband took this utterly for granted. 'But then,' she says, 'when I actually read him the first twenty pages of *Maurice Guest*, no one was more amazed than he was. He hadn't guessed I could do so well. I'll never forget that day.' Ever since, except in illness or when taking a holiday for health's sake, she has regarded every day as a working day. To live is to write.

After lunch there was still some time, and we went for a dazzling drive. Up and then past Romney Marsh, yellow and luminous with summer, inland to the old sea-cliffs of Rye. We didn't stop there for any of the 'olde' places, nor for Henry James' house, and when we drove back through little white Winchelsea, we didn't look for Beverley Nichols' thatched roof; we went into the old church, but HHR felt it cold and went outside in the sun. 'We're walking on the graves of infants,' she said in a tone of fatality when we joined her across the grass.

A swift drive back to Green Ridges, swift enough even for HHR, who's curiously modern in some of her passions, and then indoors for tea, looking out on the brilliant summer garden. Miss R. drove me to the five o'clock train—a smooth train, its quietness filled for me with the last twenty-four hours.

(1935)

Nettie Palmer
from FOURTEEN YEARS: EXTRACTS FROM A PRIVATE JOURNAL 1925–39

December 9th, 1929 This afternoon Gerald Byrne brought Shaw Neilson to see us and they stayed on till evening. Neilson could have just managed to travel alone, as he does by train and tram every day to his exacting 'sinecure' in town, but his weak eyes make it hard except on routes he knows well.

Besides, it's clear Gerald enjoys taking this little responsibility, as well as doing more serious things for JSN, even to taking down a poem if for once Neilson feels well enough to dictate it. Not that Gerald, that ruddy-faced pessimist, would once omit his formula that life's not worth living—while helping to make life distinctly easier for someone he admires.

As for Neilson, he's a grey wisp of a man now, not exhausted by violent effort as he used to be in the country but regularly tired by his daily job, tramping the corridors to conduct a deputation of Yipp Yipp shire councillors to some all-highest, tramping in another direction to bring the file relating to Yipp Yipp. Not being able to do clerical work he has this as alternative,, with the regular three weeks holiday in the year.

And with the week-ends—too short for making poetry but enough sometimes for talk—Neilson has begun to enjoy a few encounters with his more constructive admirers. Blamire Young, as decorative artist and as a manipulator of words, has written some warm pages about his poems and Neilson has been out to his home in the soft valley below the Dandenongs. And Margaret Sutherland, experimenting with combinations of instruments, has composed a setting for voice, piano and clarinet for that most atmospheric ballad 'The Orange Tree'.

When Furnley Maurice dropped in about five, Neilson was talking of the few poets he had been able to read. In his good days, he came on Padraic Colum's 'Wild Earth' and it meant a lot to him, perhaps giving him confidence to use naïve rhythms and simple themes that suit him. But through the years the bulk of his reading has undoubtedly been the letters pouring in from AGS. Blessing and cursing, admonishing, praising—and sometimes bringing models to his notice, so that he knew what Heine had written, and Victor Hugo, and something of other poets whose names meant nothing to him.

'And you've kept all those letters?' I asked anxiously, knowing Neilson had had to move about and travel light.

'I kept them for years,' he said, 'but in 1917, you know, there was the mouse-plague over the Victorian wheat country. Every scrap of paper went. The only letters of Stephens I own now came during recent years. I haven't been able to take all his advice, but he's been a wonderful friend to me—sometimes a bit awkward, though, when he knocks someone else down with the idea of building me up.'

He made this remark at large and 'to whom it might concern'. It was honourable disclaimer of agreement with all Stephens' long-standing hostilities or sudden slaughters. If there was anyone in the room who had suffered. . .Peace!

(1929)

A. B. ('Banjo') Paterson
from SYDNEY IN THE SEVENTIES

Mention of Archibald of the *Bulletin* recalls the personality of a most extraordinary man, one of the few Australians whose work was known outside this country. Jules Francis Archibald was originally a medical student, but drifted into journalism. Starting with absolutely nothing in the way of capital—he was a poorly paid reporter on an evening newspaper—he managed to scramble enough financial support together to start a struggling and highly discreditable weekly newspaper which he called the *Bulletin*. In its early days the shadow of the bailiff was seldom off the *Bulletin*'s doorstep, but Archibald had visions of founding a really influential Australian paper on the lines of the political journals that have met with the greatest success in France. Keeping this object steadily in view, and holding that such an end justified any proceedings, Archibald constituted himself the unofficial and unauthorised champion of anybody who was running in hard luck.

Just at that time, the Roman Catholic community were wild with indignation at the effect of Parkes' Education Act which (as they held) threw on them the onus of maintaining their own schools, out of their own pockets, though they paid their full share of taxation like anybody else. Quick to see an opportunity, Archibald made it his business to attack the author of the Education Act, and many a much-needed hundred pounds was forthcoming from the big Roman Catholic interests on the promise of an article that would tear the hide off old Parkes.

'Toiling, rejoicing, borrowing'—to slightly paraphrase the poet—Archibald fought his way till he had got his paper established: he went to gaol because he was unable to pay the damages which a misguided jury had given against his paper for the exposure of what was really a crying abuse: and even from the gaol itself he wrote a series of articles entitled 'In The Jug' which, to say the least of it, exhibited signs of anything but a repentant spirit. By this time he had got a big following, and articles from his paper were quoted and admired even by American editors, who probably thought that the paper was set up and printed by blackfellows.

How did he, an obscure Australian ink-slinger, manage to get his paper known and approved all over the world?

To begin with, he had great ability, and was a master of sarcasm and ridicule: also he had tireless industry, for in all the years that I had to do with Archibald I don't remember ever finding him out of his office: he had once done a little prospecting and the keenness with which he hunted for gold was only equalled by the keenness with which he hunted for good copy among the mass of articles submitted to him. His ideas may be of value to those who are plodding along the Inky Way, so here are the journalistic principles of J.F. Archibald, as sub-edited by the present writer.

'When any public question turns up, always try to be different from the other papers: some composers introduce a discord into their music, and in the volume of sound the public attention is always caught by the man who sings the discord. So be different: you may be wrong or you may be right, but at any rate be different, and even if you are wrong you will have given the unpopular side a hearing.'

'Always help the underdog in a fight: you will at least earn his gratitude, while the winner would probably bite you.'

'Never abuse anybody—laugh at them.'

'Always print the absolute truth about the shows, as nearly as you can get it. While you are struggling, they will try to break you by taking their advertisements away, but later on they will pay you a pound an inch.'

'Print all the awkward things procurable, and if you are printing a story about a mine, get it from the man working on the face: don't get it from the mine manager.'

'Most papers are edited by their advertisement canvassers, and when a paper becomes a "property" it ceases to be a paper: it is too fat to fight.'

The *Bulletin* produced another man whose name is known in other parts of the world—Henry Lawson. Some of his work has been translated into Swedish, and if a man can get by with the Swedes, there must be something more in his work than facility and local colour.

Henry was a long gangling individual with a large moustache, the insight of a seer and the mind of a child. Simple in the ways of the world, he naturally thought himself a strategist of no mean order, and he would exult over the various stunts he put up to beat publishers at their own game.

After he had made a success in Australia, he went to England and encountered his first English publisher. This is Henry's account of the interview.

'He kept me waiting for half an hour,' said Henry, 'though I could see his reflection in a glass in his room and I could see that he wasn't doing anything. So then I knew that he was going to put a bluff over me and I got ready for him.'

'"Well, Mr Lawson," he said, "if you would do us something on the lines of Rolf Boldrewood we might do business."'

'So I looked him in the eye and, "Rolf Boldrewood," I said, "Who's he?"'

Henry's bluff, however, worked a bit too well, for the English publisher didn't see that it was a bluff. He honestly thought that Henry had never heard of Rolf Boldrewood and decided offhand that Henry must be one of those impossible people with whom no firm of standing could do any business, so it was left to the Swedes to appreciate Henry's genius. Back in Australia, Henry wrote some priceless stuff for the Labour movement, but that did not last very long.

'They've declared me black,' said Henry, 'because I wrote a story disclosing some good points in a squatter.'

Henry's campaign against his Australian publishers was a bit of an epic, and was conducted on strictly original lines. Poetry, or verse in any form, was a drug on the English market and I doubt if any writer other than Kipling was making enough out of a book of verse to keep himself in bootlaces: but the Australians were reading verse, so the publishers decided to take a risk and get out a collection of my verses, giving me a royalty on each copy that was sold. Henry, meanwhile, was waiting in the offing with a collection of verses, to see how I got on.

Much to everyone's surprise my verse collection *The Man From Snowy River* ran into edition after edition and the publishers were only too anxious to get Henry's book out before the boom burst. Henry, however, would not accept a royalty—he wanted cash—and he sold his book straight out for what he afterwards stigmatised to me as 'a lousy two hundred pounds'. His book sold well, so he decided, in his curiously irresponsible way, that he would get more money out of it, and he demanded that the outright sale should be cancelled and that he should be put on a royalty. This was done, but the royalties did not come in fast enough to suit him, so he demanded that the publishers should buy his book outright for the second time: and he made himself such a nuisance by hanging about the shop, and demanding to see the principals, that they gave him another couple of hundred pounds to close all accounts between them.

Having discovered this weak point in their armour, Henry, when he was particularly desperate for money, would go down and demand something on account of royalties on his future books: he had the mind of a child, money meant nothing to him, contracts meant nothing to him, and he was not the least ashamed of his buccaneering methods. On the contrary, he would say with a chuckle of exultation, 'I'm just going down to shake those cows up for a few quid,' and the sight of this gaunt apparition with his frayed sleeves and his unfathomable eyes would so upset the high-toned clientele of the biggest bookshop in Sydney that at last it was agreed that he should be paid a certain sum weekly, such payments to cease altogether the moment that he put his nose inside the shop.

When I see the statue of Lawson in the Domain, I sometimes reflect on how little the public will do for a literary in man in his lifetime, and what a lot they will do for him when he is dead. Henry's tactics may not have been without reproach, but he faced his troubles in the only way open to him, and, as he says in his verses:

> You have to face 'em
> when your pants begin to go.

(1930s)

Henry Lawson
LETTER TO LORD BEAUCHAMP

Chaplin Cottage,
Charles Street,
North Sydney.
19th January 1900.

Dear Lord Beauchamp,

I heard that you had spoken kindly of my books—*When the World Was Wide* and *While the Billy Boils*—and as you take an interest in art and literature, I thought, as a last resource, I would confide in you and ask you to help me. The manly and independent spirit you have shown since you came to govern the colony helped to decide me. The attached article, 'Pursuing Literature', speaks for itself. All that I can say is that it is true and takes the widest possible view of the situation. The English reviews and correspondence in last part of scrap-book—if you will kindly glance at it—will explain my present position in the literary world. (I must apologize for the appearance of scrap-book, which is not very presentable; it has knocked round in camps.)

The position of purely Australian literature is altogether hopeless in Australia—there is no market. The oldest and wealthiest Daily in Australia fills its columns with matter clipped from English and American magazines. The usual answer to would-be Australian contributors is 'Very sorry, Mr So-and-So, but we have already exceeded our allowance for outside contributions.' Nothing 'goes' well here that does not come from or through England.

I have recently been obliged to sell, or, rather, sacrifice two more books in Australia, and both are larger and contain better class work than my first two. I would have waited until these books came out before writing to you, but there has been a delay in the printing. I send you specimens of the work I am doing now for £1 per column. I have been contributing to a Sydney daily, but the war news has crowded me out. I have to sell for £1 per column work that is honestly worth five.

I have never been in a position to wait until my work got home, found a market, and the money got back. I have had splendid reviews in the leading English literary journals, and letters from most of the publishers, but am tied down here because I can scarcely make a living, let alone money to go home or to keep me while I did good work and got it on the English market. I am, because of the prices paid literary men here, obliged to publish rubbish—or, at least, good ideas in a hurried and mutilated form—and, because of the reputation I have gained in Australia, I am forced to sign hurried work—else I couldn't get it published at all. That's the cruellest part of the business.

In short, I am wasting my work, wasting my life, spoiling the reputation I have gained, and wearing out my brains and heart here in Australia. If I were single I would find my way to England somehow; but I am married, have one child, and another one due this month, so I am tied hopelessly. We live comfortably on £2 per week, and it takes me all my time to make that with my pen.

I am sure that I could, in six months, command my own prices in London—but how am I to get there? In order to succeed it would be necessary for me to be in London a few months to learn the ropes. We cannot deal at this distance, as it takes 9 months at least to correspond with two magazines in succession. Or if I could have 12 months out here clear of financial worry, to do my best work and get it home, I would, I feel sure, raise myself out of this grinding, sordid life which is killing my work and me.

I send you a book by Barcroft Boake, a young Australian who, if he had lived, would have been our leading poet. While his best work was being published he hanged himself in the scrub, down Botany way—for the same reasons that I want to raise myself out of this hole of a place.

I will not appeal to the country. I can see nothing before me but years of hack-work, of sacrificing my books as soon as written—and before it— and in the end perhaps a big name in London and a chance to go there, and fancy prices, *when I have written myself out*—it was the case with Louis Becke. And all this for the want of a hundred pounds or so at the start. I have been obliged to sell all my rights as you will see by enclosed agreement—which you will kindly cause to be returned with scrap-book— everything except perhaps my soul; our newspaper proprietors would buy that if they could make anything on it.

I—how shall I put this? Will you help me out of the miserable hole I am in? I heard you were rich. All my friends are as poor as myself. I know none of our scrubby aristocracy, nor do I wish to know them. Will you—say—send me enough to hang out here for a year independent of the Australian Press—or go home? I could go in about April, but could not leave my wife behind. And I'm sure that within two years I could win fame and fortune in London and repay you. If you cannot help me, kindly destroy this. It is the first letter of this kind I have ever written in my life, and will be the last.

Yours truly,
HENRY LAWSON

Tried very hard to go as War correspondent with contingent; but could not get paper to pay expenses.

(1900)

Patrick White
from THE PRODIGAL SON

At the age of 46 I have spent just on twenty of those years overseas. During the last ten, I have hardly stirred from the six acres of 'Dogwoods', Castle Hill. It sounds odd, and is perhaps worth trying to explain.

Brought up to believe in the maxim: Only the British can be right, I did accept this during the earlier part of my life. Ironed out in an English public school, and finished off at King's, Cambridge, it was not until 1939, after wandering by myself through most of Western Europe, and finally most of the United States, that I began to grow up and think my own thoughts. The War did the rest. What had seemed a brilliant, intellectual, highly desirable existence, became distressingly parasitic and pointless. There is nothing like a rain of bombs to start one trying to assess one's own achievement. Sitting at night in his London bed-sitting room during the first months of the Blitz, this chromium-plated Australian with two fairly successful novels to his credit came to the conclusion that this achievement was practically nil. Perhaps significantly, he was reading at that time Eyre's *Journal*. Perhaps also he had the wind up; certainly he reached rather often for the bottle of Calvados in the wardrobe. Anyway, he experienced those first sensations of rootlessness which Alister Kershaw has deplored and explained as the 'desire to nuzzle once more at the benevolent teats of the mother country'.

All through the War in the Middle East there persisted a longing to return to the scenes of childhood, which is, after all, the purest well from which the creative artist draws. Aggravated further by the terrible nostalgia of the desert landscapes, this desire was almost quenched by the year I spent stationed in Greece, where perfection presents itself on every hand, not only the perfection of antiquity, but that of nature, and the warmth of human relationships expressed in daily living. Why didn't I stay in Greece? I was tempted to. Perhaps it was the realization that even the most genuine resident Hellenophile accepts automatically the vaguely comic role of Levantine beachcomber. He does not belong, the natives seem to say, not without affection; it is sad for him, but he is nothing. While the Hellenophile continues humbly to hope.

So I did not stay in my elective Greece. Demobilization in England left me with the alternative of remaining in what I then felt to be an actual and spiritual graveyard, with the prospect of ceasing to be an artist and turning instead into that most sterile of beings, a London intellectual, or of returning home, to the stimulus of time remembered. Quite honestly, the thought of a full belly influenced me as well, after toying with the soft, sweet awfulness of horsemeat stew in the London restaurants that I could afford. So I came home. I bought a farm at Castle Hill, and with a Greek friend and partner, Manoly Lascaris, started to grow flowers and vegetables, and to breed Schnauzers and Saanen goats.

The first years I was content with these activities, and to soak myself in landscape. If anybody mentioned Writing, I would reply: 'Oh, one day, perhaps.' But I had no real intention of giving the matter sufficient thought. *The Aunt's Story*, written immediately after the War, before returning to Australia, had succeeded with overseas critics, failed as usual with the local ones, remained half-read, it was obvious from the state of the pages, in the lending libraries. Nothing seemed important, beyond living and eating, with a roof of one's own over one's head.

Then, suddenly, I began to grow discontented. Perhaps, in spite of Australian critics, writing novels was the only thing I could do with any degree of success; even my half-failures were some justification of an otherwise meaningless life. Returning sentimentally to a country I had left in my youth, what had I really found? Was there anything to prevent me packing my bag and leaving like Alister Kershaw and so many other artists? Bitterly I had to admit, no. In all directions stretched the Great Australian Emptiness, in which the mind is the least of possessions, in which the rich man is the important man, in which the schoolmaster and journalist rule what intellectual roost there is, in which beautiful youths and girls stare at life through blind blue eyes, in which human teeth fall like autumn leaves, the buttocks of cars grow hourly glassier, food means cake and steak, muscles prevail, and the march of material ugliness does not raise a quiver from the average nerves.

It was the exaltation of the 'average' that made me panic most, and in this frame of mind, in spite of myself, I began to conceive another novel. Because the void I had to fill was so immense, I wanted to try to suggest in this book every possible aspect of life, through the lives of an ordinary man and woman. But at the same time I wanted to discover the extraordinary behind the ordinary, the mystery and the poetry which alone could make bearable the lives of such people, and incidentally, my own life since my return.

So I began to write *The Tree of Man*. How it was received by the more important Australian critics is now ancient history. Afterwards I wrote *Voss*, possibly conceived during the early days of the Blitz, when I sat reading Eyre's *Journal* in a London bed-sitting room. Nourished by months spent trapesing backwards and forwards across the Egyptian and Cyrenaican deserts, influenced by the arch-megalomaniac of the day, the idea finally matured after reading contemporary accounts of Leichhardt's expeditions and A. H. Chisholm's *Strange New World* on returning to Australia.

It would be irrelevant to discuss here the literary aspects of the novel. More important are those intentions of the author which have pleased some readers without their knowing exactly why, and helped to increase the rage of those who have found the book meaningless. Always something of a frustrated painter, and a composer *manqué*, I wanted to give my book the textures of music, the sensuousness of paint, to convey through the theme and characters of *Voss* what Delacroix and Blake might have seen, what Mahler and Liszt might have heard. Above all I was determined to prove that the Australian novel is not necessarily the dreary, dun-coloured offspring of journalistic realism. On the whole, the world has been convinced, only here, at the present moment, the dingoes are howling unmercifully.

What, then, have been the rewards of this returned expatriate? I remember when, in the flush of success after my first novel, an old and wise Australian journalist called Guy Innes came to interview me in my London flat. He asked me whether I wanted to go back. I had just 'arrived', who was I to want to go back? 'Ah, but when you do,' he persisted, 'the colours will come flooding back onto your palette.' This gentle criticism of my first novel only occurred to me as such in recent years. But I think perhaps Guy Innes has been right.

So, amongst the rewards, there is the refreshed landscape, which even in its shabbier, remembered versions has always made a background to my life. The worlds of plants and music may never have revealed themselves had I sat talking brilliantly to Alister Kershaw over a Pernod on the Left Bank. Possibly all art flowers more readily in silence. Certainly the state of simplicity and humility is the only desirable one for artist or for man. While to reach it may be impossible, to attempt to do so is imperative. Stripped of almost everything that I had considered desirable and necessary, I began to try. Writing, which had meant the practice of an art by a polished mind in civilized surroundings, became a struggle to create completely fresh forms out of the rocks and sticks of words. I began to see things for the first time. Even the boredom and frustration presented avenues for endless exploration; even the ugliness, the bags and iron of Australian life, acquired a meaning. As for the cat's cradle of human intercourse, this was necessarily simplified, often bungled, sometimes touching. Its very tentativeness can be a reward. There is always the possibility that the book lent, the record played, may lead to communication between human beings. There is the possibility that one may be helping to people a barely inhabited country with a race possessed of understanding.

These, then, are some of the reasons why an expatriate has stayed, in the face of those disappointments which follow inevitably upon his return. Abstract and unconvincing, the Alister Kershaws will probably answer, but such reasons, as I have already suggested, are a personal matter. More concrete, and most rewarding of all, are the many letters I have received from unknown Australians, for whom my writing seems to have opened a window. To me, the letters alone are reason enough for staying.

(1958)

THE WRITING PROCESS

84

He wishes your opinion.' So I bowed a little waist bow to Tante Rosa
and obeyed.

At last the morning came to an end and Madge and Norman arrived in
the old car. Going away for the weekend was for us both a new experience.
But no one in the house had suggested we should not go and we left with
them all smiling fondly on us.

'We do nothing here but eat,' Madge said later. 'Really it's too
terrible but what else can one do in the [coun]try?' She looked at me as
if ~~the~~ to suggest another meaning, but I ...   at her. I sat
opposite Louise shelling peas, our ...   ...with the
fresh green pods, pod snapping, sn...   ...d the
fish her husband caught. The f...
hot and, in the little oven, ...
was roasting. A tremendous ...

Norman came and went ...
moisture. He came into ...
wood. ~~And~~ Madge prep...
last, took everythin...   forks
and ~~forms~~ and glas...
I thought Louise ...   let them stand ...
of the table. On ...
simply peop...
the cold ...
Lou...
for...
front of ...
for her eating. ...
herself with her own knif...

(overlaid letter)

Dear Elizabeth Jolley,

Many thanks for sending us the two c...
We liked both, and have ultimately op...
the next issue of *Scripsi*, though we c...
if you thought this fair enough. ...
very pleased to be printing your work: ...
acknowledge the fact the the Fremantle Ar...
publishing *Milk and Honey* later in the yea...

We do have a number of queries about the text...
In the first line of p.13, can we delete the ...
As it is it looks a bit over punctuated with b...
comma. 'In the tenth line of p.18 should there ...
the close of the quotation: i.e., "Tante Rosa ma...
paté than Heloise," Louise whispered...etc.?   *Yes*

There is a problem with the Latin quotation from the...
p.19. In the Mass for the Dead the line reads "Tuba...
sonum": as you have it, it makes no grammatical sense...
course is true when the quote is repeated on p.20. We...
is just an error in transcription. Would it be best to...
the Latin lines: *Tuba mirum spargens sonum, Rex tremenda*...
let them stand out a little as signature lines, as it were...

On p.20 do you want the word "free" to stand apart from its...
as it does? "Fount of pity" on the next line we will restore...
"Fount of pity". And should the phrase "by all mean", ten li...
from the bottom of P.20 read "by all means"?   *Yes*

We're sorry to sling this list of editorial quibbl...
it's probably best to clarify these things in ...
planning to bring the issue out in March: ...
by Murray Bail and Tom Pickard (an Engl...
short story by Michel Tournier (an Engl...
in English.

While other parts of this Anthology have paid attention to the way writers deal with what used to be called 'their material' or the way in which they respond to the world or participate in it, this Section turns to the essential inwardness of writing, the process of writing. It shows how texts reflect upon their own situation; how writing is often about writing.

There is an important sense in which writing can never *actually* express a world outside of words. Language is a system of signs which stands in for 'truth', 'experience', 'reality': it is not itself 'truth', 'experience', 'reality'. Language works because words are understood as being different from other words, not because of an inevitable and direct connection with 'things'. What they refer to then is other words; other words by which other things are constructed. Literature does not reflect a reality: it creates one. When we read poetry, we may seek that transcendent meaning or truth 'behind the words' but all we can ever really engage with is the system of signs we call language, and we can only ever do so in language.

Writing must always be, in part, about writing, about the way it works in words. It is often possible to discover that, metaphorically or metonymically, texts embody images of their own construction. In some cases they may invoke an image from their own 'subject'. John Tranter's (punning) insistence on 'craft' that keeps the whole act of faith aloft is such an example; Rosemary Dobson's poem finds its inspiration in signs (literally billboards); 'Ern Malley's' 'Dürer: Innsbruck, 1495' speaks of the inevitability of what we now call intertextuality, the impossibility of writing without referring to other writing. Elizabeth Jolley's 'Woman in a Lampshade' is explicitly about a writer writing; in Michael Wilding's 'The Words She Types', a writer's absence becomes more and more marked as the story progresses (but how does the story progress without a writer?). Peter Carey's 'The Last Days of a Famous Mime' dramatises the predicament of the 'author' who seeks to ignore the distinction between text and truth.

Rosemary Dobson's 'Oracles for a Childhood Journey' seems a simple poem, concerned to find its substantive sources in the empirical world of childhood, railway journeys and advertising billboards. But that reliance on a secure, empirical set of signs begins to break down. This is not a 'Childhood Journey' but oracles for one. The oracle was not a god speaking the truth but rather a medium who spoke in (often ambiguous) code, a perfect example of the mediating contingency of language in texts. Indeed, as the poem continues, it becomes less and less direct in its communication: 'the sad old man' from Yerrinbool appears to be the Messenger but 'his tidings blew on the wind away' disrupting not only the message but also the poem's syntax. But the most potent images of clear speaking—the billboards—are also now disrupted, their 'messages' dispersed and brought into new relation with each other and with the reader. They are the oracles, and they (appropriately) speak in code. Wittily enough the poem ends '*Out of the Blue Comes...Doctor Morse!*', locating its meaning in a code (Morse code?), a set of formal conventions which are not inherently meaningful but which come 'out of the blue'.

If 'Oracles For a Childhood Journey' seemed simple enough, Paul Pfeiffer's 'At the Window' does not. Yet, in terms of what it is *about*, it is actually quite straightforward. It describes the ending of night and the moment of dawn at which thought is reordered. But its very difficulty makes it a poem about its own composition. The poem as enunciated is about that other reordering by which language replaces thought, by which poems are constructed as 'the imagination' struggles with (and in) language. 'At the Window' was published in the second *Jindyworobak Anthology* (1939) yet its affinities with that movement, which sought to connect Australian culture with a deeper understanding of the physical and social landscape and with Aboriginal articulations of it in particular, seem slight. The 'guttural goose' would have been more at home in the pages of *Angry Penguins*, the avant-garde literary journal that also originated in Adelaide, in the early 1940s: indeed Pfeiffer did publish poems in *Angry Penguins*.

Angry Penguins sought not to liberate Australian poetry from 'alien' influences but to embrace them. Edited by Max Harris and (later) John Reed, it encouraged writing and painting by those eager to experiment in form and subject. Opposed to limited versions of Australian nationalism in art, it published and commented on the work of contemporary European and American modernist writers and painters. It was, then, the antithesis of both the Jindyworobaks and the social realists. In 1944, the conservative poets James McAuley and Harold Stewart, dismayed by what they regarded as the undisciplined nature of most of what was published in th(journal, by 'the gradual decay of meaning and craftsmanship in poetry' decided to test the discrimination of the editors by sending them a bundle of factitious poems. The poems were produced in an afternoon with the aid of a random collection of reference books and, according to Stewart and McAuley, were intended to be technically crude and logically incoherent. They were sent to Harris supposedly from the recently deceased (and wholly fictitious) Ern Malley. Harris published the poems, the hoax was revealed, and the Adelaide police decided to prosecute Harris on the grounds that a couple of the poems were obscene. After an extraordinary court case, in which international witnesses were called to substantiate the 'literary merit' of the poems, Harris was fined £5 and the cause of modern poetry in Australia was discredited. But the discrediting seems to rest on the assumption that composition can only be undertaken by a single mind working towards coherent meaning, that that meaning is *given* to the text by the mind of the poet.

Clearly, 'Dürer: Innsbruck, 1495' remains, whatever the circumstances of its composition, a remarkably intelligible and moving poem. It is ironically significant—in a poem composed in collaboration—that the speaker, a single 'I', feels defeated by intertextuality, by the inability to 'be original', to be anything other than 'an interloper'. The 'I' is confronted by other writings, other readings; the essential knowledge, wittily enough, comes from yet other texts: 'I had read in books that art is not easy.' (*The Black Swan of Trespass* was used as the title for Humphrey McQueen's book on modernism in Australia.)

Dürer is also the focus of Kenneth Slessor's exploration of the possibilities of poetry, 'Nuremberg'. Albrecht Dürer (1471–1528) was the greatest artistic figure of the Renaissance outside Italy. Largely based at Nuremberg in Germany, he was an engraver, painter, woodcut and decorative designer. In Slessor's poem, it is (and the pun must be admitted) his durability that seems attractive. Much more confident of its power to order the world than the 'Malley' poem, 'Nuremberg' celebrates the power of the imagination to order and shape the past, to overcome time, just as Dürer's art ('the plates of iron') endures. This confidence fails in such late Slessor poems as 'Five Bells' and 'Beach Burial'.

The power of the imagination to draw impressions together into harmony patently fails in John Tranter's 'Lufthansa' as well. Though Tranter spoke in an earlier interview (in *Meanjin* in 1981) of 'the need to maintain some kind of control over the way I think and act and speak', this poem is unable to bring that control to bear on the phenomena that the speaker records. So, speculation about the consequences of a controlled art like Dürer's, 'the truth that holds the grey/shaking metal whole while we believe in it', the memories of Katharina, and the admiration for the cool hostess do not come together to reveal truth or even to make experience intelligible. The 'craft' which the hostess enacts, which the aircrew employ while they 'adjust the tilt of the sky', falls short of the apparent power of Dürer to change consciousness. The poem returns to 'a dictionary of shelter'. This poem won *The Australian* poetry award in 1985.

Operating within the modernist belief in the ability of the imagination to order the chaos of experience, Dimitris Tsaloumas' 'The Journey' attempts to recover something absent, a persistent project of Slessor's poetry also. The meaning of the journey is given by its destination. Defined by that which it has not yet attained, it ceases to be a journey when the goal is no longer deferred. The poem begins by defining its subject in terms of what it is not. It then seeks images which will evoke it even if its presence cannot be attained. Significantly, the subject is never named; that which is sought, the goal of the journey (a country? a person?) cannot be given presence.

An appropriate sequel to those poems that grappled with Dürer as a possible paradigm for the immortality of human endeavour, Hope's 'Pyramis or the House of Ascent', celebrates the transcendent ego. The heroes of the poem are the pyramid builders whose creations 'outlast time' and the cultures which produce them. No queasy speculation here about the social corruption, the slavery or the inequalities, but a steady admiration of the will to order of the builders. And that is what the speaker admires too in the work of the poets, in whom such hubris is redeemed by the transformative power of art.

Gwen Harwood's poem, '"Thought is Surrounded by a Halo"', is less concerned with the transformative power of art than with the way in which language gives form to thought. Thought can never present itself as it is but must always appear through the mediation of language. Ludwig Wittgenstein (1889–1951) was Professor of Philosophy at Cambridge (1939–47); *Philosophical Investigations*, a work in which his later view that philosphical problems could be addressed only by paying close attention to the language in which they were framed, was published posthumously. Language is not that in which thought is expressed but that in which thought exists. The request, to 'show me the order of the world...no model, but the truth itself', is a rhetorical one, answered in the images of the response part of the poem.

In a sense Adamson's 'Towards Abstraction/Possibly a Gull's Wing' seeks to move towards what Harwood calls 'no model, but the truth itself'. The poem seems to reach for some autonomy from the 'poet'— 'What way, who moves? ah, let's be pure/in observation, let us drop opinions.'

Finola Moorhead's 'The Landscape of the Egg' moves between a number of positions, attempting (as she does elsewhere in her work) to avoid the single speaking position and the linear logic of conventional narrative. 'Landscape' is reflexive, concerned to examine its own articulation, constantly offering a critique of its own position. It thus produces an excess of meanings which escape the control of writer and reader: no single interpretation is adequate. In Section 3 language (as it did in Gwen Harwood's poem) 'surrounds rather than is'; it is provisional, cannot even prove the existence of the perceiving 'i', which thus becomes lower case. Language is already known; therefore it cannot belong to the writer. Art takes words 'for a joy-ride'. As the text proceeds, it becomes more concerned with the problem of sorting out the gender of language. The 'already-known' language is patriarchal language, one that has been turned into weapons. Section 6 tries to reclaim the language by emphasising its lack of uniformity, its second-hand nature, by making it over to women's ends. But as that begins to sound essentialist, Section 7 turns away towards the personal. As Moorhead has said elsewhere: 'Experimentation with form is an absolute necessity for a woman writer. For what has been done and how that was done neither says what she has to say nor provides the way of saying it.'

According to ancient Greek belief there were nine muses, daughters of Mnemosyne and Zeus. Conventionally represented as nubile nymphs bestowing inspiration as a favour on artists, they have no attraction for the speaker of Sylvia Kantaris' 'The Tenth Muse'. Her muse is male and very ordinary, 'like a sack of potatoes'; he is neither attractive nor co-operative. He also insinuates the inadequacy of her gender. Terpsichore was the muse of dancing.

Marion Campbell's *Lines of Flight* experiments with language and form as is evident even from this short extract. Rita Finnerty (a punning name) is an artist who has travelled to France. There she oscillates between working on her 'serious' art in solitude and being enmeshed in a variety of social and sexual relationships in the world in which she takes on commercial art for an advertising agency ('my deadline for Julienne towels') in order to survive. In each she is constructed in a variety of ways, all of which she resists, just as the text resists simple construction by constantly adopting new roles, new modes of articulation, by switching from one register of language to another and even from English into French. It reflects on art and its relation to culture, but it never licenses one particular position, slipping endlessly from one to another. The extract concludes on a combative, transgressive note, reflected in the very utterance of the text.

Among the varieties of fiction which depart from the conventional representation of narrative realism are the fable, metafiction, and reflexive writing or literature of process. It is hard to be firm about definitions since these are, of course, all types which subvert formal conventions. Loosely speaking, though, the four remaining pieces in this Section exemplify those varieties.

Dal Stivens' 'The Gentle Basilisk' is a fable, emphasising the non-realistic elements and moving towards a moral conclusion. A basilisk was a mythic reptile whose breath and even glance were said to be fatal; it was hatched by a reptile from a cock's egg.

Elizabeth Jolley's 'Woman in a Lampshade' does not stress its non-realistic elements but nurtures them nevertheless. As in much of Jolley's work, the writer is a 'character' in the fiction and the writer's fiction interpenetrates the fiction in which she is a character. Writing is the subject and the form of the text; the fictionality of the text is correspondingly emphasised; its status as a verbal construct underlined. The notion of characters as 'real people' becomes harder to maintain.

Much of Peter Carey's work is metafiction, that is, fiction which is (though not always explicitly) about the act and materials of writing. 'The Last Days of a Famous Mime' carefully breaks up the narrative into a series of occasionally connected fragments. Miming, derived from the Greek mimesis, to imitate, is an appropriate metaphor for Carey's subversive relationship to realism. His mime does not imitate; his responses do not affirm his audience's sense of the actuality of their world. But in his final performance, he is overwhelmed by the dangers of mimesis, losing the distinction between text and truth, between representing a river and being one, between being a signifier and being a signified.

The final selection here, Michael Wilding's 'The Words She Types', epitomises in some ways the concerns of so many of the others. It investigates the relationship between writer, language and text. Flirting with the idea of the autonomy of the text, it allows its writer to disappear, his 'presence' gradually to diminish. The controlling power of the artist's imagination, so crucial in the modernist period, is neatly subverted here. The typist becomes not so much the 'transmitter' of the story as its reader and a 'character' in it.

Alan Lawson/Ken Goodwin

Rosemary Dobson
ORACLES FOR A CHILDHOOD JOURNEY

The painted billboards spoke to me,
Out of the Blue Comes the Whitest Wash
And *Doctor Morse's Indian Root*
(They Reach the Liver) Pills,
Reiterated loud and strong   5
All the way to Mittagong.

I put the question from the train
On the way to Mittagong,
What does the future hold for me?
Not Pythian snakes nor Sacred Bough   10
Gave answer more oracularly—
Doctor Morse's Indian...Rea...

All the way to Mittagong
I asked of flying cloud and sky,
And shall I then write poetry?   15
And whence shall come the words to me?
And whence the mask to speak them through?
Out of the Blue, Out of the Blue.

(At Yerrinbool a sad old man
Issued from the city's gates   20
To meet the Traveller on the train.
I think he was the Messenger.
His tidings blew on the wind away,
Peanuts, lollies, choco...lay...)

How like the Chorus in a Play   25
The billboards pointed all one way
To show the God in the Machine
Descending from the Empyrean,
And spoke with a united force—
Out of the Blue Comes...Doctor Morse!   30

(1973)

Paul Pfeiffer
AT THE WINDOW

The last dismantled star flung into space,
In swift gradations
Night ripens into day.
Thought patterns flailed like octopus
Dichotomize.
Hen-coop cocks crow up the dawn...
'The guttural goose hath ushered in the day!'

(1939)

'Ern Malley'
DÜRER: INNSBRUCK, 1495

I had often, cowled in the slumberous heavy air,
Closed my inanimate lids to find it real,
As I knew it would be, the colourful spires
And painted roofs, the high snows glimpsed at the back,
All reversed in the quiet reflecting waters—   5
Not knowing then that Dürer perceived it too.
Now I find that once more I have shrunk
To an interloper, robber of dead men's dream,
I had read in books that art is not easy
But no one warned that the mind repeats   10
In its ignorance the vision of others. I am still
The black swan of trespass on alien waters.

(1944)

Kenneth Slessor
NUREMBERG

So quiet it was in that high, sun-steeped room,
So warm and still, that sometimes with the light
Through the great windows, bright with bottle-panes,
There'd float a chime from clock-jacks out of sight,
    Clapping iron mallets on green copper gongs.   5

But only in blown music from the town's
Quaint horologe could Time intrude...you'd say
Clocks had been bolted out, the flux of years
Defied, and that high chamber sealed away
    From earthly change by some old alchemist.   10

And, oh, those thousand towers of Nuremberg
Flowering like leaden trees outside the panes:
Those gabled roofs with smoking cowls, and those
Encrusted spires of stone, those golden vanes
    On shining housetops paved with scarlet tiles!   15

And all day nine wrought-pewter manticores
Blinked from their spouting faucets, not five steps
Across the cobbled street, or, peering through
The rounds of glass, espied that sun-flushed room
    With Dürer graving at intaglios.   20

O happy nine, spouting your dew all day
In green-scaled rows of metal, whilst the town
Moves peacefully below in quiet joy....
O happy gargoyles to be gazing down
   On Albrecht Dürer and his plates of iron!   25

                      (1924)

John Tranter
LUFTHANSA

Flying up a valley in the Alps where the rock
rushes past like a broken diorama
I'm struck by an acute feeling of precision—
the way the wing-tips flex, just a little
as the German crew adjust the tilt of the the sky and   5
bank us all into a minor course correction
while the turbo-props gulp at the mist
with their old-fashioned thirsty thunder—or
you notice how the hostess, perfecting a smile
as she offers you a dozen drinks, enacts what is   10
almost a craft: Technical Drawing, for example,
a subject where desire and function, in the hands
of a Dürer, can force a thousand fine ink lines
to bite into the doubts of an epoch, spelling
Humanism. Those ice reefs repeat the motto   15
whispered by the snow-drifts on the north side
of the woods and model villages: the sun
has a favourite leaning, and the Nordic flaw
is a glow alcohol can fan into a flame.
And what is this truth that holds the grey   20
shaking metal whole while we believe in it?
The radar keeps its sweeping intermittent promises
speaking metaphysics on the phosphor screen;
our faith is sad and practical, and leads back
to our bodies, to the smile behind the drink   25
trolley and her white knuckles as the plane drops
a hundred feet. The sun slanting through a porthole
blitzes the ice-blocks in my glass of lemonade
and splinters light across the cabin ceiling.
No, two drinks—one for me, one for Katharina   30
sleeping somewhere—suddenly the Captain
lifts us up and over the final wall
explaining roads, a town, a distant lake
as a dictionary of shelter—sleeping elsewhere
under a night sky growing bright with stars.   35

                      (1984)

Dimitris Tsaloumas
THE JOURNEY

Were you a fever, I'd cure you; a woman and I'd
    forget you. But it's with other passion
that you consume me—a pining of the soul
    at the twilight summoning of angels.
That's why I bridged the winds, by-passed the times,   5
    and in landscapes where my roots
meet dawn's I wandered, in the quarters of
    oblivion, inquiring of men and others
lit by river-lotuses, on whom the lilies shine.
    And I raised you in triumph from the dead   10
naked in pride's embrace that I might worship you,
    and see you on the Doric altars of my music
that my days might prosper, though I'm counted poor
    because I spurn the trinkets others wear.

(1985)

A. D. Hope
PYRAMIS or THE HOUSE OF ASCENT

This is their image: the desert and the wild,
A lone man digging, a nation piling stones
Under the lash in fear, in sweat, in haste;
Image of those demonic minds who build
To outlast time, spend life to house old bones—   5
This pyramid rising squarely in the waste!

I think of the great work, its secret lost;
The solid, blind, invincible masonry
Still challenges the heart. Neglect and greed
Have left it void and ruin; sun and frost   10
Fret it away; yet, all foretold, I see
The builder answering: 'Let the work proceed!'

I think of how the work was hurried on:
Those terrible souls, the Pharaohs, those great Kings
Taking, like genius, their prerogative   15
Of blood, mind, treasure: 'Tomorrow I shall be gone;
If you lack slaves, make war! The measure of things
Is man, and I of men. By this you live.'

No act of time limits the procreant will
And to subdue men seems a little thing,   20
Seeing that in another world than this
The gods themselves unwilling await him still
And must be overcome; for thus the King
Takes, for all men, his apotheosis.

I think of other pyramids, not in stone,   25
The great, incredible monuments of art,
And of their builders, men who put aside
Consideration, dared, and stood alone,
Strengthening those powers that fence the failing heart:
Intemperate will and incorruptible pride.   30

The man alone digging his bones a hole;
The pyramid in the waste—whose images?
Blake's tower of vision defying the black air;
Milton twice blind groping about his soul
For exit, and Swift raving mad in his—   35
The builders of the pyramid everywhere!

(1955)

Gwen Harwood
'THOUGHT IS SURROUNDED BY A HALO'

—Ludwig Wittgenstein, *Philosophical Investigations* 97

Show me the order of the world,
the hard-edge light of this-is-so
prior to all experience
and common to both world and thought,
no model, but the truth itself.   5

    Language is not a perfect game,
    and if it were, how could we play?
    The world's more than the sum of things
    like moon, sky, centre, body, bed,
    as all the singing masters know.   10

    Picture two lovers side by side
    who sleep and dream and wake to hold
    the real and the imagined world
    body by body, word by word
    in the wild halo of their thought.   15

(1974)

Robert Adamson
TOWARDS ABSTRACTION/
POSSIBLY A GULL'S WING

The most disconcerting feature
is an absolute flatness,
especially the sand.

I've been here in love, and having
passed the perfectly calm ocean,   5

had only noticed the terns.

If there was some way back,
some winding-track to follow I might possibly
discover the elusive spirits.

As now, for instance, I'm completely   10
indifferent to the sad way
that fellow moves over the sand.

What way, who moves? ah, let's be pure
in observation, let us drop opinions.
Look, he stops, and throwing off his towel,   15
runs into the surf

where stroking out, he attracts the terns
and they curve above him.

Now look back to the beach,
it is mid-winter, the sand's deserted   20
and eddies of wind-caught grit

dance and fall about unhindered.

At the far end of the beach is a protruding object,
a rusty rifle—He comes out
from the surf, stubbing his toes   25

heading towards the place
where the rifle lies melting in salt-air.

Sand whispers under his feet as he bypasses it.
Dazed, he goes off in no particular direction.

The surf rolls a dead tern onto the sand   30
and he kicks it, wings unfold

like a fan, sea-lice fall from sepia feathers
and the feathers catch fire.

                                                          (1970)

Finola Moorhead
from THE LANDSCAPE OF THE EGG

1

There is an egg-cup behind the breastbone. It is a space of loneliness where there are vast plains and winds of their own accord reach the vibration of sound. Winds moan over the plains in this space of silence, which experiences certain weather conditions. It has an unearthly climate. Inside the upper torso, no larger than an egg, it is, for me, the seat of writing—a space of loneliness, a space of silence. [. . .]

3

Then language itself is like a shell. It surrounds rather than is the something that is. It's very symbiotic all this, open to horrific arguments and kidnappings of all kinds. But i cannot wriggle out of it by saying, indeed claiming, that, *for me*, language surrounds, language hints, language holds something else. i cannot do that, say, 'for me'. i cannot be right if i make a definition of language to suit me alone. That is a travesty of language.

For while the space of loneliness, the little potent area of unearthly climate, may be the seat of writing, for me, the words and concepts it bears forth in its primeval-like swamp are belonging to all, already.

Giving fresh birth to the already there, is this one of the dilemmas of language in its creative mode?

To make the thing an artefact in the materials of language, we use words that are understandable. Aye. Eeey. They are understandable because they are already known. They belong to the reader as much as to the writer.

Words are stolen from the common coffers by the poets, used and given back. Taken for a joy-ride. Unlike the loaves and fishes, the nature of their constant multiplication requires no miracle.

A joy-ride is a performance, an event, loaves and fishes are food. Anything, like anything, can be a metaphor for language, while language itself might be entirely metaphorical.

4

Wouldn't it be lovely to dissolve the impasse by stating, blandly, with a blush of transcendental bliss, that language is mysterious. To claim for writers that they are adepts to a mystery, transmuted Delphic oracles, priestesses of the verbal temple.

i am not speaking here of what language is to men. They made the ploughshare into a weapon; they did the same to language. i am speaking of women writers and their (y)our dilemmas in relation to language. We all know we are working with hand-me-down used and abused words for the most part. Men can try and clean them up, if they have the heart; remodel the weapons they've made back into tools of agriculture for the benefit of the earth. It's a big and boring job, and only a few ever bother to do it.

No, for women, it's the echo of silence in language. The question of silence, as the Dutch woman's movie posed it. The love of silence, as the music of the unsaid experienced in the egg-cup behind the breastbone that is given in the arrangement of words and sentences is what i am most concerned with or excited by, when i'm talking of writing. [...]

6

Yes, i like the bazaar image of women's writing. It is not factory stuff. It has not a mint condition sameness about it. One warms to the awkwardness in it, often, as if it truly were hand-done at home with secondhand materials, like a quilt made from remnants, a mat woven from torn strips of unwearable clothes, a patchwork bolero, a papier-mâché sculpture, a bubbly jumper knitted up from unravelled wools, a painted egg. i like these images very much, for how cheap and practical, how original and inventive, for the optimum creativity and skill, the humour and the 'amateurism'.

For they're like our work, rich in creativity and care, impoverished in terms of materials. We must work with very old and worn stuff, the language of our culture. Each one of us must do it differently, choose which old bits to use, what to make, how much time to put into it, whether to play with a formula or recreate lost forms.

You couldn't get more of a variety of styles. . .
all echoing
the same enchantment
of the chord
in the windswept
exiled space
inside—

7

You don't believe me. You can't believe it. She's romanticising again. She's being quasi-spiritual, and that is such a pain. Doesn't she know how cynical we've become? The wheels of this particular vehicle are egg-shaped, oval. Its movement is eccentric, handicapped—awfully uncomfortable.

Women hear everything, even the farthest, whispered criticism. The wind carries it right here, to the place behind the breastbone. And the criticism appears to come from within.

(1985)

Sylvia Kantaris
THE TENTH MUSE

My muse in not one of the nine nubile
daughters of Mnemosyne
in diaphanous nightshifts
with names that linger in the air
like scent of jasmine or magnolia   5
on Mediterranean nights.
Nor was any supple son of Zeus appointed
to pollinate my ear with poppy dust
or whispers of sea-spray.
My muse lands with a thud   10
like a sack of potatoes.
He has no aura.
The things he grunts are things
I'd rather not hear.
His attitude is 'Take it or leave it, that's   15
the way it is,' drumming his fingers
on an empty pan by way of music.
If I were a man I would enjoy
such grace and favour,

tuning my fork to Terpsichore's lyre,   20
instead of having to cope with this dense
late-invented eunuch
with no more pedigree than the Incredible Hulk,
who can't play a note
and keeps repeating 'Women   25
haven't got the knack'
in my most delicately strung and scented ear.

                                                    (1983)

Marion Campbell
from LINES OF FLIGHT

She is trying to develop a looser gestural style in these urban graffiti
drawings, working along to free jazz on the little cassette player, letting it
work through her and counter-acting it. He leaves his final draft and pokes
a wincing, loose-lipped face through the kitchen door. *Mais Rita, enfin!*
Figure-toi un peu! Just imagine trying to do academic work against that! It
might be all right with that libidinous stuff you are doing. *Ce genre*
d'expression pulsionnelle, he said.

She turns the Miles Davis off immediately. Lips pressed grimly. Almost a
pleasure in the austerity of martyrdom, the undercurrent of the rhetoric
she denies herself simply playing at her speech organs: You bastard, here I
am involved in the most Vicious Games of Capitalism at Publikon to get
some degree of autonomy—for us both—let you forget your Material
Situation so you can do your Intellectual Work; who found this place
anyhow on her own initiative and who pays the rent, you seem to think
that topping up the kitty every now and again with a few francs scrounged
from your parents is enough to share the load and set the rules of the place
and play Master when visitors come and all the time I say nothing. You
say to them: Yeah, we had quite a find, must admit I've always been lucky
in that way. And you make all the decisions on the decoration, decide
which of my paintings are *convenable* and which are too disquieting and I
say nothing. And now the aggressive rattle of the typewriter has resumed,
charging and recharging and even if I found time to work (what about my
deadline for Julienne towels?) I'd have to fight for a half-hour slot because,
after all, your Discourse Analysis is more important but only yesterday
you expressed surprise that I hadn't taken on more work this month.

Of course this is all petty and unreasonable: it's only because she's
clenched against him that she can't think against his noise. He is oblivious
to these little concerns and look who is thinking now that lunchtime is
coming up and that she'd better do something about it, make maybe a
salade niçoise and a mushroom omelette and that she'd better pack up her
gouaches. He shuts the door on her in the kitchen so that if anyone comes,
she's the one who is disturbed. Even if it's one of his own friends, he hisses
through the crack of the door: Rita, tell him that I'm on the last lap and
that I can't spare a moment and so she ends up trapped there, chatting

desultorily to some stranger who has no particular place to go and who offers her a capricious analysis of her work in progress. Here is Sébastien now asking whether she has thought about lunch.

She says: Yes, that's why I'm packing up my paints, what do you think?

You're crazy to worry, we could go to the Resto-U. I feel like a break anyhow.

But the long walk there or waiting for buses would make just one more hole in her time: Really, it's no trouble, she says. I've already chopped the mushrooms.

Then she goes down for bread and cheese and ends up washing up because, after all, she was the one who insisted on eating in the flat. Now, at three in the afternoon, when she has managed to resume painting, he wants to wash. She has his gaze from the sink where he is splashing jugsful of water over his noble body, interfering with her brush, her painted space. Or when it's her in the tub, he'll burst into the kitchen from the landing; this was a quick, mechanically executed wash she was having, but now it's being assessed as performance and sexual invitation. *Oh que c'est déli-cieux*, he says and cups her soapy buttocks¯in his hands, tries the con-sistency of the flesh and says: Oh-oh, Rita, you'd better watch out! You're actually starting to get some cellulite!

Once again, she is exposure of junkety flesh for his teasing analysis.

She tightens her muscles, tightens her throat, eats less, even though she would defy him by becoming fat. Even her painting arranges itself against his premature scrutiny. It is becoming cramped now. Or else too full of nervy attempts made too late to loosen it. Over-painted. She hears him whistling up the stairs and a mad heart jumps within her, her pulse races and she defends the painting with one annihilating swipe of the turps rag. The paintings gelled in the foetal folds of that rag, the weight of them. And then, at night, his day having been uninterrupted by idle visits and petty domestic concerns, he will stretch in the frame of the kitchen door, grunt and give that prolonged yawn of satisfaction. Just as she is setting herself up again after the washing up and taking down the garbage for the morning collection: Ah, Rita, not bad going today, got ten pages done. I'm really starting to think I'll make it!

His heavy hand works the tense muscles of her neck, *Ah ma chérie*, he says. Of course, she thinks, of course he is innocent of the prisons she secretes around herself. The smell of his salty dark skin dilates her, her hand releases the brush. They are rolling together on the bed; laughter in the tumble of canopy and cushions.

At midnight she slips from under the weight of his thigh, sheltering, not possessive, she thinks this time, but there is a groan, as if in sleep he knew her abandonment as she creeps back for some criminal activity in the kitchen. Maybe this is just perversity. Maybe she can only work through a sense of transgression. He recognizes that aspect of her painting, covets the energies he berates only half-jokingly as onanistic, developing and exploiting an excess not released in their sex together. There it is, develop-ing a tenuous line, multiplying its knots and folds now into a billowing colour field, as if some atavistic repository had been tapped, unfolding within her and at last she feels something more collective, something beyond the accidents of her specific womanhood. She will snarl and hiss if necessary to defend this chance, this space.

(1985)

Dal Stivens
THE GENTLE BASILISK

An orphan basilisk grew up alone in an African desert. He was innocent of his true malevolent nature and regarded himself—when he thought of himself at all—as an ordinary kind of serpent and not very different from the vipers with whom he shared the desert.

He was a gentle little serpent, aesthetically dispositioned and given to sniffing the flowers of the hardy desert shrubs; he was unaware that mature basilisks have breaths so poisonous they blast shrubs and burst stones asunder. Accordingly, his surprise was great when one day in young manhood he smelt one of his favourite shrubs and saw it wither under his bulging eyes.

'Astonishing!' he cried and breathed exploringly on a neighbouring shrub. It died in seconds. 'I did it, then,' said the gentle basilisk. He was so shocked he burst into tears. He retired into a cave and stayed there for three days. On the fourth he crawled out and wriggled determinedly across the desert.

'I'll seek the help of the holy man who lives in the Blue Cave,' said the young basilisk, averting his head as he approached a shrub. 'He is a wise man and may well know how to help me.'

The ancient monk listened to the basilisk and shook his head.

'There's nothing I can do,' he said. 'You are as God made you. It is not for me to doubt the wisdom of the Almighty in creating basilisks with malevolent breaths—' here the hermit scratched his bald, scaling head— 'though sometimes I almost entertain blasphemous doubts. If you were a human being with a soul, I could baptize you and enjoin you to seek salvation. But it's clear you have no soul though your sentiments of not wishing to blast trees and burst boulders asunder—'

'Trees and stones,' corrected the basilisk modestly.

'Trees and stones,' said the holy man. 'Your sentiments do your heart honour. I'm inclined to think you may have been born into a pagan state of grace—'

Here the hermit broke off in dismay at his words and crossed himself hurriedly. He resumed, 'My son, be patient and accept your lot—and, pray you, continue to keep your head averted while I give you the benefit of such wisdom as the years have brought me. It is not for you to change your lot. That has been determined.'

'Venerable father, I should like to accept your advice,' said the young basilisk, 'but I have heard it said it is possible to lift oneself by one's own shoestrings if the will is great enough—and, of course, if one wore any shoes.'

'My son, it is no more possible for you to change your physical nature than it is for that gnat which I see hovering over you.'

In that instant, the gnat perched on the basilisk's neck and stung him. The basilisk started violently, turned his head and wheezed painfully. The ancient withered into ashes.

The basilisk contemplated the tiny grey heap with tears in his eyes. 'I am sorry it happened to him for he was a good man and meant well though I did not find his philosophy attractive. It could be argued his fate was predestined. He would not have wished it otherwise.' And then added, 'Boy, did you see how swiftly he went into a crisp!'

The young basilisk set off for the Yellow Cave where he knew there dwelt an alchemist.

'I should have approached him instead of that determinist,' he told himself.

The alchemist listened to the young basilisk's story and burst into laughter when he heard of the fate of the hermit.

'Every dogma has its day even if it's a short one,' he said 'Don't worry, my boy, we'll soon cure you. Every poison has its antidote. Just be careful to keep your head turned away.'

The alchemist paced up and down the cave. 'I'll soon have the answer. Anything is possible in nature. Man has merely to find the key to uncover all secrets.'

He gestured. 'Behold that great stack of dross lead, my boy. Any day now I'll turn it into the purest of gold.' The alchemist shrugged and flung out both hands. 'Why should there be any difficulty in solving your little problem, my boy?'

'None at all,' said the young basilisk. 'Unless—'

'Unless nothing!' said the alchemist contemptuously. 'Your breath is poisonous. Find the antidote. Simple as ABC. I'll start with the premise that your breath is alkaline.'

The alchemist poured a smoking liquid from a bottle into a spoon. 'This is an acid and could well be the antidote. Swallow it down.'

'It looks as though it might burn me,' said the young basilisk doubtfully.

'Come, my boy, where's your love of experiment? Down with it. It can't burn you. Basilisks are invulnerable—or nearly so.'

'As you wish,' said the young basilisk uncertainly. 'But what's this "invulnerable" business?'

'I see you are not merely timid but uneducated,' said the alchemist. 'Basilisks can't be poisoned. They can be slain by a knight but only if he is fortunate enough to avoid their evil breath.'

'Invulnerable, just fancy that!' exclaimed the young basilisk joyfully.

'Let's waste no more time,' said the alchemist and put the spoon down on the floor of the cave and stepped back. The young basilisk crawled towards it and sipped cautiously.

The acid stung his lips, tears blinded his eyes, and he tossed his head round in agony. 'It burns,' he protested through blistered lips. 'You said it wouldn't hurt.' The young basilisk threshed about for half a minute and then demanded, 'Why don't you answer me, hey?'

His eyes cleared and he saw a small heap of ashes. The basilisk blinked. 'I'm sorry it happened but he was unpractical and obviously brought it on himself by his cocksureness.' He appraised the heap of ashes. 'Golly, I crisped him to a smaller heap than the hermit!'

The young basilisk wriggled away. He had gone only a short distance when he was challenged by an armoured knight who drew down his visor and couched his lance.

'A moment, I pray you, sir knight,' cried the young basilisk. 'I am not at all what you think I am. I am a basilisk with a gentle disposition and a genuine lover of shrubs and even boulders.'

'Prepare yourself, basilisk!' said the knight sternly. 'I am a plain man with no time for words.'

'I beg you to believe me, sir knight. Although my breath is poisonous, I would not harm any tree, crag, or living man. Indeed, I wish to render innocuous my malevolent breath.'

'Wishes aren't achievements,' said the knight shortly. 'I treat things as I find them. I am a practical man. You are a basilisk. Basilisks have venomous breaths. Basilisks should be destroyed.'

'But I wish no harm to any man,' said the basilisk.

'That is what you say now,' said the knight. 'But you have the power to blast shrubs and split stones and power—as I have heard a wise man say—power corrupts. Look to yourself, basilisk!'

And shouting, 'God be my guide', the knight drove the spurs into his horse and bore down on the basilisk. The serpent waited fearfully. Sweat started from between his scales. His heart beat rapidly. He panted and called piteously to the knight that it was unnecessary to slay this basilisk whatever others might be.

The knight thudded up to the little serpent, steel lance tip thrusting down, gleaming in the sun. Suddenly the lance head flickered with dancing blue flames. Blue fire raced up the shaft. The knight's suit shone red and blue-white. The horse dissolved into tumbling ashes. The incandescent suit of armour clanked into the horse's ashes.

'Golly!' cried the astonished basilisk. 'It was terrific! I get more and more malevolent, it seems.'

He wriggled away, meditatively slow. 'It seems I cannot escape my nature no matter how I wish it.' He gazed contemplatively at a large boulder. 'I wonder what I could do to that?' He filled his cheeks and blew hard. The great rock split with a roar.

'Oh boy!' cried the young basilisk exultantly. 'Did you see that?' He looked around him. 'Let's see what I can do to that oak.' He puffed hard. The oak shivered and then flew apart with a tumult of sound.

'I must be the most malevolent of all basilisks,' he cried wonderingly. 'What did that knight say about power? To hell with him! Now look at that mountain over there...and that army of knights at its foot. I wonder what I could do to them?'

The basilisk scratched his chin on a stone and then set off determinedly towards the flapping pennants.

(1957–8)

Elizabeth Jolley
WOMAN IN A LAMPSHADE

One cold wet night in July Jasmine Tredwell took several sheets of paper and her typewriter together with a quantity of simple food and some respectable wine and, saying good-night fondly to her dozing husband, she set off in search of solitude.

'I'm going up to the farm,' she said, 'I'll be home first thing on Monday morning,' she promised. But her husband, Emeritus Professor of Neo Byzantine Art, was encased in head-phones listening to Mahler and paid no attention to the departure.

It was not her custom to give lifts to strangers. Indeed, because of reported bashings and murders in lonely suburbs, she had, in an impulsively tender moment, promised the elderly Professor that she would never pick up from the roadside any stranger however pathetic or harmless his appearance.

She saw the young man standing in the dark. He seemed to be leaning rather than standing, the storm holding him up in its force. He was an indistinct outline, blurred because of the rain. It was as if he had come into existence simply because someone, hopelessly lost among words, had created him in thoughtful ink on the blotting paper. Immediately, forgetting her promise, she stopped the car and, leaning over, opened the door with some difficulty.

'Hop in quick young man, you're getting drowned!'

The grateful youth slipped quickly into the warm and secure fragrance. He tried, without success, not to mark the clean upholstery with the water as it ran off him in dirty little streams. Jasmine took the hills noisily, the windscreen wipers flying to and fro flinging off the splashings as if the car boasted small fountains on either side.

'Thanks,' he said, 'thanks a lot.'

'Such a terrible night,' she said, 'are you going far?'

'As far as I can get.'

'Where shall I drop you?'

'Oh, anywhere. It'll do if you drop me off when you've gone as far as you're going.' He gave a nervous little laugh. 'Tah very much,' he said. 'Thank you very much, tah!'

That the young man had no definite destination did not cause Jasmine to wish that she had not stopped to offer him a ride. They hardly spoke. Almost at once Jasmine was touched to notice that her youthful travelling companion had fallen asleep.

'He must have been exhausted,' she thought and she wondered about his ragged soaked clothes. 'He's probably hungry too,' she said to herself.

Jasmine felt safe in the lamplight. And she felt safe in the lampshade, pretty too. She was not a pretty woman, she never pretended to be. But the lampshade, when she put it on, made her feel pretty, softly so and feminine. It was the colour of ripe peaches and made of soft pleats of silk. It was light and it fitted her perfectly. It was like a garden-party hat only more foolish because it was, after all, a lampshade. To wear the lampshade suggested the dangerous and the exotic while still sheltered under a cosy domesticity.

She never guessed the first time she placed it on her head how she would feel. She had never experienced such a feeling before. It had taken her by surprise. After that first time she had looked with shy curiosity at other women in shops and at parties, at the hairdresser's and even while passing them in the street, quietly noticing the private things about them, the delicate shaping of the back of the neck or the imaginative tilt of the ears. She wondered too about all the tiny lines and folds and creases, all the secret things. So recently having discovered something about herself, she wondered what secret pleasures they had and whether they had known them long before she had discovered hers.

She sang softly,

> *I love my little lampshade*
> *So frilly and warm*
> *If I wear my silky lampshade*
> *I'll come to no harm.*

'Are you awake?' she asked the young man later that night. He was buried under a heap of old fur coats and several spoiled pages.

'Are you awake? Hey! Are you awake? God? how soundly you sleep! It's being young, I suppose, hey! wake up!'

'What's that? What the...?' he hardly moved.

'Young man, could you move over a bit, my typewriter's falling off my knee, it's giving me the most awful cramp. Also I'm getting a pain in my back. Ah! that's better. No, no further or you'll fall out. That'll do beautifully. Hey!' she laughed, pleased with the music of her own voice, 'don't roll back! You know, if you lie on the edge of the bed, you'll soon drop off!'

He drew the coats closer and made no sound.

'That was supposed to be a joke,' she said noisily rearranging the papers. 'But seriously,' she said, 'it's like this, I've got a young man, he's a bit of a nuisance really. First he's in a suburban post office in Australia. Can you imagine him behind the counter with his pale offended eyes about to burst into tears and all the little veins and capillaries flushed on his crooked boyish face, or something like that?

'Then he turns up again in a depressing hotel in Calais where two lesbians have gone to have a bit of privacy. The younger one wants to get away from her husband and the older one is the husband's secretary, a really boring stuffy old maid. She's quite empty headed and very irritating to be with for more than a few minutes as the younger one discovers quite quickly. In addition, the secretary, the boring one, drinks heavily and is not really very clean. An unfortunate situation altogether. Anyway, my young man's there at the hotel reception desk, in the night, being absolutely useless.'

'Who?' the voice muffled in furs could hardly be heard.

'My young man of course,' Jasmine, preening, fingered her peach-ripe silk pleats lovingly. 'He's left the PO to be a hotel receptionist in Calais,' she continued, 'And then, to my surprise, he moves to a cheap hotel in India, Madras to be exact, and I've got him there exactly the same, the pale offended eyes filled with tears, the same blushing capillaries, perhaps he's a bit thinner, more haunted looking and, as usual, he's no earthly use,' Jasmine sighed sadly. 'He's absolutely unable to help the guests when they arrive exhausted in the night. It's two more lesbians, younger than the others and one is very uncomfortable with an unmentionable infection. Not a very nice subject really but, as a writer, I have to look closely at *Life* and every aspect of it.' Jasmine sighed again thoughtfully, her long fingers reaching up restlessly plucked the folds of unexpected foolishness.

'*C'est un triste métier*,' she knew her pronunciation was flawless. 'In all the stories,' she said, 'one of the women is horrible to my young man. Absolutely horrible! I mean one in all three. So that's three times he has a really bad time, in all, he's despised, rejected and betrayed. But I'm glad to say that on all occasions the awful unkind behaviour is deeply regretted as soon as the resulting wretchedness is evident.'

'What's the trouble?' the young man sat up and yawned almost dislocating his lower jaw.

Jasmine banged her typewriter.

'Can't you understand, I'm stuck! I'm stuck, stuck, stuck.' She shuffled the papers across the bed. 'Oh by the way,' she said as calmly as she could, 'would you mind not smoking in bed. My husband can't stand it.'

'He's not here is he?' the young man began uneasily, 'you said, I thought...'

'No of course not,' Jasmine said, 'but the smoke hangs around and he's very sensitive, his nose I mean.' She laughed. 'But,' she said, 'whatever shall I do with them?'

'Who?'

'My characters of course. I suppose,' she paused, 'I suppose they could carry on in bed.' She began to type rapidly.

'Eh? Yeah!' He turned over.

'Mind the typewriter! Oops! I thought it was gone that time. That's better. You know I must tell you I've got a friend, Moira, well she's not a friend really, more of an enemy. Writers don't have any friends.' She settled comfortably against her mountain of pillows. 'Well Moira's trying to get a psychiatric musical off the ground. God! That woman's a Bore when she talks about her work. She never stops talking! All last week she was on about an official speech she'd been asked to write for the ceremonial opening of a deep sewerage system, I mean what is there in deep sewerage?'

'Quite a lot I should think,' he yawned again. 'Have you got going now?'

'No, not at all, it's awful!' she pulled another spoiled page from her typewriter. 'I'm afraid,' she said watching the paper as it floated to the floor, 'I'm afraid, well, you must feel so trapped and cheated. I mean, being here with me in this lonely place. Just think! I brought you all this way and then everything happening like that!'

'What d'you mean, happening,' he said patiently, 'I mean nothing has yet, has it?'

'I didn't expect my young man and the lesbians...'

'I thought they was in Madras,' he interrupted.

'Yes, yes that's right, so they should be, but my young man...'

'Well, where is he then? I thought the idea was we'd be having the place to ourselves and I'd work the farm and—' a note of disappointment replaced the impatience in his voice.

'It's such a nuisance,' Jasmine replied. 'Really I'm sorry. I was so looking forward, you know, to our getting to know each other and,' she paused, 'and there he is, stupid and useless!'

'Who? Where is he?' he sat up.

'In my brief-case. Would you mind awfully? I left it just outside in the porch, I'd be so grateful it you would.'

Reluctantly he looked at the cold floor.

'No stop!' Jasmine cried. 'Stay where you are in the warm. I must be mad! I'm the one who should go. It's my fault he's out there. I should go. I'm going out to get him. You stay in bed. I'm going!'

Jasmine slipped from the bed and pattered with quick bare feet over the boards. He heard the outside door open and slam shut. He heard the noise of plates and cups and cutlery, a plate dropped somewhere crashing and breaking.

'What's that? Who's there?' he called.

'It's nothing,' she replied through a mouthful of food, 'nothing at all to worry about. I'm just having a cheese sandwich.' She came to the bedside. 'Would you like some or are you the kind of person who doesn't like eating in bed? I've sliced up an onion and a hard-boiled egg. Do have some!'

'No thank you,' he said. 'I'm not hungry really no; no thank you, really not hungry thanks all the same.'

Jasmine ate ravenously.

'Have some Burgundy,' she said, 'or would you prefer a beer?' She poured a generous glass of wine for herself and opened a can for her guest.

'Just move over a bit,' she said with her mouth full, 'thanks.' She chewed and swallowed, 'I'm sorry, really I am,' she said, 'about these papers all over the bed. I'd like to be able to make it up to you in some way. You see I should never have picked you up. When I saw you at the side of the road absolutely drenched I simply couldn't help offering you a lift.' She studied the remains of the egg apparently lost in thoughts for which there were no words. 'Ever since I decided to become a writer,' she announced, 'I've been an absolute Pain! You hardly know me really. I mean, take tonight, I've been perfectly terrible. Please, please don't try to contradict me.'

In the silence of his obedience he hiccupped.

'Manners!' he apologized.

'Oh dear!' Jasmine was dismayed. 'Perhaps you shouldn't drink beer in bed. My husband always gets hiccups if he drinks lying down. Try walking about.'

He was not inclined to leave the bed.

'Well,' Jasmine said, 'if you're shy put this old nighty on. You walk about and I'll think up a fright for you.'

Self-conscious and solemn in brushed nylon the young man paced to and fro on the creaking floor boards. He hiccupped at regular intervals. Every minute his thin body jerked.

'Manners!' he muttered, and one minute later, 'Manners!'

Suddenly she screamed, 'Help! Help!'

'What the, who's there? Where the hell are you?' he hiccupped. 'Manners!'

'Help! Hellup!'

He hiccupped, 'Manners! Where the hell are you?'

'Under the bed silly! Help me out there's not much space.' She was out of breath. 'Such a pity it didn't work.' In the brief silence he hiccupped again.

'Look out!' she whispered. 'Look out! There's a spider behind you. A great black spider. S.P.I.D.E.R. Look behind you!'

'Manners! What? I can't hear you. Manners!'

'Oh, it's no good. You'll simply have to wait till they wear off.' She was just the tiniest bit sulky. 'I really can't help it,' she said, adjusting the lampshade with one delicate finger, 'if He visits me in the middle of the night.'

'Who? Here? Who visits you?' He began to search through the heap of furs. 'Where's my clothes? I'd better be off. Look, I shouldn't be here.'

Jasmine laughed. 'Oh relax! The Muse of course,' she said, 'perhaps I should say My Muse.' She paused. 'It's very amusing really. Oh!' Her laughter was like a shower of broken glass. 'Oh!' she said, 'I made a pun there. I wonder if I could use it somewhere in here, let me see.' She rearranged several of the papers. She laughed again. 'You look so serious walking up and down in that tatty old gown.' He turned to look at her seriously and steadily.

'I've been wondering what's that, I mean, what's that on your head?'

'It's a lampshade,' she replied.

'If you don't mind my arskin', why do you?'

'Always when I'm writing,' her voice was deep with reverence.

'But I thought we was going to have it away together.'

'Yes,' Jasmine said, 'I thought so too but it's my young man—'

'The one who was in all those places?'

'Yes.'

'Oh, I see,' he paused and said in a flat voice, 'praps I'd better go then.'

'Oh no,' Jasmine said, 'there's absolutely no need. I know,' she said, 'let's dance! My little transistor's here somewhere. I know it's here, somewhere here.' She rummaged among the bear skins and the ancient silver fox. 'Ah! here we are. If we danced, you never know, it might be better. I'll just see if I can get some music. Ah good! here's music. Listen there's a dancing teacher too. What a scream!'

The pulse of the music noticeably caused life to return and the dancing instructor's voice flowed quietly bringing shape and order into the disordered room.

'Now for the stylized step. Starting position,' the Irish voice was kind, 'beat one step up beat two step together beat three step back beat four step together up together back together and up together and back together arms loose relax and smile.'

'Come on!' Jasmine was laughing.

'I don't dance. Really, I don't dance.'

'Oh come on!'

'Not on beds. I don't dance on beds. It's too dangerous and, besides, it's rude.'

Jasmine laughing and breathless reached out and turned the volume on more.

There was a change in the music.

'Now the basic camel walk and step and kick and camel walk,' the instructor's patient voice continued. 'Beat one stub left beat two stub right

beat three stub left beat four stub right beat five stub left beat six kick left
beat seven stub right beat eight and kick and kick that's just fine you'll
make it in time beat one stub left beat two stub right think happy and
relax beat three stub left beat four stub right that's great you're great the
greatest!'

Jasmine fell off the bed with a crash.

'And now the Latin Hustle,' the dancing instructor's persistent voice
changed rhythm as the music changed. 'Touch and one and two and step
back three and four forward five and six repeat touch and one and two
and step and one and two and one.'

'Now you've properly done it!' The young man fell over the furniture.
'You've knocked over the light. Have you broke it? It's pitch dark!' He
stumbled again, knocking over a chair. 'Where are you?' he shouted. 'It's
pitch black dark. Yo' must 'ave broke the lamp.'

'Over here!' Jasmine sang, teasing through the music and the darkness.

'Where's the matches?' Panic made him angry.

'Yoo hoo! Here I am,' Jasmine was beside him, and then she was far
away. 'I'm over here,' she called, and suddenly she was close again. Both
were breathing heavily, gasping even, furniture fell and crockery crashed
as if something was rocking the cottage. Jasmine was laughing and
laughing, pleased and excited.

'Oh go on,' she cried. 'Don't stop!' she pleaded.

'Repeat these movements till you feel comfortable and confident in your
performance,' the dancing instructor's voice, keeping time perfectly, pene-
trated above and below the sound of the music. 'Follow the beat sequence
and turn and turn repeat and turn and repeat,' his patience was endless.

'I'm going outside,' the young man was polite and strained. 'If you'll
excuse me,' he said, 'I'll 'ave to go outside.'

'Yes, yes of course,' Jasmine said, 'Just through the yard and up the
back you can't miss.'

'Thanks,' he let the door slam. 'Sorry!' he called.

'You'll make it in time,' the dancing master's voice consoled. 'Try once
more beat one stub left beat two stub right.'

Jasmine switched off her tiny radio. She was laughing softly, breathlessly: 'Now where's the other lamp and the matches? Ah! here they are.'

In the soft light she made herself comfortable with three pillows at her
back. She began to type rapidly.

'My story just needs a bit of action,' she said.

A gun shot sounded close by, it was followed by a second shot.

'Splendid!' Jasmine said. 'That's just what I needed. Now I know what
happens next.' She continued to type. 'He'd better do it at once. But not in
Madras. He'd better get on a 'plane quickly.' Her typewriter rattled on.
'Oh well to save time he can do it at the airport.' She read aloud what she
had written in the mincing tones reserved for her work. *Quietly he took
the jewelled pistol from its silky case and held it to his pale crooked
forehead. His eyes were full of tears...*' She changed her voice. 'That's a
nice touch, the crooked forehead, what exquisite writing. I've never written so well before.' She read again in the special voice, as she typed,
Closing his eyes, he pulled the trigger...'

The young man came in. He hiccupped.

'Oh my God!' said Jasmine. 'What happened?'

'I missed both times,' his voice was flat.

'Oh what a nuisance. So you're still here.' She pulled the page from her typewriter and crumpled it in her hand.

'Of course I'm still here. Where should I be?'

'But the shots,' Jasmine interrupted, 'I thought—'

'Oh that! I tried to get a rabbit but it was too quick,' he gave a shy laugh. 'I've never pointed a gun at anything before.'

'Useless, absolutely useless,' Jasmine was exasperated, 'you've muffed the whole thing. You muffed it. Can't you do anything properly.'

'I don't know,' he was almost tearful, 'I've never had the chance.'

'I suppose you've never tried for long enough,' she said.

'I would be able to if I stayed here. I—' he was eager. 'I've had a look out there. I like your place. It's just beginning to get light out there, I could see all the things that need doing. I'll fix the fence posts and paint the sheds. I think I know what's up with the tractor, I'll be able to get it going. There's all the things I'd like to do out there.' He paused and then rushed on, 'on the way up here in the car you said I could stay and work the farm, you said you needed someone like me.'

'You never stay anywhere long enough, you said so yourself.' She put a fresh sheet in the typewriter.

'Well it's not my fault. Like I said, "I've had no chance."'

'What do you do?' Jasmine asked.

'What d'you mean?'

Outside a rooster crowed.

'Oh never mind!' Jasmine yawned. 'I suppose you're, how do they describe it,' she paused, 'discovering yourself.'

'I'm between jobs,' he shouted, 'That's where I've always been, between jobs. Between jobs. Between nothing!' he paused.

'But out there,' he was breathless and excited, 'I saw it all out there waiting to be done, there's everything to do out there. I'll fix everything, you'll see.'

'We like it as it is,' Jasmine said. 'My husband and I like it as it is, we don't want any change.'

'There's even a turkey yard,' he interrupted her, 'you'd like some turkeys wouldn't you, the yard only needs a bit of new wire netting. I'd have some fowls too.'

'But don't you understand,' Jasmine said, 'we only come here to get away from it all. We like the place as it is. It's only a weekender you know, we like it like this.'

'I'll measure up how much wire,' he ignored her, 'I'll need a bit of paper and a pencil. I'll work out how much paint.'

'Australia, Calais, Madras,' Jasmine said softly, 'what does it matter where I set him, London, New York, Bombay, Paris, Rome, it's all the same wherever he is. What does it matter where he pulls the trigger. First, I'll get him somewhere alone and then I'll kill him off.'

'What's that,' he said quickly, 'what did you say?'

Outside another rooster answered the first one.

'Oh, nothing,' she fussed through her papers. 'I think it's really quite light outside now. There's a bus down at the crossroads about five fifty. It should get you back to town around eight o'clock.' She paused and then said, 'I want you to know I feel really bad about the whole thing. I mean about bringing you all the way to the cottage like this,' she spoke rapidly, 'because of wasting your time like this, and I do feel bad about it, I'm going to give you this poem I've written. You can keep it. I have other copies.'

'Thank you,' he was only just polite, 'thank you very much '

'Fourteen stanzas,' Jasmine crooned, 'fourteen stanzas all with fourteen lines and every one all about my adorable little black poodles.'

'What'll I do,' the young man said, 'when I get to the empty town at eight?'

'There's a little refrain,' Jasmine murmured, 'in the middle of every stanza.'

'What'll I do,' he said, 'when I get to the empty town at eight? I mean where will I go? What can I do there?'

'All the stanzas', she continued, 'have this little refrain to include every one of my little black dogs.'

'I mean,' he said, 'where will I go when I get there? I'd rather stay here and fix the fences. Where will I go? What's there to do in the empty town at eight?' He smiled a moment at his own thoughts. 'You know,' he said, 'there's something good about putting new paint on with a new brush. Dark glossy green, I can just see it out there,' he smiled in the direction of the yard.

'When I wrote the poem,' Jasmine said, 'I knew it was good. I was really pleased with it. It's a good poem. I love my poem.'

'Where will I go in the empty town?' he whined. 'I'll have nothing to eat and nowhere to sleep. Can't I stay and paint the shed? Please?'

'I want everyone to be pleased with the poem,' she said.

'Eight's early to reach town if you've no reason,' he shouted.

'There!' Jasmine smiled, 'I've just thought of a wonderful line for a new poem. I must get it down because I forget everything I think up if I don't get it down.' She began to type, made a mistake, and pulling the spoiled page out, started a fresh page.

'I mean,' the young man cried, 'where will I go when I get there? What's there in town for me to do?'

'I never realized before', Jasmine yawned, 'that my young man in Madras is an absolute Bore!'

He went to the door and opened it. 'Well, I'd better be on my way then,' he said in a quiet flat voice. He went out carefully closing the door behind him.

Jasmine sat in bed writing her autobiography. *My father*, she typed, *was the distinguished scientist who discovered heat and light*. She stopped typing to sing to herself,

> *I love my little lampshade*
> *So frilly and warm*
> *If I wear my silky lampshade*
> *I'll come to no harm.*

He wrote, she typed, *in his lifetime, two text books, the one on light was blue and for heat, he chose red.*

(1980)

Peter Carey
THE LAST DAYS OF A FAMOUS MIME

1

The Mime arrived on Alitalia with very little luggage: a brown paper parcel and what looked like a woman's handbag.

Asked the contents of the brown paper parcel he said, 'String.'

Asked what the string was for he replied: 'Tying up bigger parcels.'

It had not been intended as a joke, but the Mime was pleased when the reporters laughed. Inducing laughter was not his forte. He was famous for terror.

Although his state of despair was famous throughout Europe, few guessed at his hope for the future. 'The string,' he explained, 'is a prayer that I am always praying.'

Reluctantly he untied his parcel and showed them the string. It was blue and when extended measured exactly fifty-three metres.

The Mime and the string appeared on the front pages of the evening papers.

2

The first audiences panicked easily. They had not been prepared for his ability to mime terror. They fled their seats continually. Only to return again.

Like snorkel divers they appeared at the doors outside the concert hall with red faces and were puzzled to find the world as they had left it.

3

Books had been written about him. He was the subject of an award-winning film. But in his first morning in a provincial town he was distressed to find that his performance had not been liked by the one newspaper's one critic.

'I cannot see,' the critic wrote, 'the use of invoking terror in an audience.'

The Mime sat on his bed, pondering ways to make his performance more light-hearted.

4

As usual he attracted women who wished to still the raging storms of his heart.

They attended his bed like highly paid surgeons operating on a difficult case. They were both passionate and intelligent. They did not suffer defeat lightly.

5

Wrongly accused of merely miming love in his private life he was somewhat surprised to be confronted with hatred.

'Surely,' he said, 'if you now hate me, it was you who were imitating love, not I.'

'You always were a slimy bastard,' she said. 'What's in that parcel?'

'I told you before,' he said helplessly, 'string.'

'You're a liar,' she said.

But later when he untied the parcel he found that she had opened it to check on his story. Her understanding of the string had been perfect. She had cut it into small pieces like spaghetti in a lousy restaurant.

6

Against the advice of the tour organizers he devoted two concerts entirely to love and laughter. They were disasters. It was felt that love and laughter were not, in his case, as instructive as terror.

The next performance was quickly announced.

TWO HOURS OF REGRET.

Tickets sold quickly. He began with a brief interpretation of love using it merely as a prelude to regret which he elaborated on in a complex and moving performance which left the audience pale and shaken. In a final flourish he passed from regret to loneliness to terror. The audience devoured the terror like brave tourists eating the hottest curry in an Indian restaurant.

7

'What you are doing,' she said, 'is capitalizing on your neuroses. Personally I find it disgusting, like someone exhibiting their club foot, or Turkish beggars with strange deformities.'

He said nothing. He was mildly annoyed at her presumption: that he had not thought this many, many times before.

With perfect misunderstanding she interpreted his passivity as disdain. Wishing to hurt him, she slapped his face.

Wishing to hurt her, he smiled brilliantly.

8

The story of the blue string touched the public imagination. Small brown paper packages were sold at the doors of his concerts.

Standing on stage he could hear the packages being noisily unwrapped. He thought of American matrons buying Muslim prayer rugs.

9

Exhausted and weakened by the heavy schedule he fell prey to the doubts that had pricked at him insistently for years. He lost all sense of direction and spent many listless hours by himself, sitting in a motel room listening to the airconditioner.

He had lost confidence in the social uses of controlled terror. He no longer understood the audience's need to experience the very things he so desperately wished to escape from.

He emptied the ashtrays fastidiously.

He opened his brown paper parcel and threw the small pieces of string down the cistern. When the torrent of white water subsided they remained floating there like flotsam from a disaster at sea.

10

The Mime called a press conference to announce that there would be no more concerts. He seemed small and foreign and smelt of garlic. The press regarded him without enthusiasm. He watched their hovering pens anxiously, unsuccessfully willing them to write down his words.

Briefly he announced that he wished to throw his talent open to broader influences. His skills would be at the disposal of the people, who would be free to request his services for any purpose at any time.

His skin seemed sallow but his eyes seemed as bright as those on a nodding fur mascot on the back window ledge of an American car.

11

Asked to describe death he busied himself taking Polaroid photographs of his questioners.

12

Asked to describe marriage he handed out small cheap mirrors with MADE IN TUNISIA written on the back.

13

His popularity declined. It was felt that he had become obscure and beyond the understanding of ordinary people. In response he requested easier questions. He held back nothing of himself in his effort to please his audience.

14

Asked to describe an aeroplane he flew three times around the city, only injuring himself slightly on landing.

15

Asked to describe a river, he drowned himself.

16

It is unfortunate that this, his last and least typical performance, is the only one which has been recorded on film.

There is a small crowd by the river bank, no more than thirty people. A small, neat man dressed in a grey suit picks his way through some children who seem more interested in the large plastic toy dog they are playing with.

He steps into the river, which, at the bank, is already quite deep. His head is only visible above the water for a second or two. And then he is gone.

A policeman looks expectantly over the edge, as if waiting for him to reappear. Then the film stops.

Watching this last performance it is difficult to imagine how this man stirred such emotions in the hearts of those who saw him.

(1975)

Michael Wilding
THE WORDS SHE TYPES

Advertised it looked an interesting job: Writer requires intelligent typist. It sounded more interesting than routine copy-typing; and the 'intelligent' held out the bait of some involvement. Amongst dreams had hung one of success as a great writer. Other dreams: but that one had hung there. So she answered.

The appointment required an old apartment block with heavy doors at the entrance, old, varnished wood, that swung to with a heavy oiled smoothness and closed off time at the street.

'What I expect is not difficult,' the writer said; 'accuracy, precision, neatness. And if you succeed in them, perhaps a little more, a little discretion. The initiative to correct, without constant recourse to me, slight carelessnesses of spelling, grammatical solecisms. But let us go along stage by stage and see how we find each other.'

And within the heavy doors, the high-ceilinged still apartment, footfalls deadened on the soft carpet, walls sealed with wooden bookshelves carrying their store of the centuries, the windows double glazed against the sounds and temperatures of the street. And a small table for the tray of coffee or fruit juice or lemon tea to be placed, soundlessly. She missed only music, would have liked the room resonant to rich cadences against the deep polished wood and leather bindings.

She would come to her desk and at the right of the typewriter would be the sheets he had put for her. And as she retyped those sheets she would place them at the left of the typewriter and as soon as she had completed a piece she would collate the sheets and the carbons and leave them in manila folders for him to collect from the drawers at the left of the desk.

The earliest days were easy, copying from typescript. No problems, no uncertainties, no ambiguities. Occasionally he had jammed the keys or jumped a space or missed off the closing quotation mark; but often he had pencilled in the corrections himself. Later, though, perhaps as he became more sure of her, he omitted to make the corrections. And his typing became less punctilious. Words were sometimes misspelt, whether through ignorance or the exigencies of typing it was not for her to ask. He would sometimes use abbreviations, not spelling out a character's name in full but giving only the initial letter. And when he began to give her manuscript sheets to type from the abbreviations increased, the effort of writing out the obvious in longhand too much for him, unnecessary.

And she always managed. It was her pride always to manage, to transliterate from his degenerating scrawl that day by day yearned towards the undifferentiated horizontal, to expand the abbreviations, to fill out the lacunae with their 'he said' or 'she replied'. Her intelligence at last being fulfilled she did not complain of the scrappier sheets that over time were presented to her. Her electric typewriter hummed quietly as ever, nothing retarded her rhythmic pressure on the keys.

He would write instructions in the margin of the drafts. Indications of where to fill out, where to add in, how to expand, interpret. And she would fulfil these instructions, incorporating them into the draft he had roughed out and presenting one whole and finished fabric. And when he offered sheets only of instruction, she knew his manner well enough to develop the sketched out plan as he required.

Was it a shock one morning to find blank sheets on the right of the typewriter? Yet her ready fingers took paper and carbons from their drawer and without hesitation touched the keys. Her eyes read over the characters as they appeared before her.

She read of a girl who saw advertised what looked an interesting job: Writer requires intelligent typist. It sounded more interesting than routine copy-typing: and the 'intelligent' held out the bait of some involvement. Amongst dreams had hung one of success as a great writer. Other dreams: but that one had hung there. So she answered.

Without prompting her fingers touch the keys and tell the story. The girl cannot tell, as she writes this story of herself, if it is indeed of herself. Always the words she has typed have been the words he has presented, suggested, required. But are the words she types now any different from other words she has typed? The girl cannot tell the truth of her situation, because for her to write is to give expression to his stories. Is this but another story she is typing for him, and the truth of her story irrecoverably lost? He has given her no notes from which to tell. And if it is not his story it is even more his story. For if she is telling the story of her story, it was he who established the story. The words she uses will be the words he has set up in sètting up her story, even if they are coincidentally her own words.

She sees only what the keys stamp out on the blank paper before her. If it is her truth no one will know. He will collect the typescript in its manila folder from the drawer on the left, and will publish it whether the words were the words he required or were her words. Readers will read and register amusement or boredom or fascination or disdain, and her truth, if it is her truth, read as fiction will never after be available as truth, whether or not it ever was.

(1975)

REALISM AND ROMANCE

Although representations of the everyday and the familiar, as distinct from
the extraordinary and the exotic, are as old as art itself, the term 'realism'
to identify these does not seem to have been used in English until 1856. In
that year, coincidentally the same that Flaubert shocked the French public
and authorities with his anti-romantic 'scenes from provincial life' in
Madame Bovary, George Eliot extended Ruskin's use of 'realism' in
Modern Painters to literature that presented social life with meticulous
attention to detail, and in the United States Emerson used the word to
describe Swift's style. As a reaction against the romanticism of the earlier
nineteenth century, realism—or a range of realistic subjects and styles—

came to characterise new developments in fiction (and later drama) in Europe, the United States and, by the last decades of the century, when a new generation of predominantly native-born writers emerged, Australia.

Even within particular countries, realism was not a single, simple movement that allowed easy definition. But perhaps the attribute most commonly shared by those who saw themselves as realists was their opposition, explicit or implicit, to 'romance'—to what they held to be not 'true to life' but rather improbable and artificial, escapist and sentimental. In the minds of many of their readers, the realists' rejection of heroes and heroines was also a rejection of idealism and morality, a rejection which was perceived as reaching scandalous extremes in the work of the French and Scandinavian naturalists who followed Zola in the 'scientific' study of the determining effects of heredity and environment on human behaviour. These naturalists were a direct influence on 'Henry Handel Richardson', the most prominent Australian novelist of the earlier twentieth century.

If European realists held that romance was inauthentic and an escape from contemporary issues, realists in new countries could see it as even more remote. When the influence of the English romantics and of Scott's novels was at its highest, it was often asserted that the United States lacked the historical 'associations', the social structure, and the 'properties' (such as ivy-coloured ruins) for literature. One way for American writers to respond to these patronising assumptions was to reject romantic literature as foreign, and literally imported. Like Walt Whitman, they could follow Emerson's call to abandon exotic themes and settings and celebrate the true romance of America, a romance that far excelled that of 'feudal' Europe. Or, like Mark Twain, they could mockingly reject the conventionally literary and present the 'local colour': the dialects, the lore, the customs, the human types of the regions they knew at first hand.

Narrated throughout in the vernacular, a technique realists frequently used to convey authenticity, Twain's *Huckleberry Finn* is a classic example of anti-literary realism, which contrasts the verisimilitude of Huck's 'scenes from provincial life' with the inauthenticity of Tom Sawyer's and other characters' literary constructions of reality. The most famous of the American 'Western humorists', Twain was admired by Lawson, Furphy and 'Steele Rudd' among Australians who were writing about the way of life in the regions that they knew from experience, not from books.

If, as in *Huckleberry Finn*, realism could accommodate romance through Huck's quest for freedom down the river, romances could also accommodate a lot of authenticating realism, in terms of closely observed details, and few major writers could be confidently designated pure realists or pure romancers. Flaubert wrote not only *Madame Bovary* and *The Sentimental Education*, but also *Salambô*, with its gorgeously exotic settings. George Eliot wrote *Romola*, set in Renaissance Italy, as well as her 'scenes of provincial life' set in the England of her youth. Among Australian writers, Henry Lawson was not alone in rejecting the falsifications of Anglo-Australian romance (directed towards a predominantly English audience), though he did not always succeed in resisting the temptations of melodrama and sentimentality.

Perhaps more illuminating than attempting to define realism and romance separately, and abstractly, would be to see them as opposing tendencies that manifest themselves (and define themselves by their differences from each other) in a variety of ways in the work of Australian writers of the later nineteenth and earlier twentieth centuries. To consider how individual writers in particular works have brought realism and romance into opposition can give readers an historical context for appreciating the writers' concern with the kinds of literature they were—or were not—writing. Such concern, often implicit, sometimes explicit, as with Lawson's enumeration in 'The Union Buries Its Dead' of all the conventional (and false) elements he has omitted, can make us aware of the writer's consciousness of the disputed issues that the realists' disparagement of romance raised, issues of which their contemporary readers would have been aware.

The fullest early discussion of Australian writing is Frederick Sinnett's 'The Fiction Fields of Australia' which appeared in the Melbourne *Journal of Australasia* in 1856, the year Ruskin, Eliot and Emerson introduced the term 'realism' into literary critical discussion. Although Sinnett does not use that word itself, his preferences are for the realistic in fiction. While a great admirer of Scott, for his discernment of human nature, Sinnett sees the age of romanticism as over and rejects its assumptions that exotic settings and heroic subjects are essential for literature. Like American critics before him—and he refers indirectly to Hawthorne, whose *The House of the Seven Gables* had been published four years before—he mounts a two-pronged defence against the charge that a new country like Australia lacks the historical 'associations' for literature: on the one hand, when the best contemporary English fiction deals with immediate, everyday circumstances, it is no disadvantage that Australia lacks such properties for romantic Gothic fiction as ivy-covered ruins; on the other hand, Australia rather than being devoid of material for the genuine 'romance of the real' offers a surfeit of 'local colour'.

For Sinnett, the true measure of fiction lies not in its settings, which are incidental, but in its presentation of human nature, which is universal. Previous Australian writing had concentrated too heavily on externals, merely documenting what was exotic for readers elsewhere, and not sufficiently on human nature in Australia. The novel he found to praise for not being 'too Australian' was Catherine Helen Spence's *Clara Morison: A Tale of South Australia During the Gold Fever* (1854). Unfortunately, Sinnett's survey could not take into account Henry Kingsley's classic Anglo-Australian 'station romance', *The Recollections of Geoffry Hamlyn*, which appeared the same year as his essay. But although Sinnett was writing before much local fiction had been published, he anticipated much subsequent discussion about the subjects and styles appropriate to a distinctively Australian literature.

Like Sinnett before him, 'Rolf Boldrewood' was a great admirer of Scott. Starlight, the bushranger hero of *Robbery Under Arms*, is an embodiment of romantic and aristocratic ideals; but the novel is narrated colloquially by the typical 'cornstalk' or native-born (and bush-born) Dick Marston. Dick's narrative is full of 'local colour', such as his description of the family farm, and in its manner as well as its details anticipates many of Lawson's descriptions of selection life. As a youth, Lawson could have read *Robbery Under Arms* in the *Sydney Mail*, where it was serialised in 1882–3. Within a few years, his own verses, stories and sketches began appearing in the Sydney *Bulletin*. By the early 1890s, a new generation of predominantly native-born writers were being published and encouraged by J.F. Archibald, one of the weekly paper's founding editors, an enthusiast for French rather than English culture, and for realistic rather than moralistic literature. The literary editor Archibald appointed, A.G. Stephens, shared similar preferences.

Lawson, 'Banjo' Paterson, 'Steele Rudd', Barbara Baynton, and Christopher Brennan were among the many writers Archibald and Stephens encouraged to write for an Australia-wide audience. One of the most prolific contributors of short stories was 'Price Warung' with his tales of the convict system. Like Marcus Clarke before him with *For the Term of His Natural Life* and his tales, Warung blended two modes of the historical, documentary realism and the 'romance of Australia'. Other aspects of the international debate over realism and romance appeared in the work of other *Bulletin* writers. In 1892, Lawson and Paterson staged their verse debate over 'the City versus the Bush', each accusing the other of not knowing the 'real' Australia (Paterson's 'An Answer to Various Bards' is from this exchange).

Towards the end of 1892, Archibald assisted Lawson to go to Bourke in the far north-west of NSW to seek work and 'copy' for his contributions to the *Bulletin*. Lawson was shocked by the disparity between the life he found in the bush and how it had been romanticised in literature. The sketch 'In a Dry Season' is his report of the trip. Compared with the many traveller's tales about the new ways of life and the new 'race' that were emerging in Australia, such as Kotze's 'Journey From Cooktown to Maytown', Lawson's is almost a parody in its matter-of-fact flatness and uneventfulness; though, as the mythological enters Kotze's verbatim recount of the coach driver's yarn with the reference to Tantalus (the son of Zeus who was punished by never being able to attain the sustenance that was just beyond his grasp), so Lawson's faithfully recorded details, such as the sight of the woman throwing out the wash-up water or the line of camels on the horizon, take on a very literary, if enigmatic, suggestiveness. One of Lawson's most celebrated stories, 'The Union Buries Its Dead', was originally sent down from Bourke to the Sydney *Truth* as 'a sketch from life', and later in his life Lawson insisted on its veracity: to him it was not a story, something 'made-up'.

Many of the successful writers of 'colonial romances' for the English market were women, among the most prominent Rosa Praed and Ada Cambridge. Miles Franklin, whose manuscript of *My Brilliant Career* Lawson took with him to London in 1900, was clearly reacting against these when she wrote in her introduction that her book was 'not a romance', nor 'a novel', but 'a *real* yarn'; that is, no fanciful fiction but a version of her own experience presented as the story of the highly imaginative Sybylla, who moves between the kinds of social settings falsified alike in 'station romances' and in tales of selection life. Written against these prevailing Australian literary conventions, *My Brilliant Career* is still intensely literary in its play with them. While Franklin's style has often been seen as overwrought, it mirrors, like James Joyce's in his later *A Portrait of the Artist As a Young Man*, the artist figure's immature feelings as it soars upwards into romantic ecstasies and then, with comic irony, plummets into the deflating depths of low-life realism.

Furphy also plays the literary against the vernacular, the romantic against the realistic, and the dialect yarn against the written fiction. In 1897, Furphy sent the manuscript of a novel, entitled *Such is Life*, to Stephens at the *Bulletin*. When it eventually appeared in the Bulletin Library series, in 1903, it constituted the most extended example of realistic 'scenes of provincial life' and dialect humour of this period. Furphy, as the author behind Tom Collins, his committedly realist narrator, ironically mocks Collins's ambitions to be an undeluded and 'scientific' observer of life in the Riverina. So dismissive is Collins of romance (which he still reads voraciously) that he fails to perceive the 'real life' romance under his nose, and the fact that the boundary rider Nosey Alf is a woman! In one of the two chapters deleted from the original manuscript, and later published separately as *The Buln-Buln and the Brolga* (the other became *Rigby's Romance*), two acquaintances of Collins, Barefoot Bob down from the country and Freddy Falkland-Pritchard up from Melbourne, compete for Mrs Falkland-Pritchard's admiration by attempting to tell (modestly, of course) the most impressive story of personal heroism. Freddy's stories, like Tom Sawyer's, have transparently been fabricated from his reading, while Bob's possibly equally mendacious reminiscences have, like Huck Finn's, a plausibility or 'authenticity' that comes from their vernacular manner and detailed 'local colour'. The fact, though, that by this time these were well established coventions in Australian literature should make the reader wary of seeing Bob's yarns as any more 'true', except imaginatively, than Freddy's.

As in Europe and (even more directly comparable for Australian readers) America, the phenomenon of the newly expanded, industrialised, and seemingly dehumanised cities called for some imaginative response: either recoil, and retreat into nostalgia for the bush of the pioneers, or a rediscovery of the communal and the traditional within the new urban patterns of living for the majority of the population. The city as subject and setting was a site of the 'real' in much late nineteenth-century writing. Louis Stone in his novel *Jonah* explores a subject that would appeal to any naturalist, the sub-culture of the larrikins (a 'social problem' in their day), yet realistic as it is in many senses it is also a relocation of traditional pastoral in a contemporary urban setting. Unlikely and untidy as it might seem to literary historians wanting to establish exclusive categories, Christopher Brennan, a poet influenced directly by French symbolism, shared with Stone, Lawson and others in Australia—and one can look ahead to later Australian writers like Christina Stead and Patrick White—an ambivalent fascination with the modern and seemingly unnatural city. 'The Yellow Gas Is Fired from Street to Street' from *Poems [1913]* is an example of the urban nocturnes that punctuate Brennan's symbolist cycle of poems: a cycle which can be read as a stylistic dialogue between romantic and realistic modes, and which ends with the poet's philosophically realistic recognition that he too lives in the garishly gas-lit city and not in some more romantic time or place that he has fondly imagined from his reading.

The continuance of, and the continuing tensions between, realistic and romantic modes can be suggested by the latest instances here, both from 1942. John Morrison, with Frank Hardy, Dorothy Hewett, Judah Waten and others, belonged to the social realist circle of writers identified with the Communist Party of Australia, and with Maxim Gorki's and other

Soviet theoreticians' prescriptions for 'socialist realism' from the mid-1930s. Yet while Morrison's stories focus on working class experience which he knew at first hand, traditional romantic elements (as in the writings of other social realists) are frequently introduced: in 'The Nightshift' the realistic and the romantic are employed to project class differences as well as to contrast young Dick's dreamy desires with the demands and dangers of the waterside workers' job. Eve Langley, while ostensibly realistic, in the sense that she is apparently writing from first-hand experience of that staple of 'social(ist) realism', the itinerant rural proletariat (the 'lower depths' that Gorki would have approved of as a subject), presents a classically picaresque romance, replete, like Furphy's *Such is Life*, with all the traditional knock-about fun of gender confusion. Stylistically, though, Langley can have her heroine, like Franklin's Sybylla, plummet back into the most deflating, and comic, realism, as when, in the extract here, Blue finds where the butter is.

While the term 'realism' may have been new in 1856, the kind of writing it referred to can be found long before then (as Emerson's use of it then to refer back to Swift suggests); and, as the screen constantly reminds us, romance continues to be as popular today as ever. As well, a number of writers, from Charles Harpur writing under the influence of the English romantic poets to Patrick White in the present (his *Voss* is a splendid example), have brought a consciously literary evocation of the heroic and transcendent spirit of European romanticism into contrast with what White has called 'the bags and iron of Australian life', the mundane and the material. The extracts in this Section have been chosen to suggest some of the ways in which such neatly opposed categories as the 'realistic' and 'romantic' define themselves, not neatly and absolutely in the hands of imaginative and conscious writers, but by opposition to each other. The intermixture of modes, and play with them, the confusion of arbitrary and absolute difference between the realistic and 'true' and the fictional and 'false' that are found in this section can be readily discerned in many other writings in other sections in this Anthology also.

Brian Kiernan

Frederick Sinnett
from THE FICTION FIELDS OF AUSTRALIA

In the first place, then, it is alleged against Australia that it is a new country, and, as Pitt said, when charged with juvenility, 'this is an accusation which I can neither palliate nor deny'. Unless we go into the Aboriginal market for 'associations', there is not a single local one, of a century old, to be obtained in Australia; and, setting apart Mr Fawkner's pre-Adamite recollections of Colonel Collins, there is not an association in Victoria mellowed by so much as a poor score of years. It must be granted, then, that we are quite debarred from all the interest to be extracted from any kind of archeological accessories. No storied windows, richly dight, cast a dim, religious light over any Australian premises. There are no ruins for that rare old plant, the ivy green, to creep over and make his dainty meal of. No Australian author can hope to extricate his hero or heroine, however pressing the emergency may be, by means of a spring panel and a subterranean passage, or such like relics of feudal barons, and refuges of modern novelists, and the offspring of their imagination. There may be plenty of dilapidated buildings, but not one, the dilapidation of which is sufficiently venerable by age, to tempt the wandering footsteps of the most arrant *parvenu* of a ghost that ever walked by night. It must be admitted that Mrs Radcliffe's genius would be quite thrown away here; and we must reconcile ourselves to the conviction that the foundations of a second 'Castle of Otranto' can hardly be laid in Australia during our time. Though the corporation may leave Collins-street quite dark enough for the purpose, it is much too dirty to permit any novelist (having a due regard for her sex) to ask the White Lady of Avenel, or a single one of her female connections, to pass that way.

Even if we survive these losses, the sins of youth continue to beset us. No one old enough for a hero can say,

I remember, I remember the house where I was born,

apropos of a Victorian dwelling. The antiquity of the United States quite puts us to shame; and it is darkly hinted that there is not so much as a 'house with seven gables' between Portland and Cape Howe.

...Here we have not been accustomed to see nature through the medium of art, but directly; and though, to the eye of genius, 'the earth and every common sight' possesses a 'glory and a freshness', and needs no abridgement or coloring, yet to possess such powers of perception is the privilege only of one among thousands. The great mass of mankind can only hope to catch glimpses of the glory of 'every common sight', when genius holds it up for them in the right light. This genius has not yet done for Australian nature. Most of us have had more than enough of positive Australian dialogue, but we have never read an Australian dialogue artistically reported. We have heard squatter, and bullock-driver, and digger, talk, and we think it would be very uninteresting, no doubt; and a verbatim report of the conversation of Brown, Jones, and Robinson, in the old world, would be equally uninteresting, but we know by experience that genius can report it so as to be interesting—yet to leave it the conversation of Brown, Jones, and Robinson still. The first genius that performs similar service in Australia will dissipate our incredulity, as to this matter, for ever.

It is not to be assumed that, if the life going on about us seems somewhat slow and tedious, the picture of it must be equally so; for the picture is microcosmic, and does not reproduce the life itself, but a compact and comprehensive likeness of it, that enables us to see, in a few minutes, and in true perspective, the scenes which, in actual existence, we plod through only in the course of years. It is, however, superfluous to deal theoretically with the objection that fiction cannot properly deal with things close upon the foreground of our observation, because it is destroyed by experience. European novelists, during one period, thought that their works acquired an extra charm by dealing chiefly with distant times and places. Scott's genius invested distant times and places with such interest that people began to fancy such distance an essential of such interest. Dickens, on the contrary, by his genius, suddenly awoke London to a perception of the artistic uses that could be made of every-day London life; and men, in the constant habit of having their boots cleaned at Borough inns, were startled to find how the 'boots' at a Borough inn might be a Sam Weller. Thackeray has, perhaps, gone still farther in selecting his characters from the precise time and circle of his readers. From his pages many old habitués of clubs first acquire a true understanding of club life, and the majority of his admirers are, perhaps, most delighted with seeing their own experiences reproduced to them by this master mind, with the exquisite and seemingly intuitive sense which belongs to him—of the manner in which true art makes keenly pleasurable the contemplation of what, in its absolute shape, we tire of every day of our lives. The most successful and delightful novels of the present day are invariably those which deal with immediately surrounding circumstances, both of time and place [...]

One word as to scenery. Many worthy people thought railways would put an end to romance in England. The new police act, it was conceived by others, would be equally destructive to the raw material of novels. The romance of robbery, some imagined, ended when robbers ceased to wear gold-laced coats and jack boots, and to do their business on horseback. The genius of fiction, however, can accommodate herself to greater changes than these, and remains just as fresh and as blooming under circumstances that make people, unacquainted with the invulnerable hardiness of her constitution, predict her immediate decline and death. For our part we hold that there is comparatively little in the circumstance, and almost all in the genius that handles it; but those who believe in mounted robbers, and mourn over the introduction of railways, should feel that in Australia the novelists' golden age is revived. When Waverley travelled up from London, to visit his northern cousins, the Osbaldistones, he went on horseback, and took a fortnight over the journey—that is the way we manage here to this very day. There was a great deal of 'sticking-up' then, and there; and there is here, and now. Sir William of Deloraine had to swim the stream that it would have spoiled a magnificent description for him to have crossed by a cast-iron bridge, as he would do in the reign of Victoria; but in the colony which bears her name, the Central Road-Board cannot be accused of having destroyed the romance of the water-courses.

How, in the name of gas-pipes and rural police, is a traveller to be lost and benighted in England now-a-days. Here he can be placed in that unpleasant but interesting predicament, without violating, in the least, the laws of perfect probability. Look at the railway map of England, and see where

> Now spurs the lated traveller apace
> To gain the timely inn.

He has no control over the iron-horse that whirls him along, and when he gets to the terminus he gains the timely inn in a Hansom cab. Here the description applies with precise accuracy. In short, the natural and external circumstances of Australia partake much more of what we used to call romance than those of England, but we refuse to claim any advantage on this score, and content ourselves with reasserting that those who know how to deal with it can extract almost as much out of one set of circumstances as out of another, wherever the human heart throbs and human society exists. [. . .]

In the first place we may remark that most Australian stories are *too* Australian, and, instead of human life, we have only local 'manners and customs' portrayed in them. The *dramatis personæ* are not people with characters and passions, but lay figures, so constructed, and placed in such attitudes, as to display the costumes of the place and period. The few Australian novels which have been written are too apt to be books of travels in disguise. The authors are but voyagers sailing under the false colors of novelists, and you might as well call the illustrations to Cook's voyages (depicting 'natives of Nootka sound', 'war dance among the Sandwich Islanders', &c.) pictures, as such works novels. They have their uses, doubtless, and are not to be despised, but they are, at best, works of simple instruction as to matters of fact, rather than works of art. If we were asked what was the first requisite of a novel, we should say human character. The second—human character. The third—human character. Even plot and incident comes afterwards, and the mere question of costume and local coloring after plot and incident. In most Australian stories the order is reversed, and Australian customs are predominant. We must be careful not to be misunderstood here, or we might be supposed to say, what would be contrary to the whole tenor of our writing, and to imply that beau ideal Australian novels would only differ in trivial and minor things from any other novels. [. . .]

Now, in the kind of novel we want to see written, but do not expect to read for some time, we want to see a picture of universal human life and passion, but represented as modified by Australian externals. The description of all these externals must then be truthful and complete, but subordinated to the larger purposes of fiction. [. . .]

We had intended, in this paper, to have reviewed some of the best Australian stories that have yet been published, but these general remarks have extended to such a length that we must postpone the fulfilment of this intention until next month. In the mean time we content ourselves with the concluding remark, that real genius is ever able to draw its inspiration from the rills that run at its own feet, and without travelling to Helicon—that everywhere nature has new beauties and truths for the eye and mind that know how to perceive and grasp them—and that, when we complain of her sterility, we should rather humbly confess our own.

The fault is ours, if, in this fresh and vast country, peopled with men of all characters, and degrees, and nations, in which all human feelings and emotions are astir, in which the pulse of existence beats with almost feverish speed, we regard the whole scene as tame and prosaic, and able to furnish the materials for no books but ledgers. What should we have made of such far more barren places as have given up hidden treasures, and been made bright and beautiful for all generations, at the touch of such genius as his, for example,

> Who trod in glory and in joy,
> Following his plough along the mountain side?

(1856)

'Rolf Boldrewood' (Thomas Alexander Browne) from ROBBERY UNDER ARMS

CHAPTER 1

My name's Dick Marston, Sydney-side native. I'm twenty-nine years old, six feet in my stocking soles, and thirteen stone weight. Pretty strong and active with it, so they say. I don't want to blow—not here, any road—but it takes a good man to put me on my back, or stand up to me with the gloves, or the naked mauleys. I can ride anything—anything that ever was lapped in horsehide—swim like a musk-duck, and track like a Myall blackfellow. Most things that a man can do I'm up to, and that's all about it. As I lift myself now I can feel the muscle swell on my arm like a cricket ball, in spite of the—well, in spite of everything.

The morning sun comes shining through the window bars; and ever since he was up have I been cursing the daylight, cursing myself, and them that brought me into the world. Did I curse mother, and the hour I was born into this miserable life?

Why should I curse the day? Why do I lie here, groaning; yes, crying like a child, and beating my head against the stone floor? I am not mad, though I am shut up in a cell. No. Better for me if I was. But it's all up now; there's no get away this time; and I, Dick Marston, as strong as a bullock, as active as a rock-wallaby, chock-full of life and spirits and health, have been tried for bush-ranging—robbery under arms they call it—and though the blood runs through my veins like the water in the mountain creeks, and every bit of bone and sinew is as sound as the day I was born, I must die on the gallows this day month.

Die—die—yes, die; be strung up like a dog, as they say. I'm blessed if ever I did know of a dog being hanged, though, if it comes to that, a shot or a bait generally makes an end of 'em in this country. Ha, ha! Did I laugh? What a rum thing it is that a man should have a laugh in him when he's only got twenty-nine days more to live—a day for every year of my life. Well, laughing or crying, this is what it has come to at last. All the drinking and recklessness; the flash talk and the idle ways; the merry cross-country rides that we used to have, night or day, it made no odds to us; every man well mounted, as like as not on a racehorse in training taken out of his stable within the week; the sharp brushes with the police, when now and then a man was wounded on each side, but no one killed. That came later on, worse luck. The jolly sprees we used to have in the bush townships, where we chucked our money about like gentlemen, where all the girls had a smile and a kind word for a lot of game upstanding chaps, that acted like men, if they did keep the road a little lively. Our 'bush telegraphs' were safe to let us know when the 'traps' were closing in on us, and then—why the coach would be 'stuck up' a hundred miles away, in a different direction, within twenty-four hours. Marston's gang again! The police are in pursuit! That's what we'd see in the papers. We had 'em sent to us regular; besides having the pick of 'em when we cut open the mail bags.

And now—that chain rubbed a sore, curse it!—all that racket's over. It's more than hard to die in this settled, infernal, fixed sort of way, like a bullock in the killing-yard, all ready to be 'pithed'. I used to pity them when I was a boy, walking round the yard, pushing their noses through the rails, trying for a likely place to jump, stamping and pawing and roaring and knocking their heads against the heavy close rails, with misery and rage in their eyes, till their time was up. Nobody told *them* beforehand, though!

Have I and the likes of me ever felt much the same, I wonder, shut up in a pen like this, with the rails up, and not a place a rat could creep through, waiting till our killing time was come? The poor devils of steers have never done anything but ramble off the run now and again, while we—but it's too late to think of that. It *is* hard. There's no saying it isn't; no, nor thinking what a fool, what a blind, stupid, thundering idiot a fellow's been, to laugh at the steady working life that would have helped him up, bit by bit, to a good farm, a good wife, and innocent little kids about him, like that chap, George Storefield, that came to see me last week. He was real rightdown sorry for me, I could tell, though Jim and I used to laugh at him, and call him a regular old crawler of a milker's calf in the old days. The tears came into his eyes reg'lar like a woman as he gave my hand a squeeze and turned his head away. We was little chaps together, you know. A man always feels that, you know. And old George, he'll go back—a fifty-mile ride, but what's that on a good horse? He'll be late home, but he can cross the rock ford the short way over the creek. I can see him turn his horse loose at the garden-gate, and walk through the quinces that lead up to the cottage, with his saddle on his arm. Can't I see it all, as plain as if I was there?

And his wife and the young 'uns 'll run out when they hear father's horse, and want to hear all the news. When he goes in there's his meal tidy and decent waiting for him, while he tells them about the poor chap he's been to see as is to be scragged next month. Ha! ha! what a rum joke it is, isn't it?

And then he'll go out in the verandah, with the roses growin' all over the posts and smellin' sweet in the cool night air. After that he'll have his smoke, and sit there thinkin' about me, perhaps, and old days, and what not, till all hours—till his wife comes and fetches him in. And here I lie—my God! why didn't they knock me on the head when I was born, like a lamb in a dry season, or a blind puppy—blind enough, God knows! They do so in some countries, if the books say true, and what a hell of misery that must save some people from!

Well, it's done now, and there's no get away. I may as well make the best of it. A sergeant of police was shot in our last scrimmage, and they must fit some one over that. It's only natural. He was rash, or Starlight would never have dropped him that day. Not if he'd been sober either. We'd been drinking all night at that Willow Tree shanty. Bad grog, too! When a man's half drunk he's fit for any devilment that comes before him. Drink! How do you think a chap that's taken to the bush—regularly turned out, I mean, with a price on his head, and a fire burning in his heart night and day—can stand his life if he don't drink? When he thinks of what he might have been, and what he is! Why, nearly every man he meets is paid to run him down, or trap him some way like a stray dog that's taken to sheep-killin'. He knows a score of men, and women too, that are only looking out for a chance to sell his blood on the quiet and pouch the money. Do you think that makes a chap mad and miserable, and tired of his life, or not? And if a drop of grog will take him right out of his wretched self for a bit why shouldn't he drink? People don't know what they are talking about. Why, he is that miserable that he wonders why he don't hang himself, and save the Government all the trouble; and if a few nobblers make him feel as if he might have some good chances yet, and that it doesn't so much matter after all, why shouldn't he drink?

He does drink, of course; every miserable man, and a good many women as have something to fear or repent of, drink. The worst of it is that too much of it brings on the 'horrors', and then the devil, instead of giving you a jog now and then, sends one of his imps to grin in your face and pull your heart-strings all day and all night long. By George, I'm getting clever—too clever, altogether, I think. If I could forget for one moment, in the middle of all the nonsense, that I was to die on Thursday three weeks! die on Thursday three weeks! die on Thursday! That's the way the time runs in my ears like a chime of bells. But it's all mere bosh I've been reading these long six months I've been chained up here—after I was committed for trial. When I came out of the hospital after curing me of that wound—for I was hit bad by that black tracker—they gave me some books to read for fear I'd go mad and cheat the hangman. I was always fond of reading, and many a night I've read to poor old mother and Aileen before I left the old place. I was that weak and low, after I took the turn, and I felt glad to get a book to take me away from sitting, staring, and blinking at nothing by the hour together. It was all very well then; I was too weak to think much. But when I began to get well again I kept always coming across something in the book that made me groan or cry out, as if some one had stuck a knife in me. A dark chap did once—through the ribs—it didn't feel so bad, a little sharpish at first; why didn't he aim a bit higher? He never was no good, even at that. As I was saying, there'd be something about a horse, or the country, or the spring weather—it's just coming in now, and the Indian corn's shooting after the rain, and *I'll* never see it; or they'd put in a bit about the cows walking through the river in the hot summer afternoons; or they'd go describing about a girl, until I began to think of sister Aileen again; then I'd run my head against the wall, or do something like a madman, and they'd stop the books for a week; and I'd be as miserable as a bandicoot, worse and worse a lot, with all the devil's tricks and bad thoughts in my head, and nothing to put them away.

I must either kill myself, or get something to fill up my time till the day—yes, the day comes. I've always been a middling writer, tho' I can't say much for the grammar, and spelling, and that, but I'll put it all down, from the beginning to the end, and maybe it'll save some other unfortunate young chap from pulling back like a colt when he's first roped, setting himself against everything in the way of proper breaking, making a fool of himself generally, and choking himself down, as I've done.

The gaoler—he looks hard—he has to do that, there's more than one or two within here that would have him by the throat, with his heart's blood running, in half a minute, if they had their way, and the warder was off guard. He knows that very well. But he's not a bad-hearted chap.

'You can have books, or paper and pens, anything you like,' he said, 'you unfortunate young beggar, until you're turned off.'

'If I'd only had you to see after me when I was young,' says I—

'Come; don't whine,' he said, then he burst out laughing. 'You didn't mean it, I see. I ought to have known better. You're not one of that sort, and I like you all the better for it.'

Well, here goes. Lots of pens, a big bottle of ink, and ever so much foolscap paper, the right sort for me, or I shouldn't have been here. I'm blessed if it doesn't look as if I was going to write copies again. Don't I remember how I used to go to school in old times; the rides there and back on the old pony; and pretty little Grace Storefield that I was so fond of, and used to show her how to do her lessons. I believe I learned more that way than if I'd had only myself to think about. There was another girl, the daughter of the poundkeeper, that I wanted her to beat; and the way we both worked, and I coached her up, was a caution. And she did get above her in her class. How proud we were! She gave me a kiss, too, and a bit of her hair. Poor Gracey! I wonder where she is now, and what she'd think if she saw me here to-day. If I could have looked ahead, and seen myself—chained now like a dog, and going to die a dog's death this day month!

Anyhow, I must make a start. How do people begin when they set to work to write their own sayings and doings? There's been a deal more doing than talking in my life—it was the wrong sort—more's the pity.

Well, let's see; his parents were poor, but respectable. That's what they always say. My parents were poor, and mother was as good a soul as ever broke bread, and wouldn't have taken a shilling's worth that wasn't her own if she'd been starving. But as for father, he'd been a poacher in England, a Lincolnshire man he was, and got sent out for it. He wasn't much more than a boy, he said, and it was only for a hare or two, which didn't seem much. But I begin to think, being able to see the right of things a bit now, and having no bad grog inside of me to turn a fellow's head upside down, as poaching must be something like cattle and horse duffing—not the worst thing in the world itself, but mighty likely to lead to it.

Dad had always been a hard-working, steady-going sort of chap, good at most things, and like a lot more of the Government men, as the convicts were always called round our part, he saved some money as soon as he had done his time, and married mother, who was a simple emigrant girl just out from Ireland. Father was a square-built, good-looking chap, I believe, then; not so tall as I am by three inches, but wonderfully strong and quick on his pins. They did say as he could hammer any man in the district before he got old and stiff. I never saw him 'shape' but once, and then he rolled into a man big enough to eat him, and polished him off in a way that showed me—though I was a bit of a boy then—that he'd been at the game before. He didn't ride so bad either, though he hadn't had much of it where he came from; but he was afraid of nothing, and had a quiet way with colts. He could make pretty good play in thick country, and ride a roughish horse, too.

Well, our farm was on a good little flat, with a big mountain in front, and a scrubby, rangy country at the back for miles. People often asked him why he chose such a place. 'It suits me,' he used to say, with a laugh, and talk of something else. We could only raise about enough corn and potatoes, in a general way, for ourselves from the flat; but there were other chances and pickings which helped to make the pot boil, and them we'd have been a deal better without.

First of all, though our cultivation paddock was small, and the good land seemed squeezed in between the hills, there was a narrow tract up the creek, and here it widened out into a large well-grassed flat. This was where our cattle ran, for, of course, we had a team of workers and a few milkers when we came. No one ever took up a farm in those days without a dray and a team, a year's rations, a few horses and milkers, pigs and fowls, and a little furniture. They didn't collar a 40-acre selection, as they do now—spend all their money in getting the land and squat down as bare as robins—a man with his wife and children all under a sheet of bark, nothing on their backs, and very little in their bellies. However, some of them do pretty well, though they do say they have to live on 'possums for a time. We didn't do much, in spite of our grand start.

The flat was well enough, but there were other places in the gullies beyond that that father had dropped upon when he was out shooting. He was a tremendous chap for poking about on foot or on horseback, and though he was an Englishman, he was what you call a born bushman. I never saw any man almost as was his equal. Wherever he'd been once, there he could take you to again; and what was more, if it was in the dead of the night he could do it just the same. People said he was as good as a blackfellow, but I never saw one that was as good as he was, all round. In a strange country, too. That was what beat me—he'd know the way the creek run, and noticed when the cattle headed to camp, and a lot of things that other people couldn't see, or if they did, couldn't remember again. He was a great man for solitary walks, too—he and an old dog he had, called Crib, a cross-bred mongrel-looking brute, most like what they call a lurcher in England, father said. Anyhow, he could do most anything but talk. He could bite to some purpose, drive cattle or sheep, catch a kangaroo, if it wasn't a regular flyer, fight like a bulldog, and swim like a retriever, track anything, and fetch and carry, but bark he wouldn't. He'd stand and look at dad as if he worshipped him, and he'd make him some sign and off he'd go like a child that's got a message. Why he was so fond of the old man we boys couldn't make out. We were afraid of him, and as far as we could see he never patted or made much of Crib. He thrashed him unmerciful as he did us boys. Still the dog was that fond of him you'd think he'd like to die for him there and then. But dogs are not like boys, or men either—better, perhaps.

Well, we were all born at the hut by the creek, I suppose, for I remember it as soon as I could remember anything. It was a snug hut enough, for father was a good bush carpenter, and didn't turn his back to any one for splitting and fencing, hut-building and shingle-splitting; he had had a year or two at sawing, too, but after he was married he dropped that. But I've heard mother say that he took great pride in the hut when he brought her to it first, and said it was the best-built hut within fifty miles. He split every slab, cut every post and wallplate and rafter himself, with a man to help him at odd times; and after the frame was up, and the bark on the roof, he camped underneath and finished every bit of it—chimney, flooring, doors, windows, and partitions—by himself. Then he dug up a little garden in front, and planted a dozen or two peaches and quinces in it; put a couple of roses—a red and a white one—by the posts of the verandah, and it was all ready for his pretty Norah, as she says he used to call her then. If I've heard her tell about the garden and the quince trees and the two roses once, I've heard her tell it a hundred times. Poor mother! we used to get round her—Aileen, and Jim, and I—and say, 'Tell us about the garden, mother.' She'd never refuse; those were her happy days, she always said. She used to cry afterwards—nearly always.

The first thing almost that I can remember was riding the old pony, 'Possum, out to bring in the milkers. Father was away somewhere, so mother took us all out and put me on the pony, and let me have a whip. Aileen walked alongside, and very proud I was. My legs stuck out straight on the old pony's fat back. Mother had ridden him up when she came— the first horse she ever rode, she said. He was a quiet little old roan, with a bright eye and legs like gate-posts, but he never fell down with us boys, for all that. If we fell off he stopped still and began to feed, so that he suited us all to pieces. We soon got sharp enough to flail him along with a quince stick, and we used to bring up the milkers, I expect, a good deal faster than was good for them. After a bit we could milk, leg-rope, and bail up for ourselves, and help dad brand the calves, which began to come pretty thick. There were only three of us children—my brother Jim, who was two years younger than I was, and then Aileen, who was four years behind him. I know we were both able to nurse the baby a while after she came, and neither of us wanted better fun than to be allowed to watch her, or rock the cradle, or as a great treat to carry her a few steps. Somehow we was that fond and proud of her from the first that we'd have done anything in the world for her. And so we would now—I was going to say—but that poor Jim lies under a forest oak on a sandhill, and I—well, I'm here, and if I'd listened to her advice I should have been a free man. A free man! How it sounds, doesn't it? with the sun shining, and the blue sky over your head, and the birds twittering, and the grass beneath your feet! I wonder if I shall go mad before my time's up.

Mother was a Roman Catholic—most Irishwomen are; and dad was a Protestant, if he was anything. However, that says nothing. People that don't talk much about their religion, or follow it up at all, won't change it for all that. So father, though mother tried him hard enough when they were first married, wouldn't hear of turning, not if he was to be killed for it, as I once heard him say. 'No!' he says, 'my father and grandfather, and all the lot, was Church people, and so I shall live and die. I don't know as it would make much matter to me, but such as my notions is, I shall stick to 'em as long as the craft holds together. You can bring up the girl in your own way; it's made a good woman of you, or found you one, which is most likely, and so she may take her chance. But I stand for Church and King, and so shall the boys, as sure as my name's Ben Marston.'

(1882)

'Price Warung' (William Astley)
HOW MUSTER-MASTER STONEMAN EARNED HIS BREAKFAST

I

An unpretentious building of rough-hewn stone standing in the middle of a small, stockaded enclosure. A doorway in the wall of the building facing the entrance-gate to the yard. To the left of the doorway, a glazed window of the ordinary size. To its right a paneless aperture, so low and narrow that were the four upright and two transverse bars which grate it doubled in thickness no interstice would be left for the admission of light or air to the interior. Behind the bars—a face.

Sixteen hours hence that face will look its last upon the world which has stricken it countless cruel blows. In a corner of the enclosure the executioner's hand is even now busy stitching into a shapeless cap, a square of grey serge. To-morrow the same hand will use the cap to hood the face, as one of the few simple preliminaries to swinging the carcase to which the face is attached from the rude platform now in course of erection against the stockade fence and barely 20 yards in front of the stone building.

The building is the gaol—locally known as the 'cage'—of Oatlands, a small township in the midlands of Van Diemen's Land, which has gradually grown up round a convict 'muster-station', established by Governor Davey. The time is five o'clock on a September evening, 55 years ago. At nine o'clock on the following morning, Convict Glancy, No. 17,927, transportee ex ship *Pestonjee Bomanjee* (second trip), originally under sentence for seven years for the theft of a silk handkerchief from a London 'swell', will suffer the extreme penalty of the law for having, in an intemperate moment, objected to the mild discipline with which a genial and loving motherland had sought to correct his criminal tendencies. In other words, Convict Glancy, metaphorically goaded by the wordy insults and literally by the bayonet-tip of one of his motherland's reformatory agents—to wit, Road-gang Overseer James Jones—had scattered J.J.'s brains over a good six square yards of metalled roadway. The deed had been rapturously applauded by Glancy's fellow-gangers, all of whom had the inclination, but lacked the courage, to wield the crowbar that has been the means of erasing this particular tyrant's name from the pay-sheets of His Britannic Majesty's Colonial Penal Establishment. Nevertheless and notwithstanding such tribute of appreciation, HBM's Colonial representatives, police, judicial and gubernatorial, have thought it rather one to be censured and have, accordingly, left Convict Glancy for execution.

This decision of the duly constituted authorities Convict Glancy has somewhat irrelevantly (as it will seem to us at this enlightened day) acknowledged by a fervent 'Thank God!'—an ejaculation rendered the more remarkable by the fact that never before in his convict history had he linked the name of the Deity with any expression of gratitude for the many blessings enjoyed by him in that state of penal servitude to which it had pleased the same Deity to call him. On the contrary, he had constantly indulged in maledictions on his fate and on his Maker. He had resolutely cursed the benignant forces with which the System and the King's Regulations had surrounded him, and he had failed to reverence as he ought the triangles, the gang-chains, the hominy, the prodding bayonet, and the other things which would have conduced to his reformation had he but manifested a more humble and obedient spirit. No wonder, therefore, as Chaplain Ford said, that it has come about that he has qualified for the capital doom.

Upon this doom, in so far as it could be represented by the gallows, Convict Glancy was now gazing with an unflinching eye. On this September evening he stands at his cell-window looking on half-a-dozen brown-clothed figures handling saw, and square, and hammer, as they fix in the earth two sturdy uprights, and to those a projecting cross-beam; as they bind the two with a solid tie-piece of knotless hardwood; as they build a narrow platform of planks around the gallows-tree; as they fasten a rope to the notched end of the cross-beam; and as they slope to the edge of the planks, ten feet from the ground, a rude ladder. All the drowsy afternoon he had watched the working party, though Chaplain Ford had stood by his side droning of the grace which had been withheld from him in life, but might still be his in death. He had felt interested, had Convict Glancy, in these preparations for the event in which he was to act such a prominent part on the morrow. He had even laughed at the grim humour of one of the brown-garbed workers who, when the warder's eye was off him, had gone through the pantomime of noosing the rope end round his own neck—a little joke which contributed much to the (necessarily noiseless) delight of the rest of the gang.

Altogether, Convict Glancy reflected as dusk fell, and the working party gathered up their tools, and the setting sun tipped the bayonets of the guard with a diamond iridescence, that he had spent many a duller afternoon. If the Chaplain had only held his tongue, the time would have passed with real pleasantness. He said as much to the good man as the latter remarked to the warder on duty in the cell that he would look in again after supper.

'You may save yourself the trouble, sir,' quoth, respectfully enough, Convict Glancy. 'You have spoilt my last afternoon. Don't spoil my last night!'

Chaplain Ford winced at the words. He was still comparatively new to the work of spiritually superintending a hundred or so monsters who looked upon the orthodox hell as a place where residence would be pleasantly recreative after Port Arthur Settlement and Norfolk Island; and the time lay still in the future when, being completely embruted, he would come to regard it as a very curious circumstance indeed that Christ had omitted eulogistic reference to the System from the Sermon on the Mount. Consequently, he winced and sighed, not so much—to do him justice—at the utter depravity of Convict Glancy as at his own inability to reach the reprobate's heart. But he took the hint; he mournfully said he would not return that evening, but would be with the prisoner by half-past 5 o'clock in the morning.

II

When Chaplain Ford entered the enclosure immediately before the hour he had named, he at once understood, from the excitement manifested by a group assembled in front of the 'cage', that something was amiss. Voices were uttering fearful words, impetuously, almost shriekingly, and hands swung lanterns—the grey dawn had not yet driven the darkness from the stockade—and brandished muskets furiously. A very brief space of time served to inform the reverend functionary what had gone wrong.

Convict Glancy had made his escape, having previously murdered, with the victim's own bayonet, the warder who had been told-off to watch him during the night. This latter circumstance was, of course, unfortunate, but alone it would not have created the excitement, for the murder of prison-officials was a common enough occurrence. It was the other thing that galled the gesticulating and blaspheming group. That a prisoner, fettered with ten-pound irons, should have broken out of gaol on the very eve of his execution—why, it was calculated to shake the confidence of the Comptroller-General himself in the infallibility and perfect righteousness of the System. And, popular and authoritative belief in the System once shattered, where would they be?

The murdered man had gone on duty at 10 o'clock, and very shortly afterwards he must have met with his fate. How Glancy had obtained possession of the bayonet could only be conjectured. As was the custom during the day or two preceding a convict's execution, he had been left unmanacled, and ironed with double leg-chains only. Thus his hands were free to perpetrate the deed once he grasped the weapon. Glancy, on his escape, had taken the instrument with him, but there was no doubt that he had inflicted death with it, the wound in the dead man's breast being obviously caused by the regulation bayonet. Possibly the sentinel had nodded, and then a violent wrench of the prisoner's wrist and a sudden stab had extended his momentary slumber into an eternal sleep. The bayonet had also been used by Glancy to prise up a flooring-flag, and to scoop out an aperture under the wall, the base-stones of which, following the slipshod architecture of the time, rested on the surface and were not sunk into the ground.

The work of excavation must have taken the convict several hours, and must have been conducted as noiselessly as the manner of committing the crime itself. A solitary warder occupied the outer guard-room, but he asserted that he had heard no sound except the exchange of whistle-signals between the dormitory guard at the convict-barracks (a quarter-of-mile away at the rear of the gaol stockade) and the military patrol. The night routine of the 'cage' did not insist upon the whistle-signal between the men on duty, but they passed a simple 'All's well' every hour. And this the guardroom-warder maintained he had done with the officer inside the

condemned cell, the response being given in a low tone, from consideration, so the former thought, for the sleeping convict so soon to die. Of
course, if this man was to be believed, Glancy must have uttered the
words. It was not the first time the signal which should have been given by
a prison officer had been made by his convict murderer.

The murder was discovered on the arrival of the relief watch at five
o'clock. The last 'All's well' was exchanged at four. Consequently the
escapee had less than an hour's start. The scaling of the stockade would
not be difficult even for a man in irons, and once in the bush an experienced
hand would soon find a method of fracturing the links.

It must be admitted that this contumacious proceeding of Convict Glancy was most vexatious. Under-Sheriff Ropewell, now soundly reposing at
the township inn, would be forthcoming at 9 o'clock with his Excellency's
warrant in his hands to demand from Muster-Master Stoneman the body
of one James Glancy, and Muster-Master Stoneman would have to apologise for his inability to produce the said body. The difficulty was quite
unprecedented, and Stoneman, as he stood in the midst of his minions,
groaned audibly at the prospect of having to do the thing most abhorrent
to the official mind—establish a precedent.

'Such a thing was never heard of!' he cried. 'A man to bolt just when he
was to be turned off! And the d—d hypocrite tried to make his Honour
and all of us think that he was only too happy to be scragged. It's too
d—d bad!'

It certainly did seem peculiar that Glancy, who had apparently much
rejoiced at the contemplation of his early decease, should give leg-bail just
when he was to realise his wishes. He had told the judge that 'he was —
glad they were going to kill him right off instead of by inches', and yet he
had voluntarily thrown off the noose when it was virtually round his neck.
Was it the mere contrariness of the convict nature that prompted the
escape? Or, was it the innate love of life that becomes stronger as the
benefits of living become fewer and fewer? Had the craving for existence
and for freedom surged over his despair and recklessness at the eleventh
hour?

Such were the inquiries which Chaplain Ford put to himself as, horrified, he took in the particulars of No. 17,927's crowning enormities from
the hubbub of the group.

'Damn it!' said the Muster-Master at last, 'we are losing time. The devil
can't have gone far with those ten-pounders on him. 'We'll have to put the
regulars on the track as well as our own men. Warder Briggs, report to
Captain White at the barracks, and—'

Muster-Master Stoneman stopped short. Through the foggy air there
came the familiar sound as of a convict dragging his irons. What could it
be? No prisoners had been as yet loosed from the dormitory. Whence
could the noice proceed?

Clink—clank—s-sh—dr-g-g—clink—clank—dr-g-g. The sound drew
nearer, and Convict Glancy turned in at the enclosure gateway—
unescorted. He had severed the leg-chain at the link which connected with
the basil of the left anklet, but had not taken the trouble to remove the
other part of the chain. Thus, while he could take his natural pace with his
left foot, he dragged the fetters behind his right leg.

A moment of hushed surprise, and then three or four men rushed towards him. The first who touched him he felled with a blow.

'Not yet,' said he, grimly. 'I give myself up, Mr. Stoneman—you don't take me! I give myself up—you ain't going to get ten quid[1] for taking me.' And then Convict Glancy laughed, and held out his hands for the handcuffs. He laughed more heartily as the subordinate hirelings of the System threw themselves upon him like hounds on their prey.

'No need to turn out the sodgers now, Muster-Master—not till nine o'clock.' Once more his hideous laugh rang through the yards. 'You had an easier job than you expected, hadn't you, Stoneman, old cove?'

Muster-Master Stoneman had been surprised into silence and into an unusual abstinence from blasphemy by the reappearance—quite unprecedented under the circumstances!—of the doomed wretch. But the desperado's jeering tones whipped him into speech.

'Curse you!' he yelled, 'I'll teach you to laugh on the other side of your mouth presently. You'd better have kept away.' He literally foamed in his mad anger.

'Do you think I couldn't have stopped away if I'd wanted to, having got clear?' A lofty scorn rang out in the words. 'But do you think I was going to run away when I was so near Freedom as that?' And the wretch jerked his manacled hands in the direction of the gallows. 'You d—d fool!'

No one spoke for a full half-minute. Then: 'Why did you break gaol then?' asked the Muster-Master.

'*Because I wanted to spit on Jones' grave!*' was the reply.

III

Muster-Master Stoneman was as good as his word. Death couldn't drive the smile from Glancy's face. That could only be done by one thing—the lash.

When next the Muster-Master spoke it was to order the prisoner a double ration of cocoa and bread. And, 'Briggs,' he continued, 'while he is getting it, see that the triangles are rigged.'

'The triangles, sir!' exclaimed Officer Briggs and Convict Glancy together.

'I said the triangles, and I mean the triangles. No. 17,927 has broken gaol, and as Muster-Master of this station, and governor of this gaol, and as a magistrate of the territory, I can give him 750 lashes for escaping. But as he has to go through another little ceremony this morning I'll let him off with a 'canary'—(a hundred lashes).'[2]

'You surely cannot mean it, sir!' exclaimed Parson Ford.

'Mean it, sir! By G—, I'll show you I mean it,' replied the MM, whose blaspheming no presence restrained save that of his official superiors. 'Give him the cocoa, Warder Tuff, give the doctor my compliments, and tell him his attendance is required here. Tell him he'd better bring his smelling

---

1. 'Ten quid': The reward of ten pounds paid by Government on the recapture of an escaped prisoner.

2. Muster-Master Stoneman had doubtless in his mind's eye when he made this remark the decision of a Sydney Court which had legalised the infliction, by an official holding a plurality of offices, of a sentence passed by him in each capacity, but for the one offence.

salts—they may be wanted,' he sneered in conclusion.

'You devil!' cried Glancy. The reckless grin passed away, and his face faded to the pallor of the death he was so soon to die.

As Muster-Master Stoneman turned on his heel to prepare the warrant for the flogging, he looked at his watch. It was half-past six.

At seven o'clock the first lash from the cat-o'-nine-tails fell upon Convict Glancy's back.

At 7.30 his groaning and bleeding body, which had received the full hundred of flaying stripes, lay on the pallet of the cell where he had murdered the night-guard but a few hours before.

At eight o'clock Executioner Johnson entered the cell. 'I've brought yer sumthink to 'arden yer, Glancy, ol' man. I'll rub it in, an' it'll help yer to keep up.' So tender a sympathy inspired Mr Johnson's words that anyone not knowing him would have thought he was the bearer of some priceless balsam. But Convict Glancy knew him; and, maddened by pain though he was, had still sensibility enough left to make a shuddering resistance to the hangman as he proceeded to rub into the gashed flesh a handful of coarse salt. 'By the Muster-Master's orders, sonny,' soothingly remarked Johnson. 'To 'arden yer.'

At 8.15 Under-Sheriff Ropewell, who had been apprised while at breakfast of the murder and escape, appeared on the scene escorted by his javelin-men. This gentleman, too, had been greatly perplexed by Convict Glancy's proceedings. 'Really it was most inconsiderate of the man,' he said to the Muster-Master. 'I do not know whether I ought to proceed to execution, pending his trial for this second murder.'

'Oh,' said the latter functionary—flicking with his handkerchief from his coat-sleeve as he spoke a drop of Convict Glancy's blood that had fallen there from a reflex swirl of the lash, 'I think your duty is clear. You must hang him at nine o'clock, and try him afterwards for the last crime.'

And as Convict Glancy, per *Pestonjee Bomanjee* (second), No. 17,927, was punctually hanged at 9.5, it is to be presumed that the Under-Sheriff had accepted this solution of the difficulty.

At 10.15 a mass of carrion having been huddled into a shell, and certain formalities, which in the estimation of the System served as efficiently as a coroner's inquest, having been duly attended to, Muster-Master Stoneman bethought himself that he had not breakfasted.

'I'll see you later, Mr Ropewell,' he said, as the latter was endorsing the Governor's warrant with the sham verdict; 'I'm going to breakfast. I think I've earned it this morning.'

(1890)

Stefan von Kotze
from JOURNEY FROM COOKTOWN TO MAYTOWN

It is incredible how ugly a bush horse can look when droughts have dried up every blade of grass, and water has disappeared; how miserably lean and hopeless such a horse can become and yet retain its usefulness. The tired eye, the rough, dirty hide, the sharply-marked ribs, and the razor-like back, added to it an old, often repaired harness and a shaky decrepit coach, the whole outfit under the command of a bearded, tanned, limping, and indescribably profane old man. No, the royal mail did not impress me favourably.

I had dressed myself in bush fashion, similar to the driver. An open-neck coloured woollen shirt, a pair of leather breeches which assume all shades before they reach the wash tub, a wide-brimmed hat, top boots without socks—that's the correct outfit. On Sundays and holidays a coloured neckerchief might be added and perhaps when it rains one might don a coat. Otherwise, the bushman never wears a coat.

On this *martyr box* we had to cover 50 miles to reach our destination, Maytown, beyond the large water divide in the centre of the old Palmer goldfield. Verily, I would have been shaken to pieces had I not covered part of the way on foot. The fare was to be 50 shillings. After everything had been stowed away in the coach, we disappeared in a cloud of dust along the winding road. Alas, this is the bush. To the right, as far as the eye can see, open country, dried-up pastures, in certain intervals small, dwarfed trees gnarled by an unmerciful sun and made sapless by hot winds. All the trees were eucalypts and their sparse foliage gave no shade— every starved branch exposing its ugly bareness in a leaf-less poverty. These grotesque tree branches appeared to me like a horror-chamber of plant life. The brooding mid-day stillness, the absence of all animal life, the fierce, uncanny white light, the scorched, thirsty soil, and the distant bare hills covered with black granite boulders, all this combined to a terrible depressing harmony whose basic note was age—soulless, unspeakable age—deprived of any hope.

The thermometer had reached almost 120°, but I shivered. The driver vouchsafed some explanations of this mute tragedy, whenever he was not engaged in bestowing the curses of Heaven in the most bloodthirsty terms on his struggling horses. At present he drove through a dried-out sandy creek bed.

'See that old trunk over there?' he asked, pointing with his whip to a fallen giant of the bush. 'That's the spot where last year we found a poor cove. And here,' he added, pulling up his horses in the shadow of an enormous Leichhardt tree (one of the few shade-spreading trees in the bush, named after the lost German explorer)—'here we buried him. See, here is the name and date.' I read 'Tantalus, 15.12.1890' in deep, already overgrown cuts in the soft bark. 'Tantalus,' I repeated in surprise. 'Funny name,' confirmed the driver. 'The passenger I had with me cut it into the tree. He didn't know his Christian name. The poor beggar had a terrible end.' And without further encouragement he started to talk, at the same time cutting a plug of tobacco and filling his pipe. 'Well, one day, same weather as we have now, we pass here when the horses suddenly shy and try to break away.' (I looked at our horses smilingly and doubtfully, but the driver did not see my point.) '"Heavens," my passenger called out. I turned. There was the corpse of a young fellow, the legs caught below the tumbled-down trunk of the big tree. We jumped from the coach. Not far from the body lay a Winchester rifle and a long knife in a sheath. Of course it is a kangaroo hunter, I said to meself. Had a nap in the shade and a tree fell on top of him. Clear enough. But alongside him lay a kind of crude lassoo, evidently made of strips from his shirt. What use would that have been to him? Suddenly I get an idea. You see,' and the driver turned to me, 'the poor cove sat there with broken thighs, without water, without help. The sun reached him at mid-day and so came the ants—yes, the ants.' Here the driver shivered and spat savagely in the sand, crushing with his foot many of the tiny, black insects that crawl about the ground in millions.

'He must have made his lassoo and tried to draw the rifle or the knife towards himself. They were mighty close by but still beyond his reach. How long he tried to reach these things which would bring him death, and how long it was before thirst and pain and ants killed him, nobody knows. But he didn't look pretty when we found him. These damned ants,' and he spat ferociously several times. 'We searched and found his tent. But there were no papers. We pulled him out from below the tree and buried him. The government pays you £5 for such a job,' remarked the driver with satisfaction, 'and since I didn't know him meself, my passenger cut this foreign word into the bark, saying that's his family name. But he smiled saying it and I fancy he pulled my leg. 'Did you ever hear of such a name?' he added, using the whip on his team of horses.

'Yes,' I answered quietly. 'It is rather a large family.'

'Be damned,' said the driver. 'Of course out here we know people only by their Christian names.' And then we drove on.

The driver of the mail coach seemed pleased with the reception of his yarn; he loosened up a bit, and treated me thereafter more like a fellow on his own intellectual level. It made me proud. But it was no time before my friend realised that I was after all only a new chum. I had asked some questions which gave me away. He must have thought he had been hasty in crediting me with intelligence. He tried to rectify it. I pondered about the fact that those who live in the bush, such hard lives like bushmen, should be so jealous of their profession. A new chum who seeks their company is treated with contempt, probably arising from an inferiority complex. How differently men in other strata of society receive new-comers...

The road got worse and worse. Without avail did the driver lose himself in a labyrinth of profanity and curse systematically every one of his horses as a whole and in parts from tail to mouth, then generalise his curses, expanding to his coach, the bush, the colony, Australia itself, the planets and all creation.

'You'll have to get off,' he exploded at last, 'otherwise we'll never get there.' I complied silently and resigned myself to the inevitable. We had reached a hilly part and long rises seemed to be too much for the unfortunate team. Besides, I was glad to stretch my legs after the long ride in the rattling box. I waded through the deep, white dust, trailing after the Royal Mail till we reached the top of the hill. I then resumed my place again and our coach descended quickly downhill, in fact too fast for our poor team of horses. But the driver explained to me that horses were very cheap in Australia. He never mentioned the risk confronting passengers and I did not dare to touch on the subject.

My friend the driver started again to tell anecdotes and jokes, but, since he attempted to adapt them to my intellectual level, he generally missed the point. At least that was my impression. By some chance they might never have had a point at all. I only listened with half an ear. I became depressed by the dust, the heat, being shaken to pieces, and the ugly dead appearance of the scenery around me. What could a human being see in such an existence? Where was the power to entice him to these bare, red-hot rocks? Where was the lure to entice him into these lean arms, to this thirsty bosom of nature? Instinctively I began to realise the true connection between bush and man. I guessed rightly, and had it confirmed later on. It was the story of the vampire and its victim. The steel-blue empty sky draws the soul out of its victims. Their individuality becomes lost in the infinity like a single tear in the ocean.

Bloodless age warms itself on the young, vital bodies of the victims. And what reward...?

I remembered the kangaroo-hunter and his sticky end. I interrupted the driver whilst he was telling one of his funny stories: 'Do such cases happen often?' 'What cases?' 'Such accidents as the one with the young fellow you buried last year.'

The driver seemed offended. He glared at me and I felt uncomfortable. But before I could apologize, he relaxed and started to grin, introductory to what he had to say. 'Hm,' he said. 'Yes, I just come to think of it, a funny thing I once experienced in South Queensland...I mean a friend of mine...or, as a matter of fact, he heard it from a man, who...but never mind. Every word is gospel truth.'

(before 1903)

Henry Lawson
IN A DRY SEASON

Draw a wire fence and a few ragged gums, and add some scattered sheep running away from the train. Then you'll have the bush all along the New South Wales Western line from Bathurst on.

The railway towns consist of a public house and a general store, with a square tank and a schoolhouse on piles in the nearer distance. The tank stands at the end of the school and is not many times smaller than the building itself. It is safe to call the pub 'The Railway Hotel', and the store 'The Railway Stores', with an 's'. A couple of patient, ungroomed hacks are probably standing outside the pub, while their masters are inside having a drink— several drinks. Also it's safe to draw a sundowner sitting listlessly on a bench on the verandah, reading the *Bulletin*.

The Railway Stores seem to exist only in the shadow of the pub, and it is impossible to conceive either as being independent of the other. There is sometimes a small, oblong weatherboard building—unpainted, and generally leaning in one of the eight possible directions, and perhaps with a twist in another—which, from its half-obliterated sign, seems to have started as a rival to the Railway Stores; but the shutters are up and the place empty.

The only town I saw that differed much from the above consisted of a box-bark humpy with a clay chimney, and a woman standing at the door throwing out the wash-up water.

By way of variety, the artist might make a water-colour-sketch of a fettler's tent on the line, with a billy hanging over the fire in front, and three fettlers standing round filling their pipes.

Slop sac suits, red faces, and old-fashioned, flat-brimmed hats, with wire round the brims, begin to drop into the train on the other side of Bathurst; and here and there a hat with three inches of crape round the crown, which perhaps signifies death in the family at some remote date, and perhaps doesn't. Sometimes, I believe, it only means grease under the band. I notice that when a bushman puts crape round his hat he generally leaves it there till the hat wears out, or another friend dies. In the latter case, he buys a new piece of crape. This outward sign of bereavement usually has a jolly red face beneath it. Death is about the only cheerful thing in the bush.

We crossed the Macquarie—a narrow, muddy gutter with a dog swimming across, and three goats interested.

A little further on we saw the first sundowner. He carried a Royal Alfred, and had a billy in one hand and a stick in the other. He was dressed in a tailcoat turned yellow, a print shirt, and a pair of moleskin trousers, with big square calico patches on the knees; and his old straw hat was covered with calico. Suddenly he slipped his swag, dropped his billy, and ran forward, boldly flourishing the stick. I thought that he was mad, and was about to attack the train, but he wasn't; he was only killing a snake. I didn't have time to see whether he cooked the snake or not—perhaps he only thought of Adam.

Somebody told me that the country was very dry on the other side of Nevertire. It is. I wouldn't like to sit down on it anywhere. The least horrible spot in the bush, in a dry season, is where the bush isn't—where it has been cleared away and a green crop is trying to grow. They talk of settling people on the land! Better settle *in* it. I'd rather settle on the water; at least, until some gigantic system of irrigation is perfected in the West.

Along about Byrock we saw the first shearers. They dress like the unemployed, but differ from that body in their looks of independence. They sat on trucks and wool-bales and the fence, watching the train, and hailed Bill, and Jim, and Tom, and asked how those individuals were getting on.

Here we came across soft felt hats with straps round the crowns, and full-bearded faces under them. Also a splendid-looking black tracker in a masher uniform and a pair of Wellington boots.

One or two square-cuts and stand-up collars struggle dismally through to the bitter end. Often a member of the unemployed starts cheerfully out, with a letter from the Government Labour Bureau in his pocket, and nothing else. He has an idea that the station where he has the job will be within easy walking distance of Bourke. Perhaps he thinks there'll be a cart or buggy waiting for him. He travels for a night and day without a bite to eat, and, on arrival, he finds that the station is eighty or a hundred miles away. Then he has to explain matters to a publican and a coach-driver. God bless the publican and the coach-driver! God forgive our social system!

Native industry was represented at one place along the line by three tiles, a chimney-pot, and a length of piping on a slab.

Somebody said to me, 'Yer wanter go out back, young man, if yer wanter see the country. Yer wanter get away from the line.' I don't wanter; I've been there.

You could go to the brink of eternity so far as Australia is concerned and yet meet an animated mummy of a swagman who will talk of going 'out back'. Out upon the out-back fiend!

About Byrock we met the bush liar in all his glory. He was dressed like—like a bush larrikin. His name was Jim. He had been to a ball where some blank had 'touched' his blanky overcoat. The overcoat had a cheque for ten 'quid' in the pocket. He didn't seem to feel the loss much. 'Wot's ten quid?' He'd been everywhere, including the Gulf country. He still had three or four sheds to go to. He had telegrams in his pocket from half-a-dozen squatters and supers offering him pens on any terms. He didn't give a blank whether he took them or no. He thought at first he had the telegrams on him, but found that he had left them in the pocket of the overcoat aforesaid. He had learned butchering in a day. He was a bit of a scrapper himself and talked a lot about the ring. At the last station where he shore he gave the super the father of a hiding. The super was a big chap, about six foot three, and had knocked out Paddy Somebody in one round. He worked with a man who shore 400 sheep in nine hours.

Here a quiet-looking bushman in a corner of the carriage grew restless, and presently he opened his mouth and took the liar down in about three minutes.

At 5.30 we saw a long line of camels moving out across the sunset. There's something snaky about camels. They remind me of turtles and iguanas.

Somebody said, 'Here's Bourke.'

(1892)

Henry Lawson
THE UNION BURIES ITS DEAD

While out boating one Sunday afternoon on a billabong across the river, we saw a young man on horseback driving some horses along the bank. He said it was a fine day, and asked if the water was deep there. The joker of our party said it was deep enough to drown him, and he laughed and rode farther up. We didn't take much notice of him.

Next day a funeral gathered at a corner pub and asked each other in to have a drink while waiting for the hearse. They passed away some of the time dancing jigs to a piano in the bar parlour. They passed away the rest of the time sky-larking and fighting.

The defunct was a young union labourer, about twenty-five, who had been drowned the previous day while trying to swim some horses across a billabong of the Darling.

He was almost a stranger in town, and the fact of his having been a union man accounted for the funeral. The police found some union papers in his swag, and called at the General Labourers' Union Office for information about him. That's how we knew. The secretary had very little information to give. The departed was a 'Roman', and the majority of the town were otherwise—but unionism is stronger than creed. Drink, however, is stronger than unionism; and, when the hearse presently arrived, move than two-thirds of the funeral were unable to follow. They were too drunk.

The procession numbered fifteen, fourteen souls following the broken shell of a soul. Perhaps not one of the fourteen possessed a soul any more than the corpse did—but that doesn't matter.

Four or five of the funeral, who were boarders at the pub, borrowed a trap which the landlord used to carry passengers to and from the railway station. They were strangers to us who were on foot, and we to them. We were all strangers to the corpse.

A horseman, who looked like a drover just returned from a big trip, dropped into our dusty wake and followed us a few hundred yards, dragging his packhorse behind him, but a friend made wild and demonstrative signals from a hotel verandah—hooking at the air in front with his right hand and jobbing his left thumb over his shoulder in the direction of the bar—so the drover hauled off and didn't catch up to us any more. He was a stranger to the entire show.

We walked in twos. There were three twos. It was very hot and dusty; the heat rushed in fierce dazzling rays across every iron roof and light-coloured wall that was turned to the sun. One or two pubs closed respectfully until we got past. They closed their bar doors and the patrons went in and out through some side or back entrance for a few minutes. Bushmen seldom grumble at an inconvenience of this sort, when it is caused by a funeral. They have too much respect for the dead.

On the way to the cemetery we passed three shearers sitting on the shady side of a fence. One was drunk—very drunk. The other two covered their right ears with their hats, out of respect of the departed—whoever he might have been—and one of them kicked the drunk and muttered something to him.

He straightened himself up, stared, and reached helplessly for his hat, which he shoved half off and then on again. Then he made a great effort to pull himself together—and succeeded. He stood up, braced his back against the fence, knocked off his hat, and remorsefully placed his foot on it—to keep it off his head till the funeral passed.

A tall, sentimental drover, who walked by my side, cynically quoted Byronic verses suitable to the occasion—to death—and asked with pathetic humour whether we thought the dead man's ticket would be recogonised 'over yonder'. It was a GLU ticket, and the general opinion was that it would be recognised.

Presently my friend said:

'You remember when we were in the boat yesterday, we saw a man driving some horses along the bank?'

'Yes.'

He nodded at the hearse and said:

'Well, that's him.'

I thought awhile.

'I didn't take any particular notice of him,' I said. 'He said something, didn't he?'

'Yes; said it was fine day. You'd have taken more notice if you'd known that he was doomed to die in the hour, and that those were the last words he would say to any man in this world.'

'To be sure,' said a full voice from the rear. 'If ye'd known that, ye'd have prolonged the conversation.'

We plodded on across the railway line and along the hot, dusty road which ran to the cemetery, some of us talking about the accident, and lying about the narrow escapes we had had ourselves. Presently someone said:

'There's the Devil.'

I looked up and saw a priest standing in the shade of the tree by the cemetery gate.

The hearse was drawn up and the tail-boards were opened. The funeral extinguished its right ear with its hat as four men lifted the coffin out and laid it over the grave. The priest—a pale, quiet young fellow—stood under the shade of a sapling which grew at the head of the grave. He took off his hat, dropped it carelessly on the ground, and proceeded to business. I noticed that one or two heathens winced slightly when the holy water was sprinkled on the coffin. The drops quickly evaporated, and the little round black spots they left were soon dusted over; but the spots showed, by contrast, the cheapness and shabbiness of the cloth with which the coffin was covered. It seemed black before; now it looked a dusky grey.

Just here man's ignorance and vanity made a farce of the funeral. A big, bull-necked publican, with heavy, blotchy features, and a supremely ignorant expression, picked up the priest's straw hat and held it about two inches over the head of his reverence during the whole of the service. The father, be it remembered, was standing in the shade. A few shoved their hats on and off uneasily, struggling between their disgust for the living and their respect for the dead. The hat had a conical crown and a brim sloping down all round like a sunshade, and the publican held it with his great red claw spread over the crown. To do the priest justice, perhaps he didn't notice the incident. A stage priest or parson in the same position might have said, 'Put the hat down, my friend; is not the memory of our departed brother worth more than my complexion?' A wattlebark layman might have expressed himself in stronger language, none the less to the point. But my priest seemed unconscious of what was going on. Besides, the publican was a great and important pillar of the Church. He couldn't, as an ignorant and conceited ass, lose such a good opportunity of asserting his faithfulness and importance to his Church. The grave looked very narrow under the coffin, and I drew a breath of relief when the box slid easily down. I saw a coffin get stuck once, at Rookwood, and it had to be yanked out with difficulty, and laid on the sods at the feet of the heartbroken relations, who howled dismally while the grave-diggers widened the hole. But they don't cut contracts so fine in the West. Our grave-digger was not altogether bowelless, and, out of respect for that human quality described as 'feelin's', he scraped up some light and dusty soil and threw it down to deaden the fall of the clay lumps on the coffin. He also tried to steer the first few shovelsful gently down against the end of the grave with the back of the shovel turned outwards, but the hard, dry Darling River clods rebounded and knocked all the same. It didn't matter much—nothing does. The fall of lumps of clay on a stranger's coffin doesn't sound any different from the fall of the same things on an ordinary wooden box—at least I didn't notice anything awesome or unusual in the sound; but, perhaps, one of us—the most sensitive—might have been impressed by being reminded of a burial of long ago, when the thump of every sod jolted his heart.

I have left out the wattle—because it wasn't there. I have also neglected to mention the heartbroken old mate, with his grizzled head bowed and great pearly drops streaming down his rugged cheeks. He was absent—he was probably 'Out Back'. For similar reasons I have omitted reference to the suspicious moisture in the eyes of a bearded bush ruffian named Bill. Bill failed to turn up, and the only moisture was that which was induced by the heat. I have left out the 'sad Australian sunset' because the sun was not going down at the time. The burial took place exactly at mid-day.

The dead bushman's name was Jim, apparently; but they found no portraits, nor locks of hair, nor any love letters, nor anything of that kind in his swag—not even a reference to his mother; only some papers relating to union matters. Most of us didn't know the name till we saw it on the coffin; we knew him as 'that poor chap that got drowned yesterday'.

'So his name's James Tyson,' said my drover acquaintance, looking at the plate.

'Why! Didn't you know that before?' I asked.

'No; but I knew he was a union man.'

It turned out, afterwards, that J.T. wasn't his real name—only 'the name he went by'.

Anyhow he was buried by it, and most of the 'Great Australian Dailies' have mentioned in their brevity columns that a young man named James John Tyson was drowned in a billabong of the Darling last Sunday.

We did hear, later on, what his real name was; but if we ever chance to read it in the 'Missing Friends Column', we shall not be able to give any information to heart-broken Mother or Sister or Wife, nor to any one who could let him hear something to his advantage—for we have already forgotten the name.

(1893)

A. B. ('Banjo') Paterson
AN ANSWER TO VARIOUS BARDS

Well, I've waited mighty patient while they all came rolling in,
Mister Lawson, Mister Dyson, and the others of their kin,
With their dreadful, dismal stories of the Overlander's camp
How his fire is always smoky, and his boots are always damp;
And they paint it so terrific it would fill one's soul with gloom—   5
But you know they're fond of writing about 'corpses' and 'the tomb'.
So, before they curse the bushland, they should let their fancy range,
And take something for their livers, and be cheerful for a change.

Now, for instance, Mr. Lawson—well, of course, we almost cried
At the sorrowful description how his 'little 'Arvie' died,   10
And we lachrymosed in silence when 'His Father's Mate' was slain;
Then he went and killed the father, and we had to weep again.
Ben Duggan and Jack Denver, too, he caused them to expire,
After which he cooked the gander of Jack Dunn, of Nevertire;

And, no doubt, the bush *is* wretched if you judge it by the groan   15
Of the sad and soulful poet with a graveyard of his own.

And he spoke in terms prophetic of a revolution's heat,
When the world should hear the clamour of those people in the
    street;
But the shearer chaps who start it—why, he rounds on them in
    blame,
And he calls 'em 'agitators' who are living on the game.   20
But I 'over-write' the bushmen! Well, I own without a doubt
That I always see a hero in the 'man from furthest out'.
I could never contemplate him through an atmosphere of gloom,
And a bushman never struck me as a subject for 'the tomb'.

If it ain't all 'golden sunshine' where the 'wattle branches wave',   25
Well, it ain't all damp and dismal, and it ain't all 'lonely grave'.
And, of course, there's no denying that the bushman's life is rough,
But a man can easy stand it if he's built of sterling stuff;
Though it's seldom that the drover gets a bed of eiderdown,
Yet the man who's born a bushman, he gets mighty sick of town,   30
For he's jotting down the figures, and he's adding up the bills
While his heart is simply aching for a sight of Southern hills.

Then he hears a wool-team passing with a rumble and a lurch,
And, although the work is pressing, yet it brings him off his perch.
For it stirs him like a message from his station friends afar   35
And he seems to sniff the ranges in the scent of wool and tar;
And it takes him back in fancy, half in laughter half in tears,
To a sound of other voices and a thought of other years,
When the woolshed rang with bustle from the dawning of the day,
And the shear-blades were a-clicking to the cry of 'Wool away!'   40

Then his face was somewhat browner, and his frame was firmer
    set—
And he feels his flabby muscles with a feeling of regret.
But the wool-team slowly passes, and his eyes go sadly back
To the dusty little table and the papers in the rack,
And his thoughts go to the terrace where his sickly children squall,   45
And he thinks there's something healthy in the bush-life after all.
But we'll go no more a-droving in the wind or in the sun,
For our fathers' hearts have failed us and the droving days are done.

There's a nasty dash of danger where the long-horned bullock
    wheels,
And we like to live in comfort and to get our reg'lar meals.   50
For to hang around the townships suits us better, you'll agree,
And a job at washing bottles is the job for such as we.
Let us herd into the cities, let us crush and crowd and push
Till we lose the love of roving, and we learn to hate the bush;
And we'll turn our aspirations to a city life and beer,   55
And we'll slip across to England—it's a nicer place than here;

For there's not much risk of hardship where all comforts are in store,
And the theatres are in plenty, and the pubs are more and more.

But that ends it, Mr. Lawson, and it's time to say good-bye,
So we must agree to differ in all friendship, you and I.   60
Yes, we'll work our own salvation with the stoutest hearts we may,
And if fortune only favours we will take the road some day,
And go droving down the river 'neath the sunshine and the stars,
And then return to Sydney and vermilionize the bars.

(1892)

A. G. Stephens
from ONE REALIST AND ANOTHER

Realistic art, as reiterated, is the universal expression of a particular impression. [. . .]

The steps of that art are thus three in number. First, there is the statement of the thing seen. Second, there is the statement of the thing seen so that it becomes a type of its class. Third, there is the statement of the type so that it is seen in relation to all things, all types; becomes universal in its reference—a key to unlock every comprehending mind. [. . .]

Barbara Baynton has taken only the first step. Her studies of some Australian people and scenes are realistic beyond anything of the kind yet written here—beyond Lawson, even beyond Miles Franklin. Bit by bit, with careful epithet after epithet, the work is built up until nothing could be closer to the life. Flaubert would have been in ecstasy over such a pupil: for minute fidelity there has been no writer anywhere to surpass this writer.

But always or nearly always Mrs Baynton remains on the first plane of realism—she describes wonderfully well the thing she sees; but that thing is not a human type, or is a human type for Australia only. So that the reader, on the third plane, has to strain his mind to an unfinished piece of realistic art, if he would receive the message which is that art's justification and climax. And, if he have not Australian knowledge, this is a task which the reader cannot achieve.

The value of *Bush Studies* for Australians is another matter. Despite inequalities and some lack of finish, they deserve the warmest praise. 'Bush Church' simply could not be set down better. 'Squeaker's Mate' lacks an ending; but as far as it goes it is almost similarly perfect. 'The Chosen Vessel' has been added to since it appeared as the 'The Tramp' in *The Bulletin*, and the additional matter has been inserted in the wrong place; but none the less it is astonishingly graphic. To 'Billy Skywonkie' and 'Scrammy 'And' the same praise applies.

The book contains only half-a-dozen sketches; and four of them are in all essentials perfect so far as they go. This is uncompromising commendation; but *Bush Studies* deserves uncompromising commendation. So precise, so complete, with such insight into detail and such force of statement, it ranks with the masterpieces of literary realism in any language.

On the first plane only.

(1903)

Miles Franklin
MY BRILLIANT CAREER

from CHAPTER 22

SWEET SEVENTEEN

Monday arrived—last day of November and seventeenth anniversary of my birth—and I celebrated it in a manner which I capitally enjoyed.

It was the time of the annual muster at Cummabella—a cattle-station seventeen miles eastward from Caddagat—and all our men were there assisting. Word had been sent that a considerable number of beasts among those yarded bore the impress of the Bossier brand on their hides; so on Sunday afternoon uncle Jay-Jay had also proceeded thither to be in readiness for the final drafting early on Monday morning. This left us manless, as Frank Hawden, being incapacitated with a dislocated wrist, was spending a few weeks in Gool-Gool until he should be fit for work again.

Uncle had not been gone an hour when a drover appeared to report that twenty thousand sheep would pass through on the morrow. Grass was precious. It would not do to let the sheep spread and dawdle at their drovers' pleasure. There was not a man on the place; grannie was in a great stew; so I volunteered my services. At first she would not hear of such a thing, but eventually consented. With many injunctions to conduct myself with proper stiffness, I started early on Monday morning. I was clad in a cool blouse, a holland riding-skirt, and a big straw hat; was seated on a big bay horse, was accompanied by a wonderful sheep-dog, and carried a long heavy stock-whip. I sang and cracked my stock-whip as I cantered along, quite forgetting to be reserved and proper. Presently I came upon the sheep just setting out for their day's tramp, with a black boy ahead of them, of whom I inquired which was the boss. He pointed towards a man at the rear wearing a donkey-supper hat. I made my way through the sheep in his direction, and asked if he were in charge of them. On being answered in the affirmative, I informed him that I was Mr Bossier's niece, and, as the men were otherwise engaged, I would see the sheep through.

'That's all right, miss. I will look out that you don't have much trouble,' he replied, politely raising his hat, while a look of amusement played on his face.

He rode away, and shouted to his men to keep the flock strictly within bounds and make good travelling.

'Right you are, boss,' they answered; and returning to my side he told me his name was George Ledwood, and made some remarks about the great drought and so on, while we rode in the best places to keep out of the dust and in the shade. I asked questions such as whence came the sheep? whither were they bound? and how long had they been on the road? And having exhausted these orthodox remarks, we fell a-talking in dead earnest without the least restraint. I listened with interest to stories of weeks and weeks spent beneath the sun and stars while crossing widths of saltbush country, mulga and myall scrubs, of encounters with blacks in Queensland, and was favoured with a graphic description of a big strike among the shearers when the narrator had been boss-of-the-board out beyond Bourke. He spoke as though well educated, and a gentleman—as drovers often are. Why, then, was he on the road? I put him down as a scapegrace, for he had all the winning pleasant manner of a ne'er-do-well.

At noon—a nice, blazing, dusty noon—we halted within a mile of Caddagat for lunch. I could have easily ridden home for mine, but preferred to have it with the drovers for fun. The men boiled the billy and made the tea, which we drank out of tin pots, with tinned fish and damper off tin plates as the completion of the *menu*, Mr Ledwood and I at a little distance from the men. Tea boiled in a billy at a bush fire has a deliciously aromatic flavour, and I enjoyed my birthday lunch immensely. Leaving the cook to collect the things and put them in the spring-cart, we continued on our way, lazily lolling on our horses and chewing gum-leaves as we went.

When the last of the sheep got off the Caddagat run it was nearing two o'clock.

Mr Ledwood and I shook hands at parting, each expressing a wish that we might meet again some day.

I turned and rode homewards. I looked back and saw the drover gazing after me. I waved my hand; he raised his hat and smiled, displaying his teeth, a gleam of white in his sunbrowned face. I kissed my hand to him; he bowed low; I whistled to my dog; he resumed his way behind the crawling sheep; I cantered home quickly and dismounted at the front gate at 2.30 pm, a dusty, heated, tired girl.

Grannie came out to question me regarding the sex, age, condition, and species of the sheep, what was their destination, whether they were in search of grass or were for sale, had they spread or eaten much grass, and had the men been civil?

When I had satisfactorily informed her on all these points, she bade me have something to eat, to bathe and dress, and gave me a holiday for the remainder of the day.

My hair was grey with dust, so I washed all over, arrayed myself in a cool white dress, and throwing myself in a squatter's chair in the veranda, spread my hair over the back of it to dry. Copies of Gordon, Kendall, and Lawson were on my lap, but I was too physically content and comfortable to indulge in even these, my sworn friends and companions. I surrendered myself to the mere joy of being alive. How the sunlight blazed and danced in the roadway—the leaves of the gum-trees gleaming in it like a myriad gems! A cloud of white, which I knew to be cockatoos, circled over the distant hilltop. Nearer they wheeled until I could hear their discordant screech. The thermometer on the wall rested at 104 degrees despite the dense shade thrown on the broad old veranda by the foliage of creepers, shrubs, and trees. The gurgling rush of the creek, the scent of the flower-laden garden, and the stamp, stamp of a horse in the orchard as he attempted to rid himself of tormenting flies, filled my senses. The warmth was delightful. Summer is heavenly, I said—life is a joy.

Aunt Helen's slender fingers looked artistic among some pretty fancy-work upon which she was engaged. Bright butterflies flitted round the garden, and thousands of bees droned lazily among the flowers. I closed my eyes—my being filled with the beauty of it all.

I could hear grannie's pen fly over the paper as she made out a list of Christmas supplies on a table near me.

'Helen, I suppose a hundredweight of currants will be sufficient?'

'Yes; I should think so.'

'Seven dozen yards of unbleached calico be enough?'

'Yes; plenty.'

'Which tea-service did you order?'

'Number two.'

'Do you or Sybylla want anything extra?'

'Yes; parasols, gloves, and some books.'

'Books! Can I get them at Hordern's?'

'Yes.'

Grannie's voice faded on my ears, my thoughts ran on uncle Jay-Jay. He had promised to be home in time for my birthday spread, and I was sure he had a present for me. What would it be?—something nice. He would be nearly sure to bring someone home with him from Cummabella, and we would have games and fun to no end. I was just seventeen, only seventeen, and had a long, long life before me wherein to enjoy myself. Oh, it was good to be alive! What a delightful place the world was!—so accommodating, I felt complete mistress of it. It was like an orange—I merely had to squeeze it and it gave forth sweets plenteously. The stream sounded far away, the sunlight blazed and danced, grannie's voice was a pleasant murmur in my ear, the cockatoos screamed over the house and passed away to the west. Summer is heavenly and life is a joy, I reiterated. Joy! Joy! There was joy in the quit! quit! of the green-and-crimson parrots, which swung for a moment in the rose-bush over the gate, and then whizzed on into the summer day. There was joy in the gleam of the sun and in the hum of the bees, and it throbbed in my heart. Joy! Joy! A jackass laughed his joy as he perched on the telegraph wire out in the road. Joy! Joy! Summer is a dream of delight and life is a joy, I said in my heart. I was repeating the one thing over and over—but ah! it was a measure of happiness which allowed of much repetition. The cool murmur of the creek grew far away, I felt my poetry books slip off my knees and fall to the floor, but I was too content to bother about them—too happy to need their consolation, which I had previously so often and so hungrily sought. Youth! Joy! Warmth!

(1901)

Joseph Furphy
from THE BULN-BULN AND THE BROLGA

'We was talkin' about blackfellers,' continued Bob, recalling himself. 'I'd jist put it this way; it's wrong to be too hard on the pore beggars; an' it don't do to be too soft with 'em. I seen one little instance, the fust time me an' Bat was up north. Tell you how it come—

'Me and Bat was ridin' in by our two selves from Drumclog, in Queensland; an' it was always safe to have a rifle with you about that quarter; an' we was layin' out to stop all night at Yandaree. Well, gittin' on in the afternoon, an' us dodgin' up to the back o' the station, we hears the crack of a gun, an' then another crack. Course, we thought nothing of it; but I'll tell you what was takin' place at the time—

'The man that owned the station—nice feller he is, as you'd meet in a week's travellin'—he'd on'y been there a couple or three months; an' he'd come from a part where the blackfellers was quiet as sheep, on account of all the rumbumptious fellers gittin' dispersed. Well, this Moorfield had jist shifted his fambly to Yandaree; an' this afternoon he was at home, doin' a bit o' carpenter work; an' his missus she was pokin' about the house; an' the kids was playin' under a tree at the back door; an' Miss Moorfield she was sittin' in the front veranda, readin' a book; an' the servant girl was moochin' round as usual; an' the couple or three hands was away that day at the joinin' station, helpin' to muster. There was a whole swag o' blackfellers had come into a deep holler, half a mile away, but they was supposed to be tame—though, mind you, they hadn't got their Marys or piccaninnies with 'em.

'Well, Miss Moorfield she hears a "Woh!" an' she sees a big buck blackfeller comin' along solitary, with three or four spears. She didn't altogether like the looks of him, bein'—well, bein' jist in his skin, so to speak; an' she was goin' inside; an' he lets fly a spear at her. It didn't hit her, but it nailed the gown-part of her frock to the wall; an' she makes a dart for the door, leaving' half her frock stickin' on the spear; an' in she bolts, an' slaps the door shut behind her. Broad daylight, if you please!

'Course, Moorfield, he got excited; an' he collars holt of his rifle, an' runs out on the veranda—

'"Clear off!" he sings cut; an' he levels his rifle at the blackfeller. The blackfeller he stopped, but he wouldn't clear off—not frightened enough. He knowed who he'd got to deal with. That's the grand secret, missus.

'"Clear off!" says Moorfield agen; an' he fires a shot over the black-feller's head. Rotten bad line. The blackfeller he runs back a bit, an' then comes forrid slowly. Moorfield he presents his rifle, an' the blackfeller laughs. Both o' them killin' time; but the blackfeller was gainin', hand over fist—on'y Moorfield couldn't see it.

'Well, this style o' thing was goin' on when me an' Bat come so as we could see across a bit of a rise at the back o' the station. We pulls up, an' looks at one another.

'"Blackfellers!" says Bat. "Jist in time."

'"There's my dream out!" says I.

'"Holy snake! you're right," says Bat. That was the pore feller's favourite word. 'Sort o' technical phrase. "If we scoot up the bed o' the creek," says he, "we'll git a sittin' shot to start with."

'So it was no time before we was dartin' up through the back garden, layin' on our horses' necks—an' the fun of it was that the blackfellers was watchin' every road but that one, in case the station hands might be turnin' up.

'"Thank God! thank God" says Mrs Moorfield, when she seen us; an' her as white as a sheet, an' her arms round the whole bunch o' kids.

'We fetches our horses right into the back veranda, behind some creep-ers, an' walks into the house, an' looks through the winder o' the front room. Moorfield he was standin' in the door; an' there was the blackfeller laughin' an' dancin'; an' ten to fifteen more blackfellers sneakin' up from one cover to another, half-game an' half-frightened. Bat he lifts the winder about two inches, an' drops on one knee—that bein' his favourite style, pore feller.

'"Don't shed blood till you can't help it," says Moorfield. "Jist keep him at a distance for one minute more, to give him a chance. I always been on the best o' terms with the blacks," says he. "If you kill that feller, we'll have to fight the whole tribe."

'"Ain't you got to fight the whole tribe now?" says Bat. "You ain't looked round yet. But you want to let this bloke hear the bizz o' the bullet. Watch here"—an' he lets drive.

'The blackfeller he jumps up about two foot, or mebbe two foot an' a half; an' flaps down on his face. Then other blackfellers that we'd never seen a sight of, not to mention the ones we had noticed, they began to show up everywhere, but they all walked off to the nearest brigalow. Fact, they run; for I lined two o' them, an' got one out o' the two; then Bat he missed the next one; an' I rolled another feller over, but he crep' away among some bushes. Then we both wasted a couple o' shots, through bein' in too great a hurry. Then Bat—he was wonderful quick, pore ole Bat!— he lames another feller; an' away scoots the rest o' the mob, takin' all the cover that come in their road. You see, missus, when the bully o' the tribe was dispersed, the others was like a swarm o' bees with no queen. Course, me an' Bat we jumped on our horses agen, an' started the whole drove across the country, till our rifles was too hot to handle—for we'd no end o' cartridges. Providence sent us round that road, for a certainty. Still, you'll hear people sayin' there's nothing in dreams.'

'Did you dream of this adventure beforehand, Mr Bruce?' asked the lady, with vivid solicitude.

'Tell you what I dreamed the very night before. I dreamed I was fishin' in a sort o' black lagoon, baitin' with bits o' water-melon, an' pullin' out fish with blackfellers' heads on 'em.'

'But wasn't there some danger of the survivors plotting revenge?' asked the lady, after a pause.

'Well, no. The fust blackfeller was dead, an' that was the main object; dead as a nit; with the hole between his shoulders where the bullet come through.' He hesitated a moment, with the uneasy consciousness of something unappetizing in this post-mortem evidence; then, turning his soft, Byronic eyes on the lady's face, he resumed in a coldly scientific spirit. 'Curious thing about the Martin-Henry—you can hardly poke your finger in the hole where the bullet goes in at, but you could shove your fist in the place where she comes out.'

Then a troubled look, and a despondent mal-du-mulga sigh, bespoke the sensitive barbarian's appreciation of the lady's half-averted face and my stony silence.

'While Mr Bruce was speaking of bullies, I thought of Wesley Tregurtha,' said Fred, turning to me. 'Do you know, I never could overcome my dislike of that boy. You may remember how I used to trounce him on the slightest possible pretext, or on no pretext whatever? Sometimes he resisted, too! I've known that boy, Mr Bruce, to fight till he could neither see nor stand. Upon my honour, I have. Poor devil! his end was a terrible one. It's a painful story, Tom, but I think it will interest you.'

'I'm sure it will,' I replied, flinching under the honest eyes of the past master.

'It was—let's see—in August '71,' continued Fred. 'I was coming back to Victoria, from England, in the *Aurungzebe*—1500 tons—George But-

terworth, master. One morning, at daylight—it was the tenth of August—
I heard a rap at my cabin door.

'"Come in," says I; and in comes Stokes, the mate, with a long face—'

'*Your* mate?' asked Bob, hiding his misery under an affectation of
critical interest.

Mrs Pritchard bent toward the last speaker while she courteously explained the rating of ships' crews; and straightway a sense of returning
self-respect threw sunshine over that incongruously lengthy effigy which
contained Bob.

'"Serious matter, Mr Falkland-Pritchard, I'm afraid," says Stokes.
"We're chased by a suspicious looking sail."

'"Probably a brother to our Mediterranean friend," says I, referring to
an incident of a few weeks before. "Don't disturb me, please. I'm sleepy
this morning. Call the old man."

'"Tanked up, as usual," says Stokes. "All the responsibility is on my
shoulders. For heaven's sake, let me have your assistance."

'I dressed myself, and went on deck. About a mile to windward, I saw a
wicked-looking craft, schooner rigged, keeping the weather gauge of us,
and decreasing her distance every moment. I should have told you that the
Aurungzebe was a sailing vessel.

'"She declines to answer our signals; what do you make of her?" says
Stokes, handing me a glass.

'Livens a man up wonderful, fust thing in the mornin,' observed Bob
approvingly.

'One look was sufficient. The long, low hull was bristling with the
muzzles of cannon, showing through the open ports,' continued Fred,
while a flash of intelligence passed over Bob's face, followed by a wave of
colour.

'"What shall we do, Mr Falkland-Pritchard?" says Stokes.

'"Call up the watch below, and batten down the hatchways," says I.
"Let us keep the passengers out of the way, and out of danger at the same
time."

'Just then a puff of smoke rose from one of the forward ports of the
schooner, and a shot whistled across our bows.

'"Couldn't the *Aurungzebe* get away from her, if you had the weather
gauge, and the wind on your quarter?" says I.

'"Not a doubt of it," says Stokes—"if we had a lead of a mile."

'"Heave to, and speak her, then," says I. "I'll be with you in a moment."

'I darted into my cabin, and slipped on an undress uniform, together
with a splendid sword, presented to me by the Emperor of the French.
Then I returned on deck. By this time, the schooner was hove to, half a
cable's length to windward, commanding us with her guns. Stokes was
waiting for me. I took the speaking-trumpet from his hand—

'"Ship ahoy!" I called out. "Who are you?"

'"Surrender, or I'll sink you!" was the answer, in a voice I thought I
recognized. It was the pirate captain—quite a young fellow. All the crew
seemed to be Malays. My resolution was taken at once.

'"I'm willing to surrender," says I, speaking through the trumpet. "As a
guarantee of good faith, I'll go on board your ship alone. Now, Stokes,"
says I, "man your halyards immediately, and the moment you see me

board that vessel, put your helm hard a-port, clap on every stitch of sail you can carry, and cross her stern. Then show her a clean pair of heels, and go like the deuce.'''

'You foolish, mad-headed thing!' murmured the desperado's wife, in a trembling voice.

'I jumped into the gig—'

'Jumped into the gig,' repeated Bob deprecatingly. Again his ministering angel explained, evidently finding relief in the distraction.

'—I jumped into the gig as she touched the water, and pulled across to the schooner. A rope-ladder was lowered, and in half a minute I was on deck. The pirate captain came forward.

'"Permit me to introduce myself," says I, with a deceit which may be forgiven under the circumstances—"Captain George Butterworth, of the ship *Aurungzebe*, at your service."

'As the words left my lips, there was a creaking, rushing, hissing sound; and the *Aurungzebe* dashed across the schooner's wake, showing one cloud of canvas from t'-galla'-m'st to deck, and every inch of it drawing hard.

'"Treachery!" yelled the pirate captain; and he rushed upon me, sword in hand. Now comes the surprising part of my story—a part which, for certain reasons, I have been in the habit of suppressing. I never forget a face I have once seen; and in the pirate captain I recognized—whom do you think, Tom?'

'I couldn't guess.'

'Then, by Jove, I recognized Wes Tregurtha! and he fairly foamed at the mouth as he recognized me.

'"I've caught you at last, Falkland-Pritchard!" he hissed through his clenched teeth.

'"And take my word for it, my good fellow, you've caught a Tartar!" says I, laughing. Then our blades crossed.

'By Jove, it was splendid! I had proved more than a match for the most skilful fencing-masters in France, but, deuce take me, I seemed to have met my equal at last.'

'The other blokes they never interfered?' suggested Bob, with docile interest.

'Asiatics are peculiarly susceptible to panic,' I remarked in explanation.

'I am no theorist,' continued Fred candidly; 'all I know is that they *didn't* interfere. They stood huddled together in the bow of the ship, watching Tregurtha and myself, as we stood, foot to foot; our blades bending and quivering, and crossing like flashes of lightning, while the spray of sparks flew like the very devil from both weapons. I soon saw that the game was in my own hands, for neither of us could gain one point on the other, and it would simply be a question of endurance. However, busy as I was, I noticed the sky turning black as ink; and, looking over Tregurtha's shoulder, I saw, along the western horizon, a thin line, like a thread of silver. Then I noticed a low, moaning sound that soon increased to a deafening roar; and the sky turned blacker, and the thin, white line grew broader and brighter; coming across the dark water with the speed of a race-horse. By Jove, it was a white squall!'

'Go to (sheol)!' murmured the rapt bushman.

'All this time, the duel went on. Tregurtha began to give way. I could

have cut him down, but, deuce take me, I thought of old times. Suddenly
the squall struck the schooner with the force of an avalanche. The sheets
snapped like threads of twine; the two masts went by the board; and I
found myself swimming for my life. I saw the mainmast floating beside me,
and I managed to get astride of it. Then, looking through the blinding
spray, I saw a man slowly drag himself out of the water and sit on the
other end of the mast. It was Tregurtha. He crept toward me without
speaking. When he approached within ten or twelve feet, we both prepared for a contest which could leave only one survivor. I saw him coolly
draw a long Venetian dagger, and throw the steel sheath into the sea. I was
unarmed. He still crept on like a tiger, watching me with murder in his
eyes. Nearer—nearer—till we were only a yard apart; then he sprung on
me. Quick as lightning, I caught his wrist, and endeavoured to wrench the
weapon from his grasp. At last, struggling desperately as we were, and the
mast pitching and rolling like the devil, his dagger-point struck him full
in the body—' here the narrator laid his hand tenderly upon his own
stomach in illustration—'the glass blade snapped off at the hilt, and the
fight was over.'

Bob drew a long breath. The lady's face was white as chalk. I was
listening with genuine admiration. You will notice that Fred's power lay
largely in the quality of compatibility, or congruity. You would never hear
him say, like your first-person-singular novelist-liar, 'my blood ran cold'—
'I was unnerved with terror'—'I never was so frightened in my life'—or
words to similar purport. He could see the inconsistency. With the instinct
of genius, he perceived that the genuine hero, relating his little adventure,
never descends to that sort of palaver, simply because attested courage
neither knows nor needs any such paltry foil. (Good counsel, marry; learn
it, learn it, marquess.) [...]

The bushman, whatever else he may be, is always a consecutive thinker,
balancing evidence with judicial circumspection; and he seldom speaks till
he has something to say. Bob turned to Mrs Pritchard.

'Curious thing how some yarns proves their own selves,' he remarked. 'I
notice that very forcible with your ole man. Now, when he said, quite
simple, about makin' observations to find out what part o' the sea he was
in, I seen the truth o' the yarn stickin' out a yard. Course, I seen the truth
of it all along; for schooners *has* on'y two masts, an' by the same token
sheets ain't sails, they're ropes. But that remark about takin' observations
sort o' clinched the yarn on the fur side.'

'You're a keen observer, Mr Bruce,' said the lady, half-suspiciously;
though she might have known that, to the barbarian's sense of propriety,
my own frivolous comment had made a clear vindication politely imperative.

'On'y some ways,' replied Bob, with a sigh. 'Most ways, I'm a more-
poke. But I can't help thinkin' about that pore outlawr layin' among the
ropes, sufferin' from pain an' agony; an' the birds pickin' his eyes out
while he's alive,' he continued thoughtfully. 'Minds me o' one time me an'
Bat was comin' home to Tarrawarra, after deliverin' a few fats at the
Palmer. Well, one night we sent Paddy O'Rafferty across the rise to look at
the horses—'

'There were three of you in the party, Mr Bruce?'

'No, missus; on'y me an' Bat. Paddy was a blackfeller. Well, he told us he seen a fire about a mile away, so us not bein' tired, we thought we'd walk across. We fetched our rifles with us for company, not expectin' any bother; but when we come near the fire, we begun to think different. Blackfellers mostly goes in for a piccaninny fire—jist three sticks, with the ends kep' together—but these fellers had a rouser; an' we begun to think they was at it agen. Cannivals. Us an' two other blokes had caught them jist finishin' off a Chow, on'y three weeks before; an' another Chow, with his legs broke, keepin' fresh for when he was wanted. Well, this time I'm tellin' you about, we seen a lot o' them in the light o' the fire; an' us about sixty yards away; an' by n' by two fellers comes out o' the dark, leadin' a lubra by both arms. They fetches her in front of the fire; an' us sneakin' a bit closer; an' another feller he grips a holt of her hair, an' drags her head down forrid, about *that* low; an' another feller he swings his nilla-nilla with both hands—

'"Fire!" says Bat, jist above his breath; an' we let fly the both of us together. Guess how many we got?'

The lady shook her head despairingly. She was in dreadful company this evening.

'Jist on'y the feller with the waddy,' continued Bob, with his melancholy smile. 'One bullet under the shoulder-blade, an' one at the butt o' the lug: But we was one second too late to save the pore lubra; her back was broke, an' her legs was useless. An' before we had time to shove in another cartridge, the blackfellers was gone like mallee-hens; an' no one was left on'y the lubra an' the corp.

'Next mornin' we passed the blackfellers' camp a bit after sunrise; an' there was the lubra ketchin' holt o' the grass an' stuff with both hands, tryin' to snake herself along the ground, to git a drink at the gilgie. I give her a drink with my pannikin, an' turned her over on her back—bein' a bit easier that way. Well, after we had went about a mile, I pulls up—

'"Bat," says I, "I'm thinkin, about that pore misfortunate. The crows'll have her eyes before she's dead."

'"Please yourself," says Bat. "I'll wait here till you come back."

'So I canters back; an' there was the lubra, layin' where I left her, pullin' up grass with her fingers, an' moanin' pitiful. I ties up my horse, an' sneaks on till I wasn't ten yards off of her; then I fires straight into the top of her head. She never knowed what put her out o' pain; an' I ain't frightened of her risin' up in judgment agen me.'

We were all silent for a minute.

(1898; published 1948)

Louis Stone
JONAH

from CHAPTER 3

CARDIGAN STREET AT HOME

Mrs Yabsley came to the door for a breath of fresh air, and surveyed Cardigan Street with a loving eye. She had lived there since her marriage twenty years ago, and to her it was the pick of Sydney, the centre of the habitable globe. She gave her opinion to every newcomer in her tremendous voice, that broke on their unaccustomed ears like thunder:

'I've lived 'ere ever since I was a young married woman, an' I know wot I'm talkin' about. My 'usband used ter take me to the play before we was married, but I never see any play equal ter wot 'appens in this street, if yer only keeps yer eyes open. I see people as wears spectacles readin' books. I don't wonder. If their eyesight was good, they'd be able ter see fer themselves instead of readin' about it in a book. I can't read myself, bein' no scholar, but I can see that books an' plays is fer them as ain't got no eyes in their 'eads.'

The street, which Mrs Yabsley loved, is a street of poor folk—people to whom poverty clings like their shirt. It tumbles over the ridge opposite the church, falls rapidly for a hundred yards, and then recovering its balance, saunters easily down the slope till it meets Botany Road on level ground. It is a street of small houses and large families, and strikes the eye as mean and dingy, for most of the houses are standing on their last legs, and paint is scarce. The children kick and scrape it off the fences, and their parents rub it off the walls by leaning against them in a tired way for hours at a stretch. On hot summer nights the houses empty their inhabitants on to the verandas and footpaths. The children, swarming like rabbits, play in the middle of the road. With clasped hands they form a ring, and circle joyously to a song of childland, the immemorial rhymes handed down from one generation to another as savages preserve tribal rites. The fresh, shrill voices break on the air, mingled with silvery peals of laughter.

> What will you give to know her name,
> Know her name, know her name?
> What will you give to know her name,
> On a cold and frosty morning?

Across the street comes a burst of coarse laughter, and a string of foul, obscene words on the heels of a jest. And again the childish trebles ring on the tainted air:

> Green gravel, green gravel,
> Your true love is dead;
> I send you a message
> To turn round your head.

They are ragged and dirty, true children of the gutter, but Romance, with the cloudy hair and starry eyes, holds them captive for a few merciful years. Their parents loll against the walls, or squat on the kerbstone, devouring with infinite relish petty scandals about their neighbours, or shaking with laughter at some spicy yarn.

About ten o'clock the children are driven indoors with threats and blows, and put to bed. By eleven the street is quiet, and only gives a last flicker of life when a drunken man comes swearing down the street, full of beer, and offering to fight any one for the pleasure of the thing. By twelve the street is dead, and the tread of the policeman echoes with a forlorn sound as if he were walking through a cemetery.

As Mrs Yabsley leaned over the gate, Mrs Swadling caught sight of her, and, throwing her apron over her head, crossed the street, bent on gossip. Then Mrs Jones, who had been watching her through the window, dropped her mending and hurried out.

The three women stood and talked of the weather, talking for talking's sake as men smoke a pipe in the intervals of work. Presently Mrs Yabsley looked hard at Mrs Swadling, who was shading her head from the sun with her apron.

'Wot's the matter with yer eye?' she said, abruptly.

'Nuthin',' said Mrs Swadling, and coloured.

The eye she was shading was black from a recent blow, a present from her husband, Sam the carter, who came home for his tea, fighting drunk, as regular as clockwork.

'I thought I 'eard Sam snorin' after tea,' said Mrs Jones.

'Yes, 'e was; but 'e woke up about twelve, an' give me beans 'cause I'd let 'im sleep till the pubs was shut.'

'An' yer laid 'im out wi' the broom-handle, I s'pose?'

'No fear,' said Mrs Swadling; 'I ran down the yard, an' 'ollered blue murder.'

'Well,' said Mrs Yabsley, reflectively, 'an 'usband is like the weather, or a wart on yer nose. It's no use quarrelling with it. If yer don't like it, yer've got ter lump it. An' if yer believe all yer 'ear, everybody else 'as got a worse.'

She looked down the street, and saw Jonah and Chook, with a few others of the push, sunning themselves in the morning air. Her face darkened.

'I see the push 'ave got Jimmy Sinclair at last. Only six months ago 'e went ter Sunday school reg'lar, an' butter wouldn't melt in 'is mouth. Well, if smokin' cigarettes, an' spittin', an' swearin' was 'ard work, they'd all die rich men. There's Waxy Collins. Last week 'e told 'is father 'e'd 'ave ter keep 'im till 'e was twenty-one 'cause of the law, an' the old fool believed 'im. An' little Joe Crutch, as used ter come 'ere beggin' a spoonful of drippin' fer 'is mother, come 'ome drunk the other night so natural, that 'is mother mistook 'im fer 'is father, an' landed 'im on the ear with 'er fist. An' 'im the apple of 'er eye, as the sayin' is. It's 'ard ter be a mother in Cardigan Street. Yer girls are mothers before their bones are set, an' yer sons are dodgin' the p'liceman round the corner before they're in long trousers.'

It was rare for Mrs Yabsley to touch on her private sorrows, and there was an embarrassing silence. But suddenly, from the corner of Pitt Street, appeared a strange figure of a man, roaring out a song in the voice of one selling fish. Every head turned.

''Ello,' said Mrs Jones, 'Froggy's on the job to-day.'

The singer was a Frenchman with a wooden leg, dressed as a sailor. As he hopped slowly down the street with the aid of a crutch, his grizzled beard and scowling face turned mechanically to right and left, sweeping the street with threatening eyes that gave him the look of a retired pirate, begging the tribute that he had taken by force in better days. The song ended abruptly, and he wiped the sweat from his face with an enormous handkerchief. Then he began another.

The women were silent, greedily drinking in the strange, foreign sounds, touched for a moment with the sense of things forlorn and far away. The singer still roared, but the tune was caressing, languishing, a love song. But his eyes rolled fiercely, and his moustache seemed to bristle with anger.

> Le pinson et la fauvette
> Chantaient nos chastes amours,
> Que les oiseaux chantent toujours,
> Pauvre Colinette, pauvre Colinette.

When he reached the women he hopped to the pavement, holding out his hat like a collection-plate, with a beseeching air. The women were embarrassed, grudging the pennies, but afraid of being thought mean. Mrs Yabsley broke the silence.

'I don't know wot ye're singin' about, an' I shouldn't like ter meet yer on a dark night, but I'm always willin' ter patronise the opera, as they say.'

She fumbled in her pocket till she found tuppence. The sailor took the money, rolled his eyes, gave her a magnificent bow, and continued his way with a fresh stanza:

> Lorsque nous allions tous deux
> Dans la verdoyante allée,
> Comme elle était essoufflée,
> Et comme j'étais radieux.

'The more fool you,' said Mrs Jones, who was ashamed of having nothing to give. 'I've 'eard 'e's got a terrace of 'ouses, an' thousands in the bank. My cousin told me 'e see 'im bankin' 'is money reg'lar in George Street every week.'

And then a conversation followed, with instances of immense fortunes made by organ-grinders, German bands, and street-singers—men who cadged in rags for a living, and could drive their carriage if they chose. The women lent a greedy ear to these romances, like a page out of their favourite novelettes.

They were interrupted by an extraordinary noise from the French singer, who seemed suddenly to have gone mad. The push had watched in ominous silence the approach of the Frenchman. But, as he passed them and finished a verse, a blood-curdling cry rose from the group. It was a perfect imitation of a dog baying the moon in agony. The singer stopped and scowled at the group, but the push seemed to be unaware of his existence. He moved on, and began another verse. As he stopped to take breath the cry went up again, the agonised wail of a cur whose feelings are harrowed by music. The singer stopped, choking with rage, bewildered by the novelty of the attack. The push seemed lost in thought. Again he turned to go, when a stone, jerked as if from a catapult, struck him on the shoulder. As he turned, roaring like a bull, a piece of blue metal struck him above the eye, cutting the flesh to the bone. The blood began to trickle slowly down his cheek.

Still roaring, he hopped on his crutch with incredible speed towards the push, who stood their ground for a minute and then, with the instinct of the cur, bolted. The sailor stopped, and shook his fist at their retreating forms, showering strange, foreign maledictions on the fleeing enemy. It was evident that he could swear better than he could sing.

'Them wretches is givin' Froggy beans,' said Mrs Swadling.

'Lucky fer 'im it's daylight, or they'd tickle 'is ribs with their boots,' said Mrs Jones.

'Jonah and Chook's at the bottom o' that,' said Mrs Swadling, looking hard at Mrs Yabsley.

'Ah! the devil an' 'is 'oof,' said Mrs Yabsley, grimly, and was silent.

The sailor disappeared round the corner, and five minutes later the push had slipped back, one by one, to their places under the veranda. Mrs Jones was in the middle of a story:

''Er breath was that strong, it nearly knocked me down, 'an so I sez to 'er, "Mark my words, I'll pocket yer insults no longer, an' you in a temperance lodge. I'll make it my bizness to go to the sekertary this very day, an' tell 'im of yer going's on." An' she sez...w'y, there she is again,' cried Mrs Jones, as she caught the sound of a shrill voice, high-pitched and quarrelsome. The women craned their necks to look.

A woman of about forty, drunken, bedraggled, dressed in dingy black, was pacing up and down the pavement in front of the barber's. She blinked like a drunken owl, and stepped high on the level footpath as if it were mountainous. And without looking at anything, she threw a string of insults at the barber, hiding behind the partition in his shop. For seven years she had passed as his wife, and then, one day, sick of her drunken bouts, he had turned her out, and married Flash Kate, the rag-picker's daughter. Sloppy Mary had accepted her lot with resignation, and went out charing for a living; but whenever she had a drop too much she made for the barber's, forgetting by a curious lapse of memory that it was no longer her home. And as usual the barber's new wife had pushed her into the street, staggering, and now stood on guard at the door, her coarse, handsome features alive with contempt.

'Wotcher doin' in my 'ouse?' suddenly inquired Sloppy, blinking with suspicion at Flash Kate. 'Yous go 'ome, me fine lady, afore yez git yerself talked about.'

The woman at the door laughed loudly, and pretended to examine with keen interest a new wedding ring on her finger.

'Cum 'ere, 'an I'll tear yer blasted eyes out,' cried the drunkard, turning on her furiously.

The rag-picker's daughter leaned forward, and inquired: ''Ow d'ye like yer eggs done?'

At this simple inquiry the drunkard stamped her foot with rage, calling on her enemy to prepare for instant death. And the two women bombarded one another with insults, raking the gutter for adjectives, spitting like angry cats across the width of the pavement.

The push gathered round, grinning from ear to ear, sooling the women on as if they were dogs. But just as a shove from behind threw Sloppy nearly into the arms of her enemy, the push caught sight of a policeman, and walked away with an air of extreme nonchalance. At the same moment the drunkard saw the dreaded uniform, and, obeying the laws of Cardigan Street, pulled herself together and walked away, mumbling to herself.

The three women watched the performance without a word, critical as spectators at a play. When they saw there would be no scratching, they resumed their conversation.

'W'en a woman takes to drink, she's found a short cut to 'ell, an' let's everybody know it,' said Mrs Yabsley, briefly. 'But this won't git my work done,' and she tucked up her sleeves and went in.

'The push, bent on killing time, and despairing of any fresh diversion in the street, dispersed slowly, one by one, to meet again at night.

(1911)

John Morrison
THE NIGHTSHIFT

Eight o' clock on a winter's evening.

Two men sit on the open section of a tramcar speeding northwards along St Kilda road. Two stevedores going to Yarraville — nightshift— 'down on the sugar'. One—old, and muffled to the ears in a thick overcoat—sits bolt upright, his tired eyes fixed on the far end of the car with that expression of calm detachment characteristic of the pipe-smoker. His companion, a much younger man, leans forward with hands clasped between his knees, as if enjoying the passing pageant of the famous road.

'It'll be cold on deck, Joe,' remarks the young man.

'It will that, Dick,' replies Joe. And they both fall silent again.

At Toorak Road a few passengers alight. A far greater number crowd aboard. Mostly young people going to dances and theatres. Smoothly groomed heads and white bow-ties. Collins Street coiffures and pencilled eyebrows and rouged lips. Creases and polished pumps. Silk frocks and bolero jackets. They fill the tram right out to the running-boards. The air becomes heavily scented.

The young wharfie, mindful of past rebuffs, keeps his seat. He can still see the road, but within twelve inches of his face a remarkably small hand is holding a pink silk dress clear of the floor. He finds it a far more interesting study than the road. Reflects that he could enclose it completely and quite comfortably within his own big fist. Little white knuckles, the fingers of a schoolgirl, painted nails—like miniature rose-petals. He sniffs gently and appreciatively. Violets. His gaze moves a little higher to where the wrist—a wrist that he could easily put thumb and forefinger around— vanishes into the sleeve of the bolero. Higher still. Violets again. Real flowers this time, to go with the perfume. From where he's sitting, a cluster of purple on a pale cheek. She's talking to a young fellow standing with her; her smile is a flicker of dark eyelashes and a flash of white teeth.

Dick finds himself contrasting his own immediate future with that of the girl's escort. Yarraville and the Trocadero. Sugar-berth and dance-floor. His eyes fall again to the little white hand so near his lips, and he sits back with an exclamation of contempt as he catches himself wondering what she would do if he suddenly kissed it. Sissy!

Old Joe's thoughts also must have been reacting to the impact of silks and perfumes.

'The way they get themselves up now,' he hisses into Dick's ear, 'you can't tell which is backside and which is breakfast.'

Dick eyes him with mild resentment. 'What's wrong with them? They look good to me.'

Joe snorts his disagreement, and the subject drops. Dick is only amused. He understands Joe. The old man has shown no disapproval of similar passengers who joined the tram at Alma Road and in Elsternwick. It's the name: 'Toorak'. It symbolizes something. Poor old Joe! Too much courage and not enough brain. Staunch as ever, but made bitter and pig-headed with the accumulation of years. Weary of 'The Struggle'. Left behind. A trifle contemptuous of the young bloods carrying the fight through its final stages. A grand mate, though. And a good hatchman. That means a lot on a sugar job. With the great bulk of the old stevedore at his elbow, and the little white hand before his face, Dick is sensitive of contact with two worlds. Shoddy and silk. Strong tobacco and a whiff of violets. Yesterday and Tomorrow.

Flinders Street-Swanston Street intersection. They get off and push through the pleasure-seeking crowd on the wide pavement under the clocks. Another tram. Contrast again. Few passengers this time. One feels the cold more. Swift transition from one environment to another. Swanston Street to Spencer Street. Play to work. Light to darkness. No more silks and perfumes. Shadowy streets almost deserted. Groups of men, heavily wrapped against the cold, tramping away under the frowning viaduct.

'It'll be a fair bitch on deck,' says Joe, quite unconscious of his lack of originality.

'Yes, you can have it all on your own.'

No offence intended; none taken. They walk in silence. Joe isn't the talking kind. Dick is, but the little white hand and the glimpse of violets on a pale cheek have set in motion a train of thought that makes him irritable. He keeps thinking: 'Cats never work, and even horses rest at night!'

Berth Six, River. Passing up the ramp between the sheds they come out on to the wharf. Other men are already there. Deep voices, and the stamping of heavy boots on wood. The mist is thick on the river, almost a fog. Against the bilious glow of the few lights over on south side dark figures converge on one point, then vanish one at a time over the edge of the wharf.

Dick and Joe join their mates on the floating landing-stage. Rough greetings are exchanged.

'How are you, Joe?'

'What the hell's that got to do with you?'

'You old nark! Got a needle on the hip?'

'I don't need no needle. How's the missus, Sammy?'

'Bit better, Joe. She was up a bit today.'

'Line up there!—here she comes.'

As the little red light appears on the river the men crowd the edge of the landing-stage, each anxious to get a seat in the cabin on such a night. The water is very black and still, and the launch moves in with hardly a ripple. The night is full of sounds. Little sounds, like the rattle of winches at the distant timber berths; big sounds, like the crash of the coal-grabs opposite the gasworks. All have the quality of a peculiar hollowness, so that one still senses the overwhelming silence on which they impinge. In some strange way sound never quite destroys the portentous hush which goes with fog. Dick feels it as he follows old Joe over the gunwale and gropes his way through the cabin to the bows.

'It's quiet tonight, Joe. Can't be many ships working.'

'Quiet be damned. There's four working on north side. Where the hell're you going, anyway?'

'I'm going to sit outside.'

'You can sit on your own, then. This ain't no Studley Park tour.'

Dick doesn't mind that; all the same he isn't left alone. Other men are forced out beside him as the cabin fills. He finds it hard to dodge conversation. Racing. Football. Now if it was politics...The Struggle! Just a humour, of course. He has no fixed antipathies to nightwork, the waterfront or his mates. Nightwork means good money; three pounds a shift. A real saver sometimes. Many a time he's stood idle for days, then picked up a single night—enough to keep landlord and tradesmen quiet, at least. Two hours less work than the dayshift too. Nevertheless it's all wrong. Surely to Christ the work of the world could be carried on in daylight. So much waste and idleness during the day, and toil at night. Only owls, rats and men work at night.

'What's wrong, Dick? You're not saying much.'

'Just a bit dopey, Bluey. Not enough shut-eye.'

Damn them!—why can't they mind their own business?

The launch travels smoothly and swiftly. Quite safe. The mist is thickening, but there's a bit of light in the river here from the ships working on north side. Small ships, as ships go, but monstrous seen from the passing launch. Beautiful in a way of their own, too, with the clusters of lights hanging from masts and derricks. Little cities of industry resting on towering black cliffs. One can't tell where the black hulls join the black water.

Nameless bows, but still familiar to the critical stevedores.

'That's the *Bundaleera*. Good job. She worked the weekend.'

'The *Era*. She'll finish tonight.'

'The *Montoro*. They say there's only one night in her.'

Strange twentieth-century code of values. A collier which works Sundays is a good ship; a deep-water liner which works only one night is a bad ship.

'They can stick their Sunday work for mine!' Joe's voice.

'I suppose you get more out of the collection-box, you bloody old criminal!'

'That's all right. I only been to church twice in my life. The first time they tried to drown me, and the second time they married me to a crazy woman.'

Dick smiles to himself. A smile of affection for the old warrior. Joe's a good Christian, whether he knows it or not. There's a word for him: 'Nature's gentleman'. A hard doer and a bit of a pagan, that's all. Three convictions: one for stealing firewood during the Depression, one for punching a policeman during the '28 strike, and one for travelling on an expired railway ticket—also during the Depression. Across one cheek the scar of a wound received on Gallipoli. A limp in his right leg from an old waterfront accident. 'Screwy' arms and shoulders from too much freezer work in the days when every possible job had to be stood up for. 'Sailor

Joe'. Dick loves him as any healthy youth can love a seasoned guide and mentor. They work together, ship after ship. They travel together, live near each other.

With a mutter of deep voices the launch chugs its way across the Swinging Basin. The mist continues to thicken. South side is just visible. Haloes of brassy yellow around lonely lights. Dismal rigging of idle coal lighters—grimy relics of the white wings of other days. North side can be heard but not seen. Beyond the veil ageing winches clatter at the coal berths and railway trucks crash against each other in Dudley Street yards. A man's voice hailing another comes across the water with extraordinary distinctness.

A few minutes later everything vanishes and the speed of the launch drops to a walking pace. Real fog now. Dick's eyes have been fixed on the ridge of water standing out from the bows. Twice since leaving Berth Six it has fallen in height; now it is but a ripple. Voices in the cabin are still cursing the cold, speculating lightly on the chances of reaching shore in the event of a collision. Dick wishes they'd all shut up. He's cold himself, but some of his irritation has gone. Here again is beauty—of a kind, like ships working at night, and the little white hand. Just three feet away the sooty water flows slowly past. It's easy to imagine that only the water moves, that the launch is motionless, a boatload of men resting in the perpetual night of a black river. To port, south side has ceased to exist; to starboard, north side is only the distant clamour of a lost world.

Nine o' clock.

The green navigation light of Coode Island.

Only the light. A bleary green eye, neither suspended nor supported. Green eye and grey fog. They pass fairly close. Too close, they realize, as the launch swings sharply off to port. New sounds come out of the night. Sounds of a working ship. Dead ahead, and not far away. Yarraville. Conversation, which has languished, flickers into life again.

'What the hell's that?'

'Don't tell me it ain't nine o'clock yet!'

'Just turned. Maybe there's a rockboat in.'

'There is. They picked up for her this morning.'

'We won't be long now—thank Christ! I'm as cold as a frog.'

'Listen to the dayshift howl when we pull in. It'll be ten o'clock when they get up the river.'

In two places, one on each bow, the fog changes colour. Two glowing caves open up, as if a giant had puffed holes in a drop-curtain. And in each cave the imposing superstructure of a ship materializes with all the bewildering play of light and shadow characteristic of ships at night. Rockboat and sugarboat. The *Trienza* and the *Mildura*. The comparatively graceful lines of the bigger ship don't interest the approaching stevedores. Their eyes are all on the *Mildura*, their minds all grappling with one question: how many nights?

'By God, she's low!'

'She's got a gutsful all right.'

'Three or four nights—you beaut!'

Under a barrage of jeers and greetings from the dayshift the launch noses in to the high wharf.

'You were a long time coming!'

'What're you growling at? You're getting paid for waiting.'

'Ho there, Bluey, you old scoundrel!'

'How are you, Jim? Left a good floor for us?'

'Good enough for you, anyhow. She ain't a bad job.'

'How many brands?'

'Five in Number Two Hatch. Grab the port-for'ard corner if you're down there. You'll get a good run till supper. Two brands.'

'Good on you, son!'

The nightshift swarms up the face of the wharf, cursing a Harbour Trust which provides neither ladder nor landing-stage. Dick is last up, for no other reason than that Joe is second last. The strain imposed on the old man to reach the top angers his young mate. Damn their hides! All ugliness again. A man can never get away from it for long. The strange charm of the fog-bound river has gone. The black beams of the wharf, with the shrouded men clinging to them like monstrous beetles, symbolize all the galling dreariness of the ten hours just beginning. Symbolism also in the tremendous loom of the coal-gantry. Toiling upwards, always toiling upwards, with just a little glimpse of beauty now and then, like the mist, and the little white hand, and the ridge of black water streaming away from the bows of the launch.

'Shake it up, old-timer!' someone cries from above.

Joe's big boots are just above Dick's head. One of them is lifted on to the next beam. He waits for the other to move, but the old man is still feeling for a higher grip for his hands. Dick's own fingers are getting numb. The beams are covered with wet coal-dust and icy cold. At either side the dayshift men are swarming down. Noise, confusion, and black shapes everywhere.

A sudden anxiety seizes Dick as Joe's higher foot comes down again to the beam it has just left.

'On top there!' he yells. 'Help this man up!'

Too late. Even as he moves to one side and reaches upwards in an endeavour to get alongside his mate, the old man's tired fingers give in. A big clumsy bundle hurtles down, strikes the gunwale of the launch with a sickening thud, and rolls over the side before anyone can lay a hand on it.

An hour later another launch noses away into the fog. Only two men. Both are within the cabin, one standing behind the little steering wheel, the other crouched near the open doorway with eyes fixed on the grey pall beyond the bows. Coode Island is astern before the boatman speaks.

'He was your mate?'

'Yes, he was my mate.'

'You got him out pretty quick.'

'Not quick enough. He hit the launch before he went into the water, you know.'

After a minute's silence. 'Does the buck know you've left?'

'I'm not worried. I wouldn't work tonight, not for King George. And somebody's got to tell his old woman.'

'I'm going right up to Berth Two. Will that do you?'

'Yes, anywhere.'

Anywhere indeed. And the further and slower the better.

Not so much different from an hour ago. Mist, black water, and the crash of trucks over in the railway yards. But no men. One of them embarked now on a longer journey than he ever dreamed of. And in a few minutes there will be lights, and more lights. And voices, and the faces of many people. And not one of them will know a thing of what has happened. Princes Bridge, and the bustle of the great intersection. Trams, and St Kilda Road. And the big cars rolling along beneath the naked elms. The other world—violets—and the little white hand.

The little white hand. Funny. She'll be dancing somewhere now, and the grand old man with whom she very nearly rubbed shoulders—

'What was that?' asks the boatman.

Dick is startled to find he has spoken aloud.

'We don't know much about each other, do we?' he says without hesitation.

'What d'you mean?'

'Oh, nothing...'

(1944)

Eve Langley
THE PEA PICKERS

from PART 1

FOR THE BEST! FOR THE BEST!

The nights grew hotter, for the bush-fire season was fuming among the rocks and trees to the north. We tossed on our beds all night, and got up now and then for a cool drink.

We were both in love. Blue's was a long-standing affair in our native town. And as we snored side by side in dreams, we toyed with each other's hands in joyful bliss. When we awoke, we recognized each other with a grunt of disgust and jumped over to the other side of the bed. Every morning we awoke pale, dispirited, ill-tempered and lazy and had frequent quarrels, after which I would go down to the almond-trees and devour nuts while I made verse.

Blue, eyeing me wonderingly, offering to share my hermit-like walks, was repulsed, and I went alone. One afternoon, in the throes of my unspoken passion, I walked far into the bush along a road to a farm called Waddel's. The road to it was set with those silent rusty flints one finds in Gippsland. There were post-and-rail fences on either side of the road, thick with lichen, and every mile or so there was an enamel placard on them, advertising soap. One of the saddest sights you could see. Another advertisement which must have driven more men to drink than the tongue can tell, was that long blue legend which affirmed that 'Reckitt's Blue is best, Melbourne 300 miles'. I met a swaggie leaning against a sign, talking to it earnestly.

'I've seen thousands of youse along this road,' he said. 'Youse have been the only living words I've known for days, and now I can hear youse chattering in me ears all the time. I can't think because of them signs. I get to wondering what the next one will have on it. If it's the same words I think I haven't moved a step; and if it's different words, I want to go back and compare them with the words on the other rails, miles behind. Why can't the city leave the bush alone? We don't go milling around in the busy streets with swags and horses and dogs.'

I shall never forget that walk to Waddel's: my mind was in that virgin condition where nature is merciless. Now she laid it on to the flesh with mystifying odours of leaves, glimpses of far-away ranges that made me tremble, sudden winds that blew gusts of loneliness into the mind, and the slow sweet divulging of a bush road, being covered by two human feet. I was in anguish and there was no escape from it. If I could have been dissolved into a flower or a pool of water it would have been all over. The late sun shivered with the lights of autumn, as I walked down to Waddel's. Hands, shares, wheels and hooves had ploughed the bush down and planted deep grass in a valley that had once been up to its neck in the sea. I wandered furtively around the heels of the deep-breathing bulls and made my way up into the chalk cliffs where the fossilized oyster shells crumbled in the open air. I picked them up and pretended to know something of conchology, in order to forget my passion and my pain; but, in reality, any sort of knowledge would have just chilled me, and made me stupid and sent me home dreaming. No, I was the victim of slow-moving time. As I went home, I climbed a little hill, thinking that if I should be able to marry Kelly I would have sons and daughters; so strong was this thought that I knew nature was thinking for me, and floundered to get out of her hands.

But she was even suggesting names for these unborn Gippslanders. 'One could be called Gauntlet,' I thought. The other might have been christened Hobnail, for all I knew, because, just as I topped that hill, I saw that which was my own, rightfully. Between us, these feelings of flesh and fancy, stood as obstructions.

I saw a miserable Gippsland township, grand with distance. It was a sultry purple day and dead and dry was the grass, but I looked from where I stood, on the side of the hill, and saw in a sudden stream of sun from a heavy cloud a few roofs magnificent with the light, miles away. Some unknown town of which I shall never know the name. It had the pathetic beauty of an old crop of unharvested wheat left to melt and moulder under the storms of the world and, while I looked, rain fell there, or I think it fell, for I saw the arms of a rainbow outstretched, as though a great head lay on them and wept for the sake of the desolation in that place.

And one white roof that I watched earnestly smote me heartward, so that I turned on my heel, in an anguish of unrest and longing. At length I went on, but would have as happily died, for my kingdom, Beauty, lay behind me for ever.

Something gleamed on the dark road, and I bent and picked up sixpence with a quick hand and a surprised heart. Consoled, I strode off to the hut, my prize in hand.

Just as well it was in my hand, because when I got home, Blue, who sat peeling apples and glowering at the fire, said, 'Did you take our milk money with you, Steve?'

Feeling pained, I felt in my pockets, saying, 'Yairs...yairs, I think I remember taking it,' while my fingers went through a hole in my trousers and found my leg.

'Oh, here it is,' and I gave her the sixpence that had delivered me from sorrow and sat down for hours, wondering on the nature of life. I was still sitting there when she came back with the milk, and I sat there still while she prepared the tea: I ate it in the moody silence of the heroic who have faced life singly for ever, and decided that my influence on Kelly must be an evil one, because of my distorted thoughts.

'I'll leave the country of Gippsland,' I cried, 'and let my lover be free. O Abnegation, how holy thou art! O Apostasia, what a nobility is in thy flying garments!'

'Where the hell did I put that butter?' Blue was grumbling, flea-ing the seats irritably in search of our fresh pound of butter. 'Is it on your seat?'

'No.'

'Get up...move aside and let me look.'

I was just rising as it decided to fall from the seat of my pants, as flat as the Russian steppes, and as greasy as a steppe's coat. 'Always dreaming,' complained Blue. She turned me around, had a look at my greasy spot and laughed.

In two days' time it would be Easter Monday, and Mrs Wilson had invited us, through Kelly, to come with them to Eagle Point, a place somewhere down the Mitchell River, to picnic there. Ah, sultry thunderous Easter Monday, come out of your tomb again, you Lazarus, and unwrap your linen windings one by one.

The first, coming off in a morning mist, revealed us crawling under the apple-trees at dawn, picking up spotted fruit to take to Mrs Wilson. On the dewy grass the sand clung, and among the silver leather of the apple leaves the ugliest spider I have ever seen rode to the death.

The smell of apples when they get into a bag is like a jovial ripe lively conversation of which one cannot understand a single word, but enjoys each alien sound. We dressed; I to my buttered seat and Blue to immaculate faded trousers. There was some beautiful heat in that girl which used to tint the clothes she wore. She would wear an old blue dress into a fairytale tint. Poetry, music and beauty came from her clothing, and in their midst she bloomed away, independent of fear and sorrow.

We sat by the side of the white clay road, waiting for Kelly to call for us, our bag of apples between us. The light of youth made him look wild and rapid as he came tearing down the rutted track in a double-seated buggy drawn by a horse that had enough legs, manes, eyes and snorts for a dozen. The yellow eagle, our friend, stood up on the seat, howling, shouting, screaming and laughing, with a black buggy whip flying from side to side. The road seemed to be coming along with him and, just as I had a sense that chasms were opening out behind him as he galloped along, he drew up about fifty yards farther on, and had to back the buggy to let us get in. Then, with a swift turn, we scampered breathlessly back to his home.

His mother came out and greeted us quietly. She was a tall thin woman with narrow brown eyes that moved softly and nervously from side to side, as though she were trapped and looking for a weak place. Her toothless mouth moved and munched as she looked, and her cheeks twitched at every sound. He handed the reins into her restless but experienced hands and, mounting the white Arab, stood in the stirrups and trotted behind us rapidly to the township.

Whenever we looked back we saw the handsome embarrassed youth standing astride animated snow, harnessed with silver buckle and oiled leather; his planet of hair bursting with the rays of movement; his thin red cheeks rumpled with laughter under his long white nose; and a couple of wolf fangs standing clean and sharp in his naked gums. Had he and his mare taken to the sky by way of a drop of dew and ascended in mist, I should not have been surprised at all.

We passed old hop kilns where the lost pea-pickers, they told us, lay on wet winter days, and saw the kingfishers wedding the waters of the river with a golden flash of their beaks and claws. Past rows of hawthorn hedges in leaf, but lacking flowers, we trolled, until a tall yellow-brown cliff stood up in the river Mitchell.

'Eagle Point,' they said.

Down we got and picnicked for hours. We swung on gum-trees and looked down into the water from the top of the yellow cliffs. Misery began to oppress me again. I lay down alone, above the grassy thunder of the racers' hooves on the sports ground below, and the wintry sound of applause, and I looked up into the filmy heavens. A large white mask of a cloud, shaped into the face of an Egyptian woman, floated over: the mutilated lips trembling into dissolution, and the eyes seeking for something. This beauty wore a storm for a dress. It was sewn with lightning and she wore it until twilight, when she dropped it on our heads.

As it struck the ground, Kelly kissed me with the furtive whiskery kiss of youth, smelling of the sun and feeling like a blow from a hairbrush.

The kiss of youth is like the sip an old man takes from a glass of wine as he sits in the twilight; sipping, touched into life by the sip; trembling a little, and looking away until it is time to sip again. By the time the bottle is empty he is under the table.

And with youth, by the time the feelings of passion have gone, we are under the coverlets, wedded, bedded, with little interminable gongs called 'offspring' that will not run down until they are jammed with bread and milk.

Kelly and I walked home together from his house that night, with the Arabian mare as chaperon. As we walked, and kissed, our blood mounted, and from the rear our staggering intoxicated gait must have been comical...the ballet legs and the bowed legs bending together.

Kelly exclaimed, 'I feel like a bottle of yeast that must soon explode.'

Afraid of desire, I tried to remember some saying of a great man's. Tolstoi. 'Women are like dogs. They have no souls,' he said. 'They have,' I cried to heaven. I caught Kelly by the arm and made him run until he laughed and the Arab mare ran after us, the stirrups hitting her flanks and the bridle rattling on her jaw. The thunderous dress of my Egyptian still rose up on the horizon in the night, and from it a few hot drops fell. Kelly tied our Arabian chaperon to the orchard gate and we made our love, timidly and shyly, fearing even to touch each other.

There was the cold but happy ideal of the virgin in my mind, for ever, a joy and a torment to me, and I laughed as we parted, saying, 'We conquered...we conquered. Hands and heart go pure to bed.'

(1942)

Christopher Brennan
THE YELLOW GAS IS FIRED FROM STREET
TO STREET

The yellow gas is fired from street to street
past rows of heartless homes and hearths unlit,
dead churches, and the unending pavement beat
by crowds—say rather, haggard shades that flit

round nightly haunts of their delusive dream,   5
where'er our paradisal instinct starves:—
till on the utmost post, its sinuous gleam
crawls in the oily water of the wharves;

where Homer's sea loses his keen breath, hemm'd
what place rebellious piles were driven down—   10
the priestlike waters to this task condemn'd
to wash the roots of the inhuman town!—

where fat and strange-eyed fish that never saw
the outer deep, broad halls of sapphire light,
glut in the city's draught each nameless maw: 15
—and there, wide-eyed unto the soulless night,

methinks a drown'd maid's face might fitly show
what we have slain, a life that had been free,
clean, large, nor thus tormented—even so
as are the skies, the salt winds and the sea.   20

Ay, we had saved our days and kept them whole,
to whom no part in our old joy remains,
had felt those bright winds sweeping thro' our soul
and all the keen sea tumbling in our veins,

had thrill'd to harps of sunrise, when the height   25
whitens, and dawn dissolves in virgin tears,
or caught, across the hush'd ambrosial night,
the choral music of the swinging spheres,

or drunk the silence if nought else—But no!
and from each rotting soul distil in dreams   30
a poison, o'er the old earth creeping slow,
that kills the flowers and curdles the live streams,

that taints the fresh breath of re-risen day
and reeks across the pale bewilder'd moon:
—shall we be cleans'd and how? I only pray,   35
red flame or deluge, may that end be soon!

(1896)

Section K

PERSON TO PERSON

When we engage in a relationship with another person in 'real life'—
whether that relationship is one of love, hate, work, play or duty— we are
often able to think simultaneously on two levels. We may be using certain
words to create an effect—such as affection, anger, co-operation, competi-
tiveness, or responsibility—but at the same time privately thinking something quite different. Comic strips represent this dual track of ideas by
balloons for spoken words and bubbles for thoughts.

Literature can present a greater complexity of thought than immediate
experience or comic strips. It can have characters saying one thing, rumi-
nating on the concepts being expressed or on the mode of expression; and

thinking many other things at the same time. It can have one or more authorial or editorial voices simultaneously operating in the same area of thought but with reinforcing or conflicting suggestions. And it can have several characters or voices (including a palpable sense of the language itself) commenting on the action.

In this Section of the Anthology many of the items are concerned with the play of moral and social ideas or the play of plot possibilities. The authorial voice is often at odds with what is being described or presented or there is a sense of providing a variety of indications of how the narrative may work itself out. Sometimes the tale seems more reliable than the teller—or, as D. H. Lawrence rather hyperbolically put the point in *Studies in Classic American Literature* (1924):

> The artist usually sets out—or used to—to point a moral and adorn a tale. The tale, however, points the other way, as a rule. Two blankly opposing morals, the artist's and the tale's. Never trust the artist. Trust the tale. The proper function of a critic is to save the tale from the artist who created it.

A fairly simple example of this is in Christina Stead's story, 'A Little Demon': the reader rapidly learns to distrust Jeanie and Mariana, two narrators within the tale, but at the very end finds some doubt cast on this comfortable judgment, which has at times been aided and abetted by the outer narrator in her reports of what Jeanie and Mariana say. A more wavering example occurs in Dick Roughsey's telling of 'Gidegal the Moon-man', where the narrator is sometimes telling a story of the Dreaming; sometimes describing how human beings can associate themselves with— even identify themselves with—the power of the Dreaming through song and ritual; sometimes giving autobiographical asides; sometimes suggesting that a degree of pragmatism, even scepticism, needs to be applied to such stories.

Most of the examples in this Section deal with varieties of love relationship, this being the commonest theme of almost every national literature. (One or two critics of Australian literature have, nevertheless, maintained that both the literature and the society were deficient in their acceptance and presentation of love relationships. This Section may suggest the untenability of such assertions.)

The moral attitudes brought to love and sex will naturally be conditioned by place, circumstance and upbringing. Roughsey's story, with its suggestions of the power and desirability of sex, emphasises different rituals from those prevailing in Rosa Praed's novel, *Lady Bridget in the Never-Never Land*. Praed's novel, set in Australia (or Leichardt's [sic] Land as she calls it), adopts several of the conventions of nineteenth-century British romantic fiction, including the fiancé's concern to find out information about the intended bride's former lovers (a convention turned to tragic import in Thomas Hardy's *Tess of the d'Urbervilles*) and the notion of a woman marrying on the rebound from rejection. The convention of the large protective male and the small compliant female is also evident: it is not only the somewhat insensitive Colin McKeith (a member of Parliament) to whom Lady Bridget seems 'such a child'; the narrator herself refers to Bridget's 'child-like shoulders'.

The play of ideas is muted in this passage, but Praed, herself a believer in reincarnation, telepathy and spiritualism, allows Lady Bridget to hint at the possibility of having 'lived a great many—perhaps naughty—lives' in the past. Bridget is also allowed to reflect silently, while talking to Colin, about the man who jilted her.

Ada Cambridge plays with opposing ideas about love in the two sonnets included here. As in many other items (notably those by Eve Langley and Kenneth Mackenzie), there is a sense of unresolved tension between body, mind and spirit in matters of love and a sense that the social conventions are restrictive or inappropriate. As the narrator says in Helen Garner's story, 'Civilisation and Its Discontents', in answer to the question 'Is it allowed?': 'Isn't that why women and men make love? to bend the bars a little, just for a little; to let the bars dissolve?'

In 'The Celtic Guest' by Eve Langley the bars between body and soul, male and female, waking and dream, good and evil, youth and ageing, all seem to be a little bent. There are hints of the entrapping mysteries of Oscar Wilde's *The Picture of Dorian Gray*. This strange meditative poem presents a flicker of half-grasped, unsettling ideas, with more than a hint of woman as unregenerate Eve, tempting her man. Kenneth Mackenzie's 'Shall then another...', with its epigraph written to the notorious Anne (or Ninon) de Lenclos (1620–1705) by one of her many infatuated lovers, presents woman as Lilith, the fabled first wife of Adam who enmeshed him with her sexuality but refused to submit to his will.

According to Talmudic lore, Lilith left Paradise for a region of the air. She is a spirit haunting the night, as she is presented in Brennan's 'She is the night', with its sense of irresistible but corrupting sexuality.

The occupation of distant countries by European settlers is a circumstance that encourages adaptations and rewritings of the myth of the Garden of Eden. The desire for a newly-wrought Paradise, a new heaven and a new earth, is especially powerful in United States literature, but also forms a strand in Australian literature. In Australia the rewriting, the wrenching away from conventional interpretation, is more dominant. 'Our Adam and Eve,' said Thomas Keneally at the launching of his novel, *The Playmaker* in 1987, 'had "crime" written all over their foreheads.'

This inversion of Edenic innocence may go part of the way to explain Australian reinterpretations of the myth. Another one occurs in the last part of A.D. Hope's 'The Planctus', a series of meditative complaints based on the rewriting of myth and legend. In Hope's 'Paradise Saved' he suggests that Adam might have resisted temptation and Eve and thus been left alone in Paradise in sterile righteousness. There are hints also of a rewriting of the myth of Tiresias, used by Tennyson, Swinburne, and T.S. Eliot as a man longing for death to escape the boredom and sameness of life. And the last word, 'justified', strongly suggests an opposition between religious notions (perhaps particularly Protestant notions) of righteousness and sexual fulfilment. Hope, like Patrick White and Manning Clark, often uses the Protestant conscience about sex as an emblem for the unadventurousness or dullness that he ascribes to Australia.

Dorothy Hewett's 'Grave Fairytale' is another rewriting of myth. Hewett inverts the story of Rapunzel escaping from the thraldom imposed by the witch by means of the heroic intervention of a handsome prince. In her retelling the witch is a savage, sexual part of Rapunzel, the prince a male sexual exploiter.

This is but one of many instances of bending the bars. McAuley's uneasiness about the sterile, dutiful uxoriousness of his parents (especially his father) can be set alongside Grenville's story about the unwitting attempts of an elderly married couple to sell a young woman into sexual bondage. The derisory treatment of woman by the husband in Baynton's 'The Chosen Vessel' contrasts sharply with the passionate abjectness of Mackenzie's speaker or the introspective superciliousness of Moorhouse's man.

The poems by Judith Wright, Vincent Buckley, Andrew Taylor, David Malouf and Gwen Harwood form a group in which there is a philosophical struggle with the nature of love and time, knowing and unknowing. In all except Gwen Harwood's 'Carnal Knowledge I' the speaker finds an image of the self in the loved one or in some image representing the loved one. Moorhouse's story does much the same, but it is more concerned with relating the man to concepts of Australia and of how the personality may be represented by or confined in a tract of land that one regards as an individual possession. It is a story much concerned with postures, game-playing and possessiveness.

Moorhouse's kind of playfulness with ideas and the facts of story-telling may seem fashionably post-modernist, but it is not dissimilar to the mode of Ethel Anderson's story, 'The Love-nest; or, Which Sin is That?', with its playful title reflecting and parodying titles from the mid-nineteenth century when the action is supposed to occur. Like Moorhouse (and Baynton and Stead for that matter), Anderson dangles various possibilities for the plot in front of the reader. These possibilities are almost all concerned with how relationships between people, particularly sexual relationships, will work out.

Anderson even manages an early tilt at the male dominance implicit in the word 'Man', when she has Aunt Loveday Boisragon use the word as if it were gender-neutral and then immediately with masculine overtones:

> 'Yes. Man does copy Nature. He does improve on Nature. His ship makes a swan look blowsy.'

The joke is partly in the love-stricken maiden's confident assertion of an improbable male superiority, a superiority which subsequent events undermine. This is a story in which most expectations are undermined, whether they are those of the reader, of Aunt Loveday or of the garrulous, impulsive Victoria McMurthie. Victoria seems quite sure that the love-nest is something like a brothel, an impression the reader is beguiled into sharing by the sailors singing a bawdy ballad and the mention of the sun as an Indian dancing girl (Nautch-girl) throwing the figure of Aunt Love-day into relief like a classical terracotta figurine from Tanagra. But nothing is what it seems at first. Loveday's former admirer, now an admiral, seems to Victoria like an unseamanlike dolt. The supposed bawdy house turns out to be the respectable cottage of the bosun and the multiple sets of bed linen (a subject which had earlier been Loveday's amorous downfall) 'nothing more wicked than the Admiral's washing'.

The tone of Anderson's story is light and frothy. But even in the love stories and poems that are tinged with melancholy or tragedy there is an authorial playfulness with ideas and with the possibilities for the working out of the plot. The puzzles of human relationships, particularly sexuality, can hardly be presented plausibly without a degree of puzzlement, doubt and alternative explanation.

Ken Goodwin/Alan Lawson

Dick Roughsey
GIDEGAL THE MOON-MAN

When Gidegal the moon-man was on earth he was a great lover of women. He was always after women and made many songs to make them fall in love with him. Gidegal made the big sacred ceremony of Jarrada and left it to us so that a man could sing a woman to be his wife. It is still used today. My older brother Burrud, or Lindsay, is the biggest song-man of the Lardil. Men often get him to sing the Jarrada songs to help them get the woman they want.

When a man wants to marry a certain women he calls on his close male relatives to help him. They go out in the bush to the sacred ground and get it ready. A big circle is cleared in the sand and smoothed off. In the centre an oval shape is painted on the ground using small balls of bird-down coloured with red ochre and white pipe-clay. It has a red centre. This represents the woman's vagina.

A tall pole is stuck in the ground just in front of the oval. The pole is decorated with paint and feathers and represents a penis. Strings covered with white bird-down hang from the top of the pole to represent the seminal flow. Oval holes are dug on each side of the central symbol and their edges painted with red-ochre feathers. These also represent vaginas.

The men decorate their bodies with red and white paint and ochred bird-down. Each paints his own *mulgri* on his chest and arms. On their thighs they paint ovals which also represent women.

When everything is ready the Jarrada man stands before the feathered pole with legs spread, knees bent and hands on thighs. His two relatives, perhaps grandfather and uncle, kneel over the holes at the side. They begin singing the cycle of love songs. As they sing they sway their hips back and forth in the rhythmical motions of love-making.

In the first song Gidegal sings his own body so that he'll be strong and attractive to the woman. Each song is sung several times before going on to the next. The songs do not have to be heard by the woman, she may be many miles away.

In the second song Gidegal sings the woman so that she will begin to dream of him. He sings *Guraday Lardimah, Guraday Lardimah,—Gura Binba-Binba*—'You will think sweet of me in your dreaming.'

He now sings *Bulgeery Rumana Mungeera Girano*—'You will dream that I am making love to you.' He sings a fourth song to make himself more attractive, and as he sings he rubs juice from the roots of a special bush over his body. The juice is mixed with goanna fat.

Gidegal sings a song so that the woman won't be able to stop looking at him. He sings again so that when the woman wakes next morning she will find herself wet as though from love-making. The last song describes the woman walking about next morning, knowing that she belongs to the man who sang in her dreaming.

Gidegal sings all night and all next day, repeating the song cycle over and over. The songs make the evening star twinkle and the woman is again reminded of her lover. He sings the lightning flash and when she sleeps she dreams of the lightning and sees the form of her lover in the flash. Her heart is warm and glad.

The Jarrada songs of Gidegal never fail. The woman can't help falling in love with the singer of Jarrada, even if she didn't like him before.

There are many secret songs to win the love of a sweetheart, and many ways to make them work. A man might put a song in feathers of a parrot or other bird and let them blow across to where the woman is sitting so that they cling to her skin and hair. He can get hold of a woman's *yamma* stick, or string bag, and put a song in it so that it will lead her to a meeting place in the bush.

The great Warrenby made a secret love song to win the love of Margura, the woman of wallaby dreaming. Warrenby put the song into a grasshopper. The grasshopper flew and hopped until it landed on the lap of Margura and clung to her hair. When she pulled the grasshopper away it left a small spot of fluid on her body. This made her itchy and when she scratched it the fluid entered her body and she fell in love with Warrenby.

The women also have songs to make men fall in love with them. They too go away into the bush to sing songs for love magic. My wife Elsie told me how she and some other women only recently tried songs to stop some trouble among our people.

A married man had sung Jarrada songs to get a married woman for his sweetheart. There were a lot of fights after people saw the two of them together, but they still kept up the relationship. Elsie went with some of the old women to sing chants to stop the affair. They went about a mile into the bush and found a place where the wind was blowing toward where the man was living. They sat in a circle and bared themselves to the waist.

They then decorated their breasts and shoulders with red and white paint. The women had strings decorated with bunches of white feathers.

When everything was ready the women stood in a circle and an old woman from the Wanyi tribe (south of Burketown) led the chanting. The women chanted and swayed back and forth. They shook their knees and beat their breasts as they sang words which mean: 'You must stop loving that man—shoo!' They kept on for a long time and then returned home.

The Jarrada songs of the man were too strong; the women's songs were no good against them, as the woman now has the man's child.

The women say they can sing a man to their blanket, and also separate a man from his wife. Elsie says she didn't use those songs to get me.

A man who sings another man's wife and then runs off with her is called *goonjawul* (run-away man). When he's caught or when he's had enough and come back, there is a big fight. The *goonjawul* man has to fight relatives of the woman until he has been punished. The woman usually gets a good belting from her husband. If she has been causing too much trouble he might decide to punish her with *mungin*.

Mungin means plenty. At night the husband orders his wife to go out in the bush and lie down in a certain place. He then sends, in turn, all the men who are not close relatives to have intercourse with her. Each man gives the husband a present. Sometimes he might get more than twenty. A wife stays quiet for a long time after *mungin*.

One of my relatives, old Charlie, tried the *goonjawul* business. He sang a widow and they used to meet out in the bush while hunting.

One time they were all camped out for the school holidays. They had tents and the widow was camped near Charlie and his wife. Charlie's wife was suspicious and stayed with him all the time. He couldn't get away from her, and he got very hungry for his sweetheart.

One night Charlie said he was very tired from hunting and went to bed early. Old Charlie was soon asleep and started snoring. He was only pretending of course, and he kept on snoring until his wife came to lie beside him and go to sleep. She started snoring after a while, so when he was sure she was sound asleep, he got up slowly, and still snoring, started to sneak away. He got a fright when his wife snorted a bit and rolled over, so he crept back, still snoring himself, and had a close look at her face. She was asleep all right so off he went, walking softly and snoring. He was bending low to go out of the tent when a *nulla-nulla* crashed down on his back—his wife was only pretending too. Poor old Charlie yelled out, 'Yackai—why did you hit me? I'm only going out to chuck water.'

But she called him *goonjawul* and a lot of other names and kept belting him with the *nulla-nulla*. Old Charlie had to run away and hide in the bush until his wife cooled down a bit.

(1971)

Rosa Praed
LADY BRIDGET IN THE NEVER-NEVER LAND

from BOOK 2, CHAPTER 3

They had only one more talk, in the real sense, before their marriage, and that was an unpremeditated but natural outrush of the vague jealousy which slumbered at the core of McKeith's love. It was on the last evening, and it made an ineffaceable impression upon him.

They were standing, after dinner, close together by the balustrade of the terrace.

It was a clear night, with a young moon, and the stars set deep in blue so dark that the sky gave an impression of solidity. The air was full of scents and of a soft balminess, with the faint nip of an early May in the Southern hemisphere.

He had folded her light scarf round the child-like shoulders. The touch of his big hand stirred her—it had not often done so in that peculiar way. It roused something in her that she had thought dead or drugged to sleep, and took her back for an emotional moment to a certain late summer evening at Hurlingham, when she and Willoughby Maule had stood in the garden together under the stars. There came to her an almost fierce reaction against that moment. She felt a distinct emotion now, but it was different—less tumultuous, and bringing her a soft sense of enfoldment.

She slipped her hand gently into McKeith's, and they remained thus for nearly a minute without speaking. He was the first to break the silence.

'Bridget,' he said impetuously, 'we're going to be husband and wife to-morrow. It makes me tremble, darling—with happiness and hope, and with fear, too. What have I done, a rough Bushy like me—to win a woman like you? Well you know how I think about that. And I don't believe in a man belittling himself to the woman he loves, though it's just because he loves her so that he feels himself unworthy of her. And then it comes again over me—badly sometimes—how little I really know of you, and of your life, and of your feelings towards the other men you must have had to do with—one other man in especial, may be, that you've loved, or may have thought you loved. That's what I want to know about, my dear.'

Her face was turned from his as she answered:

'Where's the good of your knowing, Colin? Whatever there was is past.'

'But *is* it past. Over and over again I've started to ask you and have pulled back. Now it's got like a festering sore in my heart, and I'm afraid it will go on festering unless I'm satisfied. There *was* somebody in especial—a man you cared for and might have married if he had been a finer sort of chap than he turned out to be?'

She looked at him sharply.

'How do you know? Has Rosamond Tallant been telling you?'

'No,' he said, with complete candour. 'There wasn't a word of that sort passed between us—and I wouldn't have heeded it if there had.'

'Joan, then? No, I'm sure Joan Gildea wouldn't have talked behind my back.'

'You may bet your life on that. Joan hasn't said anything about whatever love-affairs you may have had.'

'Every girl has had love-affairs. I'm no exception to the rule. There's been no real harm in them. Let them lie—buried in oblivion. They're not worth resurrecting.'

'No, but,' —he persisted—thinking all the while of that letter—'Bridget, I must ask you this one thing. Is there any man in the world you care for more than you care for me? I know,' he added sadly, 'that you don't love in the way I love you—in the way I'd like to be loved by you. I know that's too much to expect—yet.'

The melancholy note in his speech touched her.

'I told you that I do *want* to love you, Colin—only I can't help being what I am,' she said softly. She looked up at him in the pale brightness of thin moon and myriad stars. He stood with the faint illumination from the open windows of Government House upon his fine head and his neat fair beard. It intensified the gleam in his earnest blue eyes, while it softened his angularities and bush roughnesses, and as she looked up at him, she could not help feeling what a splendid fellow he was! What a *man*! So much finer than that other man to whom she had so nearly given herself! Ah, she had had an escape! Under all his show of romantic adventure, his ardent protestations, his magnetic charm, that other man had been utterly sophisticated, worldly, self-interested. He had shown this in his money-grabbing, in his disloyalty both to the woman he had professed to love, and to the woman he had married for her fortune. Thinking of him in this way, Lady Bridget felt that in time she might come to care a great deal more for Colin McKeith.

He caught up her last words.

'Yes, I know that you *want* to love me Biddy, and I hope with all my heart and soul that you will—or else—or else—' he broke off, his face darkening.

'Or else—what?'

'I don't know. It would be hell. I can't think such a thing at this moment. If it comes—well, I'll face it as I've had to face other ugly things. Don't let us speak of the possibility!'

She sensed some quality in him that she had not realised before.

'You frighten me a little, Colin. It's as if I might any day come up against something I wasn't prepared for; and yet—I rather like it.'

He smiled at her.

'I'm glad you like it, anyway. You seem to me such a child, Biddy, though you are always telling me you are such an old soul. I can't for the life of me make out what you mean by that.'

'Oh! a soul that has come back and back, and has lived a great many— perhaps naughty—lives.'

'H'm! Yes! Well, one life is good enough for me, and as we can't prove the other thing, what does it matter anyhow? I wouldn't want you in another life if you were going to be quite a different person. I want you as you are in this one. And so I reckon would every man who has ever been in love with you. Let us go back now to what I was asking you. Biddy, there *was* a man—one man that you did care for? You've admitted as much.'

'Yes—I suppose there was.'

'And not so long before you came out here?'

'I suppose that's true too.'

'Bridget!—do you know what's been festering in my mind—the thought that you might be marrying me in a fit of pique—a sort of reaction. Biddy—tell me honestly, my dear, if it's anything of that sort?'

She seemed to be considering.

'I don't quite know how to answer you, Colin—if I'm to be absolutely honest. And I'd always rather tell you the truth.'

'Thank God for that. Let there be truth between us—truth at any cost.'

'You see,' she said slowly. 'My whole coming out here—everything I've done lately, has been done in reaction against all I've done and felt before.'

'Would you have married that man—if everything had been on the square?'

'What do you mean by "on the square"? I've done nothing to be properly ashamed of!'

'No—no—I was thinking only of him, Biddy, did you love that man?— really love him?'

'I'm not sure yet whether I'm capable of what you'd call loving really. I had a violent attraction to him,'—he remembered the phrase—'I confess I did feel it dreadfully when he married someone else. Now it doesn't hurt me. And of course, he has gone out of my life altogether. I'm glad he has, and I hope he will keep on the other side of the world.'

'Well, let it stop at that.' He drew a breath of relief. 'I don't believe you really cared for him. If you had, you couldn't take it as you do. I'll never bother you again about that man. And oh, my dear—my dear—it doesn't seem to me possible that you shouldn't come to love me, when I love you as I do—with my whole heart and soul—I worship you, Biddy. And I'll not say again that I'm unworthy of you—a man who loves a woman like that *can't* be wholly unworthy.'

He took her in his arms and kissed her. And this time she did not resist the caress.

(1915)

Ada Cambridge
THE PHYSICAL CONSCIENCE

The moral conscience—court of last appeal—
  Our word of God—our Heaven-sent light and guide—
  From what high aims it lures our steps aside!
To what immoral deeds it sets its seal!
That beacon lamp has lost its sacred fire;
  That pilot-guide, compelling wind and wave,
  By slow, blind process, has become the slave
Of all-compelling custom and desire.

Not so the conscience of the body. This,
  Untamed and true, still speaks in voice and face,
In cold lips stiffened to the loveless kiss,
  In shamed limbs shrinking from unloved embrace,
In love-born passion, that no laws compel,
Nor gold can purchase, nor ambition sell.

(1887)

Ada Cambridge
AN ANSWER

Thy love I am. Thy wife I cannot be,
  To wear the yoke of servitude—to take
  Strange, unknown fetters that I cannot break
On soul and flesh that should be mine, and free.
Better the woman's old disgrace for me
  Than this old sin—this deep and dire mistake;
  Better for truth and honour and thy sake—
For the pure faith I give and take from thee.

I know thy love, and love thee all I can—
  I fain would love thee only till I die;
But I may some day love a better man,
  And thou may'st find a fitter mate than I;
Some want, some chill, may steal 'twixt heart and heart.
And then we must be free to kiss and part.

(1887)

Oodgeroo Noonuccal (Kath Walker)
GIFTS

'I will bring you love,' said the young lover,
'A glad light to dance in your dark eye.
Pendants I will bring of the white bone,
And gay parrot feathers to deck your hair.'

But she only shook her head.   5

'I will put a child in your arms,' he said,
'Will be a great headman, great rain-maker.
I will make remembered songs about you
That all the tribes in all the wandering camps
Will sing for ever.'   10

But she was not impressed.

'I will bring you the still moonlight on the lagoon,
And steal for you the singing of all the birds;
I will bring down the stars of heaven to you,
And put the bright rainbow into your hand.'   15

'No,' she said, 'bring me tree-grubs.'

                                              (1966)

Lesbia Harford
IN THE PUBLIC LIBRARY

Standing on tiptoe, head back, eyes and arm
Upraised, Kate groped to reach the higher shelf.
Her sleeve slid up like darkness in alarm
At gleam of dawn. Impatient with herself
For lack of inches, careless of her charm,   5
She strained to grasp a volume; then she turned
Back to her chair, an unforgetful Eve
Still snatching at the fruit for which she yearned
In Eden. She read idly to relieve
The forehead where her daylong studies burned,   10
Tales of an uncrowned queen who fed her child
On poisons, till death lurked, in act to spring,
Between the girl's breasts; who with soft mouth smiled
With soft eyes tempted the usurping King
Then dealt him death in kisses. Kate had piled   15
Her books three deep before her and across
This barricade she watched an old man nod
Over a dirty paper, until loss
Of life seemed better than possession. Shod
With kisses death might skid like thistle floss   20
Down windy slides, might prove at heart as gay
As Cinderella in glass slippers.

Life goes awkwardly so sandalled. Had decay
Been the girl's gift in that Miltonic strife
She would have rivalled God, Kate thought. A ray   25
Of sunshine carrying gilded flecks of dust
And minutes bright with fancies, touched her hair
To powder it with gold and silver, just
As if being now admitted she should wear
The scholar's wig, colleague of those whose lust   30
For beauty hidden in an outworn tongue
Had made it possible for her to read
Tales that were fathered in Arabia, sung
By trouvères and forgotten with their creed
Of love and magic. Beams that strayed among   35
Kate's fingers lit a rosy lantern there
To glow in twilight. Suddenly afraid
She seemed to see her beauty in a flare
Of light from hell. A throng of devils swayed
Before her, devils that had learned to wear   40
The shape of scholar, poet, libertine.
They smiled, frowned, beckoned, swearing to estrange
Kate from reflection that her soul had been
Slain by her woman's body or would change
From contact with it to a thing unclean.   45
Woman was made to worship man, they preached,
Not God, to serve earth's purpose, not to roam
The heavens of thought...A factory whistle screeched,
Someone turned up the lights. On her way home
Kate wondered in what mode were angels breeched.   50

(1912)

Jennifer Maiden
HYPOTHESIS

A woman with a fine ironic face
There in the corner sits relaxed
and she
Is acutely in-love & acutely
                    embarrassed by it.   5
The
Oblivious hero wanders
Like a legend
About the glowing pastel rug
Explaining a terse theory of McLuhan's: 10
That violence is the effort to create
A personal identity.
He pauses only when the lady sighs,
Adjusts her gentle hair,
                    smiles, stands,   15
has cracked a tumbler softly in her hands.

(1970)

Eve Langley
THE CELTIC GUEST

A gaunt rust-bearded man lies in my bed to-night.
In my red coat his chest is yellow.
Beneath my black quilt his limbs are white.
In front of my fire I drank with the fellow
And laughed and talked in seeming delight.   5
But I set my soul afar when his will began to grind.
I stared at the fire when its flames were leaping.
I looked at my wife's green-covered breast.
I shall take her to-night when we should be sleeping;
We, and our gaunt unhappy guest.   10
No, woman, no. It was you who put that in my mind.
But you cannot put anything into my soul,
For my soul no man can find.
The man lies down in my bed and dreams,
And I lie down in my wife's, and taking   15
Her breast in my hands I shadow its gleams,
I make a passion come forcing and aching.
And sad and ecstatic the moonlight beams.
At last I have drawn down oblivion's surrender.
I say to my heart as the darknesses lower,   20
'It would seem there is naught that man can render
Save, humbly, to serve the seed in its hour.'
No, woman, no. It was you who put that in my mind.
But you cannot put anything into my soul,
For my soul no man can find.   25
Huddled, I lay asleep at her side,
And I saw our bearded guest arising.
His body stood open with wounds wide
And he said, 'I am he, beyond surmising.'
As he knelt and kissed me like a bride.   30
The woman awoke and drooped her face
Between his chest and my broad shoulder.
I thrust her away and her youth and grace
Fell into age, and seemed to moulder.
No, woman, no. It was you who put that in my mind.   35
But you cannot put anything into my soul,
For my soul no man can find.

                                                                (1942)

Barbara Baynton
THE CHOSEN VESSEL

She laid the stick and her baby on the grass while she untied the rope that tethered the calf. The length of the rope separated them. The cow was near the calf, and both were lying down. Feed along the creek was plentiful, and every day she found a fresh place to tether it, since tether it she must, for if she did not, it would stray with the cow out on the plain. She had plenty of time to go after it, but then there was her baby; and if the cow turned on her out on the plain, and she with her baby,—she had been a town girl and was afraid of the cow, but she did not want the cow to know it. She used to run at first when it bellowed its protest against the penning up of its calf. This satisfied the cow, also the calf, but the woman's husband was angry, and called her—the noun was cur. It was he who forced her to run and meet the advancing cow, brandishing a stick, and uttering threatening words till the enemy turned and ran. 'That's the way!' the man said, laughing at her white face. In many things he was worse than the cow, and she wondered if the same rule would apply to the man, but she was not one to provoke skirmishes even with the cow.

It was early for the calf to go to 'bed'—nearly an hour earlier than usual; but she had felt so restless all day. Partly because it was Monday, and the end of the week that would bring her and the baby the companionship of his father, was so far off. He was a shearer, and had gone to his shed before daylight that morning. Fifteen miles as the crow flies separated them.

There was a track in front of the house, for it had once been a wine shanty, and a few travellers passed along at intervals. She was not afraid of horsemen; but swagmen, going to, or worse coming from, the dismal, drunken little township, a day's journey beyond, terrified her. One had called at the house to-day, and asked for tucker.

That was why she had penned up the calf so early. She feared more from the look of his eyes, and the gleam of his teeth, as he watched her newly awakened baby beat its impatient fists upon her covered breasts, than from the knife that was sheathed in the belt at his waist.

She had given him bread and meat. Her husband she told him was sick. She always said that when she was alone and a swagman came; and she had gone in from the kitchen to the bedroom, and asked questions and replied to them in the best man's voice she could assume. Then he had asked to go into the kitchen to boil his billy, but instead she gave him tea, and he drank it on the wood heap. He had walked round and round the house, and there were cracks in some places, and after the last time he had asked for tobacco. She had none to give him, and he had grinned, because there was a broken clay pipe near the wood heap where he stood, and if there were a man inside, there ought to have been tobacco. Then he asked for money, but women in the bush never have money.

At last he had gone, and she, watching through the cracks, saw him when about a quarter of a mile away, turn and look back at the house. He had stood so for some moments with a pretence of fixing his swag, and then, apparently satisfied, moved to the left towards the creek. The creek made a bow round the house, and when he came to the bend she lost sight of him. Hours after, watching intently for signs of smoke, she saw the man's dog chasing some sheep that had gone to the creek for water, and saw it slink back suddenly, as if it had been called by some one.

More than once she thought of taking her baby and going to her husband. But in the past, when she had dared to speak of the dangers to which her loneliness exposed her, he had taunted and sneered at her. 'Needn't flatter yerself,' he had told her, 'nobody 'ud want ter run away with yew.'

Long before nightfall she placed food on the kitchen table, and beside it laid the big brooch that had been her mother's. It was the only thing of value that she had. And she left the kitchen door wide open.

The doors inside she securely fastened. Beside the bolt in the back one she drove in the steel and scissors; against it she piled the table and the stools. Underneath the lock of the front door she forced the handle of the spade, and the blade between the cracks in the flooring boards. Then the prop-stick, cut into lengths, held the top, as the spade held the middle. The windows were little more than portholes; she had nothing to fear through them.

She ate a few mouthfuls of food and drank a cup of milk. But she lighted no fire, and when night came, no candle, but crept with her baby to bed.

What woke her? The wonder was that she had slept—she had not meant to. But she was young, very young. Perhaps the shrinking of the galvanized roof—hardly though, since that was so usual. Yet something had set her heart beating wildly; but she lay quite still, only she put her arm over her baby. Then she had both round it, and she prayed, 'Little baby, little baby, don't wake!'

The moon's rays shone on the front of the house, and she saw one of the open cracks, quite close to where she lay, darken with a shadow. Then a protesting growl reached her; and she could fancy she heard the man turn hastily. She plainly heard the thud of something striking the dog's ribs, and the long flying strides of the animal as it howled and ran. Still watching, she saw the shadow darken every crack along the wall. She knew by the sounds that the man was trying every standpoint that might help him to see in; but how much he saw she could not tell. She thought of many things she might do to deceive him into the idea that she was not alone. But the sound of her voice would wake baby, and she dreaded that as though it were the only danger that threatened her. So she prayed, 'Little baby, don't wake, don't cry!'

Stealthily the man crept about. She knew he had his boots off, because of the vibration that his feet caused as he walked along the verandah to gauge the width of the little window in her room, and the resistance of the front door.

Then he went to the other end, and the uncertainty of what he was doing became unendurable. She had felt safer, far safer, while he was close, and she could watch and listen. She felt she must watch, but the great fear of wakening her baby again assailed her. She suddenly recalled that one of the slabs on that side of the house had shrunk in length as well as in width, and had once fallen out. It was held in position only by a wedge of wood underneath. What if he should discover that? The uncertainty increased her terror. She prayed as she gently raised herself with her little one in her arms, held tightly to her breast.

She thought of the knife, and shielded its body with her hands and arms. Even the little feet she covered with its white gown, and the baby never murmured—it liked to be held so. Noiselessly she crossed to the other side, and stood where she could see and hear, but not be seen. He was trying every slab, and was very near to that with the wedge under it. Then she saw him find it; and heard the sound of the knife as bit by bit he began to cut away the wooden support.

She waited motionless, with her baby pressed tightly to her, though she knew that in another few minutes this man with the cruel eyes, lascivious mouth, and gleaming knife, would enter. One side of the slab tilted; he had only to cut away the remaining little end, when the slab, unless he held it, would fall outside.

She heard his jerked breathing as it kept time with the cuts of the knife, and the brush of his clothes as he rubbed the wall in his movements, for she was so still and quiet, that she did not even tremble. She knew when he ceased, and wondered why, being so well concealed; for he could not see her, and would not fear if he did, yet she heard him move cautiously away. Perhaps he expected the slab to fall—his motive puzzled her, and she moved even closer, and bent her body the better to listen. Ah! what sound was that? 'Listen! Listen!' she bade her heart—her heart that had kept so still, but now bounded with tumultuous throbs that dulled her ears. Nearer and nearer come the sounds, till the welcome thud of a horse's hoof rang out clearly.

'O God! O God! O God!' she panted, for they were very close before she could make sure. She rushed to the door, and with her baby in her arms tore frantically at its bolts and bars.

Out she darted at last, and running madly along, saw the horseman beyond her in the distance. She called to him in Christ's Name, in her babe's name, still flying like the wind with the speed that deadly peril gives. But the distance grew greater and greater between them, and when she reached the creek her prayers turned to wild shrieks, for there crouched the man she feared, with outstretched arms that caught her as she fell. She knew he was offering terms if she ceased to struggle and cry for help, though louder and louder did she cry for it, but it was only when the man's hand gripped her throat, that the cry of 'Murder' came from her lips. And when she ceased, the startled curlews took up the awful sound, and flew wailing 'Murder! Murder!' over the horseman's head.

'By God!' said the boundary rider, 'it's been a dingo right enough! Eight killed up here, and there's more down in the creek—a ewe and a lamb, I'll bet; and the lamb's alive!' He shut out the sky with his hand, and watched the crows that were circling round and round, nearing the earth one moment, and the next shooting skywards. By that he knew the lamb must be alive; even a dingo will spare a lamb sometimes.

Yes, the lamb was alive, and after the manner of lambs of its kind did not know its mother when the light came. It had sucked the still warm breasts, and laid its little head on her bosom, and slept till the morn. Then, when it looked at the swollen disfigured face, it wept and would have crept away, but for the hand that still clutched its little gown. Sleep was nodding its golden head and swaying its small body, and the crows were close, so close, to the mother's wide-open eyes, when the boundary rider galloped down.

'Jesus Christ!' he said, covering his eyes. He told afterwards how the little child held out its arms to him, and how he was forced to cut its gown that the dead hand held.

It was election time, and as usual the priest had selected a candidate. His choice was so obviously in the interests of the squatter, that Peter Hennessey's reason, for once in his life, had over-ridden superstition, and he had dared promise his vote to another. Yet he was uneasy, and every time he woke in the night (and it was often), he heard the murmur of his mother's voice. It came through the partition, or under the door. If through the partition, he knew she was praying in her bed; but when the sounds came under the door, she was on her knees before the little Altar in the corner that enshrined the statue of the Blessed Virgin and Child.

'Mary, Mother of Christ! save my son! Save him!' prayed she in the dairy as she strained and set the evening's milking. 'Sweet Mary! for the love of Christ, save him!' The grief in her old face made the morning meal so bitter, that to avoid her he came late to his dinner. It made him so cowardly, that he could not say good-bye to her, and when night fell on the eve of the election day, he rode off secretly.

He had thirty miles to ride to the township to record his vote. He cantered briskly along the great stretch of plain that had nothing but stunted cotton bush to play shadow to the full moon, which glorified a sky of earliest spring. The bruised incense of the flowering clover rose up to him, and the glory of the night appealed vaguely to his imagination, but he was preoccupied with his present act of revolt.

Vividly he saw his mother's agony when she would find him gone. Even at that moment, he felt sure, she was praying.

'Mary! Mother of Christ!' He repeated the invocation, half unconsciously, when suddenly to him, out of the stillness, came Christ's Name—called loudly in despairing accents.

'For Christ's sake! Christ's sake! Christ's sake!' called the voice. Good Catholic that he had been, he crossed himself before he dared to look back. Gliding across a ghostly patch of pipe-clay, he saw a white-robed figure with a babe clasped to her bosom.

All the superstitious awe of his race and religion swayed his brain. The moonlight on the gleaming clay was a 'heavenly light' to him, and he knew the white figure not for flesh and blood, but for the Virgin and Child of his mother's prayers. Then, good Catholic that once more he was, he put spurs to his horse's sides and galloped madly away.

His mother's prayers were answered, for Hennessey was the first to record his vote—for the priest's candidate. Then he sought the priest at home, but found that he was out rallying the voters. Still, under the influence of his blessed vision, Hennessey would not go near the public-houses, but wandered about the outskirts of the town for hours, keeping apart from the towns-people, and fasting as penance. He was subdued and mildly ecstatic, feeling as a repentant chastened child, who awaits only the kiss of peace.

And at last, as he stood in the graveyard crossing himself with reverent awe, he heard in the gathering twilight the roar of many voices crying the name of the victor at the election. It was well with the priest.

Again Hennessey sought him. He was at home, the housekeeper said, and led him into the dimly lighted study. His seat was immediately opposite a large picture, and as the housekeeper turned up the lamp, once more the face of the Madonna and Child looked down on him, but this time silently, peacefully. The half-parted lips of the Virgin were smiling with compassionate tenderness; her eyes seemed to beam with the forgiveness of an earthly mother for her erring but beloved child.

He fell on his knees in adoration. Transfixed, the wondering priest stood, for mingled with the adoration, 'My Lord and my God!' was the exaltation, 'And hast Thou chosen me?'

'What is it, Peter?' said the priest.

'Father,' he answered reverently; and with loosened tongue he poured forth the story of his vision.

'Great God!' shouted the priest, 'and you did not stop to save her! Do you not know? Have you not heard?'

Many miles further down the creek a man kept throwing an old cap into a water-hole. The dog would bring it out and lay it on the opposite side to where the man stood, but would not allow the man to catch him, though it was only to wash the blood of the sheep from his mouth and throat, for the sight of blood made the man tremble. But the dog also was guilty.

(1896)

Ethel Anderson
THE LOVE-NEST; OR, WHICH SIN IS THAT?

The tide of life flowed very briskly in those regions, and there was a great deal of conjecture about a new dwelling at Little Peeping in the Inlet, a cove until now uninhabited, and used merely by such small ships as put in to fill water-casks, or land merchandise on the beaches that flanked the river mouth. For the river here joined the sea.

It must be remembered that in Parramatta and its sparsely populated neighbouring villages at this period (the Crimean War was not yet over) there prevailed a general idea that the good were poor, and the bad, rich, and that money, in short, was not to be accumulated in any great quantities except by the enjoyment of the Devil's own luck or cunning, and by nefarious means.

The very reasonable sum represented by an income of two hundred pounds a year was regarded in such circles as being quite sufficiently 'warm' (enough) for the godly, or even the demi-godly.

The appearance, therefore, of violent and ebullient prosperity expressed by the almost audible chink (reported to have been heard by passers-by) of spondulix, Golden Joeys, Happy Dicks, Yellow Boys, or guineas, or any other term by which money was then designated (a sovereign in particular being considered hardly 'nice' enough for open reference), obviously tainted the lustre which shone like an aura round the cottage, reared up practically under cover of night, above the estuary of the river, a couple of miles below Doggett's Patch.

In local eyes its flamboyant well-being immediately invested it with the effluvia of sin; whether mortal or venial sin remained to be proved.

The radiant dwelling faced that estuary by means of which (of course clandestinely) contact might be made with the Pacific Ocean (here hardly wide enough, Miss Loveday Boisragon felt, for all that so palpably 'went on' there); and the fact that the minute building with its singing canaries, its muslin curtains waving like flags through every opened window, was so sweet, so gay, so airy that it might have been constructed of sugar-cane instead of cedar, further conduced to its recognition as being a love-nest, a place to be personally and religiously avoided (but nevertheless watched and gossiped about) by all decent Christians.

It was Victoria McMurthie, now seventeen, who first reported to her family the surprising existence of this debatable dwelling.

Victoria's father, Captain James McMurthie, was a shipping magnate poor enough to be considered virtuous. He owned various little ships of sixty tons and under, which sailed to Mauritius for sugar and cocoa, to Van Diemen's Land for apples and potatoes, and to 'the Islands', to garner in whatever they might yield; a certain reserve was shown in the enumeration of such cargoes.

The *Rose*, a brig of forty tons, carried the London trade, and since she was not passed by the Port authorities as being perfectly seaworthy, Captain McMurthie usually sailed her himself. She was, at the moment, a month overdue from Rio de Janeiro.

These vessels had all been named by the McMurthie family in full conclave as they sat round the red-clothed, lamp-lit table in their two-storied wooden house some way out of Parramatta.

The brig *Victoria and Alberteena* was named as a tribute to the two eldest daughters. The *Edward and Elias* was a tribute to the two eldest sons. The *Henry and Alice* in this domestic navy represented the youngest members in a family of sixteen; all hungry.

The *Fruitful Hannah* celebrated the virtues of an exemplary wife, of whom the Captain was very fond (she had been baptised 'Témeraire'); the ketch *Dainty Jane* he had himself singled out for honour; no member of the McMurthie family was called Jane.

The daily lives of these nautical children were so wrapped up in the comings and goings, the crews and cargoes of their beloved vessels, that they felt every change of weather even more acutely than the indefatigable man and girl, labelled 'wet' and 'dry', who popped in and out of the Swiss Chalet set above the dining-room mantelpiece.

Bunches of seaweed, swelling or wrinkled furbelows, dried-up scraps of arrow muzlets or dahlia wartlets, nailed to the verandah posts, reflected the emotions of these sea-changed young people as faithfully as they, in their turn, were influenced by the humidity or lack of it in the atmosphere; such things were kept for their prophetic qualities.

Should a cow lie down, or a swallow fly high, or a spider spin a web before noonday, such apparently trivial happenings would be reported as news; a black nor'-easter would keep Victoria awake all night; a southerly buster would prevent her from eating a bite of breakfast; a fair wind would send the whole McMurthie tribe scattering like gulls to watch the Heads (having begged lifts into Sydney) or inspire them to organise riding-parties to some vantage-point along the coast.

It was on one such excursion that Victoria had observed the 'Love Nest', which was not, of course, supposed to be known to her by so opprobious a title; yet she had heard the name applied to it.

She and Miss Loveday Boisragon returned to this same view-point one afternoon towards the end of winter. Having followed the rutty track that dropped down to the sea-shore from Doggett's Patch (they were staying at *The Devil's Tail*), they reined-in their horses on a convenient headland just facing the cottage, but on the far side of the river, and stopped to discuss it.

It was a Monday.

That most revealing of all betrayals, the washing, on which a curious coterie from Doggett's Patch, Hornsby Junction, and even Dural had kept an hebdomadal watch for months past, was waving in the sea-wind that, every afternoon, blew inland.

It was by this time well known that, as a rule, every Monday two sheets would wanton in the breeze for some three weeks on end; that every so often four sheets would make a snowy and irregular appearance. Very strangely, everyone thought, no saveloy-like bolsters filled with wind would flounce about on the clothes line, as they might have been observed to do in every other house-hold. Even more strangely, during those months in which a watch had been kept, sometimes as many as twenty sheets— sometimes even thirty—would flutter in the Love Nest wash.

'As for night-shirts,' Miss Loveday had reported to her sisters, 'the effect of scores of them all prancing about in mid-air was unnerving, quite. All Mallow's Marsh, Doggett's Patch, Hornsby Junction—even Parramatta itself—could hardly have produced so many.'

Loveday had several times been down to peep at the cottage and today, talking to Victoria, she again expressed wonder.

'As a revelation of the number of occupants of the cottage the number of sheets, naturally, should be perfectly revealing.'

She waved a horse-tail switch which kept the flies off—sometimes.

'But I find the whole affair baffling! We can only go by averages. As far as I can make out, one person lives there. Sometimes a second person stays a few night—under a week—and every two or three months the perma-nent resident entertains a house-party which would tax the accommoda-tion of St. James' Palace, or even Government House, Parramatta!'

'But so many people change only one sheet every week, on each bed,' Victoria protested. 'The lower sheet is put to the wash, the old upper sheet takes its place, and a clean sheet is put on top of it? Don't you agree?'

'You completely amaze me!' Miss Boisragon spoke with energy.

The astonishment in her charming voice was reflected in the grey regard which dwelt with penetration on the glowing, youthful face beside her. Victoria's eyes, sloe-black, were so shallow as to be without light; even her brothers admitted a resemblance to boot-buttons. Devoid of candour, they told one nothing of her thoughts. Her mouth, however, extremely sensi-tive, having one corner curled up more than the other, was always illumi-nating; it gave her away.

'You know so much! Yet your knowledge has not contaminated your mind. Someone in the Apocrypha says, "The knowledge of wickedness is not wisdom." Yet there seems to be, my dear child nothing you do not know. What freedom your generation is allowed!'

Miss Boisragon sighed.

'Was that want of freedom your tragedy, dear Aunt Loveday?'

'Indeed, yes! Yet times have so changed that I can speak of it without a blush—and to a girl of seventeen!'

'Tell me.'

'One Monday, long, long ago, I was so unmaidenly, and, as they thought, so depraved, as to read our family washing-list. I was sixteen, admittedly an "awkward" age. My parents, my dear father in particular, could not bring themselves to forgive me.'

'Oh, how terrible!'

'Yes! They could not forgive a trespass so degrading. It was the reason, too, that I never married.'

'Oh, surely not!'

'Indeed, yes! The story got about. So lascivious a curiosity was considered to be "fast". The fastidious gentleman who had been paying his addresses to me would not, could not, trust me.'

'You have lived it down?'

'Yes. I think I have. But I have never forgotten *him*. I did so adore him. I can never dip into a blue eye without anguish.'

Sadly the pair looked across the swirling waters, now sliding backward into the sea over rocks and sandbanks; the tide was on the ebb. It was a neap tide.

It was now at that mysterious hour of the late afternoon when the shadows, darkly crepuscular, appear to be longer than normal; when a rosy light brightens the tree-tops, emphasising the red veins in each pendant eucalyptus leaf, outlining each hissing wavelet—so fatigued after a long day's work—with a warm crease behind each breaking crest.

The gulls were wheeling far out to sea. The clouds bunched round the declining sun were apricot. Stretching beyond the estuary to a limitless horizon, the ocean, heavy, inert, as if stirred by every seventh wave alone was placid in the Greek sense, when the word means depth as well as quietude. Its colour was so ambiguous as to call to mind the phrases Amarynthine purple, Tyrian blue, or other such designations that admit of no exactitude.

There was a breeze; but it was fitful, it allowed for moments of inanition as preganant as the silence of lovers.

'A cherry tree in flower is lovely,' Victoria ventured, her soul visible in her tremulous mouth, 'a pear-tree, too, in moonlight! How bewitching! A chain of hills—how adorable!'

She paused, looking with an absent eye at what might have been a seagull on the blue, slowly-heaving ocean. A bird? Yet it seemed not to be!

'Yes? Dear child? You were saying?'

'But a ship! A ship! Aunt Loveday! How can I explain to you all that a ship means to me? A swan? A ship is lovelier!'

'Yes. Man has invented nothing. He improves. He copies. He sees a swallow's nest and builds a palace. He sees a swan, as you say, and creates a ship.'

Victoria re-established a shining top-hat, heavily veiled on her thatch of vital, short black hair.

'Yes. Man does copy Nature. He does improve on Nature. His ship makes a swan look blowsy. Oh! But do turn quite round!'

Miss Boisragon turned, horse and all.

As they looked seaward their heads were neatly inserted by their drooping mounts amongst the tops of blackened saplings and sheoaks. Three years back the bush had been burnt out and the few standing tree-trunks and even the rocks wore widow's weeds. Like figures on a Japanese screen, aunt and niece watched a small vessel which, hitherto unnoticed, except perhaps unconsciously, as being, perhaps a ship, perhaps a bird, had rounded the blue bay's furthermost island.

'It blows up the estuary like a lily before the wind.'

'How utterly I agree!' Miss Boisragon was herself excited. 'He, dear, whom I shocked so much—he was a sailor!'

A girl came out of the cottage, a girl whose possible good looks were not to be deciphered, quite, at such a distance. She stood waiting.

'A ship sailing into an arm of the sea, into a purple inlet where a gay, gay cottage, its verandah-posts made of Edinburgh Rock—'

'No! No! Of barley-sugar! No! Of something rarer—say of Marzipan!'

'Of Marzipan, then—where a girl in a pink dress is waiting for her sailor lover! Oh, what could be more romantic!'

'Romantic? Yes! I agree. But I cannot profess to guess why local opinion so insists on the *riches* of the inmates of that charming sugar-plum!'

'Man Thomas and Ike Peachy came down from Carefree Farm to have a "look-see" as they put it, and they told me with awe that they saw a bunch of bananas *as large as a chicken-coop* hanging up on the verandah to ripen! There's riches!'

'Pink, somehow,' the tone was disparaging, 'is such a plebeian colour.'

'A bit. It appeals to the masculine taste too brazenly.'

Was the ship a sloop? A brig? A ketch? A cutter?

It finally revealed itself as being a sloop, with a single mast, a fixed bowsprit, and a jib-stay—a stay running from the masthead to the bowsprit-head. She flew towards them, steering her proper course under easy sail.

The sun had dropped lower, to shoot almost vertical rays of light through the clear water. The breeze had freshened.

'She is well handled for so light an air of wind.'

Victoria spoke sagaciously. She knew a great deal about ships, having been permitted to sail her own *Victoria and Alberteena* (in which her sister, being younger, was hardly allowed to share) from Sydney to Newcastle and back.

'She's a sloop, possibly a Naval tender of some sort,' Victoria decided. 'Somewhere, out of sight, there may be a larger vessel.'

Still watching, she expressed dismay.

'They cannot be so foolish as to anchor just there, while the tide is running out, and the sand, as they must know, shifts about in the channels. The wind is freshening, too, and I think it is working up for half a gale. We may even be in for a black nor'-easter.'

But, riding with a steep shore on her larboard bow, a rock and shoal extending on both hands, the foolhardy sloop did drop anchor, with a rattle and splash, into a few fathoms of water, which, as Victoria well knew, would momentarily lessen.

'That boat will be high and dry in half an hour.'

The name *Amiable Nelly* was now to be made out on her stern, she had swung-to almost below their eyrie.

'Hail them and tell them so.'

'They would not hear! How queer the men look, foreshortened and hopping about like Jacks-in-a-box.'

'Sailors use their arms and their lungs more than their legs, don't you see, so in any case they would have chests a bit too big for them, you might say, but of course they stand firmly—don't, as people say they do, roll in their gait. Do you notice? They stump about. They spring about! They are so lively in movement, aren't they?'

'How romantic the sound of masculine voices carrying across the water! Oh, I do think we are enjoying our afternoon, don't you?'

Victoria listened, a pleased smile widening her delicious mouth. 'They are singing "Abel Brown"! We are too far off to hear the words, but I recognise the tune.'

'Oh, Victoria! That shocking chanty! Why, it's never been printed! It could *never* be!'

'Tra-la-la, Aunt Prunes and Prisms! Nowadays girls are not prudes!'

'It's the little man who seems to be ordering everyone about. He is very brisk.'

'They are putting some bundles into the dinghy. The two young men in coconut dungarees are evidently going ashore.'

Looking at the two well set-up young men, so handsome, so lissom, as, with an older man, they embarked in the dinghy, Victoria had a moment of exasperation.

'It's really not fair that men, who have everything—*everything* —who are so clever and brave and wonderful generally, should have such good looks as well! Consider their splendid physique! Their muscles! Observe, dear Aunt Loveday, the backs of their necks, even!'

'Beautiful!' Miss Loveday unbent. 'It's the splendour of perfect health and strength.'

Victoria made a decision.

'We must prevent such superb beings from adorning a ship that's high and dry on the rocks! Will you come down to the beach with me?'

Their horses slipped and slithered down the boulder-strewn, pebbly, almost precipitous river-bank. It was littered with so many broken boughs and burnt trunks of trees that their progress took some time, and when they finally arrived at the water's edge they found that the tide was indeed running out.

Yet the two men left in the sloop, leaning on the rail, were talking in perfect unconsciousness of its peril. They were quite absorbed, one oldish, blue-eyed, the other younger, brown-eyed, ruddy under a deeply burnt-in tan. They were obviously sailors—sea-dogs, almost—quite caked with salt.

Just as at a review, at some grand parade, a cur will appear from nowhere, and, running before the troops—say the Household Brigade in all its glory—bring an unwanted touch of comedy to a splendid occasion, so, apparently, to judge by their remote air, their indifference to all attempts at communication, were these two sailors accustomed to find women springing up under their noses, unwelcome beings, to be snubbed, to be ignored, like dogs at a review.

Obvioulsy aware of the fair equestriennes who so persistently hailed them, they scorned to reply.

'Really, they are too ridiculous! But a sloop is a sloop. Left as she is our *Amiable Nelly* will certainly be damaged when the tide drops even five or six feet lower. I'll edge Buttercup along to that spit of sand nearer the ship.'

Miss Boisragon, amused, waited on the sandy point a hundred yards, perhaps, from the sloop.

Victoria, forcing her mount into the river, guided it along a shallow ledge until she was a few yards—twenty or so—from the *Amiable Nelly*.

'Hi!'

No answer.

'Hey, you!'

'Ahoy!'

Victoria, raising her clear treble, became more nautical in her appeals. They were unacknowledged. Regardless of a fashionable habit that trailed from the saddle to the ground, she let her mount wade further across the deepening rocky shelf until the river flowed strongly against her stirrup, until her face was level with the averted eyes of the chatting men, who scorned, it seemed, to pay tribute to her presence by shifting their positions.

'Really!' Three yards from them, Victoria voiced her indignation. She was, after all, not only a sailor's daughter but the owner of a brig, 'Really! My good men! Unless you bestir yourselves and get into deeper water, the tide will leave you high and dry. I know this river! I tell you frankly I would not give a silver sixpence for your little tub in half an hour's time! Tide ebbing! Wind freshening! What on earth are you thinking about?'

Indeed, a strong air was now a little abaft their starboard beam.

The blue-eyed man, the small, briskly-moving one, who had, as Miss Boisragon had noticed, been 'ordering the others about'—one of those fussy people who can let nothing alone—glanced an instant at the swirling water (superficially the river looked wide enough for a safe anchorage), his companion, too, glanced; dismay was registered on his face, anger on his companion's.

'How soon do you expect the crew back?'

The three men who had toiled with their bundles up the hill to the cottage were now within doors, out of hail.

'The bosun, who knows the passage' (he had, indeed, voiced his misgivings), 'may be an hour. I'll get the anchor up and work her alongshore into deeper water.'

The tall man sprang from his lounging position on the ship's rail.

'Thank you for your warning,' he exclaimed.

The blue-eyed man, without thanks, was slackening a rope. The sails had been furled.

'I had better take the wheel—I know the channel well!'

The *Amiable Nelly* rode dangerously close to a rock that terminated sharply in deep water, and by venturing with some intrepidity to its limits, the river almost to her saddle-flaps, Victoria, leaning far out, was able to clutch a rope, gain a hanging ladder, and helped by the strong arms of the taller sailor, make the deck without disaster. Her mount, freed, was caught by Miss Boisragon who, guessing her niece's intention, had followed her along the shallows which had befriended her purpose. Withdrawing to the sandy spit of shore, where she waited with the two horses, Loveday Boisragon, having several times searchingly observed the blue-eyed man, had ceased to look amused.

'Get those sails set—and hurry up, man!'

Like a Pirate who had captured a prize, Victoria began giving her orders, and she ran gaily down the spotless deck, her dripping habit scarcely impeding her flight.

The little man obeyed her, sourly.

The anchor was weighed, with two to do the work enough sail was set to bring the sloop down-stream, and, Victoria at the wheel, a safer berth was found in deeper water. Here the sloop was again made fast under the lee of an islet, to await the dinghy's return.

'After all,' running a caressing hand along the smooth, worn surface of the mast, Victoria was gracious, 'you two work better than I had expected of you, after you had made so foolish an anchorage! I took you for a pair of guffies.'

Engaged in watching the colour of the water as she steered the sloop through a dangerous passage, Victoria had yet been dimly aware that the taller of the two men laboured under some suppressed emotion. This impression had not clearly registered itself on her attention. She had been too much absorbed. Now that she was less engrossed, however, she realised that he was agitated by suppressed laughter.

'Your skirt is trailing on the deck, Madam.'

The blue-eyed sailor spoke without suavity. Though he drew nearer, his manner was even more distant.

Unaware that his deck, not her habit, was his anxiety, the young interloper, as she became conscious of being, reassured him with a bright 'It's Dreadnaught! It's waterproofed serge! My father buys a bolt or two every year from a naval quarter-master he knows.'

Her answer brought no responsive smile.

By this time the sun, about to bed down for the night, had, like a Nautch-girl, shed its last cloud. A bright red ball of light, it stained the water's gold, splashing a dazzling glory over the ship's mast and stays and rigging; making its ropes gold, its deck agate. There was an exaltation past expression in the beauty that renewed each object on sea and shore with a parting benediction.

Miss Boisragon, sitting her drooping horse with a lissom grace, was a gold statuette, something precious from Tanagra, as she waited patiently on the radiant sands.

'Who is she?'

Leaning by Victoria's side on the rail the brown-eyed man was friendly. He had got the impression that the child was 'peaked'. She was, in fact, anxious about the *Rose*.

'It's my dearest aunt, Loveday Boisragon. Isn't she a sweet little pouter pigeon? She's always as neat as one of those wooden figures of Mrs Noah in a toy Ark.'

'When that cormorant frightened her horse she handled him well.'

'Oh, she's a wonderful rider! She's a marvellous person. But, of course, she's old.' Sweet Seventeen was cruel. 'She will be twenty-nine next birthday!' Victoria squeezed the water from a dripping skirt. 'But nothing daunts her.'

And Victoria being that kind of girl, and used to taking part with her friends in free discussions on the characters and idiosyncrasies of her acquaintances, a diffuseness rendered harmless by a general goodwill, by an instinct that recognised the basic untruth of everything everyone said, the victim of such gossip being endeared rather than otherwise by the imaginary failings laid bare, immediately embarked on the tale of Miss Loveday's broken heart.

'And, do you know,' she wound up, 'that utter idiot, who was a sailor, and sailors don't usually, do they? sheered off, just because, at sixteen, she read the family washing list? Yes, she was pierced to the very marrow of the heart. She loves him still, she says—she will always love him! To dip into a blue eye, Aunt Loveday says, is anguish! Anguish! It brings him so clearly to her mind.'

Victoria found no difficulty in catching her companion's brown regard, which remained glued on her shallow, unshadowed black eyes. Eyes as unreflecting as slabs of chocolate, and seeming, too, to be all pupil and no iris. Indeed he was most flatteringly attentive, his manner being in direct contradiction to that of his shipmate, who, from the first, had betrayed a dryness of manner, a disharmony, rivalling that, say, of a Gapelet, or even an Opelet, jettisoned on hot sand by an unkind tide; he was very stiff. Used to a neighbourly world, Victoria could not make him out.

'Oh, oh, oh! She read the family washing list!'

The brown-eyed man had found a pretext for laughter. How he laughed!

Though still standing near, the blue-eyed sailor gave no sign of having heard, though he loitered, he did not move out of earshot.

'Of course she could have married. There was a widower, for instance, but—'

Was she being indiscreet? Victoria wondered.

'About that widower?' She was not to be let off.

'It was the horsehair sofa that spoilt that match.' As Victoria explained her companion took notice of her dimples. 'When he came courting every Sunday afternoon at three o'clock, sharp, he and Aunt Loveday and the little boy sat on the horsehair sofa, and the little boy, don't you know, always cried. So Mr Tovey felt, he told my grandfather—Colonel Boisragon of the Madras Army—that perhaps the child had taken a dislike to Aunt Loveday, and he married Miss Augusta Wirraway instead.'

'Did your Aunt regret it?'

His young friend appeared to give the question her deep consideration.

'A choice that might be said to be made between the Devil and the deep sea—between making a dull marriage and living a spinster—is always difficult to make, but it rather stands out that Aunt Loveday, who perfectly well guessed the reason for the child's tears—the pricking horsehair—did not disclose it. She tells it now as a joke.'

At this moment the boat, manned by the two handsome young sailors (the Bosun, apparently, had waited with his wife) was rowed briskly round a bend, and came alongside heavily laden.

'We came down today,' Victoria remarked, watching the men make the dinghy fast alongside and begin dumping the baskets it had carried on to the deck, 'to peep at the Love Nest—that cottage on the hill about which everyone is so curious. Something *very wicked*, as far as I can make out, is going on there.'

Again the hearty laughter.

'Nothing more wicked than the Admiral's washing! And sometimes, too, the wardroom washing of any other ship in port. The bosun's wife lives there. She washes for us. And, of course, the man gets leave sometimes to wait a week with her. It's more convenient to send a boat in here than to go into Sydney Harbour.'

'Oh! Have you a ship of your own?' Victoria breathed.

'Certainly.' He was not communicative.

'Has *he*?'

No answer.

Victoria had slowly become aware of a sinking of heart. Were the two men whom she had so unceremoniously ordered about people of importance? Men she had criticised! Not reefers! Not Jack Tars! Not—above all—'*guffies*'? Not chewers of Bonded Jacky? Singers of Abel Brown?

As, trembling, Victoria mused, she looked about her at the shining brass, noticed afresh the deference of the sailors who had just come aboard, who smartly saluted, it seemed, each time her first friends drew a breath or cast an eye about them; she then observed that the trail of smoke, which had been for some time apparent as a black indignity on the golden air of evening, had chuffed itself fully into sight.

'A Man O'War!'

Her delight in it brought an answering smile.

'HMS *Grasshopper*.'

'Oh! Your ship?'

'My little ship.'

Together they watched the newcomer, smart as paint, of course! A funnel as tall as her two masts, elegant paddle wheels, adorning an iron hull.

'Oh! Have you chased the Barbary Pirates?'

'As a midshipman.'

'Have you defeated the Russian Fleet?'

'Oh, yes.'

'Have you seen the Sea-gypsies in the Selung Archipelago? My father lost a ship there three years back!'

'We have attended to them!'

He laughed at Victoria's eagerness.

'Come and say "goodbye". It's time we left.'

'Oh! Will you row me yourself?'

'Naturally.'

The blue-eyed sailor was no more cordial when Victoria gave her hand in saying 'good-bye'.

Instead of taking it, he put in it a silver crown-piece, and said, frostily, 'With my thanks.'

'Thanks?' Victoria was bewildered.

He said no more, but turned away. The series of accidents that had led to the miscarriage of his barge and had necessitated his transport to the *Grasshopper* in so menial a tender as the *Amiable Nelly* was going to make life difficult for some unhappy midshipman, that was certain. The disgrace (as he considered it) of being caught out by a girl of seventeen in making so dangerous an anchorage (for the bosun had hinted at its dangers) he knew he would never live down. In an imagination that did not usually function, he pictured the wardroom laughter—behind his back—yes—but he would be well aware of it. Remembering, too, the talk he had overheard about his first-love, Loveday Boisragon, delighted though he was to have escaped so degrading a connection, he stuck his nose in the air, he ground and gritted his teeth.

The dinghy put off, Victoria steering, and in the Seventh Heaven, her new friend (as she thought him) rowing.

They found Miss Boisragon walking the horses up and down the sand, less a woman than a silhouette outlined in a fading gold that, as the three talked, became dusk; a dusk washed with silver from a rising moon, a dusk that was the airy hunting-ground of some sort of moth—or an Evening Brown, perhaps—that, softly and quietly as an owl, now stirred in a neighbouring tree, would brush, sometimes with the most elusive of kisses, their cheeks.

The river, a moving tide, still had its facets of light, a blink, here and there, of phosphorus; sometimes a fish jumped.

'Look, Aunt Loveday! A present! A silver crown for saving a ship!'

Victoria laughed outright at the 'tip' as the man with eyes of a colour not now to be determined lifted her into the saddle.

'No-one ever gives me a present.'

Loveday Boisragon was wistful.

The sailor standing beside her, taking a small hand offered in farewell, said, as if he meant it, 'I will bring you a present. Should you like a canary? A parrot? A length of Chinese brocade? A Spanish fan, an ivory workbox from Golconda, a phial of rose-attar from Persia? Any of the things we poor sailors bring back from sea?'

Looking mischievous, Miss Boisragon leant from her saddle to smile in the luminous dusk into his eyes and say, 'I should like a canary, a parrot, a length of Chinese brocade, a Spanish fan, a workbox from Golconda, a phial of rosewater *and* a coral locket.'

The poor woman could not actually ask for a wedding-ring but the question which then hung in the air between them later resolved itself; he gave her one.

As the *Amiable Nelly* put out to sea to join the *Grasshopper*, which was beating off-shore, Captain Jahleel Brattle (whose eyes were brown), leaning in talk against the rail with a blue-eyed Sir Jason Popham (Admiral of the Red) ventured on a criticism.

'Should we, perhaps, er—' he changed his text. 'Was it entirely right, do you think, to tip Miss Victoria McMurthie five shillings—for saving the ship?'

'Perfectly correct.' Sir Jason had regained his assurance. 'That girl was a person of no family. You may trust me to be the best judge of that.'

'Oh?' Captain Brattle dared say no more.

'Yes. Did you not notice? She said my "*father*" instead of my "*papa*". Evidently a girl of no social training!'

Captain Jahleel Brattle at this moment made out the *Rose*, hull down, on the starboard bow.

(1956)

Christina Stead
A LITTLE DEMON

The Masons are one of those large inwoven families, sprung from a prolific and managing father and mother, good in business and able to provide for all. The children of this old pair, now old themselves, all married young; but they have small business ability and few children, perhaps one to a couple, no more. They all work, but after work they pass their time in the timeless land of the family, happy, active, with the same notions, friends and foes. Some of their friends were friends in youth, others were drawn in forty years ago and have remained part of the story ever since, just as if they were brothers or sisters. But they can take in new friends too; and, after a time, the figures of the new friends are drawn on the pattern, in the right colours and attitudes, with little differences embroidered and attributes given, as a man with a falcon, a woman with a bouquet in old weaves. And after this, the falcon or the bouquet or the reaping-hook, this figure too, is part of the family legend.

In this easy-going dreamy way, life is passed in houses and on properties the family have slowly acquired, based on the investment and energy of the original Mason couple. The conversation is about family affairs, old anecdotes which take the place of fairy-tales in other childhoods, witticisms invented long ago, by the dead or living, and family personalities, all briefly stylised.

The family, because it is essentially and from beginning to end a family, is radical or liberal in its political opinions; they well understand the need for a republic, free speech, free purpose. And just as in politics, caricatures emerge. Each character has a part long assigned to him, which he can never change; even when his hair changes from dark to pale, his character from bad to good, his fortune from poor to rich or the other way about, even if he changes his wife or his profession, he remains, 'Charlie the gate crasher' let us say.

But there is one thing diminishes a Mason and is quite incomprehensible to the family, frowned upon, and bitterly spoken of—it is to leave the city, county and country anciently picked upon by the founding father. He is an artist—he must go to South Africa on a tour! That is no excuse! He is an airman, a pilot and must fly to Europe every week: a very thin, unreliable and giftless thinking he must have, a shabby temperament: the Masons shrug.

Anyone admitted to the family, who have this invisible but ever valid passport, receives all their news, lore, fable. He hears of many people, all ticketed long before he meets them. He even gets to know them quite well, their route from birth to age, though they may live and die without coming face to face. So with Old Edie and her five bachelor sons, whose lives she soured and ruined, a powerful bitter self-centred woman who suckled her own youngest brother—an action described with uneasy laughter and a felt shudder, and one could be in Thebes and afraid of the oracle. Edie was a bad cook and a good contralto. Was she like that? But appeal against legend? There was Fat Harry and his joke about the five-barred gate and the five dollars on Saturday and where did you leave your uncle. Everyone laughed at this old joke and so did I; but I never understood the joke. One of the family figures was Stevie, the little demon. My friend Jeanie, one of the kindest women in the world, lively and witty, friendly and girlish, exclaimed,

'Wait till you see him—just see him! No one would want to see him. No one likes that kind of child.'

Stevie was Jeanie's grand-nephew, only child of brother Rolf's only daughter, Mariana.

'Mariana's adorable, she is adorable and she just can't understand where she got such a little demon. Oh, well, Carrie, you know Carrie' (no, I don't), 'Mariana's mother, how adorable she is, what an angel! She wouldn't say anything about a fly! Well, even she admits that Stevie is a perfect little devil. You know that cat Fluffy' (yes, I know Fluffy), 'well, Fluffy I never did care for. I think there is something wrong with Fluffy; someone put her in the garbage can and put the lid on. And I will say one thing for Stevie, he actually rescued it and brought it home. They asked him, "Where did you get that cat?" He said, "In the garbage" and of course they didn't believe it. They thought he had stolen it. But after that, he never touched it. Just hates it now. Well, that poor Fluffy—what a life she leads! You know Mariana's loving heart—with Rags and Duff and Boiled-Beef, those dogs; and Duff, that is Rags's mother, even bigger than Rags, but they're still puppies to her. Mariana of course is simply wild about Duff, but she adores Rags; she simply won't go anywhere without Rags. She says she will never let her have puppies and I quite agree, to spoil a beautiful big doll like that, what a shame! Oh, poor Mariana, the way she carried on when Duff had puppies, even though one of them was Rags, well, I thought she'd never get over it and it was after she had Stevie, too. But she was furious, really furious and wouldn't talk to her mother Carrie for six weeks, when she found out that Duff was going to have puppies. To spoil that darling Duff, she said. And now the fact is she prefers Rags to Duff.

'Well, you see this cat Fluffy upset the dogs and Stevie took her part, just for a day or two; and then he saw which way the wind was blowing and lost interest. Well, where Stevie comes in—I think Mariana resents Stevie, too. But why not? I would. A little boy, I think, with no feeling for animals and no notion that Rags and Duff have feelings like us—like us?—more than us. We become hardened I think, but dogs never. They become more sensitive to us as they love us more. Yes, I suppose, it is cupboard love, I say so to myself, they just love you for the mince and bones; but why do children love us? Well, poor Mariana, she has this lovely great big dog and this naughty little boy and I really think she prefers Rags, no wonder. Why is he so naughty? She can't love him. You'd say a devil had got into the child; an imp is no word for him. What that child will do! And nothing brilliant either, nothing witty like those sayings they put in magazine columns—I suppose they are polished up a bit; but still amusing, suitable for that age of childhood. But if Stevie does anything, it's mean, glim, scary, just ugly; he has an ugly temper. Does everything he can to be disagreeable, to annoy, to tease. You'd think he knew. I believe he does. He knows how it hurts and annoys, even adults; but not animals, not dogs. He has no feeling for dogs and that is why I know that he has no real understanding, just a kind of intuition for the bad, not even like animals, but something connected with a low grade of intelligence. He says vile things, pert and cruel. I really hate him, though he's Mariana's child. We all hate him, his grandparents, too. You know Carrie, how sweet she is—she tries to defend him: he's young, she says. But how long does a child stay as young as that? Anyhow, understanding the feelings of animals is a thing a child is supposed to know first; and then to understand its mother long before it can speak, just by looking in her face and a sort of intuition. Well, but not this beastly little rat. Oh, I hate him! We all hate him. Dirty, he smells,-ah-ha—he's dirtier than a little dog and rolls in his blankets all dirty and picks his nose and puts his finger in his ear for the wax and eats it and scratches his hair and no dog is like that.

'Mariana, she's so sweet and fair, is that the word? So sweet and fair and she can't stand this nasty smelly little brat. How can a child, think, a child, be like that, rotten as a pear? It is something missing; he must be defective; oh, we all feel he is a defective. But that's the strange thing, the worst of all, you'd say he does it just to spite them. In school he's quite normal, he's more, he's bright. After tearing the house to pieces, he goes to school and not a boo out of him. They were terrified about letting him go to school, because of his character, temperament, whatever it is; and then they knew he was backward, a cretin, and they didn't want to expose him. But at last they had to send him, just to give Mariana a little rest from him and the father had to take him. He took the morning off and took him.

'Well, his father, Glenn, understands him more, but he understands in another way how bad he is. Mariana was always so sweet, though a bit disin—indifferent would you say? She could have done anything, but she has no interest. Don't you think that's the secret, having interest?

'Well, she told Glenn he must tell the teacher about the kind of boy Stevie was, to be fair to her; and to keep her eyes peeled and to tell the teacher if he played up in school to send a note home and they'd beat him.

'For about six weeks they heard nothing. They began to worry, for they thought the teacher was afraid to complain; knowing what most parents are. So Mariana got up the courage to go to the school and told the teacher she must tell her what Stevie had been doing; for she was so worried; and if he'd been doing anything, to leave it to her and Glenn. She said, "We'll make the little monkey pay for it."

'Do you know what happened? The teacher was quite surprised. She said, "Why, he's very good in school. He never makes a noise and he's almost at the top now."

'You can imagine how they felt when they heard that. They could hardly bear it. Mariana was simply furious to think of that hypocritical little monkey making such trouble for her at home and then putting on a smooth face and sitting still in school, a regular little Uriah Heep, she said.

'Can you understand a boy that age being so deceitful, playing a double game? It's not normal, I told her; and I really think and his grandfather thinks too, there's something radically wrong. They thought right away of taking him and sending him to a school for feebleminded or retarded children; but the teacher didn't want him to leave.

'Well frankly, Mariana didn't believe the whole story; she thought it was an act he put on and she waited. But he kept it up at school—not at home, oh, no! That's another strange thing about the boy. He knows when he's fooling people and he'll act so sweetly and behave so nicely, if he thinks some stranger doesn't know his record. He'll fool them completely.

'That's incredible, isn't it? It shows something wrong. I know that boy's twisted in some way, a mental hunch-back, probably quite dangerous too; for the way he can scheme and not in an obvious way, but like that— fooling his parents, playing a double game, and no feeling for anyone at home, not even for Rags and Duff; and you know, a boy and a dog—it's abnormal. It quite frightens me.

'Oh, I hope they don't bring him here this summer. I am nice to him; but he knows at once, like an animal, that I can't stand hair or hide of him. His instinct isn't natural, it's like a dog's, but a dog is kind and humble and just slinks off—while he, he knows it too, but he won't answer, he turns his back and walks off, out of the room. A child—and at his age! No good will come of him. If they don't put him away in a feebleminded home he'll be a curse to society. I really do think that would be best, preventive arrest, best for society.

'But what gets you most is not his wits, poor boy he can't help that, though it's a tragedy for Mariana, but his slyness, the way he sees through you—a born crook. Nothing good will come. He's too quick and not in a smart way.

'Well, in a letter this morning, Mariana says they'll bring him; they have to; there's nowhere they dare leave him. You'll see him and you'll know at once, because you're quick at human beings, you will see. I'm just dying for you to see this dirty little warped thing. Oh, I can't wait for it. I hate the little wretch, but I can't wait to hear what you'll say.

'What he does, I can't begin to tell—bites, scratches, pinches. They shut him up in the toilet, so that he'll do his business and they say, "Why don't you do like Rags?" Rags does her business every morning and so she does, a cleaner dog never was. He stays in there out of obstinacy and does nothing. Mariana tells everyone how he is, hoping to shame the little devil, but she can't shame the devil out of Stevie, no she can't shame the devil out of the little pinhead.

'When he does come out, he knows he's bad and he just slinks away, not listening to the scolding; and she is so ashamed of a boy like that. He goes out and sulks all day and it's his fault, not hers. She tells me she's in despair. If I didn't have Rags, she says, I don't know what I'd do, I'd run away. She often told me, "I'd give him away. I never wanted anyone like that." I said, "Oh, no, no, no one would take him." And I heard her tell him, "No one would take you, you little devil or I'd give you away."

(I thought to ask what Stevie looked like.)

'A stick—so thin and pale and dirty, you can't bear to look at him, undernourished, although they feed him enough. Mariana's always at him, nags him, in fact. No. He just slinks off in his usual way and then he steals food! Think of that! Oh, the end is, we'll see him in jail and not so far off and not too soon either. We wouldn't even care. It's so clear.'

One Saturday morning in the summer we heard that Mariana, Glenn and their son Stevie had arrived at the grandparents' home, just down the dirt road. I passed the day in anticipation. The country life is calm and there is time for pleasurable anticipation. But Stevie did not come that day. My friend, Jeanie, his great-aunt, telephoned Mariana, saying that I was hopping with excitement to see the awful little boy, I had heard so much about the little demon. And she brought me the message, 'She won't be so anxious to see him, when she sees him.'

The next day about eleven, I saw the grandfather, Rolf, a tall, wiry goodlooking man, in this best clothes, leading by the hand a small slender boy in a new white suit. My heart began to beat hard, for though they were far off, I knew it must be Stevie. I am interested in and sympathise with turbulent children; but I am afraid, too, that they will lash out at me with their sharp tongues; and I came down the orchard path slowly and quietly.

I was exceedingly surprised to see a handsome sallow boy with thick wavy dark hair and a dissipated tormented face, yet innocently curious in expression. He was tall for his age: he was a little more than five years old.

He looked straight into my eyes, offered his little sallow hand and said goodday in a sweet voice. All went well, though his strained face did not relax. His grandfather went round the corner of the house, leading him by the hand. Soon I heard Alfred, the artist, Jeanie's brother, like Jeanie, married with no children, laughing nervously in his studio. I looked in the studio window and saw Alfred hitting Stevie on the head with a roll of paper. I went in. Alfred laughing still, said,

'You see, Stevie really is a naughty boy. He snatched the paper out of my hand when I shook it at him.'

Later, I went down into the town with Mariana, a beautiful woman of the ephebe type, with her smallboned dark young husband and Alfred, such a happy, good-natured, kind man, small, plump with nut-cracker features. In front with the couple sat Rags, a splendid fawn Great Dane who constantly licked Mariana and laid her head on her knee. Mariana sat in the car while Glenn and Alfred did the shopping. She was lively, sharp, impatient, full of elegant twitches. She kept kissing Rags on the head, nose and shoulder. 'Oh I love you, love you,' she said in the tone of a manly declaration, 'I wish I had more like you.'

'You love her more than Stevie,' said I boldly; (I had known the family for years). She said at once,

'Yes, I only wish Stevie were a bit like Rags. I hate Stevie. I'd like him a bit if he could be like Rags.'

This was on the way home. No one started or stirred: Alfred laughed and said, a family standby, 'Why don't you give Stevie away?'

She said between her teeth,

'I would. I'd have a motherly instinct if I could; but I can't with Stevie. I'm sorry he was born. I have a motherly instinct with Rags, so that just shows. It's Stevie's fault, the little damn devil. He's taking a child's place and he's no child. That's what I hate about the little damn imp. Glenn can't take him either.'

The fascinated husband did not object. I said,

'Stevie seems bright.'

'He'd seem anything just to spite us; don't make any mistake about Stevie. He isn't bright, he's stupid, a foul little brat; but he seems bright just to get back at us. He's the greatest simulator you ever saw. I never met up with such a dirty little hypocrite. But I'll pay him out yet. He won't get any mother love out of me: that's how I pay him out, the little devil.' And half-laughing, she dragged the meek dog to her and kissed it passionately.

'I love you, Rags and no one who isn't as good and sweet as you.'

In the afternoon the grandfather took Stevie to the town. The grandfather was a jokester and always had names for people in the town, or the
family; he invented them and they stuck. He was considered very smart,
the smarter perhaps because he had come from far away, from 'Liverpool,
England'; and yet he made such a go of it, became rich. People in the
family, people in politics or business, he called Coonskin, Goon, Goop,
Aky-kaky. He was fond of Stevie and took him everywhere. So the boy
heard him naming, nicknaming, joking. This summer day coming back up
from the town, where his father had given him money to put in the
juke-box, Stevie saw a milkman, one of the old native families, coming
from the hill; and he said, 'Hello, Maky-kaky, Crappy Maky;' and the
grandfather laughed. Stevie turned and said, 'What are you laughing at,
you old pisspot?' Grandfather did not laugh.

(1973)

Kate Grenville
THE SPACE BETWEEN

The banana-shaped tourists lie in chairs by the swimming pool and stocky
Tamil waiters on bare feet bring them drinks. The daring ones have ice.
The manager himself has assured us that yes, the water for the ice is
boiled. Boiled and then frozen. Oh yes yes. Boiled, of course boiled.

For myself I avoid the ice. It's not exactly that I don't believe him. But I
prefer to smile and shake my head. No ice, thank you.

Outside the cool marble corridors of this palace-turned-hotel, beyond
the graceful arches framing the sky, the streets of Madras are hot. Out
there the sun is a solid weight on the top of the head, a heavy hand across
the back of the neck, but beside the blue water of the swimming pool the
sun has been domesticated by umbrellas and palm-leaf screens. Where the
guests sit turning brown or scarlet, Madras is as far away as a travel book.

Here by the pool, under a blue umbrella, Mr and Mrs Partridge involve
me in kindly conversation.

—Travelling alone are you? You don't find it a bit . . . ?

Mrs Partridge's crepey old face puckers as if encountering a bad smell.

—A bit, you know, unpleasant?

Mr Partridge tries to clarify his wife's query. He rubs a hand over his
bald head, red from the sun, and says:

—You don't find that these chaps. Ah. They don't let their own women
out on their own. Of course.

They're kindly folk who do their best to conjure up the girl in white
frills who must be underneath my baggy shirts. They even have a go at a
little matchmaking. Mrs Partridge leans in and murmurs while Mr Partridge stares off across the pool.

—Sandra dear, we were talking last night to the young man who's here
with the tour. A very nice type of young man.

Her husband brings his stare back from the middle distance and speaks
energetically.

—Nice group of people here. The McFarlands. The Burnetts. The Pruitt
chap. Good company helps, doesn't it? In this heat?

Mrs Partridge nods and shows me the pink plastic of her gums.

—That's him. Ted Pruitt.

I've seen Ted here by the pool carefully browning himself like a chop on both sides. I've seen the way the water pools around his body on the cement and the way the hairs on his legs stay flattened to the skin even after they've dried. I've enjoyed watching the hairs on his legs, and the shell-pink soles of his feet, that the sun makes translucent. In the small of his back is a dark mole, pleasingly symmetrical, the kind that can turn into a cancer. I have avoided looking at his face, filled with too many teeth, too much flesh, eyes of too knowing a blue.

On cue, Ted appears at the edge of the pool. His muscular arms glint with ginger hairs as he hauls himself out. The water streams down his head and makes it as flat as a dog's. He flicks his head sideways and glittering drops land on the concrete. As I watch they evaporate into the dense sunshine.

—Ted, we were just talking about you, says Mrs Partridge. Come and meet Sandra.

He stands over me, blocking out the sun. I squint up at him, at his face invisible against the glaring sky.

—Hi. What was it again, Sandra?

—Sandy, actually.

He stands above me, legs apart, water running down his body and spreading in pools around his feet.

—Sandy? Used to know a bloke once called Sandy.

He runs a hand over his shoulders, where skeins of muscle lie side by side under the skin.

—I mean, no offence of course.

He gestures and grins and watches me under cover of rubbing his head with his towel. I see him looking at my baggy pants and shirt, and my face half-hidden under the hat. When he stands up to dry himself, the muscles of his chest flex as he rubs his back, and twinkling water is caught in the hairs of his curved thighs. He bulges heavily, thickly, unabashed, into the taut weight of stretched red nylon between his legs.

Mrs Partridge looks away as he rubs the water off his legs. Mr Partridge breaks the silence.

—I was just saying to Sandra...Sandy?

—Sandy.

—Ah. Just saying what a good bunch of people we've got here. Lucky, really.

Ted shakes water out of his ear.

—Too right.

He sits down, leaning back on his hands. I see his chest gleam in the sun but have to look away from the red bulge offered towards me.

—You been going around on your own all this time?

—Yes. It's been a lot of fun.

My voice sounds prissy in my own ears.

—Yeah?

He doesn't quite close his mouth after the word, so I can see blood-pink inner lip.

—Why'd a good-looking chick like you want to get around on your own?

He stares at me, waiting for an answer, but although I wet my lips with my tongue, I can't find one.

—You must have a bit of, you know, from the fellas.

He glances again at the shapeless pants and I wonder if he's thinking, on the other hand maybe she doesn't.

—Anyhow, any time you want to come around with us, just say the word. We'll look after you. No worries.

He smiles. It's the wide blank smile of a man who's looking down his own strong legs, safe in muscles and red nylon.

When the waiter comes over to pick up our glasses, I recognize him by the moustache, such a thin line on his upper lip that it might have been drawn with a ballpoint. Each morning this waiter brings my breakfast, knocking inaudibly before coming in immediatley with his tray of pawpaw and the dazzling smile that makes his moustache go crooked. I put a hand over my half-finished drink and he bows. He wonders too, when he sees me each morning lying in splendour in the canopied bed, why I'm alone. His black eyes dart from Ted to me and he bows again before padding off. He shouts in Tamil across the pool to another waiter and their laughter echoes betwen the arches.

The Partridges excuse themselves. They walk off arm-in-arm, slowly, like an advertisement for retirement. Ted and I sit in silence, and watch the waiter remove a toothpick from behind his ear and clean his fingernails with it. When he has finished, Ted sighs and says:

—Well, where you going next?

His voice seems very loud.

—I thought I might go to Bombay.

—Yeah? Look, we're all going there too, for the silver. Why don't you come with us? No good being on your own. For a girl especially.

He's watching me and I'm conscious of the size of his very white front teeth. His hair is starting to dry, fluffing out around his temples like down. I squint into the glare of light off the pool and picture myself diving in, trying to drown. Ted would rescue me, using the approved hair, chin or clothing carry to pull me to the side of the pool before administering artificial respiration. It would take determination to drown beside Ted.

—Well, thanks. But I don't think so.

Ted has not heard properly, shaking a last drop of water from his ear.

—Eh? That's settled then? We'll have a ball.

I have to raise my voice to say again:

—No. No, I don't think so. No.

Ted is in the middle of winking at me, thinking of the ball we'll have, when he understands that I have refused. The wink goes wrong and all the features of his face fight each other for a second. When they have resolved themselves into a coherent expression, it is one of suspicion and dislike.

—Okay. Suit yourself.

He gets up, flings his towel over the chair with a flourish, and dives in. He is a powerful swimmer, reaching the end of the pool in a few strokes and showing those pink soles in a flurry of water as he turns. He would hardly be able to imagine drowning.

—You've lost your young man!

Mr Partridge beams down at me. He and his wife are no longer arm-in-arm, but Mrs Partridge tweaks a thread off her husband's shoulder as he speaks. Behind the kindly uncle, winking at me from under white eye-brows, a sharp voice can almost be heard. Some people just don't want to be helped.

—We were counting on you to look after him!

Mrs Partridge's eyes disappear into a web of kindly wrinkles as she smiles teasingly. Behind the smile, embedded in the lines that pucker her mouth, is doubt. They both watch me, but I have nothing to tell them, and my smile is exhausting me.

Not far from the hotel, there is a cluster of shacks that squat in the dust, lining a path of beaten earth. Hens scatter under my feet and skeletal dogs run along nosing the ground. Pieces of cardboard cover the walls of the huts. DETER UPER WASH. They *are* the walls, I see when I look more closely. Women sit in the shade, picking over vegetables, while beside them their other sari hangs drying in the sun—tattered, dust-coloured with age, but washed. Is there another one in the dark interior of the hut? Is there, somewhere, the wedding sari, best quality cotton or maybe even silk, with the lucky elephant-border or the brocade border that reads GOOD LUCK GOOD LUCK GOOD LUCK all the way around the hem? As I pass, the women look up and stare, their lips drawn back to reveal stained teeth. They are not smiling, but only staring, and they look away when I smile.

Out of doorways a few small children appear, staring shyly, their huge dark eyes full of astonishment as they look at me. They curl one foot behind the other in embarrassment when I look at them and twist their bodies away as if fleeing, but their eyes never leave my face.

As I pass the huts the children drift out after me and at each hut more emerge. I can hear their feet padding in the dust behind me. When I turn around to smile they all stop in mid-stride. They all stare, motionless except for a hand somewhere scratching a melon-belly, a foot rubbing the back of a leg, a finger busy up a nostril.

On the fringes of the silent group the girls stand, curious but listless, holding babies on their hips. They stare blankly, shifting the baby from one hip to the other, automatically brushing away a fly.

At last one of the boys lets out a nervous giggle and the tension breaks. Suddenly they're all shrieking, dancing around me, bravely reaching out to dab my arm and springing back, squealing and giggling.

They seem to know a bit of English. They yell:

—Good morning! Good afternoon! Good night!

When I speak to them they explode and cover their mouths with their hands to keep so much laughing hidden. They don't point, but they nudge each other and gesture around themselves, miming my clothes. One boy, bigger than the rest, wearing only a tattered pair of shorts that hangs precariously under his round belly, sweeps his hands around and stands before us in baggy trousers and big shirt. He stares up at me and says:

—You boy or girl?

His voice does not prejudice the question one way or the other.

—Girl. I'm a girl.

He stares, not believing. After a moment he grins enormously and laughs in a theatrical way to show how well he understands the joke. Then doubt clouds his face. He ducks his head as if overwhelmed by his question, but pulls at my sleeve:

—You boy or girl?

He stares up at me waiting for the answer. His round head, under its short fur of hair, seems too large for his frail neck. He cranes up at me for the answer.

—Boy. I'm a boy. Like you.

He considers that, but after a moment of looking at the front of my shirt he bends over with laughter again. Now he's embarrassed and won't look at me. He says something to the other kids and they all stare at me. They're waiting for a proper answer. It's very quiet in this back lane. The horns of the taxis on the main road seem puny and very far away. It seems the kids could wait forever for an answer.

I start to walk back to the main road, but the kids follow, straggling after me along with the dogs and a hen or two. When I walk faster, some break into a run to keep up, even the girls with the babies on their hips bouncing and crying. One by one they dart around in front of me and run backwards for a few yards to watch my face as they try again.

—You boy or girl? Boy or girl?

They're all doing it together so that the words have become a chant. Bah yo gel bah yo gel bah yo gel.

At the edge of the shack village they stop as if on a line drawn on the road. I walk on until finally I can wave good-bye before turning a corner that takes me out of sight. But they are still calling out even after I've disappeared. Bahyogel bahyogel. Their voices carry a long way down the quiet street.

(1980)

Jessica Anderson
from TIRRA LIRRA BY THE RIVER

It was a red-brick house in a big flat chequerboard suburb, predominately iron-grey and terracotta in colour, and treeless except for an occasional row of tristanias, clipped to roundness and stuck like toffee apples into the pavement. 'If I had to live here I would die,' I told Colin.

'Die?'

He had just come home from work and we were getting ready to go to Una Porteous's house for dinner. While we looked for a small flat he had found board for us both in the same street. 'Die?' he said, combing his hair in the mirror.

'Oh, of course I don't mean *die*. What I mean is, it's not like Sydney.'

'What *is* like Sydney?'

'The harbour.'

'You won't find a flat near the harbour, not one I can afford.'

But he was wrong. He had never looked. I found one in an old house with a waterfront garden, and begged Colin to take it. He was in love with me then, and besides, he could save on fares by walking over Woolloomooloo and the Domain to his department in the city.

The old house was one of four on Potts Point. I remember their names. Bomera. Tarana. Crecy. Agincourt. In Sydney recently my nephew offered to take me there, but I had already looked across to Potts Point through his binoculars, and had seen Bomera and Tarana joined to Garden Island by an ugly, car-infested concrete isthmus. Garden Island was a real island then, with a few little battleships mooning about like the navy of Ruritania. The four houses stood opposite. One, Bomera, was of stone, built by convicts, and the other three were early Victorian. Ours was Crecy. I could not find it through my nephew's binoculars. Our flat was only one big room with a kitchen and bath, but the big room was very big indeed, with a high ceiling, a north aspect, and three pairs of long double windows through which one saw people, flowers, cats, water, sky, seagulls, ships. It was furnished with some old unimportant pleasant things, and it has remained for me a pattern of what a room should be.

When one falls in love with a city, it is always with only a part of it. 'My' Sydney, of which the houses on the point were the heart, was bound on the north by the harbour, on the south by Bayswater Road, on the west by the city (some of which it included), and on the east by Beach Road at Rushcutters Bay. In this Sydney I became conscious for the first time of the points of the compass, and felt for the first time the airs of three other climates, borne on to my skin by the three prevailing winds. In this limited territory I was very happy in spite of my sexual difficulties.

I do not propose to add to the documents on coition, but it does seem necessary to say that for a long time I got no more enjoyment from it than I had from the mangling and pulling about by the boys under the camphor laurels, of whose activities it seemed a simple but distressing extension. Perhaps I had waited too long. 'Do this,' Colin Porteous would say. 'Do that.' And I would do this and that, and not know whether to laugh or cry in my misery.

He was always very amiable about it. 'Well, you're frigid, and that's that. Women with your colouring are often frigid.' And he would go on to tell me about 'passionate Spanish women' and 'experienced French women' in a way that I knew perfectly well was puerile, though I would not let myself admit it lest it undermine my determination to be in love with him. The first substitute I made for him was a man I could love, and in this I was greatly supported by the happiness of my life while he was at work.

I suppose many women of my generation can recall a similar delicious period, when one's idleness and play are without guilt because 'it is only until the children come'. Bomera had a shifting population of which the two stable elements were a dressmaker, Ida Mayo, and a gentle bearded watercolourist in a grey dustcoat, whose name I have forgotten. At any given time, the rest would be mostly artists and actors, but one might also find a restaurant cook, a remittance man, a clerk or an engineer. The old carriage drive led from the gatehouse to a portico under a magnolia tree. This portico was square, with a broad balustrade suitable for sitting on, and opened on to a wide hall with a floor of white marble. Across the hall two statues faced each other. One, Wisdom, held a book in her hand, and the other, Folly, held, I think, a bunch of grapes. The double front doors stood open day and night, and at whatever time I went there, I always found someone about and was sure of a welcome. I would talk to them, pose for them, drink their coffee, listen to their music, and borrow their books. I began by trying to match their sophistication (as it seemed to me then), but they soon detected my ignorance, and took pleasure in startling and shocking me. I took the cue, and to please them, pretended to be even more ignorant than I was, covering my face and giving a dramatic cry, or putting my hands over my ears and begging them to stop. Amused by this game, they began to treat me with a sort of teasing condescension, as if I were a toy, almost a mascot. Only Ida Mayo the dressmaker refused to be amused.

'The fact is, Nora knows more about colour than any of you lot, with your daubs.'

Ida was a specialist, her card said, in evening wear. I was impressed by her skill, and enjoyed helping her. Colin held the opinion, common in those days, that a man was disgraced if his wife worked for money, and with Ida I had occupation without disgrace. Her two rooms were dimmed by a broad verandah, and I loved to go in and see the little lamps shining so privately on opulent materials while all was so sunny and windy and fresh outside. She used to let me break open the wrappings of her overseas fashion magazines, which I think excited me first by their smell, that celebrated smell of the glossy mag, the scent of twentieth-century folly.

'Have any more come, Ida?' I would always ask.

She would not let me take them away, and as I knelt on the floor of her workroom and turned the pages, I was under enchantment again. What did they make me long for? Not the clothes, exactly. Nor the life shown, exactly.

'*I* don't know,' said Ida, when I asked her.

But Lewie Johns, kneeling on the floor by my side, moved one hand to and fro and said, 'Just to somehow approximate the style, that's all. I bet it's a chimera, though, all that style. In real life, when you got close to it, it would just melt away.'

Lewie was one of the artists. 'The worst of the lot,' he said, 'and *that's* saying something.' Honesty had made him give up all notions of painting and content himself with picking up a bit of commerical art here and there.

'And I'm not much chop at that, either.'

In times of idleness he would often come to Ida's rooms. 'Oh, I like *this*.' And he would walk about, draping himself in satin or lamé and striking poses that even now, in memory, surprise me by their wit. Sometimes the three of us would sit together and sew on a rush job, and at these times Lewie usually complained about his love affairs. Colin, my only mentor in these matters, had depicted homosexuality as something vile and horrendous, but by the time I thoroughly understood that the men Lewie complained about were not friends but lovers, it was too late to be horrified, because he had become the best friend I had had since my school days. With him I never played the game of exaggerating my shock. He had given me an early warning by breaking off his narrative, pointing a needle at me, and saying bitterly, 'Look at her face.' I soon became very artful at disguising my shock, although I must say here that as he became equally artful at detecting it, many sulks and squabbles were the result. But in spite of this we were (as Fred remarked long afterwards about the group at number six) 'hopelessly simpatico', and a dozen times a day I would think, 'I must show Lewie this,' or 'I must tell Lewie that.' I had not acted on such fervent impulses of friendship since the time when Olive Partridge and I used to run across the paddocks to each other's houses with books we had just finished reading.

(1978)

Frank Moorhouse
FROM A BUSH LOG BOOK: GOING INTO THE HEARTLANDS WITH THE WRONG PERSON AT CHRISTMAS

That Christmas he went into the Sassafras bush with Belle, his decadent friend.

They had debauched in motel rooms and restaurants along the coast while he turned forty, spilling champagne on the bed sheets, games at midnight with live lobsters, and sadistic conversational games over restaurant meals because they had exhausted amiable conversation and because she was so young and did not have true empathy with his 'becoming forty'. He wanted now to be in the bush away from the clatter of breakfast trays, away from the somnolence of lying on beaches, and away from cars and roads and towns.

He also had some home-yearnings which came on at Christmas. His family was not in town for this Christmas but anyhow his home-yearnings had been displaced over the years away from his family in the town to the bush about 100 kilometres away from, but behind, the coastal town where he had grown up—the Sassafras bush in the Budawang range.

It was where the Clyde river started as a trickle and then quickly cut a steep, deep gorge and flowed down along the coast in wild country hidden from the highway until it appeared fully grown and slow, flowing into the sea at Bateman's Bay.

On Christmas day Belle and he left the motel at Bateman's Bay at the mouth of the Clyde and went up to the other end of the river. He had put the camping gear into the car when he left the city, half intending to go into the bush somewhere. They drove as deep into the bush as the road permitted and then left the car and backpacked their way, meeting up with the trail originally marked in 1939.

As they walked in the bush he kept glancing at Belle to see if she was being affected by the dull day and the bush. He knew about the creeping hysteria and dread which the Australian bush could bring about.

She saw him looking back at her and said, 'I'm coping. Stop looking back at me all the time.'

They walked into the bush for an hour or so and came to what is called Mitchell Lookout.

'This is called Mitchell Lookout,' he said, 'but as you see it is not a Lookout in the Rotary sense.'

It was just a shelf of rock.

'The growth is too thick,' he said to Belle, 'you can't see down to the river in the gorge.'

'I can see that the growth is too thick.'

'Laughably the only thing you can see clearly from Mitchell Lookout is directly across the gorge—they could have another lookout there which looked across at Mitchell Lookout.'

She looked across at the other side of the gorge and back again. She made a small movement of her mouth to show that she didn't think it was all that laughable.

'I don't go into the bush for views,' he said.

'You tell me, Frank—what do you go into the bush for?'

'I go into the bush to be swallowed whole. I don't go in to look at curious natural formations—I don't marvel at god's handiwork.'

'I don't mind looking at god's handiwork if it is theatrical enough.'

For reasons he could not explain and did not record in his log, he decided to put the tent there on the rock ledge overlooking the gorge.

'You'll find sleeping on rock okay,' he said. 'It is really much better than you imagine.'

'If you say so,' she said, dumping her backpack.

'I go for the unanalysed sensory experience,' he said. 'I don't go in for naming things geologically or birds and so on.'

'You don't have to apologise for not knowing the names of the birds and stones.'

He cut some bracken fern to lie on, more as a gesture towards the idea of what made for comfort.

He put up the tent, pinning each corner from the inside with rocks and tying the guy ropes to rocks.

'It's really okay,' he said. 'I have at times used a rock for a pillow.'

'I believe you,' she said, sitting, one leg crossed over the other, cleaning dirt from her painted finger nails with a nail file.

He instantly doubted whether he had ever used a rock for a pillow and whether sleeping on rock was okay.

'There,' he said, 'the tent is up.'

She looked across at it, got up and looked inside the tent but did not go in.

'How about a drink?' she said.

'Sure—it's the happy hour.'

She laughed at this to herself.

'I'll cook the Christmas dinner. That'll be my contribution,' she said.

'No', he said, 'that's okay—I'm used to cooking on campfires.'

'Look Frank, you're not the only one who can cook on campfires. I can cope, I grew up in Australia too, for godsake.'

As they had their bloody marys pre-mixed by the Company of Two, Fresno, California, he doubted whether she could cook on campfires.

'I came through the Australian experience,' she said, making a gesture at the bush.

Belle was a sexual friend. They saw each other now and then out of good simple lust—which was never quite enough to support their doing anything much else together. Nothing very extended. They had already over-extended this jaunt. He had never seen her cook a meal. It was always restaurants and Hilton hotels.

'I've been out in the bush quite a bit,' he said. 'It was my idea to come out here—so let me do it.'

'I'll cook the Christmas dinner,' she said. 'Don't you worry yourself about it.'

'Well okay—if you feel happy about it.'

'I feel quite happy about it, Hemingway.'

She made a low slow fire just right and rested the pannikins and camp cooking dishes on the coals. It wasn't quite the way he would have done it. He would have had stones in the fire on which to sit the pots. She sat them on the wood coals. But he didn't say anything—it was her fire.

Wood coals looked stable until things tilted and spilled as the wood burned away. Unless you kept pushing the pots down into the coals to stabilize them.

She squatted there at the fire. She put on the rabbit pieces—which they had not themselves hunted—after smearing them with mustard and muttering to herself *lapin moutarde* and laughing to herself. She wrapped them in tin foil and then wormed them down into the coals with a flat stick. Then she crossed herself. She put the corn cobs on to boil, candied the carrots with sugar sachets from the motel, put on the beans, wrapped the potatoes in foil and placed them in the coals. She then heated some lobster bisque, throwing in a dash of bloody mary.

She put the plum pudding on to be warmed and mixed a careful custard.

She did all this with the dishes right down on the coals of a slow fire, squatted there on her haunches.

She squatted there at the smoking fire stirring and moving pots as needed, throwing on a piece of wood at the right time, all with what, he thought, was a primitive control. He swigged bourbon from a World War I officer's flask and passed it to her from time to time. She squatted there in a silent trance, full of attention for what she was doing.

He swigged the bourbon and, on and off, became a World War I officer. She had slipped into postures which belonged to the primitive way of doing things back—what?—a thousand years to when the race cooked over campfires.

He sat off on a rock and took some back bearings using his Swiss Silva compass and Department of Mapping 1:25,000 topographic maps, trying to identify some of the distant peaks. He was in a different technology to her.

'We are at Mitchell Lookout,' he said, after some calculation, 'definitely.' He was not really that positive.

'Good,' she said.

He kept glancing at her, marvelling at her sure control of the fire and at the postures she had assumed from another time.

He opened a bottle of 1968 Coonawarra Cabernet Shiraz and it was in superb condition.

'It's ready,' she said, muttering something that he could not catch.

She presented the meal with perfect timing, everything right, at the right time, no overcooking, no cold food, no ash or sand in the food. It was served on the disposable plates they'd bought for the meal.

As they ate the Christmas dinner and drank the wine in the Guzzini goblets he'd bought for camping, a white mist filled up the gorge and stopped short of where they were so that they were atop of it, as if looking out the window of an aircraft above the clouds.

It came almost level with the slab where they were camped and where they were eating.

'Jesus, that's nice,' he said, staring down at the mist.

'I thought you didn't go in for god's handiwork.'

'Well I don't go searching for it. When he does it before my very eyes, I'm interested.'

She looked down at the mist while chewing the meat off a rabbit bone, as if assessing the mist aesthetically—eating mainly with her fingers, with their painted nails.

'It's all right,' she said.

It was warm and there were bush flies which worried her and she kept brushing them away with her hand.

'Piss off you bastards,' she said.

'I've made peace with the flies,' he said. 'Sooner or later in the Australian bush you have to stop shooing the flies and let them be.'

'I'm not going to make peace with the flies,' she said.

'Please yourself,' he said.

'I will.'

'You did the meal perfectly.'

'You aren't the only person in Australia who can cook a meal on a campfire.' She laughed to herself again, 'Actually it was the first time I had cooked a meal on a campfire.'

'It was perfect.'

'Thank you.'

'You looked very primitive—you went back to primitive postures.'

'I felt very primitive,' she said, 'if the truth be known.'

'I meant it in the best sense.'

'I assumed you did.'

They sat there with food-stained hands, smoky hair, food and wine on their breath and lips. She hoisted her skirt to expose her legs to the misty sun.

She stared expressionless at him, her hand methodically waving away the flies and she began to remove her clothing. They had sex there on the rock slab surrounded by the mist. They knew each other sexually and played with the idea of her naked body on the rock slab, the bruising of it and the abrasion. He held her head by the hair and pinned her arms, allowing the flies to crawl over her face. She struggled but could not make enough movement to get them off her face. She came and he came.

They drank and became drowsy around the fire.

During the night he got up because he liked to leave the tent in the dead of the night and prowl about naked. He said to himself that although he did not always feel easy in the bush, in fact he sometimes felt discordant in it, he'd rather be out in it feeling discordant than not be there.

'What are you doing out there for godsake?' Belle called from the tent.

'Having a piss.'

He crawled back into the tent.

'I thought for a moment you were communing,' she said.

In the morning he said, 'Well, it wasn't unsleepable on the rock?'

'No, not unsleepable,' she said, 'Nor unfuckable either.'

It was still misty and the air heavy with mositure but it was not cold.

Neither of them wanted to stay longer in the bush. He thought that he might have stayed on if he'd been alone.

Gritty with the night and damp, and having nothing much to say to each other, they had coffee and packed up.

'I liked having it off on the rock,' she said, 'I seem to be bruised.'

'But were you bruised enough?' he asked.

'Hah hah.'

It was a grey sky. The bush was close to Marcus Clarke's weird melancholy. The dampness quietened everything down just a little more than usual and the dull sky dulled everything just a little more.

'Just because I enjoy all that sort of stuff doesn't mean that I don't understand what's going on,' Belle said as they walked.

'On the rock?'

'Yes. I know all about punishment and esteem. But with me it's a game now.'

He shrugged indicating that he wasn't making any judgements about it.

'It's no longer the whole damned basis of my personality,' she said.

'You have to be a bit like that to go into the bush the way I do.'

'I was thinking that.'

They walked a few metres apart. They passed a stand of kangaroos some way off which speculatively watched them walk by. Belle and he indicated to each other by a glance that they had seen the kangaroos.

'More of god's handiwork,' she called.

He realised as they walked out that he had a disquiet about being there with Belle. When he looked at the Christmas they'd just had together—on paper—it was an untroubled and memorable and enriched event—the mist in the gorge, the perfect campfire-cooked meal, the good wine, Belle naked on the rock, his standing on the ledge in the middle of the night, the melancholy bush, the speculative kangaroos.

The disquiet came from having shared all this memorable experience, in a very personal district, with Belle. Belle didn't belong there. Belle and he didn't have the sort of relationship where you shared such potent emotional things. This Sassafras bush was a place of his childhood fantasies, it was overlaid with family, it was the place where he'd been tested as a child, it was the place where he'd learned his masculinity. He had taken Belle to the very centre of his emotional life and his male self.

Now she had become a photograph snapshot which did not belong in the album.

He looked at her up the trail plodding through the swampy part in her Keds, dripping wet.

Nor did he think that he was the sort of person she would have ideally chosen to share Christmas with. They were making do with each other.

By bringing Belle into his heartland and giving it to her as a gift he had left an ineradicable and inappropriate memory trace across the country-side. It was a category mistake.

These sad thoughts did not alter his fondness for her and he caught up with her and touched her fondly.

'Sorry about the mud,' he said.

'Don't think that I can't take it,' she said. 'I can take it all.'

'I'll get you a new pair of Keds.'

'They come from the States.'

'I'll get a pair sent across.'

'You probably won't.

He thought that, curiously, her tenacity in the bush was not so much to win his approval as to demonstrate her Australian spirit.

He found that curious.

In a motel on the coast they showered off the mud, dried off the dampness, turned up the air conditioner to warm, and got slowly drunk on the floor.

He spread out a map of southern New South Wales.

This is my territory, he showed her, from up here at Camden near the city, down the southern tableland through Bowral, down to the lakes and the snow of Jindabyne, to the old whaling town of Eden, up the coast along the beaches, through Bateman's Bay to Kiama where I took my girlfriend from school for an irritable, make-believe honeymoon after we had married in the hometown Church of England.

'How sweet,' Belle said.

'That's my territory,' he said, 'my heartlands.'

She looked at the map. He marked it out possessively with a felt pen.

'There—that is the boundary of my heartlands,' he said, more to himself.

He realised as he stared at the map with that alcoholic concentration which was both focused and then discursive, that it coincided with the territory his father had controlled as a farm machinery dealer and which he'd travelled with his father, and which his father had commanded as commander of coastal defence.

'It was my father's territory exactly,' he realised with wonder.

He told her how he had been a student at schools there, had been a rebellious but proficient scout, had played hard football up and down the coast, had been a soldier on manoeuvres there, had swum the rivers, surfed the whole coast, camped out in all the bush and hunted there.

'You're a very sentimental person,' she said.

'No, I don't think I am.'

'I think you are.'

'I think not.'

'Well, a sentimental drunk then.'

As he stared at the territory he'd marked out on the map he felt as if there were someone leaning over his shoulder looking at the map, like a high-spirited late arrival at a fading party. It was mortality.

'Let's go,' he said, 'let's check out now and go back to the city. I think it's over. I'm forty now. That's over. Christmas is over. Let's drive back to the city.'

'Sure,' she said, 'that's okay with me.'

Two weeks later he went to the Sassafras bush along the trail and camped in the same place—alone. It was a trip to erase the mistake of having gone there with Belle.

After a couple of days of being in the bush he realised that it was a misguided effort. He was making too much of having gone there with 'the wrong person' and coming back to erase it had only more deeply inscribed it—and the inscription had been added to.

Now whenever he passed the place he would think of having gone there with the wrong person and of having attempted to erase it. He would laugh about Belle squatting there cooking, about the flies on her face, and her saying, 'I feel quite happy about it, Hemingway.'

(1981)

Helen Garner
CIVILIZATION AND ITS DISCONTENTS

Philip came. I went to his hotel: I couldn't get there fast enough. He stepped up to me when I came through the door, and took hold of me.

'Hullo,' he said, 'my dear.'

People here don't talk like that. My hair was still damp.

'Did you drive?' he said.

'No. I came on the bus.'

'The *bus*?'

'There's never anywhere to park in the city.'

'You've had your hair cut. You look like a boy.'

'I know. I do it on purpose. I dress like a boy and I have my hair cut like a boy. I want to *be* a boy. So I can have a homosexual affair with *you*.'

He laughed. 'Good girl!' he said. At these words I was so flooded with well-being that I could hardly get my breath. 'If you were a boy some of the time and a girl the rest,' he said, 'I'd be luckier. Because I could have both.'

'No,' I said. 'I'd be luckier. Because I could *be* both.'

I scrambled out of my clothes.

'You're so thin,' he said.

'I don't eat. I'm sick.'

'Sick? Are you?' He put his two hands on my shoulders and looked into my eyes like a doctor.

'Sick with love.'

'Your eyes are healthy. Lustrous. Are mine?'

His room was on the top floor. Opposite, past some roofs and a deep street, was the old-fashioned tower of the building in which a dentist I used to go to had his rooms. That dentist was so gentle with the drill that I never needed an injection. I used to breathe slowly, as I had been taught at yoga: the pain was brief. I didn't flinch. But he made his pile and moved to Queensland.

The building had a flagpole. Philip and I stood at the window with no clothes on and looked out. The tinted glass made the cloud masses more detailed, richer, more spectacular than they were.

'Look at those,' I said. 'Real boilers. Coming in from somewhere.'

'Just passing through,' said Philip. He was looking at the building with the tower. 'I love the Australian flag,' he said. 'Every time I see it I get a shiver.'

.'I'm like that about the map.' Once I worked in a convent school in East London. I used to go the library at lunchtime, when the nuns were locked away in their dining room being read to, and take down the atlas and gaze at the page with Australia on it: I loved its upper points, its vast inlets, its fat sides, the might of it, the mass from whose south-eastern corner my small life had sprung. I used to crouch between the stacks and rest the heavy book on the edge of the shelf: I could hardly support its weight. I looked at the map and my eyes filled with tears.

'Did I tell you she's talking about coming back to me?' said Philip.

'Do you want her to?'

'Of course I do.'

I sat down on the bed.

'We'll have to start behaving like adults,' he said. 'Any idea how it's done?'

'Well,' I said, 'it must be a matter of transformation. We have to turn what's happening now into something else.'

'You sound experienced.'

'I am.'

'What can we turn it into?'

'Brother and sister? A lifelong friendship?'

'Oh,' he said, 'I don't know anything about that. Can't people just go on having a secret affair?'

'I don't like lying.'

'You don't have to. I'm the liar.'

'What makes you so sure she won't find out? People always know. She'll take one look at you and know. That's what wives are for.'

'We'll see.'

'How can you stand it?' I said. 'It's dishonourable. How can you lie to someone and still love her?'

'Forced to. Forced by love to be a hypocrite.'

I thought for a second he was joking.

'We could drop it now,' I said.

'What are you *saying*?'

'I don't mean it.'

Not yet. The sheets in those hotels are silky, but crisp. How do they get them like that? A lot of starch, and ironing, things no housewife in her right mind could be bothered doing. The bed was wide enough for another two people to have lain in it, and still none of us would have had to touch sides. I don't usually go to bed in the daylight. And as if the daylight were not enough, the room was full of lamps. I started to switch them off, one after another, and thinking of the phrase 'full of lamps' I remembered something my husband said to me, long after we split up, about a Shakespearean medley he had seen performed by doddering remnants of a famous British company that was touring Australia. 'The stage,' he said, 'was covered in *thrones*,' and his knees bent with laughter. He was the only man I have ever known who would rejoice with you over the petty triumphs of the day. I got under the sheet. I couldn't help laughing to myself, but it was too complicated to explain why.

Philip had a way of holding me, when we lay down: he made small rocking movements, so small that I sometimes wondered if I were imagining them, if the comfort of being held were translating itself into an imaginary cradling.

'I've never told anyone I loved them, before,' said Philip.

'Don't be silly,' I said.

'You don't know anything about me.'

'At your age?' I said. 'A married man? You've never loved anyone before?'

'I've never *said* it before.'

'No wonder she went away,' I said. 'Men are really done over, aren't they. At an early age.'

'Why do you want to fuck like a boy, then?'

'Just for play.'

'Is it allowed?' he said.

'Who by?' I said. I was trying to be smart; but seriously, who says we can't? Isn't that why women and men make love? To bend the bars a little, just for a little; to let the bars dissolve? Philip pinched me. He took hold of the points of my breasts, between forefingers and thumbs. I could see his teeth. He pinched hard. It hurt. I liked it. And he bit me. He *bit* me. When I got home I looked in the mirror and my shoulders and arms were covered in small round bruises.

I went to his house, in the town where he lived. I told him I would be passing through on my way south, and he invited me, and I went, though I had plenty of friends I could have stayed with in that city.

There was a scandal in the papers as I passed through the airport that evening, about a woman who had made a contract to have a baby for a childless couple. The baby was born, she changed her mind, she would not give it up. Everyone was talking about her story.

I felt terrible at his house, for all I loved him, with his wife's forgotten dressing gown hanging behind the door like a witness. I couldn't fall asleep properly. I 'lay broad waking' all night long, and the house was pierced by noises, as if its walls were too flimsy to protect it from the street: a woman's shoes striking the pavement, a gate clicking, a key sliding into a lock, stairs breathing in and out. It never gets truly dark in cities. Once I rolled over and looked at him. His face was sleeping, serene, smiling on the pillow next to mine like a cherub on a cloud.

He woke with a bright face. 'I feel unblemished,' he said, 'when I've been with you.' This is why I loved him, of course: because he talked like that, using words and phrases that most people wouldn't think of saying. 'When I'm with you,' he'd say, 'I feel happy and free.'

He made the breakfast and we read the papers in the garden.

'She should've stuck to her word,' he said.

'Poor thing,' I said. 'How can anyone give a baby away?'

'But she promised. What about the couple? They must be dying to have a kid.'

'Are you?'

'Yes,' he said, and looked at me with the defiant expression of someone expecting to be crossed. 'Yes. I am.'

The coffee was very strong. It was bad for me in the mornings. It made my heart beat too fast.

'I think in an ideal world everone would have children,' I said. 'That's how people learn to love. Kids suck love out of your bones.'

'I suppose you think that only mothers know how to love.'

'No. I don't think that.'

'Still,' he said. 'She signed a contract. She *signed*. She made a promise.'

'Philip,' I said, 'have you ever smelled a baby's head?'

The phone started to ring inside the house, in the room I didn't go into because of the big painting of her that was hanging over the stereo. Thinking that he loved me, though I understood and believed I had accepted the futurelessness of it, I amused myself by secretly calling it The Room In Which the First Wife Raved, or Bluebeard's Bloody Chamber: it repelled me with an invisible force, though I stood at times outside its open door and saw its pleasantness, its calm, its white walls and wooden floor on which lay a bent pattern of sunlight like a child's drawing of a window.

He ran inside to answer the phone. He was away for quite a while. I thought about practising: how it is possible to learn with one person how to love, and then to apply the lesson learnt to somebody else: someone teaches you to sing, and then you wait for a part in the right opera. It was warm in the garden. I dozed in my chair. I had a small dream, one of those shockingly vivid dreams that occur when one sleeps at an unaccustomed time of day, or when one ought to be doing something other than sleeping. I dreamed that I was squatting naked with my vagina close to the ground, in the posture we are told primitive women adopt for childbearing ('They just squat down in the fields, drop the baby, and go on working.'). But someone was operating on me, using sharp medical instruments on my cunt. Bloody flesh was issuing from it in clumps and clots. I could watch it, and see it, as if it were somebody else's cunt, while at the same time experiencing it being done to me. It was not painful. It didn't hurt at all.

I woke up as he came down the steps smiling. He crouched down in front of me, between my knees, and spoke right into my face.

'You want me to behave like a married man, and have kids, don't you?'

'*Want* you to?'

'I mean you think I should. You think everyone should, you said.'

'Sure—if that's what you want. Why?'

'Well, on the phone just now I went a bit further towards it.'

'You mean you *lined* it *up*?'

'Not exactly—but that's the direction I'm going in.'

I looked down at him. His forearms were resting across my knees and he was crouching lightly on the balls of his feet. He was smiling at me, smiling right into my eyes. He was waiting for me to say, *Good boy*!

'Say something reassuring,' he said. 'Say something close, before I go.'

I took a breath, but already he was not listening. He was ready to work. Philip loved his work. He took on more than he could comfortably handle. Every evening he came home with his pockets sprouting contracts. He never wasted anything: I'd hear him whistling in the car, a tiny phrase, a little run of notes climbing and falling as we drove across the bridges, and then next morning from the room with the synthesiser in it would issue the same phrase but bigger, fuller, linked with other ideas, becoming a song: and a couple of months after that I'd hear it through the open doors of every cafe, record shop and idling car in town. 'Know what I used to dream?' he said to me once. 'I used to dream that when I pulled up at the lights I'd look into the cars on either side of me and in front and behind, and everyone would be singing along with the radio, and they'd all be singing the same song. Even if the windows were wound up we'd read each other's lips, and everyone would laugh, and wave.'

I made my own long distance call. 'I'll be home tonight, Matty,' I said.

His voice was full of sleep. 'They rang up from the shop,' he said. 'I told them you were sick. Have you seen that man yet?'

'Yes. I'm on my way. Get rid of the pizza boxes.'

'I need money, Mum.'

'When I get there.'

Philip took me to the airport. I was afraid someone would see us, someone he knew. For me it didn't matter. Nothing was secret, I had no-one to hide anything from, and I would have been proud to be seen with him. But for him I was worried. I worried enough for both of us. I kept my head down. He laughed. He would not let me go. He tried to make me lift my chin; he gave it soft butts with his forehead. My cheeks were red.

'I'm always getting on planes with tears in my eyes,' I said.

'They'll be getting to know you,' he said. 'Are you too shy to kiss me properly?'

I bolted past the check-in desk. I looked back and he was watching me, still laughing, standing by himself on the shining floor.

On the plane I was careful with myself. I concentrated on the ingenuity of the food tray, its ability to remain undisturbed by the alterations in position of the seatback to which it was attached. I called for a scotch and drank it. My mistake was to look inside a book of poems, the only reading matter I had on me. They were poems so charged with sex and death and longing that it was indecent to read them in public: I was afraid that their power might leak out and scandalise the onlookers. Even as I slammed the book shut I saw '*I want to know, once more,/how it feels/to be peeled and eaten whole, time after time.*' I kept the book turned away from two men who were sitting between me and the window. They were drinking German beer and talking in a European language of which I did not recognise a single word. One of them turned his head and caught my eye. I expected him to look away hastily, for I felt myself to be ugly and stiff with sadness; but his face opened into a dazzling smile.

My son was waiting for the plane. He had come out on the airport bus. He saw how pleased I was, and looked down with an embarrassed smile, but he permitted me to hug him, and patted my shoulder with little rapid pats.

'Your face is different,' he said. 'All sort of emotional.'

'Why do you always pat me when you hug me?' I said.

'Pro'ly cause you're nearly always in a state,' he said.

He asked me to wait while he had a quick go on the machines. His fingers swarmed on the buttons. *Death By Acne* was the title of a thriller he had invented to make me laugh: but his face in concentration lost its awkwardness and became beautiful. I leaned on the wall of the terminal and watched the people passing.

A tall young man came by. He was carrying a tiny baby in a sling against his chest. The mother walked behind, smooth-faced and long-haired, holding by the hand a fat-nappied toddler. But the man was the one in love with the baby. He walked slowly, with his arms curved round its small bulk. His head was bowed so he could gaze into its face. His whole being was adoring it.

I watched the young family go by in its peaceful procession, each one moving quietly and contentedly in place, and I heard the high-pitched death wails of the space creatures my son was murdering with his fast and delicate tapping of buttons, and suddenly I remembered walking across the street the day after I brought him home from hospital. The birth was long and I lost my rhythm and made too much noise and they drugged me, and when it was over I felt that now I knew what the prayerbook meant when it said *the pains of death gat hold upon me*. But crossing the road that day, still sore from knives and needles, I saw a pregnant woman lumbering towards me, a woman in the final stages of waiting, putting one heavy foot in front of the other. Her face as she passed me was as calm and as full as an animal's: 'a face that had not yet received the fist'. And I envied her. I was stabbed, pierced with envy, with longing for what was about to happen to her, for what she was ignorantly about to enter. I could have cried out, Oh, let me do it again! Give me another chance! Let me meet the mighty forces again and struggle with them! Let me be rocked again, let me lie helpless in that huge cradle of pain!

  'Another twenty cents down the drain,' said my son. We set out together towards the automatic doors. He was carrying my bag. I wanted to say to him, to someone, 'Listen. Listen. I am *hopelessly in love*.' But I hung on. I knew I had brought it on myself, and I hung on until the spasm passed. And then I began to recreate from memory the contents of the fridge.

(1985)

James McAuley
BECAUSE

My father and my mother never quarrelled.
They were united in a kind of love
As daily as the *Sydney Morning Herald*,
Rather than like the eagle or the dove.

I never saw them casually touch,   5
Or show a moment's joy in one another.
Why should this matter to me now so much?
I think it bore more hardly on my mother,

Who had more generous feeling to express.
My father had dammed up his Irish blood   10
Against all drinking praying fecklessness,
And stiffened into stone and creaking wood.

His lips would make a switching sound, as though
Spontaneous impulse must be kept at bay.
That it was mainly weakness I see now,   15
But then my feelings curled back in dismay.

Small things can pit the memory like a cyst:
Having seen other fathers greet their sons,
I put my childish face up to be kissed
After an absence. The rebuff still stuns   20

My blood. The poor man's curt embarrassment
At such a delicate proffer of affection
Cut like a saw. But home the lesson went:
My tenderness thenceforth escaped detection.

My mother sang *Because*, and *Annie Laurie*,   25
White Wings, and other songs; her voice was sweet.
I never gave enough, and I am sorry;
But we were all closed in the same defeat.

People do what they can; they were good people,
They cared for us and loved us. Once they stood   *30*
Tall in my childhood as the school, the steeple.
How can I judge without ingratitude?

Judgment is simply trying to reject
A part of what we are because it hurts.
The living cannot call the dead collect: *35*
They won't accept the charge, and it reverts.

It's my own judgment day that I draw near,
Descending in the past, without a clue,
Down to that central deadness: the despair
Older than any hope I ever knew.   *40*

(1968)

Judith Wright
WOMAN TO MAN

The eyeless labourer in the night,
the selfless, shapeless seed I hold,
builds for its resurrection day—
silent and swift and deep from sight
foresees the unimagined light.   5

This is no child with a child's face;
this has no name to name it by:
yet you and I have known it well.
This is our hunter and our chase,
the third who lay in our embrace.   10

This is the strength that your arm knows,
the arc of flesh that is my breast,
the precise crystals of our eyes.
This is the blood's wild tree that grows
the intricate and folded rose.   15

This is maker and the made;
this is the question and reply;
the blind head butting at the dark,
the blaze of light along the blade.
Oh hold me, for I am afraid.   20

(1946)

Vincent Buckley
from LATE WINTER CHILD

XXV
1

Standing, naked, feet apart,
you are an athlete in triumph
and in the bed's proposed light
the grain of your skin tells me
what it was like in the old days   5
when all night we'd lie,
limbs twined in each other's smell,
loved, and betraying no-one.

2

Then, gradually, the years of part love
when you learned, as you grew desolate,   10
how the language runs out like milk
to waste and dry along your body.
The soul wears out. And the eyes.
Another skin drifts in the mirror.
Alarmed, you call out your name   15
hesitantly to the blurred bones.

3

Worst of all, because we expected them
so humbly, the years of nothingness
when, separate, more and more slowly,
we both fought against age   20
with childless poems, dance classes,
images of cities built on journeys,
counting as triumphs every chance
of laughter, each fresh nuance of dress.

4

We kept one power, the shared pulse   25
across gaps and continents, version
of the dolphin's whistle. If we lost that
our skins would dry out like bark,
and if I rang you, it would be
a no-face pressed to the phone,   30
struggling to believe one cadence
of your voice floating with static.

5

It was so tempting to construct
an angry, taut 'I', spinning out
lifetimes of poems. My passivity saved me.   35
Your touch (was) the heat that upheld me.
Believing nothing, I could hope
to see, not a god, but a child,
a place: sunrise: a whistle: bird on stem:
a low sky, downy with rednesses.   40

(1979)

Andrew Taylor
DEVELOPING A WIFE

In the one cool room in the house
he held her face two inches under the water
rocking it ever so gently
ever so gently. Her smile
of two hours earlier came back to him   5
dimly at first through the water, then with more
boldness and more clarity.
The world is too much with us
on a hot day (he thought); better
this kind of drowning into a new degree,   10
a fraction of a second infinitely
protracted into purity. Her smile
free now of chemical and the perverse
alchemy of heat dust and destroying wind
free from the irritation, the tears   15
and the anger that had finally driven him
down to this moment,
was perfect, was
irreversible, a new reality.
Is it, he thought, that there is truth   20
here which she imperfectly embodies?
Or is it I that I'm developing here—
my dream, my vision of her,
my sleight of hand?
Perhaps, he thought, our marriage is like this?—   25
flimsy, unreal, but in its own way real:
a moment, a perfection glimpsed, then gone, gone utterly,
yet caught all the same, our axis, stationary,
the other side of drowning?
                              He bore
her smile out in the heat to her, as a gift.   30

(1970)

David Malouf
from THE CRAB FEAST

V

I watch at a distance
of centuries, in the morning
light of another planet
or the earliest gloom

of this one, your backward   5
submarine retreat,
as hoovering across
the seabed—courtly,

elate, iron-plated—
you practice the Dance.   10
I watch and am shut out.
The terrible privacies!

You move slow motion sideways,
an unsteady astronaut:
step and counter   15
step, then the clash,

soundless, of tank engagement;
you might be angels
in the only condition
our senses reach them in. I observe   20

your weightless, clumsy-tender
release. I observe
the rules; cut off
here in the dimension

of pure humanity, my need for air   25
a limiting factor,
I look through into
your life. Its mysteries

disarm me. Turning
away a second time   30
to earth, to air, I leave you
to your slow-fangled order,

taking with me
more than I came for
and less. You move back into   35
my head. No, it does not finish here.

VI

We were horizons
of each other's consciousness. All transactions
at this distance are small,
blurred, uninsistent. Drawn   *40*
by unlikeness, I grew
like you, or dreamed I did, sharing your cautious
sideways grip on things not to be broken,
your smokiness of blood, as kin

to dragons we guarded   *45*
in the gloom of mangrove trunks
our hoard. I crossed the limits
into alien territory. One of us

will die of this, I told myself; and one of us
did. The other   *50*
swam off to lick warm stones and sulk with clouds along
    a shoreline;
regretting the deep

shelves and downward spaces,
breathing easy,
but knowing something more   *55*
was owed and would take place. I go down

in the dark to that encounter, the sun
at my back. On the sea-bed
your eyes on their sticks
click white in the flattened shadow of my head.   *60*

(1980)

Gwen Harwood
CARNAL KNOWLEDGE I

Roll back, you fabulous animal
be human, sleep. I'll call you up
from water's dazzle, wheat-blond hills,
clear light and open-hearted roses,
this day's extravagance of blue   5
stored like a pulsebeat in the skull.

Content to be your love, your fool,
your creature tender and obscene
I'll bite sleep's innocence away
and wake the flesh my fingers cup   10
to build a world from what's to hand,
new energies of light and space

wings for blue distance, fins to sweep
the obscure caverns of your heart,
a tongue to lift your sweetness close   15
leaf-speech against the window-glass
a memory of chaos weeping
mute forces hammering for shape

sea-strip and sky-strip held apart
for earth to form its hills and roses   20
its landscape from our blind caresses,
blue air, horizon, water-flow,
bone to my bone I grasp the world.
But what you are I do not know.

(1972)

Kenneth Mackenzie
SHALL THEN ANOTHER...

*'C'est vous perdre une seconde fois, que de croire qu'un autre vous
possède...'*

—Villarceaux à Ninon de Lenclos

Shall then another do what I have done—
be with those legs and arms and breasts at one?
Shall the warm silken skin, that I alone knew,
be for another's couching, and shall he own new
gestures of hers—some subtle modification   5
of that loose drop of the head, of that dilation
amorous yet brutal of her pupils' caverns?
Shall he bait beasts and halt at the white taverns
and scale those purple climaxes, half-sleeping,
knowing not what he's accomplished? Shall the weeping   10

of that warm womb, the sobbing of its throat
be music to him, till by note by note
it's lost and wasted, as he grows there—too
used and occasion-hardened, and the brew
of love sours in his belly?   15
How can I think that he between her knees
shall at length find time to think, or hawk, or sneeze,
go over the day's event, yet up and down,
plan for tomorrow, cool above her frown
and tighter arms, as in the pleasure-pain   20
she parts from beauty, and becomes huge and plain
and draws him deeper—a Demeter's sigh
sealing the spasm. Tell me—how shall I,
who always knew these monstrous movements of her,
dream and know now she has let another love her?   25
How shall I bear or dare to bring to mind
memory's cheap coin, finding it unrefined
by the heat of mental passions and sharp fires?
Or how, in her importunate desires
being somehow re-embraced, shall I go on,   30
saying, 'These contacts have been, but are gone
into the void of all such,' and not fling
back to her, roused to frenzy by the sting
of knowing my own demise was not my end?
There are some women who would have a friend   35
out of a vanquished lover; but not she—
'Get off,' she said; 'you are an enemy.'
And so the gate of returning was left unlocked
though closed; however called against and mocked,
the enemy can return, but the friend's bound   40
by welcome's pleasant-coloured chains, and ground
under the heel of mighty unsuspicion.

This is a murderous and foul condition!
I love the woman. Let me forget my fear
and find a courage such as harlots wear   45
who stultify the mind till the body looms
merry and dominating in their rooms
and fills out space and squashes memory
by frequent repetition. Let me be
all body, and mindless.   50

How warm and dry her skin was! It outglowed
the single candle flame whose colour flowed
up to her overleaning face like a flower.
She never made one move to test her power,
but, with a smile as happy as a child's,   55
blew out the golden light.

                                                    (1934)

A. D. Hope
from THE PLANCTUS

IX (EPIGRAPH)

PARADISE SAVED

(another version of the Fall)

Adam, indignant, would not eat with Eve,
They say, and she was driven from his side.
Watching the gates close on her tears, his pride
Upheld him, though he could not help but grieve

And climbed the wall, because his loneliness
Pined for her lonely figure in the dust:
Lo, there were two! God who is more than just
Sent her a helpmeet in that wilderness.

Day after day he watched them in the waste
Grow old, breaking the harsh unfriendly ground
Bearing their children, till at last they died;
While Adam, whose fellow God had not replaced,
Lived on immortal, young, with virtue crowned,
Sterile and impotent and justified.

(1969)

Christopher Brennan
SHE IS THE NIGHT

She is the night: all horror is of her
heap'd, shapeless, on the unclaim'd chaotic marsh
or huddled on the looming sepulchre
where the incult and scanty herb is harsh.

She is the night: all terror is of her   5
when the distemper'd dark begins to boil
with wavering face of larve and oily blur
of pallor on her suffocating coil.

Or majesty is hers, when marble gloom
supports her, calm, with glittering signs severe   10
and grandeur of metallic roof of doom,
far in the windows of our broken sphere.

Or she can be all pale, under no moon
or star, with veiling of the glamour cloud,
all pale, as were the fainting secret soon   15
to be exhaled, bride-robed in clinging shroud.

For she is night, and knows each wooing mood:
and her warm breasts are near in the charm'd air
of summer eve, and lovingly delude
the aching brow that craves their tender care.   20

The wooing night: all nuptials are of her;
and she the musky golden cloud that hangs
on maiden blood that burns, a boding stir
shot thro' with flashes of alluring pangs,

far off, in creeks that slept unvisited   25
or moved so smoothly that no ripple creas'd
their mirror'd slip of blue, till that sweet dread
melted the air and soft sighs stole, releas'd;

and she the shame of brides, veiling the white
of bosoms that for sharp fulfilment yearn;   30
she is the obscure centre of delight
and steals the kiss, the kiss she would return

deepen'd with all the abysm that under speech
moves shudderingly, or as that gulf is known
to set the astonied spouses each from each   35
across the futile sea of sighs, alone.

All mystery, and all love, beyond our ken,
she woos us, mournful till we find her fair:
and gods and stars and songs and souls of men
are the sparse jewels in her scatter'd hair.   40

(1898–9)

Dorothy Hewett
GRAVE FAIRYTALE

I sat in my tower, the seasons whirled,
the sky changed, the river grew
and dwindled to a pool.
The black Witch, light as an eel,
laddered up my hair   5
to straddle the window-sill.

She was there when I woke, blocking the light,
or in the night, humming, trying on my clothes.
I grew accustomed to her; she was as much a part of me
as my own self; sometimes I thought, 'She *is* myself!'   10
a posturing blackness, savage as a cuckoo.

There was no mirror in the tower.

Each time the voice screamed from the thorny garden
I'd rise and pensively undo the coil,
I felt it switch the ground, the earth tugged at it,   15

once it returned to me knotted with dead warm birds,
once wrapped itself three times around the tower—the tower
  quaked.
Framed in the window, whirling the countryside
with my great net of hair I'd catch a hawk, a bird, and once a bear.
Once night I woke, the horse pawed at the walls,   20
the cell was full of light, all my stone house
suffused, the voice called from the calm white garden, 'Rapunzel'.
I leant across the sill, my plait hissed out and spun like hail;
he climbed, slow as a heartbeat, up the stony side,
we dropped together as he loosed my hair,   25
his foraging hands tore me from neck to heels:
the witch jumped up my back and beat me to the wall.

Crouched in a corner I perceived it all,
the thighs jack-knifed apart, the dangling sword thrust home,
pinned like a specimen—to scream with joy.   30
I watched all night the beasts unsatisfied
roll in their sweat, their guttural cries
made the night thick with sound.
Their shadows gambolled, hunch-backed, hairy-arsed,
and as she ran four-pawed across the light,   35
the female dropped coined blood spots on the floor.

When morning came he put his armour on,
kissing farewell like angels swung on hair.
I heard the metal shoes trample the round earth about my tower.
Three times I lent my hair to the glowing prince,   40
hand over hand he climbed, my roots ached,
the blood dribbled on the stone sill.
Each time I saw the framed-faced bully boy sick with his triumph.

The third time I hid the shears,
a stab of black ice dripping in my dress.   45
He rose, his armour glistened in my tears,
the convex scissors snapped,
the glittering coil hissed, and slipped through air to undergrowth.
His mouth, like a round O, gaped at his end,
his finger nails ripped out, he clawed through space.   50
His horse ran off flank-deep in blown thistles.
Three seasons he stank at the tower's base.
A hawk plucked out his eyes, the ants busied his brain,
the mud-weed filled his mouth, his great sword rotted,
his tattered flesh-flags hung on bushes for the birds.   55

Bald as a collaborator I sit walled in the thumb-nosed tower,
wound round three times with ropes of autumn leaves.
And the witch. . . sometimes I idly kick
a little heap of rags across the floor.
I notice it grows smaller every year.   60

(1972)

WRITING THE SELF

One of the commonest ways of trying to distinguish human beings from other creatures is to emphasise the human uniqueness of the faculties of deliberate or willed self-examination, self-consciousness, self-awareness, and self-identification. Human beings have a sense of superiority when they see other animals (typically dogs, cats, farm animals, and birds) appear to act as if they thought themselves human—ignoring the fact that the reverse delusion is sometimes suffered by human beings themselves. Behind this sense of superiority lies the assumption that the interpretation of reality, including the definition of what is human, is essentially and uniquely a human preserve.

Associated with this definition, at least in European thinking, is the definition of the self, the unique, differentiated individuality that is considered to reside in each human person. European notions of capitalism could hardly have emerged without a prior belief in the identity and potential power of the individual. European notions of democracy are often expressed in terms of co-operation between individuals for mutual benefit.

An alternative way of looking at individuality and its potential power would, of course, be to say that it was a creation of the identity of the group or clan or society. It is not implausible to say that a collective identity, necessary for survival and protection, preceded the notion of individuality or even that excessive individuality (as found, for instance, in the figure of the hermit or recluse) is something of an aberration. Even the notion of a society, separate from its environment, may be largely a lately developed European notion. Aboriginal Australians frequently coalesce the white notions of individual, society, culture and environment into a single identity. Oodgeroo Noonuccal, for instance, says

> We are the corroboree and the bora ground,
> We are the old sacred ceremonies, the laws of the elders.
> We are the wonder tales of Dream Time, the tribal legends told.

The verb is 'are'—identity with—not 'are associated with' as a white speaker might have expected.

It is significant that this Section of the Anthology has no Aboriginal voices. The self is largely a European construction. Since at least the time of Rousseau and the beginnings of European Romanticism towards the end of the eighteenth century, it has also been an absorbing subject for writers. Wordsworth's *The Prelude*, for instance, is about the poet examining his identity with growing self-awareness. The novels that we call *Bildungsromanen*, concerned with growing up or gaining an education, are characterised by increasing self-awareness (and self-criticism): they include Goethe's *The Sorrows of Young Werther,* Dickens' *David Copperfield* and *Great Expectations*, Joyce's *A Portrait of the Artist as a Young Man*, Miles Franklin's *My Brilliant Career*, Henry Handel Richardson's *The Getting of Wisdom*, Christina Stead's *For Love Alone*, and Doris Lessing's *Children of Violence* series.

Defining the self understandably invokes its differentiation from otherness. The other against which the self is defined may be a parent or parents, a strange land, a strange people or a strange language. A hostile environment of any one of these kinds sharpens the perception of self. Further sharpening may occur through exaggerating the nature of the environment by using a Gothic or melodramatic mode or by emphasising the relative strangeness of the contrasted elements (e.g., by exaggerating the harshness and emptiness of the outback by contrast with a city-nurtured self).

Writing the self often creates the impression of mimeticism. It seems to the reader as if the writer is trying to describe what the self is 'really' like. But the veracity of the impression can rarely be checked. The 'real self' is not in the language available to the reader; that language purports to represent the 'real self', but it neither is the real self nor does it offer the real self for comparison.

At times, of course, it is evident to the reader that the real self is either a creation of the writer (or the writing) or else is more a process of search or discovery than an essence or object. The writer may seem to be seeking to discover the self, perhaps trying on mask after mask (as Yeats and Pound said) to see which one fitted best. Or the mask may be a form of defence against the reader and against the world or, as Yeats also said, a self with which to confront the beloved.

The texts in this Section offer a variety of modes of writing about the self. Some may seem identifiably Australian; others are not bound by any national considerations.

Neilson's 'The Orange Tree' presents two opposing concepts of the young girl's self, the one that she believes lies in or is symbolised by the orange tree and the conventionally romantic one that the speaker tries to foist on to her. Ivan Southall's *Josh* (an early example of a book for adolescent readers using interior monologue') is a *Bildungsroman* in which Josh's growing identification of himself operates largely through contrast with Aunt Clara's, Bill's and Rex's attempts to regulate and identify his personality.

Both these texts make play with awakening sexuality, but it is muted. In Glenda Adams' short story, 'A Snake Down Under', the title and most of the story operate through a punning symbol. The snake in the Garden of Eden, the concept of sexuality being evil, and the phallus are intertwined in this symbol. Even the gym mistress's advice on the treatment of snake-bite (now disparaged by medical experts, incidentally) is couched in terms that refer tangentially to menstruation and wariness of sex.

Despite its title, Olga Masters' story 'A Good Marriage' is more about the narrator Ellen and her growing understanding than it is about either her parents' or the Pattersons' marriage. She is fascinated by Clarice Patterson, almost totally absorbed in her as a positive role-model for herself as she grows up. By contrast, her mother and her father have quite different ideas about her upbringing.

Henry Handel Richardson's short stories (mostly involving female sexuality) have been comparatively neglected. In 'Three in a Row' the battle for dominance between Tetta, May and Patty resolves itself into a communal assertiveness against the unfairness and oppressiveness imposed by Miss Ethel who boards them for a night on their way to spend the holidays with May's mother. At the end, however, it is Tetta who, lying awake rather daringly on the verandah, contemplates her own unique identity against the infinity of the stars.

In the chapter from Christina Stead's *For Love Alone*, Teresa, from whose point of view the story is narrated, is captured in the process of defining herself by reference to the Watson's Bay environment where she lives, her brother Lance who has more freedom than she, and the girls he feels passion for. Her final statement, '"No, someone was watching"', clearly relates not just to the actual circumstances of her night-time swimming in the Bay but also to her sense of being constrained in her actions by the opinions of the members of her family.

In Lesbia Harford's poem 'Periodicity' the struggle for self-identification involves a kind of mediation between the demands of the body and the soul, the insistent pain of the body being so fierce that it almost defies and denies meaning.

The lost child is a recurring image in Australian literature and painting—in Henry Kingsley's *The Recollections of Geoffry Hamlyn* and his story 'Pretty Dick', in Lawson's 'The Babies in the Bush' and in Frederick McCubbin's painting, *The Lost Child*, for instance. In the chapter from Christopher Koch's *The Boys in the Island*, however, it is childhood itself that is lost, as Francis realises when recuperating from head injuries sustained in a car accident. His mind roves over images of 'otherness and nearness' in coming, rather uncomfortably, to acceptance of the 'iron bonds of his imminent adulthood'.

Judith Wright's 'Two Songs for the World's End' differs from most of the other items in this Section in so far as it looks from outside at the awakening self-consciousness of another, the beloved child of the speaker. Love, time and death, as often in Wright's work, are interwoven in an uneasy, complex relationship.

The contemplation of the possibility of death in the two songs is taken further into the contemplation of the actual death of a stillborn child in Gwen Harwood's 'Dialogue'. Both poets write about what might have been, but for Harwood there is no life beyond memory re-created in 'dactylic rhetoric'.

Les Murray's 'The Steel' recounts a long-suppressed story of the author's feelings of guilt about the death of his mother following a miscarriage. The self is here identified by comparison with the brothers and sisters he might, had not his own birth been induced, have expected to know. His mother's death, so devastating for the selfhood of his father, proved her a victim of injustice. In a conclusion that provided a title for the volume, *The People's Otherworld*, in which this poem appeared, Murray comments on the yearning for justice as an ideal, despite its denial by death.

Rodney Hall's 'Mrs Macintosh' uses a symbol of the subject's conception of her own selfhood, cages empty of birds—a life guiltless of oppressing others. This too, like the following one, is a poem in which selfhood is observed from outside the subject.

Thomas Shapcott's 'The Elegy Fires' closes this section with a depiction of the disintegration of personality. Memory, like an unconsuming fire, blurs, exchanges and coalesces incidents in a woman's life. The poem is, in a sense, an elegy or lament for the decay of the self.

This Section has, then, followed constructions of the self through examples from childhood to old age. Some constructions are from within the self being constructed, others from outside it. All involve opposition, or at least contrast, some benign, some of a violent, even hyperbolic form. None are totally self-absorbed versions; there is always an indication of values beyond the individual subject, always at least a slight recognition of the values of communality. Both the subject of this Section and, inevitably, the language through which it emerges are fugitive and shifting. One indication of the difficulty of the task is that, even in prose, authors resort to symbolism or repeated motifs as indirect but productive means of approaching the self.

Ken Goodwin/Alan Lawson

John Shaw Neilson
THE ORANGE TREE

The young girl stood beside me. I
   Saw not what her young eyes could see:
—A light, she said, not of the sky
   Lives somewhere in the Orange Tree.

—Is it, I said, of east or west?   5
   The heartbeat of a luminous boy
Who with his faltering flute confessed
   Only the edges of his joy?

Was he, I said, borne to the blue
   In a mad escapade of Spring   10
Ere he could make a fond adieu
   To his love in the blossoming?

—Listen! the young girl said. There calls
   No voice, no music beats on me;
But it is almost sound: it falls   15
   This evening on the Orange Tree.

—Does he, I said, so fear the Spring
   Ere the white sap too far can climb?
See in the full gold evening
   All happenings of the olden time?   20

Is he so goaded by the green?
   Does the compulsion of the dew
Make him unknowable but keen
   Asking with beauty of the blue?

—Listen! the young girl said. For all   25
   Your hapless talk you fail to see
There is a light, a step, a call,
   This evening on the Orange Tree.

—Is it, I said, a waste of love
   Imperishably old in pain,   30
Moving as an affrighted dove
   Under the sunlight or the rain?

Is it a fluttering heart that gave
   Too willingly and was reviled?
Is it the stammering at a grave,   35
   The last word of a little child?

—Silence! the young girl said. Oh, why,
   Why will you talk to weary me?
Plague me no longer now, for I
   Am listening like the Orange Tree.   40

                     (1919)

Ivan Southall
from JOSH

CHAPTER 27

Sneaking down the passage with the empty shopping-basket, wondering how late it was, feeling downright irritable, spoiling for an argument. Floorboards creaking.

'Is that you, Josh?' Her voice coming sharply.

'Yes, Aunt Clara.'

The kitchen door suddenly shutting, shutting him out, like curtain-fall on a half-finished performance. Aunt Clara's voice issuing from beyond it. 'Put the shopping in the laundry. I'll sort it out later. And close the door in case the cat gets at it.'

'Wouldn't it be handier in the kitchen?'

'No, it wouldn't.'

The brush-off again!

Josh going through the motions of Aunt Clara's deception, picking things up and banging them down, slamming doors, maybe carrying it farther than Aunt Clara intended. Laura somewhere in the offing. That was obvious. Though there wasn't a sight of her.

'Josh.'

'Yes, Aunt Clara.'

'Dress for cricket, then come through for lunch. Bill brought your clothes over. They're waiting in the bedroom.'

'It's not lunchtime, is it?'

'It will be. There's a good lad. Do as I ask you.'

It will be! Yeh, and in a year it'll be Christmas. Heck, Aunt Clara, there are things that have got to be put straight between us and now I'm shut out of the kitchen as if I had the measles. Blooming Laura! How long does it take her to do the scrubbing? You'd think she was scrubbing St Paul's Cathedral. Look, I'm not leaving this house again until we come to an understanding. Last night you knew everything but reckoned you knew nothing. Fighting off people coming here to flatten me and not even telling me. That's deceiving me, Aunt Clara. There I was trying to protect you and all the time you knew it. One thing on top of another. Shooting your mouth off about my poems. Forcing me into cricket; for your private information, Aunt Clara, I'm a dead-rotten player. Kicking me out of the house when I should have bally well stayed here and sorted it out with Laura. And what have my cousins been up to? I don't get it. Even if they are a bunch of so-and-so's how can it be my fault, how could it? I've behaved myself in this town like an angel because Dad threatened to kill me if I didn't. So saint-like I don't even know me. Maybe you're the trouble. Kids telling me you're mortgaged to the eyebrows. What a load of rubbish. Everyone in the family knows you could buy and sell the King of England. That's why Mum won't have a bar of you. Because of your blinking money. And then they say I'm sponging. Living on the smell of an oily rag! Have you ever heard such nonsense? House full of furniture. More furniture in the bathroom than we have in our living-room. What are they talking about? More books in the bedrooms than we've got in the public library. Carpets from Persia. Glass from Bohemia. Chelsea china.

Strike me, she could start a museum. Sponging on her. What a lot of hogwash. Everyone in town must be a born liar. Living in the sun, you call it. It's like living down a drainpipe. What's wrong with my stupid cousins? They never told me Ryan Creek was a mad-house, and even Dad reckons it only wakes itself on Sundays for staggering off to church and staggering home again. By crikey, Great-grandfather, you've no idea what you started. A place like this is a national disaster. No wonder they stuck a slab of granite on you big enough to sink a warship. They had to put it there to stop you from leaping out again.

Someone ringing at the front doorbell shattering Josh's magnificent oration.

Bedroom door wide open. Josh half-naked in the middle of the carpet still wagging a finger at Great-grandfather's portrait. Footsteps coming up the passage. Josh making a snap decision to pull his pants on. Aunt Clara trotting past pretending not to notice, but stopping suddenly as if she'd met a barrier. 'Good heavens, Josh, now I've seen everything.' Then trotting on again. A remark, Aunt Clara, that I would not have expected from a lady. But feeling sort of peculiar as if he was waiting for some other fellow to climb in alongside him. Gathering up the waistband by the handful and shuffling to the mirror to check on the scenery. Standing there blinking as if he had never seen his own reflection. Then swearing. 'The dirty dog. That lousy Bill. What's he done to me?'

Josh viewing himself from several angles letting go the waistband and watching it drop to his ankles, pulling it up again and sighting his legs bare from the calves downwards. Pants made for a dwarf with a belly like an elephant. Josh, Josh, have you ever seen anything like it? If you hitch 'em up you'll need a periscope. If you drop 'em down you'll be indecent. Aunt Clara, they're trying to turn me into a monkey. Great-grandfather, don't you look at me or that slab of granite won't be heavy enough, you'll come shrieking up through the middle of it. Betsy, if you come to cricket I'll drop dead of mortification. I'll never catch the ball, I'll never bally well reach it, I'll have to run a yard before my pants start moving.

'Josh, may I come in without fear of embarrassment?'

'The door's open, Aunt Clara.' A heart-rending voice of quiet desperation. 'Everyone welcome. Be my guest.'

'That's a strange thing to say, Josh, and a strange way to say it.'

'It's a strange sight you're seeing, Aunt Clara. Whose clothes are they? I mean, what could wear them? It'd have to be an animal. A wombat maybe.'

Aunt Clara taking off her spectacles and giving them a polish.

'All right,' Josh adding. 'Laugh your head off. It's got to start sometime. I might as well get used to it.'

'They must be Freddie's. I'm surprised that Bill bothered to bring them.'

'I'm not.'

'He must have ridden out miles to get them.'

'That figures.'

Aunt Clara smiling. 'We'll put a few pins in them, dear. Perhaps no one will notice.'

'It'll need to be a very dark afternoon, Aunt Clara.'

'You're a funny boy, Josh. You're really very funny.'

'Thanks.'

'I mean it as a compliment. You're quite an entertainment.'

'Yeh.'

'You are, dear. I judged you hastily. I'm going to miss you for more than your earnestness.'

'I haven't gone yet, Aunt Clara.'

'That was Rex at the door.'

'Was it? If it had been Bill I'd have strangled him.'

'The match is starting early. The boys from Croxley are here already. Rex thought you might not be able to make it. He wanted to know if your stomach-ache was worse.'

'Haven't got a stomach-ache.'

'He said you were sick in the cemetery.'

'I wasn't.'

'What were you doing in the cemetery?'

'Reading tombstones.'

'And Rex. Was he reading them?'

'Rex and I had a difference of opinion.' Why hide it any longer?

'Are you in trouble, Josh? Why don't you tell me? You're not getting on very well with people, are you?'

'You might say that, Aunt Clara.'

'Whose fault is it?'

'Couldn't be theirs, could it? I mean, it would have to be mine, wouldn't it?'

'I didn't say that.'

No, Josh, no, you're not to bring her into it. You don't cry for yourself, you cry for other people. She can't know everything. How could she? Button up the lip, Josh. 'Please, Aunt Clara, have you got the pins handy? I can't hold these pants up much longer.'

(1971)

Glenda Adams
A SNAKE DOWN UNDER

We sat in our navy blue serge tunics with white blouses. We sat without moving, our hands on our heads, our feet squarely on the floor under our desks.

The teacher read us a story: A girl got lost in the bush. She wandered all day looking for the way back home. When night fell she took refuge in a cave and fell asleep on the rocky floor. When she awoke she saw to her dismay that a snake had come while she slept and had coiled itself on her warm lap, where it now rested peacefully. The girl did not scream or move lest the snake be aroused and bite her. She stayed still without budging the whole day and the following night, until at last the snake slid away of its own accord. The girl was shocked but unharmed.

We sat on the floor of the gym in our gym uniforms: brown shirts and old-fashioned flared shorts no higher than six inches above the knee, beige

ankle socks and brown sneakers. Our mothers had embroidered our init-
ials in gold on the shirt pocket. We sat cross-legged in rows, our backs
straight, our hands resting on our knees.

The gym mistress, in ballet slippers, stood before us, her hands clasped
before her, her back straight, her stomach muscles firm. She said: If ever a
snake should bite you, do not panic. Take a belt or a piece of string and tie
a tourniquet around the affected limb between the bite and the heart. Take
a sharp knife or razor blade. Make a series of cuts, criss-cross, over the
bite. Then, suck at the cuts to remove the poison. Do not swallow. Spit out
the blood and the poison. If you have a cut on your gum or lip, get a friend
to suck out the poison instead. Then go to the nearest doctor. Try to kill
the snake and take it with you. Otherwise, note carefully its distinguishing
features.

My friend at school was caught with a copy of *East of Eden*. The
headmistress called a special assembly. We stood in rows, at attention,
eyes front, half an arm's distance from each other.

The headmistress said: One girl, and I shan't name names, has been
reading a book that is highly unsuitable for high school pupils. I shan't
name the book, but you know which book I mean. If I find that book
inside the school gates again, I will take serious measures. It is hard for
some of you to know what is right and what is wrong. Just remember this.
If you are thinking of doing something, ask yourself: could I tell my
mother about this? If the answer is no, then you can be sure you are doing
something wrong.

I know of a girl who went bushwalking and sat on a snake curled up on a
rock in the sun. The snake bit her. But since she was with a group that
included boys, she was too embarrassed to say anything. So she kept on
walking, until the poison overcame her. She fell ill and only then did she
admit that a snake had bitten her on a very private part. But it was too late
to help her. She died.

When I was sixteen my mother encouraged me to telephone a boy and ask
him to be my partner for the school dance. She said: You are old enough
to decide who you want to go out with and who you don't want to go out
with. I trust you completely.

After that I went out with a Roman Catholic, then an immigrant
Dutchman, then an Indonesian.

My mother asked me what I thought I was doing. She said: You can go
out with anyone you like as long as it's someone nice.

In the museum were two photographs. In the first, a snake had bitten and
killed a young goat. In the second, the snake's jaws were stretched open
and the goat was half inside the snake. The outline of the goat's body was
visible within the body of the snake. The caption read: Snake trying to eat
goat. Once snake begins to eat, it cannot stop. Jaws work like conveyor
belt.

A girl on our street suddenly left and went to Queensland for six months.
My mother said it was because she had gone too far. She said to me: You

know, don't you, that if anything ever happens to you, you can come to me for help. But of course I know you won't ever have to, because you wouldn't ever do anything like that.

Forty minutes of scripture a week was compulsory in all state schools. The Church of England girls sat with hands flat on the desk to preclude fidgeting and note passing. A lay preacher stood before us, his arms upstretched to heaven, his hands and voice shaking. He said: Fornication is a sin and evil. I kissed only one woman, once, before I married. And that was the woman who became my wife. The day I asked her to marry me and she said yes, we sealed our vow with a kiss. I have looked upon no other woman.

I encountered my first snake when I went for an early morning walk beside a wheat field in France. I walked gazing at the sky. When I felt a movement on my leg I looked down. Across my instep rested the tail of a tweedy-skinned snake. The rest of its body was inside the leg of my jeans, resting against my own bare leg. The head was at my knee.

I broke the rules. I screamed and kicked and stamped. The snake fell out of my jeans in a heap and fled into the wheat. I ran back to the house crying.

My friend said, 'Did it offer you an apple?'

(1979)

Olga Masters
A GOOD MARRIAGE

My Father sat at the kitchen table much longer than he should have talking about Clarice Carmody coming to Berrigo.

My mother got restless because of the cigarettes my father was rolling and smoking. She worked extra fast glancing several times pointedly through the doorway at the waving corn paddock which my father had come from earlier than he need have for morning tea.

He creaked the kitchen chair as he talked especially when he said her name.

'Clarice Carmody! Sounds like one of them Tivoli dancers!'

My mother put another piece of wood in the stove.

'God help Jack Patterson, that's all I can say,' my father said. My mother's face wore an expression that said she wished it was.

'A mail order marriage!' my father said putting his tobacco tin in his hip pocket. Suddenly he laughed so loud my mother turned around at the dresser.

'That's a good one!' he said, slapping his tongue on his cigarette paper with his brown eyes shining.

My mother strutted to the stove on her short fat legs to put the big kettle over the heat.

'It might be too,' she said.

'Might be what too?' my father said, almost but not quite mocking her.

'A good marriage,' my mother said, emptying the teapot into the scrap bucket which seemed another way of saying morning tea time was over.

'They've never set eyes on each other!' my father said. 'They wouldn't know each other's faults...'

'They'll soon learn them,' my mother said dumping the biscuit tin on the dresser top after clamping the lid on.

The next sound was a clamping noise too. My father crossed the floor on the way out almost treading on me sitting on the doorstep.

'Out of the damn way!' he said, quite angry.

My mother sat on a chair for a few moments after he'd gone watching through the doorway with the hint of a smile which vanished when her eyes fell on me.

'You could be out there giving him a hand,' she said.

My toe began to smart a little where his big boots grazed it.

I bit at my kneecaps hoping my mother would say no more on the idea.

She didn't. She began to scrape new potatoes splashing them in a bowl of water.

Perhaps she was thinking about Clarice Carmody. I was. I was seeing her dancing on the stage of the old School of Arts. I thought of thistle-down lifted off the ground and bowling along when you don't believe there is a wind. In my excitement I wrapped my arms around my knees and licked them.

'Stop that dirty habit,' my mother said. 'Surely there is something you could be doing.'

'Will we visit Clarice Carmody?' I asked.

'She won't be Clarice Carmody' my mother said, vigorously rinsing a potato. 'She'll be Clarice Patterson.'

She sounded different already.

She came to Berrigo at the start of the September school holidays.

'The spring and I came together!' she said to me when at last I got to see her at home.

She and Jack Patterson moved into the empty place on the Patterson's farm where a farm hand and his family lived when the Patterson children were little. When the two boys left school they milked and ploughed and cleared the bush with old Bert Patterson the father. The girl Mary went to the city to work in an office which sounded a wonderful life to me. Cecil Patterson the younger son married Elsie Clark and brought her to the big old Patterson house to live. Young Mrs Patterson had plenty to do as old Mrs Patterson took to her bed when another woman came into the house saying her legs went.

My father was always planning means of tricking old Mrs Patterson into using her legs, like letting a fire get out of control on Berrigo sports' day, or raising the alarm on Berrigo picture night.

For old Mrs Patterson's disability didn't prevent her from going to everything that was on in Berrigo carried from the Patterson's car by Jack and Cecil. Immediately she was set down, to make up for the time spent in isolation on the farm where Elsie took out her resentment with long sulky silences, she turned her fat, creamy face to left and right looking for people to talk to.

Right off she would say 'not a peep out of the silly things' when asked about her legs.

My father who called her a parasite and a sponger would sit in the kitchen after meals and roll and smoke his cigarettes while he worked out plans for making her get up and run.

My mother sweeping his saucer away while his cup was in midair said more than once good luck to Gladdie Patterson, she was the smartest woman in Berrigo, and my father silenced would get up after a while and go back to work.

Jack Patterson went to the city and brought Clarice back. My father said how was anyone to know whether they were married or not and my mother said where was the great disadvantage in not being married? My father's glance fell on the old grey shirt of his she was mending and he got up very soon and clumped off to the corn paddock.

I tried to see now by looking at Clarice whether she was married to Jack Patterson. She wore a gold ring which looked a bit loose on her finger. My father having lost no time in getting a look at Clarice when she first arrived said it was one of Mrs Patterson's old rings or perhaps he said one of old Mrs Patterson's rings. He described Clarice as resembling 'one of them long armed golliwog dolls kids play with'. Then he added with one of his short quick laughs that she would be about as much use to Jack Patterson as a doll.

The wedding ring Clarice wore didn't seem to match her narrow hand. I saw it plainly when she dug her finger into the jar of jam I'd brought her.

Her mouth and eyes went round like three O's. She waggled her head and her heavy frizzy hair shook.

'Lovely, darlink,' she said. 'You must have the cleverest, kindest mother in the whole of the world.'

I blushed at this inaccurate description of my mother and hoped the two would not meet up too soon for Clarice to be disappointed.

Sitting there on one of her kitchen chairs, which like all the other furniture were leftovers from the big house, I did not want ever to see Clarice disappointed.

My hopes were short-lived. Jack Patterson came in then and Clarice's face and all her body changed. She did look a little like a golliwog doll although her long arms were mostly gracefully loose. Now she seemed awkward putting her hand on the kettle handle, looking towards Jack as if asking should she be making tea. Both Jack and I looked at the table with several dirty cups and saucers on it. Jack looked over my head out the window. Clarice walked in a stiff-legged way to the table and picked up the jam.

'Look!' she said holding it to the light. 'The lovely colour! Jam red!' Jack Patterson had seen plenty of jam so you couldn't expect him to be impressed. He half hung his head and Clarice tried again.

'This is Ellen from across the creek! Oh, goodness me! I shouldn't go round introducing people! Everyone knows everyone in the country!'

Jack Patterson took his yard hat and went out.

'Oh, darlink!' Clarice said in a defeated way putting the jam on the shelf above the stove. I wanted to tell her that wasn't where you kept the jam but didn't dare.

She sat on a chair with her feet forward, the skirt of her dress reaching to her calves. She looked straight at me, smiling and crinkling her eyes.

'I think, darlink,' she said, 'you and I are going to be really great friends.'

People said that in books. Here was Clarice saying it to me. She had mentioned introducing me too, which was something happening to me for the first time in my life. I was happy enough for my heart to burst through my skinny ribs.

But I had to get off the chair and go home. My mother said I was to give her the jam and go.

But she asked me about Clarice and Jack Patterson as if she expected me to observe things while I was there. 'What's the place like?' she said.

I remembered the dark little hall and the open bedroom door showing the bed not made and clothes hanging from the brass knobs and the floor mat wrinkled. And Clarice with her halo of frizzy hair and her wide smile drawing me down the hall to her.

'She's got it fixed up pretty good,' I lied.

'The work all done?' my mother asked.

I said yes because I felt Clarice had done all the work she intended to do for that day anyway.

I felt unhappy for Clarice because the Berrigo women most looked up to were those who got their housework done early and kept their homes neat all the time.

I next saw Clarice two months later at Berrigo show.

She wore a dress of soft green material with a band of the same stuff holding her wild hair above her forehead.

'Look!' said Merle Adcock, who was eighteen and dressed from Winn's mail order catalogue. 'She's got her belt tied round her head!'

Clarice had her arm through Jack Patterson's which also drew scornful looks from Berrigo people. When Jack Patterson talked to other men about the prize cows and bulls Clarice stayed there, and watching them I was pretty sure Jack would have liked to have shaken Clarice's arm off.

My mother worked all day in the food tent at the show but managed to get what Berrigo called 'a good gander' at Clarice with Jack.

'A wife hasn't made a difference to Jack Patterson,' she said at home that afternoon. 'He looks as hang dog as ever.'

My father, to my surprise and perhaps to hers too, got up at once and went off to the yard.

The sports' day was the week after the show and that was when my father and Clarice met.

Clarice saw me and said 'Hello, darlink' and laid a finger on my nose to flatten the turned up end. She laughed when she did it so my feelings wouldn't be hurt.

My father suddenly appeared behind us.

I was about to scuttle off thinking that was why he was there, but he stood in a kind of strutting pose looking at Clarice and putting a hand on the crown of my hat.

'I'm this little one's Dad,' he said. 'She could introduce us.'

I was struck silent by his touch and by his voice with a teasing note in it, so I couldn't have introduced them even if practised at it.

'Everyone is staring at me,' Clarice said. 'So they know who I am.'

'Berrigo always stares,' said my father taking out his tobacco tin and cigarette papers and staring at Clarice too.

She lifted her chin and looked at him with all her face in a way she had. 'Like the cows,' she said and laughed.

Her glance fell on his hands rolling his smoke, so different from my mother's expression. I thought smoking was sinful but started to change my ideas seeing Clarice's lively interested eyes and smiling mouth.

'Your father was talking to Clarice Carmody,' my mother said at home after the sports as if it was my fault.

I noticed she said Clarice Carmody, not Clarice Patterson and perhaps she read my thoughts.

'I doubt very much that she's Clarice Patterson,' my mother said, hanging up the potholder with a jab.

I felt troubled. First it was my father who seemed opposed to Clarice. Now it was my mother. I wondered how I would get to see her.

My chance came when I least expected it. My mother sent me with the slide normally used to take the cans of cream to the road-side to be picked up by the cream lorry, to load with dry sticks to get the stove and copper fire going.

The shivery grass was blowing and I was imagining it was the sea which I had never seen, and the slide was a ship sailing through it.

Clarice was standing there in the bush as if she had dropped from the sky.

'Darlink!' she called stalking towards me holding her dress away from the tussocks and blackberries sprouting up beside the track which led down to the creek separating Patterson's from our place.

'It's so hot, darlink isn't it?' she said lifting her mop of hair for the air to get through it.

No one else looked at me the way Clarice did with her smiling mouth, wrinkling nose and crinkling eyes. I hoped she didn't find me too awful with straight hair and skin off my sunburned nose and a dress not even fit to wear to school.

She put out a finger and pressed my nose and laughed.

'Why don't we go for a swim, darlink?' she said.

Behind her below the bank of blackberries there was a waterhole. A tree felled years and years ago and bleached white as a bone made a bridge across the creek. The water banked up behind it so it was deep on one side and just a trickle on the other.

I wasn't allowed to swim there. In fact I couldn't swim and neither could any other girls in Berrigo my age. The teacher at school who was a man took the boys swimming in the hole but there was no woman to take the girls so we sat on the school verandah and read what we liked from the school bookshelf supervised by Cissy Adcock the oldest girl in the school.

But how could I tell Clarice I couldn't swim much less take my clothes off? I would certainly be in for what my mother called the father of a belting for such a crime.

'I'll swim and you can cool your tootsies,' Clarice said throwing an arm around me.

We walked down the track crushed together, me thinking already of looking back on this wonderful change of events, but worried about my bony frame not responding to her embrace.

She let go of me near the bank and stepping forward a pace or two began to take off her clothes.

One piece after another.

She lifted her dress and petticoat over her head and cast them onto the branch of a sapling gum. Her hands came around behind her unhooking her brassiere which was something I dreamed of wearing one day and threw it after her other things. When she bent and raised one leg to take off her pants I thought she looked like a young tree. Not a tree everyone would say was beautiful but a tree you would look at more than once.

She jumped into the water ducking down till it covered her to the neck which she swung around to look at me.

'Oh, you should come in, darlink!' she said. She lifted both her arms and the water as if reluctant to let go of her flowed off them.

'Watch, darlink,' she said and swam, flicking her face from side to side, churning up the water with her white legs. She laughed when she reached the other bank so quickly because the hole was so small.

She sat on a half submerged log and lifting handfuls of mud rubbed it into her thighs.

'Very healthy, darlink,' she said without looking at my shocked face.

She rubbed it on her arms and shoulders and it ran in little grey dollops between her breasts.

Then she plunged in and swam across to me. She came up beside me slipping a bit and laughing.

'That was wonderful, darlink,' she said a little wistfully though, as if she doubted she would ever do it again.

The bush was quiet, so silent you could hear your own breath until a bird called and Clarice jumped a little.

'That's a whip bird,' I said hearing it again a little further away, the sound of a whip lashed in the air.

'Oh darlink, you are so clever,' she said and began to get dressed.

No one at home noticed I'd been away too long. My father was dawdling over afternoon tea just before milking and my mother bustling about made a clicking noise with her tongue every time a cow bellowed.

'It's no life for a girl,' my father said referring to Clarice and making me jump nervously as if there was a way of detecting what we'd been up to.

'She took it on herself,' said my mother, prodding at some corned beef in a saucepan on the stove.

'I'll bet they never let on to her about old lolly legs,' said my father slapping away almost savagely with his tongue on his cigarette paper. 'Landing a young girl into that! They'll expect her to wait on that old sponger before too long.'

He put his tobacco away. 'I'll bet Jack Patterson hardly says a word to her from one week's end to the next.' He stared at his smoke. 'Let alone anything else.'

My mother straightened up from the stove. Her sweaty hair was spikey around her red face which wore a pinched and anxious expression, perhaps because of the late start on the milking. She crushed her old yard hat on.

'I'll go and start,' she said.

My father smoked on for a minute or two then got up and looked around the kitchen as if seeing it for the first time.

He reached for his yard hat and put it on.

'What do you think of Clarice?' he said.

I laid my face on my knees to hide my guilt.

'She's beautiful,' I said.

When he stomped past me sitting on the step he kept quite clear to avoid stepping on me.

I got a chance to go and see Clarice one day in the Christmas holidays when my mother went into Berrigo to buy fruit for the Christmas cake and cordial essence.

Clarice put her arm around me standing at the window watching Elsie Patterson at the clothesline.

Elsie was football shaped under her apron and she carefully unpegged shirts and dresses, turning them around and pegging them again. She took the sides of towels and tea towels between her hands and stretched them even.

'Why does she do that, darlink?' Clarice asked me.

Berrigo women were proud of their wash, but I found this hard to explain to Clarice.

She laughed merrily when we turned away. 'People are so funny, aren't they darlink?'

She suggested going for a swim because the day was what my mother called a roaster.

This time she took off all her underwear at home leaving her thin dress showing her shape.

'Oh, darlink!' she said when I looked away.

I followed her round bottom with a couple of lovely little dents in it down to the waterhole.

The bush was not as quiet as before. Someone is about, I thought with a bush child's instinct for such things.

'I'll go and watch in case someone comes,' I said, and she threw a handful of water at me for my foolishness.

I ran a little way up the track and when I lifted my head there shielded by some saplings astride his horse was my father.

I stopped so close the flesh of the horse's chest quivered near my eyes.

'Don't go any further,' I said. 'Clarice is swimming.'

My father jumped off the horse and tied the bridle to a tree.

'Go on home,' he said. But I didn't move.

'Go on!' he said and I moved off too slowly. He picked up a piece of chunky wood and threw it.

The horse plunged and the wood glanced off my arm as I ran.

At home I beat at the fire in the stove with the poker and put the kettle over the heat relieved when it started to sing.

I went to the kitchen door and my mother was coming down the track from the road. I heard Tingle's bus which went in and out of Berrigo every day go whining along the main road after dropping her off.

She had both arms held away from her body with parcels hanging from them.

I went to meet her not looking at her face but seeing it all the same red under the grey coloured straw hat with the bunch of violets on the brim. She had had the hat a long time.

String from the parcels was wound around her fingers and it was hard to free them.

'Be careful!' she said, hot and angry. 'Don't drop that one!'

When she was inside and saw the fire going and the kettle near the boil she spoke more gently.

'It's a shaving mug,' she said, hiding the little parcel in the back of the dresser. 'For your father for Christmas.'

(1982)

'Henry Handel Richardson'
(Ethel Florence Robertson)
THREE IN A ROW

Miss Ethel marched ahead carrying the candle, and so cupping it with her hand that the light fell full on her round, horn-rimmed spectacles, making these look like gigantic eyes.

'I'm sorry, girls,' said she, throwing open a door, 'this is the best I can do for you—every other room's full. But I know you won't mind turning in together. May's such a shrimp that you can put her between you and never know she's there.'

Dutifully the three who followed at her heels chorused: 'Oh, not at all,' 'We shall manage,' 'Very good of you to have us, Miss Ethel,' as instructed by their respective Mammas.

But once the door had shut on their hostess they gathered round the bed—a narrow half-tester—in which they were expected to lie three in a row, and let their real feelings out.

'The old toad! Playing us such a scurvy trick!'

'On such a night, too!'

'And when she wrote she'd have heaps of room!'

'It's those Waugh girls from Bendigo that've done it. *Their* father's a judge! But anything's good enough for us.'

'I wish I hadn't come,' piped Patty, the youngest, a short, fat girl of eleven.

'Oh, you!—with your bulk you're safe for the lion's share. But what did the old hag mean by her cheek about me?' snapped May, who had come to the age of desiring roundnesses. 'A shrimp, indeed!'

'Don't know I'm sure,' said thirteen-year-old Tetta, not quite truthfully. (May's was just a case of the 'girls from Bendigo' over again.) Tetta was getting rid of her clothes at top speed, peeling off her stockings, leaving one here, one there, her combinations on the floor where they fell. Then, holding her nightdress like a sail above her, she shot her arms into the sleeves, and was ready for bed while Patty was still conscientiously twisting a toothbrush round her gums, and May had got no further than loosening the buttons of her frock.

'Tetta!—you haven't done your teeth...or anything.'

'Don't want to. And I'm giving my teeth a rest. A dentist told some one I know it wore teeth out if you were always brushing them,' gave back Tetta easily.

The 'Lazy Liar!' this evoked was cut through by her shrill: 'Oh Lord, girls, *feathers*!' as she stooped to examine the build of the bed. This was that the bed had a distinct slope, out from the centre and down at the sides—she tried each in turn. And having let a few seconds elapse, for fear the others had noticed her wrigglings, she said mildly: 'Look here, Mabs, if you like I'll take the middle. I don't mind being a bit crushed.'

'Oh, no, you don't!' retorted May suspiciously, suspending her hair-brush. 'I know what it means, my dear...when you're so willing to oblige.' May was ratty with herself for being behindhand—even that stupid Pat had raced her. But to go to bed *properly* meant almost as much work as getting up in the morning.

'Well, for goodness' sake, put some biff into it. The mean bit of candle she's given us won't last for ever.'

'No, I promised my mother to brush my hair twenty times every night and morning, and I'm not going to break my word for anyone,' said May dourly; and pounded away with upraised arm. At which young Patty, who in her efforts to come in second had rather scamped the prescribed 'folding' of her clothes, suffered a pang of conscience, and turned back to refold them. But Tetta thought: though she brushed it a hundred times it would never be anything but bristly. Yes, that was just what it was like—the bristles in a brush.

Now she and Pat lay stretched out, a sheet drawn over them, a hump of feathers between. Oh, it was a shabby pretence at a 'double'—why, there was really hardly room for two. And when at last May came to join them—she had gargled her throat and cleaned her nails (just as if she was going to a party)—the rumpus began.

For Tetta said: 'Blow out the candle first.' This stood on the dressing-table, and it would have fallen to her, who lay on that side, to rise and extinguish it. May, the goose, doing as she was told, had then to climb over and in between them in the dark. There was a moment of wild confusion: dozens of legs, a whole army of them, seemed to be trampling and kicking in an attempt to sort themselves out. Tetta had taken a grip of the head-curtain, and so kept her balance, but Patty, unprepared, found nothing to hold to on the bare side of the bed, and, as May finally and determinedly squeezed herself in, slid to the floor with a cry and a thump.

'You pig!' from Tetta. 'You did that on purpose.'

'Well, what next I wonder!...after you two had taken all the room. Anyhow, now you'll just *have* to get up and make a light again.'

Grumblingly Tetta swung out her feet and groped her unknown way. 'Now where has that table gone to? Oh, *damn*!' For, coming suddenly and unexpectedly upon it, her elbow caught the candlestick and sent this flying. There was a crash; and the candle could be heard rolling over the bare boards.

'Now you've done it, you clumsy ass! Ten to one old Ethel'll come pouncing in on us.'

'If I get a bit of china in my foot it'll be me who pounces.' Tetta was on her knees, cautiously fumbling for the matches. These found and one struck, the candle was recovered; but the candlestick lay in fragments.

'Spill some grease on the floor and stick the candle to it,' suggested May.

With some difficulty Tetta contrived this hold, clutching her nightgown to her out of reach of the flame. Then she crossed to the other side of the bed to see to Patty, who still lay where she had fallen, snivelling over a bruised arm and a hefty bump on the forehead.

As there was no butter handy, Tetta poured water into the basin, soaked a sponge and held it to the wounded place, to keep it from swelling—and over this the floor got rather wet and messy, for the half-burnt, guttering candle, some three inches high, shed its meagre circle of light only on the opposite side of the room—then prodded the bruised arm to try for a broken bone. Patty was *quite* sure she had.

'Nonsense, Pat, it's only been your funny-bone,' and Tetta rose to her feet.

But the sight of May sprawling meanwhile at her ease in the centre of the bed was too much for her. 'It's all your greedy fault, pushing and shoving like that so that *you* can lie on your back. Well, you can't! There's only one way to lie and that's spoons—on our same sides. Now then, Pat!'

But Pat whimpered, if she had to sleep on the outside she'd never sleep at all, she'd always be expecting the whole night to fall out again. She'd rather lie on the floor.

'Well, why not? That's quite a good idea,' struck in May brightly. 'Then we should all have room.'

'I wouldn't, Pat,' said Tetta emphatically, with another glance at May's luxurious recumbency. 'At least not if you don't want tarantulas crawling over you in the night...and perhaps centipedes, too. There's sure to be squads about this dirty old house.'

Before she finished speaking, Patty had leapt on to the bed, her bare feet drawn up out of danger's way.

'Now then, Mabs milady, shunt! You've just *got* to let her in the middle. Are you ready?'—and with the same breath Tetta puffed out the candle and sprang to secure what little space was left.

With due care they arranged themselves, back fitted to front; and for a few seconds, tightly wedged though they were, it seemed as if there might be peace.

Then May said: 'My mother always says it's dangerous to go to sleep on your left-hand side. It makes your heart swell up. And you could die in the night.'

There was a faint squeal from Patty. 'Here, let me...I'm not going to'—and the bed rocked under her determined efforts to turn to her right.

'Well, if she does, we've all got to. *Are* you ready?' sighed Tetta once more.

Gingerly and in unison they heaved.

But: 'Tetta, you've taken every bit of sheet!' from May.

'I haven't!'

'You have!' And the sheet, reduced to a rope, was tugged violently to and fro. 'If you think I'm going to lie with my back all bare...It's bad enough to have it hanging out over the edge.'

'The answer to that is, you shouldn't have such a big behind.'

'It's not! I haven't!' cried May, justly indignant. 'It's not a scrap bigger than your own. Now if you had Pat's running into you, you *might* talk! Hers is simply enormous; it reaches down to my legs.'

'Oh, it *doesn't*!' wailed Patty, on the verge of tears again. 'It's *not* true—it's *not* enormous.'

'Oh, shut up, you blubberer! What's the matter if it is?' snapped Tetta, losing patience. 'And anyhow the Turks admire them.' But the Turks were heathens, and Patty was not consoled. She lay chewing over her injuries, to which another was now added: 'It's no good...I simply can't...I'm suffocating,' she said in a weak voice. 'My head's right down in the crack between the pillows. I haven't *any* of my own.'

'Here, take half mine,' said Tetta, and shoved it towards her. May, who liked a pillow to herself, gave hers a hasty pull, which over-shot the mark. Down and out it slid, she, attempting a rescue, after it. 'Ooh! I'm standing in water. The whole floor's swimming.'

Said Tetta when order was once more restored: 'The only thing to do'll be hold on. Here, Pat, you put your arm over me and round my stomach, and May hers round you. That's it.'

In her case it answered. But May, seeking an extra firm grip, was unlucky enough to let her fingers stray on Patty's front, and this was too much for the fat girl, who was ticklish. She began to squirm, and the more May tried to hold her fast the more she wriggled, screwing herself up, defending her middle with arms and elbows, fighting with her knees, all to the accompaniment of a shrill and unconquerable giggle.

The result was that May and Tetta found themselves standing one on each side of the bed.

'You'll have to take the fool round her bally neck.'

'Well, then I shall probably strangle her in her sleep,' said May darkly as she climbed in again.

They linked themselves anew, and once more there was a brief spell of drowsy silence.

But it was, oh, such a hot night, and before long, out of the heat and the darkness, May's voice was heard in a distracted: 'But Pat!...you're all wet.'

'I'm not, oh, I'm *not*!' tragically protested the one thus accused. Called abruptly back from a half-slumber, her mind in its confusion had jumped to the day of infant peccadilloes.

'Idiot! I didn't mean that. But we're simply sticking together like melting jellies.'

'And oh, I do want a drink so dreadfully badly! I think I'll die soon if I don't have one,' moaned Patty.

'That comes of being so fat.—Fetch her one, Mabs,' ordered Tetta, stifling the girlish equivalent of an oath, as she applied yet another match to the stub of candle.

But May tilted the jug in vain. 'I believe...yes, you *have*!...you've used up every drop. Well, Tetta Riley, if you don't deserve to come to want some day!'

'There couldn't have been more than a cupful to start with. I suppose the tank's going dry. Besides, who cleaned their teeth I'd like to know?— Well, Pat, there's nothing else for it, you'll have to suck the sponge.'

And this Patty did, to the encouraging remark from Tetta that it was only her own dirt she was eating.

But the problem of sleep had become a very real one. And the night seemed to grow hotter with every minute that passed.

Here Tetta had a new idea: they should try one of them lying crossways at the foot. Yes...that was all very well...but which? And over this there ensued a wordy dispute. Patty was too fat; she'd stick out too much...besides being so hot to put your feet against. Tetta, on the other hand, or so she argued, was too tall: 'My head'd hang over one side, my legs the other.' No, it must be May or no one, and sourly and unwillingly the victim dragged herself to the bottom of the bed and lay athwart it. But she couldn't possibly sleep without a pillow...what was she to do for a pillow?

'Why, make a bundle of your clothes and ram them under your head.'

'My clothes? That I've got to wear to-morrow? All crumpled and creased? Think I see myself!'

'Oh very well then, take mine! Thank the Lord I'm not such a darned old fad as you.' And by the last flicker of the dying candle, Tetta darted round the room, redeeming her scattered undergarments, her skirt, her petticoat...and not omitting her prickly suspenders.

'There. Now turn over so that you face the foot.'

'No, I mustn't do that. It'd mean lying on my left side.'

'What tommyrot! Not if you put your blinking head the other way round!' cried Tetta in exasperation.

But this May could not be got to see; or else she would not see it; and, by now both dog-tired and half-silly for want of sleep, they barked and bit their way through what gradually deteriorated into a kind of geometrical wrangle, and ended by Tetta snarling: 'It's easy to see *you've* never done any Euclid!'

This was a spiteful thrust; for May had failed at close of term to get her remove, and so to reach a class in which she, too, would have been held capable of writing *Quod erat demonstrandum.* And ordinarily, for decency's sake, you did not allude to her misfortune. But to-night bonds were loosed.

After this a silence fell...but not the silence of peace. May, galled to the quick, lay revolving a means of revenge.

Presently to ejaculate: 'Oh, Tetta...oh, your feet!...take them away...oh, *puh!*'

'What the ...what in the name of Christmas do you mean by that? When I have had two baths today!'

'Then all I can say is, your *shoes* must be high!'

In answer to this, involuntarily, but very fiercely, the libelled foot shot out in a straight kick. It landed on May's nose—the soft and gristly part that is so tender. With a scream May sat up and clapped her hands to it, and now, thoroughly hurt and unnerved, fell to sobbing: 'Oh, my nose, my nose! You've broken it, you beast—you dirty beast! It's bleeding...I can feel the blood dripping from it.'

Yet another of the precious matches went in verifying this. True enough a few drops of blood *were* oozing, and the upper lip had had a nasty jab against the top teeth. Once more the sponge was requisitioned, and its last remaining moisture squeezed from it.

In compensation for her injuries May now demanded to be allowed to occupy Tetta's place at the head of the bed.

'Wait. First I'm going to find out what the time is. We seem to have been here for years. It must surely be nearly morning now;' and with this, Tetta opened the door and crept on tiptoe into the passage, where a clock hung.

Returning, she said hoarsely and dramatically: 'Look here, you two, it's not even half-past twelve yet? There's still six blooming hours before we can get up...can possibly get up. And the candle's done, and there's no more water, and only two matches left. I'm fed up to the neck...I can't stick it a minute longer. I'm going out.'

'Going out? What do you mean?'

'Where to? What for?'

'What do you think? On the verandah, of course. To get cool. This room's as hot as...yes, as hot as *hell*...when you come back into it.'

'Tetta Riley!...your language! If only my mother could hear you!'

'Oh, bing, bang and bung your mother! I'm sick of the very sound of her.'

'I'll tell her every word you've said.'

'Oh, go to—to Sunday School!'

'I do. And I will. And I'll tell them, too. And you can just *get* out on your old verandah, and stop there. It'll be jolly good riddance to bad rubbish.'

'I'm going. But you're coming, too. Think I mean to leave you two snoring here while I kick my heels outside? Oh, no, my dears, not me! Up you get—and double-quick! Both of you.'

And meekly, without a further word, the two so commanded obeyed. For when Tetta, the easy-going, spoke like this—in what was known as her 'strong-minded' voice—they were her humblest servants. Nor did they resent her mastery. Patty the sheep invariably trotted tail-down after her elders; but May, for all her spirit, was at heart Tetta's devoted crony; and as a rule each made a friendly allowance for the other's failings; a slommicky laziness on the one hand, an ultra-prim exactitude on the other.

Now, at Tetta's direction, skirts were slipped over nightdresses, jackets buttoned on top. And turning their backs on the hideously crumpled battlefield of the bed, they spread a blanket on the verandah's edge, laid pillows and bolster on this, and stretched themselves out, three in a row, with a sheet atop of them.

Oh! the relief was, to escape from those fondly clinging feathers, those steep, sloping sides. Hard the boards might be, as hard as your own bones, but they were at least dead level. Besides that, you were free from the heat of your neighbour's body, and could toss and turn as you chose.

The sweetness, too, of the summer-night air, after the shut-upness of the stuffy room. Pat, who had staggered tipsily in her companions' wake, drew but a couple of full breaths and was fast asleep. May, correctly arranged on her right side, took longer: privately, she thought what they were doing not quite *nice*, and wondered what her mother would say when told of it.

But Tetta lay wakeful. For one thing, it was so light. Not from the moon, for there wasn't any; it was the stars that did it. The sky was as thick with stars as...well, she who lived on the sea-board had never seen anything like this bush sky: it was just as if some one had taken diamonds by the handful, no, the bucketful, and flung them out without caring— hundreds and thousands of diamonds, all sharp and white and glittering, with hardly an inch of space between, and what there was, gone a pale dove-grey.

'Oh, gosh, what tons! I never knew there *were* so many stars, did you?'

But there was no reply. So she just lay there, with her hands clasped under her neck, and stared up at the sky till her eyes smarted. And then something else came into her head—a familiar thought, and one she often amused herself with. It had to do with her own identity. Did there, she was given to wondering, somewhere or anywhere on earth exist a replica of herself? Was there, hidden away in some corner of the globe, another girl called Tetta Riley, thirteen years old, with a stub nose with freckles on it, and all her other little funniosities, who had grown up as she grew up, and who felt and thought like her? Herself, finding it hard to believe in her own uniqueness, she was inclined to think there might, there must be; and when, as now, she had nothing better to do, she would send her mind round the world in a fanciful search after her second self. To-night, in face of this starry splendour, she let it stray to what she believed to be 'other worlds', as well, chasing her thought among the stars and planets and the Milky Way, leaping from star to star...over gaps of palest grey...till her head spun, her eyes dazzled; and sleep, descending, gathered her too into the fold.

(1934)

Christina Stead
from FOR LOVE ALONE

CHAPTER 5

IT WAS HIGH TIDE AT NINE-THIRTY

It was high tide at nine-thirty that night in February and even after ten o'clock, the black tide was glassy, too full for lapping in the gullies. Up on the cliffs, Teresa could see the ocean flooding the reefs outside, choking the headlands and swimming to the landing platforms of jetties in the bays. It was long after ten when Teresa got to the highest point of the seaward cliffs and turning there, dropped down to the pine-grown bay by narrow paths and tree-grown boulders, trailing her long skirt, holding her hat by a ribbon. From every moon-red shadow came the voices of men and women; and in every bush and in the clumps of pine, upon unseen wooden seats and behind rocks, in the grass and even on open ledges, men and women groaned and gave shuddering cries as if they were being beaten. She passed slowly, timidly, but fascinated by the strange battlefield, the bodies stretch-ed out, contorted, with sounds of the dying under the fierce high moon. She did not know what the sounds were, but she knew children would be conceived this night, and some time later, women would marry hurriedly, if they could, like one of her cousins, who had slept the night with a man in one of these very grottoes; and perhaps one or two would jump into the sea. There were often bodies fished up round here, that had leapt when the heart still beat, from these high ledges into waters washed round these rocks by the moon.

Some fishermen came slowly up through the rocks to the edge of the curved lipped platform over which they began casually to drop down by the iron footholds to the lowest ledges, wet by the unusual tides, and from these they waded out smoothly to their fishing posts on the edge of the square-cleaving shale. The bay, the ocean, were full of moonstruck fish, restless, swarming, so thick in places that the water looked oily; their presence, the men thought, with other signs, meant storms at hand.

Terry, who knew them all and to whom they said: ''Lo,' in their meditative voices, watched them go over, some by the front cliff, shining blue, some by a small funnel where volcanic rock had crumbled in the sandstone. She went up to watch the latter and stood against a giant boulder staring out to sea. Nothing was between her and a two-hundred-foot plunge from the pale rock but a hand's breadth. She knew the funnel too. She had climbed in it as a child, but now she was even less sure-footed than then, a powerful, full-blooded young woman whose head turned easily. If she could only go to the bottom of the dike now, with the men, and spend the night with them, thigh-deep in the sweet water, catching fish, saying nothing, looking out to sea!

In the quiet harbours of the coast, the unfrequented estuaries, full of beaches of white sand and tangled scrub, she had often seen the lucky women, fishers' women, picnic women, holiday women, the wives of workers and loafers and misanthropes, who lived on boats and beaches, in shacks by the shoaling sand, with their men moving about them, free by the campfire and burning hearth, easy-going, tattered, ugly, very likely starved, beaten, but embraced by men and endowed with men's children. She had seen, the last summer, a dark-haired woman, at the bottom of a huge cliff, near Barrenjoey, at dawn. There were two boatloads of fishermen with her, Australians of Italian and English blood. They put in to shore about six in the morning, after the night's fishing. Some of them had already got there and lighted a fire, on which was a large iron pot. The woman, in black clothes, with high cheek-bones, and thin, was helped on shore by the men from the stern of the boat where she sat and she went calmly to the pot in which they were throwing fish which they brought from the boat. She said something, a man brought a piece of wood; she said something else, they laughed all about her.

Teresa came down to the foot of the cliff. Below the cliff was a lane unknown to most of the inhabitants of the Bay, although lovers walked through it, the lane where Mr Manoel lived. The wooden cottages in it faced the steep cutting where hardy trees grew twisted out of split rocks and rough grass had spun over the bores of the dynamite charges. The dirt lane was flooded with light. The blinds were not drawn and weak lamps shone out. In a room stood a double bed with a honeycomb quilt thown back over its foot. A foxy yellow, bloated little woman stood on the far side in an old-fashioned camisole and bloomers. A high chest of drawers with a crocheted cover was behind her. In another part of the cottage, men were talking. A window on the veranda with a single bulb behind it showed sticks of chocolate, bunches of carrots and cans of milk. There was worn oilcloth in the hall inside the netted door, a mop and bucket stood on the wooden veranda. A woman with grey hair moved round the kitchen table at the end of the passage. The woman was Queenie, a one-time school-mate of Teresa, who had disappeared from school and married a man twice her age, in her fifteenth year. Now she had a long married life already behind her. The dirty back yard with the Datura tree, the broken flooring, a rag on the window and even the strange old clothing the girl wore, filled Terry with languor. She regretted now that, like them all, she had despised this miserable, plain child. She went on along the row of houses with their sway-backed roof-trees. All the time, the moon, rising higher, reduced her shadow until it was at her feet; shadows began to move out of the cottages and at the sound of her footfalls, a blind was drawn somewhere along the lane.

In this hot night, not only the rocks above her, half-naked among twisted, tooth-leaved trees and spiney bushes, but the little open park she was now approaching, the grass above the dripping rocks of the military reserve, and the tram-shelters, were full of semitones and broken whispers. The roots, the trees, the timbers of the houses, strained by storms, the back yards full of plasterers' rubbish, the niches in the stony undercliff were refuges of love.

She came out from the lane, crossed the road and skirted the park. Near the seesaw, on the short grass, lay a black shape, unmoving. When she passed it, she saw it was a man over a woman, the woman's white gloves and bag lay on the grass beside them. They caught pickpockets in the Bay. Near the Old Hotel two more, the woman on her back and the man on his elbow, lay looking into each other's eyeballs, reflecting the moon. There were·none of them on the beach to-night, drowned under the high tide; none in the boats drawn up across the footpath. People sat in their moist warm gardens, talking and hitting out at the mosquitoes; the smell of eucalyptus oil and pipe-smoke reached out. Across the harbour, on the oyster-coloured water, a large Manly ferry full of lights moved southwards toward the city. She felt the swarm of lovers thick as locusts behind her when she turned into the beach path. Tied up to the fourth pile of the wharf was a rowing-boat covered with a tarpaulin. Under the tarpaulin was a woman's body; she had been fished out of the sea just outside of the cliffs that afternoon; it did not cause much comment. They lived there, among the gardens of the sea, and knew their fruits; fish, storms, corpses, moontides, miracles.

In between Teresa and her house, on the beach path, lay the old park which she had skirted on the far side, the wharf, and a few cottages. The young girl walked gravely, with a balanced stride, her back and neck straight, pretending she had a basin of water on her head. She was so intent on this as she came down by the park that at first she did not hear the people splashing in the Old Baths, now dismantled and which were no more than three strips of narrow boardwalk, awash in the present high water. But the shouts and splashes stopped as she came abreast of them, under the light of the lamp on the promenade, and in surprise she looked. She saw her brother, Leo, a seventeen-year-old, with three girls standing about or sitting in the water in careless attitudes. She did not know the girls, some girls from the Bay, in school after her time.

Leo grinned in his endearing, shamefaced way: 'Hello, Tess.'

'Hello,' said a girl's voice, satirically.

The others said nothing. One of the girls, dragging her legs through the water, was absorbed in looking down at them; the other, standing up in a wrestling attitude, cast back her tousled dark-red hair. A second lamp shone on the beach path between the Old Baths and the Old Hotel. The Old Hotel had ceased to be a hotel, but stood in the park without fence or outbuildings, a white-painted two-storey building with trees topping it, as old as the Hawkins' house, but dating from the military settlement of the Bay. Someone lived there in the Old Hotel. There were no lights there nor anywhere in the Bay, except the street lights. From the open back windows came voices. In a bush near at hand in the park a boy's voice said: 'I seen your sister; black man kissed her.'

The girls langhed.

'Lady Vah de Vah!' said the voice.

Leo laughed in a troubled way. Teresa had not stopped walking. Glancing quickly behind her, she saw Leo take a step towards the red-haired girl, who was standing in an arc, shaking the water out of her curls. She sprang upwards and wrestled with him in a beautiful bold way, the two of them winding in each other's arms, conscious of Teresa who had just gone by, excited by the boy hidden in the bush. Something hurled them at each other.

Coolly, Teresa walked on till she passed the wharf, glanced at the water and came to the first of the fishermen's cottages, Joe Martin's, it was. There the light falling through a few inches to the submerged sand showed three sting-rays swimming in a row. Some man was sitting on a boat near, stuffing his pipe.

'Sting-rays,' she said. 'And I was just going to paddle.'

'I seen three caught round in the Cove,' said the man. 'This morning when the tide was out. I suppose it's the same three.'

'They give you a nasty wound.'

'We got one in the boat with us yesterday,' said the man. 'It was dashing round like a mad cat. Your brother Lance picked it up and threw it out. I thought it would get us all.'

She went on. She thought: 'To-morrow, the night after and the next will be the three nights of full moon, the time I dream of blood, too.' The tide would be higher still. A man's voice called out. She muttered: 'Hello,' and went past. She wished she had stepped into the bay back there; it would have been queer to feel the long wet skirt round her, like sea-weed. But the sting-rays, the possible sharks which could come in close at such a time? She did not care if the dress were spoiled, she now had no use for it; but the hat? And of course they would think her a freak. Already, there was the Green Dress. The green dress was an old wool dress she had embroidered with all kinds of things, pagodas, butterflies, geraniums. She wore it only at home on Sundays, in the mornings, because it was thick and she need wear nothing under it; but Leo's friends, the Bay children, had seen it, touched it, asked her about it. She did not know herself why she kept this dress and wore it. She did not want to be eccentric, but on the contrary, to be noble, loved, glorious, admired; perfection as far as she could be perfect.

The tide still washed the kerb in front of the Hawkins's house at the end of the beach path. She could bathe there still. She rushed breathlessly up into the garden, holding up her dress, and through the wire-netted door, up the uncarpeted staircase to her room, which was at the back of the house. In the front were her father's two rooms, his bedroom and his study in which he studied nothing, but which contained the out-of-date textbooks, grammars, and botanies which he had once used, Wood's *Natural History*, the prizes of his poor youth. The south-eastern room was Kitty's, the north-eastern, Teresa's. In between was a long corridor in which a small flight of stairs led to one of the turreted attics. This corridor was also a kind of dais. One stepped down from it to reach the stairhead. All about, there were wooden passages, open windows and light and air streaming in. It was a spacious stone building, which had once been a military stables. The floors were always gritty with sand and stone-dust, as well as dirt from the hill which rose just behind them. At night, on this dust, lay the moonlight and starlight; in rains, streaks and pools of water lay about. It was rarely that Teresa put on her light to go to bed or to dress, only on dark nights of smother and storm; but Kitty was usually there, the 'woman of the house', under a lamp lingering over some sewing, visible through the half-open door, bowed close, looking like an old mother, except for her short dark hair. Kitty's room to-night for the first time was dark. Teresa leaned out of one of the back openings and called to the yard: 'Where's Kit?'

Her father's voice answered her from the shed: 'Is that you, Terry? Isn't Kit with you?' She heard him cross the flagged yard and enter the kitchen. She came across to the stairhead and shouted: 'Kit went somewhere with Sylvia.'

'Sylvia who?'

'Sylvia Hawkins. You know.'

'By herself?'

He reproved her for leaving Kitty, standing at the bottom of the stairs and looking up. Then seeing her long dress in the luminous shadow, he began to laugh. 'You two girls were figures of fun to-day running for the boat.'

'I'm going for a swim,' she said, retiring.

'Don't swim alone,' said he.

'Just in front.'

She shed her clothes hastily and ran downstairs, barefooted, dragging on a black bathing-suit she had grown out of, too small to wear in the daytime, but sleek and fishy to swim in. A tall, dark form slouched through the mosquito-door, grumbling.

'Come for a swim?' she asked her brother Lance.

'Too tired,' he said. 'Don't swim alone, and look out, there are rays and Portuguese man-of-wars about.'

'I'll stay in the light. You come and be look-out.'

'Not on your tintype.'

Her father, sitting on a stone bench in the garden, slapping mosquitoes, said: 'Have you got a look-out?'

'You come and watch,' she said.

'Nuh,' said he. 'Too tired. Been making Kitty's hope chest all the afternoon. More hope than chest.'

Lance from behind the door said: 'Hmff,' disgustedly.

'Lance doesn't care for women,' laughed the father in his soft voice.

'Really?' cried Teresa. 'Really! Doesn't he? Oh, no!'

The father laughed. Teresa dropped her towel on the steps and splashed into the water; it was so still that the splash could be heard all over the bay.

'Not out of the light,' called her father. 'I saw a large basking shark up Parsley Bay yesterday.' The basking shark was pale, changing colour with the bottom and all but invisible.

She was loafing about under a street lamp just where the beach path ended. Swimming here, she could see anyone coming either from the wharf or from the little end village of several streets arranged in a square of green called the Lawny. She floated in the water and thought she would not be afraid to go down at sea. To burn at sea—yes! But to go down! People had floated for thirty-six hours on a smooth ocean. You just let yourself go—you can even sleep floating, but the ocean she dreamed 'about under her lids was a wide smooth expanse under the moon, a halcyon sea. A man approached from the wharf way. She turned on her front and began to crawl about aimlessly, like a young prawn, over the sand. The water was only a foot or so deep. It was Georgie Martin going home. They exchanged hellos.

'See what Leo caught on the reef?' asked the big young man shyly.

'Kelpfish. We ate them,' she said, wishing him to go. As soon as he mounted the grass slope towards the street where he lived with his fat, timid wife, she turned back and began floating. It was impossible to swim in the shallows. The sky above was blond and delicate and the water far and wide was pale; she could see the bottom sand to a certain distance and it was too shallow for a shark in there.

'I'd like to sleep out to-night,' thought she. The moon gave her ghastly dreams which she enjoyed. She remembered school-yard tales: 'You will go mad, if you sleep with the moon on your face.' She had a cousin who took fits at full moon; she turned blood-red also at full moon. That was some story she had heard. Likewise, this cousin had a great charm, men ran after her; she was not precisely 'no good', but she was fly.

Voices came from the baths, saying good-bye. She even heard Leo's voice faintly calling: 'So long, so long.' Then she heard him nearer, his young baritone talking to the men, his whistling as he approached. She floated feet first to the edge of the path under the lamp and looked at him over her feet. His voice was full of delighted surprise. 'I say, why didn't you come in with us?'

She did not reply, only grinned at him. Leo flung his towel on the path and sat down with his toes in the water.

'That was Marion Josephs,' he said in a low voice.

'Which one?'

'The one with red hair.'

There was a silence in which Leo wordlessly implored Teresa not to mention his romping with girls in the Old Baths; and in which Teresa, by suddenly turning over in the water and swimming a few strokes out and back again, answered that she would not.

'Come in, come in,' said Teresa, pulling at his leg. He went in, but came right out again, because he had been playing football, fishing, and swimming all day.

'Moon's nearly full,' said he.

'Next day too,' answered Teresa.

'It's a pity you can't go swimming in trunks like I can,' he said, considerately. Teresa swam a few strokes.

'You look nice in that bathing suit,' Leo continued with an eager, timid smile, looking into her face. She lay on her back looking up dreamily at the Milky Way: 'I'd like to swim all night.'

Leo ducked his head and murmured: 'Do they hurt really?'

'What?' said Teresa, looking round for jelly-fish. Then his tone recalled her. She stared at him. He flushed but said mildly:

'Your—those,' he pointed at her breasts.

'Don't be silly.'

'I don't know,' he murmured. 'I thought perhaps.'

'How?' She plunged into the dark.

'I say, Tess,' he pursued in a clear voice, 'I say, what's your feller like?' he laughed. 'Your boy?'

'I haven't got one.'

'You must have.'

'I haven't.'

'Yes, you have,' he persuaded her, laughing gaily. 'What does he say to you, uh?' He was very eager. 'What sort of things, huh?'

'Nothing. I haven't one.'

He laughed, knowing better.

'I say, can I take you to the Maroubra Motordrome on Saturday?' he asked. It was a long trip, but she knew he had a girl down there, an Italian, black-eyed, pasty-faced, with a long English jaw and thick eyelashes; he had shown Tesesa the photomaton picture begging for her opinion; her name was Eunice. She despised Eunice, the latest of Leo's succession of black-eyed girls and she disdained Leo, this loving, handsome seventeen-year-old who already wanted to get married.

'I'm out,' she suddenly cried, bending upwards and getting to her feet. The sky behind the high attics of the old house was bubbling with radiant air. The water was receding fast. A curious flattening of the light had been coming in quick pulsations for minutes from the east and now a faint, very wide ring appeared round the moon, but the disk sailed free, without a cloud. She ran up the steps.

The bay, the headlands for miles, and all the districts of suburbs with their deep-etched gardens, the pallid streets, the couples walking, the parked cars, every buoy and rowboat, even flotsam and crabs stiffly promenading on rocks were intensely visible, and yet had dulled since half an hour ago. In the garden the trees were black against the flown moonscarves. Leo followed her in.

'Where've you been?' enquired his father.

'Swimming,' said Leo.

'Alone?'

'No, someone was watching.' Leo sprinted for the house.

(1944)

Lesbia Harford
PERIODICITY

My friend declares
Being woman and virgin she
Takes small account of periodicity

And she is right.
Her days are calmly spent   5
For her sex-function is irrelevant.

But I whose life
Is monthly broke in twain
Must seek some sort of meaning in my pain.

Women, I say,   10
Are beautiful in change,
Remote, immortal, like the moon they range.

Or call my pain
A skirmish in the whole
Tremendous conflict between body and soul.   15

Meaning must lie,
Some beauty surely dwell
In the fierce depths and uttermost pits of hell.

Yet still I seek,
Month after month in vain,   20
Meaning and beauty in recurrent pain.

(1917)

C. J. Koch
from THE BOYS IN THE ISLAND

CHAPTER 10

THE LOST CHILD

Francis woke up so slowly this morning that he was not sure for some moments who he was. He had come from a place of sleep so remote, so depthless, that now he lay in a becalmed surprise at finding himself not dead.

But he was at home, in his bedroom. It was the second week back from Melbourne.

His legs felt too weak to move, and his whole body was infantile with a feebleness almost pleasant, yet shameful. In fact he was filled with shame, waking: a helpless and almost pleasant shame. What for? For being back from the Mainland?

Lying here in the areas of waking, he knew that he had returned from somewhere more greatly remote than usual, in the dark fathoms of night-dream; he had been involved in a life locked off from this one, where every atom of his energy had been spent, and he wondered with a deep curiosity what had happened there. But it was no use to try to remember, he knew: he had come up like a fish from those black depthless fathoms; and once the night-dream had let him go, there was no going back.

Instead he slipped back into the different, easier areas of morning-dream, just below the surface, where the light of the day continued to filter, and where if he dreamed, he would know that he dreamed.

But he did not actually dream. Instead, his head was invaded by voices, and a smell. He moved in a tan vacuum where (thinking rather than dreaming, calculating with a deep interest) he tried to identify the voices, to decide where or what the vacuum was; and he found that the voices were everyone's, everyone he had ever known, and the place was Everywhere. It was Everywhere, and it was everything: and it smelt of childhood: a pleasant smell, flat and clean, like paper.

Through his own head, a little boy went running: himself, five years old. It was in the sunny playing-time, before school began. Through the tan ether which began to sprout grass and flowers he saw himself running, enthralled, possessed, calling. It was the cry of great child-excitement, of the Game he was playing. 'Oooh...'—long and dying, the drawn-out exclamation of surprise at what he had seen: the world, and the Otherland's nearness.

Then Francis woke again, to final, full waking, and a regret stabbed him as profound as the exhaustion of the night-dream.

And with this, the iron bonds of his imminent adulthood relaxed from around his head: he submitted to the paper-smell of everything so long gone away. He had woken this morning the way he used to wake at five years old. It had been gone, but it had come again: the scent and climate of the childish Everything, when the world bathed you, and forgave you.

And I am a fool, Francis Cullen told himself. This was both his discovery and his shame. He knew now, almost grown up, that he had been a fool. Nothing had happened, as Shane had said: and a time had ended, broken itself up in Melbourne, and he lay in his bed in Elimatta in his pyjamas and knew himself a fool.

You are a fool, Lad said, *because you listened to the story of childhood. Others forget it, they lock it behind their eyes, but you did not. That is why you are a fool. It is a story which begins, but the end does not arrive: you lose it. Into the paper-sweet smell of everything comes the tang of enemy iron. And you are supposed to forget it, the thing the cry was for, the surprise at the Otherland's nearness. But you did not forget it: that was your foolishness.*

Even now he was not cured of that story. Because, hearing outside the window a car's sleepy hum down the road, dying away with a serene yet urgent core of sound, long persistent, he heard the dream-shrunk voices speak of it, murmuring:

It was no car of today at all, it travels to the areas of otherness and nearness, here in the island if you could only find them, out past the Rise where Terry O'Brien still roams in gay and innocent badness with his uncles, through the heady air of the special place of suburb heights where it all begins, always. He could hear the car for a long time.

He adjusted his bandaged head carefully on the pillow. His memory had a memory which lay lost: and he knew (a fool) he would always yearn for that fool's journey down the passage of the cry and the lost car's sound, looking for the memory of a memory.

Shane had been right. They had been going nowhere. After his discharge from hosptial, Francis had come back home, not just to recover from his concussion, but to ask his father to send him back to school, to try again for his Leaving. Shane plucked at Francis's work-shirt again. '*What's this? What's this?*' It had been just a fool's fancy dress: Shane had been right.

The Game had ended, because it was suddenly no longer a game. It had killed poor George, who had never had much to do with it except to watch, and who had been too old for it: he had died in hospital of his head injuries.

It was silly that George was dead; Francis had not known George very well, but it had shocked him because it was so silly: a silly mistake. And the mistake was theirs, he knew that, although no one had been convicted of it. They had not begun to drink that morning, and so Lewie could not be convicted of drunken driving, although there had been some talk of it.

It was over, and no more a game, because George had been killed and because Keeva (Lewie told him in a letter) was getting engaged to a fairly prosperous small business man none of them knew, and whom she had apparently been stringing along for some time.

They were growing up. It was what Shane had seen, before any of them. It was a thing that happened when you did not want it, and sooner than you expected.

He went out alone at dusk and walked down Station Street towards Gooree. The low-crouching houses of Elimatta seemed to breathe gently, like sleepers, in the late winter air. He walked with a tired indifference. But when he turned the bend, the lights of Lutana Rise had come out, wild and white, by the spaces of the eastern distance, chattering their enormous secret as though day never made it dim. Between the forming and re-forming structures of winter mist, they glared in a cool fury. It was as though, across the intervening spaces of the valley, where only the moving red tail-light of a car was definite, like the sullen beginning of some perilous expedition, they dared him to come again. Against that prospect, a wind-tormented young eucalypt in a garden tossed its thin body back-wards and forwards, as though trying to break free from its roots.

And at the bend of the road, in the dusk, Francis seemed to see (without surprise, it was what he had come here for) Shane again, standing with one hand raised in the gesture he had made often, in the time when they had believed that everything would happen: it was the gesture he had made at Essendon airport, a sort of salute, half joking, half not—and how would he ever know now how much had been joke and game to Shane?

'It wouldn't have happened, boy,' Francis whispered, standing by the bend. 'When you grow up there's nowhere it can happen.'

(1958)

Gwen Harwood
DIALOGUE

If an angel came with one wish
I might say, deliver that child
who died before birth, into life.
Let me see what she might have become.
He would bring her into a room   5
fair skinned   the bones of her hands
would press on my shoulderblades
in our long embrace
                       we would sit
with the albums spread on our knees: 10
now here are your brothers   and here
your sister   here the old house
among trees and espaliered almonds.
   —But where am I?
                       Ah my dear   15
I have only one picture
               here
in my head   I saw you lying
still folded   one moment   forever

your head bent down to your heart
eyes closed on unspeakable wisdom
your delicate frog-pale fingers
                                             spread   20
apart as if you were playing
a woodwind instrument.
     —My name?   25
                   It was never given.
     —Where is my grave?
                in my head   I suppose
the hospital burnt you.   30
     —Was I beautiful?
                To me.
     —Do you mourn for me every day?
Not at all   it is more than thirty years
I am feeling the coolness of age   35
the perspectives of memory change.
Pearlskull   what lifts you here
from night-drift to solemn ripeness?
Mushroom dome? Gourd plumpness?
The frog in my pot of basil?   40
     —It is none of these, but a rhythm
        the bones of my fingers   dactylic
        rhetoric smashed from your memory.
        Forget me again.
                      Had I lived   45
no rhythm would be the same
nor my brotters and sister feast
in the world's eternal house.

Overhead   wings of cloud
     Burning   and under my feet   50
        stones marked with demons' teeth.

                            (1980)

Les A. Murray
THE STEEL

    I am older than my mother.
    Cold steel hurried me from her womb.
    I haven't got a star.

    What hour I followed
    the waters into this world   5
    no one living can now say.
    My zodiac got washed away.

    The steel of my induction
    killed my brothers and sisters;
    once or twice I was readied for them   10

and then they were not mentioned
again, at the hospital
to me or to the visitors.
The reticence left me only.

I think, apart from this,   15
my parents' life was happy,
provisional, as lives are.

Farming spared them from the war,
that, and an ill-knit blue shin
my father had been harried back   20

to tree-felling with, by his father
who supervised from horseback.
The times were late pioneer.

So was our bare plank house
with its rain stains down each crack   25
like tall tan flames,
magic swords, far matched perspectives:

it reaped Dad's shamed invectives—
Paying him rent for this shack!
The landlord was his father.   30

But we also had fireside ease,
health, plentiful dinners, the radio;
we'd a car to drive to tennis.

Country people have cars
for more than shopping and show,   35
our Dodge reached voting age, though,
in my first high school year.

I was in the town at school
the afternoon my mother
collapsed, and was carried from the dairy.   40
The car was out of order.

The ambulance was available
but it took a doctor's say-so
to come. This was refused.
My father pleaded. Was refused.   45

The local teacher's car was got finally.
The time all this took didn't pass,
it spread through sheets, unstoppable.

Thirty-seven miles to town
and the terrible delay.   50
Little blood brother, blood sister,
I don't blame you.
How can you blame a baby?
or the longing for a baby?

Little of that week   55
comes back. The vertigo,
the apparent recovery—
She will get better now.
The relapse on the Thursday.

In school and called away   60
I was haunted, all that week,
by the spectre of dark women,
Murrays dressed in midday black

who lived on the river islands
and are seen only at funerals;   65
their terrible weak authority.

Everybody in the town
was asking me about my mother;
I could only answer childishly
to them. And to my mother,   70

and on Friday afternoon
our family world
went inside itself forever.

Sister Arnall, city girl
with your curt good sense   75
were you being the nurse
when you let them hurry me?
being responsible

when I was brought on to make way
for a difficult birth in that cottage hospital   80
and the Cheers child stole my birthday?

Or was it our strange diffidence,
unworldly at a pinch, unresentful,
being a case among cases,

a relative, wartime sense,   85
modern, alien to fuss,
that is not in the Murrays?

I don't blame the Cheers boy's mother:
she didn't put her case.
It was the steel proposed   90
reasonably, professionally,
that became your sentence

but I don't decry unselfishness:
I'm proud of it. Of you.
Any virtue can be fatal   95

In the event, his coming gave no trouble
but it might have, I agree;
nothing you agreed to harmed me.

I didn't mean to harm you
I was a baby.   *100*

For a long time, my father
himself became a baby
being perhaps wiser than me,
less modern, less military;

he was not ashamed of grief,   *105*
of its looking like a birth
out through the face

bloated, whiskery, bringing no relief.
It was mainly through fear
that I was at times his father.   *110*
I have long been sorry.

Caked pans, rancid blankets,
despair and childish cool
were our road to Bohemia
that bitter wartime country.   *115*

What were you thinking of,
Doctor MB, BS?
Were you very tired?
Did you have more pressing cases?

Know panic when you heard it: *120*
Oh you can bring her in!
Did you often do
diagnosis by telephone?

Perhaps we wrong you,
make a scapegoat of you;   *125*
perhaps there was no stain
of class in your decision,

no view that two framed degrees
outweighed a dairy.
It's nothing, dear: *130*
just some excited hillbilly—

As your practice disappeared
and you were cold-shouldered in town
till you broke and fled,
did you think of the word Clan?   *135*

It is an antique
concept. But not wholly romantic.
We came to the river early;
it gives us some protection.

You'll agree the need is real.   *140*
I can forgive you now
and not to seem magnanimous.

It's enough that you blundered
on our family steel.

Thiry-five years on earth: *145*
that's short. That's short, Mother,
as the lives cut off by war

and the lives of spilt children are short.
Justice wholly in this world
would bring them no rebirth   *150*
nor restore your latter birthdays.
How could that be justice?

My father never quite
remarried. He went back
by stages of kindness to me   *155*
to the age of lonely men,
of only men, and men's company

that is called the Pioneer age.
Snig chain and mountain track;
he went back to felling trees   *160*

and seeking justice from his
dead father. His only weakness.
One's life is not a case

except of course it is.
Being just, seeking justice: *165*
they were both of them right,
my mother and my father.

There is justice, there is death,
humanist: you can't have both.   *170*
Activist, you can't serve both.
You do not move in measured space.

The poor man's anger is a prayer
for equities Time cannot hold
and steel grows from our mother's grace.
Justice is the people's otherworld.   *175*

                                                        (1982)

Rodney Hall
MRS MACINTOSH

Mrs Macintosh so simply
has reduced the world's dilemmas
to her fixed obsession, birdcage buying.
Now exhibits fill her rooms:
some are miniature pagodas,   5
and one a jail of cells.
The smallest, made from a lost

girl's hand, is bones enmeshed
in silver wire. The largest
looks an anarchy of cleverness   10
the total snub to cage-convention
a cloud so frail and knobbled
it dangles crazily askew, high
against the inconvenience of a wall.

These, her eccentricities,   15
are cherished catalogued
paraded for the delectation
of any visiting evangelist
salesman or charity collector.
Her cages, Mrs Macintosh   20
is careful to point out, are empty.
Birds revolt her—frighten
her wrinkled eye with theirs
and mock her ways with harsh high
female voices; or sing so sweetly   25
they could almost lure her back
to join the world. Unbearable.
No, she likes her symbolism:
cages free of birds, pure captivity
that's innocent of pain.   30

All day her hymns escape the house.

                                    (1967)

Thomas Shapcott
THE ELEGY FIRES

The old woman does not tell the nurse
but she has had to reach out
to touch the flames upon her wardrobe.
The wood is uncharred. Around the bed, too,
flames. And last night a hand   5
beside her own. Eyesight failing,
and the ghost fires, she stared again
to make sure—the hand of her own mother.

With her own unfamiliar hands, lost
for words, she begins the letter   10
to her son and the date she writes
is ten years out. Ten years, burnt out
as if they had never mottled her
and no ash. Ten years
ten leaves out of a diary   15
and her palms are the colour of old newsprint.
'Why do you never write?' one page,
one line of script, ten years, forty years.

Abridgements, she made her virtue out of discarding things.
The bookcase to one daughter, the Doulton to another.   20
She rid herself of a lifetime's possessions. Her children
have weathered, squinting faces, ash-grey hair.
In the unconsuming fire what may return in a vortex?
    Two children
splashing, green woollen bathers hugging into the creases.
Even the sudden gust of shoreline seaweed that made her hurry
    them on   25
to somewhere cleaner, how could that come back? Each grain
in her ocean-damp sandshoes bound again, knotted tight,
as if she still had young feet.

Where is the nurse? She has let go everything
but the ring on her strong, useless, mottled hand.   30
The bitter arguments of those middle years have been let go,
the long sea-trip back home with little Grace
when she had to discover finally there was nothing left
in Andover. The fretting over money. Parched summers
year after year. Not all things return.   35
The flames caress her hands
they hover round her body as if she had no body.
This is not her body, this parody crumpled under sheets.
Flames without heat. Years of purpose drawn up,
hours of waiting.   40
Hours of work in kitchens, committees,
minutes alone with dew speaking down by the fowl-run,
    minutes.
She stares for focus, she will outstare flames.
Focus is difficult now, rainbow. She is betrayed
as once in childhood she was mocked   45
by a fractured spectrum.

Is this memory? Out loud her voice is a phone-call,
close but cupped in. 'What parts of our brain function
to achieve this? I know the flames are hallucination.'
No, she will not disturb the nurses.   50
The flames are visible. The hand of her mother
is visible. She knows, soon, there will be the voices.

Fifty years since her mother whispered. Things that come back
to choose her are not of her deciding. Must she now
endure everything?   55
Her son, who came this morning, has not returned
for ten years, forty years. That person is not her daughter.
Updraught. If only her mother's hand were comforting:
it is another claimant. If you do not give
it shall be taken. What you give away   60
shall return a thousandfold.

                                                            (1982)

BIOGRAPHICAL INFORMATION

ADAMS, Glenda (1940–   ) b Sydney, moved to New York to write and study 1964; 2 vols short fiction, 2 novels including *Hottest Night of the Century* (1979) and *Dancing on Coral* (1986); Miles Franklin Award 1988.

ADAMSON, Robert (1943–   ) spent several periods of youth in gaols; 8 vols poetry; leading figure in 'New Australian Poetry' movement, editor *New Poetry* in early 1970s.

ANDERSON, Ethel (1883–1958) b England, educated Sydney, lived in India; 2 vols poetry, 2 essay collections, 3 vols short fiction, including *At Parramatta* (1956).

ANDERSON, Jessica (1925–   ) 5 novels, including *Tirra Lirra by the River* (1978), 2 vols short fiction, including *Stories from the Warm Zone and Sydney Stories* (1987); Miles Franklin Award 1978, 1980, NSW Premier's Award 1980.

ASTLEY, Thea (1925–   ) teacher, novelist, writer of short fiction, editor; 10 novels, including *A Kindness Cup* (1974), 2 vols short fiction, including *It's Raining in Mango* (1987); 3 times winner Miles Franklin Award, Steele Rudd Award 1988.

ATKINSON, Caroline (1834–72) first Australian-born woman novelist; 2 novels, including *Gertrude the Emigrant* (1857).

BAIL, Murray (1941–   ) 1 vol. short fiction, 2 novels, *Homesickness* (1980) and *Holden's Performance* (1987); National Book Council Award, *Age* Book of the Year Award 1980, Victorian Premier's Award 1988.

BANDLER, Faith (1918–   ) b Murwillumbah, father a Vanuatuan; 2 semi-autobiographical novels, *Wacvie* (1977) and *Welou My Brother* (1984); strongly identified with struggle for Aboriginal rights.

BAYNTON, Barbara (1857–1929) b Scone, NSW; 1 vol. short fiction, *Bush Studies* (1902), 1 novel; after 1904 alternated residence between Australia and England.

'BOLDREWOOD, Rolf' (Thomas Alexander Browne) (1826–1915) b London, arrived Australia 1831; farmer, police magistrate; 17 novels including *Robbery Under Arms* (1882–3), short fiction, articles, agricultural manuals.

BÓSTOCK, Gerald (1942–   ) leading figure in Aboriginal drama and film production; play, *Here Comes the Nigger*, 1 vol. poetry.

BOYD, Robin (1919–71) leading figure in Australian architecture as practitioner, writer, critic, lecturer; 12 books, including *The Australian Ugliness* (1960).

BRENNAN, Christopher (1870–1932) 5 vols poetry, including *Poems [1913]* (1914), 1 vol. prose published posthumously; taught modern languages at University of Sydney; literary affinity with French Symbolist writers.

BRETT, Lily (1946–   ) b Melbourne of Polish Jewish refugees; won Mattara Poetry Prize for *The Auschwitz Poems* (1986).

BUCKLEY, Vincent (1925–88) b Romsey, Vic. of Irish Catholic lineage; poet, critic, academic, editor; 7 vols poetry, including *The World's Flesh* (1954), 4 critical works, 2 autobiographical works, including *Cutting Green Hay* (1983).

CAMBRIDGE, Ada (1844–1926) b Norfolk, migrated 1870; 3 vols poetry, including *Unspoken Thoughts* (1887), 17 novels, 1 vol. short fiction, 2 vols autobiography.

CAMPBELL, Marion (1948–   ) writer of short fiction and 2 novels, *Lines of Flight* (1985) and *Not Being Miriam* (1988); lived for several years in France.

CAPPIELLO, Rosa (1942–   ) *b* Naples, migrated 1971; 2 novels, including *Paese fortunato* (1981), translated as *Oh Lucky Country* (1985).

CAREY, Peter (1943–   ) advertising agency principal, novelist, writer of short fiction; 3 novels including *Bliss* (1981) and *Oscar and Lucinda* (1988), 2 collections short fiction; Booker Prize 1988.

CLARKE, Marcus (1846–81) *b* London, migrated 1863; leading Melbourne journalist; 5 published plays, 3 novels including *His Natural Life* (serialised 1870–2), 19 vols short fiction/articles, including *Old Tales of a Young Country* (1871).

COOK, James (1728–79) commanded HMS *Endeavour* in expedition to search for the Great South Land, reached Botany Bay, 28 April 1770 and named whole of east coast 'New South Wales', claiming possession for Britain.

COSTELLO, Moya (1952–   ) part-time tutor in adult education, associated with collective producing *Womenspeak*; first prose collection *Kites in Jakarta* (1985).

COUANI, Anna (1948–   ) *b* Sydney of Greek-Polish descent; poet and editor, 3 vols short fiction including *Italy* (1977) and *The Train* (1983); edited *Telling Ways: Australian Women's Experimental Writing* (1988); joint founder of Sea Cruise Books.

CURLEWIS, Jean (1899–1930) daughter of Ethel Turner and Judge H. R. Curlewis; 3 novels, 5 children's books, collaborated with mother on *The Sunshine Family* (1923).

DAMPIER, William (1652–1715) naval trader and privateer; in 1688 explored north-west coast of Western Australia; notable writer of voyage narratives.

DAVIS, Jack (1918–   ) Noongah people, WA; author, actor, director; 2 vols poetry including *The First-Born and Other Poems* (1970); 5 plays including *Kullark* and *Barungin* (1988); ed. *Identity* 1973–9.

DAVISON, Frank Dalby (1893–1970) 5 novels including *Man-shy* (serialised 1923–5), 2 travel books, 2 collections shorter fiction.

DAWE, Bruce (1930–   ) 11 vols poetry including *No Fixed Address* (1962), poems collected as *Sometimes Gladness* (1978, 1983, 1988), 1 vol. short fiction; Patrick White Literary Award 1980.

DOBSON, Rosemary (1920–   ) poet, publisher, translator from Russian, artist; 10 volumes of poetry including *Cock Crow* (1965), editor of *Sisters Poets 1* anthology (1979).

DRANSFIELD, Michael (1948–73) associated with neo-Romanticism and drug culture; 6 vols poetry (3 published posthumously), including *Streets of the Long Voyage* (1970).

EE TIANG HONG (1933–   ) *b* Malacca (now Malaysia), migrated to Western Australia 1975; 3 vols poetry including *Myths for a Wilderness* (Kuala Lumpur 1976).

FARMER, Beverley (1941–   ) spent 3 years in Greece; 1 novel *Alone* (1980), 2 vols short fiction, *Milk* (1983) and *Home Time* (1985); NSW Premier's Award 1984.

FARRELL, John (1851–1904) son of Irish immigrants to goldfields 1852; contributor to *Boomerang*, *Worker*, *Bulletin*; 2 vols poetry including *My Sundowner and Other Poems* (1904).

FIELD, Barron (1786–1846) migrated 1819–24 as NSW Supreme Court judge; *First Fruits of Australian Poetry* (1819) first book of poems published in Australia.

FITZGERALD, R. D. (1902–87) poet, literary commentator, surveyor; 10 vols poetry, including *Moonlight Acre* (1938), 1 vol. prose (1976).

FOOTT, Mary Hannay (1846–1918) *b* Glasgow, migrated 1853; literary editor *Queenslander* for a decade; 2 vols poetry, including *Where the Pelican Builds and Other Poems* (1885).

FRANKLIN, Miles (1879–1954) grew up in Monaro and Goulburn regions of NSW;

1906–32 lived in England and USA; 12 novels including *My Brilliant Career* (1901), some published as by 'Brent of Bin Bin'.

FURPHY, Joseph ('Tom Collins') (1843–1912) 1 vol. poetry, 3 novels, including *Such is Life* (1903); poor sales and little recognition in his lifetime but promoted afterwards by Kate Baker who provided Miles Franklin with material for a biography.

GARDNER, Silvana (1942–   ) *b* Dalmatia, migrated with parents as refugees; 5 vols poetry including *When Sunday Comes* (1982).

GARNER, Helen (1942–   ) 2 novels, including *Monkey Grip* (1977), 2 vols short fiction including *Postcards from Surfers* (1985), film scripts.

GENCER, Gün (1944–   ) *b* Turkey; poet, playwright, dramaturge, director; graduated from NIDA 1976.

GERSTAECKER, Friedrich (1816–72) *b* Hamburg, spent less than a year in Australia in 1851; handbook for German immigrants, 2 fictional works including *The Two Convicts* (1857), travel narrative.

GIBSON, G. H. ('Ironbark') (1846–1921) *b* Plymouth, migrated NZ 1869, Australia 1874; 3 vols verse, including *Southerly Busters* (1878).

GILBERT, Kevin (1933–   ) Irish father, mother of Aboriginal descent; established Kalari Aboriginal Art Gallery; 2 vols poetry, including *People ARE Legends* (1978), 2 prose works, collection of interviews; play 'The Cherry Pickers' first contemporary work by Aboriginal playwright performed in Australia; ed., *Inside Black Australia* (1988).

GILMORE, Dame Mary (1865–1962) 6 vols poetry, including *Marri'd and Other Verses*, 3 vols prose; ed. Women's Page of Sydney *Worker* 1908–31; joined William Lane's New Australia venture in Paraguay 1896.

GORDON, Adam Lindsay (1833–70) came to South Australia 1853, mounted policeman and property owner, author of many stories and poems about horses including the poems in *Bush Ballads and Galloping Rhymes* (1870); committed suicide because of financial failure 1870.

GRENVILLE, Kate (1950–   ) 3 novels, including *Lilian's Story* (1985) which won the *Australian*/Vogel Award and *Joan Makes History* (1988); 1 vol. short fiction, *Bearded Ladies* (1984).

HALL, Rodney (1935–   ) *b* England, migrated after 1939–45 War; 11 vols poetry including *Selected Poems* (1975), 5 novels including *Just Relations* (1982); poetry editor *The Australian* 1967–78, edited 3 posthumous vols of Dransfield's poetry; Miles Franklin Award 1982.

HARDY, FRANK (1917–   ) 6 novels, including *Power Without Glory* (1950) which was subject of defamation action and *But the Dead are Many* (1975), 6 vols short fiction/yarns; also journalist, songwriter, and writer for radio and TV.

HARFORD, Lesbia (1891–1927) 1 novel, 2 vols poetry including *The Poems of Lesbia Harford* (1941), all published posthumously.

HARPUR, Charles (1813–68) 3 vols poetry, including *The Tower of the Dream* (1865), 3 pamphlets poetry, 1 play; suffered from many corrupt editions until *Poetical Works* (1984) edited by Elizabeth Perkins.

HARWOOD, Gwen (1920–   ) poet, musician; 4 vols poetry, including *Poems* (1963), librettos; Patrick White Literary Award 1978.

HERBERT, Xavier (1901–84) 3 novels, including *Capricornia* (1938) and *Poor Fellow My Country* (1975), 1 novella, 1 vol. short fiction, autobiography; Miles Franklin Award 1975.

HEWETT, Dorothy (1923–   ) 1 novel, 6 vols poetry including *Alice in Wormland* (1987), 8 published plays including *The Chapel Perilous* (1972).

HOPE, A. D. (1907–   ) poet and academic; 11 vols poetry including *The Wandering Islands* (1955), *Collected Poems* (1972) and *Antechinus* (1981); 3 vols essays, various critical and dramatic works; Ingram Merrill Award, New York 1969, Robert Frost Award 1976.

HOWITT, Richard (1799–1870) *b* England, migrated 1840–44; account of experience in colony includes selection of verse, *Impressions of Australia Felix during four years' Residence in that Colony* (1845).

HUMPHRIES, Barry (1934–   ) revue artist whose characters include Dame Edna Everage, Sandy Stone, Sir Les Patterson (film 1987); collaborated with Nicholas Garland on Barry McKenzie comic strip; published under various characters' names, including *A Nice Night's Entertainment* (1981).

INGAMELLS, Rex (1913–55) founder of Jindyworobak movement and editor of *Jindyworobak Anthologies* (1938–53); 7 vols poetry including *Gumtops* (1935) and *The Great South Land* (1951) which won Grace Leven Prize, 1 novel, 1 children's story.

IRELAND, David (1927–   ) 7 novels, including *The Chantic Bird* (1968), *A Woman of the Future* (1979) and *City of Women* (1981); Miles Franklin Award 1971, 1976, 1979.

JACKEY JACKEY (*d* 1854) Aborigine from near Muswellbrook NSW who accompanied Edward Kennedy in expedition to Cape York Peninsula 1848, burying Kennedy after he had been fatally speared and returning with bravery and superb bushcraft to report events.

JOHNSTON, George (1912–70) series of thriller novels under pseudonym 'Shane Martin', 4 accounts of war experiences, 3 collaborative novels with wife, Charmian Clift, semi-autobiographical trilogy including *My Brother Jack* (1964).

JOLLEY, Elizabeth (1923–   ) *b* Birmingham, migrated to WA 1959; 3 vols short fiction including *Woman in a Lampshade* (1983), 8 novels, including *Mr Scobie's Riddle* (1982) and *The Sugar Mother* (1988); *Age* Book of the Year Award 1982.

KANTARIS, Sylvia (1936–   ) *b* England, lived in Australia 1962–73; 5 vols poetry including *The Sea at the Door* (1985).

KEFALA, Antigone (1935–   ) *b* Romania of Greek parents; lived in Romania, Greece, NZ, Australia; 2 vols poetry, including *The Alien* (1973), 2 novellas under title *The First Journey* (1975), novel *The Island* (1984).

KENDALL, Henry (1839–82) *b* Milton, NSW; spend childhood in Illawarra and Clarence River districts, NSW; 3 vols poetry including *Leaves from Australian Forests* (1869).

KENEALLY, Thomas (1935–   ) 18 novels including *Bring Larks and Heroes* (1967), *The Chant of Jimmie Blacksmith* (1972) and *Schindler's Ark* (1982); film and TV adaptations and script writing; Miles Franklin Award 1967, 1968; Cook Bicentenary Award 1970; Booker Prize 1982.

KINGSLEY, Henry (1830–76) *b* Northamptonshire, migrated 1853–58; brother of English novelist Charles Kingsley; Australian material in 3 vols short fiction and 4 novels, including *The Recollections of Geoffry Hamlyn* (1859).

KOCH, C. J. (1932–   ) *b* Hobart, lived for extensive periods in Europe and America, travelled in Asia; 4 novels, including *The Year of Living Dangerously* (1978) and *The Doubleman* (1985), 1 collection of essays; *Age* Book of the Year Award 1978; National Book Council Award 1979.

KOTZE, Stefan von (1869–1909) *b* Germany, migrated 18??; 1 vol. short fiction, *Australian Sketches* (1945) translated from 1903 German version, which was translated from English originals in Australian press.

LANG, John Dunmore (1799–1878) *b* Scotland, migrated 1823 as Sydney's first Presbyterian minister; 4 vols history, 3 vols poetry.

LANGLEY, Eve (1908–74) 2 novels, *The Pea Pickers* (1942) and *White Topee* (1954); spent later life as recluse in Blue Mountains.

LAWLER, Ray (1921–   ) actor, producer, playwright; prize-winning play *Summer of the Seventeenth Doll* (1955, published 1957), several other plays for stage and television; now lives in Europe.

LAWSON, Henry (1867–1922) *b* Grenfell, son of Louisa Lawson, moved to Sydney, 1883; wrote extensively in verse, short fiction, sketches and essays for *The*

Bulletin, Boomerang, Worker, Truth; periods in New Zealand and England; writing declined after about 1902.

LAWSON, Louisa ('Dora Falconer') (1848–1920) *b* Mudgee, NSW; separated from husband and moved to Sydney with children, 1883; active in spiritualist, republican and feminist movements, founded *The Dawn* (1888), first Australian feminist journal; 1 novel, 1 vol. poetry.

LINDSAY, Norman (1879–1969) painter, etcher, illustrator, cartoonist; 11 novels, including *Redheap* (1930), 2 children's novels, including *The Magic Pudding* (1918), 4 vols aesthetic/philosophical writing, autobiography *My Mask* (1970).

LOWER, Lennie (1903–47) humorous columnist with various newspapers; novel, *Here's Luck* (1930), 5 vols short fiction.

MACKENZIE, Kenneth ('Seaforth') (1913–55) 4 novels, including *The Young Desire It* (1937), 4 vols poetry, 2 published posthumously.

MAIDEN, Jennifer (1949–   ) 8 vols poetry, including *The Border Loss* (1979), 1 novel, and a major collection of poetry and prose, *The Warm Thing* (1983).

'MALLEY, Ern' the supposed author of 16 avant-garde poems sent to Max Harris, co-editor of *Angry Penguins* in 1944; actually written as a hoax against modernism by James McAuley and Harold Stewart.

MALOUF, David (1934–   ) *b* Brisbane, alternates residence between Australia and Tuscany; 6 vols poetry, including *First Things Last*, 1 vol. short fiction, 3 novels, including *Johnno* (1975), 4 novellas, 1 vol. autobiography, *12 Edmonstone St* (1984); opera libretto of *Voss*; Pascall Prize 1988.

MARTIN, Arthur Patchett (1851–1902) editor *Melbourne Review*; edited 3 anthologies; 3 vols poetry, 2 vols history, biography; *The Beginnings of an Australian Literature* (1898) one of earliest Australian literary surveys.

MARTIN, David (1915–   ) *b* Hungary, Jewish family, grew up in Germany, migrated 1949; 8 vols poetry, 2 vols short fiction, including *Foreigners* (1982), *The Hero of Too* (1965), numerous children's books, plays and travel books.

MASTERS, Olga (1919–86) after working as a journalist on south coast NSW turned to fiction late in life; 2 novels, including *Loving Daughters* (1984), 3 vols short fiction, including *The Home Girls* (1982); 1 vol. short fiction, 1 novel published posthumously.

McAULEY, James (1917–76) 9 vols poetry, including *Under Aldebaran* (1946), 4 vols prose; founding editor *Quadrant* (1956), 4 vols literary criticism; with Harold Stewart perpetrated 'Ern Malley' hoax (1944).

McKELLAR, Hazel (1930–   ) Kooma clan, south-west Queensland, founding member of Cunnamulla Australian Native Welfare Association; author of *Matya-Mundu* (1984).

MODJESKA, Drusilla *b* England, came to Australia 1971; historian and feminist, author of *Exiles at Home: Australian Women Writers 1925–1945* (1981), co-editor of *The Poems of Lesbia Harford* (1984).

MOORE, George Fletcher (1798–1886) *b* Ireland, migrated 1830; 2 vols journals/letters, Aboriginal vocabulary (1842).

MOORHEAD, Finola (1947–   ) full-time writer of novels, short fiction, plays since 1973; author of *Quilt: A Collection of Prose* (1985), *Remember the Tarantella* (1987).

MOORHOUSE, Frank (1938–   ) 8 vols short fiction ('discontinuous narratives'), including *The Americans, Baby* (1972), *Tales of Mystery and Romance* (1977) and *Forty Seventeen* (1988), 1 novel, screenplays; associated with radical group of writers, artists, film makers, academics gathered in Balmain in late 1960s; *Age* Book of the Year Award 1988.

MORGAN, Sally (1951–   ) grew up in Perth unaware until about the age of 15 of her Aboriginal descent; subsequent investigation uncovered her family and a relationship with the Drake-Brockmans, a pioneering white family; painter, and author of *My Place* (1987).

MORRISON, John (1904–   ) *b* England, migrated 1923; member Realist Writers

Group; 2 novels, 1 vol. essays/memoirs, 5 vols short fiction, including *Twenty-Three* (1962).

MUDIE, Ian (1911–76) 9 vols poetry, including *Corroboree to the Sun* (1940) and *Selected Poems* (1976), 2 histories; edited numerous anthologies; associated with Jindyworobak movement.

MUDROOROO NAROGIN (Noongah people, WA; formerly known as Colin Johnson) (1939–   ); 2 vols poetry, 4 novels, including *Wild Cat Falling* (1965), which was first novel published by an Aboriginal writer, and *Doin Wildcat* (1988).

MURDOCH, Sir Walter (1874–1970) *b* Scotland, migrated 1884; weekly columnist on *Argus, Herald, Australian*; 1912–39 Professor of English, University of WA; 17 vols essays, biography Alfred Deakin, numerous school texts.

MURRAY, Les A. (1938–   ) *b* Nabiac, north coast NSW; 9 vols poetry, including *The Ilex Tree* (1965, with Geoffrey Lehmann) and *The Vernacular Republic: Poems 1951–1981*, 2 vols essays including *The Peasant Mandarin* (1978), 1 verse novel, edited 2 anthologies.

NEILSON, John Shaw (1872–1942) 8 vols poetry (3 published posthumously), including *Heart of Spring* (1919); literary career strongly influenced by editor A. G. Stephens.

NOWRA, Louis (1950–   ) 8 plays including *Inner Voices* (1977) and *The Golden Age* (1985), 3 novels, including *Palu* (1987), collaborated as lyricist with composer Sarah de Jong; screenplays and film scripts.

O'DOWD, Bernard (1866–1953) 5 vols poetry, including *Dawnward?* (1903), 1 vol. essays; part of radical nationalist movement.

OODGEROO NOONUCCAL (Noonuccal clan, Stradbroke Island; formerly known as Kath Walker) (1920–   ) leading figure in Aboriginal activist movement; 1 vol. short fiction, *Stradbroke Dreamtime* (1972), 3 vols poetry, including *We Are Going* (1964).

PALMER, Nettie (1885–1964) wife of Vance Palmer; prolific literary journalist; 2 vols poetry, journal, 4 critical prose works, including first full-length study of Henry Handel Richardson.

PALMER, Vance (1885–1959) husband of Nettie Palmer; 2 vols poetry, 2 vols plays, 4 vols short fiction, 16 novels, including *Golconda* trilogy (1948, 1957, 1959), 5 vols essays, including influential *The Legend of the Nineties* (1954); abridged Furphy's *Such Is Life* (1937).

PATERSON, A. B. ('Banjo') (1864–1941) raised on sheep station near Yass, NSW; solicitor and journalist, Sydney; best-known as balladist and sporting writer; engaged in *Bulletin* debate, 1892–93, about representation of bush life.

PENTON, Brian (1904–51) journalist; 2 novels, including *Landtakers* (1934), 3 polemical/iconoclastic works, including *Advance Australia—Where?* (1943).

PFEIFFER, Paul   Adelaide poet, contributor to *Jindyworobak Anthologies* and *Angry Penguins* magazine.

PHILLIPS, A.A. (1900–85) *b* Melbourne; schoolmaster, Wesley College 1925–71; editor numerous collections of Australian writing; critical articles, 2 collections criticism, including *The Australian Tradition* (1958).

Π O (Peter Oustabasidis) (1951–   ) *b* Greece, migrated in infancy; draughtsman; 7 vols poetry, including *Fitzroy Brothel* (1974) and *Re: The National Neurosis: Ockers* (1983); editor of and contributor to, various underground magazines.

PORTER, Hal (1911–84) raised Bairnsdale, Vic.; schoolteacher, librarian, theatrical producer; in Japan 1949–50; 3 novels, 3 plays, 3 vols poetry, 3 autobiographies including *The Watcher on the Cast Iron Balcony* (1963), theatrical biography; won many Australian literary awards.

PORTER, Peter (1929–   ) *b* Brisbane, left for England 1951; 14 vols poetry, including *The Last of England* (1970) and *Collected Poems* (1983), 2 collaborations with painter, Arthur Boyd.

PRAED, Rosa (1851–1935) *b* Queensland, moved to England 1875; author of over 40 works of fiction, almost half associated with Australia, including *Policy and*

Passion (1881); 2 vols of reminiscences, including *My Australian Girlhood* (1902).

PRICHARD, Katharine Susannah (1883–1969) *b* Fiji; founding member of Communist Party of Australia; 2 plays, 2 vols poetry, 5 vols short fiction, 12 novels including *Working Bullocks* (1926), *Coonardoo* (1929).

'RICHARDSON, Henry Handel' (Ethel Robertson) (1870–1946) moved to Germany in 1888, then to England in 1903; 6 novels, including *The Fortunes of Richard Mahony* (1917, 1925, 1929), unfinished autobiography, *Myself When Young* (1948).

ROBINSON, Roland (1912–   ) associated with Jindyworobak movement; 9 vols poetry, including *Selected Poems* (1983), 5 vols prose reflecting interest in Aboriginal lore, 3 vols autobiography.

ROUGHSEY, Dick (1924–   ) *b* Langunarnji Island, Gulf of Carpentaria; painter using both Aboriginal and Western methods; 3 vols Aboriginal legend, 1 vol. autobiography.

'RUDD, Steele' (Arthur Hoey Davis) (1868–1935) *b* Drayton, Darling Downs, Qld; moved to Brisbane, 1885; public servant; frequent contributor to *Bulletin*; founded *Steele Rudd's Magazine* (1904); 10 vols of Rudd family sketches, 6 plays, and 14 other vols fiction.

SHAPCOTT, Thomas (1935–   ) *b* Ipswich, Qld; 13 vols poetry, including *Shabby-town Calendar* (1975), 5 novels, including *White Stag of Exile* (1984), 1 vol. short fiction; edited several anthologies; Director, Literature Board, Australia Council (1983–9).

SINNETT, Frederick (1830–66) *b* Germany, migrated 1849; helped found *Melbourne Punch* (1855) and wrote for other papers; 2 vols historical accounts; first extended essay on Australian literature.

SKRZYNECKI, Peter (1945–   ) *b* Germany, of Ukrainian-Polish descent, migrated 1949; 5 vols poetry, including *Immigrant Chronicle* (1975), 1 vol. short fiction, 1 novel; edited anthology of multicultural writing.

SLESSOR, Kenneth (1901–71) *b* Orange, NSW, lived in Sydney; Australian Army Official War Correspondent, 1940–44; 9 vols poetry, including *One Hundred Poems 1919–1939* (1944); notable journalist, critic and reviewer.

SOUTHALL, Ivan (1921–   ) prolific writer of fiction and non-fiction for children; 3 vols based on war experiences; Children's Book of the Year Award, 1966, 1968, 1971, 1976.

SPENCE, Catherine Helen (1825–1910) *b* Scotland, came to Australia 1839; 7 novels including *Clara Morison: A Tale of South Australia during the Gold Fever* (1854) and *Handfasted* (not published until 1984); tracts on social reform, feminism (including women's right to vote), religion; autobiography (unfinished).

STEAD, Christina (1902–83) went abroad 1928, returned 1974; 11 novels, including *For Love Alone* (1944), 2 vols short fiction, including *Ocean of Story* (1985); none of her work published in Australia until 1965; Patrick White Award 1974.

STEPHENS, A. G. (1865–1933) *b* Toowoomba, Qld; wrote for *Boomerang*; sub-editor and later literary editor of *Bulletin*, founder of 'Red Page' (1896), manager *Bulletin* publishing section, 1897–1906; 1 vol. essays, *Red Pagan* (1904), 2 vols poetry, 2 novels, 2 plays; founded *Bookfellow* (1899–1926).

STEPHENSEN, P. R. ('Inky') (1901–65) *b* Biggenden, Qld; assoc. with London literary circles and Left-wing politics in 1920s, founded isolationist-nationalist Right-wing Australia First movement in 1941, interned until 1945; as publisher and publicist, influential in Australian literary circles in 1930s.

STEWART, Douglas (1913–85) *b* New Zealand, migrated 1938, editor of *Bulletin's* 'Red Page' (1940–61), literary editor for publishers Angus & Robertson (1961–71); 11 vols poetry including *Collected Poems* (1967), 6 verse plays, including *Fire on the Snow* (1944), 1 vol. short fiction.

STIVENS, Dal (1911–   ) founding President Australian Society of Authors (1963); 8 vols short fiction, including *The Unicorn* (1976), 4 novels including *Jimmy Brockett* (1951); Miles Franklin Award 1970, Patrick White Award 1981.

STONE, Louis (1871–1935) *b* England, migrated 1884; 2 novels, *Jonah* (1911) and *Betty Wayside* (1915), 2 plays, including *The Lap of the Gods* (1923).

STOW, Randolph (1935–   ) *b* WA, lived in England since 1966; 7 novels, including *To The Islands* (1958, revised edition 1982) and *Visitants* (1979), 4 vols poetry, popular children's novel *Midnite* (1967), libretti; numerous literary awards.

'TASMA' (Jessie Couvreur) (1848–97) *b* London, came to Australia as child with her family, lived later years in Brussels; 6 novels including *Uncle Piper of Piper's Hill* (1889), short fiction.

TAYLOR, Andrew (1940–   ) poet and academic; 7 vols poetry, including *The Invention of Fire* (1976) and *Selected Poems* (1982).

TENCH, Watkin (?1758–1833) *b* England; travelled with First Fleet; in expeditions which discovered Nepean/Hawkesbury River; 2 accounts of colony, republished as *Sydney's First Four Years* (1961).

TRANTER, John (1943–   ) poet, editor, critic; 6 vols poetry, including *Crying in Early Infancy* (1977) and *Selected Poems* (1982); edited *The New Australian Poetry* (1979).

TSALOUMAS, Dimitris (1921–   ) *b* Greek island of Leros, migrated 1952; 3 vols poetry, including *The Observatory* (1983); several vols poetry in Greece; National Book Council Award 1983.

WALWICZ, Ania (1951–   ) *b* Poland, migrated 1963; 1 vol. poetry *Writing* (1982), numerous public and radio performances of poetry, exhibitions of painting.

'WARUNG, Price' (William Astley) (1855–1911) radical journalist, prolific *Bulletin* short-story contributor, 5 vols short fiction including *Tales of the Convict System* (1892).

WATEN, Judah (1911–85) *b* Russia, Jewish family, migrated 1914; 7 novels, including *The Unbending* (1954), 2 vols short autobiographical fiction including *Alien Son* (1952).

WEBB, Francis (1925–73) 6 vols poetry including *A Drum for Ben Boyd* (1948); some composition during (frequent) periods in hospital for schizophrenia.

WELLER, Archie (1958–   ) *b* Perth, Noongah people; 1 novel *The Day of the Dog* (1981), 1 vol. short fiction *Going Home* (1986), co-editor vol. of Aboriginal writing; runner-up *Australian*/Vogel Award 1980.

WENTWORTH, William Charles (1793–1872) 1 historical account, poem *Australasia* (1823); published *Australian* newspaper; instrumental in gaining self-government for NSW, chairman of Constitution-drafting committee.

WENZ, Paul (1869–1939) *b* France, migrated 1892 after extensive travels; 2 vols short fiction, 4 novels, only work in English is *Diary of a New Chum* (1908).

WHITE, Patrick (1912–   ) 12 novels, 2 vols short fiction, 2 vols poetry, 8 published plays, autobiography *Flaws in the Glass* (1981), Nobel Prize 1973 (used to establish Patrick White Literary Award), Miles Franklin Award 1957, 1961.

WILDING, Michael (1942–   ) *b* England, migrated 1969; 4 vols short fiction, account of Australian 'Utopia' in Paraguay, 4 novels, including *Pacific Highway* (1982); established publishers Wild & Woolley; associated with *Tabloid Story*.

WILLIAMSON, David (1942–   ) 12 published plays including *The Removalists* (1972) and *Emerald City* (1987), filmscripts including *Gallipoli, Travelling North*.

WRIGHT, Judith (1915–   ) *b* Armidale; poet, literary critic, editor, anthologist, conservationist; 14 vols poetry, including *The Moving Image* (1946) and *Phantom Dwelling* (1985), 2 vols family history, 1 vol. essays, seminal book of Australian poetry criticism.

CHRONOLOGICAL TABLE OF AUSTRALIAN LITERARY HISTORY

(Abbreviations: *b* born; *d* dies; D drama; F fiction; P (non-fictional) prose; V verse)

DATE	HISTORICAL/CULTURAL EVENTS
40 000 years BP (before the present)	Aborigines living in Australia (earliest site so far dated is on Swan River, Western Australia)
12 000 years BP	Tasmania separated from continent by rise in sea level
8 000– 6 500 years BP	New Guinea separated from continent by rise in sea level
1521–24	Portuguese explorer, Mendonça, sails east from Malacca and then south along east coast of Australia and passes through Bass Strait (?)
1606	Dutch explorer, Willem Jansz, in *Duyfken* explores Cape York Peninsula, but does not recognise it as part of another continent Spanish explorer, De Quiros, reaches Vanuatu, naming it Austrialia del Espiritu Santo; his second-in-command, Torres, sails through Torres Strait
1616	Dutchman Dirk Hartog in *Eendracht* nails pewter dish to a pole on island off WA coast
1627	*Batavia* wrecked on Houtman's Abrolhos; mutiny and massacre by crew
1642	Abel Tasman in *Heemskerk* and *Zeehan*, commissioned by the Dutch Governor General of the East Indies, explores south-west Tasmania
1688	William Dampier in *Cygnet* explores north-west coast; book published 1697; further exploration of west coast in 1699
1770	Captain Cook 'discovers' Australia and takes possession of the eastern coast (named New South Wales) for King George III
1774	Matthew Flinders *b*
1776	J.H. Tuckey *b*
1778	Gregory Blaxland *b*
1779	Captain James Cook *d*
1782	James Hardy Vaux *b* (?) Thomas Wells *b*
1786	Barron Field *b*
1788	First Fleet arrives in Australia with convicts; Captain Arthur Phillip formally proclaims the colony of New South Wales at Sydney Cove; Count de la Perouse arrives in Botany Bay; first conflict between Aborigines and settlers at Rushcutters Bay; penal station established at Norfolk Island

Date	Publications	Literary/Cultural Events
1789	Anon (ed.), *The Voyage of Governor Phillip to Botany Bay* (also contains Erasmus Darwin's 'A Visit of Hope to Sydney Cove near Botany Bay') (P) Tench, Watkin (1758?), *A Narrative of the Expedition to Botany Bay* (P)	*The Voyage of Governor Phillip* is the first book about Australia to be published in London First dramatic production in Australia (George Farquhar's *The Recruiting Officer*) performed by convicts in Sydney Many Aborigines die of smallpox, introduced by Europeans
1790	White, John (1756?), *Journal of a Voyage to New South Wales* (P)	W. C. Wentworth *b*
1791		Henry Savery *b*
1792		William Howitt *b*
1793	Hunter, John (1737), *An Historical Journal of the Transactions at Port Jackson and Norfolk Island* (P) Tench, Watkin (1758?), *A Complete Account of the Settlement at Port Jackson and Norfolk Island* (P)	William Charles Wentworth *b* The first book to deal solely with the natural history of Australia (*Zoology and Botany of New Holland and the Isles Adjacent*, by George Shaw and James Edward Smith) published in London
1794	Johnson, Richard (1753), *An Address to the Inhabitants of the Colonies, established in New South Wales and Norfolk Island* (P)	
1795		First Fleet wooden printing press used for first time by George Hughes
1796		First theatre opened in Sydney by Robert Sidaway
1798	Collins, David (1756), *An Account of the English Colony in New South Wales*, Vol. 1 (Vol. 2, 1802) (P)	George Fletcher Moore *b* Charles Rowcroft *b*
1799		Richard Howitt *b* John Dunmore Lang *b* 'Henry Melville' *b* 6 years of Aboriginal resistance to white settlement in Hawkesbury and Parramatta districts begins ('The Black War')
1801		'Ticket-of-leave' system introduced, enabling convicts to work for themselves

DATE	PUBLICATIONS	LITERARY/CULTURAL EVENTS
1802	The first book published in Australia, the *New South Wales General Standing Orders*, issued in Sydney by George Howe, the 'father' of printing in Australia	R. H. Horne *b*
1803		Settlement established on Derwent River; shifted to site of Hobart 1804
		Sydney Gazette and New South Wales Advertiser (−1842) founded by Governor King, edited and printed by George Howe
1804	'CS' (?), 'The Vision of Melancholy, A Fragment' (V)	John Gould *b*
		'The Vision of Melancholy' is first poem published locally (*Sydney Gazette*, 4 March)
		Van Diemen's Land settlers authorised to shoot about 50 Aborigines
		Castle Hill 'rebellion' by about 300 Irish convicts who marched on Parramatta; Roman Catholic church services prohibited
1805	Tuckey (1776), *An Account of a Voyage to Establish a Colony at Port Phillip in Bass's Strait* (P)	Alexander Harris *b*
1807		Charles Tompson *b*
1808		Anna Maria Bunn *b*
		W. H. Christie *b*
		James Tucker *b* (?)
1810 ·	Robinson, Michael Massey (1744), *Odes* (V), in *Sydney Gazette*	C. T. Knowles *b*
		David Collins *d*
		Lachlan Macquarie begins term of office as Governor (1810−21)
1811	Mann, David Dickinson (?1775), *The Present Picture of New South Wales* (P)	
1812		Louisa Anne Meredith *b*
		British suppliers withdraw credit to colony; liquidity crisis and recession (−1815)
1813		Charles Harpur *b*
1814	Flinders (1774), *A Voyage to Terra Australis* (P)	William Woolls *b*
		Matthew Flinders *d*

Date	Publications	Literary/Cultural Events
1815		Henry Parkes *b*
		Mary T. Vidal *b*
1816		Friedrich Gerstaecker *b*
		John George Lang *b*
		J. H. Tuckey *d*
1818	Thomas Wells (1782), *Michael Howe, the Last and Worst of the Bushrangers of Van Diemen's Land* (P)	William Forster *b*
1819	Field (1786), *First Fruits of Australian Poetry* (V)	First book of verse locally published by George Howe
	Wentworth (1790), *A Statistical, Historical and Political Description of the Colony of New South Wales and its Dependent Settlements in Van Diemen's Land* (P)	
1820	Oxley, John (?1785), *Journals of Two Expeditions into the Interior of New South Wales* (P)	Raffaello Carboni *b*
1821		John Hunter *d*
		The first locally produced magazine, *Australian Magazine*, 1821–22, published in Sydney by George Howe
		Port Macquarie opened as a penal settlement for incorrigible convicts
1822		J. R. Houlding *b*
		George French Angas *b*
		Macquarie Harbour on west of Van Diemen's Land opened as a penal settlement for incorrigible convicts
		Convict shepherds strike for more money; organiser, James Straiter, brutally punished
1823	Blaxland (1778), *A Journal of a Tour of Discovery across the Blue Mountains* (P)	
	Wentworth (1790), *Australasia* (V) first book of verse by an Australian-born author to be published in Britain	
1824		J. L. Michael *b*
		Australian (Sydney, 1824–48) founded, the first privately-owned newspaper in the colony
		Penal settlement established at Moreton Bay; trading settlement established at Melville Island (abandoned 1829)
		Jack Donohoe sentenced in Dublin to transportation

DATE	PUBLICATIONS	LITERARY/CULTURAL EVENTS
1825		Catherine Helen Spence *b*
		Australian Subscription Library and Reading Room established in Sydney
		Military settlement established at King George Sound (Albany, WA)
		Norfolk Island penal settlement revived
1826	Tompson (1807), *Wild Notes, from the Lyre of a Native Minstrel* (V)	T. A. Browne ('Rolf Boldrewood') *b*
		Rachel Henning *b*
		Michael Massey Robinson *d*
		Tompson's *Wild Notes* (published in Sydney) was first book of verse of a native-born poet
1827	Cunningham (1789), *Two Years in New South Wales* (P) 'Pindar Juvenal', *The Van Diemen's Land Warriors* (V)	Caroline Leakey *b* Richard Johnson *d*
1828		D. H. Deniehy *b*
		Richard Rowe *b*
		John Oxley *d*
		David Burn, *The Bushrangers* (D), produced in Edinburgh
		White population shown as 36 595 in first official Census in NSW
1829	Savery (1791), *The Hermit in Van Diemen's Land* (F)	Sydney Shipwrights' Association formed (first trade union in NSW)
		First direct mail to England on *Thomas Laurie*
1830	Savery (1791), *Quintus Servinton* (F)	Henry Kingsley *b*
		Frederick Sinnett *b*
		Quintus Servinton was the first novel written in Australia to be published in book form (in Hobart)
		Governor Arthur attempts to drive all remaining Tasmanian Aborigines across the island by a 'Black Line' of some 2000 men
		Port Arthur penal station established near Hobart
1831		Robert Sealy *b*
		Charles Thatcher *b*
		Sydney Herald begins (since 1842 titled *Sydney Morning Herald*)

Date	Publications	Literary/Cultural Events
1832	Woolls (1814), *The Voyage* (V)	John White *d*
1833	Sturt (1795), *Two Expeditions into the Interior of South Australia* (P) Woolls (1814), *Australia* (V)	Adam Lindsay Gordon *b* George Gordon McCrae *b* Watkin Tench *d* Theatre Royal (Sydney) founded (1833–38) Governor Stirling leads attack on about 80 Aborigines at Pinjarra, Western Australia
1834	'Melville' (1799), *The Bushrangers* (D)	Caroline Atkinson *b*
1835	Thomas, E. H. (1801?), *The Bandit of the Rhine* (D)	James Brunton Stephens *b* *The Bandit of the Rhine* (now lost) was the first Australian play published in book form John Batman arrives at Port Phillip Bay and signs 'treaty' with Aborigines for ceding of 243 000 hectares of land
1836	Martin (*c* 1803), *History of Australasia* (P)	G. B. Barton *b* Charles Darwin in Australia South Australia proclaimed colony Select Committee of the British House of Commons (1836–7) acknowledges Aborigines' 'plain and sacred right' to their land
1837	Lang, John Dunmore (1799), *Transportation and Colonisation* (P)	E. H. Thomas *d*
1838	Bunn (1808), *The Guardian* (F) Martin, James (1820), *The Australian Sketch Book* (P) Woolls (1814), *Miscellanies in Prose and Verse* (P, F, V)	*The Guardian* was first novel printed and published in New South Wales and first written by a woman to be published in Australia 'Myall Creek Massacre' in north-central NSW in which 12 whites kill 28 Aborigines in reprisal for killing some whites; 7 white men subsequently found guilty of the murder of an Aboriginal child and hanged End of system of assigning convict labour to settlers in NSW First German Lutheran settlers, fleeing religious persecution, arrive at Port Adelaide Caroline Chisholm arrives in Sydney Severe drought in NSW (–1840)
1839		Henry Kendall *b*

Date	Publications	Literary/Cultural Events
1840	Hill, Fidelia (?1790), *Poems and Recollections of the Past* (V)	First book of verse written by a woman published in Australia
		Transportation of convicts to NSW ends
		Depression of 1840s begins
1841	Christie (1808), *A Love Story* (F)	*A Mother's Offering to her Children* 'by a Lady Long Resident in NSW' (Charlotte Barton), first children's book
1842	Burn (1799?), *Plays and Fugitive Pieces* (D)	Henry Savery *d*
	Lang, John George (1816), *Legends of Australia* (F)	*Plays and Fugitive Pieces* the first collection of plays to be published in Australia
	Parkes (1815), *Stolen Moments* (V)	*Legends of Australia* the first extended piece of fiction by a native-born writer
1843	Hill, S. P. (1821), *Tarquin the Proud* (D)	Joseph Furphy *b*
	Rowcroft (1798), *Tales of the Colonies* (P)	Edward E. Morris *b*
1844	Meredith, Louisa A. (1812), *Notes and Sketches of NSW* (P)	Ada Cambridge *b*
		J.B. O'Reilly *b*
		C.T. Knowles *d*
		Edward Geoghegan's *The Currency Lass* produced in Sydney
1845	Harpur (1813), *Thoughts: A Series of Sonnets* (V)	Ernest Favenc *b*
	McCombie, Thomas (1819), *Arabin, or the Adventures of a Colonist in New South Wales* (F)	
	Tucker (1808), *The Adventures of Ralph Rashleigh* (F)	
	Vidal (1815), *Tales for the Bush* (F)	
1846	Rowcroft (1798), *The Bushranger of Van Diemen's Land* (F)	Marcus Clarke *b*
		Mary Hannay Foott *b*
		G.H. Gibson ('Ironbark') *b*
		Barron Field *d*
		Argus (Melbourne, 1846–1957) founded
1847	Harris (1805), *Settlers and Convicts* (P/F)	Catherine Martin *b*
		T. H. Huxley in Australia
1848	Gould (1804), *The Birds of Australia*, completed (36 parts in 7 vols, 1840–48; supplementary vol. 1869)	Jessie Catherine Couvreur ('Tasma') *b*
		Louisa Lawson *b*

Date	Publications	Literary/Cultural Events
1848	Nathan (1790), ed., *The Southern Euphrosyne and Australian Miscellany* (F/V/P) Vidal (1815), *Esther Merle* (F)	Edward Kennedy and Jackey Jackey explore Cape York peninsula Ludwig Leichhardt disappears on third expedition, setting out from Moreton Bay Revolutions in Europe lead to migrants from Hungary, Germany, etc. First foreign-language newspaper, *Die Deutsche Post für die Australischen Kolonien*, produced in Adelaide
1849	Harris (1805), *The Emigrant Family* (F)	Gold found in substantial quantity near Melbourne by a boy named Chapman
1850	Vidal (1815), *Cabramatta, and Woodleigh Farm* (F)	
1851		Arthur Patchett Martin *b* John Farrell *b* Rosa Praed *b* First of the goldrushes begin with the discovery of gold at Bathurst in New South Wales and at Ballarat and Bendigo in Victoria; goldrushes result in waves of immigration during the 1850s
1852	Meredith (1812), *My Home in Tasmania* (P) Mundy (1804), *Our Antipodes* (P) West (1809), *The History of Tasmania* (P)	University of Sydney library established
1853	Clacy (18??), *A Lady's Visit to the Gold Diggings of Australia* (P) Harpur (1813), *The Bushrangers, and Other Poems* (D, V) Lang (1816), *The Wetherbys, or Chapters of Indian Experience* (F)	Gregory Blaxland *d* Melbourne's public library established
1854	Howitt (1792), *A Boy's Adventures in the Wilds of Australia* (F) Spence (1825), *Clara Morison* (F)	Fidelia Hill *d* Jackey Jackey *d* Uprising of miners at the Eureka Stockade (Ballarat) *Age* (Melbourne) founded
1855	Carboni (1820), *The Eureka Stockade* (P) Howitt (1792), *Land, Labour and Gold* (P)	William Astley ('Price Warung') *b* Louis Becke *b* Catherine Stow (Mrs Langloh Parker) *b* (?)

Date	Publications	Literary/Cultural Events
1855	Lang, John George (1816), *The Forger's Wife* (F)	Lola Montez performs Spider Dance in Sydney
		Victorian government imposes head-tax of £10 on each arriving Chinese gold-miner
		Some Sydney stone-masons win 8-hour working day
1856	Sinnett (1830), *The Fiction Fields of Australia* (P)	J. F. Archibald *b*
		Charles Rowcroft *d*
	Spence (1825), *Tender and True* (F)	The first account of Australian literature, *The Fiction Fields of Australia*, published in *Journal of Australasia*, 1856
		Manhood suffrage for Lower House of Parliament introduced in South Australia; other states followed
1857	Caroline Atkinson (1834), *Gertrude the Emigrant*, first novel by Australian-born woman (F)	Barbara Baynton *b*
		The Month: A Literary and Critical Journal founded
	Gerstaecker (1816), *The Two Convicts* (F)	
	Howitt (1792), *Tallangetta, the Squatter's Home* (F)	
	Michael (1824), *Songs Without Music* (V)	
	Thatcher (1831), *Colonial Songster* (V)	
1858	Michael (1824), *Sir Archibald Yelverton* (V)	Victor Daley *b*
	Rowe (1828), *Peter Possum's Portfolio* (F, V)	Non-Aboriginal population reaches 1 million
1859	Atkinson (1834), *Cowanda* (F)	Fergus Hume *b*
	Fowler (1833), *Southern Lights and Shadows* (P)	Rabbits released as game in Victoria
	Kingsley (1830), *The Recollections of Geoffry Hamlyn* (F)	
	Lang, John George (1816), *Botany Bay* (F)	
	Leakey (1827), *The Broad Arrow* (F)	
1860	Deniehy (1828), *How I Became Attorney-General of New Barataria* (F)	F. J. Broomfield *b*
		A. A. G. Hales *b*
	Michael (1824), *John Cumberland* (V)	Ethel Pedley *b* (?)
	Vidal (1815), *Bengala* (F)	
1861	Meredith (1812), *Over the Straits* (P)	William Lane *b*
		Anti-Chinese riots at Lambing Flat goldfields, NSW

Date	Publications	Literary/Cultural Events
1862	Harpur (1813), *A Poet's Home* (V)	Francis Adams *b*
	Kendall (1839), *Poems and Songs* (V)	Cobb & Co begin operating coach service in NSW
1863		Daisy Bates *b*
		George Essex Evans *b*
		Pacific Islanders ('Kanakas') first brought to Queensland as labourers
1864	Gordon (1833), *The Feud* (V)	A. B. ('Banjo') Paterson *b*
	Horne (1802), *Prometheus the Firebringer* (V)	John George Lang *d*
		Australasian (1864–1946) founded
	Thatcher (1831), *Colonial Minstrel* (V)	Major national drought (–1866)
1865	Harpur (1813), *The Tower of the Dream* (V)	E. G. Dyson *b*
		Mary (Cameron) Gilmore *b*
	Kingsley (1830), *The Hillyars and the Burtons* (F)	A. G. Stephens *b*
	Spence (1825), *Mr Hogarth's Will* (F)	D. H. Deniehy *d*
		Australian Journal: A Weekly Record of Amusing and Instructive Literature, Science and the Arts (1865–1958) founded
1866	Barton (1836), *The Poets and Prose Writers of New South Wales* and *Literature in New South Wales* (P)	Barcroft Boake *b*
		Bernard O'Dowd *b*
		Frederick Sinnett *d*
	Horne (1802), *The South Sea Sisters* (D)	James Tucker *d*
		Barton's books (published in Sydney) were the first book-length studies of Australian writing
1867	Gordon (1833), *Sea Spray and Smoke Drift* (V)	Henry Lawson *b*
		Roderic Quinn *b*
	Houlding (1822), *Australian Capers* (F)	Goldrushes in Queensland (1867–86) begin
	McCrae, G. G. (1833), *Mamba and the Story of Balladeadro* (V)	
1868	McCombie, Thomas (1813?), *Frank Henly, or Honest Industry Will Conquer* (F)	Randolph Bedford *b*
		A. H. Davis ('Steele Rudd') *b*
		Charles Harpur *d*
	Spence (1825), *The Author's Daughter* (F)	J. L. Michael *d*
	Yarrington (18??), ed., *Prince Alfred's Wreath* (V)	Transportation of convicts ends
		Aboriginal cricket team tours England
		Maria Ann Smith propagates 'Granny Smith' apple
1869	Clarke (1846), *The Peripatetic Philosopher* (P) and *Long Odds* (F)	E. J. Brady *b*
		Stefan von Kotze *b*

Date	Publications	Literary/Cultural Events
1869	Kendall (1839), *Leaves From Australian Forests* (V) Kingsley (1830), *Tales of Old Travel Renarrated* (F) Rowe (1828), *The Boy in the Bush* (F)	W. H. Ogilvie *b* Paul Wenz *b* Thomas McCombie *d* Charles Sturt *d* Mary T. Vidal *d* Darwin surveyed Suez Canal opened
1870	Clarke (1846), *His Natural Life* (F), in the *Australian Journal* Gordon (1833), *Bush Ballads and Galloping Rhymes* (V) Houlding (1822), *Rural and City Life* (F)	C. J. Brennan *b* Jeannie Gunn (Mrs Aeneas Gunn) *b* Ethel Robertson ('Henry Handel Richardson') *b* Adam Lindsay Gordon *d* Richard Howitt *d* Construction of Overland Telegraph line begins; completed 1872 Mail steamer service between Sydney and San Francisco begins
1871	Clarke (1846), *Old Tales of a Young Country* (P) Kingsley (1830), *Hetty, and Other Stories* (F) Stephens, James Brunton (1835), *Convict Once* (V)	J. Le Gay Brereton *b* Louis Stone *b* Anthony Trollope's first visit to Australia (1871–2)
1872	Kingsley (1830), *Hornby Mills and Other Stories* (F) Lang, John Dunmore (1799), *Poems Sacred and Secular* (V)	A. H. Adams *b* John Shaw Neilson *b* Ethel Turner *b* Caroline Atkinson *d* Friedrich Gerstaecker *d* W. C. Wentworth *d*
1873	Clarke (1846), *Holiday Peak* (F) McCrae, G. G. (1833), *The Man in the Iron Mask* (V) O'Reilly (1844), *Songs from the Southern Seas* (V) Stephens, James Brunton (1835), *The Godolphin Arabian* (V)	Dora Wilcox *b* David Unaipon *b* W. H. Christie *d* 'Henry Melville' *d* Anthony Trollope's *Australia and New Zealand* and *Harry Heathcote of Gangoil* published in London Edward William Cole opens first 'book arcade' in Melbourne Palmer River goldrush begins
1874	Angas (1822), *The Wreck of the Admella* (V)	Edith Joan Lyttleton ('G. B. Lancaster') *b*

Date	Publications	Literary/Cultural Events
1874	Clarke (1846), *His Natural Life* (F), in book form Kingsley (1830), *Reginald Hetherege* (F) Ranken, W. L. (1839), *The Dominion of Australia* (P)	Walter Murdoch *b* Alexander Harris *d* J. C. Williamson and his wife Maggie begin theatrical tour of Australia
1875	Cambridge (1844), *The Manor House* (V) and *Up the Murray* (P) Clarke (1846), *'Twixt Shadow and Shine* (F) Swan (1835), *Tales of Australian Life* (F)	William Gosse Hay *b* David Burn *d* Raffaello Carboni *d* Havelock Ellis in Australia (1875–79) Anthony Trollope's second visit
1876	Forster (1818), *The Weirwolf* (D) Stephens, James Brunton (1835), *A Hundred Pounds* (F)	C. J. Dennis *b* Hugh McCrae *b* Henry Kingsley *d* Truganini, the last full-blood Tasmanian Aboriginal, dies in Hobart, aged 73 *Melbourne Review* founded by George Robertson Stump-jump plough invented
1877	Clarke (1846), *Four Stories High* (F) Forster (1818), *The Brothers* (D) Manning (1845), *The Balance of Pain* (V)	May Gibbs *b* Caroline Chisholm *d* Shearing machine patented by Frederick York Wolseley
1878	'Boldrewood' (1826), *Ups and Downs* (F) Farrell (1851), *Ephemera: An Iliad of Albury* (V) Gibson (1846), *Southerly Busters* (V)	John Dunmore Lang *d* Charles Thatcher *d*
1879	Martin (1830), ed., *An Easter Omelette of Prose and Verse* (P/V) O'Reilly (1844), *Moondyne* (F)	C. E. W. Bean *b* Louis Esson *b* Miles Franklin *b* Norman Lindsay *b* William Howitt *d* Richard Rowe *d* Anthony Trollope's *John Caldigate* published in London Joseph Conrad in Australia 1879 (and 1880, 1887, 1892, 1893)
1880	Kendall (1839), *Songs from the Mountains* (V) Praed (1851), *An Australian*	J. F. Archibald and John Haynes begin publishing the *Bulletin* Australia's most notorious bushranger,

Date	Publications	Literary/Cultural Events
1880	*Heroine* (F) Rowe (1828), *Roughing it in Van Diemen's Land* (F)	Ned Kelly, captured at Glenrowan and hanged Second wave of immigration during 1880s Melbourne Telephone Exchange Co begins operation with 44 subscribers Major national drought (–1886) Frozen meat successfully exported to London, using refrigeration plant developed by T.S. Mort and E.D. Nicolle
1881	Clarke (1846), *The Conscientious Stranger* and *The Mystery of Major Molineux and Human Repetends* (F) Kendall (1839), *Orara* (V) Praed (1851), *Policy and Passion* (F) Spence (1825), *Gathered In* (F)	E. F. O'Ferrall ('Kodak') *b* Frank Wilmot ('Furnley Morris') *b* E. Morris Miller *b* Marcus Clarke *d* John Gould *d* Caroline Leakey *d* Henry Kendall appointed first forest inspector in NSW
1882	'Boldrewood' (1826), *Robbery under Arms* (F) in the *Sydney Mail* Farrell (1851), *Two Stories* (V) O'Reilly (1844), *Songs, Legends and Ballads* (V)	Frederic Manning *b* William Forster *d* Henry Kendall *d*
1883	Curr (1820), *Recollections of Squatting in Victoria* (P) Harpur (1813), *Poems* (V) McCrae, G. G. (1833), *A Rosebud from the Garden of the Taj* (V) Twopeny (1857), *Town Life in Australia* (P)	Ethel Anderson *b* William Blocksidge ('Baylebridge') *b* Katharine Susannah Prichard *b* Charles Tompson *d*
1884	Clarke (*d* 1881), *The Marcus Clarke Memorial Volume* (F, P) Forster (*d* 1882), *Midas* (D) Moore (1798), *Diary of Ten Years' Eventful Life of an Early Settler in Western Australia* (P)	R. H. Horne *d* N.W. Swan *d*
1885	Clarke (*d* 1881), *For the Term of his Natural Life* (first edition to be so titled; F) Foott (1835), *Where the Pelican Builds* (V) Praed (1851), *The Head Station* (F)	Dorothea Mackellar *b* Nettie Palmer *b* Vance Palmer *b* Italian settlers arrive on Richmond River, NSW Tom Roberts, Frederick McCubbin, and Louis Abrahams establish artists' camp near Melbourne

Date	Publications	Literary/Cultural Events
1886	Adams, Francis (1862), *Australian Essays* (P) Clarke (*d* 1881), *Sensational Tales* (F) Hume (1859), *The Mystery of a Hansom Cab* (F) Kendall (*d* 1882), *Poems* (V) Praed (1851), *Miss Jacobsen's Chance* (F)	George Fletcher Moore *d* George French Angas *d* J. F. Archibald editor of *Bulletin* 1886–1902 Shearers' Union formed at Ballarat, precursor of Australian Workers' Union George Chaffey's Mildura irrigation scheme adopted by Victorian Government
1887	Adams, Francis (1862), *Poetical Works* (V) Cambridge (1844), *Unspoken Thoughts* (V) Farrell (1851), *How he Died, and Other Poems* (V) O'Reilly (1844), *The Golden Secret* (F)	F. T. Macartney *b* Jack McLaren *b* The *Boomerang* (−1892), a radical weekly edited by William Lane and J. G. Drake Henry Lawson's first published poem, 'Song of the Republic', in the *Bulletin*
1888	Adams, Francis (1861), *Songs of the Army of the Night* (V) Finn ('Garryowen') (1819), *The Chronicles of Early Melbourne* (P) Sladen (1856), ed., *Australian Ballads and Rhymes* (V); *A Century of Australian Song* (V); *Australian Poets 1788–1888* (V)	Arthur Upfield *b* James Tucker *d* (?) 'Rolf Boldrewood's' *Robbery under Arms* published as a book in London Henry Lawson's first story, 'His Father's Mate', published in the *Bulletin* Louisa Lawson's *Dawn: A Journal for Australian Women* begins monthly publication (−1905) Angus & Robertson begins publishing
1889	Giles (1835), *Australia Twice Traversed* (P) Praed (1851), *The Romance of a Station* (F) 'Tasma' (1848), *Uncle Piper of Piper's Hill* (F)	Anna Maria Bunn *d* '9 × 5' Exhibition in Melbourne (Roberts, Streeton, Conder)
1890	Archibald (1856) and Broomfield (1860), eds, *A Golden Shanty: Prose and Verse by Bulletin Writers* (F, V) 'Boldrewood' (1826), *A Colonial Reformer, The Miner's Right* and *The Squatter's Dream* (F) Cambridge (1844), *A Marked Man* (F) Clarke (*d* 1881), *The Austral Edition* (F) Hales (1860), *The Wanderings of a Simple Child* (F) Martin, Catherine (1847), *An Australian Girl* (F)	Zora Cross *b* James Devaney *b* Ion Idriess *b* J. B. O'Reilly *d* Australian Labor Federation Queensland Provincial Council plans for a political Labor Party, formed at Blackall *The Worker*, edited by William Lane begins monthly publication (Brisbane) Great maritime strike defeated, despite support from other unions

Date	Publications	Literary/Cultural Events
1890	Praed (1851), *The Head Station* (F) 'Tasma' (1848), *In her Earliest Youth* (F); *A Sydney Sovereign* (F) Vogan (18??), *The Black Police* (F)	Victorian land boom collapses; depression and company failures in eastern states (through 1890s) Robert Louis Stevenson in Australia 1890, 1891, 1893 Blue-speckle cattle-dog ('Blue heeler') established as a pure breed
1891	'Boldrewood' (1826), *A Sydney-side Saxon* (F) Cambridge (1844), *The Three Miss Kings* (F) Evans (1863), *The Repentance of Magdalen Despar* (V) 'Tasma' (1848), *The Penance of Portia James* (F)	Lesbia Harford *b* The *Australasian Critic: A Monthly Review of Literature, Science and Art*, edited by T. G. Tucker and W. Baldwin Spencer, with E. E. Morris as literary editor First Federal Convention (including New Zealand) meets in Sydney to draft Constitution Queensland shearers' strike First Labor Electoral League candidates contest elections (NSW), winning 35 seats Rudyard Kipling in Australia
1892	Adams, Francis (1861), *Australian Life* (F); *The Melbournians* (F) 'Boldrewood' (1826), *Nevermore* (F) Cambridge (1844), *Not All in Vain* (F) Lane (1861), *The Workingman's Paradise* (F) 'Tasma' (1848), *A Knight of the White Feather* (F) 'Warung' (1855), *Tales of the Convict System* (F)	John Tierney ('Brian James') *b* Barcroft Boake *d* Lane's *The Workingman's Paradise* (published in Brisbane) written to raise funds for the families of unionists imprisoned during the shearers' strike John (Jacky) Howe shears 321 merino sheep in a day Gold found at Coolgardie (and Kalgoorlie 1893)
1893	Adams, Francis (1861), *The Australians* (P) Clarke (*d* 1881), *Chidiock Tichbourne* (P) Favenc (1845), *The Last of Six* (F) Gibson (1846), *Ironbark Chips and Stockwhip Cracks* (V) Praed (1851), *Outlaw and Lawmaker* (F)	Martin Boyd *b* Frank Dalby Davison *b* Francis Adams *d* William Woolls *d* Adult suffrage (enfranchisement of women) introduced for Lower House in South Australia; other states and the Commonwealth (1902) followed First public telephone in NSW at Sydney GPO
1894	Becke (1855), *By Reef and Palm* (F) Lawson (1867), *Short Stories in Prose and Verse* (F, V) Neilson (1872), *The Tales We Never Hear* (V)	Jean Devanny *b* H. V. Evatt *b* A. B. Facey *b*

Date	Publications	Literary/Cultural Events
1894	Stephens, A.G. (1865), *A Queenslander's Travel-notes* (P) Turner, Ethel (1872), *Seven Little Australians* (F) 'Warung' (1855), *Tales of the Early Days* (F)	
1895	'Boldrewood' (1826), *The Sphinx of Eaglehawk* (F) Cambridge (1844), *Fidelis* (F) Paterson (1864), *The Man from Snowy River* (V) Praed (1851), *Mrs Tregaskiss* (F) 'Tasma' (1848), *Not Counting the Cost* (F)	Leonard Mann *b* Mark Twain in Australia Words and music of 'Waltzing Matilda' first sung in public; the words were written by 'Banjo' Paterson Angus & Robertson begin regular publishing with *The Man from Snowy River* Major national drought (−1903): the '1902' drought
1896	Brereton (1871), *The Song of Brotherhood* (V) and *Perdita* (V) Dyson (1865), *Rhymes from the Mines* (V) Favenc (1845), *The Moccasins of Silence* (F) Lawson (1867), *While the Billy Boils* (F); *In the Days When the World was Wide* (V) Parker (1855?), *Australian Legendary Tales* (F)	Joan Lindsay *b* Sir Henry Parkes *d* A. G. Stephens editor of *Bulletin* 'Red Page', 1896–1906 Public cinematography screenings in Sydney and first films made by Marius Sestier Queensland Agricultural Lands Purchase Act begins Australia-wide policy of breaking up large estates for closer settlement NSW introduces first old age pension scheme
1897	Boake (*d* 1892), *Where the Dead Men Lie* (V) Brennan (1870), *XVIII Poems* and *XXI Poems (1893–1897): Towards the Source* (V) Brereton (1871), *Sweetheart Mine* (V) Cambridge (1844), *At Midnight* (F) Farrell (1851), *Australia to England* (V) Praed (1851), *Nulma* (F) Quinn (1867), *Mostyn Stayne* (F) 'Tasma' (1848), *A Fiery Ordeal* (F) 'Warung' (1855), *Tales of the Old Regime* (F)	Marjorie Barnard *b* Flora Eldershaw *b* Helen Simpson *b* Jessie Catherine Couvreur ('Tasma') *d*
1898	Cambridge (1844), *Materfamilias* (F) Daley (1858), *At Dawn and Dusk* (V)	Keith Hancock *b* Ethel Pedley *d*

DATE	PUBLICATIONS	LITERARY/CULTURAL EVENTS
1898	Dyson (1865), *Below and On Top* (F) Evans (1863), *Loraine, and Other Verses* (V) Morris (1843), *Austral English: A Dictionary of Australasian Words, Phrases and Usages* (P) Ogilvie (1869), *Fair Girls and Gray Horses* (V) 'Warung' (1855), *Tales of the Isle of Death* (F); *Half-Crown Bob and Tales of the Riverine* (F)	A. C. Rowlandson founds NSW Bookstall Company to publish cheap paperback novels The Australian Constitution approved by referendum
1899	Brady (1869), *The Ways of Many Waters* (V) Brereton (1871), *Landlopers* (F) Favenc (1845), *My Only Murder* (F) Pedley, Ethel (?1860), *Dot and the Kangaroo* (F) Quinn, (1867), *The Hidden Tide* (V) 'Rudd' (1868), *On Our Selection* (F)	Jean Curlewis *b* Ernestine Hill *b* *The Bookfellow* (–1925) founded by A. G. Stephens Formation of the Australian Literature Society Pigeon and 19 other Aboriginal prisoners whom he had freed shot in Kimberley region after being at large for several years
1900	'Boldrewood' (1826), *The Babes in the Bush* (F) Lawson (1867), *On the Track and Over the Sliprails* (F); *Verses, Popular and Humorous* (V)	Jack Lindsay *b* A.A. Phillips *b* British Parliament passess an Act to constitute the Commonwealth of Australia; all states join the Federation Two Aboriginal brothers, Jimmy and Joe Governor, and Jackie Underwood kill 7 whites in New South Wales (see Keneally's *The Chant of Jimmie Blacksmith*, 1972)
1901	'Boldrewood' (1826), *In Bad Company* (F) Dyson (1865), *The Gold Stealers* (F) Franklin (1879), *My Brilliant Career* (F) Hay (1875), *Stifled Laughter* (F) Lawson (1867), *Joe Wilson and His Mates* (F); *The Country I Came From* (F) Quinn (1867), *The Circling Hearths* (V) Stephens, A. G. (1865), ed., *The Bulletin Story Book* (F); *The Bulletin Reciter* (V)	Eleanor Dark *b* Henrietta Drake-Brockman *b* Xavier Herbert *b* Kenneth Slessor *b* P. R. ('Inky') Stephensen *b* G. B. Barton *d* Proclamation of the Federal Constitution; first national election Legislation enacted to prohibit permanent settlement by non-Europeans ('White Australia' policy)

Date	Publications	Literary/Cultural Events
1902	Baynton (1857), *Bush Studies* (F)	Dymphna Cusack *b*
	'Boldrewood' (1826), *The Ghost Camp* (F)	Robert D. FitzGerald *b*
	Brereton (1871), *Oithona* (V)	Thistle Y. Harris *b*
	Lawson (1867), *Children of the Bush* (F)	Florence James *b*
		Alan Marshall *b*
	Paterson (1864), *Rio Grande's Last Race* (V)	Christina Stead *b*
		Edward E. Morris *d*
	Praed (1851), *Dwellers by the River* (F)	Arthur Patchett Martin *d*
	Stephens, A.G. (1865), *Oblation* (F)	James Brunton Stephens *d*
	Stephens, James Brunton (1835), *Poetical Works* (V); *My Chinee Cook and Other Humorous Verses* (V)	
1903	Bedford (1868), *True Eyes and the Whirlwind* (F)	Robert Close *b*
		Lennie Lower *b*
	Cambridge (1844), *Thirty Years in Australia* (P)	
	Furphy (1843), *Such is Life: Being Certain Extracts from the Diary of Tom Collins* (F)	
	O'Dowd (1866), *Dawnward?* (V)	
	Praed (1851), *Fugitive Anne* (F)	
	'Rudd' (1868), *Our New Selection* (F)	
1904	Farrell (*d* 1904), *My Sundowner, and Other Poems* (V)	John Morrison *b*
		Brian Penton *b*
	Praed (1851), *Nyria* (F)	John Farrell *d*
	'Rudd' (1868), *Sandy's Selection* (F)	*Steele Rudd's Magazine* founded (−1926)
	Stephens, A.G. (1865), *The Red Pagan* (P)	Commonwealth Conciliation and Arbitration Act establishes Arbitration Court
1905	Bedford (1868), *The Snare of Strength* (F)	Victor Daley *d*
	'Boldrewood' (1826), *The Last Chance* (F)	Lothian Publishing Co. founded in Melbourne
	Favenc (1845), *Voices of the Desert* (V)	
	Furphy (1843), *Rigby's Romance* (F)	
	Lawson (1867), *When I was King* (V)	
	Lawson, Louisa (1848), *The Lonely Crossing* (V)	
	Paterson (1864), ed., *Old Bush Songs* (V)	
	Praed (1851), *The Maid of the River* (F)	

Date	Publications	Literary/Cultural Events
1906	Cambridge (1844), *A Happy Marriage* (F)	Cyril Pearl *b*
	Dyson (1865), *Fact'ry 'Ands* (F); *In the Roaring Fifties* (F)	A. H. Adams editor of *Bulletin* 'Red Page' 1906–09
	Evans (1863), *The Secret Key and Other Verses* (V)	*The Story of the Kelly Gang*, one-hour narrative film, shown in Melbourne
	O'Dowd (1866), *The Silent Land* (V)	
	Paterson (1864), *An Outback Marriage* (F)	
	Praed (1851), *The Lost Earl of Ellan* (F)	
	'Rudd' (1868), *Back at our Selection* (F)	
1907	Baynton (1857), *Human Toll* (F)	Ralph de Boissiere *b*
	Hay (1875), *Herridge of Reality Swamp* (F)	Gavin Casey *b*
	O'Dowd (1866), *Dominions of the Boundary* (V)	A.D. Hope *b*
	Praed (1851), *The Luck of the Leura* (F)	Gwen Meredith *b*
		John O'Grady ('Nino Culotta') *b*
		Lone Hand (1907–21) founded
		Mr Justice Higgins's decision in Harvester Case establishes concept of a 'basic wage'
1908	Banfield (1852), *The Confessions of a Beachcomber* (P)	Eve Langley *b*
	Brereton (1871), *Sea and Sky* (V)	Colin Simpson *b*
	Daley (1858), *Poems* (V)	Ernest Favenc *d*
	Gunn (1870), *We of the Never Never* (F)	Commonwealth Literary Fund founded
	'Richardson' (1870) *Maurice Guest* (F)	
	'Rudd' (1868), *Dad in Politics* (F)	
	Sorenson (1869), *The Squatter's Ward* (F)	
1909	Franklin (1879), *Some Everyday Folk and Dawn* (F)	Ronald McKie *b*
	McCrae, Hugh (1876), *Satyrs and Sunlight: Silvarum Libri* (V)	George Essex Evans *d*
	O'Dowd (1866), *The Seven Deadly Sins* (V)	Stefan von Kotze *d*
	'Rudd' (1868), *Stocking our Selection* (F)	
1910	Bean (1879), *On the Wool Track* (F)	Alan Moorehead *b*
	Blocksidge (1883), *Moreton Miles; Southern Songs; A Northern Trail* and *The New Life* (V)	Catherine Spence *d*
		Mitchell Library (Sydney) opens

Date	Publications	Literary/Cultural Events
1910	Brereton (1871), *To-morrow* (D)	Cozens Spencer produces *The Life and Adventures of John Vane, the Notorious Australian Bushranger*, beginning prolific three years of film production
	Bruce (1878), *A Little Bush Maid* (F)	
	Esson (1879), *Bells and Bees* (V)	
	Gilmore (1865), *Marri'd* (V)	
	Lawson (1867), *The Rising of the Court* (F)	
	Praed (1851), *Opal Fire* (F)	
	'Richardson' (1870), *The Getting of Wisdom* (F)	
	Spence (*d* 1910), *An Autobiography* (P)	
1911	Bean (1879), *The Dreadnought of the Darling* (P)	William Hart-Smith *b*
	Bedford (1868), *Billy Pagan, Mining Engineer* (F)	Ian Mudie *b*
		Hal Porter *b*
	Daley (*d* 1905), *Wine and Roses* (V)	Olaf Ruhen *b*
	Dyson (1865), *Benno and Some of the Push* (F)	Dal Stivens *b*
		Judah Waten *b*
	Lawson (1867), *Mateship* (F)	William Astley ('Price Warung') *d*
	Stone (1871), *Jonah* (F)	Up to 300 000 migrants, mostly British, arrive 1911–4
		Major national drought (–1916): the '1914' drought
1912	Cambridge (1844), *The Retrospect* (F)	Sidney J. Baker *b*
	Esson (1879), *Red Gums* (V); *The Time is not yet Ripe* and *Three Short Plays: The Woman Tamer, Dead Timber, The Sacred Place* (D)	George Johnston *b*
		Roland Robinson *b*
		Kylie Tennant *b*
	Gibson (1846), *Ironbark Splinters from the Australian Bush* (V)	Patrick White *b*
		Joseph Furphy *d*
	Gordon (*d* 1870), *Poems* (V)	
	Hay (1875), *Captain Quadring* (F)	
	O'Dowd (1866), *The Bush* (V)	
1913	Brennan (1870), and Brereton (1871), *A Mask* (D)	John Blight *b*
		Mary Durack *b*
	Cambridge (1844), *The Hand in the Dark* (V)	Rex Ingamells *b*
	Dennis (1876), *Backblock Ballads* (V)	Kenneth Mackenzie *b*
	Lawson (1867), *Triangles of Life* (F)	Barbara McNamara ('Elizabeth O'Conner') *b*
	Lindsay, Norman (1879), *A Curate in Bohemia* (F)	Douglas Stewart *b*
	Prichard (1883), *Clovelly Verses* (V)	Donald Stuart *b*
	Stephens, A. G. (1865), *Bill's Ideas* (F)	Louis Becke *d*

Date	Publications	Literary/Cultural Events
1914	Adams, A. H. (1872), *Three Plays for the Australian Stage: The Wasters, Galahad Jones, Mrs Pretty and the Premier* (D)	Peter Cowan *b*
		Margaret Kiddle *b*
		Russel Ward *b*
	Blocksidge (1883), *Life's Testament* (V)	Rachel Henning *d*
	Brennan (1870), *Poems 1913* (V)	Workers' Educational Association formed in Australia
	Dyson (1865), *Spat's Fact'ry* (F)	Australia joins Britain in World War I, 1914–18
1915	Dennis (1876), *The Songs of a Sentimental Bloke* (V)	David Campbell *b*
		C.M.H. (Manning) Clark *b*
	McCrae, G. G. (1833), *The Fleet and Convoy* (V)	T.A.G. Hungerford *b*
	Mawson (1882), *The Home of the Blizzard* (P)	John Manifold *b*
		David Martin *b*
	Palmer, Vance (1885), *The Forerunners* (V); *The World of Men* (F)	Judith Wright *b*
		T.A. Browne ('Rolf Boldrewood') *d*
	Praed (1851), *Lady Bridget in the Never-Never Land* (F)	Australian and New Zealand Army Corps (ANZACs) at Gallipoli
	Prichard (1883), *The Pioneers* (F)	
	Stone, Louis (1871), *Betty Wayside* (F)	
1916	Blocksidge (1883), *A Wreath* (V)	George R. Turner *b*
	Dennis (1876), *The Moods of Ginger Mick* (V)	Morris West *b*
	Furphy (*d* 1912), *Poems* (V)	*Birth* (ed. Bernard O'Dowd, Vance Palmer and others, 1916–22, founded
	Neilson (1872), *Old Granny Sullivan* (V)	Roy Rene (Harry van der Sluys or 'Mo') opens in comedy duo, Stiffy and Mo, in Sydney
	Praed (1851), *Sister Sorrow* (F)	Conscription referendum lost
	Ogilvie (1869), *The Australian* (V)	Returned Soldiers' and Sailors' Imperial League of Australia (RSL) founded
1917	Baynton (1857), *Cobbers* (F)	Nancy Cato *b*
	Bedford (1868), *The Silver Star* (F)	Jon Cleary *b*
	Dennis (1876), *Doreen and The Glugs of Gosh* (V)	Frank Hardy *b*
		Sumner Locke-Elliott *b*
	'Maurice' (1881), *To God: From the Weary Nations* (V)	James McAuley *b*
	Paterson (1864), *Saltbush Bill, JP* (V); *Three Elephant Power* (F)	William Lane *d*
		Second conscription referendum lost
	'Richardson' (1870), *Australia Felix* (F)	
1918	Brennan (1870), *A Chant of Doom* (V)	Faith Bandler *b*
	Dennis (1876), *Digger Smith* (V)	Jack Davis *b*
	Gibbs (1877), *Snugglepot and Cuddlepie* (F)	Mary Hannay Foott *d*

Date	Publications	Literary/Cultural Events
1918	Gilmore (1865), *The Passionate Heart* (V)	Non-Aboriginal population reaches 5 million
	Hay (1875), *The Escape of the Notorious Sir William Heans* (F)	Major national drought (−1920)
	Lindsay, Norman (1879), *The Magic Pudding* (F)	
	McCrae, G. G. (1883), *John Rous* (F)	
1919	Bedford (1868), *Aladdin and the Boss Cockie* (F)	Robin Boyd *b*
		Nene Gare *b*
	Brereton (1871), *The Burning Marl* (V)	Olga Masters *b*
	Dennis (1876), *Jim of the Hills* (V)	J. F. Archibald *d*
	Neilson (1872), *Heart of Spring* (V)	*Smith's Weekly* (−1950) founded
		The Sentimental Bloke, film produced by Raymond Longford
		Soldier settlement begins in Murrumbidgee Irrigation Area and elsewhere; many farms fail over next 20 years
		Female wage set at 54 per cent of (male or 'family') basic wage
		Influenza epidemic (1917−19) kills almost 12 000 in one year
1920	Boyd, Martin (1893), *Retrospect* (V)	Donald Horne *b*
	Esson (1879), *Dead Timber* [*The Drovers* and three earlier plays] (D)	Rosemary Dobson *b*
		Gwen Harwood *b*
	Kendall (*d* 1882), *Poems* (V)	Colin Thiele *b*
	McCrae, Hugh (1876), *Colombine* (V)	Kath Walker (Oodgeroo Noonuccal) *b*
	'Maurice' (1881), *Eyes of Vigilance* and *Ways and Means* (V)	Louisa Lawson *d*
	Palmer, Vance (1885), *The Camp* (V); *The Shantykeeper's Daughter* (F)	*The Man from Snowy River*, film produced by Beaumont Smith
	Quinn (1867), *Poems* (V)	*On Our Selection*, film produced by Raymond Longford
1921	Bean (1879), *The Story of the Anzac, The Official History of Australia in the War of 1914−18*, Vol. 1 (P)	Eric Lambert *b*
		Ray Lawler *b*
	Bruce (1878), *Back to Billabong* (F)	Ivan Southall *b*
	Dennis (1876), *A Book for Kids* (V)	Dimitris Tsaloumas *b*
	'Maurice' (1881), *Arrow of Longing* (V)	Patricia Wrightson *b*
	O'Dowd (1866), *Alma Venus!* (V)	G. H. Gibson ('Ironbark') *d*
	O'Ferrall (1881), *Bodger and the Boarders* (F)	Pioneer Players formed in Melbourne by Vance Palmer, Louis Esson, and Stewart Macky; performed Australian plays, 1922—6
		While the Billy Boils, film produced by Beaumont Smith
		First Archibald Prize for portraiture

DATE	PUBLICATIONS	LITERARY/CULTURAL EVENTS
1921	Paterson (1864), *Collected Verse* (V) Prichard (1883), *Black Opal* (F)	
1922	Gilmore (1865), *Hound of the Road* (F) McCrae, Hugh (1876), *Idyllia* (V) Palmer, Vance (1885), *The Boss of Killara* (F)	Geoffrey Dutton *b* Henry Lawson *d* Legislation for assisted passage leads to a further 300 000 migrants during the 1920s Melbourne University Press established
1923	Martin, Catherine (1847), *The Incredible Journey* (F) Neilson (1872), *Ballad and Lyrical Poems* (V) Palmer, Vance (1885), *The Enchanted Island* (F)	Dorothy Hewett *b* Elizabeth Jolley *b* Eric Rolls *b* D. H. Lawrence's *Kangaroo* published in London *Vision*, ed. Jack Lindsay, Kenneth Slessor and others, (1923–24), founded Opening of first public radio station, 2SB Sydney First subscriber (sealed-set) wireless station begins in Sydney
1924	Brereton (1871), *The Carillon Poems* (V) Dennis (1876), *Rose of Spadgers* (V) Palmer, Vance (1885), *Cronulla* and *The Outpost* (F); *The Black Horse* (D) Slessor (1901), *Thief of the Moon* (V)	Dick Roughsey *b* David Rowbotham *b* D. H. Lawrence and M. L. Skinner, *The Boy in the Bush* published in London
1925	Boyd, Martin (1893), *Love Gods* (F) Gilmore (1865), *The Tilted Cart* (V) Lawson (*d* 1922), *Poetical Works* (V) 'Richardson' (1870), *The Way Home* (F)	Thea Astley *b* Vincent Buckley *b* Jessica Anderson *b* Francis Webb *b* E. F. O'Ferrall ('Kodak') *d* *The Australian Encyclopaedia*, ed. Arthur Jose, 2 vols (Angus & Robertson, 1925–26) First Australian radio play, *The Barbarous Barber*, broadcast by 3LO (written J. H. Booth, produced Stanley Brooks)
1926	Boyd, Martin (1893), *Brangane* (F) McLaren (1887), *My Crowded Solitude* (F) Prichard (1883), *Working Bullocks* (F) Slessor (1901), *Earth Visitors* (V)	Patsy Adam-Smith *b* Ada Cambridge *d* *The Moth of Moonbi*, first feature film directed by Charles Chauvel Anna Pavlova dances in Australia

Date	Publications	Literary/Cultural Events
1927	Devaney (1890), *The Currency Lass* (F)	David Ireland *b*
	FitzGerald (1902), *The Greater Apollo* (V)	Alan Seymour *b*
		Lesbia Harford *d*
	Neilson (1872), *New Poems* (V)	G. G. McCrae *d*
1928	Boyd, Martin (1893), *The Montforts* (F)	Bruce Beaver *b*
	Brereton (1871), *Swags Up!* (V); *The Temple on the Hill* (D)	Richard Beynon *b*
		Doreen Clarke *b*
	Evans (*d* 1909), *Collected Verse* (V)	Elizabeth Harrower *b*
	Franklin (1879), *Up the Country* (F)	*London Aphrodite*, eds Jack Lindsay and P. R. Stephensen (1928–29), founded in London
	McCrae, Hugh (1876), *Satyrs and Sunlight* (V)	*For the Term of His Natural Life*, film directed by Norman Dawn
	Palmer, Vance (1885), *The Man Hamilton* (F)	Formation of the Fellowship of Australian Writers
	Prichard (1883), *The Wild Oats of Han* (F)	Charles Kingsford Smith makes first trans-Pacific flight in the 'Southern Cross'
1929	Devaney (1890), *The Vanished Tribes* (F)	Ray Mathew *b*
		Peter Porter *b*
	Dyson (1865), *The Golden Shanty* (F)	R. A. Simpson *b*
	'Eldershaw, M. Barnard', *A House is Built* (F)	Barbara Baynton *d*
	FitzGerald, (1902), *To Meet the Sun* (V)	James Joyce's *Ulysses* banned in Australia
	Hay (1875), *Strabane of the Mulberry Hills* (F)	The Great Depression (1929–34) begins
	Manning (1882), *The Middle Parts of Fortune: Somme and Ancre* [abridged edn 1930 titled *Her Privates We*] (F)	
	Prichard (1883), *Coonardoo* (F)	
	'Richardson' (1870), *Ultima Thule* (F)	
	Unaipon (1873), *Native Legends* (P)	
1930	Franklin (1879), *Ten Creeks Run* (F)	Geoffrey Blainey *b*
	Gilmore (1865), *The Wild Swan* (V)	Bruce Dawe *b*
	Hancock (1898), *Australia* (P)	Peter Kenna *b*
	Lindsay, Norman (1879), *Redheap* (F)	Hazel McKellar *b*
	Lower (1903), *Here's Luck* (F)	Jean Curlewis *d*
	Palmer, Vance (1885), *Men are Human* and *The Passage* (F)	Radio telephone link to Britain and New Zealand
	Prichard (1883), *Haxby's Circus* (F)	
	'Richardson' (1870), *The Fortunes of Richard Mahony*: three novels published in 1917, 1925, 1929 (F)	

Date	Publications	Literary/Cultural Events
1931	Brereton (1871), *So Long, Mick* (D)	Shirley Hazzard *b*
	Davison (1893), *Forever Morning* and *Man-shy* (F)	Peter Mathers *b*
		Barry Oakley *b*
	'Eldershaw, M. Barnard', *Green Memory* (F)	Edward Dyson *d*
	Franklin (1879), *Old Blastus of Bandicoot* (F); *Back to Bool Bool* (F)	*Manuscript: A Miscellany of Art and Letters* (Geelong 1931–35), founded
	Gilmore (1865), *The Rue Tree* (V)	
	Idriess (1890), *Lasseter's Last Ride* (P)	
	Palmer, Vance (1885), *Separate Lives* (F)	
	Upfield (1888), *The Sands of Windee* (F)	
1932	Dark (1901), *Slow Dawning* (F)	Christopher Koch *b*
	Gilmore (1865), *Under the Wilgas* (V)	C. J. Brennan *d*
	Idriess (1890), *Flynn of the Inland* (P)	Fergus Hume *d*
	Lindsay, Norman (1879), *The Cautious Amorist* (F)	Australia's national broadcasting network, the ABC, begins
	Mann, Leonard (1895), *Flesh in Armour* (F)	Aborigines excluded from Federal pastoral industry award conditions (–1966)
	Palmer, Vance (1885), *Daybreak* (F)	
	Prichard (1883), *Kiss on the Lips* (F); *The Earth Lover* (V)	Sydney Harbour Bridge opened
	Slessor (1901), *Cuckooz Contrey* (V)	
1933	Davison (1893), *The Wells of Beersheba* (P)	Kevin Gilbert *b*
		Fay Zwicky *b*
	Franklin (1879), *Bring the Monkey* (F)	John Le Gay Brereton *d*
	Lindsay, Norman (1879), *Saturdee* (F)	A. G. Stephens *d*
	O'Ferrall (*d* 1925), *Stories* (F)	
	Slessor (1901), *Darlinghurst Nights* (V)	
1934	'Baylebridge' (1883), *Love Redeemed* (V)	Barry Humphries *b*
		James McQueen *b*
	Boyd, Martin (1893), *Scandal of Spring* (F)	David Malouf *b*
	Dark (1901), *Prelude to Christopher* (F)	Chris Wallace-Crabbe *b*
	Lindsay, Norman (1879), *Pan in the Parlour* (F)	Regular airmail service between Australia and England begins; USA service from 1937
	'Maurice' (1881), *Melbourne Odes* (V)	
	Neilson (1872), *Collected Poems* (V)	
	Palmer, Vance (1885), *The Swayne Family*; *Sea and Spinifex* (F)	
	Penton (1904), *Landtakers* (F)	

Date	Publications	Literary/Cultural Events
1934	'Richardson' (1870), *The End of a Childhood* (F) 'Rudd' (1868), *Green Grey Homestead* (F) Stead (1902), *The Salzburg Tales* (F); *Seven Poor Men of Sydney* (F)	
1935	Boyd, Martin (1893), *The Lemon Farm* (F) Dennis (1876), *The Singing Garden* (P, V) Mann, Leonard (1895), *Human Drift* (F) Palmer, Vance (1885), *Hurricane* (F) Tennant (1912), *Tiburon* (F) White, Patrick (1912), *The Ploughman, and Other Poems* (V)	Rodney Hall *b* Antigone Kefala *b* Thomas Keneally *b* Thomas Shapcott *b* Randolph Stow *b* A. H. Davis ('Steele Rudd') *d* Frederick Manning *d* Rosa Praed *d* Louis Stone *d*
1936	Boyd, Martin (1893), *The Painted Princess* (F) Dark (1901), *Return to Coolami* (F) Davison (1893), *Children of the Dark People* (P) Devanny (1894), *Sugar Heaven* (F) 'Eldershaw, M. Barnard', *The Glasshouse* (F) Franklin (1879), *All That Swagger* (F) Ingamells (1913), *Forgotten People* (V) Paterson (1864), *The Shearer's Colt* (F) Stead (1902), *The Beauties and the Furies* (F) Stivens (1911), *The Tramp* (F)	'B. Wongar' (Sreten Bozic) *b* Judith Rodriguez *b* A. H. Adams *d* A. A. G. Hales *d* National Library begins issuing *Annual Catalogue of Australian Publications* (1936–60)
1937	Boyd, Martin (1893), *The Picnic* (F) Dark (1901), *Sun across the Sky* (F) 'Eldershaw, M. Barnard' (1897), *Plaque with Laurel* (F) Hay (1875), *The Mystery of Alfred Doubt* (F) Mackenzie (1913), *Our Earth* (V); *The Young Desire It* (F) Mann, Leonard (1895), *A Murder in Sydney* (F) Palmer, Vance (1885), *Legend for Sanderson* (F) Prichard (1883), *Intimate Strangers* (F)	Colleen McCullough *b* Catherine Martin *d* *Venture*, ed. Rex Ingamells, Adelaide, (1937–40), founded Radio serial *Dad and Dave* begins (–1953) Beginning of recovery from Depression as prices for exported primary products improve

Date	Publications	Literary/Cultural Events
1938	Boyd, Martin (1893), *Night of the Party* (F)	Sara Dowse *b*
	Brennan (*d* 1932), *Twenty-three Poems* (V)	Robert Hughes *b*
		Colin Johnson (Mudrooroo Narogin) *b*
	Dark (1901), *Waterway* (F)	Morris Lurie *b*
	Evatt (1894), *Rum Rebellion* (P)	Frank Moorhouse *b*
	FitzGerald (1902), *Moonlight Acre* (V)	Les A. Murray *b*
	Herbert (1901), *Capricornia* (F)	C. J. Dennis *d*
	Ingamells (1913), *Sun-Freedom* (V)	*The Australian Abo Call*, first newspaper written by and for Aborigines begins publication, edited by Jack Patten (6 issues)
	Lindsay, Norman (1879), *Age of Consent* (F)	
	Mackenzie (1913), *Chosen People* (F)	*Jindyworobak Anthology* (1938–53) begins
	Mann, Leonard (1895), *The Plumed Voice* (V)	Playwrights' Advisory Board established (–1963)
	Neilson (1872), *Beauty Imposes* (V)	
	Ratcliffe (1904), *Flying Fox and Drifting Sand* (F)	Albert Namatjira's first exhibition held
	Stead (1902), *House of All Nations* (F)	
1939	'Baylebridge' (1883), *Sextains* and *This Vital Flesh* (V)	Germaine Greer *b*
		Barbara Hanrahan *b*
	Boyd, Martin (1893), *A Single Flame* (F)	Gerald Murnane *b*
	Franklin, Miles (1879) and Cusack (1902), *Pioneers on Parade* (P)	Paul Wenz *d*
		Australia at war, 1939–45
	Gilmore (1865), *Battlefields* (V)	*Southerly*, edited by R. G. Howarth, founded
	McCrae, Hugh (1876), *Poems* (V)	
	Mann, Leonard (1895), *Mountain Flat* (F)	Douglas Stewart literary editor (–1961) of the *Bulletin*
	Miller (1881), *Australian Literature* (P)	Contemporary Art Society founded
	'Richardson' (1870), *The Young Cosima* (F)	Major national drought (–1945)
	Slessor (1901), *Five Bells* (V)	
	Tennant (1912), *Foveaux* (F)	
	White, Patrick (1912), *Happy Valley* (F)	
1940	Boyd, Martin (1893), *Nuns in Jeopardy* (F)	Glenda Adams *b*
		Jack Hibberd *b*
	Davison (1893), *The Woman at the Mill* (F)	Manfred Jurgensen *b*
	Ingamells (1913), *Memory of Hills* (V)	Andrew Taylor *b*
	Neilson (1872), *To the Men of the Roads* (V)	Mrs K. Langloh Parker *d*
		Helen Simpson *d*
	Palmer, Vance (1885), *National Portraits* (P)	*Angry Penguins*, ed. Max Harris and others (1940–6), founded

Date	Publications	Literary/Cultural Events
1940	Prichard (1883), *Brumby Innes* (D)	*Meanjin* (Brisbane, then Melbourne) begins, with C. B. Christesen as first editor
	Stead (1902), *The Man who Loved Children* (F)	
	Stewart (1913), *Elegy for an Airman* (V)	*40 000 Horsemen,* film directed by Charles Chauvel, starring Chips Rafferty
1941	Dark (1901), *The Timeless Land* (F)	Murray Bail *b*
	Gilmore (1865), *The Disinherited* (V)	Beverley Farmer *b*
	Macartney (1887), *Preferences* (V)	Roger McDonald *b*
	Manifold (1915), *The Death of Ned Kelly* (V)	Randolph Bedford *d*
	Mann, Leonard (1895), *Poems from the Mask* (V)	F.J. Broomfield *d*
	O'Dowd (1866), *Poems* (V)	A. B. ('Banjo') Paterson *d*
	Prichard (1883), *Moon of Desire* (F)	*Coast to Coast* (1941–73, 1986) founded
	Stewart (1913), *Sonnets to the Unknown Soldier* (V)	*Poetry: A Quarterly of Australian and New Zealand Verse*, ed. Flexmore Hudson (1941–7), founded
	Tennant (1912), *The Battlers* (F)	ABC inaugurates the Argonauts' Club for children
	White, Patrick (1912), *The Living and the Dead* (F)	
1942	Casey (1907), *It's Harder for Girls* (F)	Ron Blair *b*
	Ingamells (1913), *News of the Sun* (V)	Gerry Bostock *b*
	Langley (1908), *The Pea Pickers* (F)	Rosa Cappiello *b*
	Mann, Leonard (1885), *The Go-Getter* (F)	Silvana Gardner *b*
	Porter, Hal (1911), *Short Stories* (F)	Helen Garner *b*
	Stewart (1913), *Ned Kelly* (D)	Serge Liberman *b*
		Humphrey McQueen *b*
		Michael Wilding *b*
		David Williamson *b*
		William Blocksidge ('Baylebridge') *d*
		John Shaw Neilson *d*
		Frank Wilmot ('Furnley Maurice') *d*
1943	Barnard, Marjorie (1897), *The Persimmon Tree* (F)	Robert Adamson *b*
	Casey (1907), *Birds of a Feather* (F)	Peter Carey *b*
	Hart-Smith (1911), *Columbus Goes West* (V)	Robert Drewe *b*
	Ingamells (1913), *Content are the Quiet Ranges* and *Unknown Land* (V)	John Tranter *b*
	Neilson (d 1942), *Lines Written in Memory of Adam Lindsay Gordon* (V)	Louis Esson *d*
	Stewart (1913), *Ned Kelly* (D)	*Australian New Writing* (annual), edited by K. S. Prichard, George Farwell and Bernard Smith (–1946)
	Tennant (1912), *Ride on Stranger* and *Time Enough Later* (F)	*Barjai* (1943–47) founded

DATE	PUBLICATIONS	LITERARY/CULTURAL EVENTS
1944	Cowan (1914, *Drift* (F)	Alex Buzo *b*
	Dobson (1920), *In a Convex Mirror* (V)	Blanche d'Alpuget *b*
		David Foster *b*
	Dutton (1922), *Night Flight and Sunrise* (V)	Gün Gencer *b*
	McCrae, Hugh (1876), *Forests of Pan* (V)	The 'Ern Malley hoax' against *Angry Penguins*, ed. Max Harris
	Mackenzie, Kenneth (1913), *The Moonlit Doorway* (V)	
	'Ern Malley', *The Darkening Ecliptic* (V)	
	Manifold (1915), *Trident* (V)	
	Mann, Leonard (1895), *The Delectable Mountains* (V)	
	Marshall (1902), *These are my People* (P)	
	Prichard (1883), *Potch and Colour* (F)	
	Slessor (1910), *One Hundred Poems* (V)	
	Stewart (1913), *A Girl with Red Hair* (F); *The Fire on the Snow* and *The Golden Lover* (D)	
1945	Baker (1912), *The Australian Language* (P)	John Docker *b*
		Robert Gray *b*
	Blight (1913), *The Old Pianist* (V)	John Romeril *b*
	Casey (1907), *Downhill is Easier* (F)	Peter Skrzynecki *b*
	Close (1903), *Love Me Sailor* (F)	William Gosse Hay *d*
	Dark (1901), *The Little Company* (F)	The Australian Book Council, later National Book Council, formed in Sydney
	Gilmore (1865), *Pro Patria Australia* (V)	
	Hart-Smith (1911), *Harvest* (V)	Australian National Film Board established
	Lindsay, Norman (1879), *The Cousin from Fiji* (F)	
	McCrae, Hugh (1876), *Voice of the Forest* (V)	War Service Land Settlement Scheme begins
	West (1916), *Moon in my Pocket* (F)	
1946	Boyd, Martin (1893), *Lucinda Brayford* (F)	Lily Brett *b*
	Davison (1893), *Dusty* (F)	Ethel Robertson ('Henry Handel Richardson') *d*
	Esson (*d* 1943), *The Southern Cross* (D)	Children's Book of the Year Award begins
	Franklin (1879), *My Career Goes Bung* (F)	Georgian House and Robert Close found guilty of obscene libel over publication of *Love Me Sailor*
	McAuley (1917), *Under Aldebaran* (V)	
	Manifold (1915), *Selected Verse* (V)	Post-war assisted passage scheme for migrants from UK begins (−1955)

Date	Publications	Literary/Cultural Events
1946	Marshall (1902), *Tell us the about the Turkey, Jo* (F)	Woomera rocket range established in South Australia
	Prichard (1883), *The Roaring Nineties* (F)	
	Stead (1902), *Letty Fox: Her Luck* (F)	
	Stewart (1913), *The Dosser in Springtime* (V)	
	Stivens (1911), *The Courtship of Uncle Henry* (F)	
	Tennant (1912), *Lost Haven* (F)	
	Wright (1915), *The Moving Image* (V)	
1947	Casey (1907), *The Wits are Out* (F)	Peter Kocan *b*
	'Eldershaw, M. Barnard', *Tomorrow and Tomorrow* (F)	Finola Moorhead *b*
		Lennie Lower *d*
	Lindsay, Norman (1879), *Halfway to Anywhere* (F)	Post-war European immigration programme begins; £10 fares for UK ex-servicemen and families
	Morrison (1904), *Sailors Belong Ships* (F)	
	Neilson (*d* 1942), *Unpublished Poems* (V)	
	Palmer, Vance (1885), *Hail Tomorrow* (D); *Cyclone* (F)	
	Stewart (1913), *Glencoe* (V); *Shipwreck* (D)	
1948	Dark (1901), *Storm of Time* (F)	Marion Campbell *b*
	Dobson (1920), *The Ship of Ice* (V)	Anna Couani *b*
	Drake-Brockman (1901), *Sydney or the Bush* (F); *The Lion Tamer* (D)	Michael Dransfield *b*
		Alan Wearne *b*
	Furphy (*d* 1912), *The Buln-Buln and the Brolga* (F)	*Rusty Bugles* censored by NSW Chief Secretary
	Gilmore (1865), *Selected Verse* (V)	First Holden cars produced
	Harpur (*d* 1868), *Rosa: Love Sonnets to Mary Doyle* (V)	
	McCrae, Hugh (1876), *Story Book Only* (F)	
	Marshall (1902), *Ourselves Writ Strange* (P)	
	Palmer, Vance (1885), *Golconda* (F)	
	Park (?1923), *The Harp in the South* (F)	
	Prichard (1883), *Golden Miles* (F)	
	Stead (1902), *A Little Tea, a Little Chat* (F)	
	Webb (1925), *A Drum for Ben Boyd* (V)	
	White, Patrick (1912), *The Aunt's Story* (F)	

Date	Publications	Literary/Cultural Events
1949	Boyd, Martin (1893), *Such Pleasure* (F)	Jennifer Maiden *b*
	Campbell (1915), *Speak with the Sun* (V)	Roderic Quinn *d*
	FitzGerald (1915), *Heemskerck Shoals* (V)	*Blue Hills* (−1976), radio serial written by Gwen Meredith, begins on ABC
	Marshall (1902), *How Beautiful are thy Feet* and *Pull down the Blind* (F)	Snowy Mountains Authority established to provide electricity and irrigation along Murray and
	Morrison (1904), *The Creeping City* (F)	Murrumbidgee Rivers; many migrants work on its setting up
	Park (?1923), *Poor Man's Orange* (F)	
	Wright (1915), *Woman to Man* (V)	
1950	Casey (1907), *City of Men* (F)	Brian Castro *b*
	Franklin (1879), *Prelude to Waking* (F)	Kate Grenville *b*
	Hardy (1917), *Power without Glory* (F)	Louis Nowra *b*
	'James, Brian' (1892), *The Advancement of Spencer Button* (F)	*Smith's Weekly* (1919−) closes
	Lindsay, Norman (1879), *Dust or Polish?* (F)	Australia enters Korean War (−1953)
		Female rates of pay reach 75 per cent of male rates
	Marshall (1902), *Bumping into Friends* (F)	Myxomatosis virus kills millions of rabbits
	Morrison (1904), *Port of Call* (F)	
	Prichard (1883), *Winged Seeds* (F)	
1951	Cusack (1902) and Florence James (1902), *Come in Spinner* (F)	Ania Walwicz *b*
		Angelo Loukakis *b*
	Ingamells (1913), *The Great South Land* (V)	Sally Morgan *b*
	McCrae, Hugh (1876), *The Ship of Heaven* (D)	Π O (Peter Oustabasidis) *b*
		Daisy Bates *d*
	Mackenzie, Kenneth (1913), *Dead Men Rising* (F)	Brian Penton *d*
	Stivens (1911), *Jimmy Brockett* (F)	Defamation suit over Frank Hardy's *Power without Glory*
1952	Boyd, Martin (1893), *The Cardboard Crown* (F)	Moya Costello *b*
		E. J. Brady *d*
	Braddon (1921), *The Naked Island* (F)	*Ern Malley's Journal* (ed. Max Harris and others, 1952−5) founded
	De Boissiere (1907), *Crown Jewel* (F)	
	FitzGerald (1902), *Between Two Tides* (V)	*The Realist Writer* (ed. Bill Wannan, subsequently Stephen Murray-Smith, 1952−4) founded
	Henning (1826), *The Letters*, ed. David Adams (F)	
	Hungerford (1915), *The Ridge and the River* (F)	
	Marshall (1902), *People of the Dreamtime* (P)	
	Stead (1902), *The People with the Dogs* (F)	

Date	Publications	Literary/Cultural Events
1952	Stewart (1913), *Sun Orchids* (V)	
	Tennant (1912), *Tether a Dragon* (D)	
	Waten (1911), *Alien Son* (F)	
	Webb (1925), *Leichhardt in Theatre* (V)	
1953	Brennan (d 1932), *The Burden of Tyre* (V)	Steven Sewell *b*
		Bernard O'Dowd *d*
	'Caddie', *Caddie, a Sydney Barmaid* (F)	Dora Wilcox *d*
	Dark (1901), *No Barrier* (F)	
	FitzGerald (1902), *This Night's Orbit* (V)	
	Martin, David (1915), *From Life* (V)	
	Stivens (1911), *The Gambling Ghost* (F)	
	Tennant (1912), *The Joyful Condemned* (F)	
	Webb (1925), *Birthday* (V)	
	Wright (1915), *The Gateway* (V)	
1954	Blight (1913), *The Two Suns Met* (V)	Miles Franklin *d*
	Buckley (1925), *The World's Flesh* (V)	Jack McLaren *d*
	Franklin (1879), *Cockatoos* (F)	*Overland* (Melbourne, ed. Stephen Murray-Smith) founded
	Gilmore (1865), *Fourteen Men* (V)	
	Langley (1908), *White Topee* (F)	*Poetry Magazine* (Sydney, 1954–71; later *New Poetry*) founded
	Mackenzie (1913), *The Refuge* (F)	
	Palmer, Vance (1885), *The Legend of the Nineties* (P)	*Jedda*, Charles Chauvel's last feature film
	Waten (1911), *The Unbending* (F)	Australian Elizabethan Theatre Trust founded
		Assisted Passage Scheme to help migrants from USA and Northern Europe
1955	Boyd, Martin (1893), *A Difficult Young Man* (F)	Rex Ingamells *d*
	Hope (1907), *The Wandering Islands* (V)	Kenneth Mackenzie ('Seaforth Mackenzie') *d*
		Molly Skinner *d*
	Marshall (1902), *I Can Jump Puddles* (P)	First performance of Ray Lawler's *Summer of the Seventeenth Doll*
	Morrison (1904), *Black Cargo* (F)	
	Niland (1917), *The Shiralee* (F)	
	Palmer, Vance (1885), *Let the Birds Fly* (F)	
	Stewart (1913), *The Birdsville Track* (V)	
	Stivens (1911), *Ironbark Bill* (F)	

Date	Publications	Literary/Cultural Events
1955	White, Patrick (1912), *The Tree of Man* (F) Wright (1915), *The Two Fires* (V)	
1956	Anderson, Ethel (1883), *At Parramatta* (F) Campbell (1915), *The Miracle of Mullion Hill* (V) De Boissiere (1907), *Rum and Coca-Cola* (F) Franklin (d 1954), *Gentlemen at Gyang Gyang* (F) McAuley (1917), *A Vision of Ceremony* (V) Marshall (1902), *How's Andy Going?* (F) Porter, Hal (1911), *The Hexagon* (V) Stow (1935), *A Haunted Land* (V) Tennant (1912), *The Honey Flow* (F) Upfield (1888), *Man of Two Worlds* (F)	Flora Eldershaw *d* *Quadrant* (Sydney), ed. James McAuley, begins *Westerly* (Perth) begins Regular television broadcasting begins in Sydney with ABC and TCN9
1957	Boyd, Martin (1893), *Outbreak of Love* (F) Harrower (1928), *Down in the City* (F) Lawler (1921), *Summer of the Seventeenth Doll* (D) Mann, Leonard (1895), *Elegiac, and Other Poems* (V) Palmer, Vance (1885), *Seedtime* and *The Rainbow Bird* (F) Slessor (1910), *Poems* (V) Stivens (1911), *The Scholarly Mouse* (F) Stow (1935), *Act One* (V); *The Bystander* (F) Waten (1911), *Shares in Murder* (F) White, Patrick (1912), *Voss* (F)	*Australian Letters,* ed. Max Harris, Geoffrey Dutton and others, founded (–1968) Miles Franklin Award begins; first winner Patrick White's *Voss*
1958	Astley (1952), *Girl with a Monkey* (F) Cato (1917), *All the Rivers Run* (F) Cowan (1914), *The Unploughed Land* (F) O' Grady, John ('Nino Culotta') (1907), *They're a Weird Mob* (F) Hardy (1917), *The Four-legged Lottery* (F) Koch (1932), *The Boys in the Island* (F)	Archie Weller *b* Ethel Anderson *d* Mary Grant Bruce *d* Hugh McCrae *d* Ethel Turner *d* *Melbourne Critical Review* begins, since 1965 titled *Critical Review* *Nation* (1958–72) begins

Date	Publications	Literary/Cultural Events
1958	Martin, David (1915), *Poems 1938–1958* (V)	*Realist Writer* (Sydney) founded; later *Realist* (–1970)
	Pearl (1906), *Wild Men of Sydney* (F)	National Institute of Dramatic Art (NIDA) established at University of New South Wales
	Phillips (1900), *The Australian Tradition* (P)	
	Porter, Hal (1911), *A Handful of Pennies* (F)	Equal pay for women legislation in NSW (followed by long-standing disputes about what 'equal work' was)
	Ruhen (1911), *Naked under Capricorn* (F)	Major national drought (–1968)
	Stewart (1913), *Four Plays* (D)	
	Stivens (1911), *The Wide Arch* (F)	
	Stow (1935), *To the Islands* (F)	
	Ward (1914), *The Australian Legend* (P)	
1959	Campbell (1915), *Evening Under Lamplight* (F)	Vance Palmer *d*
	Durack (1913), *Kings in Grass Castles* (F)	Antipodean Group of artists, including Boyd, Brack, Blackman, Perceval, Pugh, Dickerson, and critic Bernard Smith, formed in Melbourne
	FitzGerald (1902), *The Wind at your Door* (V)	Non-Aboriginal population reaches 10 million
	Hart-Smith (1911), *Poems of Discovery* (V)	
	Herbert (1901), *Seven Emus* (F)	
	Hewett (1923), *Bobbin Up* (F)	
	Mann, Leonard (1895), *Andrea Caslin* (F)	
	Palmer, Vance (1885), *The Big Fellow* (F)	
	Prichard (1883), *N' Goola* (F)	
	Stuart (1913), *Yandy* (F)	
	Wallace-Crabbe (1934), *The Music of Division* (V)	
	West (1916), *The Devil's Advocate* (F)	
	Wright (1915), *The Generations of Men* (P)	
1960	Astley (1925), *A Descant for Gossips* (F)	Tim Winton *b*
	Beynon (1928), *The Shifting Heart* (D)	National Library of Australia becomes an autonomous body
	Boyd, Robin (1919), *The Australian Ugliness* (P)	Adelaide Festival of the Arts established
	Harrower (1928), *The Catherine Wheel* (F)	First performance of Alan Seymour's *One Day of the Year*
	Hope (1907), *Poems* (V)	*Summer of the Seventeenth Doll,* film
	'O' Conner' (1913), *The Irishman* (F)	*Lady Chatterley's Lover* banned in Australia
	Stewart (1913), *Fisher's Ghost* (D); ed *Voyager Poems* (V)	Economic recession

Date	Publications	Literary/Cultural Events
1961	Beaver (1928), *Under the Bridge* (V)	Mrs Aeneas Gunn *d*
	Buckley (1925), *Masters in Israel* (V)	*Australian Book Review,* ed. Geoffrey Dutton and Max Harris (–1974; revived 1978)
	Cook (1929), *Wake in Fright* (F)	
	Gare (1919), *The Fringe Dwellers* (F)	*Australian National Bibliography* begins
	Hall (1935), *Penniless Till Doomsday* (V)	
	Herbert (1901), *Soldier's Women* (F)	All TV commercials to be of Australian origin from this year
	Manifold (1915), *Nightmares and Sunhorses* (V)	
	Mathew (1929), *A Bohemian Affair* (F)	
	Porter, Hal (1911), *The Tilted Cross* (F)	
	Porter, Peter (1929), *Once Bitten, Twice Bitten* (V)	
	Shapcott (1935), *Time on Fire* (V)	
	Stuart (1913), *The Driven* (F)	
	Waten (1911), *Time of Conflict* (F)	
	Webb (1925), *Socrates, and Other Poems* (V)	
	White, Patrick (1912), *Riders in the Chariot* (F)	
1962	Astley (1925), *The Well Dressed Explorer* (F)	Paul Radley *b*
		Jean Devanny *d*
	Boyd, Martin (1893), *When Blackbirds Sing* (V)	Dame Mary Gilmore *d*
	Campbell (1915), *Poems* (V)	H.M. Green *d*
	Casey (1907), *Amid the Plenty* (F)	*Makar* (St Lucia, 1962–79) founded
	Clark (1915), *A History of Australia,* Vol. 1 (Vol. 6, 1987) (P)	*The Sundowners,* film
		First chair of Australian Literature established at Sydney University, inaugurally held by G. A. Wilkes and, from 1968, by Dame Leonie Kramer
	Dawe (1930), *No Fixed Address* (V)	
	Dutton (1922), *Flowers and Fury* (V)	
	FitzGerald (1902), *Southmost Twelve* (V)	Australia joins USA in Vietnam War (1962–72)
	Martin, David (1915), *The Young Wife* (F)	
	Morrison (1904), *Twenty-three* (F)	
	Porter, Hal (1911), *A Bachelor's Children* (F)	
	Seymour (1927), *The One Day of the Year* (D)	
	Stewart (1913), *Rutherford* and *The Garden of Ships* (V)	
	Stow (1935), *Outrider* (V)	
	Turner, George (1916), *The Cupboard Under the Stairs* (F)	
	Wright (1915), *Birds* (V)	

Date	Publications	Literary/Cultural Events
1963	Blight (1913), *A Beachcomber's Diary* (V)	W. H. Ogilvie *d*
	Hall (1935), *Forty Beads on a Hangman's Rope* (V)	*Australian Literary Studies* (ed. L. T. Hergenhan) founded
	Hardy (1917), *Legends from Benson's Valley* (F)	*Arena* (Fitzroy) founded
	Harwood (1920), *Poems* (V)	*Southern Review* (Adelaide) founded
	Hazzard (1931), *Cliffs of Fall* (F)	*Oz*, ed. Richard Walsh and Richard Neville (−1965), founded
	Herbert (1901), *Larger than Life* and *Disturbing Element* (F)	*Art and Australia* founded
	Locke-Elliott (1917), *Careful, He Might Hear You* (F)	Australian Society of Authors formed, with Dal Stivens as President
	Moorehead (1910), *Cooper's Creek* (F)	Penguin Australia founded
	Porter, Hal (1911) *The Watcher on the Cast-iron Balcony* (F); *The Tower* (D)	First Aboriginal graduate from an Australian university, Charles Perkins
	Prichard (1883), *Child of the Hurricane* (F)	First data transmission service, between Sydney and Melbourne
	Stow (1935), *Tourmaline* (F)	Australia signs Nuclear Test Ban Treaty
	Thiele (1920), *Storm Boy* (F)	
	West (1916), *The Shoes of the Fisherman* (F)	
	Wright (1915), *Five Senses* (V)	
1964	Beaver (1928), *Seawall and Shoreline* (V)	Gavin Casey *d*
	Cato (1917), *The Sea Ants* (F)	E. Morris Miller *d*
	Cowan (1914), *Summer* (F)	Nettie Palmer *d*
	Davison (1893), *The Road to Yesterday* (F)	Walker's *We Are Going*, first full volume of published verse by an Aboriginal writer
	Horne, Donald (1921), *The Lucky Country: Australia in the Sixties* (P)	*Australian* founded
	Johnston (1912), *My Brother Jack* (F)	*Poetry Australia* (Sydney) founded
	Keneally (1935), *The Place at Whitton* (F)	Selective conscription for overseas service begins (−1972)
	McAuley (1917), *Captain Quiros* (V)	
	Shapcott (1935), *The Mankind Thing* and *Sonnets 1960−63* (V)	
	Walker (Oodgeroo) (1920), *We are Going* (V)	
	Waten (1925), *Distant Land* (F)	
	Webb (1925), *The Ghost of the Cock* (V)	
	White, Patrick (1912), *The Burnt Ones* (F)	
	Wright (1915), *City Sunrise* (V)	

Date	Publications	Literary/Cultural Events
1965	Astley (1925), *The Slow Natives* (F)	P. R. ('Inky') Stephensen *d*
	Boyd, Martin (1893), *Day of my Delight* (F)	Johnson's (Mudrooroo's) *Wild Cat Falling*, first published novel by an Aboriginal writer
	Cowan (1914), *The Empty Street* (F)	
	Dawe (1930), *A Need of Similar Name* (V)	Sun Books begins
	FitzGerald (1902), *Forty Years' Poems* (V)	'Last' independent traditional groups, of Pintubi people 'brought in' to settlements
	Johnson (Mudrooroo) (1938), *Wild Cat Falling* (F)	Australian troops sent to Vietnam
	Keneally (1923), *The Fear* (F)	
	Koch (1923), *Across the Sea Wall* (F)	
	Martin, David (1915), *The Hero of Too* (F)	
	Murray (1938) and Lehmann (1940), *The Ilex Tree* (V)	
	Porter, Hal (1911), *The Cats of Venice* (F)	
	Porter, Peter (1929), *Poems Ancient and Modern* (V)	
	Southall (1921), *Ash Road* (F)	
	Stow (1935), *The Merry-go-round in the Sea* (F)	
	White, Patrick (1912), *Four Plays* (D)	
1966	Beaver (1928), *You Can't Come Back* (V)	Eric Lambert *d*
	Blainey (1930), *The Tyranny of Distance* (P)	*Australian Dictionary of Biography* begins
	Buckley (1925), *Arcady and Other Places* (V)	*Two Ways Meet: Stories of Migrants in Australia*, edited by Rorabacher
	Cowan (1914), *Seed* (F)	*They're a Weird Mob*, film
	Harrower (1928), *The Watch Tower* (F)	Gurindji Aboriginals strike for land rights (−1973) at Wave Hill
	Hazzard (1931), *The Evening of the Holiday* (F)	Aboriginals no longer excluded from Federal and Queensland rural awards but covered as 'slow workers'
	Hope (1907), *Collected Poems 1930–65* (V)	Aboriginal population estimated at 102 000 (estimate subsequently raised)
	Lurie (1938), *Rappaport* (F)	Japan displaces UK as Australia's major overseas market
	Mathers (1931), *Trap* (F)	
	Porter, Hal (1911) *The Paper Chase* (F); *The Professor* (D)	Decimal currency introduced
	Stead (1902), *Dark Places of the Heart* (F)	R. G. Menzies resigns after 16 years as Prime Minister
	Walker (Oodgeroo) (1920), *The Dawn is at Hand* (V)	

Date	Publications	Literary/Cultural Events
1966	White, Patrick (1912), *The Solid Mandala* (F) Wright (1915), *The Other Half* (V); *The Nature of Love* (F)	
1967	Beaver (1928), *Open at Random* (V) Dutton (1922), *Poems Soft and Loud* (V) Hall (1935), *Eyewitness* (V) Hazzard (1931), *People in Glass Houses* (F) Keneally (1935), *Bring Larks and Heroes* (F) Lindsay, Joan (1896), *Picnic at Hanging Rock* (F) Prichard (1883), *Happiness* and *Subtle Flame* (F) Shapcott (1935), *A Taste of Salt Water* (V)ᵥ Stead (1902), *The Puzzlehead Girl* (F) Stewart (1913), *Collected Poems* (V) Tennant (1912), *Tell Morning This* (F) Wallace-Crabbe (1934), *The Rebel General* (V)	Cecil Mann *d* D'Arcy Niland *d* La Mama theatre opened in Melbourne Open-line radio begins Referendum to amend Constitution, thus giving Federal government power to legislate for Aborigines, and including full-blood Aborigines in Census, passed by record 90 per cent vote Uniform censorship agreement between states and Commonwealth government Ronald Ryan last person to be hanged in Australia
1968	Astley (1925), *A Boat Load of Home Folk* (F) Blight (1913), *My Beachcombing Days* (V) Davison (1893), *The White Thorntree* (F) Dawe (1930), *An Eye for a Tooth* (V) Hall (1935), *An Autobiography of a Gorgon* and *The Law of Karma* (V) Ireland (1927), *The Chantic Bird* (F) Keneally (1935), *Three Cheers for the Paraclete* (F) Lehmann (1940), *A Voyage of Lions* (V) Lindsay, Norman (1879), *Rooms and Houses* (F) Martin, David (1915), *The Idealist* (V) Porter, Hal (1911), *Elijah's Ravens* (V) Stivens (1911), *Three Persons Make a Tiger* (F) West (1916), *The Tower of Babel* (F)	C.E.W. Bean *d* Henrietta Drake-Brockman *d* Dorothea Mackellar *d* *The Drover's Wife*, film

Date	Publications	Literary/Cultural Events
1969	Beaver (1928), *Letters to Live Poets* (V)	May Gibbs *d*
	Boyd, Martin (1893), *The Tea Time of Love* (F)	Norman Lindsay *d*
		Katharine Susannah Prichard *d*
	Dawe (1930), *Beyond the Subdivisions* (V)	*Australian Author* (Sydney) founded
	Hope (1901), *New Poems: 1965–1969* (V)	
	Keneally (1945), *The Survivor* (F)	
	Johnston (1912), *Clean Straw for Nothing* (F)	
	Lurie (1938), *Happy Times* (F)	
	McAuley (1917), *Surprises of the Sun* (V)	
	Moorhouse (1938), *Futility and Other Animals* (F)	
	Murray (1938), *The Weatherboard Cathedral* (V)	
	Rolls (1925), *They All Ran Wild* (F)	
	Shapcott (1935), *Inwards to the Sun* (V)	
	Webb (1925), *Collected Poems* (V)	
	West (1916), *The Heretic* (F)	
1970	Adamson (1944), *Canticles on the Skin* (V)	Frank Dalby Davison *d*
	Campbell (1915), *The Branch of Dodona* (V)	James Devaney *d*
		George Johnston *d*
	Davis (1918), *The First-Born and Other Poems* (V)	Walter Murdoch *d*
	Hall (1935), *Heaven, in a Way* (V)	University of Queensland Press begins extensive publishing of Australian literature
	Hazzard (1931), *The Bay of Noon* (F)	The Pram Factory in Melbourne becomes the home of the Australian Performing Group
	Hope (1907), *Dunciad Minor* (V)	
	Oakley (1931), *A Salute to the Great McCarthy* and *Let's Hear it for Prendergast* (F)	Nimrod Theatre founded in Sydney by John Bell and Ken Horler
	McQueen, Humphrey (1942), *A New Britannia* (P)	Experimental Film Fund and Australian Film Development Corporation established
	Porter, Hal (1911), *Mr Butterfry and Other Tales of New Japan* (F)	
	Serventy (19?), *Dryandra* (P)	
	Stivens (1911), *A Horse of Air* (F)	
	Walker (Oodgeroo) (1920), *My People* (V, P)	
	White, Patrick (1912), *The Vivisector* (F)	

Date	Publications	Literary/Cultural Events
1971	Adamson (1944), *The Rumour* (V)	Robin Boyd *d*
	Buzo (1944), *Macquarie* (D)	Frank Clune *d*
	Dawe (1930), *Condolences of the Season* (V)	Kenneth Slessor *d*
		John Tierney ('Brian James') *d*
	Hardy (1917), *The Outcasts of Foolgarah* (F)	*LinQ* (Townsville) founded
	Ireland (1927), *The Unknown Industrial Prisoner* (F)	*Aboriginal and Islander Identity* (Perth) founded
	Johnston (*d* 1970), *A Cartload of Clay* (F)	Currency Press, the first company to publish only Australian plays, founded in Sydney by Katharine Brisbane and Philip Parsons
	Keneally (1935), *A Dutiful Daughter* (F)	
	McAuley (1917), *Collected Poems 1936–1970* (V)	
	Porter, Hal (1911), *The Right Thing* (F)	
	Wright (1915), *Collected Poems 1942-1970* (V)	
1972	Astley (1925), *The Acolyte* (F)	Martin Boyd *d*
	Dransfield (1949), *Drug Poems* and *The Inspector of Tides* (V)	*Refractory Girl* (Sydney) founded
		Tabloid Story founded
	Hewett (1923), *The Chapel Perilous* (D)	National Black Theatre's all-Aboriginal production, *Basically Black,* opens in Sydney
	Hope (1907), *Collected Poems 1930–1970* (V)	
	Ireland (1927), *The Flesheaters* (F)	First Labor Party government for 23 years formed by E. G. Whitlam
	Keneally (1935), *The Chant of Jimmie Blacksmith* (F)	Aboriginal flag designed by Gary Foley and Harold Thomas
	Kenna (1930), *The Slaughter of St Teresa's Day* (F)	'Aboriginal Embassy' set up opposite Parliament House, Canberra
	Mathers (1931), *The Wort Papers* (F)	Assisted passages for non-Europeans (Vietnamese, East Timorese) introduced
	Moorhouse (1938), *The Americans, Baby* (F)	
	Murray (1938), *Poems against Economics* (V)	
	Porter, Peter (1929), *After Martial* and *Preaching to the Converted* (V)	
	Tranter (1943), *Red Movie* (V)	
	Wilding (1942), *Aspects of the Dying Process* (F)	
	Williamson (1942), *The Removalists* (D)	
1973	Buzo (1944), *Norm and Ahmed, Rooted, The Roy Murphy Show: Three Plays* (D)	Michael Dransfield *d*
		Francis Webb *d*
	Cowan (1914), *The Tins* (F)	Patrick White awarded Nobel Prize for Literature
	Hibberd (1940), *A Stretch of the Imagination* (D)	

Date	Publications	Literary/Cultural Events
1973	Kenna (1930), *A Hard God* (D)	Literature Board (subsequently within Australia Council) replaces the Commonwealth Literary Fund
	Romeril (1945), *I Don't Know Who to Feel Sorry For* (D)	
	Stead (1902), *The Little Hotel* (F)	National Book Council founded
	West (1916), *The Salamander* (F)	National Playwrights' Conference founded
	White, Patrick (1912), *The Eye of the Storm* (F)	Australian Film and Television School established
	Williamson (1942), *Don's Party* (D)	Opening of Sydney Opera House
	Wright (1915), *Alive: Poems 1971–72* (V)	Aboriginal Legal Service established
	Wrightson (1921), *The Nargun and the Stars* (F)	Preferential tariff arrangements with UK end as UK joins EEC
1974	Astley (1925), *A Kindness Cup* (F)	Eve Langley *d*
	Beaver (1928), *Lauds and Plaints* (V)	Wild and Woolley (Sydney) begin publishing new Australian writing
	Carey (1943), *The Fat Man in History* (F)	C. B. Christesen retires as editor of *Meanjin*
	Docker (1945), *Australian Cultural Elites* (P)	
	Foster (1944), *The Pure Land* (F)	*Mother I'm Rooted*, an anthology of women's writing edited by Kate Jennings
	Hibberd (1940), *Dimboola* (D)	
	Ireland (1927), *Burn* (F)	The *Age* Book of the Year Award begins
	Keneally (1935), *Blood Red, Sister Rose* (F)	National Book Council Awards begin
	McKie (1909), *The Mango Tree* (F)	Patrick White Award begins
	Malouf (1934), *Neighbours in a Thicket* (V)	*SPAN* founded
	Moorhouse (1938), *The Electrical Experience* (F)	Public Lending Right scheme introduced
	Murray (1938), *Lunch and Counter Lunch* (V)	*The Cars that Ate Paris*, first feature film by Peter Weir
	Porter, Hal (1911), *Fredo Fuss Love Life* (F)	New Labor government introduces immigration policy which effectively ends 'White Australia' policy
	Stuart (1913), *Prince of my Country* (F)	Cyclone Tracy destroys Darwin
	Viidikas (1948), *Wrappings* (F)	
	West (1916), *Harlequin* (F)	
	White, Patrick (1912), *The Cockatoos* (F)	
	Wilding (1942), *Living Together* (F)	
1975	Bail (1941), *Contemporary Portraits* (F)	*Hecate: A Women's Interdisciplinary Journal* (St Lucia) founded
	Beaver (1928), *Odes and Days* (V)	*New Literature Review* founded
	Blight (1913), *Hart* (V)	Public Lending Right introduced
	Campbell, David (1915), *Deaths and Pretty Cousins* (V)	First access and ethnic radio station (3ZZ Melbourne) opened (closed 1977)

Date	Publications	Literary/Cultural Events
1975	Dawe (1930), *Just a Dugong at Twilight* (V)	Whitlam government dismissed by Governor-General Kerr
	Dransfield (*d* 1973), *Memoirs of a Velvet Urinal* (V)	International Women's Year
	Hall (1935), *A Place among People* (V)	
	Hardy (1917), *But the Dead are Many* (F)	
	Herbert (1901), *Poor Fellow my Country* (F)	
	Hope (1907), *A Late Picking* (V)	
	Keneally (1935), *Gossip from the Forest* (F)	
	Malouf (1934), *Johnno* (F)	
	Oakley (1931), *Bedfellows* and *The Feet of Daniel Mannix* (D)	
	Romeril (1945), *The Floating World* (D)	
	Summers (1945), *Damned Whores and God's Police* (P)	
	Tranter (1943), *The Alphabet Murders* (V)	
	Wilding (1942), *The Short Story Embassy* and *The West Midland Underground* (F)	
1976	Blair (1942), *The Christian Brothers* (D)	Sidney J. Baker *d*
	Buzo (1944), *Martello Towers* (D)	James Devaney *d*
	Buckley (1925), *Golden Builders* (V)	Ian Mudie *d*
	Drewe (1943), *The Savage Crows* (F)	James McAuley *d*
	Ireland (1927), *The Glass Canoe* (F)	*Theatre Australia* founded (−1982)
	Keneally (1935), *Season in Purgatory* (F)	*Caddie*, first feature film by Donald Crombie
	Oakley (1931), *A Lesson in English* (D)	*The Devil's Playground*, first feature film by Fred Schepisi
	Stead (1920), *Miss Herbert (The Suburban Wife)* (F)	
	Stivens (1911), *The Unicorn* (F)	
	West (1961), *The Navigator* (F)	
	White, Patrick (1912), *A Fringe of Leaves* (F)	
	Williamson (1942), *A Handful of Friends* (D)	
	Wright (1915), *Fourth Quarter* (V)	
1977	Adamson (1944), *Cross the Border* (V)	*Journal of Australian Studies*, ed. Bob Bessant, founded
	Dutton (1922), *A Body of Words* (V)	

Date	Publications	Literary/Cultural Events
1977	Elliott (1917), *Water under the Bridge* (F)	Hale and Iremonger begin publishing Australian literature
	FitzGerald (1902), *Product: Later Verses* (V)	Association for the Study of Australian Literature (ASAL) founded
	Hanrahan (1939), *The Albatross Muff* (F)	Special Broadcasting Service established to provide multilingual radio and TV services (reinforced by the *Galbally Report*, 1978)
	Keneally (1935), *A Victim of the Aurora* (F)	
	Marshall (1902), *The Complete Stories of Alan Marshall* (F)	Films include *The Getting of Wisdom* (Bruce Beresford) and *The Last Wave* (Peter Weir)
	McCullough (1937), *The Thorn Birds* (F)	
	Moorhouse (1938), *Tales of Mystery and Romance* (F)	
	Oakley (1931), *Walking through Tigerland* (F)	
	Park (?1923), *Swords and Crowns and Rings* (F)	
1978	Anderson, Jessica (1925), *Tirra Lirra by the River* (F)	*Australian Book Review,* 2nd series
	Beaver (1928), *Death's Directives* (V)	*The Chant of Jimmie Blacksmith,* film by Fred Schepisi
	Dawe (1930), *Sometimes Gladness* (V)	*Mattoid* (Geelong) founded
	Dransfield (d 1973), *Voyage into Solitude* (V)	
	Garner (1942), *Monkey Grip* (F)	
	Gilbert (1933), *People ARE Legends* (V)	
	Hanrahan (1939), *Where All the Queens Strayed* (F)	
	Koch (1932), *The Year of Living Dangerously* (F)	
	Lehmann (1940), *Ross' Poems* (V)	
	Malouf (1934), *An Imaginary Life* (F)	
	Murray (1938), *Ethnic Radio* (V)	
	Nowra (1950), *Inner Voices* (D)	
	Π O (Peter Oustabasidis) (1951), *Panash* (V)	
	Porter, Peter (1929), *The Cost of Seriousness* (V)	
	Tranter (1943), *Crying in Early Infancy: One Hundred Sonnets* (V)	
	White, Patrick (1912), *Big Toys* (D)	
1979	Adams (1940), *The Hottest Night of the Century* (F)	David Campbell d
		Ion Idriess d
	Astley (1925), *Hunting the Wild Pineapple* (F)	*Island Magazine* founded

Date	Publications	Literary/Cultural Events
1979	Beaver (1928), *As it was...* (F); *Selected Poems* (V)	New South Wales Premier's Literary Awards begin
	Buckley (1925), *The Pattern* and *Late Winter Child* (V)	*My Brilliant Career*, first feature film by Gillian Armstrong
	Buzo (1944), *Makassar Reef* (D)	
	Carey (1943), *War Crimes* (F)	
	Cowan (1914), *Mobiles* (F)	
	Drewe (1943), *A Cry in the Jungle Bar* (F)	
	Hanrahan (1939), *The Peach Groves* (F)	
	Ireland (1927), *A Woman of the Future* (F)	
	Johnson (Mudrooroo) (1938), *Long Live Sandawara* (F)	
	Keneally (1935), *Confederates*; *Passenger* (F)	
	McDonald (1941), *1915* (F)	
	Nowra (1950), *Visions* (D)	
	Stow (1935), *Visitants* (F)	
	Tranter (1943), *Dazed in the Ladies Lounge* (V)	
	White, Patrick (1912), *The Twyborn Affair* (F)	
1980	Anderson (1925), *The Impersonators* (F)	*The Australian*/Vogel National Literary Award begins
	Bail (1941), *Homesickness* (F)	Multicultural television (SBS) begins in Sydney and Melbourne
	Blight (1913), *The New City Poems* (V)	
	Dransfield (d 1973), *The Second Month of Spring* (V)	*Picnic at Hanging Rock*, film by Peter Weir
	Farmer (1941), *Alone* (F)	*Breaker Morant*, film by Bruce Beresford
	Garner (1942), *Honour and Other People's Children* (F)	
	Hanrahan (1939), *The Frangipani Gardens* (F)	
	Hazzard (1931), *The Transit of Venus* (F)	
	Keneally (1935), *The Cut-rate Kingdom* (F)	
	Kocan (1947), *The Treatment* (F)	
	Malouf (1934), *First Things Last* (V)	
	Moorhouse (1938), *The Everlasting Secret Family and Other Stories* (F)	
	Murray (1938), *The Boys who Stole the Funeral: A Novel Sequence* (V)	

DATE	PUBLICATIONS	LITERARY/CULTURAL EVENTS
1980	Oakley (1931), *The Great God Mogadon and Other Plays* (D)	
	Radley (1962), *Jack Rivers and Me* (F)	
	Stow (1935), *The Girl Green as Elderflower* (F)	
1981	Carey (1943), *Bliss* (F)	Dymphna Cusack *d*
	D' Alpuget (1944), *Turtle Beach* (F)	Leonard Mann *d*
	Facey (1894), *A Fortunate Life* (P)	John O'Grady ('Nino Culotta') *d*
	Foster (1944), *Moonlite* (F)	*The Macquarie Dictionary*, the first general dictionary compiled in Australia, published
	Hall (1935), *The Most Beautiful World: Fictions and Sermons* (V)	
	Harwood (1920), *The Lion's Bride* (V)	*Oxford History of Australian Literature* published
	Hope (1907), *Antechinus: Poems 1975–1980* (V)	*Scripsi* (Melbourne), ed. Peter Craven, founded
	Ireland (1927), *City of Women* (F)	*Art and Text* founded
	Kenna (1930), *Furtive Love* (D)	*Gallipoli*, film by Peter Weir
	Lehmann (1940), *Nero's Poems* (V)	*Puberty Blues, Mad Max 2, Winter of Our Dreams*, films
	Loukakis (1951), *For the Patriarch* (F)	
	Lurie (1938), *Dirty Friends* (F)	Australian population reaches 15 million
	Martin, David (1915), *Foreigners* (F)	
	Modjeska, *Exiles at Home* (P)	
	Nowra (1950), *Inside the Island* and *The Precious Woman* (D)	
	Oakley (1931), *Marsupials and Politics: Two Comedies* (D)	
	Porter, Hal (1911), *The Clairvoyant Goat* (F)	
	Porter, Peter (1929), *English Subtitles* (V)	
	Rolls (1923), *A Million Wild Acres* (P)	
	Weller (1958), *The Day of the Dog* (F)	
	White, Patrick (1912), *Flaws in the Glass: A Self-portrait* (P)	
1982	Adamson (1944), *The Law at Heart's Desire* (V)	Jim McNeil *d*
		Albert Facey *d*
	Astley (1925), *An Item from the Late News* (F)	Thomas Keneally awarded Booker Prize
	Couani (1948), *Were All Women Sex-Mad? and Other Stories* (F)	*Australian Short Stories*, ed. Bruce Pascoe, begins
	Hall (1935), *Just Relations* (F)	*Australasian Drama Studies* (St Lucia) founded
	Hanrahan (1939), *Dove* (F)	
	Keneally (1935), *Schindler's Ark* (F)	*The Man from Snowy River*, film
	Lee (1951), *True Love and How to Get It* (F)	Australian National Gallery opens in Canberra

Date	Publications	Literary/Cultural Events
1982	McDonald (1941), *Slipstream* (F)	
	Malouf (1934), *Child's Play with Eustace and the Prowler* and *Fly Away Peter* (F)	
	Masters (1919), *The Home Girls* (F)	
	Morrison (1904), *North Wind* (F)	
	Murnane (1939), *The Plains* (F)	
	Radley (1962), *My Blue Checker Corker and Me* (F)	
	Robinson (1912), *Selected Poems* (V)	
	Romeril (1945), *Bastardy* (D)	
	Shapcott (1935), *The Birthday Gift* (F)	
	Walwicz (1951), *Writing* (F)	
	Waten (1911), *Scenes of Revolutionary Life* (F)	
	Wilding (1942), *Pacific Highway* (F)	
	Winton (1960), *An Open Swimmer* (F)	
	Zwicky (1933), *Kaddish* (V)	
1983	Blair (1942), *Marx* and *Last Day in Woolloomooloo* (D)	Colin Simpson *d*
	Buckley (1925), *Cutting Green Hay* (P)	Christina Stead *d*
	Castro (1950), *Birds of Passage* (F)	Alan Moorehead *d*
	Cato (1917), *Forefathers* (F)	*Australian Journal of Cultural Studies* (Perth) founded (since 1986, titled *Journal of Cultural Studies*)
	Davis (1918), *Kullark and The Dreamers* (D)	
	Dawe (1930), *Sometimes Gladness*, 2nd edn (V); *Over Here, Harv!* (F)	
	Drewe (1943), *The Bodysurfers* (F)	
	Farmer (1941), *Milk* (F)	
	Foster (1944), *Plumbum* (F)	
	Hanrahan (1939), *Kewpie Doll* (F)	
	Johnson (Mudrooroo) (1938), *Doctor Wooreddy's Prescription for Enduring the Ending of the World* (F)	
	Jolley (1923), *Woman in a Lampshade*, *Mr Scobie's Riddle* and *Miss Peabody's Inheritance* (F)	
	Kefala (1935), *The Island* (F)	
	Kocan (1947), *The Cure* (F)	
	Liberman (1942), *A Universe of Clowns* (F)	
	Murray (1938), *The People's Otherworld* (V)	

Date	Publications	Literary/Cultural Events
1983	Nowra (1950), *Sunrise* (D)	
	Porter, Peter (1929), *Collected Poems* (V)	
	Sewell (1953), *Traitors* (D)	
	Shapcott (1935), *Welcome!* (F)	
	Tennant (1912), *Tantavallon* (F)	
	Tsaloumas (1921), *The Observatory* (V), tr. Philip Grundy	
	White, Patrick (1912), *Signal Driver* (D)	
	Williamson (1942), *The Perfectionist* (D)	
	'B. Wongar' (Sreten Bozic) (1936), *Walg* (F)	
1984	Cappiello (1942), *Oh Lucky Country* (F)	A. Bertram Chandler *d*
	Docker (1945), *In a Critical Condition* (P)	Joan Lindsay *d*
		Alan Marshall *d*
	Garner (1942), *The Children's Bach* (F)	Hal Porter *d*
	Gray (1945), *The Skylight* (V)	Xavier Herbert *d*
	Grenville (1950), *Bearded Ladies* (F)	*Outrider* (ed. Manfred Jurgensen) founded
	Harford (*d* 1927), *The Poems of Lesbia Harford* (V)	
	Ireland (1927), *Archimedes and the Seagle* (F)	
	Jolley (1923), *Milk and Honey* (F)	
	Kefala (1935), *The Island* (F)	
	McQueen, James (1934), *Uphill Runner* (F)	
	Malouf (1934), *Harland's Half Acre* (F)	
	Masters (1919), *Loving Daughters* (F)	
	Shapcott (1935), *The White Stag of Exile* (F)	
	Stow (1935), *The Suburbs of Hell* (F)	
	Winton (1960), *Shallows* (F)	
1985	Astley (1925), *Beachmasters* (F)	Eleanor Dark *d*
	Benterrak, Muecke and Roe, *Reading the Country* (F/P)	John Manifold *d*
		A.A. Phillips *d*
	Campbell (1948), *Lines of Flight* (F)	Douglas Stewart *d*
	Carey (1943), *Illywhacker* (F)	Judah Waten *d*
	Costello (1952), *Kites in Jakarta* (F)	Allan Yates ('Carter Brown') *d*
	Farmer (1941), *Home Time* (F)	Victorian Premier's Literary Award begins
	Garner (1942), *Postcards from Surfers* (F)	

Date	Publications	Literary/Cultural Events
1985	Grenville (1950), *Lilian's Story* (F)	
	Hanrahan (1939), *Annie Magdalene* (F)	
	Hart-Smith (1911), *Selected Poems 1936–1984* (V)	
	Hope (1907), *The Age of Reason* (V)	
	Jolley (1923), *Foxybaby* (F)	
	Koch (1932), *The Doubleman* (F)	
	Lurie (1938), *The Night We Ate the Sparrow* (F)	
	Malouf (1934), *Antipodes* (F); *12 Edmonstone Street* (P)	
	Masters (1919), *A Long Time Dying* (F)	
	Moorhead, Finola (1947), *Quilt: A Collection of Prose* (F)	
	Moorhouse (1938), *Room Service* (F)	
	Nowra (1950), *The Golden Age* (D)	
	Slessor (d 1971), *The War Diaries of Kenneth Slessor* (P)	
	Stead (d 1983), *Ocean of Story* (F)	
	Tsaloumas (1921), *A Book of Epigrams* (V)	
	Williamson (1942), *Sons of Cain* (D)	
	'B. Wongar' (Sreten Bozic) (1936), *Karan* (F)	
1986	Adams (1940), *Dancing on Coral* (F)	Olga Masters *d*
	Beaver (1928), *Headlands* (V)	*Coast to Coast* revived
	D'Alpuget (1944), *Winter in Jerusalem* (F)	*Australian Feminist Studies* begins
	Brett (1946), *The Auschwitz Poems* (V)	
	Dawe (1930), *Towards Sunrise* (V)	
	Gray (1945) *Selected Poems 1963–83* (V)	
	Grenville (1950), *Dreamhouse* (F)	
	Jolley (1923) *The Well* (F)	
	Papaellinos, *Ikons* (F)	
	Shapcott (1935), *Hotel Bellevue* (F)	
	Wearne (1948), *The Nightmarkets* (V/F)	
	Weller (1958), *Going Home* (F)	
	White (1912), *Memoirs of Many in One* (F)	
	Winton (1960), *That Eye, The Sky* (F)	

Date	Publications	Literary/Cultural Events
1987	Astley (1925), *It's Raining in Mango* (F)	
	Bail (1941), *Holden's Performance* (F)	Marjorie Barnard *d*
	Clark (1915), *A History of Australia*, vol 6 (P)	Kenneth Cook *d*
		R. D. FitzGerald *d*
	Drewe (1943), *Fortune* (F)	Cyril Pearl *d*
	Hall (1953), *Kisses of the Enemy* (F)	Grace Perry (founder of *Poetry Australia*) *d*
	Harford (*d* 1927), *The Invaluable Mystery* (F)	
	Hewett (1923), *Alice in Wormland* (V)	Niels Stevns (founder of *The Australian*/Vogel Awards) *d*
	Hughes, Robert (1938), *The Fatal Shore* (P)	
	Keneally (1935), *The Playmaker* (F)	
	Koch (1932), *Crossing the Gap* (P)	
	McCullough (1937), *The Ladies of Missalonghi* (F)	
	Masters (*d* 1986), *Amy's Children* (F)	
	Moorhead, Finola (1947), *Remember the Tarantella* (F)	
	Morgan (1951), *My Place* (P)	
	Murnane (1939), *Landscape with Landscape* (F)	
	Nowra (1950), *Palu* (F)	
	Skrzynecki (1945), *I'm Dying Laughing* (F)	
	Wright (1915), *Phantom Dwelling* (V)	
1988	Anderson (1925), *Stories from the Warm Zone and Sydney Stories* (F)	Vincent Buckley *d*
		Sir Keith Hancock *d*
	Carey (1943), *Oscar and Lucinda* (F)	Stephen Murray-Smith *d*
	Davis (1918), *John Pat and Other Poems* (V)	Kylie Tennant *d*
	Foster (1944), *The Pale Blue Crochet Coathanger Cover* (F)	*The Australian National Dictionary: A Dictionary of Australianisms on Historical Principles*, ed. W. S. Ramson
	Grenville (1950), *Joan Makes History* (F)	Inaugural Pascall Prize awarded to David Malouf
	Hope (1907), *Ladies from the Sea* (D)	Peter Carey wins Booker Prize for *Oscar and Lucinda*
	Hall (1935), *Captivity Captive* (F)	
	Hanrahan (1939), *A Chelsea Girl* (F)	
	Jolley (1923), *The Sugar Mother* (F)	
	Masters (*d* 1986), *The Rose Fancier* (F)	
	Moorhouse (1938), *Forty-Seventeen* (F)	
	Johnson (Mudrooroo) (1938), *Dalwurra, the Black Bittern* (V); *Doin Wildcat* (F)	

Date	Publications	Literary/Cultural Events
1988	Murnane (1939), *Inland* (F)	
	Murray (1938), *The Daylight Moon* (V)	
	Shapcott (1935), *Limestone and Lemon Wine* (F)	
	Skrzynecki (1945), *The Beloved Mountain* (F)	
	Slessor (d 1971), *The War Despatches of Kenneth Slessor* (P)	
	Stewart (d 1985), *Garden of Friends* (P)	
	Tranter (1943), *Under Berlin: New Poems 1988* (V)	
	Tsaloumas (1921), *Falcon Drinking* (V)	
	Winton (1960), *In the Winter Dark* (F)	

INDEX